Mrs Dalgairns's Kitchen

CARLETON LIBRARY SERIES

The Carleton Library Series publishes books about Canadian economics, geography, history, politics, public policy, society and culture, and related topics, in the form of leading new scholarship and reprints of classics in these fields. The series is funded by Carleton University, published by McGill-Queen's University Press, and is under the guidance of the Carleton Library Series Editorial Board, which consists of faculty members of Carleton University. Suggestions and proposals for manuscripts and new editions of classic works are welcome and may be directed to the Carleton Library Series Editorial Board c/o the Library, Carleton University, Ottawa K1S 5B6, at cls@carleton.ca, or on the web at www.carleton.ca/cls.

240 *Tax, Order, and Good Government*
A New Political History of Canada, 1867–1917
E.A. Heaman

241 Catharine Parr Traill's *The Female Emigrant's Guide*
Cooking with a Canadian Classic
Edited by Nathalie Cooke and Fiona Lucas

242 *Tug of War*
Surveillance Capitalism, Military Contracting, and the Rise of the Security State
Jocelyn Wills

243 *The Hand of God*
Claude Ryan and the Fate of Canadian Liberalism, 1925–1971
Michael Gauvreau

244 *Report on Social Security for Canada* (New Edition)
Leonard Marsh

245 *Like Everyone Else but Different*
The Paradoxical Success of Canadian Jews, Second Edition
Morton Weinfeld with Randal F. Schnoor and Michelle Shames

246 *Beardmore*
The Viking Hoax That Rewrote History
Douglas Hunter

247 *Stanley's Dream*
The Medical Expedition to Easter Island
Jacalyn Duffin

248 *Change and Continuity*
Canadian Political Economy in the New Millennium
Edited by Mark P. Thomas, Leah F. Vosko, Carlo Fanelli, and Olena Lyubchenko

249 *Home Feelings*
Liberal Citizenship and the Canadian Reading Camp Movement
Jody Mason

250 *The Art of Sharing*
The Richer versus the Poorer Provinces since Confederation
Mary Janigan

251 *Recognition and Revelation*
Short Nonfiction Writings
Margaret Laurence
Edited by Nora Foster Stovel

252 *Anxious Days and Tearful Nights*
Canadian War Wives during the Great War
Martha Hanna

253 *Take a Number*
How Citizens' Encounters with Government Shape Political Engagement
Elisabeth Gidengil

254 *Mrs Dalgairns's Kitchen*
Rediscovering "The Practice of Cookery"
Edited by Mary F. Williamson

Mrs Dalgairns's Kitchen

Rediscovering *The Practice of Cookery*

Edited by

Mary F. Williamson

With modernized recipes by

Elizabeth Baird

Carleton Library Series 254

McGill-Queen's University Press

Montreal & Kingston • London • Chicago

ISBN 978-0-2280-0533-9 (cloth)
ISBN 978-0-2280-0788-3 (ePDF)

Legal deposit first quarter 2021
Bibliothèque nationale du Québec

Printed in Canada on acid-free paper that is 100% ancient forest free (100% post-consumer recycled), processed chlorine free

This book has been published with the help of a grant from the Canadian Federation for the Humanities and Social Sciences, through the Awards to Scholarly Publications Program, using funds provided by the Social Sciences and Humanities Research Council of Canada.

Funded by the Government of Canada | Financé par le gouvernement du Canada | Canada | Canada Council for the Arts | Conseil des arts du Canada

We acknowledge the support of the Canada Council for the Arts.

Nous remercions le Conseil des arts du Canada de son soutien.

Library and Archives Canada Cataloguing in Publication

Title: Mrs Dalgairns's kitchen : rediscovering the practice of cookery / edited by Mary F. Williamson ; with modernized recipes by Elizabeth Baird.
Names: Dalgairns, Mrs., author. | Williamson, Mary F., editor.
Series: Carleton library series ; 254.
Description: Series statement: Carleton Library series ; 254 | This edition of the Practice of Cookery is an adaptation of the 1830 third edition published by Robert Cadell in Edinburgh and London. | Includes bibliographical references and index.
Identifiers: Canadiana (print) 2020038662X | Canadiana (ebook) 20200386727 | ISBN 9780228005339 (cloth) | ISBN 9780228007883 (ePDF)
Subjects: LCSH: Cooking. | LCGFT: Cookbooks.
Classification: LCC TX717 .D142 2021 | DDC 641.5942—dc23

This book was designed and typeset by studio oneonone in Minion 11/13.5

Contents

Acknowledgments

It has been almost twenty years since I first became intrigued by Mrs Dalgairns's *The Practice of Cookery*. I first acquired the third Edinburgh-London edition of 1830, but such was my enthusiasm that I went on to buy five more editions.

Many individuals on both sides of the Atlantic, in their personal and institutional capacities, have made this reprint edition possible.

Elizabeth Baird, whose name resonates among Canadian cooks, and indeed among culinary historians, eagerly accepted the challenge of turning two-hundred-year-old recipes into doable twenty-first-century "to-do" dishes, from appetizers through main courses, desserts, and special day presentations. Elizabeth was also helpful earlier in this project, sharing her connections with heritage promoter friends on Prince Edward Island. I can't thank her enough. Elizabeth herself appreciates the generous contributions to modernizing Mrs Dalgairns's recipes from Bridget Wranich, program officer at Fort York National Historic Site, and editor Julia Armstrong.

On Prince Edward Island itself, I owe a debt of gratitude to ex-premier and retired senator Catherine Callbeck, Elizabeth Boswall, and Richard Savidant of the Prince Edward Island Genealogical Society. There would have been no book if not for the abundant and generously offered services of Charlotte Stewart, heritage officer of the Public Archives and Records Office of Prince Edward Island. John Boylan, public services archivist, instinctively knew that I would appreciate seeing recipes found in the Lieutenant John MacDonald collection. I am also beholden to Amy (Tinker) McKay of St Paul's Anglican Church Archives in Halifax, Nova Scotia, a parish of the Diocese of Nova Scotia and Prince Edward Island, for thorough searches of the Callbecks going back to the mid-eighteenth century.

And none of this could have happened without full access to the comprehensive archives of Mrs Dalgairns's publisher, Robert Cadell (and potential publisher, James Murray), in the National Library of Scotland, Edinburgh, with my personal gratitude on site and via email to Olive Geddes, then senior curator of the Manuscripts Division.

I always knew that a visit to the town of Dundee was essential, if only to try to follow in the footsteps of my protagonist. In March 2005 it was with an overwhelming sense of connection that I was able to make a first visit to the City of Dundee Archives which itself is on Shore Terrace, just a few buildings west of the Dalgairnses' home and wine business. Christopher McKinlay devoted considerable time to addressing my email enquiries until his retirement from the archives in 2004. Previous to a 2015 visit to Dundee I was updated on local archival sources by Richard Cullen.

Captain Basil Hall was "the power behind the throne" in ensuring publication of *The Practice of Cookery.* Without the advice and assistance of his biographer, James McCarthy, whom I was delighted to meet in Edinburgh, details of the Dalgairns/Hall relationship and Hall's influence with publisher Robert Cadell would have been yet another – but in this case major – "unknown." In his *That Curious Fellow: Captain Basil Hall, R.N.* (2011), McCarthy details Hall's involvement with every aspect of *The Practice of* Cookery, noting that Hall had "spent an inordinate amount of time on the Dalgairns cookbook."

On a personal level I am grateful to my friend the late Pamela DeBulnes Dodds, who while on an architectural research trip to Bath Abbey in 2004 spotted the plaque erected in memory of Mrs Dalgairns's mother, Anne Callbeck.

The expertise of Joan Winearls in the worlds of cartography and in particular Canadian maps is widely known. I was much relieved when as a longtime friend she offered to assist in scouting out two era-appropriate maps of Prince Edward Island and eastern North America as illustrations for the introduction.

I very much appreciate the Thomas Fisher Rare Book Library of the University of Toronto for having digitized my copy of the third (1830) edition of *The Practice of Cookery*. In particular Elizabeth Ridolfo, who oversaw the digitization process, deserves my sincere thanks, as does Pearce J. Carefoot, head of the Department of Rare Books and Special Collections at the Fisher Library, who visited his library during early COVID-19 times to retrieve and send me the two maps of eastern Canada.

The following deserve my hearty thanks for their expertise, and often their enthusiasm for the idea of the book, over the almost twenty years since all of this began: Sandra Alston, Noreen Aubertin-Potter (Codrington Library, All Souls College, Oxford), Patricia Belier (University of New Brunswick), Helen Billing, Lucille Campey, Nathalie Cooke, Elizabeth Driver, Catherine

Hennessey, Ruth Jennings, Patricia Kennedy (Library and Archives Canada), Fiona Lucas, Warren McDougall (Centre for the History of the Book, University of Edinburgh), George Parker, Bonnie Schepers (UELAC), and many others whose help has been invaluable. The work of professional genealogists Helen Curtis and Caroline Makein was much needed in the pursuit of the primary events in the lives of both Catherine and Peter Dalgairns.

And considerable financial research assistance has been received via the York University Professional Expense Reimbursement plan.

Jonathan Crago of McGill-Queen's University Press was extraordinarily encouraging and helpful beginning with my publication proposal. His suggestions regarding what readers and cooks would be expecting and support through the readers' reports and the grant application to the Aid to Scholarly Publications Program of the Federation for the Humanities and Social Sciences have been invaluable in shepherding this book through to publication. Working with the exceedingly competent members of MQUP's editorial and marketing staff has been a pleasure.

Above all I am profoundly grateful to Susan E. Houston, without whom I would never have pursued my ambition, near obsession, with telling the true story of Catherine Emily Callbeck Dalgairns. In addition to acting as my personal editor, Susan accompanied me all the way to London, Edinburgh, Dundee, and Prince Edward Island.

Introduction

In March 1829, fifteen hundred copies of Mrs Dalgairns's *The Practice of Cookery, Adapted to the Business of Every Day Life* were released to the public by an impatient author and her obliging publisher Robert Cadell of Edinburgh, along with his London agents Simpkin and Marshall. Its publication was preceded by notices in the leading newspapers of Edinburgh, Dublin, and London, with a series of ever larger advertisements in the *Times*.[1]

The cookbook, priced at 7s 6d, was an immediate commercial and critical success, and Cadell and his successors were to benefit from thirty years of steady sales of more than sixteen editions from 1829 until 1861.[2] In that year, Mrs Beeton's *Book of Household Management* was first published, crushing the competition with a plethora of colour plates. While the celebrated Mrs Beeton compensated for her ignorance of cookery by cutting and pasting from the work of her predecessors, Mrs Dalgairns was an original.

All sources, whether library catalogues, reviews, or discussions of nineteenth-century cookery or cookery books, referred to Mrs Dalgairns as a Scottish cookbook author. None disclosed, or seemed aware of, her biography, which begins in Charlottetown, Prince Edward Island, where she was born in 1788 when the Island bore the name St John's Island. She was raised there, and was married in Charlottetown in 1808. I, too, had assumed Mrs Dalgairns was Scottish, being attracted

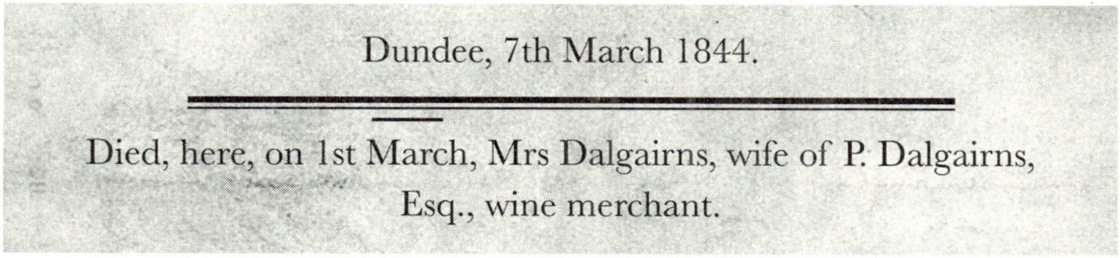
Dundee, 7th March 1844.

Died, here, on 1st March, Mrs Dalgairns, wife of P. Dalgairns, Esq., wine merchant.

Fig. 1 Mrs Dalgairns's death notice as it appeared in the *Dundee Courier* (Dundee, Scotland), 12 March 1844, Gale Primary Sources, British Library Newspapers.

to her cookbook simply because I was looking for old Scottish recipe sources. But much genealogical research has determined that Catherine Emily Callbeck Dalgairns was Canadian, although being Canadian was not a reality until Canadian Confederation in 1867. The key was the surname Callbeck – a name that resonates today in Prince Edward Island. The genealogy of the Callbeck family has been well documented, but no one had followed up on one Catherine Emily who, two years after marrying Peter Dalgairns, departed for England in 1810. In reality, Mrs Dalgairns had lived in Scotland fewer than seven years when her cookbook first appeared in 1829. That the author was Scottish stuck to her throughout all editions of her cookbook. Her death in 1844 was announced in the *Observer* (London) and in at least three local newspapers: "Died, here, on 1st March, Mrs Dalgairns, wife of P. Dalgairns, Esq., wine merchant." No mention of her birthplace, nor her authorship of a close to bestselling cookbook.[3] The story of *The Practice of Cookery* and its author Catherine Emily Callbeck Dalgairns presented here has as much to do with the cookbook's place in that academic enterprise known as "The History of the Book" as with her biography or cookery itself.[4] The field is not limited to the book as we know it; rather, it encompasses newspapers, magazines, forms, and related manuscripts as well as authorship and publishers.

In over fourteen hundred recipes in twenty-five chapters, plus a thorough index not found in the cookbooks of her contemporaries, and with almost all chapters preceded by useful preparatory remarks, the author offers readers-cooks lesser known ethnic recipes from three continents. As well, Mrs Dalgairns pulls examples from sources familiar to her audience, comprised largely of middle-class women whose households include at least one cook. Along with an unusually wide variety of seasonings and flavourings, all of this innovation does honour to the Canadian Mrs Dalgairns.

This edition of the *Practice of Cookery* is an adaptation of the 1830 third edition published by Robert Cadell in Edinburgh and Simpkin and Marshall in London. It offers the complete text; however, the suggested corrections noted in the errata slip have been corrected here, along with several typographic errors that appear in a very few mangled sentences. The much-lauded original twenty-seven-page index, which appears at the front of the text and just after the prefaces of the original book, has been inserted here in full with the new page numbers at the back of *Mrs Dalgairns's Kitchen*, along with, but separate from, the general index, which itemizes important terms in the introduction and glossary. On the whole, older cookbooks provided readers with a simplified index, merely citing the names of the recipes or listing them under categories such as "Pork" or "Puddings." At the time, Mrs Dalgairns's index set a helpful precedent for her reader/cooks as well as for cookbook indexes published throughout the nineteenth century up to the present. Recipes are usually indexed under two, or exceptionally three, headings – for example "Currie of veal, rabbit or fowl … 172"; "Fowl, veal, or rabbit, currie of … 172"; and "Veal, currie of rabbit, fowl, or …172."

In presenting Mrs Dalgairns's *The Practice of Cookery* to today's readers/cooks we are including the final eight chapters, which do not specifically address recipes for cooking foods. These chapters, albeit with a few recipes related to food, are headed "Domestic Wines," "Poultry Yard," "Dairy," "Brewing," "Kitchen Garden," "Bees," and "Pigs," plus a "Miscellany."[5] All of the more than sixteen editions of *The Practice of Cookery* conclude with an appendix, with later editions stretching to three appendices, two of them offering additional recipes not found in the general index. Anna Prophet's Oxtail Soup begins Appendix No. II, first seen in 1840s editions. We know from the 1841 Dundee census that, at that time, Anna Prophet was the resident cook in the Dalgairns household.

The Callbecks of Prince Edward Island

At this point I should explain how I settled on what forenames to call our author Mrs Dalgairns. In Prince Edward Island she is Catherine Emily Callbeck. In Scotland she signed her letters "E. C. Dalgairns." But with marriage notices clearly stating "Miss Catherine Callbeck" and a Dundee census record "Catherine Dalgairns," "Catherine" is the name that I have adopted as having the highest legitimacy.

When in 1788 Catherine was born in Charlottetown (known then as Charlotte Town) the colony was known as Saint (or St) John's Island. Her father, Phillips (*sic*) Callbeck, had been an attorney to the King's Bench Court in Dublin when, in 1770, he was appointed by King George III to the post of attorney general of the Island, maintaining his entry in Dublin directories under "Attornies" until his death in 1790. In 1772, he married Ann (or Anne, also known to her familiars as "Nancy") Coffin of Boston, who was born into a prominent Massachusetts Mayflower family, several of whose members pursued the Loyalist cause to what are now known as Canada's Maritime Provinces.[6] Ann's father, Nathaniel, had been a recruiting agent for the British in the Boston area.[7] Her daughter Catherine, the future author of a cookbook, was the youngest of six Callbeck children: two boys and four girls.

Fig. 2 Charlotte Town as in 1779, Hillsborough River, St John's Island and Prince Edward's. Gulph St Lawrence. "Charlotte Town as in 1779." Watercolour by Charles Randle, 1813. Object number 954.100.4. Gift of the Sigmund Samuel Endowment Fund, Royal Ontario Museum.

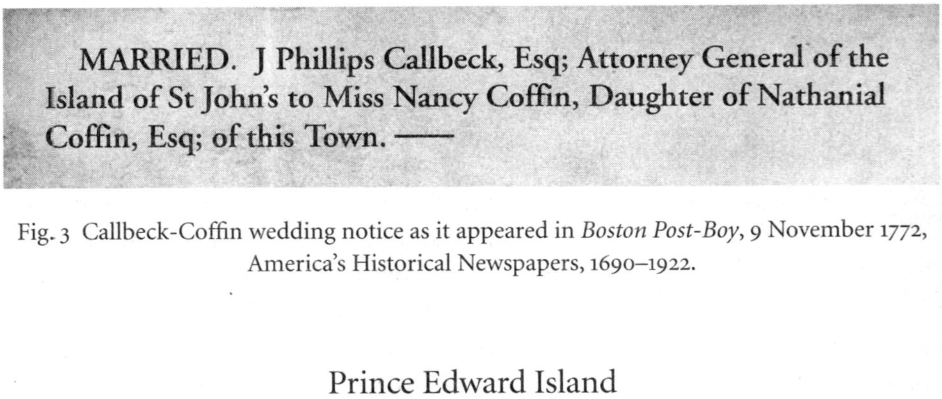

MARRIED. J Phillips Callbeck, Esq; Attorney General of the Island of St John's to Miss Nancy Coffin, Daughter of Nathanial Coffin, Esq; of this Town. ——

Fig. 3 Callbeck-Coffin wedding notice as it appeared in *Boston Post-Boy*, 9 November 1772, America's Historical Newspapers, 1690–1922.

Prince Edward Island

Situated in the Gulf of St Lawrence, separated from Nova Scotia and New Brunswick by the Northumberland Strait, Prince Edward Island (PEI) is found at Latitude 46′ 14″, which is equivalent to southern France and northern Oregon, United States. The British colony was incorporated into Canada in 1873, just six years after Confederation. When Jacques Cartier arrived in 1534, claiming the island as a colony of France, he declared the Island to be "the fairest land that may possibly be

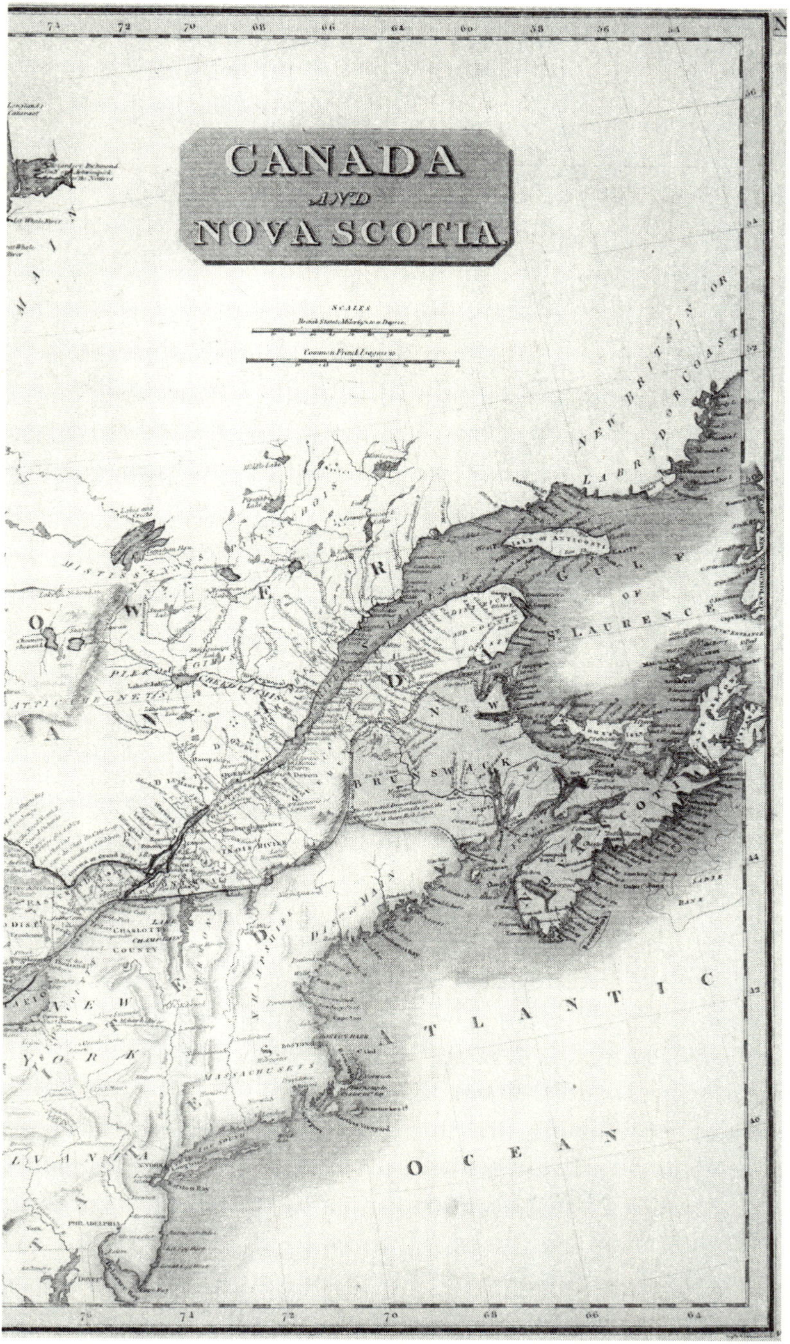

Fig. 4 Part of *Canada and Nova Scotia* [map] from John Thomson, *A New General Atlas* (Edinburgh, 1821), showing the Atlantic provinces with Prince Edward Island, and south to Boston and New York. Reproduced with permission of the Thomas Fisher Rare Book Library, University of Toronto.

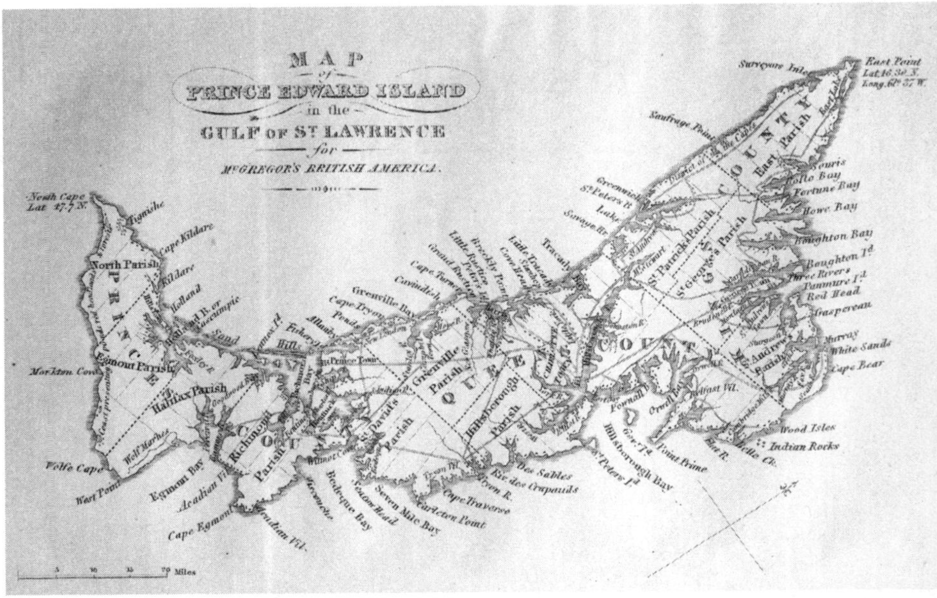

Fig. 5 *Map of Prince Edward Island in the Gulf of St. Lawrence for McGregor's British America*, in John MacGregor's *British America: in two volumes* (Edinburgh: William Blackwood; London: T. Cadell, 1832). vol. 1, opp. p. 283. Reproduced with permission of the Thomas Fisher Rare Book Library, University of Toronto.

seen." He would have been greeted by the Mi'kmaqs, who called themselves the *Abegweit*, meaning "cradle in the waves." It is thought they occupied sites on PEI as early as ten thousand years ago by crossing from Nova Scotia and New Brunswick via the Northumberland Strait. Mi'kmaq peregrinations among the future Maritime provinces continued into the 1800s. In PEI the Mi'kmaqs chose to live on Lennox Island, although ownership of the island was disputed and repeatedly changed hands among the Europeans. The town of Bedeque on the south coast of the Island, facing New Brunswick, was part of Mi'kmaq territory until European settlement, with many generations of Callbecks, for over two centuries, calling Bedeque home. Interactions between Europeans and Mi'kmaqs in the Atlantic region were frequent, often in the context of who owned what land, with European self-sufficiency often depending upon Mi'kmaq assistance. Today, on their website, the Mi'kmaqs declare themselves to be the "Lennox Island Mi'kmaq First Nation, Prince Edward Island, Canada."[8]

French settlement on the island, which the French had named Île St Jean, was not permitted until the 1720s, with the Acadian emigrants arriving from France. The number of Acadians is estimated to have been five thousand persons at most. However, the Island was ceded in 1763 to Great Britain under the Treaty of Paris, and its name anglicized to Island of St John. Not surprisingly, the French-speaking Islanders were expelled by the British, although many families made their way back in later years. With the two warring European countries carrying their disputes overseas into the Gulf of St Lawrence, it was inevitable that the Island's newer populations ebbed and flowed. As early as 1758 the Island was governed as part of Nova Scotia, and in 1769 a separate colonial administration was established. The fertile land of PEI was allocated by lottery to members of the British elite, with the entire Island divided into sixty-seven townships, or lots, with each lot encompassing twenty thousand acres.

In 1799 the Island once again was renamed, this time Prince Edward Island to honour the son of King George III, and its population was back to a little over five thousand. From the outset, immigration from Britain was dominated by Gaelic-speaking Scots Highlanders. In 1803, with the encouragement of Lord Selkirk, some eight hundred Highlanders and Scottish Islanders, who were not impoverished, nor had suffered seizures of their land, sought an economically advantageous life on PEI. In 1770, when Phillips Callbeck arrived, the British population amounted to just fifteen hundred families. In addition to holding the position of attorney general, and treasurer of the Island, Phillips Callbeck was the principal merchant, owning a store where he stocked fishing supplies. Extant correspondence reveals that expeditions were frequently made across the narrow straight to Halifax and Pictou in Nova Scotia – a matter of two days and 445 nautical miles – for shopping, entertainment, social events, and political and religious occasions. On Prince Edward Island in the 1770s and 1780s, the ownership of black slaves was not uncommon among the upper classes. Phillips Callbeck is inaccurately recorded in early nineteenth-century Loyalist muster rolls as not owning slaves. Possibly Callbeck treated his slaves as unpaid "indentured servants who worked inside the house, possibly as cooks in the kitchen rather than out in the fields."[9]

As attorney general of the Island of St John's in the early 1770s, when Governor William Patterson returned to England, Phillips Callbeck was appointed Administrator of the Island (officially President of His Majesty's Council) at the outbreak of "the American Rebellion" of the Thirteen Colonies to the south.[10] The Callbeck family home in Charlottetown was twice invaded by New England privateers.

Letters survive between Phillips Callbeck and Thomas Wright, an Island magistrate, and General George Washington that provide gripping details of the invasion of December 1775, when the privateers, who were also captains in the American forces, looted the Callbeck house, taking not only Ann Callbeck's jewellery and household furnishings but also all alcoholic beverages and "stores of Vinegar, Oil, Candles, Fruit, sweetmeats, Hams, Bacon &c." In other words, they seized all the provisions that would have provided winter support for the Callbecks and "between 70 and 80 people who were latterly arrived on the Island and depended on Mr. Callbeck." Mr Callbeck had received advance warning of the raid and his wife was escorted to their country farm. By Callbeck's own account the privateers threatened to cut Mrs Callbeck's throat if they could catch her. Callbeck was taken aboard one of the invading ships and delivered to George Washington in Cambridge, Massachusetts, and after three days was released with apologies and returned to the Island.[11] George Washington himself wrote: "As the captains acted without any warrant for such conduct, I have thought it but justice to release these gentlemen, whose families were left in the utmost distress."[12] Having lost the thirteen colonies, Britain simply lost interest in the Island of St John, which embodied no strategic importance.[13]

It must be said that, while the surname "Callbeck" survives and is historically recognized today on the Island, Ann Coffin is not the progenitor of those residents bearing the Callbeck name. Before he married Ann Coffin, Phillips Callbeck had a son named Phillips Morris Callbeck with Catharine Morris of Halifax. When as a young man Phillips Callbeck Jr moved from Halifax to the Island, his half-brothers and sisters stated firmly that his surname should be "Morris," but he insisted that he was Phillips Callbeck. Thus, "Phillips Morris Callbeck became the ancestor of all the Callbecks, both the proud and the humble, that have lived on this Island since 1792."[14]

Attorney General Phillips Callbeck died at age forty-six on 21 February 1790, just two years after Catherine was born. The Island's assembly voted to set up a monument in the city graveyard in his memory, and it even approved the wording for a long inscription. But nothing happened until 1946, when his descendant William Callbeck erected a monument in the Old Protestant Burying Ground in Charlottetown, which can be seen today.[15]

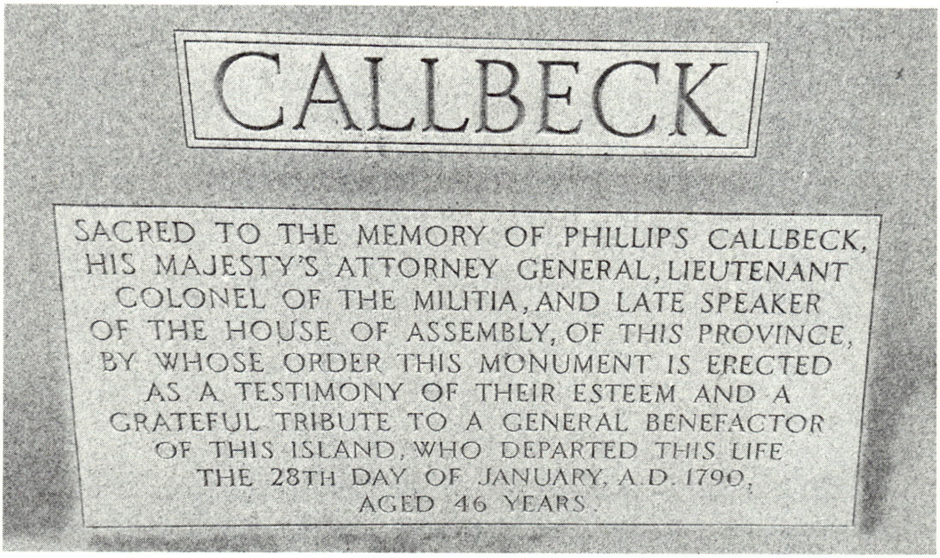

Fig. 6 Gravestone of Phillips Callbeck in the Old Protestant Burying Ground, Charlottetown. Photograph by Mary F. Williamson.

"Beautiful and Accomplished"

In Charlottetown, on 11 September 1808, in a double ceremony with her sister Sophia Maria and her new husband George Irving, Catherine married Peter Dalgairns, a Scot of the Forfarshire landed gentry who had immigrated to Pictou in Nova Scotia. A contemporary English newspaper account focuses on Catherine's uncle, Vice-Admiral Sir Isaac Coffin, Bart., who commanded His Majesty's ten-gun schooner *Porgey*, and who visited Prince Edward Island to attend the wedding of his nieces, "two beautiful and accomplished girls."[16]

When he married Catherine, Peter Dalgairns intended to settle on the Island and had purchased a house in Charlottetown. But he was soon embroiled in PEI Supreme Court actions, owing his new brother-in-law substantial sums, with debts to be settled by the sale of timber rights on lands he had purchased. Multiple further actions against "absent debtor and absconder" Peter Dalgairns were charged by other Islanders between 1811 and 1814. These included the assertion that the timber was in a perishable state and would likely go "adrift" and that an

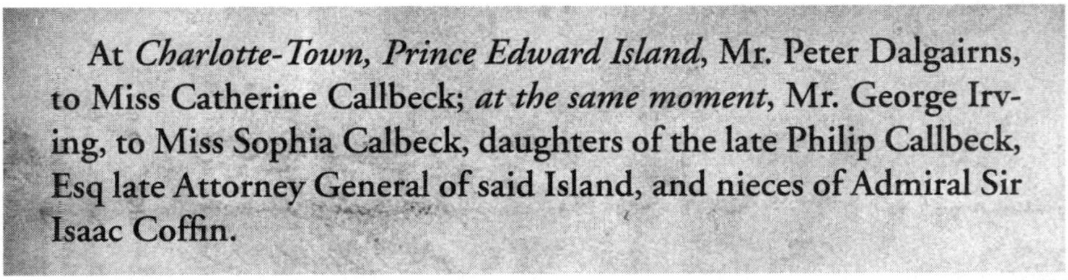

At *Charlotte-Town, Prince Edward Island*, Mr. Peter Dalgairns, to Miss Catherine Callbeck; *at the same moment*, Mr. George Irving, to Miss Sophia Calbeck, daughters of the late Philip Callbeck, Esq late Attorney General of said Island, and nieces of Admiral Sir Isaac Coffin.

Fig. 7 Newspaper notice of the double wedding as it appeared in the *Lancaster Gazette and General Advertiser* (Lancaster, England), 29 October 1808, Gale Primary Sources, British Library Newspapers.

English Bill of Exchange for over £1,800 had proved to be worthless.[17] The couple clearly was obliged to leave Prince Edward Island. One could say they "fled" PEI for England, first to Liverpool and then to London for twelve years. What Catherine was not to know was that Peter would turn out to be a serial bankrupt in his various seemingly respectable endeavours as a ship and insurance broker, and then wine and liquor merchant, both occupations being vulnerable to business cycles. But Peter Dalgairns appears especially unlucky, surviving bankruptcy proceedings in every decade of his adult life during their years in England and finally, from the 1820s until his wife's death in 1844, in Dundee, fifty-six road miles (ninety kilometres) north of Edinburgh on the west coast of Scotland.[18]

At this point it is hard to imagine how Catherine Dalgairns could have moved from one of the most unknown, isolated, and least populated British colonies to London, virtually the centre of the world (plus being dependent on a man who was being criminally prosecuted) without suffering from an overwhelming case of anxiety and self doubt. And yet, among bestselling female British cookbook authors of the time, such as Hannah Glasse, Elizabeth Raffald, Maria Rundell, Meg Dods, and Eliza Acton, only Catherine Dalgairns brought to her successful authorship a diverse background, having experienced a wide variety of culinary traditions. Today, Prince Edward Island continues to celebrate its cultural and food heritage, embracing a rich and varied ethnic past: Mi'kmaq, Acadian, Scottish, and, to a lesser extent, English. In addition, Catherine Callbeck would draw on her Irish and American heritage.

That Catherine did suffer through her husband's bankruptcy cycles we know from correspondence in the papers of her Edinburgh publisher Robert Cadell. In

1830, Catherine Dalgairns wrote to Cadell to say she had set up a trust fund for her royalties, with her brother-in-law Andrew Dalgairns of Ingleston as trustee along with C. Guthrie, a London banker.[19] In this way she shielded her royalties from being seized in legal actions against her husband. On 11 November 1833, she wrote to Cadell to thank him for sending along two cookbooks she had requested, noting: "The two Volumes that came to hand with your letter I have not been able to examine owing to a long illness that I have suffered from and which has debilitated me so much that it will be some time before I am able to study even a Cookery Book." Could it be that the long illness stemmed from her husband's long-standing financial misfortunes and their unsettling effect on their daily lives in Dundee?

Unlike the majority of cookbook authors, Mrs Dalgairns was not a professional cook, a teacher of cookery, or a cook in an aristocratic household. But she clearly harboured more than a housewife's interest in food and cooking, and, of course, she was born into what might be termed British North American aristocracy. The question is: Why compile this cookbook? It may be that the unhappy circumstances that embroiled her family before she was born and undoubtedly afterwards, and her husband's business failures, bent her mind towards the cookbook project, which appears to have captivated her imagination and energy several years before the book was eventually published.

"That very curious fellow"[20]

The saga of the publication of *The Practice of Cookery* sheds invaluable light on the highly personal and flexible world of early nineteenth-century publishing in Britain. The first and dominant voice we hear is that of Captain Basil Hall, whose involvement at every stage of the production and publicity of the cookbook was essential to its eventual publication. The son of Sir James Hall of Dunglass, Scotland, a baronet of Nova Scotia, Basil joined the Royal Navy as a midshipman at the young age of fifteen. His on-board travels took him to Halifax, where, on several occasions in the early 1800s, he was posted for several weeks. During one such sea trip in 1803 he made "a deliberate jaunt in North America … and a small trip to Prince Edward's Island, in the Gulf of St. Lawrence, to which I shall possibly advert again."[21] We suspect that he met young Catherine Callbeck on Prince Edward Island. The two, as social equals, were likely thrown together on festive occasions, and surviving letters suggest that their relationship went further than a warm acquaintanceship.[22]

In a letter written in January of 1808 to Mrs General Martin Hunter of New Brunswick, Basil's mother wrote: "I wish I had heard of Basil's return from that island he has gone to … and blabbing his intentions all over Halifax." This was just three months before Catherine Callbeck would marry Peter Dalgairns. And just a month later Basil Hall wrote to Mrs Hunter, suggesting that a young lady used to send him "wishes" in her letters. "If my memory deceives me and such things did take place in sly corners and some matrimonial engagements which it were safer perhaps to make in New Scotland (i.e. Nova Scotia) than old Scotland …etc."[23]

Fast forward twenty years. As Hall's biographer observes, Basil Hall became obsessed with persuading his own two publishers to take on the cookbook, which had taken up an inordinate amount of his time.[24] Could Hall have taken a shine to Catherine Callbeck, just his age, and might this explain his outside commitment to her cookbook project? Without hesitation it can be said that, without Basil Hall's interventions, the cookbook would never have been published.

The Cook's Companion, or, *A New System of Cooking*, or, *The Practice of Cookery*?

In the year leading up to his tour of North America with his wife and daughter in 1827–28, Basil Hall focused on Mrs Dalgairns's cookbook and its potential publication. He had spoken to his well-regarded publisher John Murray about the preface, making changes to it in the "spirit" of Murray's recommendations. Writing at length to Murray on 1 November 1826, going into every conceivable detail of the content of the cookbook, Hall asks for proofs and assures Murray that the manuscript had been "read and compared repeatedly by the parties who understand the subject." Hall then continues somewhat aggressively: "I shall be glad if you can make up your mind about this subject with as little delay as possible, as it will be of consequence to all parties that some final arrangement be entered into before I leave this part of the country [for North America]." His suggested title: "What do you think of the 'Cook's Companion – by another Lady' or 'A New System of Cooking adapted to Persons of Moderate Income'?" By 13 April 1827, Basil Hall appreciates that once an agreement is secured Mrs Dalgairns will own one half of the copyright and Murray the other half. In this last letter to John Murray, Hall concludes: "I hope and trust that you mean to keep to your sagacious flair of making it as cheap as possible — & I have no doubt of its immense success."

At this point Mrs Dalgairns herself intervenes with firm ideas about various aspects of her cookbook. In a letter dated 1 April 1827 to Basil Hall from her home at Shore (Terrace) in Dundee, she expresses delight with the wording of his preface – "it is certainly much improved" – but there is a misspelling! Surely "refered" in the first line of the preface should be spelled "referred" with two "rs." As for the title page, she wishes that Mr Murray would not give her name as "Mrs. E.C.D." but, rather, "Mrs. Dalgairns." She is expecting proofs, and because their house is being repainted she is worried that they will have to move while the work is being done. "I cannot bear the smell of Paint." The concern is that the package may be misdirected!

At this point this editor is inclined to intervene to provide a little context for publisher John Murray's thoughts and concerns as he began to deal with Mrs Dalgairns and her cookbook. Basil Hall, and Mrs Dalgairns herself, would have been fully aware of a bestselling cookbook that had been published by John Murray beginning in 1806 and that would appear in sixty-seven editions into the late nineteenth century, with each edition printed in hundreds of thousands of copies.[25] This was *A New System of Domestic Cookery, by a Lady* (Maria Eliza Rundell), an old family friend of the publisher. From the beginning, *Domestic Cookery* was embraced by cookbook readers and users as the last word on domestic cookery, and over many ensuing decades it more than secured John Murray of Albermarle Street's bottom line. But success had come at a cost. It was just two years earlier than the Hall-Dalgairns-Murray contractual discussions that a prolonged court case about copyright brought by Mrs Rundell against John Murray was resolved. In 1824 she was judged to be the winner, with her costs paid plus an out-of-court settlement of £2,000.

In taking on this new cookbook was John Murray simply doing a favour for Basil Hall? Hall had earlier expressed favourable expectations based on a longstanding friendship. Or did Murray assume that, in comparison with Mrs Rundell, Mrs Dalgairns would be relatively docile and compliant with regard to any suggestions for improvements or changes? It appears that Murray was unfamiliar with cookbooks, in which adherence to detail is essential, and this embroiled him in disputes with both cookbook authors.

According to Maria Rundell's entry in the *Dictionary of National Biography*, "as the earliest manual of household management with any pretensions to completeness it called forth many imitations."[26] In the previous century, and throughout the nineteenth and into the twentieth century, copying recipes, making small changes, and even outright plagiarism was not uncommon, but Mrs Dalgairns was not guilty on any count. And while *Domestic Cookery* was embellished with a number of engravings in the meats sections – the firm commonly presented illustrations, occasionally engaging well known artists such as J.M.W. Turner – Murray must have trusted that the absence of illustrations, along with a low price, would not detract from sales of this new cookbook.

On 13 April 1827, we read in a letter from Basil Hall to John Murray that Mr and Mrs Dalgairns had signed a publication agreement. We shall see that Catherine Dalgairns wouldn't be satisfied with her cookbook until the publisher agreed to add further receipts that occupied her mind and time in the kitchen. Mr Murray had sent her a copy of Ude's *The French Cook*, which, according to her letter to him of 10 May, inspired her to produce, but not copy, more French recipes for her cookbook, even after the proofs had been delivered. Back in 1806, Mrs Rundell had been eager to include French and other continental recipes, and she, too, had received gifts of other cookbooks from Murray. And she had asked for the inclusion of further recipes, as well as the deletion of others, for the second edition of *Domestic Cookery*.

But Mrs Dalgairns's response may have led to the *paille* that broke the camel's back for a publisher who regarded cookbooks as light, unserious reading, in comparison with works by Charles Darwin, Lord Byron, Jane Austen, and his many other authors of note. In no time *The Practice of Cookery* – or whatever title had been decided – was no longer on John Murray's publication schedule. We can well imagine that he anticipated a never-ending insistence on more recipes. After all, *Domestic Cookery* by Mrs Rundell, without any further actions or complaints by its author, would keep the publisher afloat for many decades to come.

In August 1828, Edinburgh publisher Robert Cadell was in discussion with Basil Hall regarding publication of *Travels in North America in the Years 1827 and 1828*, based on Hall's journals written in the United States and Canada.[27] At the same time there were frequent asides about Mrs Dalgairns and her cookbook. A few days later, on 7 August 1828, to be precise, Cadell wrote to Basil Hall enclosing a publication agreement to be passed on to Mrs Dalgairns in Dundee. Was this identical to the agreement signed the year before with John Murray? It reads: "We most cheerfully agree to take all the risks of One Thousand copies of Mrs. Dalgearns [*sic*] Cookery Book and pay one half of the gain of said 1000 books 12 mos from publication or when we have only 100 or 50 unsold as you may decide – we also agree to make Mrs. Dalgearns a distinct offer for all future editions prior to going to proofs; you deciding on the number to the printer – £50 to a/c and at Mrs. Dalgearns service whenever she likes. &c &c &c. The Book to go to press immediately

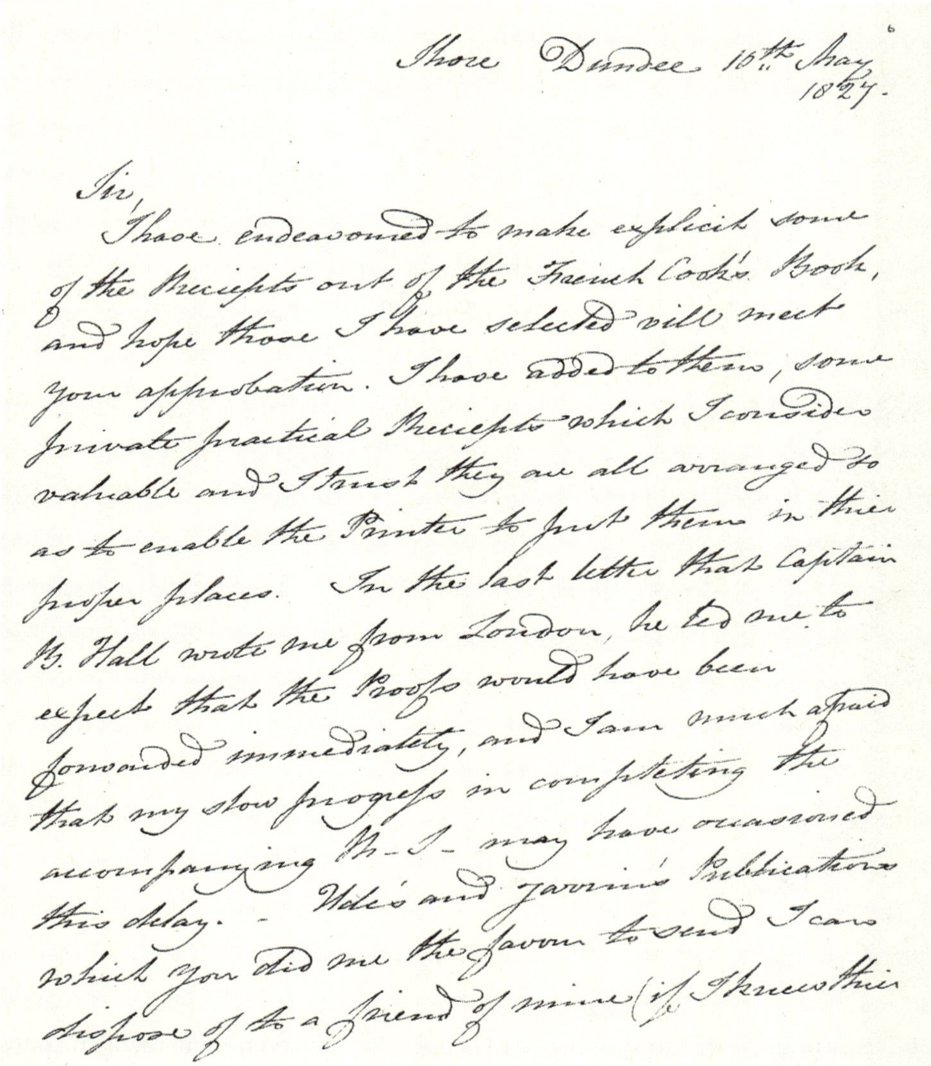

Shore Dundee 10th May 1827.

Sir,

I have endeavoured to make explicit some of the Receipts out of the French Cook's Book, and hope those I have selected will meet your approbation. I have added to them, some private practical Receipts which I consider valuable and I trust they are all arranged so as to enable the Printer to put them in their proper places. In the last letter that Captain B. Hall wrote me from London, he led me to expect that the Proofs would have been forwarded immediately, and I am much afraid that my slow progress in completing the accompanying M.S. may have occasioned this delay. – Ude's and Jarrin's Publications which you did me the favour to send I can dispose of to a friend of mine (if I knew this

Fig. 8 Mrs Dalgairns writing from her home on Shore Terrace, Dundee, to the eminent publisher John Murray on 10 May 1827, beginning: "I have endeavoured to make explicit some of the Receipts out of the French Cook's Book, and hope those I have selected will meet your approbation. I have added to them, some private practical Receipts which I consider valuable and I trust they are all arranged so as to enable the Printer to put them in their proper places." Letter from Mrs Dalgairns to John Murray, 10 May 1827, National Library of Scotland, Archive of John Murray, publishers, MS 40404, acc.12604/1504.

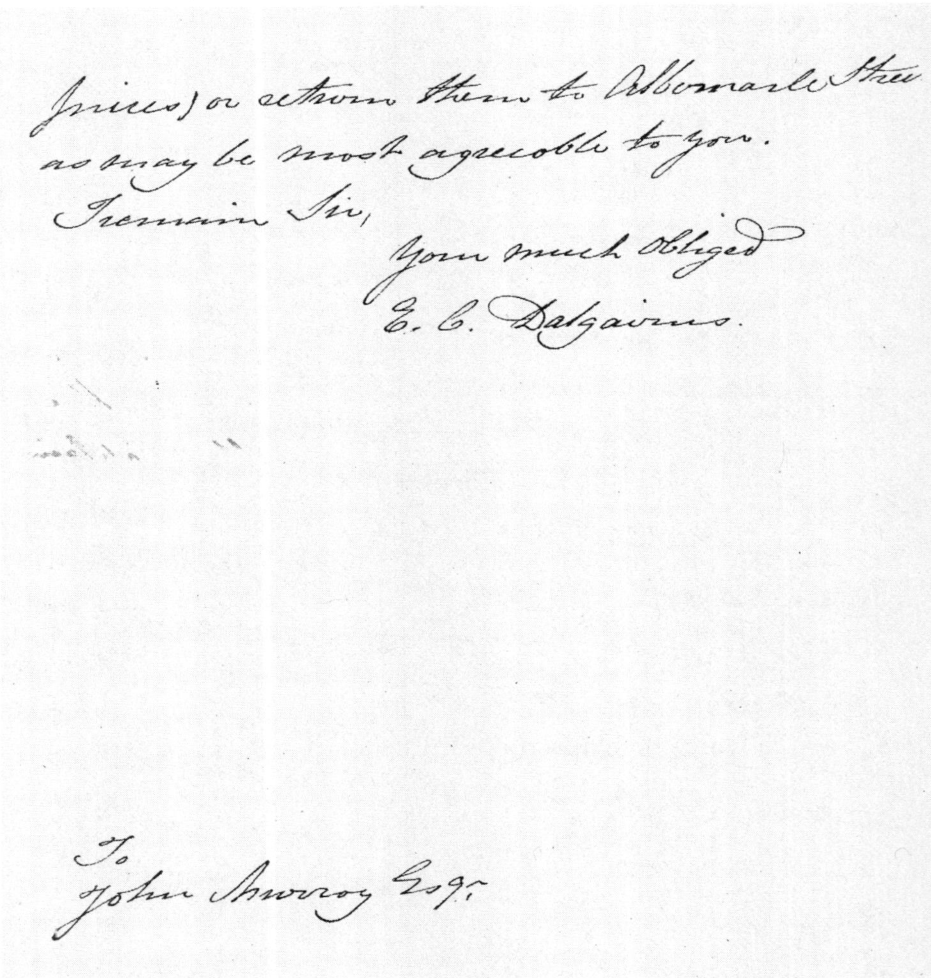

prices) or return them to Albemarle Street
as may be most agreeable to you.
I remain Sir,
Your much Obliged
E. C. Dalgairns.

To
John Murray Esq.

and to be published as soon as ready. RC." Robert Cadell rejoiced in being the publisher of the celebrated author, Sir Walter Scott, whose Waverley Novels were issued with frequency and much fanfare from Cadell's printer Ballantyne and Company. By then he was also Basil Hall's publisher and instinctively knew that promising cookbooks were "a sure thing."[28]

Hall's response arrived immediately, striving to assure Cadell: "[I am] glad to see you so hearty about Mrs. Dalgairns' Book, & I can only assure you that you cannot oblige me more than by putting your shoulders to the wheel on its behalf." He continues with suggestions for its publication, such as its size and an index, "a copious Index, however, with the same article inserted under half a dozen differed heads, if possible, in order to prevent the possibility of disappointment in the search." The project, it seems, was well under way, even though the publisher had not yet seen the author's name in writing and had misspelled it. From then on Hall corresponded with Cadell weekly, and sometimes daily, on some aspect of the work from his residence in Idol Lane, London; from his father's house at Dunglass; and his own house at Craigie, Dundee. As to the title of the cookbook, he suggests "Practical Cookery by Mrs. Dalgairns" – "simple – sufficiently comprehensive – easily remembered – & contains all that is true & in point." Five days later Hall sent Cadell his final decision for the title: "You know there is the Practice of Medicine, The Practice of Seamanship & other things & 'what for no' – The Practice of Cookery?" It seems that Hall was unaware of Mrs Frazer's *The Practice of Cookery*, published in Edinburgh, with numerous editions coming out from 1791 into the early 1800s.

Earlier cookbooks normally presented a chapter on medicine and medical treatments. From 1769 up to the last edition in 1834, Elizabeth Raffald had been an exception to the rule, stating in her preface to *The Experienced English Housekeeper*: "neither have I meddled with physical receipts, leaving them to the physician's superior judgement, whose proper province they are." Hall, too, believed that there was little reason for keeping such a chapter, although Mrs Dalgairns had already composed one. "Surely nothing can be worse than encouraging people to do without medical advice in such a country as this … Possibly a few of the most commonplace antidotes to the most ordinary poisons might be useful – but certainly, to my taste, a chapter on medicine is a disagreeable appendage to a cookery Book." Nonetheless, a few medical prescriptions were sneaked into two pages of the "Miscellany," with treatments for stomach ache, ear-ache, burns, and bleeding.

By November 1828, Basil Hall is poised to write the new preface, and proofs of parts of the book are ready for his inspection. Questions about whether to use stereotype rather than old-fashioned type-setting arise. These are early days for stereotyping versus typecasting. A cheaper printing process, stereotyping involves creating a metal plate or mould that assumes no changes. Cadell opted for typesetting, although for later editions stereotyping was acceptable, easily enabling the addition of further recipes to *The Practice of Cookery*. Cadell had already noted in his London diary: "Capt. Hall advocates stereotype – advised against this for a Cookery Book in a first attempt, to stereotype this the first 100 would cost £196."[29]

One senses that Mrs Dalgairns herself was at a loss in the world of book publication. Hall advises Cadell that he should see her and persuade her to stay in Edinburgh "to correct one or two sheets ... that she may learn the Printer's marks & other points of information." In fact, she did spend nearly a week at the end of August 1828 in Edinburgh, "engaged in revising her ms." On 1 September, Mr Cadell received Mrs Dalgairns in his offices in St Andrew Square, Edinburgh, and the next day she and her husband dined with Cadell.

By late August, Robert Cadell had shared his own ideas with Basil Hall about how the cookbook should be presented, and yet he is still eager for Hall's opinions. He is unconcerned about the length of the book, advocating not for 12mo (about 5.5 x 7.5 inches) but rather a kind of foolscap that could amount to 6 ¾ x 4 ¼ inches or more. Ultimately, 12mo prevails. It seems that Mrs Dalgairns had given him a full list of contents, which was "quite unnecessary." "I hear many ladies say that they never look at them. They invariably refer to the Index." It makes perfect sense to Cadell that the index should follow the preface and come "before the body of the Book, not after." He goes on about the arrangement of the chapters. A final decision about the title with numerous variations is swirling through his head.

At the end of August, Cadell assures Basil Hall that Mrs Dalgairns "is greatly delighted that her book is at last seriously going to Press. Rely on it, no whim wham shall now lose it. I have no doubt of the book being a good one – no unusual exertion will be required to bring it into notice." Given that Cadell was the publisher of William Kitchiner's *The Cook's Oracle*, for which each new edition since the first in 1817 had been received with exuberant praise in Britain and North America, these expectations for *The Practice of Cookery* were high indeed. "Few read cookery books end on. It is all reference, more especially when the Book acquires an established reputation." The few he was thinking about may have been reviewers for newspapers and magazines. Cadell was already thinking about further editions, beyond a second edition in six months' time, and the risks involved. But the price, 7s 6d, would remain the same, with Mrs Dalgairns receiving one shilling per book.

By January 1829, Hall is working on a puff and asks Cadell about its length: "Well known established works are improved by puffs." Impatient as ever, he asks Cadell to "send me Mrs. Dalgairns' Preface when it is set up – with any remarks of your own - & the sooner the better." He returns the preface to Cadell "much doctored & cut down." Hall has tried his hand at an extension of the wording of the title, with "expressly adapted to the business of every day life" to be added to "The Practice of Cookery."

Inside his letter he includes "an additional receipt for which there is room at page 444. Don't tell Mrs. Dalgairns any thing about it – till she sees it." Sure enough, a recipe for "Captain Hall's Sandwiches for Travellers" does appear in chapter 19, the "Miscellany," on page 444 of the first edition. It seems that Cadell pressed him to explain the sandwich recipe and soon after received instructions: "You will discover by trial – or by reflecting a little that if the loaf be not quite circular, the two slices of both buttered on the top &, then turned down face to face, would not fit. You must therefore butter one on the top & the other on the under side, to make them fit." In the "Poultry" chapter there is already a sandwich recipe, calling for fowl and ham, plus a little mustard and salt. The word "sandwich" is often sourced today to the 4th earl of Sandwich in the late 1700s, but by the early 1800s the sandwich had become a reasonably familiar article of food.

On 13 January 1829, Cadell forwarded proofs of Hall's puff for the cookbook.[30] When not having to shepherd Sir Walter Scott's latest novel through to publication, and Basil Hall's travels in North America, Cadell had focused his attention on creating proofs for the cookbook, ensuring that advertisements were placed in the London newspapers. By late April he had despatched multiple copies of *The Practice of Cookery* to Hall and six copies to the author herself.

A Cookbook Manuscript Springs to Life

It was while Catherine Dalgairns was living in London from about 1811 to 1822 that much of the cookbook we know today gradually came together, but it is frustrating that we know very little about her life in that city. Her husband Peter conducted his ship insurance business in partnership with Edward Winslow at 36 St Mary-at-Hill in the Parish of Billingsgate, just five streets east of London Bridge. Descended from the Puritans who founded Plymouth, Massachusetts, in 1776, Winslow's father, Loyalist judge Edward Winslow fled first to Halifax and then to the newly established Province of New Brunswick. Edward Winslow had been a close friend of Catherine's father Phillips Callbeck, which is confirmed by correspondence between the two men.[31] The Dalgairns couple lived briefly in Liverpool, where Peter, merchant, and his partner Murdock Tolme suffered their first British bankruptcy in 1811.[32] After moving to London, Peter's bouts of bankruptcy continued. It must be said that the Napoleonic Wars raging at the time wreaked damage on many industries, including insurance. Peter Dalgairns and Edward Winslow split their ship insurance partnership of six years amidst bankruptcy proceedings in 1818.[33] In May of 1819, Edward Winslow was drowned in the wreck of his brig *William and Matthew* in the seas near Shelburne, Nova Scotia. Edward's sad demise caused much tumult in New Brunswick, where the prominent Winslow family was expecting one of its sons to return to the province in the spring of that year.

By 1822 Peter Dalgairns, now a wine and brandy merchant, is listed at 5, Martin's lane, Cannon Street, a little to the west of London Bridge.[34] It is likely that the building served as both the home and wine store of Peter and Catherine. In any case, living in this area Catherine would have had easy access to markets and the docks, where ships arrived from other parts of Europe and East India bearing exotic foods and spices.

The bankruptcies occurred with increasing regularity after the Dalgairns family moved to Dundee, Scotland. Peter had grown up just north of Dundee in Ingliston in Forfarshire, where the family home, Ingliston House, still stands. In Dundee, Catherine and Peter lived above his wine and liquor shop on Shore, or Shore Terrace, on the edge of the city harbour, where Peter Dalgairns offered a generous stock of alcoholic beverages listed in contemporary advertisements. By the early 1840s he was also selling vegetable seeds. The particular legal procedures in Scotland, termed "Sequestrations," involved handing over all of one's assets to creditors, but the consequences of fault were less severe than those of traditional bankruptcies. For Peter these judgements occurred in 1824, 1827, 1833, and 1835.[35]

Catherine's mother Ann was living (briefly?) in London, England, in 1804 but made a final departure from Prince Edward Island for London in 1817, domiciled at 86 Great Portland Street. In both years she wrote letters to the Earl of Liverpool with increasing urgency, asserting that her husband, Phillips Callbeck, as attorney general of the Island of St John, was owed an arrears in payment of his salary. Alas, her claim was rejected on the grounds that the money was owed to Mr Desbrisay, and not to Philip (*sic*) Callbeck.[36] On the surface it seems that Ann Callbeck did not have access to the financial assets that would have been expected by one of her class. We know she moved on to Bath, where she died on 15 October 1826.[37] But surely mother and daughter shared recipes from the old days in Boston and PEI when both were living in London. We are made aware of her mother's interest in cooking by means of a letter she wrote in Charlottetown on 29 September 1800 to Mrs John Macdonald of Tracadie, also on the Island. She talks about the cheapness and abundance of meat in Halifax, she also comments that "rye flour which makes excellent Brown Bread is selling at 45/ per Barrel."[38] Her daughter's Brown Bread calls for a mixture of wheat, barley, and rye flour.

To gain some sense of what life was like for an economically insecure but socially well connected family in London at that time I am indebted to the extraordinarily

Fig. 9 Martin's Lane, Cannon Street, in 1829, where Peter and Catherine Dalgairns had a home in the early 1820s, close to the end of their years in London. Plate and description of "Church of St. Martin Orgar, Martin's Lane, Cannon Street," from *London and the Environs in the Nineteenth Century Illustrated by a Series of Views from original drawings by Thomas H. Shepherd* (London: Bracken Books, 1983 [Reprint of London: Jones & Co., 1829, 108]).

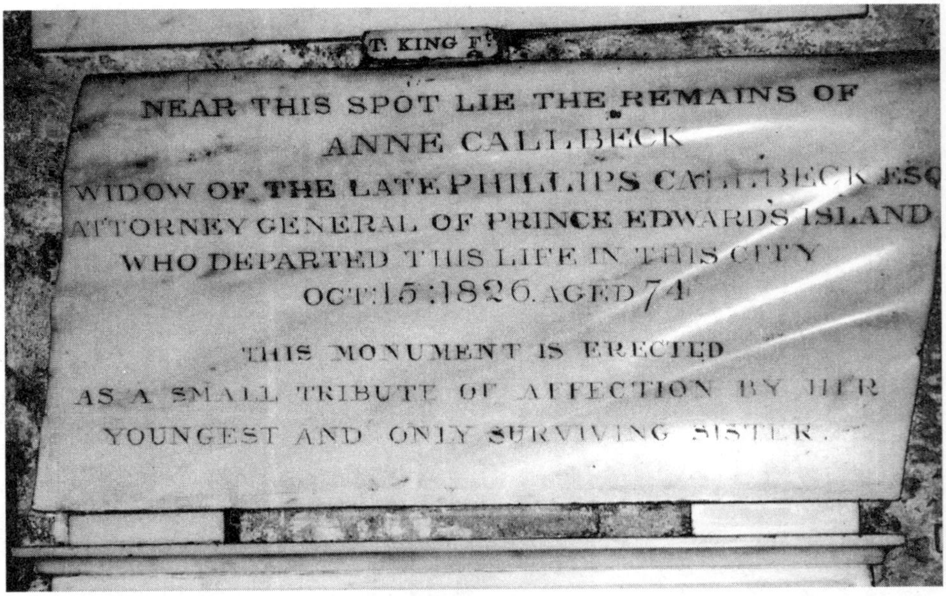

Fig. 10 Plaque on south side, second bay west of transept, of Bath Abbey, Bath, Somerset: "Near this spot lie the remains of Anne Callbeck widow of the late Phillips Callbeck, Esq. Attorney-General of Prince Edward Island who departed this life in this city Oct: 15: 1826. Aged 74. This monument is erected as a small tribute of affection by her youngest and only surviving sister" [Christian Lewis]. Photograph by Pamela Dodds.

detailed diary (1809–1832) of a property-owning working man named William Feltuss, who lived on the south side of the Thames, a mile from London Bridge. It is of considerable interest to learn that the Feltuss property included a kitchen garden, where the family grew fruits, vegetables, and herbs, raised pigs and hens, and bred rabbits. Mr Feltuss's diary confirms my suspicion that the Dalgairns family in London, and in Dundee, may well have established such a kitchen garden for growing vegetables and raising livestock and poultry.[39] If Catherine and Peter Dalgairns had kept diaries in 1815 and 1816 they undoubtedly would have recorded the dire outcomes of the harvest failures in "the year without summer," when Mount Tambora in the Dutch East Indies blew its top. The resulting violent volcanic eruption deeply affected agriculture all over the world, including in Europe and North America.

Fig. 11 "Entrance to the Port of Dundee," from *Finden's Views of the Ports, Harbours, Watering Places & Coastal Scenery of Great Britain* (London: George Virtue, 1842). Drawn by W.H. Bartlett and engraved by E. Benjamin. Shore Terrace can be seen on the right, overlooking the harbour.

Advertising *The Practice of Cookery* throughout the Empire

On 9 April 1829, Robert Cadell recorded in his diary: "Busy all day walking out and entering Advertisement of the Practice of Cookery also the Waverley Novels for the London newspapers."[40] It has to be said that *The Practice of Cookery* was a bit of an afterthought to Sir Walter Scott's Waverly Novels, which over the years were individually greeted by a devoted following in Britain and across the ocean in North America. Thus a series of newspaper advertisements cited Scott's latest title along with the cookbook and Captain Basil Hall's *Travels in North America* in Dublin, London, and Edinburgh and other cities.[41]

That twenty-five copies of *The Practice of Cookery* were forwarded to Paris booksellers Messrs Galignani makes perfect sense. Galignani had enjoyed an international reputation as both a publisher and seller of English-language books. Beginning with the fall of Napoleon's empire in 1815, the English returned to Paris in force, and by 1831 both the upper class and worker English populations had doubled in size.[42] In fact, the cookbook could be purchased throughout the English-speaking world. Advertisements in Australian newspapers were posted into the 1860s, after the date of the final sixteenth edition, and in New Zealand into the 1870s.[43] The copy of the 1845 edition now owned by the University of Guelph Library is inscribed by Mrs Maclean, the wife of a surgeon who was attached to the Hyderabad Residency in India.[44]

At this time in the Canadas English-speakers tended to favour American cookbooks, which dealt more usefully with products and foods common in North America, but booksellers also advertised much-admired British titles, which undoubtedly appealed to recent immigrants from the British Isles.[45] Advertisements for *The Practice of Cookery* appear to have been confined to Montreal and Quebec City.[46] Armour and Ramsay of Montreal, in its *Catalogue of Books* for 1836, lists "The Practice of Cookery. By Mrs. Dalgairns. 1 vol.," along with cookbooks by the Scottish Megs Dods, English authors William Kitchiner and Mary Holland, plus the Americans Eliza Leslie and Lydia Child. There can be little doubt that our cookbook was obtainable from at least one of the admirable York (Toronto) bookstores praised by Ontario pioneer and author Catharine Parr Traill. In her *The Backwoods of Canada* (1835), Traill presents readers with an anecdote, declaring that the roads were so bad that when she sends to the nearby town for her groceries, and the team of horses brings them up, she finds "rice, sugar, currants, pepper and mustard all jumbled into one mess." She goes on: "I think the recipe would cut quite a figure in Mrs. Dalgairns' Practice of Cookery under the original title of a 'bush pudding.'"[47] It's good to know that back then many readers of *The Backwoods of Canada,* whether in England or Canada, would have been familiar with, and may even have owned, *The Practice of Cookery.*

The publisher John Neilson of Quebec City, in his correspondence with Carey of Philadelphia, asked whether American editions of British books could be purchased more cheaply than copies from Britain, and the reply was "yes!"[48] Copyright was largely ignored in those days. In the early 1830s, residents of British North America would have found far less expensive American editions for sale in bookstores rather than pricier British productions, but that the 1830 Boston/New York edition of the cookbook was printed on cheaper paper is a factor to be taken into account.

"The very best compilation"

On 10 April 1829, with an eye to attracting the attention of the most widely read magazines, Robert Cadell wrote to his London co-publishers Messrs Simpkin and Marshall: "We enclose also sundry copies for reviews, etc. and 12 extra for you to give to such others as you think will do the book good, but you may increase this quantity if you think fit – push this book in all ways. Our friend Capt Hall takes

> Early in June will be published, in 3 vols. post octavo with a coloured Map,
>
> TRAVELS IN NORTH AMERICA in 1827 and 1828. By Captain Basil Hall, R.N. Printing for Cadell and Co., Edinburgh; and Simpkin and Marshall, London.
>
> Of whom may be had-
>
> 1. Anne of Gelerstein. By the Author of Waverley. 3 vols., price of £1 11s. 6d. (Just published.)
> 2. St. Valentine's Day; or, the Fair Maid of Perth. By the author of Waverley, &c. 3 vols. £1 11s. 6d. 2d edition.
> 3. Chronicles of the Canongate. By the author of Waverley. First series, 2 vols., £1 1s. Second edition. Contents:-Tale 1. The Highland Widow. -2. The Two Drovers. -3 The Surgeon's Daughter.
> 4. Tale of a Grandfather; being Stories from the History of Scotland. By Sir Walter Scott, Bart. First Series. A new Edition. 3 vols. 19s.6d.
> 5. The Practice of Cookery, adapted to the Business of Every-day Life. By Mrs. Dalgairns. In one thick vol., price 7s.6d. "This is by far the most complete and truly practical work which has yet appeared upon this subject. Mrs. Dalgairns is not one of those imaginative and flowery preceptors who think it necessary to call in the aid of fiction and fine writing to give an interest to the engrossing and important matters of which she treats – she proceeds to business at once. Her book will be found an infallible Cook's Companion, and a treasure of great price to the mistress of a family. It is stuffed choke-full of the most important gastronomical information. It contains 1,434 receipts, 95 of which are for soups, 115 for fish, 70 for beef, 60 for veal, 31 for pork, 41 for poultry, 14 for curries, 104 for gravies, sauces, &c., 68 for vegetables, 263 for puddings, pies, and tarts, 134 for creams, custards, &c., 100 for cakes, &c., 82 for preserves, 61 for domestic wines, 15 for the dairy, and 88 miscellaneous. Then we have rewards, besides, on the poultry yard, brewing, the kitchen garden, bees, pigs, &c. With so many arguments in its favour, we cannot doubt that the "Practice of Cookery" will soon find its way into a wide and useful circulation." – Edinburgh Literary Journal, 18th April.

Fig. 12 Advertisement for the cookbook as it appeared in the *Times* (London), 29 May 1829, Gale Primary Sources, Times Digital Archive, 1785–2014.

The Practice of Cookery. By Mrs. Dalgairns. 1 vol.
Modern Domestic Cookery. By Elizabeth Hammond. 1 vol.
Two Hundred Receipts for French Cookery. By Miss Leslie. 1 vol.
The Cook's Oracle, containing Receipts for Plain Cookery. By Dr. Kitchiner. 1 vol.
The Frugal Housewife. By Mrs. Child. 1 vol.
The Grocer and Distiller's Useful Guide, containing many Important Receipts. 1 vol.

Fig. 13 *The Practice of Cookery* seen in the catalogue of books for sale by Armour and Ramsay of Montreal, 1836. *Catalogue of Books in the Various Departments of Science and General Literature, for Sale by Armour & Ramsay* (Montreal: *Montreal Gazette*, 1836), 26. www.canadiana.ca.

a great interest in it." Cadell's salesman's instincts produced the desired favourable results, undoubtedly surpassing his, and Mrs Dalgairns's, hopes. Previous to publication of the first edition, as noted above, advertisements were inserted in the leading English, Scottish, and Irish newspapers, and in magazines directed at women readers in England and North America. While the academic establishment today may find it bizarre, in the nineteenth century literary reviewers treated cookbooks as "gastronomical information" worthy of critical attention. A close association of cookery with literature was articulated by the much admired gourmand and cookbook author Eustache Ude, who, in referring to the "twin stars of literature and cookery," insisted that "the two must be considered as necessarily parallel." "Cookery is the highest of physical arts. And literature of metaphysical."[49]

Fortunately for Robert Cadell and Mrs Dalgairns, several Scottish and English newspapers, literary magazines together with representatives of the "ladies" press, took notice of this new title. Most male reviewers – and virtually all reviewers were male – admired the author's science, her authority, her practicality, her succinct directions, her avoidance of literary fripperies, and her lack of extravagance. James Ballantyne of the *Edinburgh Weekly Journal* began his review confessing a certain ennui with cookery books; but, having heard that the prolific travel writer Captain Basil Hall had "good-naturedly" written the preface to Mrs Dalgairns's work, his curiosity had been piqued. "We have little doubt of this work taking the lead of all its companions, and maintaining its ascendancy after wards." Two other Scottish papers, the *Caledonian Mercury* and the *Scots Times*, went out of their way to bestow extravagant praise: "The Practice of Cookery is a book worthy of all acceptance, and we recommend it accordingly to every one who wishes to dine comfortably at a moderate cost" … "She is, and we mean it, *par excellence*, a *most sensible lady*. Her volume does not contain the poetry of cookery, like Kitchener's [*sic*] Oracle[,] nor does it sparkle with the literature of the culinary art, like the Manual of our friend of the Cleikum Inn [Meg Dods]; but it is more practical, more varied, and more suited to what we may call the practical readers of such works, than either of its predecessors. It is this character of utility which appears to us to constitute its value, and we have no doubt will prove its passport to extensive circulation."

The reader is advised in the *Spectator* (London) that "Mrs. Dalgairns' *Practice of Cookery* is a work on the old system. The course of improvement in these works has been immense." After looking back briefly on the old standards – Mrs Glasse of the mid- to late 1700s, Meg Dods, Mrs Rundell and William Kitchiner of the early 1800s – reviewer Charles Rintoul continues: "We think – we are not sure – that we shall put away Rundell and Kitchener [*sic*] for Mrs. Dalgairns. She is far more copious than they are, far more various, and to us more novel. It is not a gourmand's book neither does it pretend to be."[50]

With regard to novelty, it is useful to remember that eighteenth-century cookbook authors regularly borrowed from and even plagiarized their "renowned" predecessors, a custom that was generally accepted when the authors, or rather compilers, claimed to have selected the very best recipes. They didn't even try to pretend that they had tested them, while Mrs Dalgairns assiduously tested, altered, and, in her mind, improved upon recipes that were already widely known and part of the English-language culinary repertoire.

An enthusiastic reviewer in the *Edinburgh Literary Journal* began by applauding the author, writing: "This is by far the most complete, and truly practical work, which has yet appeared upon this subject … Mrs. Dalgairns is not one of those imaginative and flowery preceptors, who think it necessary to call in the aid of fiction and fine writing, to give an interest to the engrossing and important matters of which she treats." After a summary of the chapters and individual recipes in the cookbook, he concludes: "With so many arguments in its favour, we cannot doubt that the Practice of Cookery will soon find its way into a wide and useful circulation." The *Gentleman's Magazine* assured its readers that "The Practice of Cookery by Mrs. Dalgairns, is a truly practical and cheap system of Cookery… It is a valuable present for Cooks, or for young mistresses of families, where economy in domestic arrangements is necessary."

A reviewer in *La Belle Assemblée* (London) "begs leave to assure [Mrs Dalgairns] that, agreeably to his estimate of gastronomic science – especially with a view to economy as well as to epicurean indulgence – it is the very best compilation that he has ever had the pleasure of meeting with." Readers of *The Ladies' Museum* are told: "The wisest man must sometimes dine; and if he deserves a good dinner he will recommend to his housekeeper's notice Mrs. Dalgairns' "Practice of Cookery," the most practical and useful book on culinary science which we have met for some time." Under "Cookery" in an 1838 issue of Quebec City's the *Literary Transcript and General Intelligencer*, a writer embraces Mrs Dalgairns's declaration that she presents recipes not for new dishes but, rather, for how to make those dishes already established in public favour. "None but the most thankless *gourmands*, or the *gourmet*," he writes, "would sit down and weep for new worlds of luxury. Good cookery is too rarely understood and practiced to justify any such wishes." Reflecting a distinctive American perspective on the proper audience for such a cookbook, the *Ladies Magazine and Literary Gazette* of Boston was inclined to rate the recipes as not all economical. But "there is much in it which may be advantageous to housekeepers," while those looking for extravagance might consider Kitchiner's *The Cook's Oracle*.[51] In newspaper advertisements for future editions of *The Practice of Cookery*, Cadell inserted review extracts as a come-on to future sales.

In 1844, in a seventeen-page article titled "The Rise and Progress of Culinary Literature and Cookery," a writer for the *Foreign Quarterly Review* rated the ten top cookery books of his time. The majority had been published in Paris, but the 1829 edition of Mrs Dalgairns appears as number eight, ahead of Ude's *The French Cook* and Mrs Rundell's *A New System of Domestic Cookery*. "Mrs. Dalgairns," he wrote, "is one of the best of cookery books we know for persons of the upper class of life not overburthened with wealth. It ought to be an invaluable book to the middle classes. We have heard, and believe that Sir Walter Scott contributed largely to this work." (There is no evidence for this assertion.) The reviewer continues with one caveat, which is that the author "exhibits too palpable an addiction to Scotch dishes. This is a prevailing peccadillo – if not the heinous fault of all Picts, old or young, male or female."[52] We are again confronted by a false assumption, given that Catherine Dalgairns was not a Pict (i.e., a Scot) and that her cookbook had been largely compiled before she had moved to Scotland and at a time when she had no idea of when and where it would be published. While Robert Cadell would have rejoiced in this article, Mrs Dalgairns, alas, had died a month earlier and was unable to take pride in the compliments bestowed on *The Practice of Cookery*.

While Robert Cadell made a note in his diary of the death of Basil Hall in September 1844, there is no mention of Mrs Dalgairns's decease in March or in any entry later that year. It is difficult to imagine that, in spite of the admiration for *The Practice of Cookery* expressed in the *Foreign Quarterly Review*, Mrs Dalgairns would be so out of mind with her publisher. And Cadell would go on to publish three more editions of the cookbook, the first the very next year.

An American Edition of *The Practice of Cookery* in 1830

While there is no discussion of American rights in the surviving correspondence between Robert Cadell in Edinburgh and his co-publisher Simpkin and Marshall in London, nor anywhere in Cadell's letters, diaries, or accounts, it is likely the London publisher independently conveyed publication rights to Munroe and Francis in Boston. We owe a glimmer of a possible explanation to Captain Basil Hall, who cited an example of copyright evasion, or piracy, by American publishers in an article published in the *Prince Edward Register* for 6 October 1829. In "Printing in America" Hall was specifically addressing the complex fate of Sir Walter Scott's Waverley Novels, but it is useful to remember that Sir Walter was a client of Robert Cadell, one whose writings figured in making Cadell a rich man.[53] On the other hand, Charles Francis of Munroe and Francis was known to frown on the activities of American "pirate" publishers.[54] More than likely, Hall's exposé does not apply to *The Practice of Cookery*, which undoubtedly formed part of a package deal for a variety of Cadell/Simpkin and Marshall books of which Kitchiner's *The Cook's Oracle* was another beneficiary.

In early December 1829, the Boston and New York publishers suspected they had a winner when they began to advertise *The Practice of Cockery* by Mrs Dalgairns. For the Boston booksellers' auction sale of 29 June 1832, Munroe and Francis offered three cookbooks, including twenty-five copies of *The Practice of Cookery*, which were listed to retail at one dollar.[55]

Various changes from the British editions were designed to ensure the cookbook would appeal to American readers, but there was no mention of this either on the title page or in advertisements as there had been for British predecessors Mrs Glasse, Susannah Carter, Mrs Rundell, and William Kitchiner. The publishers' confidence is apparent in what must have been a costly six-inch advertisement in the *Boston Courier*, with the preface reproduced in full. However, the tone of the preface would have inadvertently appealed to American cooks by its

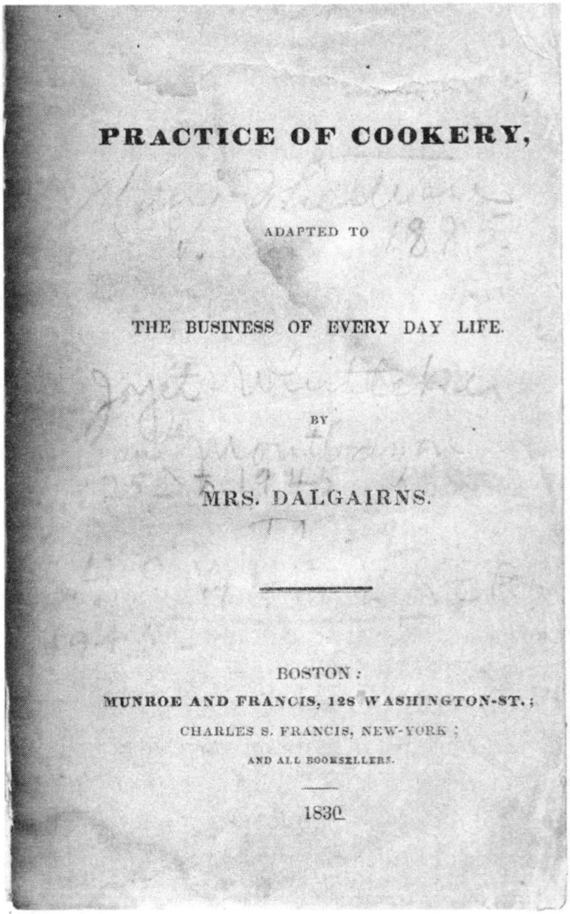
PRACTICE OF COOKERY,

ADAPTED TO

THE BUSINESS OF EVERY DAY LIFE.

BY

MRS. DALGAIRNS.

BOSTON:
MUNROE AND FRANCIS, 128 WASHINGTON-ST.;
CHARLES S. FRANCIS, NEW-YORK;
AND ALL BOOKSELLERS.

1830.

Fig. 14
Title page of the Boston and New York edition of 1830.

emphasis on practicality, clarity, and economy. Mrs Dalgairns's name would already have been familiar to readers of popular British periodicals sold by booksellers throughout New England, with their glowing reviews of her cookbook. Munroe and Francis hustled to make the cookbook available up and down the eastern seaboard. Notices appeared in newspapers from Maine to South Carolina.[56] At a price of one dollar, it was an attractive buy in comparison with other British and American cookbooks.

In addition to its practicality, users of the cookbook would have responded to specified ingredients associated with the New World and foods of New England origin. A few recipe names are prefixed by "American" or "North American," such as "American Snowballs" and "American Blancmange." Potted lobster and "Capillaire," a syrup based on maiden-hair fern, are "North American." But you also find the basic English cookbook repertoire that was still being followed in the United States.

The changes from the second and third Edinburgh/London editions are not immediately obvious, but someone in the New York office reviewed the book carefully, deleting here and adding there, substituting terminology, correcting the errata in the Edinburgh 1830 edition, and making index corrections. The index was moved from the front to the back. Right off it was decided to exclude the chapters on poultry, the dairy, kitchen garden, brewing, bees, and pigs, as well as appendices dealing with income and expenses and foods in season. By 1829, publisher Robert Cadell in Edinburgh had yet to be persuaded that stereotyping made sense, and for the American edition a longer and wider format was typeset, although printed on cheaper paper. A useful "Table of Weights and Measures" readily converts from British weights into American measures. A few recipe names were changed, for example, "Finnan or Aberdeen Haddocks" was renamed "Smoked Haddocks," and "Sally Luns or Bath Breakfast Cakes" was turned simply into "Breakfast Cakes." In the British edition each meat chapter begins with a list of names of the various cuts as they are known in England and in Scotland, but in the US edition "America" is linked with England to read "in England and America."

A writer with the *New York Evening Post* pounced on the final recipe in the collection, which was "Captain Basil Hall's Travelling Sandwiches." He undoubtedly had in mind Captain Basil Hall's visit to the United States the year before, which is described in full in Hall's published journal of the tour, which had raised the ire of Americans. In a convoluted way the New York writer suggests that, in the United States, Hall's reputation in the kitchen may far outlive the reputation of his books![57]

It was hardly a coincidence that just two years after *The Practice of Cookery* was issued by Munroe and Francis in a scant 750 copies, the Boston publisher brought out an encyclopaedic collection of recipes titled *The Cook's Own Book: Being a Complete Culinary Encyclopedia.* This is subtitled *By a Boston Housekeeper*, a reference to an anonymous author who subsequently was identified by the Library of Congress as Mrs N.K.M. Lee. Its full text can be searched and read on the website "Feeding America: The Historic American Cookbook Project" of Michigan State University. In their introduction to *The Cook's Own Book* the editors ascribe many of the recipes to Dr William Kitchiner, Richard Dolby, Mrs Rundell, and Mrs Raffald, all British cookbook authors. Mrs Lee herself admits to copying large sections on Roasting and Boiling to *The Cook's Oracle* by Kitchiner, who was one of Robert Cadell's bestselling authors. But there is no mention of Mrs Dalgairns, whose *The*

Fig. 15 An 1830s Staffordshire chamber pot depicting the likeness of Basil Hall uncovered in a pit near Rome, New York. In 1827–28, travelling with his wife and child, Hall was feted by Americans as a celebrated travel writer of high social status. And yet, throughout his *Travels in North America*, published in 1830, he frankly criticized American customs and culture. Chamber pot by Staffordshire Potteries, in the collections of Fort Stanwix National Monument in Rome, New York.

Practice of Cookery was sourced (plagiarized?) for well over one hundred recipes. The editors used the example of Mrs Lee's Indian Pudding as evidence that she could be original, and American, this time employing cornmeal as an ingredient. This was a grossly inaccurate claim. Mrs Lee's second recipe for Indian Pudding follows Mrs Dalgairns's "Indian Meal, or Maize, Pudding" word for word, even to the use of "Indian meal" as an ingredient rather than "cornmeal." Benefiting from at least a dozen printings from 1832 to 1865, *The Cook's Own Book* was, as noted in the entry for Mrs Lee in *Feeding America*, one of the most popular cookbooks of nineteenth-century America, thanks, in part, to the unacknowledged contributions of Mrs Dalgairns.[58]

Mrs Dalgairns strenuously maintained her own originality, assuring the readers of the second edition of 1829 that: "A considerable number of new Receipts has been added; but only such as the Author has had adequate means of asserting to be valuable – a principle which has been scrupulously adhered to throughout the volume."

Royalties, Sales, New Editions, and MORE Recipes

Signing himself "Rob Cadell," in a letter dated 1 May 1830, Cadell informed Mrs Dalgairns: "I now have the pleasure of handing you on the other side of this a receipt for £75, being the amount due to you for the second edition of your Practice of Cookery of which 1500 copies were printed. The Edition now at press will be ready in about a fortnight … I shall send you some copies of the Third Edition the moment it is ready." And, indeed, it is the third edition of 1830 that is presented here.

Mrs Dalgairns's four surviving letters to Robert Cadell date from 1833 to 1839, all of them addressing the transmission of royalties to her trust account and her heart-felt concern about sales: "I wish that our Book would circulate more readily than it seems to do – upon comparison with others of the same description it ought to be more valued" (16 August 1833). To the latter, Cadell replies: "By all means continue to improve your Book, but I do not think I shall have to call upon you for material for a New Edition till some time next year. I have 800 unsold of the last edition which will take nearly a year to exhaust." He continues with further unwelcome news, which is that he plans to reduce the price to five shillings from seven shillings and sixpence, but "in the present taste for cheap books I would indulge it and lead off at a low rate; the apparent gain will come down, but I have not a doubt of increasing the sale in this way, and thus really increasing the emolument." Cadell's decision appears justified, given that, even with 145 additional recipes, the fifth edition of 1835 reduced the complement of the first seventeen chapters from 419 pages to 361 pages, largely through the use of stereotyping.

Mrs Dalgairns had assigned not only her royalties to a trust fund managed by her brother-in-law, Andrew Dalgairns, but also the copyright of her cookbook.[59] Regarding copyright, as a publisher Robert Cadell was sustained by many successful book titles. Just two years before Mrs Dalgairns died, the copyright act of 1842, stemming from literary copyright reform in Victorian England, greatly changed

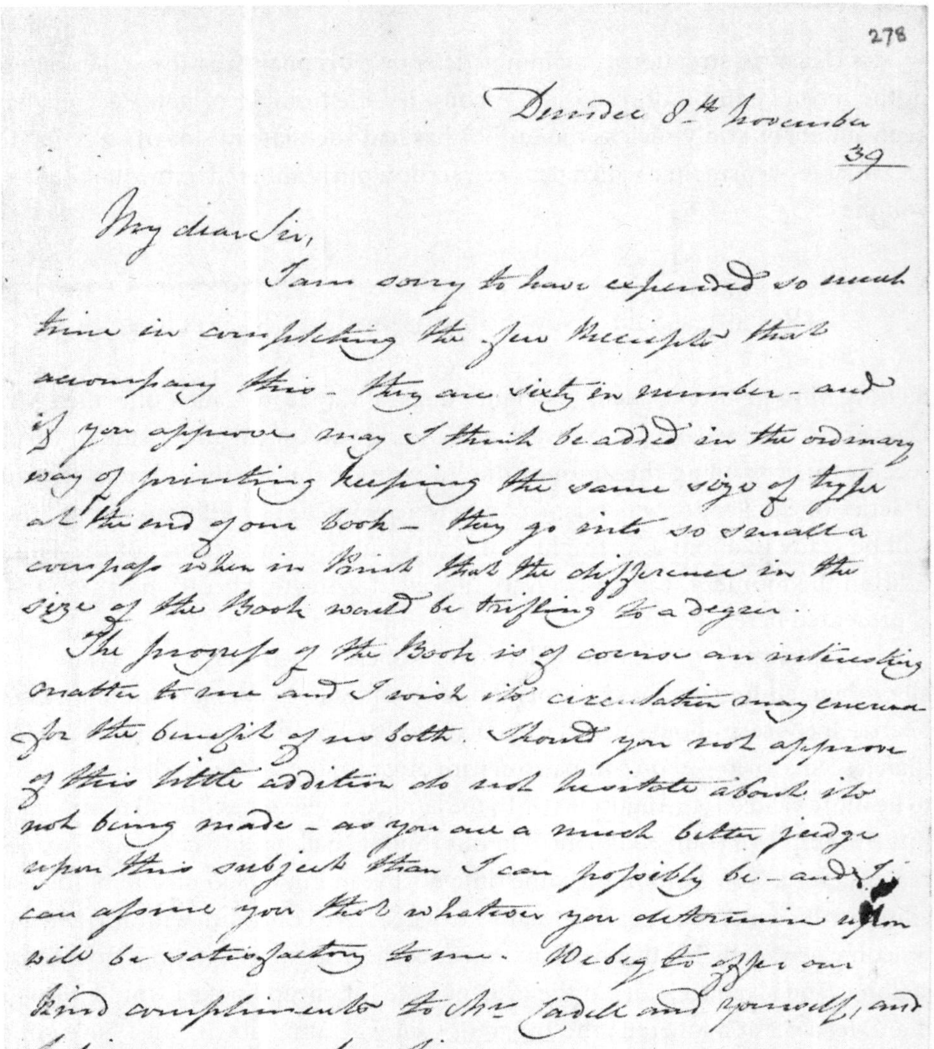
278

Dundee 8th November
39

My dear Sir,

I am sorry to have expended so much time in completing the few Receipts that accompany this - they are sixty in number - and if you approve may I think be added in the ordinary way of printing keeping the same size of type at the end of your book - they go into so small a compass when in Print that the difference in the size of the Book would be trifling to a degree.

The progress of the Book is of course an interesting matter to me and I wish its circulation may ensure for the benefit of us both. Should you not approve of this little addition do not hesitate about its not being made - as you are a much better judge upon this subject than I can possibly be - and I can assure you that whatever you determine upon will be satisfactory to me. We beg to offer our kind compliments to Mrs Cadell and yourself, and believe me my dear Sir

Yours with sincere regard
E. C. Dalgairns

Fig. 16 The final surviving letter from Mrs Dalgairns to Robert Cadell, 8 November 1839: "I am sorry to have expended so much time on completing the few receipts that accompany this – they are sixty in number – and if you approve may I think be added in the ordinary way of printing keeping the same size of type at the end of your book – they go into so small a compass when in Print that the difference in the size of the Book would be trifling to a degree." Mrs Dalgairns's letter to Robert Cadell of 8 November 1839, National Library of Scotland, correspondence and papers of the publisher Robert Cadell, MS. 21004, p. 278.

the copyright landscape. In March 1848, four years after her death, Cadell virtually shouted in a letter to an unknown recipient: "I am purchasable! that is my entire business – Stock, Series & Copyrights are in the market. I wish to retire." But a twelfth edition under his name did appear in 1850. Thereafter, other publishers, among them Houlston & Stoneman and R. Griffin of London, and finally Charles Griffin, followed through to what we assume is a final edition in 1861. This assumption is based on advertising eighteen years later (i.e., in 1889), when Charles Griffin and Co. of London issued *A Catalogue of Standard Works* in which is listed "Dalgairns (Mrs.): The Practice of Cookery ... the best book for Scotch dishes. About Fifty new Recipes have been added to the present Edition, but only such as the Author has had adequate means of ascertaining to be valuable. *Seventeenth Edition.* (In preparation.)" While a seventeenth edition was "in preparation," it clearly was never published.[60]

Posthumous Editions and Sales

Posthumous editions of successful cookbooks were de rigueur in the eighteenth and nineteenth centuries, given that their authors, such as Hannah Glasse, Mrs Rundell, Elizabeth Raffald, and Eliza Acton, would enrich their publishers well beyond their deaths. Even before Catherine Dalgairns died at age fifty-six on 4 March 1844, the evolution of at least seven posthumous editions of *The Practice of Cookery* involved two different publishers declaring on title pages questionable edition numbers, with their dates of publication moving ahead and then to earlier years than their stated edition numbers. Houlston & Stoneman of London co-published with Cadell in the 1840s. However, beginning in 1836, London publisher Richard Griffin, who had co-published the cookbook with Robert Cadell, took it up with even greater enthusiasm, going out on his own somewhat later to issue what we assume are the final five editions. Although he would not have been personally acquainted with Mrs Dalgairns, he must have recognized that he had the rights to an in-demand although not necessarily bestselling cookbook.

It is not possible to claim there were sixteen editions when there could have been as many as twenty, some of them undated. Griffin's final edition of 1861 was just one of the many cookbooks in which further editions were dropped after the appearance of Mrs Beeton's colourfully illustrated *Book of Household Management.* It was a revelation to most of us when we learned that Mrs Beeton's recipes had been plagiarized from the most popular cookbooks of the mid- to late nineteenth century, although Mrs Dalgairns appears not to have been one of the all-time best-selling cookbook author's sources.[61]

It was unexpected to find that the Schlesinger Library at Harvard University owns a copy of the 1850 twelfth edition of *The Practice of Cookery*, which is inscribed thus: "Mrs. B. Whishaw from her Affectionate God-father M. G. Calbeck, Dundee April 1851." Montague Calbeck is a brother of Catherine Callbeck Dalgairns, and from the 1851 Dundee census we are aware that Montague G. Calbeck, a wine merchant, origin "Prince Edward Island, British Subject," was a visitor to his brother-in-law Peter Dalgairns that year, eight years after his sister's death in that city.[62] In 1851 he was living in Bath, the city where his mother had died twenty-five years earlier.

"Valuable criticisms"

It is unusual for a cookbook author to both acknowledge criticisms of her recipes and positively confront them in future editions. In her "Preface to the third edition," Mrs Dalgairns addresses her readers: "Every Receipt in this work has been carefully revised for this Edition, in order that advantage might be taken of the numerous valuable criticisms by which it has been honoured in all parts of the Empire." We know of at least a couple of instances in which she addressed criticisms by making alterations to her text. One literary reviewer was inclined to think that there was too much acid in her recipe for Soda Water, addressing the issue with "If Mrs. Dalgairns will favour him with a note, previous to the publication of the next edition, the editor [of *La Belle Assemblée*] will be most happy to transmit to her the copy of a much superior recipe for the instantaneous production of soda water, with another for aerated ginger beer, &c."[63] A second recipe for Soda Water was inserted into the "Domestic Wines" chapter of the third edition.

On 30 August 1833, her publisher Robert Cadell wrote her to complain: "My ladies doubt your preserving recipes, they do not find them to answer, how would it do to give a few nice ones in their way."[64] It seems that some of her preserving recipes didn't work! Mrs Dalgairns had a come-back: "I regret to hear that your Lady friends find any inaccuracies in my Preserving receipts as I have thought a great deal of them particularly, and have always found them answer as I have many others who highly approve of them." Brushing off the implied criticism, she thanked Cadell effusively, taking this as an opportunity to press for the new edition when any improvements and additions thought to be necessary could be made.

On a more positive side, Basil Hall's wife Margaret, in an 1829 letter to her mother, noted that the cookbook is "selling remarkably well." She continues: "I recommend 'Lemon Pudding' & 'Rich Pudding' to your notice, with half the quantity of butter mentioned in the receipt, and 'Apple Pudding' without any butter at all. We have tried those three in this way and found them excellent."[65]

Was it in response to criticism, or did Mrs Dalgairns gradually appreciate that she had misspelled – or had used old spellings for some food words which she then updates in the third edition, such as "potatoe" to "potato," and "hamburg" to "hamburgh," and "harricot" to "harico." "Sauce piquant" has been correctly "frenched" to "sauce piquante," and "velouté sauce" to "veloutée sauce." Oddly, "tomata" as in "tomata catsup" and several other tomato recipes persists through the final edition in 1861. While the spelling "tomato" had been a common spelling for several decades, there were exceptions. Eliza Acton (just eleven years younger than Mrs Dalgairns), in her bestselling *Modern Cookery for Private Families*, first published in 1845 with further editions into the 1900s, calls for "tomatas" in numerous recipes. "Tomatas" is the spelling of choice by Anne Cobbett in her *The English Housekeeper*, published in numerous editions through the 1830s to 1860.

Diversity, Multicultural, Fusion – Whatever!

Mrs Dalgairns may have been deemed sensible, economical, practical, copious, and various, but reviewers of *The Practice of Cookery* seem not to have picked up on the wide-ranging geographical and ethnic sources of her recipes. The reviewer for the *Spectator* came close when he credited her with being "more novel," for, indeed, other cookbooks of the late eighteenth and mid-nineteenth centuries tended to narrowly reflect their respective authors' geographical circumstances while at the same time identifying ways of cooking associated with other European countries that had influenced British cookery. The Scottish food historian Marion McNeill tells us that "it is not surprising that in the earliest Scottish cookery-books we learn to dress cod in the Dutch way, lobsters in the Italian way, a nowt's tongue in the Polish way, and so forth, as well as numerous dishes *à la française*."[66] In *The Practice of Cookery* nine recipes are described as "Dutch" and five as "Italian." But at least ten are given Scottish names (e.g., Scotch Pancakes, Caledonian Cream,

Montrose Cakes, Aberdeen Crulla, and Scots Christmas Bun and Seed Cakes). Haggis was as common in northern England as in Scotland.

With few surviving issues of any Prince Edward Island newspapers from the late 1700s and early 1800s, it is difficult, but not impossible, to gain a sense of interactions among the various peoples on the Island and their daily lives. A detailed picture of food resources available to the Callbeck family on PEI can be gleaned from John Stewart, a contemporary (1806) source who just two years before Catherine Callbeck's marriage published an account of the Island. Not only did PEI support a wide variety of fruits, including berries of all kinds, but also cherry and plum trees, and apple trees that had been planted by the earlier French settlers and were still bearing. Of fish and shellfish he writes: "Oysters are in great plenty." "Muscles" (i.e., mussels) could be found in large beds in harbours, and lobsters, then as now, were there to be harvested. Shrimps were "large and fine." Other common fish were cod, haddock, flounder, halibut, hake, sea perch, trout, smelt, herring, and skate. "Wheat, barley, oats, rye and pease are cultivated," and, in fact, barley and oats were being exported to the continent of Europe. Prince Edward Island, he claimed, was the "first country in North America for both." And the renowned PEI potatoes even then were "raised in great abundance." For the Islanders, Indian corn, or maize, was "a valuable grain."[67] When Mrs Dalgairns arrived in Scotland these fruits, fish, and oats and barley were staples of the Scottish diet. With little written or printed evidence, it is impossible to know whether the presence of the Mi'kmaq people, who had made the Island their headquarters, exerted an Indigenous influence on food choices and cooking.

At the beginning of the British regime in 1770, most French Acadians had been removed, with a few families returning to the Island in later years. However, by the late 1770s, the timber trade had gradually attracted a sizeable group of immigrants who began to arrive in droves from the Scottish Highlands and Western Isles, and then other parts of Scotland. When Mrs Dalgairns took up residence in Dundee and perhaps hastily added some Scottish recipes to her manuscript cookbook to satisfy a local audience, she would already have been aware of a noteworthy Scottish culinary heritage.

Mrs Dalgairns's mother, Ann Coffin, married Phillips Callbeck in 1772, undoubtedly bringing with her from Boston a mind full of New England ways of cooking, or she may even have brought handwritten family recipes. It was not until 1796 that the first American cookbook was published, although English cookbooks, with minor alterations suited to American foods and tastes, were for sale at booksellers in Boston. With only 150 families living on the Island in 1770, it is unlikely that the abundance extolled in Stewart's 1806 account could be found in the early years of the Callbeck marriage.

Were the various Irish dishes in the cookbook drawn from Catherine's Irish heritage through her father? A Stew, Puffs, Black Puddings, Rock and Seed Cake recipes in the cookbook are all preceded by "Irish."

Her Sources and the French Connection

We know about a few of the cookbooks Catherine consulted as sources both before and after new editions of her own cookbook would be issued. In 1833, Catherine wrote to Cadell asking him to send her copies of two cookbooks, "if these Books could be got second hand so much the better." The two are *Cookery and Confectionary* by John Conrad Cooke (1824) and *The Lady's Own Cookery* "by a Lady of distinction" (i.e., Lady Catherine Campbell Bury). The latter cookbook she assumed had been published the year before, or in early 1833. It is of interest that the three-hundred-page *The Lady's Own Cookery Book and New Dinner-Table Directory* was published anonymously by H. Colburn of London in February 1832, except that high society knew that Lady Bury hid behind numerous titles in which the author was not named.[68]

While in Paris in October of 1829, Basil Hall writes to Cadell: "I picked up the other day in a stall in the Boulevards, the accompanying Book of Cookery – 'La Cuisiniere Bourgeoise' – at the Citizens Cookery & paid 2 francs for it, & send it to you, as I think it cannot fail to furnish some useful hints for the next Edition of Mrs. Dalgairns."[69] The names of some of the receipts in *La Cuisiniere Bourgeoise*, first published in 1746, crop up in *The Practice of Cookery*. For Mrs Dalgairns, reading French would not have presented difficulties. Given that no publicly funded schools existed in PEI at the time, presumably her early education, including instruction in the French language, was by tutor. The copy of *La Cuisinière Bourgeoise* might well have been welcomed as a source, although an old source, given that it had been published over fifty years earlier. Its directions for the cooking of fish, meats, eggs, and vegetables are basic, and the seasonings recommended are largely restricted to common herbs such as parsley and chervil, and a *bouquet garni*, plus onion and garlic.

As noted in figure 8, back on 10 May 1827, Mrs Dalgairns wrote to publisher John Murray about being inspired by the much-applauded *French Cook's Book* by Louis Eustache Ude (London, 1813), which Murray had obliged her by forwarding a copy. She had added yet more recipes, while making others more "explicit." She was already expecting proofs of her cookbook, but delving into Ude had convinced her that she needed even more recipes, a mindset that eventually killed her prospects of being published with John Murray. In comparing her cookbook with Ude's it is difficult not to conclude that her copy of the French cook's magnum opus would have been more than a little dog-eared, given that she clearly had leafed through it page by page, rewording and simplifying a substantial number of its recipes. Three weeks earlier, on 1 April, she had complained to Basil Hall that Ude had been a challenge: "I find the French man's receipts very up hill work and hope in what I am attempting I may succeed in enabling the Dishes to be more. I have just the French names, as a matter of necessity and have had to refer to the Sauces so often which <u>mess</u> up all the Dishes that I think they should succeed the made Dishes." It should be noted here that while Ude had been an experienced cook in France, his cookbook was compiled in London, England, where he was chef at a gentlemen's gambling and eating club. A close study of Ude is reflected in the ingredients and methods of preparing and cooking various dishes in several chapters – for example, Sauce d'Attelets; Another Cressy Soup, with a slice of ham added; Soft Roes of Herrings in Cases; Capons à la Turque; and Neck of Veal à la Barbarie. It should not be forgotten that, as Catherine Callbeck, Mrs Dalgairns may well have been exposed to French cookery traditions by the Acadians on Prince Edward Island. While deported in the early 1700s under British colonial rule, many returned, and for over four centuries the francophone Acadians have made the Maritime provinces their homeland.[70]

Looking through the index and pages of *The Practice of Cookery*, the reader may be struck by a surprising number of recipe titles suggesting a French style of cooking, such as à la Crême, or à la Turque, à la Hollandaise, à la Condé, à la Vénitienne, à la Reine, à la Richelieu, à la Ste. Menoult, and so forth.[71] Many recipes simply bear French names, such as Croquettes de Pommes, Fromage Cuit, Sauce d'Attelets, and Un Turban de Ris et de Pommes. To assume that recipes not bearing recognizable French names are not French is to ignore the influence of French culinary terminology on English, Scottish, and even Canadian and American recipe names, together with cookery methodology that can be traced back to medieval times. Long before Mrs Dalgairns, the authors of cookbooks in Britain were styling recipes as "of" or "on" the French fashion.

The noble houses and men's clubs of Britain often attracted French cooks to preside over their kitchens, with slavish attention and flamboyance, often hallmarks of what would be known as the French style of cooking. In her "To the

Reader" in her *The Art of Cookery* Hannah Glasse poured scorn on this practice and on French cookery itself: "So much is the blind Folly of this Age, that they would rather be impos'd on by a *French* Booby, than give Encouragement to a good *English* Cook!"[72] Many of the most important French cookbooks of the time were immediately translated for a more than willing English-speaking audience. In the second edition of Mistress Margaret Dods's *The Cook and Housewife's Manual* of 1827, the Scottish author, otherwise known as Christian Isobel Johnstone, advises readers that she has added a new feature – that is, "A Compendium of French Cookery." In 1844, Thomas Webster devoted considerable space to a comparison of French and English cooking, observing that "French dishes have always had a decided advantage over the English in appearance; they are made to please the eye as well as the taste."[73] Those who trace the evolution of British recipes in early published cookbooks for their ingredients as well as the style of cooking are able to follow what are sometimes small changes up to the nineteenth century. Food terms that today we assume are English have simply been "englished" (or "scottished") from French terms, such as "tourtes" into "tart,""hochepot" into "hotch potch," "mouton" into "mutton,""porc" into "pork," and "ragoust" into "ragout." A "gigot" in both French and English is a leg of mutton.

Often these recipes made their first appearance not in France or in any other part of Europe but, rather, in Arabic countries, where the copious use of spices provides a clue as to origin. Even "blancmange" is an Arab chicken-based sweetened dish. In England it soon became meatless, perfumed with rosewater. By the early nineteenth century an American version of blancmange thickened with arrowroot from the West Indies, and then cornmeal, gained popularity across the Atlantic. In *The Practice of Cookery* we are offered American Blancmange, thickened with arrowroot, flavoured with laurel water, cinnamon, and lemon, and turned out of a mould.

In Scotland the "Auld Alliance," which began with Mary of Guise, second wife of James V (1538), is often lauded as the time when French cooking merged with Scottish traditions. In any case, a Scottish style of cookery was established as distinctive from English cookery, although such distinctions over time have gradually mingled. The "Highland Lady," Elizabeth Grant of Rothiemurchus, had her own disapproving views on the Scottish-French connection in the early 1800s: "in a real old fashioned Scotch house, where no dish was attempted that was not national, the various abominations served up in corner dishes under French names were merely libels upon housekeeping."[74]

The menus for special dinners in Canada and in the United States in much of the nineteenth century indicate a predilection for French names for various dishes. In Canada, British expats regularly staged elaborate banquets in honour of their patron saints' special days. Without actually giving us menus, going back to the late 1700s, the newspapers of the time provide sketchy details. In this context, one mid-nineteenth-century Toronto caterer stands out: a free African American man named Beverly Randolph Snow. At his Epicurean Recess he sold exotic foodstuffs, but Snow also catered banquets on a sumptuous scale rarely witnessed by that city. One of these was a Masonic Ball with over seven hundred guests, staged by the St Andrew's Lodge on 16 November 1848. Accompanied by a full range of French wines the menu provides glimpses of multiple courses and, as was common at the time, dishes bearing French names. Among those are Croquettes, Charlotte Russe, and Blanc Mange, plus further familiar dishes, such as Mock Turtle Soup, that could have come straight out of *The Practice of Cookery*.[75] In New York in the 1830s, francophilia reigned in high-end restaurants, with French menus, French dishes, French ingredients, and the French style of service resulting in the best possible dining experience.[76]

On 29 January 1830, Robert Cadell noted in his diary that he had sent Mrs Dalgairns a "French Cookery book." Could this have been yet another copy of Ude, or *The French Family Cook* of 1793, the English translation of Menon's *La Cuisinière bourgeoise* given to Mrs Dalgairns by Basil Hall?[77] Or even *The Art of French Cookery* by Antoine Beauvilliers, with at least three English-language editions from a London publisher in the 1820s? A substantial number of recipes included in each subsequent edition of Mrs Dalgairns's cookbook reveal the extent to which she pushed her publisher Robert Cadell to include more recipes. The first edition of 1829 offers 1,434 recipes. For the 1830 edition, forty-eight have been added for a total of 1,482 but without further French recipes. By 1835 the number has risen to 1,597. Posthumous editions add forty more in a third appendix.

Curries and All Things Spicy

That a whole chapter – albeit a short one – is devoted to Curries is unusual in a British cookbook of the early 1800s. The first of many Anglo-Indian cookbooks, Robert Riddell's *Indian Domestic Economy and Receipt Book* of 1849 was published in Madras two decades later. It would be a mistake to assume that all of Mrs Dalgairns's curries and highly spiced Indian dishes are confined to that chapter.

In almost all sections, except those devoted to Creams and Custards, can be found recipes for foods from South-East Asia, albeit anglicized, such as Mullagatawny Soups in the Soups chapter; Bradu Fagadu (lobster, spinach, and curry powder) and Indian Fagadu (spinach, lobster or shrimps, onion and spices) in the Fish chapter; Kebabbed Veal, Cutcharee, and Pillau under Veal; Coratch (garlic, cayenne, Indian soy, walnut catsup, cochineal, and vinegar) under Gravies and Sauces; Indian Pancake (eggs, milk, rice, sugar, and cinnamon) in Puddings, Pies and Tarts; Indian Gingerbread under Cakes and Biscuits (ginger, cloves, and cinnamon); and Indian Pickle (multiple vegetables and garlic) in Pickles. A total of twenty-one spices are called for in the cookbook. That over forty recipes call for garlic may come as a surprise, even a shock, given that, in the early 1800s, garlic was treated as a herb, occupying a prominent place in the medicine cupboard.

Like so many of her countrypeople in the British Isles, Mrs Dalgairns employed spices as the ideal solution to transforming salted, smoked, pickled, and dried foods such as cod and herring, and various meats, into dishes fit for a gentleman's table, especially during the winter. The practice of adding spices to overcome rancid tastes and smells was centuries old. As we know from a ledger kept by Bedeque, PEI, merchant and store-keeper William Schurman, various spices, such as cinnamon, nutmeg, pepper, ginger, and allspice were being sold in 1795, clearly seen as luxuries for which Schurman commanded high prices.[78]

Indeed, an escalating interest in anglicized Indian foods throughout the British domination of India, beginning with the East India Company, and then the colonial administration, is reflected in many British cookbooks. The wives of British officers and government administrators posted to India returned to England and Scotland with an acquired taste for what would be labelled Anglo-Indian dishes, often made with commercial ready-mixed pastes and powders. We know that Mrs Dalgairns approved the substitution of curry paste, or at least "Cooke's Currie Paste," made by the London cookbook author and provisioner at 99, Hatton Garden, whose product she blatantly advertises in these pages.[79] The first known reference to curry, a word that derives from the Tamil *kari*, meaning sauce, dates to the end of the sixteenth century. Curry powders were concocted from an indefinite mixture of spices as required. Back in 1747, Hannah Glasse called for curry "The Indian way." In 1817, and again in 1831, William Kitchiner shares with readers his recipe for curry powder that had been selected by a friend at India House.[80] In Britain some curry powders would have been imported from India, and, as both Colleen Taylor Sen and Clarissa Dickson-Wright have stated, by the 1780s commercial ready-mixed curry powder was freely available. There was always the danger of adulteration or simply poor quality. Mrs Dalgairns offers readers three recipes for Currie Powder plus a further recipe in a later edition. She calls for such spices as coriander seed, ginger, black pepper, fenugreek seed, mustard seed, cumin seed, turmeric, and cayenne. Several of her recipes for spicy dishes call for currie (curry) powder, but there is always the assumption that it was freshly ground and hadn't languished on a kitchen shelf for months.

Spices had been introduced to Europe during the age of exploration and, initially, were used in medicines rather than in cookery. The spice trade blossomed in the early nineteenth century, with the British East India Company taking the initiative in ensuring the production and export of pepper, nutmeg, cloves, coriander, fennel, cassia, cardamom, turmeric, and chilis from Indonesia and Malaysia as well as India. It should be noted that Captain Basil Hall had visited and written about his adventures in those parts of the world. His published anecdotes of food and cookery – and even how he made a curry – undoubtedly were shared orally with his old friend Mrs Dalgairns.[81] Other possible sources for these recipes are three brothers-in-law whose careers were spent in India with the British East India Company beginning in the early 1800s, two in military service and one as a surgeon. Major Robert Dalgairns, at one time aide-de-camp to the governor general of India, was married to an English woman by whom he had several children. In his will, Colonel James Dalgairns left significant bequests to his two "reputed" daughters born in Java and Nagpore, respectively. It is tempting to ascribe some of the curry recipes in the cookbook to the two mothers – or even the men – living halfway around the world.[82]

By the late 1700s, vanilla had arrived in Britain, having been imported from the other side of the Atlantic. The product of the vanilla plant was soon prized as a food flavouring and perfume agent in Europe. According to various accounts, by the 1790s and into the 1800s the Marquis of Blandford was growing vanilla plants in a greenhouse in the garden of his Reading estate.[83] In the 1758 edition of Hannah Glasse's *The Art of Cookery*, in "Another Way to make Chocolate," the author instructs the cook to "put in three good Vanelas, or more or less as you please." And Richard Dolby, in his *The Cook's Dictionary* of 1830, under "Vanilla," lists six recipes, without specifying the form of vanilla (e.g., "two drachms of vanilla," "half an ounce of vanilla," and "a quarter of a pound of vanilla"). In *The Practice of Cookery* there is no mention of vanilla as beans, or ground up, or in liquid form, until it is referenced in Appendix III of the posthumous editions. There we see a recipe for a pudding, Pommes à la Dauphin, with the anonymous author declaring that vanilla was present in this pudding eaten by Queen Victoria when she and Prince Albert were dining in September 1843 at Château d'Eu with Louis-Philippe of France. Accompanying the recipe is the statement that the English Queen "sent her plate twice for it." Both rosewater and orange flower water were common flavourings, and they almost totally disappeared once vanilla was introduced.

The Preparatory Remarks

It would be a mistake to slide through Mrs Dalgairns's Preparatory Remarks at the beginning of most chapters and go straight to the recipes. The modern term for these remarks is "headnotes," and these are highly prized by cookbook admirers when they are present. They often reveal the personality of the author, her or his authority, and sometimes take the form of exhortations. In her Preparatory Remarks Mrs Dalgairns debates the quality of particular joints of meats and the best ways of cooking them, and the need for meats to be fresh – "they cannot be too fresh." In the case of lobsters a surprising "barnacles and other marine animals adhering to it are certain indications of superior goodness." She advises on the proper utensils for each kind of dish, recommending a slab of marble, stone, or slate for rolling out paste, rather than wood. She is particularly insistent on the timing of dishes, which often should be prepared a day or many days before being eaten. In the case of preserves, they must be looked at occasionally lest they ferment and need to be reboiled. There is considerable personal experience here. Persistence – even obsession – pervades her Remarks, complemented by the strong tone of her letters to her publisher.

Chefs or cookbook authors today would be stunned by the immense variety of fish, meats, vegetables, and fruits called for in *The Practice of Cookery*, besides an impressive range of spices and herbs: 21 spices (as noted earlier); 24 herbs; 28 species of fish; and 21 of meats, including game; 61 different vegetables; and 22 varieties of fruits.

The **oils and fats** she used in cooking and in dressings are rarely named. Olive oil is specified only three times, but that is likely because most of the olive oil imported from Italy was cheaply made and quickly spoiled.[84] She calls for salad oil three times, "fine oil," "sweet oil," and butter of course. Beef suet and the fat of veal and mutton, and pork lard, are common, as is clarified dripping.

While the **adulteration** of foodstuffs is not mentioned in *The Practice of Cookery*, this scourge was prevalent at the time. The issue was firmly addressed by Frederick Accum in his influential *A Treatise on Adulterations of Food*, first published in London in 1820. Here we learn about the universal colouring of cheese and how alum was added to baked goods. When we read about the inclusion of beer and wine (which were frequently faked) we have to wonder about Peter Dalgairns's business line as a wine merchant. By his second edition of the same year, Accum had added the adulteration of milk, isinglass, and cinnamon to his earlier list. Then, as today, it was all due to "the eager and insatiable thirst for gain."

Leavening or raising agents such as baking powder, which are commonplace today, had not yet been invented. English and Scottish cooks at the time were dependent on multiple eggs and yeast as rising agents for cakes. For Mrs Dalgairns, the large numbers of eggs called for in many of her cake recipes were undoubtedly plucked from her own henhouse. The yeasts specified in *The Practice of Cookery* are beer yeast, bran yeast, baker's yeast, and potato yeast, or just "fresh sweet yeast." However, in the United States and Canada, more advanced raising agents had been in use for cake baking as far back as the late 1780s. It began with pearlash, chemically known as potassium carbonate. The earliest recorded mention of pearlash use in American cookbooks is found in Amelia Simmons's *American Cookery*, first published in 1796. German bakers were known throughout Europe in the 1700s to be successfully using a "secret" ingredient: "pottasche" and pearlashes, which were a purified form of pot ashes. In Canada pot ashes, albeit largely employed in farming and industrial (principally soap) operations rather than for cooking, were regularly exported to England and Scotland from Quebec, beginning in the early 1800s. William Lyon Mackenzie, noted Canadian politician and future rebel, as editor of the Toronto newspaper the *Colonial Advocate*, on 2 January 1826 importunes his readers to share "useful information" that could be included in his forthcoming "Treatise on Pot and Pearl Ashes." Alas, it seems that the book never went to press. As early as 1828, the *St Catharines Farmers Journal* (twenty kilometres or just over twelve miles west of Niagara Falls), in its 2 July issue, published "Receipts for the Ladies" with Tea Cakes, Pint Cake, Dough Cake, and Cream Cake requiring a "small lump," or "one tea-spoonful" of pearlash.

In England and Scotland, pearlash was a late arrival, soon to be replaced by bicarbonate of soda, or baking soda.[85] But Mrs Dalgairns had been quick off the mark in foreseeing the possibilities posed by pearlash, with two recipes calling for this new leavening agent: Gingerbread Cake ("half an ounce of pearl ashes") and another for Parliament Cakes ("a bit of pearl ash about the size of a nut"). By the 1840s, with further refining, "saleratus" was introduced in North America. And finally, by the 1850s, baking powder was commonly used for baking on both sides of the Atlantic. In England, from 1806 through dozens of editions, in Mrs Rundell's *A New System of Domestic Cookery* (with a Boston edition in 1807) the pages devoted to cakes often call for yeast and many eggs, with the addition of a glass of sweet wine or a large glass of brandy. The previous year an American edition of Mrs Glasse's *The Art of Cookery* was published in Alexandria, Virginia, despite excellent sales of the English editions from the mid-1750s onwards. But Hannah Glasse was beginning to be seen as old-hat. In both Rundell and Glasse, for cakes it is still eggs and yeast, without a nod to pearlash and new American ways of baking cakes.

Breakfast, Dining …

Breakfast was the favourite meal of Sir Walter Scott and of many Scots of that time. In writing to his wife on 1 February 1838, Charles Dickens gloried in a breakfast he enjoyed at a Yorkshire inn: "We have had for breakfast, toasts, cakes, a Yorkshire pie, a piece of beef about the size and much the shape of my portmanteau, tea, coffee, ham and eggs."[86] Somerset Maugham has often been quoted as saying: "To eat well in England you should have breakfast three times a day." Back in the 1820s, Mrs Dalgairns obliges with suggestions that today would be seen by most people as inappropriate at the beginning of a work day, or even on a weekend: various kinds of dried, smoked, and salted fish; sheep's kidneys broiled ("an excellent breakfast for a sportsman"); calf's liver; pig's head; pork pies; and cold mutton. More approachable is a range of breakfast cakes cooked on the stove with a waffle iron or baked in the oven as yeast-raised rolls.

As for Scottish dining customs at the time when Mrs Dalgairns was in the final stages of composing *The Practice of Cookery*, there had been a revolution from old ways, when men, consuming multiple bottles of alcohol throughout an evening, would have dominated the room devoted to dining. Gradually, dining rooms became larger, as did dining tables, which often could accommodate twenty or more guests. By the late eighteenth century, with men and women dining together, the dining room assumed the air of the most sumptuous room in the house, even among the middle ranks, with attendant attention to tableware, silverware, cutlery, glassware, and china.[87]

Unlike most cookbook authors of her time, Mrs Dalgairns does not suggest menus for each meal of the day, nor does she provide illustrations of place settings appropriate to each meal.[88] In fact, we see no plates or illustrations of any kind.

She does not offer advice as to the healthiest diet. However, when it comes to the presentation of foods on the table, Mrs Dalgairns has an eye for their decorative effect. For Another Raised Crust she suggests "ornament according to fancy with leaves, festoons, or chains of rings made of the paste." For Irish Rock "ornament with a sprig of myrtle," and Egg Marmalade when quite cold may be "garnished with flowers." A Ratafia Cream is decorated with sweetmeats cut out like flowers and harlequin comfits are strewn over the top. For tartlets "make ornaments of paste, roll it quite thin, and as even as possible; cut it with tin stars, leaves, or any other form." A Solid Veal Pie "if right done will have a glazed appearance and the variety of colours looks well by candlelight." For meat pies, but not fruit pies, puff pastry may be ornamented with shapes resembling leaves cut out with a pastry-cutter. Her attention to the appearance of food in a dish or on a plate is not unlike the outlook of chefs today, who perceive the presentation of food as akin to art.

The Early Nineteenth-Century Kitchen

A Dutch oven is called for in thirty-four recipes in *The Practice of Cookery* and clearly was an indispensable cooking pot in Mrs Dalgairns's kitchen. The Dutch oven has enjoyed a long history, stretching back to a brass version in the early eighteenth century. By the early 1800s, brass had been replaced by iron, with three legs, which allowed it to stand over coals in front of a hearth. The shape and appearance of Dutch ovens have evolved over the years, even into the twenty-first century when recipes still specify a Dutch oven, or large casserole pot. The early versions usually sported a long handle and a concave lid, which was designed to hold coals. Mrs Dalgairns employed her Dutch oven for roasting, browning, toasting, heating, drying (herbs), and baking. In the case of Ramakins, the cook bakes them "in small paper cases in the Dutch oven." Besides a hearth, Mrs Dalgairns likely kept a stove fuelled by wood. However, beginning in the 1820s, her stove may have been fuelled by coal when railway trains cleared the way for the transportation of coal all over Great Britain.[89] She uses the top of a stove to stew soup, to boil jelly, to bake Flemish Wafers, and to make Pommes à la Dauphin, and she advises that a stove, or iron plate, is preferable to fire for preserving. In cases where foods prepared at home needed to be baked, these were normally delivered to a commercial baker, usually found close by.

As for cooking stoves, or kitchen ranges, Peter Brears writes that the "Leamington," incorporating a practical roasting range, a large boiler, and an oven heated

Fig. 17
Frontispiece to *Modern Domestic Cookery, and Useful Receipt Book. Containing Approved Directions for Purchasing, Preserving, and Cooking, Meat, Fish, Poultry, Game, &c. The Art of Trussing and Carving: Preparing Soups, Gravies, Sauces, and Made Dishes. Potting, Pickling, &c. The Branches of Pastry and Confectionary; a Complete Family Physician; Instructions to Servants, for the Best Method of Performing Their Various Duties: The Art of Making British Wines, Brewing, Baking &c.*, by Elizabeth Hammond, 6th edition (London: Dean and Munday, Threadneedle Street; and A.K. Newman and Co., Leadenhall Street, 1828). Wellcome Library. Original book in University of Leeds Library.

by its own separate fireplace, was in common use in Britain from the 1820s onwards. The Leamington illustrated by Brears is taken from Thomas Webster's *An Encyclopaedia of Domestic Economy* of 1844, in which (without a mention of Leamington) the woodcut of a "Kitchen Range" is accompanied by a compilation of its features, including a revolving trivet; a drawer below to hold dripping pans, dishes, or anything requiring heat; a series of hooks; spits that are carried by a jack and jack chain; and beside the range an iron oven that can be used to bake pastry.[90]

Kitchen utensils included a girdle and griddle, both being types of frying pans, and skewers, rolling pins, and sieves. Among unfamiliar items are an earthen pipkin, a small pot used for cooking directly on a stove or by a hearth, and a tammy, a piece of woollen cloth that could be used in place of a sieve. See the glossary for various unfamiliar kitchen tools rarely seen today.

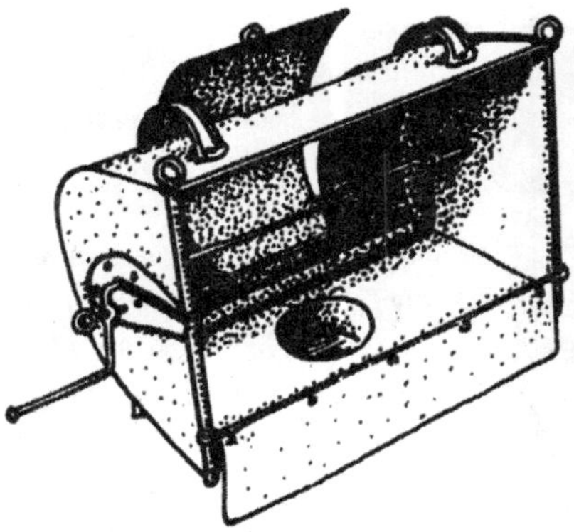

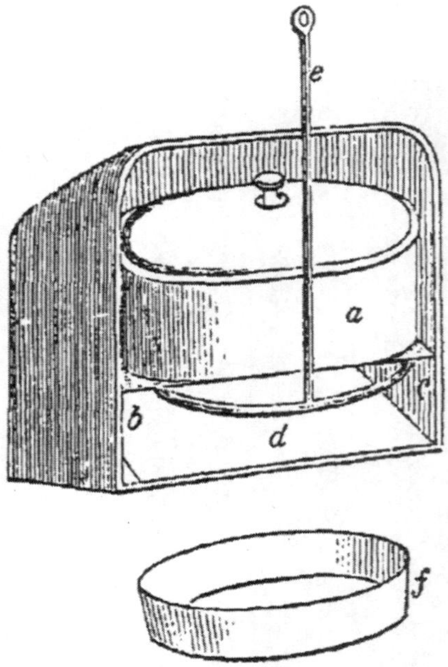

Fig. 18, 19, and 20 The uses and appearance of Dutch ovens have evolved through the centuries from the late 1700s up until today. Illustrated here is an early late eighteenth-century example; another from the 1840s; and finally a 6.5-quart cast iron Dutch oven, advertised by the Paderno factory in Prince Edward Island since 1979. Dutch oven in *Food & Cooking in 18th Century Britain: History & Recipes*, by Jennifer Stead ([London]: English Heritage, 1985), 103. Dutch oven in *An Encyclopaedia of Domestic Science* by Thomas Webster (London: Longman, Brown, Green and Longmans, 1844), bk. XI, p. 826, fig. 656. Facsimile edition, nl: Elibron Classics, 2005. One of six Dutch ovens advertised on website of Paderno factory in Prince Edward Island. www.paderno.com.

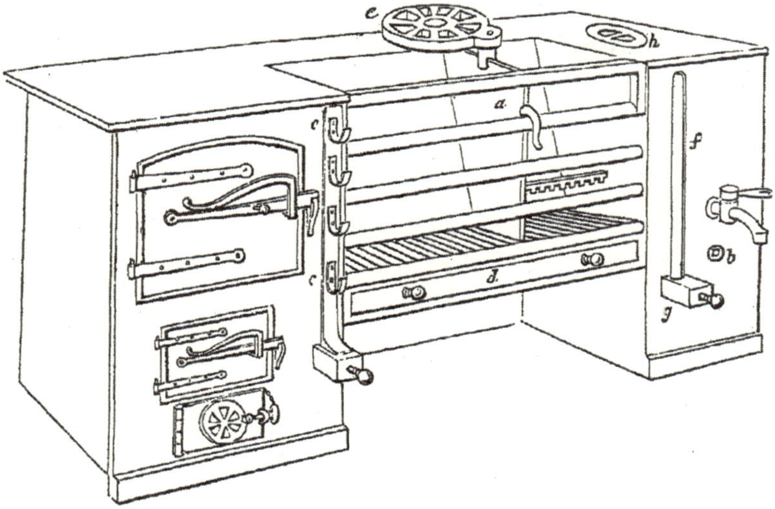

Fig. 21 A "Leamington" kitchen range. Simply styled a "Kitchen Range," in *An Encyclopaedia of Domestic Science* by Thomas Webster (London: Longman, Brown, Green and Longmans, 1844), bk. XI, p. 813, fig. 629. Facsimile edition, nl: Elibron Classics, 2005.

One tends to think of skewers in connection with kebabs, or skewered marinated meats for roasting on the barbecue sold in supermarkets today. But skewers are not cooking utensils invented for a modern summer outdoors lifestyle, and, indeed, they go back centuries. In the midst of the massive invasion of England by the Normans in the 1060s, as depicted in the seventy-metre Bayeux Tapestry, scenes of meats and poultry on skewers being cooked over a fire, or served in a manor house, are prominently displayed in more than two panels. Mrs Dalgairns specifies skewers: sometimes small, in one instance to be made of silver, for roasting or frying various fish and meats.

Recipe Highlights for Cooks Today and *The Practice of Cookery*

Dear reader/cook: do not be too shocked when you plunge into the first chapter on Soups and find "take 12 quarts of water," or "clean a calf's head nicely," or "pick out the black part of the eyes." It is true that many of Mrs Dalgairns's recipes are directed at homes where families of ten or more might be sitting around the table.

And the kind of meat preparation we associate with a butcher, and not a home cook, two hundred years ago was often taken on by a butcher but, at other times, assumed by a servant or the woman of the house.[91]

SOUP and FORCEMEAT

Mrs Dalgairns offers a wide range of soups. She expressly warns the reader/cook that "utensils employed in the kitchen must be kept scrupulously clean." Soups are better when made the day before they are eaten, and meat "cannot be too fresh." At Campbell House Museum in Toronto, director/curator Elizabeth Driver has on several occasions recreated dishes out of *The Practice of Cookery*. One is the **Soup Cressy**, with its fresh seasonal vegetables plus sweet herbs, mace, and cloves added to the broth, a carrot soup that is happily consumed at any time of year. Driver finds that the **Mullagatawny**, or **Currie Broth**, is flavourful and makes a colourful meal in itself. *The Practice of Cookery* is found in the old kitchen at Fort York National Historic Site in Toronto, where Elizabeth Baird has followed Mrs Dalgairns's recipes, among them **Cocky Leeky Soup**.

Is it possible that Mrs Dalgairns was able wrestle with a 120-pound turtle in her kitchen for **Turtle Soup**? Or rather a turtle stew. As Clarissa Dickson Wright tell us, "Soup is a bit of a misnomer: turtle soup was more a stew, really, since it had different cuts of the turtle floating around in it." It seems that real turtle soup was fashionable in the great houses up until the late 1800s. In Toronto, the African American provisioner and caterer Beverly R. Snow of the Epicurean Recess advertised a "Splendid Green Turtle weighing 125 lbs. The turtle will be served up in all the various modes of English and French cookery."[92] Because of the expense ordinary people resorted to mock turtle soup, based on a calf's head.[93] Sure enough, Mrs Dalgairns provides her readers with the "ordinary" alternative, with a **Calf's-head Soup, or Mock Turtle,** early in the Soups chapter.

Forcemeat, from the French *farcir*, is a food term rarely encountered in cookbooks of our era, but it can be translated simply as stuffing comprising bread crumbs, chopped cooked vegetables, mushrooms, or combinations of various cut-up meats or fish such as oysters, crab, lobster, or haddock, with added seasonings. *The Practice of Cookery* is awash in references to forcemeat balls, and even as stuffing in connection with soups, beef, mutton, veal, pork, chickens, pigeons, partridges, and fish. Further forcemeat recipes are found in the Gravies and Sauces chapter.

FISH and SEAFOOD

F. Marian McNeill confidently advises her readers that, "relatively speaking, the Scots were always a piscivorous, the English a carnivorous race … Despite the excellence of their beef and mutton, the Scots have never been great meat-eaters."[94] Charles Mackie, in his 1836 book about the Town of Dundee, on a single page offers "piacatorial description" of fifteen species of fish caught in lakes and rivers, and off the seashore, of which ten are addressed by Mrs Dalgairns.[95] Back in Prince Edward Island, "the fruits of the sea, which were mainly cod, herring and shellfish, had been the mainstays of the Acadian diet." "Just as the British came to be beef eaters, the Acadians became known as fish eaters."[96] In *The Practice of* Cookery, the Fish chapter vastly outweighs each of the meat chapters, with almost half the number of pages in total that are assigned to Beef, Mutton, Lamb, Veal, and Pork. In considering oysters and lobsters, it is hardly surprising that a child of Prince Edward Island would exhibit a fondness for both. Today half of the oysters eaten in Canada come from that Island, most drawn from Malpeque Bay on the north shore of the Island and simply designated "Malpeques." Oysters creep into several chapters of the cookbook, with **Oyster Soup** (calling for "half a hundred"), **Oyster Sauce**, oysters baked in savoury pies, added to an omelette, and the foundation of a catsup. For Mrs Dalgairns, living in both England and Scotland, those bivalves from the coast of the County of Kent or the Firth of Forth "are the most esteemed." As in New York harbour, in England oysters ceased to be a food of the masses by the mid-800s, evolving into a costly delicacy when native oyster beds suffered serious declines. In Scotland, by the early 1900s, pollution and overfishing had virtually wiped out all signs of an oyster industry.[97]

Lobster is at the heart of numerous recipes following a paragraph devoted to advice on what the buyer should look for when purchasing lobsters. **Lobster sauce** is popular as a garnish for other fish dishes, but on its own lobster is boiled, fricasseed, potted, and made into pies. In a later edition of *The Practice of Cookery* she adds **To Pot, a North American Receipt.** In Britain lobster is associated with Scotland, where it is in plentiful supply. In the early nineteenth century lobster was taken up by gourmets, as Meg Dods footnoted in 1827: "Lobsters are held in great esteem by gastrologers for the firmness, purity, and flavour of their flesh."[98] A one-sentence recipe for **Lobster Salad** provides all the instructions you need – although it may blow a hole in your pocketbook! – for an unexpected but delicious side or main dish. Besides lobster it calls for minced onions, pickled green apples, green capsicums (i.e., bell peppers), lemon juice, and salt. Mrs Dalgairns would have fondly recalled the lobsters caught around her home Island. Centuries ago, seafood of all kinds, including lobster, was being exported by Atlantic Canadians to many European nations. In 1972, Sondra Gotlieb noted that, while the demand for lobsters from PEI was increasing, the lobster population was threatened due to the raking of Irish moss, a medical ingredient, resulting in the disturbance of lobster beds.[99] In recent years PEI lobsters have regularly been marketed in the United States as "Maine" lobsters.[100]

The reader is offered six recipes for **eels.** Excessive pollution of the Thames River in the early nineteenth century threatened traditional fisheries, promoting the introduction of eels. In a population explosion, eels, and other cheap seafoods, were considered suitable foods for the working poor.

Otherwise among the fish and seafood recipes those for salmon reflect traditional and yet not too onerous ways of dealing with a very familiar species, albeit usually with a sauce. In Canada, we have ready access to salmon from both our west and east coasts – not necessarily wild salmon – and can only sigh to think of the salmon that long ago graced the rivers of provinces that are far from the sea. Janet Chute makes a well-documented case for the importance, and relevance for Europeans, of fishing by the Mi'kmaq in the Maritime provinces during the 1700s and early 1800s. With the arrival of Europeans, fish became significant items of trade, and evidence has emerged for a commercial salmon fishery. It is indeed possible that, on Prince Edward Island, the Callbecks partook of Mi'kmaq salmon and eels, just two of several species caught by the Mi'kmaqs in the seas around Nova Scotia and New Brunswick.[101] According to Judith Comfort, even today Maritimers "roast salmon the traditional Mi'kmaq way, planking it next to an open fire."[102]

In her Toronto diary entry for 13 August 1793, Mrs Simcoe, the wife of the first lieutenant-governor of Upper Canada (the future province of Ontario), living far away from any evidence of salt water, wrote: "An Indian named Wable Casigo supplies us with Salmon which the Rivers & Creeks on this shore abound with."[103] Today we are advised that salmon are increasingly smaller than less than a half century ago, and much smaller than 150 years ago, when, as Thomas Webster wrote in 1844, "When the salmon runs from six to ten pounds they are very good fish but by a late act of parliament no salmon is permitted to be sold by the fishmonger of less than 6 lbs. weight, to prevent the destruction of the breed."[104] This would have been true in Scotland in the early nineteenth century, given that the ten salmon recipes in *The Practice of Cookery* assume a whole salmon of considerable proportions. **Caveach Salmon,** meaning the raw fish pickled in vinegar, its name deriving from the Spanish *escobeche*, is a less common way of dealing with salmon that may not be overly fresh. Mrs Dalgairns fries slices of salmon, then adds boiled vinegar, shallots, and spices, which are poured over the cold fried fish. Back in 1813, Ude, in *The French Cook*, wrote that salmon from the Thames River in London were the most esteemed.

MEAT

When observing the large quantities called for in many of the meat recipes, a rump of beef, or eighteen pounds of ham, or a suckling pig, it is useful to know that, traditionally, large joints, and whole animals, were prepared and served on Sundays, with the bulk in the form of leftovers recycled into "made" dishes throughout the following weekdays.

Mrs Dalgairns offers readers thirty-four recipes for Mutton and only eight for Lamb. "Lamb" covers a multitude of sins when naming the meat of the sheep today. If the animal is more than twelve months old it should be labelled "mutton," but by the mid-nineteenth century, with much older (and tougher) animals coming on the market, the term "mutton" suggested to customers meat not fit for human consumption, and the term fell out of favour and, eventually, was simply dropped from the vocabulary of most butchers.

While the dark, squishy, for some the unspeakable inner parts of an edible animal strike us as suitable only as animal feed (except for liver or kidneys), in Mrs Dalgairns's time no part of the animal was discarded or simply not considered to be suitable food for human beings. These parts were often gathered under such terms as "offal," or "lights," and included entrails, tongue, bladder, brains, lungs, skirts (harslet), gizzards, pinions, chitterlings or guts, pluck, heart, feet, head, snout, melt, throats, windpipe, tripe, sweetbreads, thymus, pancreas, and stomach.

CURRIES

There are so many foods in the cookbook that involve curry or curry powder it is difficult to suggest – "try this" – or "this." David Burnett and Helen Saberi, in their *The Road to Vindaloo*, consulted several old cookbooks, choosing two of Mrs Dalgairns's recipes as illustrations of curry dishes for private families. **Kebobbed Currie** is well worth a try, with any kind of meat anointed with onions, apples, garlic, curry powder plus turmeric, bay leaves and lemon juice, and grilled on skewers. Curry has a long history in North America. In an early example, in

Fig. 22 Frontispiece showing a cook dealing with a roast of beef. Designed by Joseph Fussell and engraved by Samuel Davenport for the *Complete Economical Cook and Frugal Housewife, a New System of Domestic Cookery; An Entire New System of Domestic Cookery; Containing Approved Directions for Purchasing, Preserving, and Cooking. Also, Trussing and Carving; Preparing Soups Gravies, Sauces, Made Dishes, Potting Pickling, &c. with Directions for Pastry and Confectionary. Likewise the Art of Making British Wines, Brewing, Baking, Gardening, &c.*, by Mrs Mary Holland, 6th edition (London: Thomas Tegg, Cheapside; Glasgow: R. Griffin & Co.; Dublin: J. Cumming, 1827). Multiple digitized editions over several decades with the same frontispiece. For example, 1837, 14th edition, New York Public Library; 1843, "A New Edition": Internet Archive, Wellcome Library, University of Leeds Library; 1853, 16th edition: Hathi Trust, University of Michigan.

1833 William Lyon McKenzie noted that packets sailing between London and New York served passengers a lunch of meats and fish prepared in various ways, among them curried.[105]

GRAVIES, SAUCES

The gravies and sauces dealt with here apply primarily to meats, poultry, fish, and game, and normally would be served in a sauce tureen. Few require extensive preparation, for example, the **Mint Sauce** that is put together in just a few minutes: minced young mint leaves, vinegar, and brown sugar. As an aside, it should be noted that when sugar is called for it is either brown sugar (now known as Demerara sugar – that is, white sugar with added molasses) or white sugar, which would have been purchased in a loaf and then pounded. In the early 1800s, Maria Rundell had remarked that "Sugars, being an article of considerable expense in all families, the purchase demands particular attention," but by 1830 the price of sugar had precipitously decreased.[106]

VEGETABLES

In the late 1700s, horticulturists and gardeners had embarked on various schemes to develop different kinds of fruits and vegetables that would supplement the common varieties found in kitchen gardens and markets. Among those vegetables considered to be unusual were French beans, artichokes, and celery. Besides giving us several cooking recipes for each of these new varieties in the "Vegetables" and "Preserves" chapters in the "Kitchen Garden," we are given instructions for growing all three. As noted earlier, sixty-one varieties of vegetables are addressed by Mrs Dalgairns. The favourite vegetable among the Scots at that time, a staple of the kitchen garden, was kale, the equivalent among the peasant population of potatoes in Ireland. In Meg Dods (1826), Scotland is referred to as "The Land o' Kail." It is a hardy plant that can survive and even benefit from periods of frost. Samuel Johnson was totally dismissive of kale, or perhaps his derision was simply directed at the Scots, writing: "They [the Scots] cultivate hardly any other plant for common tables, and when they had not kail then probably had nothing."[107] With the addition to the kale of a little barley, leeks, and a broth based on either salted beef or cooked fresh beef, a cook has concocted Mrs Dalgairns's **Scots Kale.**

Tomatoes, which actually are a fruit, were always cooked, given that many believed that uncooked tomatoes were poisonous. Cucumbers were stewed, or made into soup, or preserved, a practice that could be wisely followed today, given that many people suffer from the relative indigestibility of fresh cucumbers.

SALADS

Mrs Dalgairns offers only two salads: **A Summer Salad** and **A Winter Salad**, with the Winter Salad based on a head of celery. This would suggest a "salad" as we know it today was uncommon back then, but that would be a mistake. More than a 130 years earlier, in 1699, John Evelyn had issued his *Acetaria: A Discourse of Sallets*, offering multiple salad ingredients such as carrots, lettuce, cucumbers, endive, scallions, and even "garlick"! The Summer Salad in the Vegetables chapter, as replicated at Campbell House Museum in Toronto, consists of lettuce, mustard greens and cresses, a little sorrel, and young onions. Spring onions would do the trick. It is an easy course on a bright summer day, especially when garnished with nasturtium flowers. Mrs Dalgairns's Winter Salad calls for endive as a substitute for lettuce, with the addition of red cabbage and slices of boiled beets. A **Salad Sauce,** or dressing, has a basic and familiar ring with olive oil, vinegar, a little mustard and salt plus the option of adding a mashed hard-boiled egg yolk. A further recipe for Winter Salad suggests the addition of anchovies, cayenne, black pepper, and a little thick cream. At Campbell House Museum the suggested dressing is generously applied to enhance the taste. See above under Fish and Seafood regarding **Lobster Salad**.

PUDDINGS, PIES & TARTS; CREAMS, CUSTARDS, &C

In many households of the time, puddings and other sweet dishes would have been consumed by family members only on Sundays, the pre-eminent meal of the week. The cook – whether a servant or the mother or other female – focused her culinary efforts on that one meal, enjoyed after the morning church service.

Puddings, Custards, Cakes, and Biscuits are likely the recipes that would most entice the cook of today into recreating choice dishes of old. *The Practice of Cookery* is brimming with promising sweet recipes, most of them stalwarts of the late eighteenth- and early nineteenth-century culinary repertoire. How about **Burnt Cream**, otherwise known as Crème Brûlée? The dessert enjoyed in restaurants everywhere today can be produced using her recipe, with the top scorched by a handy kitchen blow-torch rather than a salamander. Two recipes for **Bread and Butter Pudding** hark back to Mrs Glasse, and even earlier to the seventeenth century. In her second

Fig. 23. Frontispiece designed by Richard Corbold and engraved by Francis Kearny for *The Complete Confectioner, or, the Whole Art of Confectionary Made Easy; Containing, Among a Variety of Useful Matter, the Art of Making the Various Kinds of Biscuits, Drops, Prawlongs, Ice Creams, Water Ices, Fruits Preserved in Brandy, Preserved Sweetmeats (wet) Dried Fruits, Cordials, &c. &c. as also the Most Approved Method of Making Cheeses, Puddings, Cakes &c. in 250 Cheap and Fashionable Receipts. The Result of Many Years Experience with the Celebrated Negri and Whitten*, by Frederic Nutt, 4th edition, with considerable additions. London printed. New York reprinted for Richard Scott and sold at his bookstore, no. 243 Pearl-Street, 1807. Courtesy Schlesinger Library, Harvard College Library, bequest of Mrs Charles N. Greenough, 20 September 1926.

recipe, Mrs Dalgairns requires the cook to add "half of pint of brandy or rum, or currant wine." In her early years in Prince Edward Island, she was undoubtedly familiar with rum distilled from molasses, the most popular alcoholic beverage of North Americans at the time.

The Trifle dessert has a long history. Mrs Dalgairns's **Whim Wham**, which can be traced back to the eighteenth century, is part of that tradition. A Whim Wham is defined by the Oxford English Dictionary as a fanciful or fantastic object, or a trifling object, hence the use of the name for a dessert. Mrs Dalgairns's recipe for Whim Wham was chosen by Helen Saberi and Alan Davidson in a book titled *Trifle* as an illustration of the genre. With whipped cream, red currant jelly, a little white wine and biscuits – Naples biscuits, a biscuit flavoured with rosewater with origins in the seventeenth century, are suggested – or plain biscuit or sponge cake can be substituted. Mrs Dalgairns comes up with a colourful garnish of candied orange peel cut into straws.

Another kind of trifle is the **Floating Island**, which tourists in France regularly encountered as *Île flottante* on the ubiquitous "Tourist Menu" offered in late twentieth-century restaurants. Printed recipes for Floating Island go back to Hannah Glasse and *The Art of Cookery* of 1747. Mrs Dalgairns's recipe is a somewhat toned down, and easily constructed, version of Glasse, calling for cream or milk, whipped egg whites and yolks cooked up with lemon peel and cinnamon, with the option of a little wine plus a fruit jelly piled up over the custard.[108]

The majority of Mrs Dalgairns's pies fall under the heading of "savoury," many for seafood, which accounts for the several variations on the pastry required. Among her pastries are those that call for suet and beef dripping, hot water pastry, and puff pastry. Also short crust pastry with sugar, and chou (choux) pastry, which can serve as the perfect surround for a modern Gâteau Saint-Honoré.

In her chapter on "Ice Cream: Cold Comfort" in *Much Depends on Dinner*, Margaret Visser traces the long history of harvesting and creating blocks of ice, and ice cream, back to the Greeks and yet again the early Arabs with their *sharbia* (i.e., sherbert), Italian *gelati*, and French *glaces* until the present day. In New York, ice-cream vending is recorded as early as 1828, and "Italians had introduced the idea to Britain by 1850 at the latest."[109] There are ice cream makers today who still rely on old-fashioned churning machines, which call for ice and salt. Mrs Dalgairns's **Raspberry Iced Cream** presents a modest challenge with its reliance on a "freezing-pot." She suggests freezing in moulds, and adds that "water ices are made in this way, substituting water for cream."

Fig. 24 Woodcut in an advertisement for the St Catharines Coffee and Spice Manufactory from the *St Catharines Journal, and Welland Canal, Niagara District, General Advertiser* (St Catharines, Ontario), 27 November 1843. From microfilm of original newspaper in Library and Archives Canada, Ottawa.

BISCUITS and CAKES

Mrs Dalgairns offers her version of Sally Lunn, here titled **Sally Luns, or Bath Breakfast Cakes.** Even today British cookbooks regularly include recipes for Sally Lunn, a light yeast cake that is a specialty of the town of Bath. The Oxford Dictionary of English notes that Sally Lunn is a sweet, light teacake, typically served hot. The name of the cake is said to derive from the name of a woman selling such cakes at her tea-shop in Bath at the end of the eighteenth century. Others say that this story is a myth and that Sally Lunn derives from the French *soleil lune*, meaning sun and moon.

Caraway, possibly the most popular spice of the eighteenth-century British kitchen, is a distinctive ingredient in all seed cakes, often with the addition of nuts and candied peels. Seed cakes go back to printed cookbooks of the seventeenth century and were considered by many to be "rich." They were egg-based or yeast-based until the early twentieth century, when baking powder came into general use.[110] Mrs Dalgairns's recipes for **Scots Seed Cake** and **Irish Seed Cake** call for large numbers of eggs plus brandy, spices, and various sweetmeats.

An example of how Mrs Dalgairns not only tweaked time-honoured recipes but also improved upon the basic deliciousness of the dish is her recipe – actually two recipes – for **Shrewsbury Cakes.** Caraway seeds are the customary flavouring beyond the usual butter, flour, sugar, and eggs, as seen in Raffald's *The Experienced English Housekeeper*, first published in 1769. In 1806, Mrs Rundell added cinnamon, nutmeg, and rosewater. Mrs Dalgairns, in **Another way to make Shrewsbury Cakes**, further enhanced Mrs Rundell's mixture with currants, resulting in even tastier cookies or small cakes.[111]

American Gingerbread is just one of several gingerbread recipes. Gingerbread, as in cookies, is found in five versions in the first American cookbook by Amelia Simmons published in 1796. Apart from the essential ginger, Simmons employs coriander, cinnamon, allspice, mace, rosewater, and regular sugar or brown sugar or molasses. But not wine. Nonetheless, Mary Randolph's *The Virginia* Housewife of 1824 offers three recipes for Ginger Bread, one of which calls for brandy. Gingerbread has a long history in virtually all European countries going back to the Middle Ages. Besides wine, Mrs Dalgairns calls simply for ginger and rosewater as flavouring, and brown sugar. With the dough "the thickness of a penny-piece" spread out with a spoon over flat tin pans, and "while warm cut into oblong pieces," these are easy-to-make-and-bake crisp gingerbread cookies.

Readers may notice that a small number of commercially available products are employed as ingredients, such as Harvey's Sauce, patent cocoa, Indian soy, rosewater, and orange flower water. And of course Cooke's Currie Paste, which is given a boost at the end of the Curries chapter. **Oliver's Biscuits** are undoubtedly her version of Bath Olivers, or Oliver's, named after a Dr William Oliver who lived mostly in Bath.

FRUITS and PRESERVES

With regard to strawberries, until the seventeenth century only wild strawberries were sold. Over many decades, even centuries, new varieties were gradually introduced into England from the New World, including Virginia, and only then could they be cultivated or grown in commercial and domestic kitchen gardens.[112] In the first volume (1826) of John Loudon's *The Gardener's Magazine*, English and Scottish plant sellers offer several new species of strawberries, accompanied by wood-engraved illustrations. Among the new varieties: Bishop's Orange ("belonging to that class called Scarlet"), Early Globe, Cinnamon, and Virginian. In another, J. Wilmot of Isleworth, Middlesex, "has raised a new and very superior strawberry named Wilmot's Superb." For two different recipes **To Preserve Strawberries** Mrs Dalgairns calls for "rose" and "large scarlet pine."

We tend to think of marmalade as a member of the family of jams put on toast for breakfast or scones for tea, simply not thinking about the long history of marmalade.[113] For Mrs Dalgairns **Orange Marmalade** is more often an aggressive yet delicious addition to various puddings and tarts, and even pancakes. With three recipes for orange marmalade, and one for lemon marmalade, Mrs Dalgairns is

Fig. 25
Early James Keiller and Sons marmalade jar, said to be made 1862 to 1873, owned by Mary F. Williamson.

simply following a Scottish tradition and, more specifically, the Dundee and Keiller dynasty methods of treating the peels of the oranges. Back in 1736 and Scotland's first cookbook, Mrs McLintock, in her *Receipts for Cookery and Pastry-Work*, specified the way "To Make Orange Chips," while later Mrs Frazer (first edition 1791) offered "Chip Orange Marmalade," using the Scottish designation "chip," meaning shredded, as did the Keillers. Mrs Dalgairns instructs the cook to "cut the peel into thin chips." In **Another way to make Orange Marmalade** the peels are to be minced. Either way these marmalade recipes are easily followed today, with the marmalade in *The Practice of Cookery* used as an ingredient in various types of sweet foods such as tarts, cheesecakes, puddings, and pancakes. Bitter or Seville oranges are usually available in stores in late January and through February.

DOMESTIC WINES, THE POULTRY YARD, THE DAIRY, BREWING, THE KITCHEN GARDEN, BEES, PIGS, & ETC.

The final eight chapters, while not an afterthought, did not fully engage Mrs Dalgairns, nor her reviewers. To add more recipes was not a priority. For each new edition she concentrated on coming up with more cooking recipes for the first seventeen chapters. While she never ceased to push Robert Cadell into adding more and more, with each new edition up to the fifth in 1835, she came up with only six new "receipts" for the later chapters. The American edition of 1830 omits all but two of the final non-cookery chapters and offers American readers "Wines." And of course **Captain Hall's Sandwiches for Travellers** was tucked in by Robert Cadell on the final page of the "Miscellany."

It is impossible to know why Mrs Dalgairns chose these particular five new recipes – for example, in "Domestic Wines" **Another Way to make Noyau** (when there was already Another Way), and **Arrow-Root Water** and **La Tire, or London Candy** (a kind of taffy), in the "Miscellany." **Auchtertyre Stilton Cheese** (a cheese specific to the Scottish Highlands) has been added to "The Dairy."

Mrs Dalgairns's husband Peter was, of course a wine dealer in the later years of their residence in London, and then in Dundee, and would not have been troubled by a chapter on "Domestic Wines." Non-commercial wines made in Britain were concocted from a variety of fresh fruits, including ripe and unripe grapes, and were hardly a challenge to wines imported from France or southern Europe, even gooseberry wine said to "resemble Champagne." In her *The Scots Cellar*, Marian McNeill gives readers four recipes from "Domestic Wines" for Caledonian Liqueur, Birch Wine, Hawthorne Liqueur, and Spruce Beer, a favourite of many North Americans.

Catherine Parr Traill, living in the backwoods of Ontario from 1832 to the 1850s, in a letter written on 22 January 1838, promises herself to try spruce beer since she has received a good recipe.[114] For several legitimate reasons, Mrs Dalgairns does not agree with others that brandy should be added to the mixture, but adding brandy is "an established practice."

Much of the "Miscellany" is given over to instructions for polishing, scrubbing, and cleaning various articles, such as clothing, the furnishings in a house, and jewellery. There are a few "recipes": three for Coffee (one with an egg added and another with milk).[115] Also Cocoa and various hot drinks, many of them recommended for invalids.

Under "Poultry Yard" the reader is presented with instructions for raising hens, turkeys, bustards, guinea and pea fowls, ducks, geese, and pigeons. For **Brewing** the brewer requires only hops, malt, and wort, together with vats and casks, to make table-beer and table-ale. In four pages "The Dairy" tells us how to make butter. Among seven pages devoted to cheese, Mrs Dalgairns guides cheesemakers through the long process, and many weeks, involved in creating a blue coat, or blue mould, followed by two recipes for making Stilton Cheese.

It is possible that the original buyers of *The Practice of* Cookery were seduced by the chapter on the "Kitchen Garden." Most gardening books of the day assumed gardeners would own a greenhouse – for example, *The Scotch Forcing and Kitchen Gardener* by Walter Nicol, published in Edinburgh in 1798. William Speechley's *Practical Hints in Domestic Rural Economy* (London, 1820) offers readers an engraved frontispiece titled "Plan of a kitchen garden." In any case, Mrs Dalgairns appears to target readers in Britain, mentioning "the climate of Britain," meaning England, Wales, and Scotland. Her kitchen garden grows (with her spellings) different kinds of cabbage, kale, brussels sprouts, cauliflower, broccoli, kohl-rabbi, turnip, carrots, parsnips, scorzonera, salsify, skirret, red beet, white beet, Jerusalem artichokes, beans, and kidney or French beans, spinach, asparagus (two kinds), sea-kale, onions, leeks, cibol, chives, garlic, shalot, artichokes, cardoon, Roman and ice lettuce plus other types of lettuce, endive, celery, garden cress and mustard, French and common sorrel, radish, Indian cress or nasturtium, burnet, horseradish, parsley, angelica, and rhubarb. The Kitchen Garden doesn't include Indian corn, or maize, although her Indian Meal, or Maize Pudding, does of course call for Indian (corn) meal. In volume 6, 1830, *The Gardener's Magazine* of London offers two articles with five engravings of Indian corn and details of several varieties of American corn being grown through the 1820s by English gardeners. Three pages following rhubarb in Vegetables deal with herbs: sage, clary, mints, thyme,

120 *Design for a Kitchen-Garden,*

16

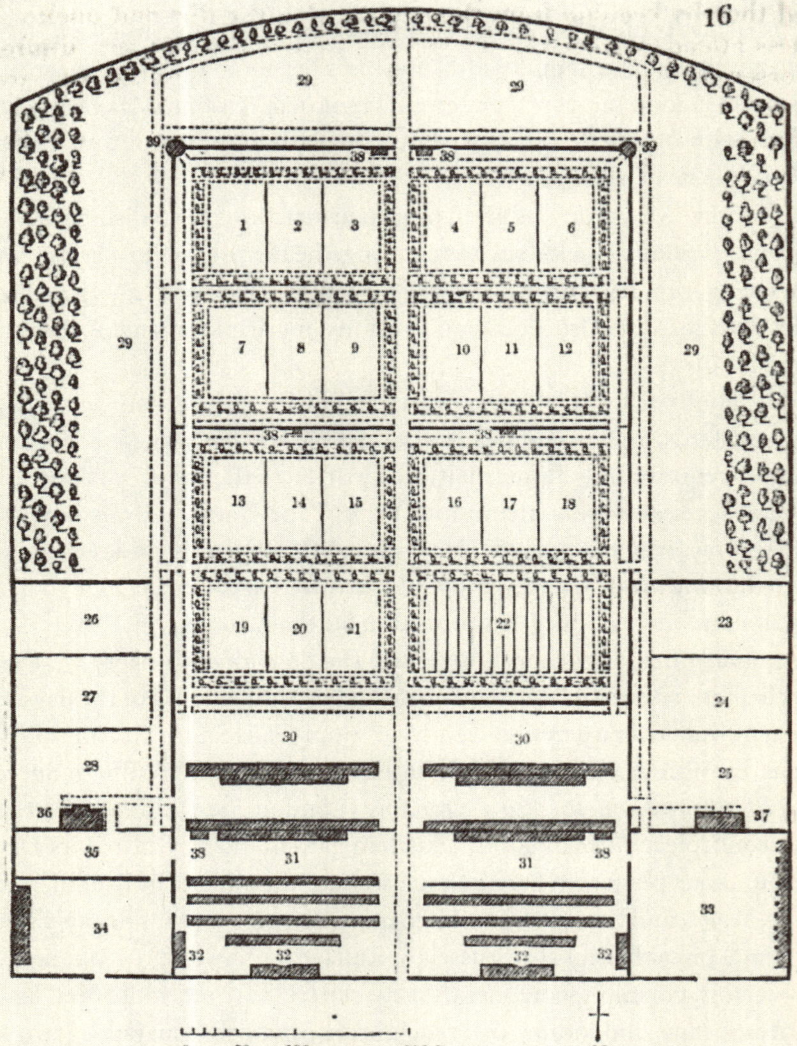

1. to 21, Culinary departments for a rotation of crops. 22, Asparagus. 23, Artichokes. 24, Rhubarb. 25, Sea-kale. 26, Jerusalem artichokes, which may be divided into several sections, for alternate cropping with other vegetables. 27, Horseradish. 28, Herb beds. 29, Fruit garden. 30, Forcing department. 31, Frame-ground, with dwarf wall for training, five ranges for frames, cucumber ridge, &c., and two pits. 32, Sheds for mushrooms, tool-house, and other purposes. 33, Department for mixing and turning dung, with open shed. 34, Compost department, with open shed. 35, Yard to gardener's house. 36, Gardener's house. 37, Fruit, onion, and seed-rooms, with lodging-room over. 38, Water tanks. 39, Rotundas, for lodging-rooms for under-gardeners.

Fig. 26 A design for a kitchen garden. Illustration on p. 120 (fig. 16.) of "A Series of Designs for laying out Kitchen-Gardens," by Mr. T. Rutger of Shortgrow, Essex. *The Gardener's Magazine.* vol. 11, March 1835, p. 118–22. Original owned and digitized by University of Michigan. Accessible at Hathi Trust.

marjoram, savory, tarragon, tansy, hyssop, costmary, rosemary, lavender, balm, coriander, caraway, and samphire, with parsley found under "Vegetables."

Most readers were (and are) unlikely to carry on to the final chapters "On Bees" and "On Pigs," plus an "Appendix." The appendix begins with "A Rule by which any gentleman may be enabled to establish a practical system of domestic economy, according to his income," with a table of household expenses for servants, clothes, rent, and so on based on one's annual income in seven stages from £1,000 to £10,000. The table is followed by "ESTIMATE of EXPENSES for a Family of Five persons" with an annual income of £500, with lists under "weekly" and "annually." The details of expenses include not only various foods such as bread, butter, cheese, meat and fish, vegetables, and beer but also miscellaneous items such as candles, clothes, "Extra for entertainments, medicine, and other incidents" plus "Two maid-servants" and "One Man-servant (out of the house)." With no children, but at least one or two servants, the Dalgairns household would indeed qualify as a "Family of Five Persons," but one assumes with an income higher than £500. Through various editions, and at least up until the posthumous eighth edition in 1849, this section of the appendix remains unchanged, with identical amounts in pounds. "A NOTE" follows, telling readers when various species of fish, meats, poultry, game, and vegetables are in season, with no qualifiers as to the geographical locations where the readers might live. As noted earlier, in 1840 a second appendix is added, this time with forty-nine additional recipes. For the "15th" edition of 1860, the index is banished to the end and a further twenty-two recipes added, with the names of the new recipe authors unknown.

Not content with putting down her pen and sitting back (saying to herself "finished!"), in a final paragraph Mrs Dalgairns writes a short table: "The Weights and Measures in this book are: 16 ounces to a pound; 4 quarts to a gallon; Two Scots pints make one English gallon; One mutchkin a pint." With "mutchkin" – a Scottish liquid measure (not used in *The Practice of Cookery*) – Mrs Dalgairns ends her cookbook with a flourish and a nod to Sir Walter Scott, who, in his various works, was prone to writing about mutchkins of brandy.

Catherine Emily Callbeck Dalgairns's Culinary Legacy to the New and Old Worlds

To sum up Catherine Dalgairns's achievement in serving readers and cooks with cookery recipes that "meet the taste of the majority" it is best to return to the original preface of *The Practice of Cookery*. Convinced that "a perfectly original book

The Practice of Cookery adapted to the Business of Every Day Life. By Mrs. DALGAIRNS. Thirteenth Edition, Enlarged.

London, &c. : Griffin & Co.

It is related of a certain Prince, that he never set out upon a journey, without sending his cook in advance, so that ample provision might be made for the gratification of his gastronomical propensities, on his arrival at each halting place ; and that upon one occasion, being alarmed by a report that a serious accident had happened to the advance party, he was at last agreeably relieved from a feverish state of excitement, by being informed that it was only the chaplain, and not the indispensable cook who had been injured. There may be few who are so devoted gastronomists as the Prince in question ; but there are as few – we doubt if there be any – who are indifferent either regarding the quality of their food, or the way in which it is cooked. A book on practical cookery, therefore can be criticized by all ; and it is only by its receipts being successfully experimented on, that it will become popular. When a volume upon this subject passes through a number of editions, it is evident that the information contained in it is of a thoroughly useful kind, and easily applicable in the arrangements of ordinary households. Mrs. Dalgairns' Complete System of Practical Cookery has stood this test, having passed through no fewer than thirteen editions, during which its popularity has been increased rather than diminished. And as each successive edition has appeared, new receipts for making favourite dishes which experience may have suggested, have been added. In the work there are twenty-five chapters, each being devoted to a different branch of the subject, and being preceded by very useful preparatory remarks. And there are contained in it nearly 1600 recipes, selected because economical, easy to follow, and calculated to furnish the dishes required for daily use as well as those for occasions of ceremony. Every one of them too "has either been actually tried by the author, or by persons whose accuracy in the various manipulations could be safely relied upon." Indeed the great object has been – and it seems to have been most successfully carried out – to produce such as work as might be of daily use in any household. We may merely add that while the present is the most complete edition of this very useful work yet published, it is also by far the cheapest.

Fig. 27 An 1854 Encomium, or advertisement, for a 13th edition of *The Practice of Cookery*. Advertisement placed by Griffin and Co. of London in the *Dundee Courier* (Dundee, Scotland), 22 March 1854. Gale Primary Sources, British Library Newspapers.

of Cookery would neither meet with, nor deserve, much attention; because what is wanted is not receipts for new dishes," her ambition was to issue "clear instructions how to make those already established in public favour." She had her eye on composing a work "having, in all respects, a practical character," and this was a positive outlook in the eyes of many reviewers, especially those in North America. The most prominent authors among her cookbook predecessors were not focused on "the mistress of a family" but, rather, on more than one well-paid servant, or more likely a bevy of cooks and sub-cooks in grand houses.

Unlike eighteenth-century cookbook authors, Mrs Dalgairns never copied word for word, nor did she make minuscule changes to recipes in the cookbooks that she studied. In almost every case she makes a choice, and then tests the ingredients and methods of cooking. Whether to include a recipe inspired her to make alterations that she trusted were improvements, often by adding a bit of spice or other flavourful ingredients.

From the point of view of a Canadian or North American cook in the twenty-first century, one is struck by her success in corralling recipes from the variety of mostly English-speaking cultures with which she had interacted throughout her life, creating a collection that recalls the roots of her family and her husband's family in British North America, Ireland, the United States, England and Scotland, and India. Clearly seen is more than a *soupçon* of the French dishes that graced the dining tables of ordinary and yet open-minded families of her day in all those countries. Her ingredients and clear instructions invite the cooks of today to replicate in their own kitchens dishes that were broiled, stewed, boiled, baked, preserved, ornamented, or simply assembled for families living almost two hundred years ago.

It is puzzling that *The Practice of Cookery* is little known among today's culinary historians, in spite of high praise in its own day. With a final edition in 1861, for over forty years copies had been sold all over the English-speaking world. Perhaps it is simply seen as a Scottish cookbook and as not relevant to cooks who are looking for recipes to be found in a broader geographical context. Meg Dods's *The Cook and Housewife's Manual* is the only Scottish cookbook that maintains steady widespread recognition, in part because of its association with Sir Walter Scott.

The strong "Canadian" connection of its author is not the only reason Canadian readers and cooks should embrace this antiquarian work. The existence of archival manuscripts in several repositories related to the Callbeck and Coffin families, together with the various Dalgairns family members, and details of the cookbook's publication, have made this introduction possible. The print history of *The Practice of Cookery* is illustrative of the intimate yet sophisticated business arrangements that characterized the publishing industry in the early decades of the nineteenth century. To be able to read letters written by Mrs Dalgairns, and Cadell's letters to and from Basil Hall, together with correspondence and diaries recording the process of publication, advertising, and sales, has presented an almost unprecedented opportunity.

Can we say that Mrs Dalgairns's cookbook is based on a multicultural or diverse culture? Perhaps not in today's terms, but the precisely 1,482 early nineteenth-century recipes included here were drawn from a wider sphere of international cookery than is found in the cookbooks of her English-speaking contemporaries. Most important, the fact that *The Practice of Cookery* was reissued in multiple editions from 1829 to 1861 suggests that at least three generations of cooks were inclined to regard this collection of recipes to be an indispensable asset in the kitchen. Just try the Soup Cressy, or Kebabbed Currie, or Whim Wham, and you will see why.

NOTES

1 The *Times*, 11 March 1829, a single line; 7 lines on 1 March; on 4 June an excerpt from a positive review in the *Edinburgh Literary Journal*; and finally, on 20 July from the *Spectator* of 13 June: "We consider we have reasons strongly to recommend Mrs. Dalgairns as an economical, useful, and practical system of cookery, adapted to the wants of all families, from the tradesman to the country gentleman. It is not a gourmand's book, nor does it pretend to be." With the publication of new editions, Cadell pays for the *Times* advertisements in 1830, 1832, 1837, 1841, 1842, and 1846. Ads in the the *Examiner* (London) for 15 March and 26 April 1829 present The PRACTICE OF CROOKERY in caps. In 1829, ads also appeared in numerous English provincial newspapers, for example the *Leeds Intelligencer*, *Aris's Birmingham Gazette*, and *Manchester Courier and Lancashire General Advertiser*.

2 While I have been unable to identify a copy of the 1861 edition, a 15th edition, published by Charles Griffin and dated 1861, is listed in *The English Catalogue of Books Published from January 1835, to January 1863* (London: Sampson Low, 1864), 185.

3 The death notice with identical wording appears in the *Dundee Courier* of 12 March 1844; the *Dundee, Perth and Cupar Advertiser* of 15 March; the *Dundee Warder and Arbroath and Forfar Journal* of 19 March, and in the *Observer* (London) on 18 March

1844. No records exist for Mrs Dalgairns's place of burial, nor for a surviving gravestone.

4 The history of the book – a discipline now taught in universities in several countries, including Canada. Following two conferences devoted to the subject, three publications titled *History of the Book in Canada* were published by the University of Toronto Press, covering "Beginnings to 1840" (2004); "1840–1918 (2005); and "1918–1980" (2007).

5 The 1830 Boston/New York edition omits these final chapters except for "Wines" and the "Miscellany."

6 The Loyalists, now known as the United Empire Loyalists of Canada, were the people who fled north during the American Revolution to various parts of British North America. The Callbeck-Coffin marriage was reported in American newspapers, including the *New London Gazette* (New London, Connecticut) on 13 November 1772. Ann's name is given there as "Nancy."

7 The Coffins were descended from Sir Richard Coffyn, who accompanied William the Conqueror from Normandy in 1066, and a descendant who immigrated to New England in the 1600s.

8 In Canadian newspapers, stories about the Mi'kmaq and Sipekne'katik exercising Indigenous historical rights to fish for lobster, mostly in Nova Scotia, have appeared almost daily, beginning in the autumn of 2019. Some local non-Indigenous commercial fishers question First Nations rights to fish "out of season." Negotiations are currently ongoing to determine a precise interpretation of the Supreme Court of Canada's ruling in 1999 that under Indigenous treaty rights, deemed "real and substantial," First Nations are granted the right to earn a "moderate living." Coverage of the lobster dispute ignores the Minigoo Fisheries, operated by the Mi'kmaq on Lennox Island, PEI, beginning in 2010. As a federally licensed seafood processing plant it offered fresh and frozen lobster until bankruptcy forced it to close.

9 A surviving PEI court case from 1785, *King v. Jupiter Wise* (Executive Council Minutes, 1 July 1786, RG2, PAPEI) involves two slaves, Mingo and Guy, both belonging to "Captain Callbeck." See Holman, "Slaves and Servants on Prince Edward Island: The Case of Jupiter Wise," *Acadiensis* 12, 1 (1982): 100–1; Jim Hornby, *Black Islanders: Prince Edward Island's Historical Black Community* (Charlottetown: Institute of Island Studies, 1991), 3, 10, 16–19 (also with the story of *King v. Wise*). In Harvey Armani Whitfield and Barry Cahill, "Slave Life and Slave Law in Colonial Prince Edward Island, 1769–1825," *Acadiensis* 38, 2 (2009): 29–51, Whitfield states that "Attorney-General Phillips Callbeck, an Irish lawyer … was also a slave-holder" (11).

10 In The National Archives Kew (UK) there are numerous official records with regard

to Phillips Callbeck and the defence of Prince Edward Island, e.g.: 5785, PRO 30/55/51/16, to Major General James Paterson: Callbeck raised eighty-five men, and "the company have been constantly doing duty in the garrison of Charlotte Town"; 817, PRO 30/55/88/25, from Thomas Wright, etc. asking for postponement of Clinton's order to disband Phillips Callbeck's company, which the council is "persuaded is so essentially necessary for the safety and protection of the colony"; T 1/545/6 Loyalist claims.

11 The original letters and copies are held by the Library of Congress, George Washington Papers, series 4. These can be accessed at http://founders.archives.gov/documents/Washington/03-02-02-0456.

12 Lorne C. Callbeck, *The Cradle of Confederation: A Brief History of Prince Edward Island from Its Discovery in 1534 to the Present Time* (Fredericton, NB: Brunswick Press, 1964), 80.

13 J.M. Bumsted, *Land, Settlement, and Politics on Eighteenth-Century Prince Edward Island* (Montreal and Kingston: McGill-Queen's University Press, 1987), 14.

14 Lorne, C. Callbeck, *My Island, My People* (Charlottetown: The Prince Edward Island Heritage Foundation, 1979), 49.

15 George Wright, *Who Departed This Life: A History of the Old Protestant Burying Ground, Charlottetown, Prince Edward Island* (Charlottetown: Acorn Press, 2005), 31–6, 160; Orlo Jones and Doris Haslam, eds., *An Island Refuge: Loyalists and Disbanded Troops on the Island of Saint John* (Charlottetown: Abegeweit Branch of the United Empire Loyalists Association of Canada, 1983), 52.

16 See full account of Sir Isaac Coffin's visit to Prince Edward Island in *Lancaster Gazette and General Advertiser* (Lancashire, Westmoreland), 29 October 1808. In gratitude for his loyalist activities on behalf of the British government, Sir Isaac Coffin was granted possession of the Magdalen Island (Îles de la Madeleine). A record of the marriage by licence of Peter Dalgairns and Miss Catherine Emily Callbeck on 11 September 1808 is with St Paul's Anglican Church in Charlottetown (acc. 3069/1) and in records of "Prince Edward Island, Canada, Baptisms, Marriages, Burials, 1780-1983" in the Public Archives and Record Office of Prince Edward Island (PAPEI). The double wedding was reported in the *New-England Palladium* (Boston) on 1 November 1808 and in the *New Brunswick Royal Gazette* for 10 October 1808, where it is noted that the Reverend Theophilus Desbrisay presided over the weddings. At the age of twenty, by royal warrant, the Reverend Desbrisay was appointed minister of the Parish of Charlotte. See *Past and Present of Prince Edward Island, Embracing a Concise Review of Its Early Settlement, Development and Present Conditions, Written*

by the Most Gifted Authors of the Province, under the advisory editorship of Hon. D.A. MacKinnon, LLB, KC, and Hon. A.B. Warburton, DCL, KC (Charlottetown: B.F. Bowen, [1906?]), 248, https://books.google.ca/books?id=KxA1AQAAMAAJ.

17 As Lucille Campey notes in her *A Fine Class of Immigrants: Prince Edward Island's Scottish Pioneers, 1770–1850* (Toronto: Dundurn, Natural Heritage Books, 2001), for Scottish immigrants "the key to this better life was timber. The Scots who came to Prince Edward Island were some of the earliest settlers to exploit the benefits to be had from the rapidly expanding timber trade with Britain" (xi). Peter Dalgairns was one of those Scottish timber buyers and exploiters!

18 Despite being a bankrupt, in Dundee Peter Dalgairns appears to have been accorded the honourable status of a burgess – that is, a freeman and member of the merchant class – with his name appearing in the *The Dundee Lockit Book: Burgess Roll of Dundee, 1513–2009*, for 16 August 1827 as follows: Dalgairns, Peter, Wine Merchant.

19 In a letter dated 23 August 1833, Andrew Dalgairns writes to Cadell from Ingliston to acknowledge receiving "seventy-five pounds sterling being in full payment of the sum you agreed to pay Mrs. Dalgairns for printing fifteen hundred copies of the fourth edition of her book." See Robert Cadell Papers, National Library of Scotland, MSS 21003, 235.

20 "That curious fellow, who takes charge of everyone's business without neglecting his own." This was Sir Walter Scott's comment on Basil Hall. See James McCarthy, *That Curious Fellow: Captain Basil Hall, R.N.* (Caithness, SCT: Whittles Publishing 2011), iii.

21 See Basil Hall, *Fragments of Voyages and Travels of Captain Basil Hall* (Edinburgh: R. Cadell, 1831), 1:93.

22 See correspondence involving Basil Hall, Basil's wife Margaret Hunter Hall, and Mrs Martin Hunter (his sister-in-law) in Public Archives of New Brunswick, Martin Hunter Colonial Administrator, RS333, record series A, correspondence. It is worth noting that Basil and Catherine were both born in 1788 and that both died in 1844.

23 Basil Hall and Mrs General Hunter correspondence, National Library of Scotland, MS 14196, Margaret Hall to Mrs Hunter, January 1808, 75; Basil Hall to Mrs Hunter, 5 February 1808, 1.

24 McCarthy, *That Curious Fellow*, 132–3, 136.

25 For details of the litigation between Mrs Rundell and John Murray, see Sarah Benjamin, "The Author, the Bookseller and the Court Case: Maria Rundell vs. John Murray," *Petiits Propos Culinaires* 14 (June 2019): 70–85. Another invaluable source has been Janet Morgan's preface to a reprint of the 1816 edition of *Domestic Cookery*, published by Persephone Books in 2009.

26 "Maria Rundell," in *Dictionary of National Biography*, vol. 49 (London: Smith, Elder and Co., 1897), 403.

27 During Basil Hall's travels in 1827 to North America, at the Fair and Show of the Agricultural Society in Brighton, Massachusetts, he would have run into two of Catherine Dalgairns's uncles: Sir Isaac Coffin and his brother General John Coffin. In the *American Mercury* (Hartford, CT) for 30 October 1827, General Coffin is described as "a liberal benefactor of the Society," and it is noted that "Capt. Basil Hall, of the British Navy, who in his travels in the United States omits no opportunity of making himself acquainted with all our institutions, and who has expressed his high satisfaction he has derived from his knowledge of them." The president of the society proposed a vote of thanks to General Coffin and his brother Admiral Sir Isaac Coffin, "which was carried by a spontaneous show of hands from every person present."

28 Correspondence and papers of the publisher Robert Cadell, National Library of Scotland, accounts 21056. The agreement is found in Cadell to Hall, 7 August 1828, MS 21007. The one thousand copies were quickly raised to fifteen hundred copies, with subsequent editions also fifteen hundred. The selling price was 7s 6d, with one shilling per copy to Mrs Dalgairns.

29 An early newspaper article in which the stereotype process is described in detail appeared in the *Kingston Chronicle and Gazette* (Ontario), 23 November 1833, copied from *Chamber's Edinburgh Journal.*

30 Basil Hall's wife Margaret was in denial about the puff when writing to her mother in London. "I can assure you Basil is guiltless about any puff in any newspaper, regarding Mrs. Dalgairns." Xerox copies of letters to Jean, Lady Hunter, from members of the family of Sir James Hall of Dunglass, National Library of Scotland, MS 14196, 51.

31 In a letter dated 25 November 1783 to "My Dear Winslow," Phillips Callbeck signs off as "Ever your Faithful and affectionate Phillips Calbeck." See Winslow Papers, University of New Brunswick Archives, vol. 3-31.

32 Reports of the 1811 bankruptcy appeared in the *Hull Packet*, 4 June 1811; *Cheltenham Chronicle*, 6 June 1811; *Caledonian Mercury*, 6 June 1811; the *Tradesman: or, Commercial Magazine* (London), 1 July 1811; *Lincoln, Rutland, Stanford Mercury*, 8 August 1811.

33 The *Times* reported the dissolution of the partnership of Dalgairns and Winslow on 29 March 1819, with sales beginning on 6 April. Two attorneys supported them in the proceedings at the Guildhall.

34 The 1819 directory listing is found in *The Post Office London Directory for 1819*, 88. For 1822, the listing is in *History, Directory and Gazetteer of the County of York; with Select*

Lists of the Merchants and Traders of London. vol. 1, West Riding, lvii. This address can be associated with the present Cannon Street underground station.

35 Newspapers reporting the various Scottish bankruptcies include *Aris's Birmingham Gazette*, 11 March 1824; *Caledonian Mercury* (Edinburgh), 17 March 1827; *Times*, 24 April 1833; *Fife Herald, Kinross, Strathcona and Clackmannan Advertiser*, 19 March 1835; and *Perry's Bankrupt and Insolvent Gazette* (London), 26 September 1835.

36 See "Correspondence and papers, official and private of the first three Earls of Liverpool," British Library, 1, Callbeck (Ann), widow of P. Callbeck, Attorney General of Prince Edward Island, add. 38266 (ff.105), 38367 ff.33, ff.66–68, ff.70–. ff.73 (ff.105). In his will, made out in 1790, Phillips Callbeck appointed his wife "my Sole Executive of this my last Will" but without any indication of his assets at that time. See National Archives Kew, Prob 11/1202/272.

37 Notice of Ann's death at Bath, "relict of the late Philips Callbeck, Esq. many years Attorney General of this Island," was published in the *Prince Edward Island Register* of 2 February 1827.

38 Dated 29 September 1800, the letter is in Macdonald Papers (Z664), PAPEI.

39 The diary is owned by well-known culinary historian Peter Brears, who in his 2018 series of articles in *Petits Propos Culinaires*, 110–12, gives readers the minutiae of the contents of the diary.

40 Papers of Robert Cadell, publisher, diaries, National Library of Scotland, MS 21018 – 1.

41 *Dublin Evening Post*, 7 July 1829; *Times* 20 April 1829; *Scotsman*, 29 April 1829.

42 See Diana Cooper-Richet and Emily Borgeaud, *Galignani*, English version by Iain Watson (Paris: Galignani, 1999), 9–10.

43 "Mrs. Dalgairn's Cookery" was offered by bookseller James W. Waugh in the *Sydney Morning Herald* for 30 May 1861. The *Bruce Herald* of Otago, New Zealand, featured advertisements for the cookbook from 8 September 1874 well into 1875. Given that Mrs Beeton's *Book of Household Management* had put an end to new editions of the most popular British cookbooks that had preceded it, the fact that both Dalgairns and Beeton appear alongside each other in a single advertisement is a wonder to behold.

44 While there were undoubtedly earlier advertisements in India, D'Rozario and Co. of Calcutta offered for sale on 24 April 1845 "Dalgairn's Practice of Cookery, adapted to the business of every day life" in the *Friend of India* newspaper.

45 Most of these cookbooks were published and advertised over several decades in ongoing editions. Among American cookbooks offered by Canadian booksellers were

Mrs Lydia Child's *The American Frugal Housewife* (Boston, 1829); Mary Randolph's *The Virginia Housewife or Methodical Cook* (Washington, 1824); and *Seventy-five Receipts, for Pastry, Cakes, and Sweetmeats, by a Lady of Philadelphia* [Eliza Leslie] (Boston, 1828). British titles popular in the Canadas included Meg Dods's *Cook and Housewife's Manual* (Edinburgh, 1826); Mary Holland's *The Modern Family Receipt Book* (London, 1825); William Kitchiner's *The Cook's Oracle* (London, 1817); David Hughson's *The New Family Receipt Book* (London, 1811); Mrs Rundell's *A New System of Domestic Cookery* (London/Edinburgh,1806); and Eustache Ude's *The French Cook* (London, 1813).

46 An advertisement placed by Neilson and Cowan for "Dalgairn's Practice of Cookery" appeared in the *Quebec Gazette/Gazette de Québec* on 31 December 1829. In issues ranging through 1834, the *Montreal Herald and Daily Commercial Gazette* told readers that "Mrs. Dalgairn's 'Practice of Cookery'" was available from the newspaper office.

47 Catherine Parr Traill, *The Backwoods of Canada: Being Letters from the Wife of an Emigrant Officer, Illustrative of the Domestic Economy of British America* (London: C. Knight, 1836), 124. Traill's observation was copied word for word by W.P. Willis for a chapter titled "Impressions of Canada among Immigrants," in *Canadian Scenery Illustrated: From Drawings by W.H. Bartlett, the Literary Department by N.P. Willis Esq.*, vol. 1 (London: George Virtue, 1842), 76.

48 Library and Archives Canada, Neilson Printing firm, MG 24, B1.

49 The quotations are taken from "A Happy Transition from Cookery to Literature," in *The Lady's Magazine* for July 1829, 372–73.

50 *Scots Times*, 25 April 1829; *Spectator*, 13 June 1829.

51 Between early March and late November of 1830 advertisements for the third (1830) edition appeared in over a dozen English and Scottish newspapers, including the *Times*.

52 *Foreign Quarterly Review* 33 (1844): 98–114.

53 According to Basil Hall, by means of a fast ship from Liverpool, a courier galloping at break-neck speed from New York to Philadelphia, and dozens of printing presses "kept in motion day and night," ten thousand copies of Sir Walter's latest novel were published in North America before its appearance in Great Britain.

54 See Scott E. Casper, *Perspectives on American Book History* (Boston: University of Massachusetts Press, 2002), 522.

55 American Antiquarian Society, *Third Boston Trade Sale: Catalogue of Books to Be Sold to Booksellers Only, on Tuesday July 21, 1829* (Boston), BDSDS 1829 F.

56 Beginning in September 1829, advertisements, usually placed by the publisher or a

bookseller, appeared regularly in newspapers – for example, in the *Christian Register* (Boston, 19 and 26 September 1829), the *Christian Examiner and General Review* (New York, March 1830), the *Charleston Courier* (South Carolina), the *Portland Advertiser* (Maine), the *New Hampshire Patriot and State Gazette* (Concord, New Hampshire), the *National Gazette* (Philadelphia), the *Baltimore Patriot*, the *Boston Courier*, and the *Evening Post* (New York), plus many other newspapers in several States of the Union. Monroe and Francis were the publishers of one of North America's most popular cookbook authors: Eliza Leslie. At the end of the fourth edition of *Seventy-Five Recipes for Pastry, Cakes, and Sweetmeats*, published in 1832 by Monroe and Francis, a list of books for sale includes "The Practice of Cookery, adapted to the business of Every-Day Life. By Mrs. Dalgairns. Containing 1419 of the most useful receipts."

57 From the *Charleston Courier*, 25 December 1829: "It seems that the laurels of the worthy Captain may continue to be verdant in the pantry after they have withered in the library, that his name may still live in the mouths of scullions when it is forgotten by scholars, and that it may be associated with the agreeable ideas of bread and butter, ham and mustard, long after it has ceased to stir the bile of the over sensitive citizen of these states."

58 *Feeding America* is an online collection of the most important and influential early American cookbooks, created and sponsored by Michigan State University.

59 What happened to that trust fund, and the royalties, we shall never know, given that Mrs Dalgairns did not make out a duly registered will. And there is no public account of how the trust fund was concluded.

60 It seems that Griffin's *A Catalogue of Standard Works* was not issued from time to time on its own but, rather, as an appendix (up to thirty-six pages long) to books published by Griffin and Co. In this case, it is found at the back of *A Manual of Nursing, Medical and Surgical* by Laurence Humphry, published in 1889. A similar listing appears at the back of a Charles Griffin and Co. book published five years earlier in 1884, and back then it was the same situation, with a seventeenth edition of Mrs Dalgairns "in preparation."

61 See Kathryn Hughes, *The Short Life and Long Times of Mrs. Beeton* (London: Fourth Estate, 2006).

62 It should be noted here that, after his wife's death, Peter Dalgairns remarried in 1854, this time to Ann Will, and the two became the parents (he at age seventy-two!) of Mary Graham, known as "May," on 23 December 1855. Peter died of "Paralysis" at the age of seventy-three on 25 March 1857, while still living at Shore Terrace in Dundee. He was buried in the Dalgairns family graveyard in the Eassie Burying Ground in the County of Angus.

63 *La Belle Assemblée*, June 1829, 277–8.
64 Cadell Papers, National Library of Scotland, MS 21003, 234.
65 Ibid., MS 14196, photocopies, 51
66 F. Marian McNeill, *The Scots Kitchen: Its Traditions and Lore with Old-Time Recipes* 2nd ed. (Glasgow and London: Blackie and Son, 1963 [1929]), 34. It is worth mentioning that, in this book, McNeill provides readers with several of Mrs Dalgairns's recipes: Montrose Cakes, 198; Scots Seed Cake, 198; Honey Cakes, 200; The Queen's Tea Cakes, 203; Caledonian Liquor, 249; Deer Horns, 194; Scots Pancakes, 195; Aberdeen Crulla, 193; Whim Wham, 174; Fairy Butter, 175; Mrs Dalgairns's Scots Pudding, 169; Aunt Mary's Pudding, 164; and Nun's Beads, 162.
67 John Stewart, *An Account of Prince Edward Island in the Gulph of St Lawrence, North America* (London: W. Winchester and Son, 1806). Two other early nineteenth-century British authors addressed the bounty found in and on the Island: James Asperne, *Information to Emigrants: An Account of the Island of Prince Edward with Practical Advice to Those Intending to Emigrate* (London: James Asperne, 1819), 14; and John Cambridge, *A Description of Prince Edward Island in the Gulph of Saint Laurence, North America*, 3rd ed. (Bristol: Jonathan Baller, 1818), 6–7.
68 The cookbook was advertised in the *Observer* for 20 and 21 January 1832, said to be published in February at a price of ten shillings sixpence, bound.
69 A Quebec edition of *La Cuisinière Bourgeoise* appeared in 1825, and in London in 1793 an English translation was published as *The French Family Cook: Being a Complete System of French Cookery.*
70 Archive of John Murray, publishers, National Library of Scotland, MS 40307, fols. 59–62.
71 See C. Ann Wilson's articles on "The French Connection" in *Petits Propos Culinaires* 2 (August 1979) and 4 (February 1980).
72 Hannah Glasse, *The Art of Cookery, made Plain and Easy; Which Far Exceeds any Thing of the Kind yet Published* (London: A. Millar, and T. Trye, 1758), iv.
73 Thomas Webster, *An Encyclopaedia of Domestic Economy* (London: Longman, Brown, Green and Longmans, 1844), book 14, chap, 2, item 5301, 916.
74 This reminiscence of Elizabeth Grant dates to 1818–19 in *Memoirs of a Highland Lady* (Edinburgh: Canongate Classics, 1988 [1898]), 2:90. Corner dishes – that is, dishes that were placed at the corners of the table – played an essential role in the fashion of "French service" (*service ä la française*), which later in the century was replaced by *service à la russe*.
75 Snow had operated the Epicurean Eating House at 601 Pennsylvania Avenue in Washington. During the race riots of 1835 Snow was forced to flee a mob that burned

down his restaurant, and he made his way to Toronto. In Washington there is a historic plaque at 601 Pennsylvania Avenue commemorating, among others, Beverly Snow. For the full story of Beverly Snow in Washington and Toronto, see Jefferson Morley, *Snow-Storm in August: Washington City, Francis Scott Key, and the Forgotten Race Riot of 1835* (New York: Nan A. Talese/Doubleday, 2012). The menu was first published in the *British Colonist* (Toronto) for 17 November 1848. It was forwarded to Morley by Mary Williamson and reprinted by Morley on page 259.

76 Mark Kurlansky, *The Big Oyster: History on the Half Shell* (New York: Ballantine Books, 2006), 109–10.

77 *The French Family Cook*, published in London in 1793, was a translation of Menon's *La Cuisinière bourgeoise*, originally published in Paris in 1746.

78 See George Leard, "Rum 'N' Ribbons," *Loyalist Gazette* 21, 1 (Spring 1983): 23.

79 In a London newspaper advertisement headed INDIAN CURRIES and MULLIGATAWNIES, Cooke and Co., of 99 Hatton Garden, offers a substantial range of Indian condiments, among them Curry Paste, Curry Powders, Bengal Chattney, Indian Fish Sauce, and Indian recipes for meats and game, all to be had at Fortnum and Mason at 182 Piccadilly. See the *Examiner*, 26 April 1829, 272. And, quite by coincidence, on the previous page (271) appears an ad for *The Practice of Cookery* … by Mrs Dalgairns, "just published in 1 thick volume."

80 See William Kitchiner in his *The Cook's Oracle: Containing Receipts for Plain Cookery, on the Most Economical Plan for Private Families*. A new edition (London: Robert Cadell of Edinburgh, 1831), 358–59, where he observes: "This recipe was an attempt to imitate some of the Best *Indian Curry Powder*, selected for me by a friend at the India House: – the flavour approximates to the Indian Powder so exactly, the most profound Palaticians have pronounced it a perfect copy of the original *Curry Stuff*."

81 See Hall, *Fragments of Voyages and Travels*, 21: "I think upon a pinch, I could make a tolerable curry myself."

82 Excellent modern sources for the history of curry include: Colleen Taylor Sen's *Curry: A Global History* (London: Reaktion Books, 2009); and Lizzie Collingham's *Curry: A Tale of Cooks and Conquerors* (New York: Oxford University Press, 2006).

83 Joseph Burnett, in *About Vanilla* (Boston: The Joseph Burnett Company, 1900), 21, claims that, "as early as 1610, two or three vanilla beans were received in England by one Hugh Morgan, pharmacist to Queen Elizabeth."

84 Fabrizia Lanza, in her *Olive: A Global History* (London: Reaktion Books, 2011), 64, notes that, in addition to the reality of imported olive oil's having a rancid taste, "it was also a question of palate" and social rank as to whether one leaned towards olive oil or butter.

85 There were "exceptions to the rule." For example, in his *The Complete Confectioner and Family Cook, Including All the Late Improvements* (Edinburgh: John Anderson, 1809), John Caird, a confectioner who owned a shop on the east coast of Scotland, lists six ounces of Pot, or Pearl Ashes, for "Fine Gingerbread" and "German Gingerbread" but not for cakes. Another unusual exception is "American Potash Cakes," published in Duncan Macdonald's *The London Family Cook* (London: James Cundee, 1808), 289. 8. The recipe requires the cook to "make a solution of about a half a tea-spoonful of salt of tartar, crystal of soda, or any purified potash."

86 See Charles Dickens, *Life, Letters and Speeches of Charles Dickens, with Biographical Sketches of the Principal Illustrators of Dickens's Work.* Ed. Edwin Percy Whipple and others, vol. 1 (Boston and New York: Houghton Mifflin and Co., 1894), 114.

87 See Stana Nenadic, "Middle-Rank Consumers and Domestic Culture in Edinburgh and Glasgow, 1720–1840," *Past and Present* 145 (1994): 122–54.

88 Anne C. Wilson, in her *Eating with the Victorians* (UK: Stroud: Sutton Publishing Ltd., 2004), 58, notes that, like Maria Rundell, Mrs Dalgairns "is concerned with food within the general requirements of housekeeping, not with meals as such." The final (1834) edition of Elizabeth Raffald's *The Experienced English Housekeeper* (Derby: Henry Mozley and Sons, 1834) continues (since the first edition in 1769) the inclusion of two folding copper-plates illustrating the first and second courses served *à la française* for "young housekeepers." Raffald, whose recipes were copied by Queen Victoria, writes that she deliberately omitted a plate demonstrating the third course, which normally would have shown desserts and patisseries. Largely because hot dishes, served together with cold dishes, quickly turned into cold dishes themselves, by the 1860s service *à la russe*, which involves serving dishes sequentially, as practised today, took over from service *à la française*.

89 In the United States, with plentiful wood, it was only when the price of wood increased that "anthracite coal which burned more steadily and less smokily than wood" became more popular as fuel. See Andrew F. Smith, ed., *The Oxford Encyclopedia of Food and Drink in America* (New York: Oxford University Press, 2004), 2:500.

90 See Brears in Pamela A. Sambrook and Peter Brears, eds., *The Country House Kitchen, 1650–1900* (London: Alan Sutton Publishing in Association with National Trust Enterprises, 1996), 110; and Webster, *Encyclopaedia of Domestic Economy*, bk. 11, chap. 3, 813–14.

91 Here it is worth noting a comment by Margaret Hunter Hall, the wife of Basil Hall, during their 1827 tour of the United States. In her letters to her sister she observes that, while visiting a lady in Boston, she had been kept waiting for an hour. "I think this may in part arise from the want of good servants, which makes it necessary for

the ladies to assist in many menial offices, particularly in cooking." See Una Pope-Hennessy, *The Aristocratic Journey: Being the Outspoken Letters of Mrs. Basil Hall, Written during a Fourteen Months Sojourn in America, 1827–1828* (New York: Knickerbocker Press, 1931), 84.

92 See the *Globe* (Toronto) newspaper for 5 June 1847.

93 Clarissa Dickson Wright, *A History of English Food* (London: Arrow Books, Random House, 2012), 283.

94 McNeill, *Scots Kitchen*, 23.

95 See Charles Mackie, *Historical Description of the Town of Dundee* (Glasgow: Joseph Swan; London: Smith, Elder and Co., 1836), 165.

96 See Marie Nightingale, "The Enduring Influences on Today's East Coast Cooking," in *Northern Bounty: A Celebration of Canadian Cuisine*, ed. Jo Marie Powers and Anita Stewart (Toronto: Random House, 1995), 210.

97 For New York harbour, see Kurlansky, *Big Oyster*, in particular the chapter "Eggocentric New Yorkers." In their *The Englishman's Food: A History of Five Centuries of English Diet*, rev. Dorothy Hollingsworth (London: Pimlico 1991 [1939]), J.C. Drummond and Anne Wilbraham note on page 309 that, in Charles Dickens, "poverty and oysters seem to go together"; however, late in the 1840s "they were so dear as to be a luxury only the wealthy could afford." In Laura Mason and Catherine Brown's *The Taste of Britain* (London: Harper Press, 2006), 88 and 335, it is said that in England up until the 1860s there had been an oversupply of oysters, but disease and bad weather led to significant increases in their price. In Georgian and Victorian Scotland, a plenitude of oysters had made them the subject of celebration by poets and writers.

98 Mistress Margaret Dods of the Cleikum Inn, St Ronan's, *The Cook and Housewife's Manual: A Practical System of Modern Domestic Cookery and Family Management*, 4th ed., revised and enlarged (Edinburgh: Oliver and Boyd, 1829 [Reprint with Introduction by Glynn Christian (London: Rosters, 1988)]), 193.

99 See Sondra Gotlieb, *The Gourmet's Canada* (Toronto: New Press, 1972), 39.

100 See Julie V. Watson, "Global Marketing of Lobster: A Prince Edward Island Success Story," in *Northern Bounty: A Celebration of Canadian Cuisine*, ed. Jo Marie Powers and Anita, 203–8 (Toronto: Random House, 1995).

101 Janet E. Chute, "Mi'kmaq Fishing in the Maritimes: A Historical Overview," in *Earth, Water, Air and Fire: Studies in Canadian Ethnohistory*, edited by David McNab for Nin. Da.Waab.Jig (Group), 95–113 (Waterloo, ON: Wilfrid Laurier University Press, 1998).

102 Judith Comfort, "Some Good! The Maritime Harvest," in *Northern Bounty: A Celebration of Canadian Cuisine*, ed. Jo Marie Powers and Anita (Toronto: Random

House, 1995), 199. Comfort continues: "This ingenious method was developed before the introduction of metal cooking pots … a good thick hardwood board and a criss-cross of alder twigs pinned with small nails. We prop the plank in front of our fire-place and the heat reflected by the fire wall sears the fish. The delectable juices are sealed in behind a golden smoky crust."

103 Mary Quayle Innis, *Mrs. Simcoe's Diary* (Toronto: Macmillan of Canada, 1965), 104.

104 Webster, *Encyclopaedia of Domestic Economy*, bk. 5, chap. 6, 425, item 2218.

105 William L. Mackenzie, *Sketches of Canada and the United States* (London: Effingham Wilson, 1833), 214.

106 Mrs Rundell, *A New System of Domestic Cookery: Formed on Principles of Economy and Adapted to the Use of Private Families, By a Lady* (London: J. Murray, 1806), xvi.

107 Samuel Johnson, *A Journey to the Western Islands of Scotland* (London: W. Strahan and T. Cadell, 1775), 238.

108 Helen Saberi and Alan Davidson, *Trifle* (Totnes, UK: Prospect Books, 2001), 19–20.

109 See Margaret Visser, *Much Depends on Dinner: The Extraordinary History and Mythology, Allure, and Obsessions, Perils and Taboos, of an Ordinary Meal* (Toronto: McClelland and Stewart, 1986), 303.

110 Mason and Brown, *Taste of Britain*, 422–3.

111 Raffald, *Experienced English Housekeeper*, 270. In a second way of making Shrewsbury Cakes Raffald adds "a little mace." Rundell, *New System of Domestic Cookery*, 238.

112 I am indebted to Clarissa Dickson Wright's *History of English Food* for the history of vegetables and fruit in England.

113 Marmalade first arrived in England in the late Middle Ages from Portugal (*marmelada*) and later from other southern European countries. Back then it was made from peaches, apricots, or figs, and other fruits. For the early history of marmalade, see Anne C. Wilson, *The Book of Marmalade* (UK, Totnes: Prospect Books, 1999), and for the world-famous Keiller brand of marmalade, see W.M. Mathew, *Keiller's of Dundee: The Rise of the Marmalade Dynasty, 1800–1879* (Dundee: Abertay Historical Society, 1998).

114 See Nathalie Cooke and Fiona Lucas, eds., *Catharine Parr Traill's "The Female Emigrant's Guide": Cooking with a Canadian Classic* (Montreal and Kingston: McGill-Queen's University Press, 2017), 382.

115 In his 1825 *La physiologie du goût*, the renowned French gastronome Jean-Anthelme Brillat-Savarin devotes a short chapter in "Meditation VI" to coffee, its culinary history, and his experiences of the beverage. In the 1854 English translation, titled *The Physiology of Taste,* he observes: "The unanimous opinion was that coffee which had

been beaten in a mortar was far better than that which had been ground." Apparently, "during the Regency [chocolate] was more universally used than coffee … coffee was esteemed a luxury." In her recipe for "Milk Coffee for Breakfast" was Mrs Dalgairns offering us a *café au lait* Brillat-Savarin style? With sugar, "mingled with *café au lait*, a light pleasant aliment is produced, precisely suited to those who have to go to their offices immediately after breakfast." See Jean-Anthelme Brillat-Savarin, *The Physiology of Taste, or Meditations on Transcendental Gastronomy* (Philadelphia: Lindsay and Blakiston, 1854), 135–45.

The Practice of Cookery

THE PRACTICE OF COOKERY

ADAPTED TO

THE BUSINESS OF EVERYDAY LIFE

BY

MRS DALGAIRNS

CONTENTS

PREFACE

This Volume contains a Complete System of Practical Cookery, so carefully adapted to the purposes of every-day life, that although a person totally unacquainted with the art here treated of may not be able at first to dress a dinner, merely by referring to this book, any Cook or Housekeeper, possessed of ordinary experience, will certainly have the means of knowing, without further help than what these pages afford, how to prepare, in the best manner, every dish at present in general use.

There are Twenty-five Chapters in all, arranged in the order of the following List, each of which is preceded by those useful Preparatory Remarks, which are usually kept at the beginning of the volume, at a most inconvenient distance from the subject treated of. This is often embarrassing; and, it is believed, the novelty in arrangement here adopted, will be found advantageous to all parties concerned.

A copious alphabetical Table of Contents will be found at the beginning of the volume.* Great pains have been taken to compose a work having, in all respects, a practical character. Care has also been used to collect valuable materials from various authentic sources, the chief object being the composition of a treatise which might be called with truth, the Cook's Companion in the practice of Cookery; and at the same time, be no less useful to the mistress of a family, if required for occasional reference.

The chief requisites, in a work of this kind, are first, the intrinsic excellence of the precepts it contains; next, their economical adaptation to the habits and tastes of the majority of its readers; and, lastly, such a distinct arrangement of the various parts, that no difficulty can arise in searching for what is wanted, nor any ambiguity in the meaning of the directions when found.

* The 1830 edition included a detailed alphabetical index of recipes following the preface (and a small table of contents listing the twenty-five chapters – "In all 1482 Receipts" – just above this paragraph.

A perfectly original book of Cookery would neither meet with, nor deserve, much attention; because what is wanted in this matter, is not receipts for new dishes, but clear instructions how to make those already established in public favour. The study, therefore, of the author has been to consult the best authorities; to compare different receipts with care and impartiality, and afterwards to select for publication those only which appeared economical, easy to follow, and calculated to furnish the dishes required for daily use, as well as those for occasions of ceremony. But nothing has been considered worthy of adoption, however high its pretensions, without some specific and substantial recommendations. Every receipt, therefore, has either been actually tried by the author, or by persons whose accuracy in the various manipulations could be safely relied upon.

The defects usually complained of in most cookery books are their extravagance, and their want of distinctness in the directions. In many cases, they are perversely adapted exclusively to the finances of persons who never think of reading receipts at all, but who overcome the whole difficulty by keeping highly-educated, and, of course, expensive Cooks. Such works, therefore, afford little assistance to the young mistress of a family, to country servants, or even to persons who live in towns, but whose circumstances are so limited, that, with all the disposition in the world to learn the art of Cookery, they have no means of putting such costly lessons in practice.

It is hoped that such criticisms will not apply to this work: as the author has used every effort of industry and patience, to arrive at the truth, and to impart it clearly and forcibly to others, so that correct knowledge and judicious economy might go hand in hand, in this important branch of housekeeping.

PREFACE

TO THE THIRD EDITION

Every Receipt in this Work has been carefully revised for this Edition, in order that advantage might be taken of the numerous valuable criticisms by which it has been honoured in all parts of the Empire.

A considerable number of new Receipts have also been added; but only such as the Author has had adequate means of ascertaining to be valuable – a principle which has been scrupulously adhered to throughout the volume.

THE

PRACTICE OF COOKERY

CHAPTER 1
SOUPS

PREPARATORY REMARKS ON SOUPS AND GRAVIES

EVERY utensil employed in a kitchen must be kept scrupulously clean, and a cook ought to take especial care that all her sauce-pans be in good order. Brass pans are preferable for preserving in, and cast-iron and double block-tin are the best sort in use for every other purpose; their covers should be made to fit closely, and the tinning of the cast-iron pots and pans always renewed as soon as it is observed to be wearing off. While new, they may be easily kept clean by washing them regularly with hot water, and rubbing on them when quite dry, a little whitening with leather or flannel. After long use, they will require occasional scouring with fine sand; and before they're used, they ought always to be rinsed out with hot water, and wiped with a clean cloth. A landlady will find it good economy, and for her advantage in other respects, to provide plenty of stone-ware and earthen vessels, and also common dishes for the kitchen, that the table-set may not be used to keep cold meat on.

In boiling soup, less water is used in a digester than in a common pot, as in the digester no steam can escape.

To extract the strength from meat, long and slow boiling is necessary, but care must be taken that the pot is never off the boil. All soups are the better for being made the day before they are to be used, and they should then be strained into earthen pans. When soup has jellied in the pan, it should not be removed into another, as breaking it will occasion its becoming sour sooner than it would otherwise do; when in danger of not keeping, it should be boiled up. It never keeps long with many vegetables in it. The meat used for soups or broths cannot be too fresh. When any animal food is plain boiled, the liquor, with the addition of the trimmings of meat and poultry, makes good soups and gravies, as do also the bones of roasted or broiled meat. The gravies left in the dishes answer for hashes, and the liquor in which veal has been boiled, may be made into a glaze by boiling it with a ham bone till reduced to a third or fourth part, and seasoning it with the necessary herbs and spices.

In boiling weak soups, the pan should be uncovered that the watery particles may escape. Cow-heel jelly improves every sort of rich soup; and for thickening, truffles, morels, and dried mushrooms, may be used with advantage.

Directions are given with each of the following soups for thickening with flour and butter, cream and eggs; after the cream and eggs are added, the soup must not be allowed to boil.

Should brown gravy or mock-turtle soup be spoiling, fresh-made charcoal, roughly pounded, tied in a little bag and boiled with either, will absorb the bad flavour, and leave it sweet and good. The charcoal may be made by simply putting a bit of wood into the fire, and pounding the burnt part in a mortar.

Mullagatawny Soup

PUT half a pound of fresh butter, with six large onions sliced, three cloves of garlic, some chopped parsley, and sweet marjoram, into a stew-pan, let it stew over a slow fire till of a light brown colour; cut in small pieces five pounds of lean beef, and let that stew till the gravy be extracted, and then put in three quarts of boiling water, and half a pound of Scotch barley, and let it simmer four hours very slowly; mix four table spoonfuls of currie-powder with cold water, and add it to the stock; take out the beef, and rub the barley through a sieve, to thicken the soup. Cut a fowl in joints, skin it, and put it in a stew-pan with a piece of butter, and let it stew till quite tender; the stew-pan must be kept closely covered: this to be added to the soup, the last thing, with a pint of boiling milk, and the juice of two lemons. Boiled rice must always be served with this soup.

Another Mullagatawny Soup

MAKE a strong stock of the bones of roasted beef, mutton, and fowl; while it is preparing, put into a stew-pan, with six ounces of butter, three quarts of sliced turnip, two quarts of carrots, and eight large onions also sliced; let them stew upon the stove till tender; then add three quarts of the prepared stock, a large slice of the crumb of bread, and two table-spoonfuls of currie-powder; let them stew four or five hours; strain it through a tammy cloth, with two wooden spoons, taking care that no bones be left amongst the vegetables; if too thick to go through, add more stock. Then cut a fowl in pieces, fry it in a frying pan with butter, and add it to the soup; after it has boiled a little, draw it to the side of the stove, and let it simmer, that the grease may be taken off. A little good beef stock, in addition to that made of the bones, will be an improvement. It is sometimes thickened with whole or ground rice, instead of bread, and ought to be made upon a stove.

Mullagatawny, or Currie Broth

Make about two quarts of strong veal broth, seasoned with two onions, a bunch of parsley, salt and pepper; strain it, and have ready a chicken, cut in joints and skinned; put it into the broth, with a table-spoonful of currie-powder; boil the chicken till quite tender, and a little before serving, add the juice of a lemon, and stir in a tea-cupful of cream. Serve boiled rice to eat with this broth.

Mullagatawny

Boil slowly in two quarts of water one pound of split peas, half an ounce of butter, two onions sliced, a little salt, cayenne, and two blades of mace. When the peas are tender put in a large fowl, cut in joints and skinned, two quarts of boiling water, or stock, if the soup be required very rich; twenty minutes before serving, add a large table-spoonful of currie-powder, and the same of ground rice.

Calf's-Head Soup, or Mock Turtle

Parboil a calf's head, take off the skin and cut it in bits about an inch and a half square, cut the fleshy parts in bits, take out the black part of the eyes, and cut the rest in rings, skin the tongue, and cut it in slices, add it all to three quarts of good stock, and season it with cayenne, two or three blades of mace, salt, the peel of half a lemon, and half a pint of white wine, with about a dozen of forcemeat balls; stew all this an hour and a half, rub down with a little cold water, two table-spoonfuls of flour, mix well amongst it half a pint of the soup, and then stir it into the pot; put in the juice of half a large lemon, and the hard-boiled yolks of eight eggs; let it simmer for ten minutes, and then put it all in the tureen. When eggs are scarce, boil two eggs hard, pound the yolks in a mortar with a pinch of salt, adding the yolk of a raw egg; when well mixed together, put them on a table dusted with flour, roll them in the form of a small sausage, and cut them into very small equal parts; round every piece in the palm of the hand with a little flour, and put them on a plate as they are done; give them a boil in boiling water, then put in fresh cold water, drain them through a tammy before putting them into the soup, ragout, or any dressed dish.

Another Calf's-Head Soup

SCALD and clean thoroughly a calf's-head with the skin on, boil it an hour gently in three quarts of water, and parboil it with some sweetbreads. Cut off the meat, slice and fry of a light brown in butter two pounds of gravy beef, one of veal, and one of mutton, with five onions cut small; put all into the liquor, adding the bones of the head broken; rinse the frying-pan with two quarts of boiling water, and put it to the meat, and other things, with two whole onions, a bunch of sweet herbs, and twice their quantity of parsley; the peel of one lemon, four cloves, a little all-spice, salt, and black pepper, with a slice of the crumb of bread dried before the fire; let all this stew slowly for five hours, strain it, and when cold, take off all the fat. Cut the meat of the calf's-head, tongue, and sweetbreads, in small square bits, add them to the soup, and when it has boiled, mix very gradually with a large table-spoonful of flour, a cupful of the soup, and stir it gently into the pot; twenty minutes before serving, add a small tea-spoonful of cayenne, the yolks of eight or ten hard-boiled eggs and the same number of forcemeat balls; a pint of white wine, – madeira is the best, – and just before serving, add the juice of a lemon. Forcemeat balls for this soup are made as follows: Mix the brains with five table-spoonfuls of grated bread, the same of finely minced beef suet, a tea-spoonful of salt, one of white pepper, the grated peel of a lemon, some nutmeg, and boiled parsley chopped; beat the yolks and white of two eggs, roll the balls the size of the yolk of an egg, and fry them of a light brown in boiling dripping.

Another Calf's-Head Soup

TAKE as much as is required of not very strong veal, or beef stock, in which six onions have been boiled, brown two ounces of butter, and thicken it well with flour, then add the stock by degrees; when it boils, put in the calf's-head cut in small pieces, and some fried forcemeat balls; season it with salt and pepper. The peel of half a lemon improves it. When it has boiled twenty minutes, add two table-spoonfuls of catsup, three of essence of anchovies, and as much lemon pickle as will make it a pleasant acid. To give the soup a good colour, and to enrich the flavour, may be added a large table-spoonful of flour, mixed perfectly smooth in a tea-cupful of cold water, and stirred gradually into the soup, after which let it boil a few minutes.

Another Calf's-Head Soup

CUT half a pound of lean veal in small pieces, fry it of a light brown in butter; cut off the meat in small pieces from the bones of a cow-heel that has been boiled tender, put it into a stew-pan with the veal and two quarts of beef gravy, one anchovy, and a bit of butter, some cayenne, a blade of mace, and three cloves; stew it slowly an hour, then add a large glass of madeira, or any white wine, the green part of a leek, some parsley, and lemon thyme chopped small, lemon peel shred fine, and the juice of half a lemon. Let it stew very gently an hour and a half. Serve it with forcemeat balls, and the yolks of hard-boiled eggs.

Brown Gravy Soup

TAKE fifteen pounds of a leg or shin of beef, cut off the meat in bits, rub the bottom of the pot with butter, put in the meat, let it brown for nearly an hour, turning it constantly; break the bone, and take out the marrow, which may be kept for a pudding, but it is considered better than butter to brown the meat with; put to the meat fourteen quarts of cold water, and the bones; when it boils, skim it perfectly clean, and add six good-sized red onions, one carrot cut in three, one head of celery, a good handful of whole black and Jamaica pepper mixed; let this boil very gently ten or twelve hours closely covered, if upon a fire, but if done upon a hot plate not to be covered; strain it through a cullender, and then through a hair sieve, into a large pan to be kept for use. Return the meat and bones into the pot with three or four quarts of hot water; let it boil nearly two hours, and strain it off. This makes good stock for gravies, stews, or any made dishes.

This gravy soup keeps perfectly good for three or four weeks. When it is to be boiled to send to table, first boil vermicelli, or macaroni, in a little salt and water, till tender; strain it, and add it to the soup just before serving. This soup is quite pure, and requires no clearing. It is a most convenient thing to have in a house in cold weather, as it is always ready for use; and, served with dry toast to eat with it, makes an acceptable luncheon.

The trimmings of meat, giblets, and bones, may he boiled with the beef for this soup.

Another Brown Gravy Soup

CUT down three pounds of gravy-beef, and put it on in a stew-pan with three onions cut small, and two ounces of butter; let it brown well, stirring it to prevent the onions from burning; then add four quarts of water, one head of celery, of carrots and turnips two each, with some whole black pepper and salt; boil it gently for four hours; strain it; and the next day take off the fat. When it is heated, add some vermicelli, previously boiled in water, and serve it after boiling ten minutes.

Currie Soup

MINCE small three or four onions, according to their size, put them into a sauce-pan with two ounces of butter, dredge in some flour, and fry them till of a light brown, taking care not to burn them; rub in by degrees a large table-spoonful and a half of currie-powder, till it be quite a paste; gradually stir in three quarts of gravy soup, mixing it well together; boil it gently till it be well flavoured with the currie-powder; strain it into another sauce-pan, and add a fowl skinned and cut in small pieces, dividing each joint; stew it slowly an hour. In half a pint of the soup put a large table-spoonful of tamarinds, and stew them so as to separate the stalks and stones; strain and stir it into the soup with half a tea-spoonful of salt, and boil it for fifteen minutes before serving.

Soup Cressy

SLICE twelve large onions, and fry them pretty brown in a quarter of a pound of fresh butter; scrape and clean two dozen of good red carrots, boil them in four quarts of water till quite soft; pound them in a marble mortar, mix them with the onions, and add the liquor in which the carrots were boiled, a bunch of sweet herbs, pepper, salt, a blade of mace, and two or three cloves; let them all boil about an hour, then rub them through a hair sieve; put it on again to boil rather quickly, till it be as thick as rich cream. Put a little dry boiled rice in the tureen, and pour the soup over it. If the carrots are large, one dozen will be found sufficient.

Another Soup Cressy

WASH clean, and cut small, eight carrots, eight turnips, three heads of celery, and six onions; put them in a stew-pan with a quarter of a pound of butter and a slice of ham, stew them gently for an hour, stirring them constantly; when they begin to brown add as much gravy soup as will fill the tureen, let it boil till the vegetables are sufficiently tender to pulp with a spoon through a sieve, after which put it on the fire and boil it half an hour, skim, and season it with pepper and salt. This soup should be as thick as melted butter. Two pounds of beef boiled in four quarts of water till reduced to three, will answer for the soup.

Scotch Hare Soup

SKIN the hare, taking care to preserve the blood; cut the hare in pieces, wash it clean, cut off the fleshy parts of the back and hind legs; put all the rest on in a stew-pan with a table-spoonful of butter; keep the cover on close, and let it stew half an hour; stir it now and then. In another sauce-pan put about two ounces of butter, and three table-spoonfuls of flour; brown it nicely. Mix the blood with four quarts of cold water, strain it, and with the rest of the meat add it to the browned butter; stir it constantly, and when it boils put it to the hare which is stewing, and add one carrot, one head of celery, and three large onions cut small; season with pepper and salt. Let it boil from two hours to two hours and a half, according as the hare may be young or old. Just before serving, pick out all the bones, the carrot, and celery.

Another Scotch Hare Soup

CUT off all the meat in large pieces; stew the bones in three quarts of water with two heads of celery, five or six onions, some black pepper, salt, and cold-meat bones. Have ready half a pound of rice, well browned, and add to it two ounces of browned butter; break the blood of the hare well in water, strain and add it cold to the browning, stir it constantly till it boils, then add the stock strained, and the pieces of the hare, and stew it all together till sufficiently done.

Hare Soup

CUT the hare in joints as for a fricassee, and put it in a stew-pan, with a little allspice, three blades of mace, some salt, and whole black pepper, a bunch of parsley, a sprig of lemon thyme, one of winter savory, four quarts of water, a slice of ham, and four pounds of lean beef, two carrots, and four onions cut down; let it boil till it be reduced to three quarts; separate the hare, and strain the soup over it, and add a pint of port wine; boil it up before serving.

French Hare Soup

SKIN and wash perfectly clean two young hares, cut them into small pieces, and put them into a stew-pan, with two or three glasses of port wine, two onions stuck with two cloves each, a bunch of parsley, a bay leaf, of thyme, sweet basil, and marjoram, two sprigs each, and a few blades of mace; let the whole simmer upon a stove for an hour. Add as much boiling broth as will entirely cover the meat, simmer till it be soft enough to pulp through a sieve, then strain it and soak the crumb of a twopenny loaf in the strained liquor; separate the bones from the meat, pound the meat in a mortar, and rub it along with the liquor through a sieve; season with pepper and salt, and heat the soup thoroughly, but do not let it boil. Forcemeat balls, made of the hare, may be added to this soup.

Jugged Hare

In five quarts of water, put a pound of scrag of mutton, one of gravy beef, one of a shank of veal, and a slice of ham, all cut small; two turnips, two carrots, three onions chopped, a little mace, salt, and pepper; stew these ingredients for three or four hours, and strain the soup. The next day cut a hare in small pieces, season it with pepper, salt, half a grated nutmeg, and the peel of a small lemon; put it into a stone jar, and fill it up with the prepared soup; put a bung in the jar, tie a bladder and a bit of linen over, and set it in a pot of cold water; as it wastes, fill it up with more boiling water, and let it boil three hours. When cold, take off the fat and pick out the lemon peel. This quantity will make two tureens full, and when to be used is thickened with a table-spoonful of flour, kneaded with a small bit of butter, and half a pint of port wine to each dish. It will keep perfectly good for a fortnight.

Venison Soup

Boil down in five quarts of water two pounds of a shank of veal, or a fowl, and five pounds of the breast of venison cut small; two or three onions chopped, some whole white pepper and salt, with a quarter of a pound of lean ham. Let it stew till it be completely boiled down, when all the strength will be extracted; rub it through a sieve, thicken it with a little butter, kneaded in flour, and add a pint of madeira, and boil it for a quarter of an hour, or twenty minutes.

Brown Venison Soup

Cut in small pieces six or seven pounds of the breast of venison, put it in a stew-pan with two or three ounces of butter; cover it closely, stir it once or twice, and let it stew an hour. Mix four quarts of cold water with a pint and a half of the blood, put it on the fire in another stew-pan, and stir it constantly till it boil; then add the stew to it with an onion minced small, and a whole carrot, some salt, black and Jamaica pepper. If the meat be young, let it boil gently for two hours; if old, two and a half will be necessary. A little before serving, take out the carrot and all the bones, leaving a little of the meat; mix in half a pint of port wine, and let it boil a short time. It may be thickened with a little flour and butter.

White Soup

Blanch in cold water for twelve hours two pounds of very lean beef, put it into a pot, with a knuckle of veal, five quarts of water, two carrots, two turnips, and four middling-sized onions, a table-spoonful of white pepper, a little mace and salt; let this boil four hours, or till the strength be extracted, strain it, and the next day take off all the fat. Blanch half a pound of sweet almonds, pound them in a mortar, with a little water to prevent their oiling, mix them with the soup, and let it boil for a short time, and just before serving, add a pint of rich cream; do not allow the soup to boil after the cream is stirred in. A good substitute for cream is the same quantity of milk, boiled and mixed with a dessert-spoonful of arrow-root.

Another White Soup

Boil together a knuckle of veal, a fowl, or two chickens skinned, a carrot, a turnip, an onion, some salt, and a little whole white pepper; take out the chickens when tender, cut them in joints, and add them to the soup when strained, beat up the yolks of nine eggs, mix them with a pint of cream and a table-spoonful of well-boiled rice stir it gradually into the soup, and heat it gently before serving. A cow heel that has been previously boiled, cut up in pieces, may be used instead of the chickens.

Another White Soup

Take a good knuckle of veal, or two or three short shanks, boil it about four hours, with some whole white pepper, a little mace, salt, two onions, and a small bit of lean ham; strain it, and when cold take off all the fat and sediment; beat up the yolks of six eggs, and mix them with a pint of good cream, then pour the boiling soup upon it by degrees, stirring it well, and if it is liked, add the best part of the gristles.

Another White Soup

Put on in four quarts of water, a knuckle of veal, six pounds weight, a quarter of a pound of lean ham or bacon, two slices of the crumb of bread, one ounce of blanched sweet almonds, put in whole; six middling-sized onions, two heads of celery, some whole white pepper, three blades of mace, a bunch of parsley, and a sprig of thyme; stew all these gently for eight hours, strain it, and when cold take off all the fat; boil it, and, just before serving, take it off the fire, and stir in very gradually a pint of thick cream.

Another White Soup

Boil in four quarts of water four pounds of veal, and a fowl, with some whole white pepper, a little mace, and three middling-sized onions whole, and a bunch of parsley; let it boil three hours, strain it, and put it on again to get quite hot, and, just before serving, stir in gradually half a pint of cream with the yolks of three eggs well beaten. Do not let it boil, as that will make the eggs curdle.

Another White Soup

Stew in three quarts of boiling water, till quite tender, a knuckle of veal, with a quarter of a pound of whole rice, three whole onions, a bunch of parsley, a little sweet marjoram, and two or three blades of mace, and some salt; a little before the soup is strained, add two anchovies; strain through a hair sieve and then through a silk one, or tammy, put it again upon the fire, and stir in half a pint of rich cream, or a pint of milk with the yolks of two eggs beat up in it; let it be hot, but not boiling. If it is required to be richer, boil a fowl in the stock, with two ounces of pounded blanched sweet almonds.

Another White Soup

Put on in five quarts of water four pounds of a shank of veal, break the bone well, let it simmer till it be reduced nearly half; boil a tea-cupful of whole rice till very tender, pulp it through a cullender, strain the liquor, and add the rice, season with salt and white pepper, let it simmer for nearly an hour, and add, a little before serving, the yolks of six eggs, beaten extremely well.

Moor-Fowl Soup

It may be made with or without brown gravy soup; when with the former, six birds are sufficient, when with moor-fowl only, boil five in four quarts of water, pound the breasts in a mortar and rub it through a sieve, put it with the legs, backs, and three more moor-fowl, cut down in joints, into the liquor, season with a pint of port wine, pepper, and salt, and let it boil an hour. When only six birds are used, pound the breasts of three or four.

Pigeon Soup

Make a strong beef stock, highly seasoned as if for brown soup, take six or eight pigeons according to their size, wash them clean, cut off the necks, pinions, livers, and gizzards, and put them into the stock; quarter the pigeons and brown them nicely; after having strained the stock, put in the pigeons; let them boil till nearly ready, which will be in about half an hour, then thicken it with a little flour, rubbed down in a tea-cupful of the soup, season it with half a grated nutmeg, a table-spoonful of lemon juice or of vinegar, and one of mushroom catsup; let it boil a few minutes after all these ingredients are put in, and serve it with the pigeons in the tureen; a better thickening than flour is, to boil quite tender two of the pigeons, take off all the meat and pound it in a mortar, rub it through a sieve, and put it, with the cut pigeons, into the strained soup.

To make partridge soup, partridges may be substituted for pigeons, when only four birds will be required; pound the breast of one.

Another Pigeon Soup

TAKE eight pigeons, cut down two of the oldest, and put them, with the necks, pinions, livers, and gizzards of the others, into four quarts of water; let it boil till the substance be extracted, and strain it; season the pigeons with mixed spices and salt, and truss them as for stewing; pick and wash clean a handful of parsley, chives, or young onions, and a good deal of spinach, chop them; put in a frying-pan a quarter of a pound of butter, and when it boils, mix in a handful of bread crumbs, keep stirring them with a knife till of a fine brown; boil the whole pigeons till they become tender in the stock with the herbs, and fried bread. If the soup be not sufficiently high seasoned, add more mixed spices and salt.

Giblet Soup

CLEAN very nicely two sets of giblets, parboil them. Take the skin off the feet; cut the gizzards in quarters, the necks in three bits, the feet, pinions, and livers, in two, the head in two also, first taking off the bill; boil them till nearly done enough in a quart of weak gravy soup with an onion. Have ready boiling some rich highly seasoned brown gravy soup; add the giblets and the liquor they have been boiled in, with some chopped parsley; take out the onion, and thicken the soup with a bit of butter kneaded in flour. If the giblets are not perfectly sweet and fresh, do not add the weak soup they were boiled in. Half a pint of white wine may be added a little before serving, but it is very good without.

Kidney Soup

CUT down two kidneys, fry them a little in butter and flour, stew them in a quart of highly seasoned gravy soup till tender, then add two quarts more of the soup, and thicken it with browned flour and butter.

Ox Cheek Soup

SEPARATE the bones from the meat, and break the bones, cut the meat into pieces the length of a finger and the breadth of two, put a quart of water to every pound of meat, with a little salt, set it on a gentle fire, and skim it well during the first boiling; after it has stewed gently two hours, add carrots, turnips, onions, celery, a head or two of cabbage, and a bunch of sweet herbs, pepper, salt, and a quarter of a pound of vermicelli; let it stew two hours and a half longer, skim it, and take out the herbs and bones. Chesnuts are a good substitute for vermicelli.

Another Ox Cheek Soup

WASH the cheek clean, and cut it in small pieces, stew it till tender, in four or five quarts of water, with turnips, thyme, parsley, black-pepper-corns, and a few peas; strain off the gravy and let it stand till the next day, then take off the fat, and cut the meat in small pieces from the bones, and stew it a little longer in the gravy with six or seven onions sliced and fried a light brown, some carrots and celery cut small, a little salt, and cayenne.

Sheep's Head Broth

AFTER having the sheep's head and trotters singed, which is done with a red-hot iron, (the head and trotters are usually sent for this purpose to a blacksmith's forge,) split the head, and take out the brain, which is not used, cut out the white of the eye, and rub the head and feet well over with it; let them lie for two hours, then wash them very well in lukewarm water, and rinse them thoroughly. Cut out the tough membrane from between the toes, and lay them in cold water for two hours. Put on two gallons of water, and three quarters of a pound of Scotch barley; when it boils put in the head, trotters, and neck of the sheep, of carrots and turnips, a quart; when cut down in dice, add a little salt, cover the pot closely, and let it boil four hours; take off the scum as it rises; put in some chopped onions about an hour before serving. Boil some whole carrots and turnips, or cut them in half, to put round the head, trotters, and neck in the dish. In summer, green peas are a great improvement to this broth.

Scotch Barley Broth

IN two gallons of cold water, boil six ounces of barley; when it boils skim it, and put in a fowl and one pound of beef, or three pounds of the beef without the fowl; add three pounds of carrots and turnips, and three onions, cut very small. If greens are to be used, they will only require to be boiled an hour, and one ounce more of barley is requisite. Skim it when the vegetables come to a boil, and keep the pot boiling constantly for five hours. The fowl ought to be taken out when boiled enough, and heated in the broth, so as to be served up with it, or in another dish.

Or it may be made exactly in the same manner as the sheep's head broth of the last receipt, substituting for the head, ribs of mutton, beef, veal, or fowl, and is better to be composed of a variety of these meats.

Scots Kale

PUT barley on in cold water, and when it boils take off the scum, put in any piece of fresh beef, and a little salt; let it boil three hours, have ready a cullender full of kale, cut small and boil it till tender. Two or three leeks may be added with the greens, if the flavour is approved of. This broth is also made with salted beef, which must be put in water over night to soak.

Leek Soup, which in Scotland is called Cocky Leeky

WASH and clean three or four dozen leeks, cut the white and tender green part in bits, about an inch long, and wash them again, and put them to drain in a cullender or sieve. Have ready boiling four quarts of stock, made from beef, seasoned with pepper and salt; put in the leeks, and boil them gently for three hours, adding a fowl time enough to allow it to be well boiled, and serve it in the tureen.

Beef Brose

AFTER any large piece of beef has been taken out of the pot it was boiled in, skim off the fat with part of the liquor, and boil it in a sauce-pan. Have ready in a bowl oatmeal that has been toasted brown before the fire, pour in the boiling liquor and stir it a little; if too thick, add more liquor, and send it to table quite hot.

Rice Veal Broth

WASH clean six pounds of a knuckle of veal, and cut it in two; put it into a saucepan with four quarts of boiling water, half a pound of rice well washed, a little mace, white pepper, and salt, and a handful of chopped parsley; let it boil for three hours. Serve part of the meat in the tureen with the broth. The thick part of the knuckle may be sent up as a separate dish, with parsley and butter poured over it.

Thick Beef Soup

IN eight quarts of water boil gently for seven hours, skimming it well, eight or ten pounds of a shin or leg of beef, and a bunch of sweet herbs; strain it; the next day, take off the fat, and cut all the gristly and sinewy parts from the bones, add them to the soup, with some leeks, onions, celery, pepper, salt, and ten or twelve ounces of Scotch barley parboiled; boil it gently for two or three hours. This stock or jelly will keep good for weeks in cold weather.

Beef or Mutton Soup

Boil very gently in a closely covered sauce-pan, four quarts of water, with two table-spoonfuls of sifted bread raspings, three pounds of beef cut in small pieces, or the same quantity of mutton chops taken from the middle of the neck; season with pepper and salt; add two turnips, two carrots, two onions, and one head of celery, all cut small; let it stew with these ingredients four hours, when it will be ready to serve.

Rice Soup

Boil in four quarts of water the scrag end of a neck of veal and one pound of lean ham, till it be reduced nearly half, skimming it carefully; season with white pepper, and two blades of mace; strain it, and boil in it till tender three quarters of a pound of rice, which has been well washed.

Veal Soup

Skin four pounds of a knuckle of veal, break, and cut it small, put it in a stew-pan with two gallons of water; when it boils skim it, and let it simmer till reduced to two quarts; strain, and, when required for the table, season it with white pepper, salt, a little mace, a dessert-spoonful of lemon juice, and thicken it with a large table-spoonful of flour kneaded with an ounce of butter.

Soup Maigre

Cut small four ounces of sorrel, sixteen ounces of celery, and six or eight onions. Fry them in six ounces of butter, and stew them three or four hours in three quarts of water. Season with pepper, salt, and a little mace, and thicken it with a large table-spoonful of flour, mixed in a tea-cupful of the soup. Beat up the yolks of two eggs in half a pint of cream, put it into the tureen, with a large slice of bread toasted and cut in dice, and then pour in the stewed ingredients.

Another Soup Maigre

Brown half a pound of butter in a sauce-pan, and stew it for a quarter of an hour with the following ingredients, all washed clean and chopped small, – four cabbage lettuces, two handfuls of spinach, the same of chervil, one handful of white beet leaves, and one of sorrel, three carrots scraped down, some pepper and salt; add five pints of boiling water, and a large slice of the crumb of bread cut thin and dried before the fire. Stew it gently for two hours; and a little before serving thicken it with the beaten yolks of three eggs, with half a pint of cream or good milk. A pint of green peas and the tops of asparagus may be added.

Soup Santé

STEW four large onions, peeled and cut small, with four white lettuces, a handful of spinach, and a slice of grated bread, for an hour, in a quart of broth and a quarter of a pound of butter, then add three pints more of broth, skim off all the fat, and boil it a quarter of an hour; season with pepper and salt. Before serving, add half a pint of good cream. A pint of green peas, added with the other vegetables, is a great improvement.

Old Peas Soup

PUT a pound of split peas on in four quarts of water, with roast beef or mutton bones, and a ham bone, two heads of celery, and four onions; let them boil till the peas be sufficiently soft to pulp through a sieve, which may be in two or three hours; strain it, put it into the pot with pepper and salt, and boil it nearly an hour. Two or three handfuls of spinach, well washed and cut a little, added when the soup is strained, are a great improvement; and in the summer young green peas in place of the spinach. A tea-spoonful of celery seed, or essence of celery, if celery is not to be had.

Another Old Peas Soup

BOIL in five quarts of water one pint of split peas, an ounce of butter, four pounds of beef, two carrots, three turnips, four heads of celery, three onions, some salt and black pepper; boil them till the peas are dissolved and will easily pulp; put it all through a sieve, then put the soup over the fire with three ounces of butter and a table-spoonful of flour, and boil a small bit of lean ham in it, till it is time to serve; take it out before dishing, and have ready some celery stewed in butter, and fried bread cut in dice, and dried mint rubbed very fine, to send to table with it.

Another Old Peas Soup

BOIL in four quarts of water a shank of ham, or a piece of bacon, and about half a pound of mutton or salt beef, and a pint of split peas; boil all together very gently till the peas are quite soft, strain them through a hair sieve, and bruise them with the back of a spoon till all is pulped through; then boil the soup gently for one hour before serving.

Thin slices of bread toasted and cut in dice to be served with it, either upon a dish or in the soup; if in the soup, it should be fried in butter, and dried mint rubbed fine sent to table in a small dish. It may be also made with fourpence worth of bones, boiled for some hours in four quarts of water, with a carrot, a head of celery, three onions, some pepper and salt, strained, and the next day the fat taken off, and the peas boiled in the liquor with a little bit of butter, till sufficiently tender to pulp through a sieve.

Green Peas Soup

PUT a pint of old green peas into three quarts of water, a slice of the crumb of bread, two onions, a sprig of mint, some salt and pepper; boil them till the peas are perfectly soft, and then pulp them through a sieve; have ready two lettuces stewed tender in butter, and a pint and a half of young green peas boiled; put them into the soup with a little spinach juice, and a quarter of a pint of the juice of the youngest pea pods, and boil it all together before serving.

Another Green Peas Soup

SHELL a quart of green peas not very old, put the shells into a gallon of cold water, with a bit of bacon or mutton, boil them till very soft, pour the liquor through a hair sieve, and bruise the shells with a spoon till nothing remains but the skin. Pound in a marble mortar a handful of spinach, mix it with a little of the liquor, and strain it through a sieve, and boil it gently with the rest of the liquor for half an hour; then put in the quart of peas, and when they are boiled the soup is ready.

Another Green Peas Soup without Meat

PUT into a gallon of water a quart of old green peas, and boil them till they are perfectly soft; pulp them through a sieve; slice seven or eight onions, and fry them in butter; put them to the liquor that has been pulped, add a large lettuce, and a little mint cut very small, and a pint of young green peas; boil all together till the peas are tender, then stir in a table-spoonful of butter till it is quite melted, and put pepper and salt to season it.

Spring Soup

PUT on in four quarts of water a knuckle of veal cut down, and a quarter of a pound of lean ham, or a gammon of bacon; a quart of green split peas; cut small three or four onions, three turnips, a little parsley, thyme, celery, and one leek; stew them all together till the peas are very soft; take out the meat, and press the remainder through a fine sieve; season the soup with pepper and salt. Cut small like peas a bunch of the tops of asparagus, the hearts of two or three cabbages, cutting off the top part and the outside leaves, and a little green mint; stew them till tender, keeping them of a good green, and add them to the soup a quarter of an hour before serving. If it should not be green enough, pound some spinach, squeeze the juice through a cloth, put about a quarter of a pint into the tureen, and pour in the soup. This is the best method to make green peas soup of a good colour.

Cucumber Soup

MAKE some broth with a neck of mutton, a thick slice of lean bacon, an onion stuck with three cloves, a carrot, two turnips, some salt, and a bunch of sweet herbs; strain it; brown with an ounce of butter the crumb of a French roll, to which put four large cucumbers, and two heads of lettuce cut small; let them stew a quarter of an hour, and add to them a quart of the broth; when it boils put in a pint of green peas, and as it stews, add two quarts more of the broth.

Beet Root Soup

BOIL till tender two roots of beet, and rub off the skin with a coarse towel, mince them finely, as also two or three onions; add this to five pints of rich gravy soup, so as to make it rather thick, then stir in three or four table-spoonfuls of vinegar, and one of brown sugar; let it boil, and throw in some fricandellans made up in the form of corks, and rolled in flour.

Herb Soup

WASH and cut small twelve cabbage lettuces, a handful of chervil, one of purslane, one of parsley, eight large green onions, and three handfuls of sorrel; when peas are in season omit half the quantity of sorrel, and put a quart of young green peas; put them all into a sauce-pan, with half a pound of butter and three carrots cut small, some salt and pepper; let them stew closely covered for half an hour, shaking them occasionally to prevent their adhering to the pan; fry in butter six cucumbers cut longways in four pieces; add them, with four quarts of hot water, half a French roll, and a crust of bread toasted upon both sides; and let the whole boil till reduced to three quarts, then strain it through a sieve; beat up the yolks of four eggs with half a pint of cream, and stir it gently into the soup just before serving.

Tomata Soup

WASH, scrape, and cut small the red part of three large carrots, three heads of celery, four large onions, and two large turnips; put them into a sauce-pan, with a table-spoonful of butter, and half a pound of lean new ham; let them stew very gently for an hour, then add three quarts of brown gravy soup, and some whole black pepper, with eight or ten ripe tomatas; let it boil an hour and a half, and pulp it through a sieve; serve it with fried bread cut in dice.

Vegetable Soup

PARE and cut small one dozen of common-sized onions, five large yellow turnips, two heads of celery, and the red part of three large carrots; wash and put them in a stew-pan with two ounces of butter, cover it closely; and when the vegetables are a little soft, add to them four quarts of well-seasoned gravy soup made of roast beef bones, and let it stew four or five hours; rub it through a tammy, put it on the fire, boil and skim it before serving.

Another Vegetable Soup

BOIL in two quarts of water till reduced to one, a quart of old green peas, a few of the pea shells, a sprig of mint, and two or three onions; strain and pulp it through a sieve. Stew the following ingredients in as much water as will cover them, and season with pepper and salt; a pint of young peas, two or three onions sliced, the same number of cucumbers cut into square pieces, some lettuce stalks, scraped and cut into bits about an inch long, and two ounces of butter; add this to the pulped liquor, and boil it up. To improve the colour of the soup, half a tea-cupful of spinach juice may be added before taking it off the fire.

Winter Vegetable Soup

To every gallon of water allow, when cut down small, a quart of the following vegetables: equal quantities of turnips, carrots, and potatoes, three onions, two heads of celery, and a bunch of sweet herbs; fry them brown in a quarter of a pound of butter, add the water with salt and pepper, and boil it till reduced to three quarts, and serve it with fried toasted bread.

Another Winter Vegetable Soup

PEEL and slice six large onions, six potatoes, and four turnips; fry them in half a pound of butter or very fresh dripping; toast a crust of bread brown and hard, put it, with two or three heads of celery cut small, some herbs, pepper and salt, with the fried vegetables, into five pints of water, to stew gently for four hours, then strain it through a sieve, add a little carrot and celery cut small, and some chopped parsley, one anchovy or a red herring, and a little cayenne; boil it till the vegetables are tender.

Onion Soup

STEW till perfectly tender, in about five pints of weak veal or beef stock, two dozen of onions, peeled and sliced, three turnips, one parsnip, two carrots, two heads of celery, without the green part, a bunch of sweet herbs, half an ounce of white pepper, a little salt, and a quarter of a pound of ham; when sufficiently tender, press all the ingredients through a tammy, and let the soup stand till cold: pound the yolks of three hard-boiled eggs, mix them with a pint of thick cream, and stir it into the soup and heat it, but be careful not to boil it; new milk and the yolks of six eggs will answer instead of cream. Toast a piece of bread the size of a small roll, and put it into the soup before serving it.

Another Onion Soup

BOIL in four quarts of water six pounds of a knuckle of veal, with a dessert-spoonful of whole white pepper, and a few blades of mace; when the meat is so much boiled as to leave the bone, strain off the stock. The following day boil nine or ten large Spanish onions in milk and water, till sufficiently tender to pulp through a sieve; take the fat off from the top of the stock, boil it up, and add the onions with about a quarter of a pound of fresh butter worked with two heaped table-spoonfuls of sifted flour of rice, and a little salt; boil it gently for half an hour, stirring it constantly, and, a little before serving, stir in half a pint of rich cream.

Carrot Soup

MAKE a rich stock with a shin of beef, a quarter of a pound of lean ham, a fowl, or a piece of veal, a bunch of sweet herbs, two onions, a carrot, black and Jamaica pepper, salt, and three cloves; strain it, and when cold take off all the fat; clean and boil, till they become very tender, the red part of twelve or thirteen carrots, according to their size, and two turnips; pound them in a mortar; pound half a pound of cold roast beef, or beef steak; warm it, and rub it with the carrots through a tammy or sieve; add this to the soup, and serve it boiling hot.

Stock made with bones may be substituted for fresh beef stock.

Another Carrot Soup

WASH, scrape, and slice ten or twelve carrots, put them, with an ounce and a half of butter, into a stew-pan, cover it closely, and let them stew till sufficiently soft to press through a tammy or hair sieve; add the pulp to as much well-seasoned stock as will make it of the thickness of rich cream, and boil it for twenty or thirty minutes.

Hotch Potch

CUT in dice a good quantity of young turnips and carrots, and with one or two lettuces cut very small, the tops of some cauliflower, and a pint of full-grown peas; boil them gently in four quarts of boiling water for two hours; cut in neat chops a loin, or the best end of a neck of mutton, add them to the vegetables, with salt, pepper, and some onions cut small; let them boil an hour and a half, then add three pints of green peas, and boil half an hour longer, when it is ready to serve.

Another Hotch Potch

PUT on, in three quarts of water, a small bit of the neck of mutton, or any scraps, one quart of carrots and turnips when cut in dice, and some salt; boil them gently for an hour, then add a little cauliflower, lettuce, parsley, and onions cut small; boil a quart of full-grown peas in another sauce-pan, till sufficiently tender to press through a sieve; add it to the soup, taking out the bits of mutton, with three pints of young peas, and some nice mutton chops, and let it all boil till they are done enough. If the soup be too thick, a little before serving pour in some boiling water.

Winter Hotch Potch

BOIL in two quarts of water, for two hours or more, if not perfectly tender, one pound of peas with half an ounce of butter, or a little fat; pulp them through a sieve; put on, in a separate sauce-pan, a gallon of water, three pounds of mutton chops, some salt and pepper, a pound and a half of carrots, the same of turnips, cut small; boil till the vegetables become tender, which may be in about two hours; then add the strained liquor, and let it boil a quarter of an hour.

Soup Lorrain

Boil in four quarts of water till reduced to three, a knuckle of veal, one pound of lean beef, and one pound of mutton, a carrot, a turnip, a bunch of parsley, and a little lemon thyme, some salt and white pepper; then strain the liquor; pound very finely in a marble mortar all the white meat of a large roasted fowl, with a quarter of a pound of blanched almonds, and the yolks of four hard-boiled eggs; boil in milk the crumb of a French roll, and pound it with the other ingredients, and stir it all well into the soup; let it boil gently for ten minutes before serving.

Vermicelli Soup

The day before it is required, make four quarts of good stock, and boil in it one carrot, one turnip, four onions, one or two parsley roots, three blades of mace, salt, and some white pepper; strain it, and before using, take off all the fat; boil in some of the liquor the crumb of three French rolls till soft enough to mash smooth; boil the soup and stir well in the mashed rolls; boil it for a quarter of an hour, and before serving, add the yolks of two eggs beaten with three table-spoonfuls of cream; boil in water two or three ounces of vermicelli for fifteen or twenty minutes, strain and put it into the tureen, and pour the soup upon it.

Vermicelli à la Reine

Blanch about a quarter of a pound of vermicelli in boiling water, drain it, and throw it into some rich well-seasoned stock; when tender, take it out of the soup, and put it into the tureen; thicken the soup with eight well-beaten eggs, mixed with half a pint of cream, and pour it, when quite hot, upon the vermicelli.

Macaroni Soup

Make a good stock with a knuckle of veal, a little sweet marjoram, parsley, some salt, white pepper, three blades of mace, and two or three onions; strain and boil it. Break in small bits a quarter of a pound of macaroni, and gently simmer it in milk and water till it be swelled and is tender; strain it, and add it to the soup, which thicken with two table-spoonfuls of flour, mixed in half a pint of cream, and stirred gradually into the soup. Boil it a few minutes before serving.

Another Macaroni Soup

Boil for three hours very quickly, in five quarts of water, seven pounds of veal, a little salt, a dessert-spoonful of white pepper, and three or four blades of mace; strain it off, put it into a sauce-pan, and keep it hot upon a stove. Mix five table-spoonfuls of flour with two ounces of butter, put it into an iron-tinned saucepan, and stir it over the fire till it be melted; add half a pint of the strained stock, and then gradually mix the whole together, and keep stirring constantly till it thickens, and then add two ounces and a half of macaroni, previously boiled in milk and water for eight minutes; stir it again till it boil. Take the pan off the stove, and stir in by degrees about three quarters of a pint of rich sweet cream, and just let it boil before serving.

Soup à la Reine

POUND in a marble mortar the white meat of three cold roasted fowls, and half a pound of sweet almonds blanched; add a little cream whilst pounding. Boil this with four quarts of well-seasoned veal stock, then strain it, and just before serving, stir in a pint of cream.

Potage à la Reine

DRAW, wash, and clean three chickens, or young fowls; put them into a stewpan with a bunch of parsley, and some well-seasoned boiling veal stock; let it stew for an hour; take out the fowls, and pound all the meat to a fine paste in a marble mortar, with the crumb of two penny loaves, previously soaked in the soup, and the yolks of three or four hard-boiled eggs; rub all through a sieve, and add it to the soup, stirring it well. Put a quart of rich cream on the fire, and stir it till it boils, and then mix it with the soup, and serve it quite hot.

Potage à la Vierge

BOIL a piece of the crumb of bread about the size of an egg in a quart of rich stock, pound in a mortar the white meat of a cold roasted fowl and a few sweet almonds, put these together, and rub them through a tammy, adding a little cream, or half a pint of milk; season it well and keep it hot in a water-bath till it is to be served, when two quarts of stock made quite hot, but not boiling, may be added.

A Simple Soup

CUT small one pound of carrots, one pound of turnips, half a pound of onions, one lettuce, a little celery, and a handful of parsley; stew them for twenty minutes with a quarter of a pound of butter, some salt and pepper; then put them into three quarts of stock, made with two pounds of veal, and add one quart of green peas, and let it stew for three hours. Press it through a sieve, and boil it up before sending it to table.

Prussian Soup

IN seven pints of water boil, till reduced to five, one pound of lean beef, cut in small bits, one pint of split peas, three quarters of a pound of potatoes, three ounces of ground rice, two heads of celery, three leeks, or onions, seasoned with pepper, salt, and a little dried mint; strain it through a cullender.

Stove or Spinach Soup

BOIL in two quarts of water three sliced onions. Pick and clean as much spinach as will make two large dishes, parboil and put it in a cullender, to let the bitter water drip from it; let cold water run upon it for a minute or two, and then press out the water. Knead two ounces of fresh butter, with a table-spoonful and a half of flour, mix it with the spinach, which boil for fifteen minutes in the water and onions, then put in half a pint of cream, or good milk, some salt and pepper, boil it for fifteen minutes more. In the season of green peas, a quart added with the spinach is a great improvement. It is common to boil a lamb's head and pluck with the soup, and send them to table in the tureen. The soup is then called lamb's stove; but with the peas it is quite as good without.

Potato Soup

POTATO soup is made with beef or mutton scraps, boiled in water till the strength be extracted; strain the liquor, and put it into the pot; after washing some potatoes, scrape off the skin, cut them into quarters with some onions, season with pepper and salt, and boil them an hour and a half in the strained liquor, then press them through a cullender, and put the soup on to boil a little time. It may be made very good with butter only, a quarter of a pound of which is added after the potatoes have been put through the cullender.

Potato Flour Soup

HAVE three pints of gravy soup boiling on the fire. Mix in half a pint of cold soup six spoonfuls of potato flour, and stir it into the sauce-pan, first drawing it to a side, put it on the fire again and continue to stir it till it becomes thick, and in five minutes serve it.

For the gravy soup, water may be substituted, to which a bit of fresh butter, a little salt, and the beaten yolks of two eggs may be added or milk may be used, seasoning it with sugar, a spoonful of orange-flower water, and, if liked, the beaten yolks of eggs.

Oyster Soup

BOIL in water the crumb of two twopenny rolls, with a few blades of mace, a tea-spoonful of whole white pepper, and four onions cut small. Pick out the spice, and rub the bread and onions through a hair sieve, then add it to three quarts of well-seasoned strong veal stock. Rub down three ounces of butter, with a table-spoonful of flour, and mix it gradually with half a pint of the soup, and then stir all well together. When it has boiled a short time, add with their liquor half a hundred or more of fine oysters, and let the whole simmer for ten or fifteen minutes.

If the soup is not quite salt enough with the liquor of the oysters, a little salt may be added.

Lobster Soup

CUT small a dozen of common-sized onions, put them into a stew-pan with a small bit of butter, a slice or two of lean ham, and a slice of lean beef; when the onions are quite soft, mix gradually with them some rich stock; let it boil, and strain it through a fine hair sieve, pressing the pulp of the onions with a wooden spoon; then boil it well, skimming it all the time. Beat the meat of a boiled haddock, the spawn and body of a large lobster, or of two small ones, in a marble mortar; add gradually to it the soup, stirring it till it is as smooth as cream; let it boil again and scum it. Cut the tail and claws of the lobster into pieces, and add them to the soup before serving it, and also some pepper, cayenne, white pepper, and a glass of white wine.

Forcemeat balls may be added to oyster soup and lobster soup, made as directed under the article "Forcemeat for Fish."

Crappet Heads, or Fish Soup

PUT on in boiling salt-and-water two haddocks, and the tails, fins, and roes of six; in a quarter of an hour take out the roes and fish; let the liquor boil for an hour longer, and strain it. When cold, pick all the fish from the bones, and pick out the strings and skin from the roes; peel and chop two onions, put them on the fire in cold water, and when it boils pour off the water; take half a pound of shortbread in crumbs, two tea-spoonfuls of salt, one and a half of white pepper, and one of grated nutmeg – mince all these ingredients, mix them together thoroughly, and bind them with two beaten whites of eggs. Have ready six heads of haddocks, skinned, and the eyes taken out; make up a large ball of the forcemeat; stuff the heads, and tie them round with a coarse thread. Boil the liquor; thicken it with flour kneaded in butter; add some parsley and a little pepper, two table-spoonfuls of mushroom, the same quantity of walnut catsup, and half a pint of white wine. Skin and cut two haddocks in three or four pieces each, and put them with the heads into the stock, and boil them till they are sufficiently done, which may be in about a quarter of an hour.

Hard biscuit pounded may be used in place of shortbread, when a little fresh butter must be added. If any of the forcemeat is over, make it up in small balls.

Water Souchy

MAKE a stock with three or four flounders, two onions, and a bunch of parsley boiled in three quarts of water till they are soft enough to pulp through a sieve; then season the liquor with pepper, salt, and some parsley chopped, and boil in it a few flounders, with the brown skin taken off, or some nicely-cleaned perch or tench. Serve in a tureen, and with slices of bread and butter to eat with it.

Pepper Pot in a Tureen

STEW gently in four quarts of water, till reduced to three, three pounds of beef, half a pound of lean ham, a bunch of dried thyme, two onions, two large potatoes pared and sliced; then strain it through a cullender, and add a large fowl, cut into joints and skinned, half a pound of pickled pork sliced, the meat of one lobster minced, and some small suet dumplings, the size of a walnut. When the fowl is well boiled, add half a peck of spinach, that has been boiled and rubbed through a cullender; season with salt and cayenne. It is very good without the lean ham and fowl.

Soup for the Poor

WASH an ox head very clean; break the bones, and cut the meat in pieces; put it on in thirteen gallons of water, with a peck and a half of potatoes, half a peck of turnips, the same quantity of onions, and some carrots; peel and cut them all down. A handful of pot-herbs, and two quarts of oatmeal; season with pepper and salt. Cover the pot closely, and let it stew till the next morning; add as much hot water as may have wasted in boiling, letting it stew for some hours longer, when it will be fit for use. This soup will be found very good for a family dinner.

Soup for an Invalid

CUT in small pieces one pound of beef or mutton, or part of both; boil it gently in two quarts of water; take off the scum, and when reduced to a pint, strain it. Season with a little salt, and take a tea-cupful at a time.

Chicken Panada

SKIN a fowl; cut it in pieces, leaving the breast whole; boil it in three pints of water till perfectly tender; pick off all the meat, and pound it finely in a mortar, and mix it with the liquor it was boiled in; rub it through a sieve, and season it with salt.

Rice and Milk

To every quart of good milk allow two ounces of rice; wash it well in several waters; put it with the milk into a closely-covered sauce-pan, and set it over a slow fire; when it boils take it off; let it stand till it be cold, and simmer it about an hour and a quarter before sending it to table; and serve it in a tureen.

Cream of Rice Soup

MIX one or two table-spoonfuls of sifted flour of rice with a little good stock, rather cold than hot; add this to some boiling stock, and keep stirring till it boils; and let it boil till sufficiently thick.

The flour of rice may be made as follows: – Wash in several waters a pound of rice; wipe it in a clean towel, and when perfectly dry, pound and sift it through a sieve.

Friars' Chicken

PUT four pounds of a knuckle of veal into four quarts of water; boil it gently for two hours; strain it off; cut three chickens, or two young fowls, into joints; skin them, and when the broth boils put them in; season with white pepper and salt; let them boil a short time, and add a handful of parsley chopped small; when the chickens are boiled tender, have ready six or seven well-beaten eggs; stir them quickly into the broth one way, immediately before taking it off the fire.

This broth may be made entirely of veal, instead of chickens.

Another Friars' Chicken

CLEAN and wash three chickens; skin and cut them into joints; put them, with the livers and gizzards, on in two quarts of cold water; when it boils skin it; season with salt and white pepper. In half an hour add a handful of chopped parsley, and let it boil for half an hour longer. Beat well the whites and yolks of four or six eggs, and, just before serving, stir them very quickly one way into the broth.

Portable Soup

PUT on, in four gallons of water, ten pounds of a shin of beef, free from fat and skin, six pounds of a knuckle of veal, and two fowls; break the bones and cut the meat into small pieces, season with one ounce of whole black pepper, a quarter of an ounce of Jamaica pepper, and the same of mace; cover the pot very closely, and let it simmer for twelve or fourteen hours, and then strain it. The following day, take off the fat, and clear the jelly from any sediment adhering to it; boil it gently upon a stove, without covering the sauce-pan, and stir it frequently till it becomes very thick and in lumps about the pan. Put it into saucers about half full, and when cold lay the cakes upon flannel to dry before the fire or in the sun; keep them in a tin box, with white paper between each cake. About an ounce weight will make a pint of rich soup; pour boiling water upon it with a little salt, and stir it till it dissolves. It also answers well for gravies and all brown sauces.

Ox Tail Soup

STEEP in cold water, for some hours, two ox tails cut into bits; put them into a sauce-pan with four quarts of cold water, a bunch of sweet herbs, a dessert-spoonful of whole black pepper, three onions, two carrots, and one turnip; cover it closely, and when it boils skim it, and let it simmer for three hours; carefully take off all the fat; add a table-spoonful of vinegar and half a pint of port wine. Take out the vegetables and herbs before serving.

Rabbit Soup

CUT one or two rabbits into joints, lay them for an hour in cold water; dry and fry them in butter till about half done, with four or five onions, and a middling-sized head of celery cut small; add to this three quarts of cold water, a pound of split peas, some pepper and salt; let it stew gently for four or five hours, then strain and serve it.

Meg Merrilies' Soup

CUT a hare in pieces, and save the blood, reserve some hits of the meat and the liver to make forcemeat balls of, and put the rest of the hare into a sauce-pan with six quarts of water; season with four onions, a bunch of sweet herbs, pepper, and salt, stew it gently for two hours; in another sauce-pan put the blood and the water the hare was washed in, stir in two heaped table-spoonfuls of rice flour, to make it the consistence of gruel, and when it boils mix it with the stock. Take two partridges, or moor-fowl, if they are fresh, or part of both, skin and cut each of them into four pieces, brown them in butter in a frying-pan, and add them to the soup, with about three pints of carrots and turnips neatly cut and parboiled. Make the forcemeat balls as follows: mince the liver and meat very finely with rather more than half its quantity of fat bacon or butter, one anchovy, a little lemon-peel, and lemon-thyme, pepper and salt, grated nutmeg, and crumbs of bread; make up the balls the size of a nutmeg, with a well-beaten egg, fry them of a light brown in clarified beef dripping, fresh lard, or butter, drain them before the fire, and add them to the soup half an hour before serving, and pick out all the loose bones of the hare.

To Dress a Turtle weighing one hundred and twenty pounds

Turtle Soup

HAVING cut off the head close to the shell, hang up the turtle till next day, then open it, bearing the knife heavily on the back of the animal in cutting it off all round; turn it on its end, that all the water and blood may run out, then cut the flesh off along the spine, sloping the knife towards the bones so as to avoid touching the gall, and having also cut the flesh from the legs and other members, wash the whole well and drain it. A large vessel of boiling water being ready on the fire, put in the breast shell, and when the plates will separate easily, take them out of the water; boil the back and belly in water till the softer parts can be taken off easily; but before they are sufficiently done, as they are to be again boiled in the sauce, lay them to cool singly in earthen vessels that they may not stick together; let the bones continue to stew for some time, as the liquor must be used for moistening the sauces.

All the flesh cut from the body, the four legs and head, must be stewed in the following manner: Lay a few slices of ham on the bottom of a large stew-pan, and over the ham two or three knuckles of veal, then above the veal, the inside flesh of the turtle, and that of the members over the whole, adding a large bunch of sweet herbs, such as sweet basil, sweet marjoram, lemon-thyme, a handful of parsley, and green onions, and a large onion stuck with six cloves. Then partly moisten it with the water in which the shell is boiling, and when it has stewed some time, moisten it again with the liquor in which the back and belly have been boiled. When the legs are tender, take them out, drain, and put them aside to be afterwards added to the sauce; and when the flesh is completely done, drain it through a silk sieve, and mix with the sauce some very thin white roux; then cut all the softer parts, now sufficiently cold, into pieces about an inch square, add them to the sauce, and let them simmer gently till they can be easily pierced; skim it well.

Next chop a small quantity of herbs, and boil them with a little sugar in four bottles of madeira till reduced to two, then rub it through a tammy, mix it with the turtle sauce, and let it boil for a short time. Make some forcemeat balls as follows: cut off about a pound of meat from the fleshy part of a leg of veal free from sinews or fat, soak in milk about the same quantity of crumbs of bread; when quite soft, squeeze and put it into a mortar together with the veal, a small quantity of calf's udder, a little butter, the yolks of four hard-boiled eggs, a little cayenne, salt, and spices; pound the whole very finely, then thicken the mixture with two whole eggs and the yolk of a third, throw a bit into boiling water, and if not sufficiently firm, add the yolk of another egg, and for variety some chopped parsley may be mixed with half of the forcemeat. Let the whole cool, so that it may be formed into balls about the size of the yolk of an egg, poach them in boiling water, and add them to the turtle. Before serving, mix a little cayenne with the juice of two or three lemons, and add it to the soup. It is generally preferable to prepare the soup the day before it is required for use, and it will be best heated in a water bath, or flat vessel containing water, which is kept always very hot, but not allowed to boil. By the same method, sauces, stews, and other made dishes, may be kept hot.

When the fins of the turtle are to be served as a side dish, they must be first parboiled, then skinned, and stewed in a little turtle sauce, with some port wine, and seasoned with cayenne, salt, and a little lemon juice, and thickened with butter and flour.

Fricandeaux and blanquettes may also be made of the flesh of the turtle, in the same way as those of veal.

CHAPTER II
FISH

PREPARATORY REMARKS ON FISH

TURBOT; – a good one is thick, and the belly cream-coloured. If the belly and fins be streaked with red, it is certainly fresh. When it must be kept, it should be hung up by the tail in a cool place. The same directions apply to soles and flounders.

Cod; – when good, has a small head, broad shoulders, and a hollow at the back of the neck, and a small and stiff tail.

Salmon, haddocks, mackerel, whiting, herring, and sprats, should all be firm, and chosen with small heads, thick shoulders, and small tails.

Smelts; – when perfectly fresh, smell like a newly-cut cucumber.

Carp, tench, pike, and perch; – when fresh, the eyes are bright, the body stiff, the gills red, and hard to open.

The silver eel, so called from the bright colour of the belly, is the most esteemed.

Skate; – the female is the best, and when good is thick, and has a very white belly, tinged with lilac. That with large thorns is a very inferior fish.

A lobster should be rather heavy, in proportion to its size. When in perfection, the shell on the side will not yield to moderate pressure. Barnacles and other marine animals adhering to it are certain indications of superior goodness. If the berries appear large and brownish, it will be found watery and poor. The cock lobster is in general better than the hen, and is distinguished by its narrow tail.

Crabs; – the male is the best, and may be known by its narrow breast. When light, they are watery; which may more easily be detected after they are boiled; by then holding them firmly and shaking them, the rattling of the water will be heard.

Prawns and shrimps are good when their tails turn strongly inwards, and when they have no unpleasant smell. When oysters are alive and strong, the shell, in opening them, will close upon the knife. Those from the coast of Kent, and those called pandore, from the Firth of Forth, are the most esteemed.

On Dressing Fish

Fish must by no means be allowed to remain in the water after it is boiled; if, therefore, it should be ready before it can be sent to table, it must be dished, the cover put on, and a cloth put over it. The dish is then to be set across the fish-kettle.

Fish should be fried over a clear quick fire, and with dripping, or hog's lard, in preference to butter. The pan should be deep; and to ascertain that it is clean, a little fat is first fried in it, poured out, and the pan wiped with a clean cloth; as much dripping or lard is then put in as will entirely cover the fish. When it is boiling hot, and begins to smoke, the fish is put in; if small, they may be turned in three or four minutes, by sticking in a fork near the head with the one hand, and with the other supporting the tail with a fish-slice. When they are done, they should be laid before the fire upon an old soft towel, and turned now and then till they are dry upon both sides; or they may be put upon a large sieve, turned upwards, and which is kept for the purpose, or put on the underside of a dish.

The fire for broiling fish must be very clear, and the gridiron perfectly clean, which, when hot, should be rubbed with a bit of suet. The fish, while broiling, must be often turned.

Berwick Receipt for Boiling Salmon

THE tail of the salmon is first cut off near and below the last fin, the fish is then cut up the back, keeping the bone on one side, and then cut up into pieces of half a pound each, the blood well washed out of the fish in cold water, but the scales not to be removed; a pickle to be made of salt and water, strong enough to bear an egg, and, when boiling, the fish to be put in, and boiled very quickly for fifteen minutes. During the boiling, the scum to be taken off carefully as soon as it rises. Sauces; – lobster, melted butter, and anchovy sauce.

N.B. The hardest water is preferable for boiling salmon.

A Receipt for Boiling Salmon, by an Aberdeen Fisherman

WHEN the water is hot, put salt into it, and stir it well; taste it; when strong enough to force you to cast it from your mouth, it will do; when the water boils put in the fish; when it boils again, give twenty minutes for a salmon, and sixteen for a grilse. When salmon is cut in slices an inch thick, let them boil from ten to fifteen minutes. Serve with it a sauce tureen of the liquor the fish was boiled in.

To Broil Salmon Steaks

CUT the steaks from the thickest part of the fish, nearly an inch thick; butter pieces of white paper; fold the steaks in them, and broil them over a slow fire for ten or twelve minutes. Take off the paper; serve and garnish with plenty of fried parsley. Dressed in this way, they may be put round salmon boiled, in slices. Sauces; – melted butter, lobster, or shrimp sauce.

To Bake Salmon

CLEAN and cut the fish into slices, put it in a dish, and make the following sauce: melt an ounce of butter, kneaded in flour, in a pint and a half of gravy, with two glasses of port wine, two table-spoonfuls of catsup, two anchovies, and a little cayenne. When the anchovies are dissolved, strain and pour the sauce over the fish, tie a sheet of buttered paper over the dish, and bake it in an oven.

Trout answer well dressed in this way.

To Stew Salmon

CLEAN and scrape the fish; cut it into slices, and stew it in a rich white gravy. A little before serving, add two table-spoonfuls of soy, one of essence of anchovy, a little salt, some chopped parsley and chives.

Kipper, or Dried Salmon

CUT the fish up the back, and take out the bone; wipe it very clean with a cloth; score it, and put a handful of salt on each side, and let it lie for three days; then hang it up to dry, and it will be fit for use in two days, and eats well with a little pepper put over it, and broiled.

To Salt a Salmon

CUT the fish up the back, and cut out the bone; wipe it clean, and sprinkle it with salt; let it lie a night to drain off the liquor; wipe it dry; rub on it two or three ounces of pounded saltpetre; cut it into pieces; pack it close in a pot, with a thick layer of salt between each layer of fish. If the brine does not rise in a few days, boil a strong one, and pour it, when cold, upon the salmon, which must always be covered with it.

The bone, or chine of salmon, as it is called in Leith, eats well with salt and pepper strewed over it, cut in bits of three or four inches, and broiled over a clear fire.

Salmon Fritters

CUT small some cold boiled salted salmon; pound some boiled potatoes, moistened with cream, and the yolk of an egg beaten; mix them together, and make it into small fritters, and fry them of a light brown in fresh lard, or beef dripping; serve them with hard-boiled eggs, cut in quarters. For sauce, melt two ounces of butter, with a little cream and flour mixed, and add, when it is hot, a dessert-spoonful of soy, and two of mushroom catsup.

Caveach Salmon

BOIL in two quarts of vinegar three heads of shalots, half an ounce of whole black pepper, three cloves, two blades of mace, and a little salt. Cut the fish in slices, and fry them of a light-brown colour in fine oil, or clarified dripping; put them, when cold, into a pan, pour over them the vinegar and spices, and put on the top eight or ten spoonfuls of oil.

Soles may be done in this way, only lay over them sliced onions instead of shalots.

To Pot Salmon

TAKE off the head; cut the salmon in thick slices; wipe it dry, but do not wash it; pound half an ounce of nutmeg, mace, and cloves, the least part of cloves, half an ounce of white pepper, and some salt; chop fine one onion, six bay leaves, and six anchovies; with this season each slice; put them into a pan, with very thin slices of butter between each layer; bake it; when well done, drain off the butter, and, when cold, pour over it some clarified butter.

Spiced Salmon

MIX together, in the proportion of one-third of salt-and-water to one pint of vinegar, one ounce of whole black pepper, and one ounce of cinnamon. Cut the salmon into slices, and boil it in this; when cold, pack it close in a pan, and pour over it the liquor it was boiled in, with the spices, so as to cover it completely; cover the pan closely, to exclude the air.

Pickled Salmon

CUT the salmon into pieces; boil it as for eating, and lay it on a dry cloth till the following day; boil two quarts of good vinegar with one of the liquor the fish was boiled in, one ounce of whole black pepper, half an ounce of allspice, and four blades of mace. Put the salmon into something deep, and pour over it the prepared vinegar when cold. A little sweet oil put upon the top will make it keep a twelvemonth.

Another Pickled Salmon

To a quart of the liquor the fish has been boiled in, put rather more than half a pint of good vinegar, and half an ounce of whole black pepper; boil it, and when it is cold pour it over the fish, previously laid in a deep dish.

To Boil Turbot

Pour into the turbot kettle, with the water, two large handfuls of salt, and a teacupful of vinegar; when it boils very fast, take off the scum, put in the turbot, and when it boils again, keep it boiling fast till the turbot rises from the drainer, when it is sufficiently done. Dish and garnish it with a fringe of curled parsley and cut lemon. Sauces; – lobster and melted butter.

Cold boiled turbot heats well with salad sauce.

Turbot is generally considered best perfectly fresh; but some people prefer it kept for a few days, hung up by the tail in a cool place.

To Boil a Cod's Head and Shoulders

WASH it clean; tie it up, and dry it with a cloth. Allow, in the proportion of every three measures of water, one of salt; when it boils, take off the scum, put in the fish, and keep it boiling very fast for twenty-five or thirty minutes. Serve with it the roe cut into slices and fried with the chitterlings; and garnish with curled parsley and horse-radish. Sauces; – oyster, melted butter, or anchovy and butter.

To Dress a Cod's Head and Shoulders

WASH the cod's head and shoulders well; cut off the fins; lay it on a dish; pour some boiling water over part of the fish, and instantly scrape off all the black scales, taking care not to break the skin; repeat this till every part of the fish looks white, and then wash it in cold water. Put it on in boiling salt-and-water, and boil it for a quarter of an hour; then lay it on a dish, and rub it all over with the yolks of two or three beaten eggs, and strew it thickly with grated bread crumbs, mixed with pepper and minced parsley. Stick it all over with little bits of butter, and put it in an oven to brown. Mix a large table-spoonful of flour with a quarter of a pound of butter, a quart of gravy, a tea-cupful of white wine, some pepper, salt, and a little grated nutmeg. Mince the white meat of a lobster; slightly brown three dozen of oysters in a frying-pan, and put them with half their liquor and the lobster to the gravy, and other things; heat it up, and pour it round the fish. Garnish with cut lemon. It is not necessary to have lobster and oysters, but it is the better for both.

To dress the same dish with a white sauce, the stock should be made of veal, or an old fowl, and seasoned with white pepper and mace.

Another way to Dress a Cod's Head and Shoulders

PARBOIL the head and shoulders; drain and put it on in some rich gravy, made with meat and fish; season it with pepper and salt, a little mace, one or two onions chopped, two table-spoonfuls of catsup. Any other seasoning may be added, such as coratch, anchovy, and lemon pickle. Care must be taken not to let it boil too long. A few minutes before serving, mix smooth in a little cold water two table-spoonfuls of flour, and add it to the sauce.

Haddocks may be dressed in the same manner.

To Bake Cod, or Haddock

TAKE the middle piece of the fish, and skin it; make a stuffing with a little of the roe parboiled, a piece of butter, the yolks of two hard-boiled eggs, some grated bread crumbs, pepper, salt, grated lemon-peel, and nutmeg; bind it with the beaten white of an egg; put it into the fish, and sew it up. Place the whole in a tin dish, with bits of butter over the top of it, and bake it for an hour in a Dutch oven; turn and baste it frequently. Garnish with fried roe, or oysters. Sauces; – melted butter, oyster, or shrimp sauce.

To Crimp Cod

Cut a fresh cod into slices or steaks; lay them for three hours in salt-and-water, adding a glass of vinegar; when they may be boiled, fried, or broiled.

To Dress and keep Dry Salted Tusk, Ling, or Cod Fish

CUT into square bits, or put one large piece into cold water over night; wash it clean in fresh water, and put it on to boil in cold water for one hour and a half; then cool the water, so that the fish may be easily handled; take it out of the saucepan, and pick out the loose bones, and scrape it clean, without taking off the skin. Put it on in boiling water; and if the fish is too fresh, add a little salt with it, and let it boil gently from one hour to one and a half. The very thick part will take this time, the thin bits less, to dress. When dished, garnish with hard-boiled eggs and parsley.

Plain boiled parsnips, and a butter tureen of egg sauce, served with it.

When the fish is put on the second time, some people prefer boiling it in milk-and-water. To keep any of this sort of fish for winter use, it ought to be cut or sawed in pieces, and, when perfectly dry, laid in a small cask or wooden box, with oatmeal, oatmeal seeds, or malt dust, between each layer.

Dried Fish Pudding

BOIL the fish, take off the skin, and take out the bones, pound it, and add to it an equal quantity of mashed potatoes moistened with good milk and a bit of butter; put it in a dish, smooth it with a knife, and stick here and there little bits of butter, and brown it in a Dutch oven; serve it with egg sauce; round the edge of the dish may be put a potato paste.

Barrelled Cod Fish

To a barrel that will contain four or five fish, allow three pounds of salt, and a quarter of a pound of sugar, thoroughly mixed; split the fish, wash and clean them extremely well, and let the water drain from them; strew over them the mixed salt and sugar, and pack them into the barrel, with the skin side down, till the last fish, which put with the skin side up.

Cod Sounds Roasted or Baked

WASH and clean four or five cod sounds, and boil them till nearly done in milk-and-water; when cold, make a forcemeat of bread crumbs, a piece of butter, salt, nutmeg, white pepper, and some chopped oysters; beat up the yolks of two eggs to bind it, lay it over the sounds, roll them up, and fasten them with a small skewer, baste them with melted butter, and roll them in finely-grated bread crumbs seasoned with pepper and salt; put them on a tin in a Dutch oven, turn and baste them with a feather dipped in melted butter, and strew over bread crumbs as before; when done, and of a nice brown, serve them with oyster sauce in the dish.

Cod Sounds Broiled

LET them lie in boiling water till it is nearly cold, rub them with salt, and pull off the black and dirty skin, boil them in hot water, drain, and dust them with flour, rub them over with butter, season with white pepper and salt, and broil them. Put a table-spoonful of catsup, half a one of soy, and a little cayenne, into melted butter, heat and pour it over them.

Cod Sounds Fricasseed

WHEN cleaned as above, boil them in milk and water, drain, and put them into a sauce-pan with some white stock seasoned with mace, salt, and white pepper; thicken it with a bit of butter kneaded in flour, and, just before serving, stir in a table-spoonful of lemon pickle; garnish with sippets of thin toasted bread.

To Crimp Skate

SKIN the skate on both sides, cut it an inch and a half broad, and as long as the skate, roll up each piece, and tie it with a thread; lay them for three hours in salt and water, and a little vinegar; boil them fifteen minutes in boiling salt and water; before serving, cut off the threads. Sauces; – shrimp, butter, and anchovy. When skate are very small, they are preferable broiled.

Large Skate dressed like Veal Cutlets

CRIMP or cut the skate in square pieces, roll them in beaten eggs, and then in grated bread, mixed with chopped parsley, pepper, and salt; fry them of a nice brown colour, and serve with a rich brown gravy.

Stewed Skate

SKIN the skate, and cut it into square pieces, and brown it with butter in a frying-pan; make a rich sauce with the skin and parings, to be boiled in three pints of water; with an onion, some pepper and salt; strain and thicken it with a little butter mixed with flour, add some very finely chopped parsley, and chives; of hot vinegar, mushroom catsup, and Harvey sauce, a table-spoonful each, and a little cayenne; boil it up, and put in the skate five minutes before serving it.

Dressed Skate

CUT the skate into pieces, make a stock of the skin and fins with a haddock or a bit of veal, the shell of a lobster or crab washed, two or three onions, and a bunch of sweet herbs; boil it one hour, strain, and thicken it with flour and butter browned, a little soy, catsup, and a glass of white wine, some salt, and pepper; put in the skate, simmer it a quarter of an hour or twenty minutes, and serve it as a side dish, or as soup, when a few oyster loaves may be put in the tureen.

To Fry Small Skate

CLEAN, wash, and lay them one or two hours in vinegar, or vinegar and water, with a sliced onion, some chopped parsley, pepper, and salt; drain, and dry them well, dip them into beaten eggs, dredge them with flour, and fry them of a fine brown colour; garnish with fried parsley. Sauces; – melted butter, and shrimp sauce.

Skate with Liver Sauce

CRIMP or cut the skate into pieces, boil, and serve on it a sauce made as follows: put into a sauce-pan, parsley, cibol, mushrooms, a clove of garlic, all finely minced, and a little butter; give it a turn or two on the fire, and add a good dust of flour, then a bit of butter, capers, and a minced anchovy; the liver of the skate, first boiled and bruised, pepper, and salt; moisten it with gravy or water, and thicken it on the fire.

To Clean and Prepare Skate for Keeping

WASH them thoroughly, and rub them over with a handful of salt, rinse them, cut off the tail, and pare off the fins all round, hang them upon a fish-hake in the open air, and they will keep good for several days.

Boiled Carp

SCALE and clean a brace of carp, reserving the liver and roe; take half a pint of vinegar, or a quart of sharp cider, add as much water as will cover the fish, a piece of horse-radish, an onion cut in slices, a little salt, and a fagot of sweet herbs; boil the fish in this liquor, and make a sauce as follows: strain some of the liquor the fish has been boiled in, and put to it the liver minced, a pint of port wine, two anchovies, two or three heads of shalots chopped, some salt and black pepper, a little cayenne, a table-spoonful of soy; boil and strain it, thicken it with flour and butter, pour it over the carp hot, garnish with the roe fried, cut lemon, and parsley.

To Stew Carp

SCALE and clean a brace of carp, reserving the liver and roe; pour over the fish in a deep pan a pint of vinegar, which may be elder vinegar, if the flavour is preferred, with a little mace, three cloves, some salt and Jamaica pepper, two onions sliced, a fagot of parsley, basil, thyme, and marjoram; let them soak an hour, then put them in a stew-pan with the vinegar, and other things, the liver chopped, a pint of madeira, and three pints of veal stock; stew them an hour or two, according to their size; take out the fish and put them over a pan of hot water, to keep warm while the following sauce is made: strain the liquor, and add the yolks of three beaten eggs, half a pint of cream, a large spoonful of flour and a quarter of a pound of butter; stir it constantly, and just before putting it over the carp, squeeze in the juice of a lemon. Boil or fry the roe.

Plain boiled carp may be served with this sauce, and is dished in a napkin.

Another way to Stew Carp

CLEAN a brace of carp, save the blood and roes; fry the fish slightly in fresh lard; mix the blood well with some cold highly-seasoned beef or mutton stock, strain it, and add as much port wine as there is of broth; when it boils, put in the fish, which must be covered with the liquor; let them stew gently till sufficiently done; take them out, and keep them hot before the fire; put to the liquor two table-spoonfuls of catsup, the same of lemon pickle, and thicken it with a bit of butter kneaded in a table-spoonful of flour, boil it up and pour it over the carp; garnish the dish with the fried roes, and sippets of fried bread.

Fish Pudding

BONE and skin two raw fresh haddocks, pound them in a marble mortar, and rub them through a hair sieve; then put the fish again into the mortar with two eggs, a little parsley, and an onion cut small, some white pepper and salt, a slice of bread in crumbs, a quarter of a pound of veal suet, or marrow. Pound all well together, put it into a shape, and boil it an hour. The veal suet, or marrow, may be omitted.

Sauce for the Fish Pudding

MAKE a sauce with brown soup, in which boil the heads and fins of the haddocks, strain and thicken it with a little butter mixed with flour, and just before taking it off the fire add a tea-spoonful of anchovy sauce, and the same of essence of lobster, and of Harvey sauce; let it boil, and pour it round the pudding.

Little Fish Puddings

BONE and skin two haddocks, pound them smooth. Boil the same quantity of bread and milk as there is of fish, with a little parsley, mix it with the fish, and rub it through a sieve; put in two eggs and the yolk of a third, some salt and pepper; stir them very well together, and add the white of the third egg well beaten; roll them into the form of small sausages, flour and boil them fifteen minutes in boiling salt-and-water. Have ready the following brown sauce to serve in the dish with them. In a pint and a half of water boil the heads, fins, and bones of the haddocks, with a bunch of parsley, an onion, salt, pepper, and a bit of toasted bread; when it has boiled nearly an hour, strain it, and thicken it with flour and butter; add a table-spoonful of catsup, half a one of soy, and a little cayenne.

White Fish and Sauce

MAKE a rich gravy with a bit of veal, the heads and fins of four or five haddocks, three or four onions, some parsley, a little cayenne, black pepper, and salt, the juice of a lemon, half the peel, a table-spoonful of catsup, half a pint of white wine, and two quarts of water; simmer them for an hour, strain, and put to it the meat of a lobster or crab minced, and forcemeat balls; thicken it with half a pint of cream, the yolks of three beaten eggs, and a bit of butter kneaded in flour. Have ready boiled three haddocks skinned and without their heads, pour the sauce over them in a deep dish. Make the forcemeat balls of a small boiled haddock finely minced, grated bread crumbs, butter, pepper, salt, grated nutmeg, and parsley; bind them with the whites of two eggs beaten; and fry them in fresh lard of a light brown.

Brown Fish and Sauce

WASH them clean, take off the heads, skin and cut them into two or three pieces; boil the heads and fins in water, with a large onion cut small, for half an hour; strain it, and add some brown gravy soup; brown four ounces of butter kneaded well with two table-spoonfuls of flour; add it to the liquor, with the peel of half a lemon, two blades of mace, some salt and pepper. Boil all these, and having put in the pieces of fish, let them boil fifteen minutes, and add, just before dishing, a glass of white wine, and a little mushroom catsup and soy. Pick out the lemon-peel and mace.

Another Fish and Sauce with White Sauce

PREPARE the fish as in the receipt for brown fish and sauce, substituting veal broth for the gravy soup, and adding minced parsley with the onions; omit the catsup and soy, and do not brown the butter. It will improve the fish to soak them for half an hour in sour beer, or vinegar and water; more particularly whitings, which may be dressed as the haddocks, and the sauce enriched by just adding, before serving, two yolks of eggs beat up in three spoonfuls of cream, after which the sauce must not be allowed to boil. The stock is frequently made without meat.

To Clean and Prepare Haddocks for Keeping

SCRAPE them, and take out the entrails; cut them open considerably below the vent, so that the blood may be entirely scraped from the back bone; cut off the points of the tails, take out the eyes and gills, wash the fish, and put some salt into the bodies; let them lie till next day, then place them upon a fish hake, or a wooden rod put through the eyes, and hang them up in a cool place in the open air. They may be boiled or broiled, taking off the heads and skin.

To Boil Fresh Haddocks

CLEAN them as above directed, take off the heads and skin; when the water boils up, throw in two large handfuls of salt; put in the haddocks, boil them as fast as possible till they rise to the surface of the water, which will be from ten to fifteen minutes, according to their size; take off the scum as it rises. Sauces; – melted butter, and oyster sauce.

Baked Haddocks

MAKE a pint and a half of gravy with the heads and trimmings of three haddocks, one onion, some parsley, salt; pepper, and two anchovies cut small; strain and heat it again with an ounce of butter kneaded in a table-spoonful of flour, add two of catsup, one of vinegar, one of soy, and a small tea-cupful of white wine; have the fish ready skinned and cut into pieces; lay them into a deep dish, pour over them the sauce, and bake them in an oven.

Another way to Bake Haddocks

WASH and scrape off the scales of three large fine haddocks, leaving on the heads; make a sauce with the heads of some haddocks, two onions sliced, a bunch of parsley, and season it with pepper and salt; boil in this a small haddock, strain it, and then make a stuffing with the boiled fish picked from the bones, a few bread crumbs, chopped parsley, and some butter, and season it with salt and pepper; stuff the haddocks, and put them with the sauce into a deep dish, and bake them. A pie is made in the same way, taking off the skin and the heads of the fish, cutting them in two, and adding a glass of white wine.

Another way to Bake Haddocks

CLEAN, skin, and take off the heads of three good-sized haddocks; season grated bread crumbs with pepper, salt, and finely-minced parsley; strew some over the bottom of a dish; put in the fish, and strew more seasoned bread crumbs all over them, then put a little bit of butter here and there, and pour in as much gravy or water as the dish will hold. They will take an hour to bake, and when they begin to look brown, strew over them a few more bread crumbs, seasoned as at first.

To Fry Small Fresh Haddocks

CLEAN and scrape off the scales; cut off the fins and tails, the heads may be taken off or not, wipe them dry, rub them over with the yolk of an egg beaten, and dust them with flour; fry them in boiling lard or beef dripping; when one side is of a brown colour, turn them, and when done, lay them upon the back of a sieve before the fire to drain; garnish with fried parsley.

Another way to Fry Haddocks

WHEN perfectly fresh, take off the heads and skins, and cut out the bones very carefully; divide each side in two, wash them well, and lay them in a cloth to dry; have the yolk of an egg beat up in a plate, dip the fish into it, and strew over them sifted bread crumbs mixed with chopped parsley that has been boiled, and fry them in fresh beef dripping or lard; garnish the dish with fried parsley.

Haddocks dressed in this way make a nice garnish for boiled cod fish, or plain boiled haddocks.

To Fry Haddocks in Sauce

SKIN and cut off the heads of three or four haddocks, divide each into four pieces, wash them clean. Put a large table-spoonful of butter, with two spoonfuls of flour, into a frying-pan, and brown it; mince small two onions, and put pepper and salt upon them, and add them to the browned butter, and pour in as much boiling water as will nearly cover the pieces of fish; let it boil, put in the fish, and where one side is done, turn the other; dish it out, and pour the sauce over it; garnish with parsley. Omit the onions if the flavour is not liked, and substitute a table-spoonful of mushroom catsup, and one of lemon pickle.

Finnan or Aberdeen Haddocks

CLEAN the haddocks thoroughly, and split them, take off the heads, put some salt on them, and let them lie two hours, or all night, if they are required to keep more than a week; then, having hung them two or three hours in the open air to dry, smoke them in a chimney over peat or hardwood saw-dust. Where there is not a chimney suitable for the purpose, they may be done in an old cask open at both ends, into which put some saw-dust with a red-hot iron in the midst; place rods of wood across the top of the cask, tie the haddocks by the tail in pairs, and hang them on the sticks to smoke; the heat should be kept as equal as possible, as it spoils the fish to get alternately hot and cold; when done, they should be of a fine yellow colour, which they should acquire in twelve hours at farthest. When they are to be dressed, the skin must be taken off. They may be boiled, or broiled; and are generally used for breakfast.

To Fry Whiting

SCRAPE off the scales and cut off the fins, wipe them dry with a clean cloth; dredge them with flour, or beat up the yolk of an egg, and with a feather rub them over with it, and sprinkle them with finely-grated bread crumbs. Fry them of a nice brown in boiling fresh lard or dripping. If small and used as a garnish, they should be curled.

To broil them, they are previously prepared in the same way.

If boiled, the gut is drawn out, but they must not be washed.

To Boil Mackerel

CLEAN them well, and let them lie in vinegar and water for a short time, put them on in boiling salt-andwater for a quarter of an hour. Serve garnished with fennel. Sauces; – fennel and butter, and green gooseberry sauce.

To souse them; – put in the proportion of half a pint of vinegar to a quart of the liquor the fish has been boiled in, half an ounce of whole black pepper, a little mace, two or three bay leaves; and when cold, cover the mackerel completely with it, picking out the bay leaves.

To Broil Mackerel

CLEAN and split them open, wipe them dry, rub them over with butter, and sprinkle them with pepper and salt.

To Bake Mackerel

CLEAN them; cut off the heads and tails; put them into a deep dish, and pour over them equal quantities of water and vinegar, some whole black pepper, a little mace, salt, one or two bay leaves, and a small quantity of port wine; tie over the dish a sheet of thick white paper buttered. Another way is to season them with pepper, salt, and a little mace, all finely powdered, putting bits of butter into the bottom of the dish, and a little more butter upon the mackerel. They may be eaten hot or cold; if cold, with vinegar. If hot, serve with parsley and butter; and melted butter with catsup and soy.

Caveach Mackerel

CLEAN and cut each mackerel into four or five pieces; to six large-sized fish, pound and mix well together one ounce of black pepper, three nutmegs, six blades of mace, and a handful of salt; rub each bit of fish extremely well with the spices, and fry them brown in oil; when they are cold, put them into a jar; fill it up with the best vinegar, and pour oil upon the surface; tie it down closely. They are best to be done in the height of the season, and will keep good a twelvemonth, if not opened too soon, and answer well for a winter or spring dish.

To Fry Herrings

SCRAPE off the scales; cut off the fins; draw out the gut, keeping in the roes and milts; wipe them in a clean cloth; dredge them with flour, and fry them in boiling dripping; put them before the fire to drain and keep hot. Sauces; – melted butter, and parsley and butter.

When herrings are to be broiled, they are prepared in the same manner, and done upon the gridiron. They must not be washed.

Red Herrings

PLAIN broil them, or pour over them some beer made hot, and when it is cold drain and wipe them dry; heat them thoroughly, and rub over them a little butter, and sprinkle them with pepper.

To Bake Herrings

THEY must be perfectly fresh, and well cleaned, but not washed; the heads and fins cut off, and the bones cut out; strew over them pepper, salt, and a slice of onion minced very finely, to each; roll them up tight; pack them into a jar, and pour over them in the proportion of a pint of vinegar to two of water, with half an ounce of whole black pepper; tie over the jar a piece of bladder or paper, and bake them in an oven for an hour. Take off the cover when they are cold, and pour over them a little cold vinegar, and tie them up.

Soft Roes of Herrings in Cases

RUB butter over a round or square paper-case; its size must be according to the dish it is to be served in. Boil eight very fresh, soft-roed herrings; when done, take out the roes carefully, and put them whole into the case; sprinkle them over with a little pepper, salt, grated bread, and finely-chopped parsley. Put some little bits of butter here and there upon them, and bake them in a hot oven. When done, put a little "Maitre d'Hotel Sauce Maigre" into the case, with the juice of a lemon. Serve them quite hot and firm.

To Salt Herrings

CUT them open carefully, separating the guts from the milts and roes; throw away the milts, and leave the roes in the fish; wash them, and then put them into brine, strong enough to bear an egg; let them lie in that from twelve to sixteen hours; take them out and drain them well. In the bottom of a keg or jar, strew a good deal of salt; lay a row of herrings, and then sprinkle over them more salt, and repeat this till all are packed. Cover the top with salt, and stop it very closely, to exclude the air. When to be dressed, put them on in cold water, and when it boils let them boil for ten minutes. Serve them with mashed potatoes.

To Smoke Herrings

LAY them in salt and a little saltpetre for ten or twelve hours, and follow the same directions as for smoking Finnan Haddocks. – (see page 54.)

To Broil Sprats

CLEAN them well; dredge them slightly with flour, and put them in rows upon small skewers run through the heads; or they may be fried like herrings, and served hot and hot. Sauce; – melted butter, with catsup, soy, and lemon pickle, a spoonful of each, in it

To Bake Sprats

CLEAN them; take off the heads; put them into a deep dish, and cover them with vinegar and water, equal quantities of each. To a quart of liquid, put half an ounce of whole black pepper, a little allspice, two or three bay leaves, some salt, and an onion. Tie paper over the dish and bake them in a cool oven, or do them over a slow fire in water bath. Herrings may be done in this way. Both will keep good some weeks.

To Fry Smelts

THIS delicate little fish, when perfectly fresh, must not be washed, but wiped with a clean cloth, and dredged with flour, or brushed over with a feather, dipped into the yolk of an egg beaten, and rolled in a plate of finely-grated bread crumbs, and fried in boiling dripping, or fresh lard. They vary in size, and some will be done sooner than others. When of a clear yellow brown, take them out carefully, and lay them before the fire upon the back of a sieve to drain and keep hot. Dish them, heads and tails alternately. Garnish with fried parsley. Sauce; – melted butter. They may also be broiled.

To Fry Soles

TAKE off the brown skin, and scrape the other side; wash well, wipe, and lay them in a clean cloth to dry; beat up in a plate the yolks of one or two eggs; take the fish by the eyes, and draw them through the eggs, then sprinkle them over with finely-grated bread crumbs on both sides, never touching the fish but by the eyes; or they may be dredged with flour; slip them into a frying pan full of boiling fresh lard, or good dripping; when they become of a clear yellow brown, lay them carefully upon the back of a sieve or cloth before the fire. Serve them with plenty of fried parsley. Sauces; – shrimp sauce and melted butter.

To Boil Soles, Brill, or any other Flat Fish.

CLEAN them, cut off their fins, and put them on in boiling salt-and-water, and let it boil fast till the fish rises to the surface; when they will be done enough. Sauce; – anchovy, and shrimp sauce.

To Boil Trout

CLEAN and gut them; make the water as salt as for boiling salmon in, and when it boils, put in the trout, and let them boil fast from fifteen to twenty minutes, according to their size. Sauce; – melted butter.

To Fry Trout

CUT off the fins, clean, and gut them; dust them with flour, and dip them into the yolk of an egg beaten; strew grated bread crumbs over them, and fry them in fresh dripping; lay them upon the back of a sieve before the fire to drain. Sauce; – melted butter, with a table-spoonful of catsup, and one of lemon pickle, in it.

When they are small, roll them in oatmeal before they are fried.

To Broil Trout

CUT off the fins, and cut the fish down the back, close to the bone, and split the head in two.

Another way is after they have been cut open, to rub a little salt over them; let them lie three or four hours, and then hang them up in the kitchen. They will be ready to broil the next morning for breakfast.

To Collar Trout

WASH them clean, split them down the back, bone, and dry them well in a cloth; season them well with finely-pounded black pepper, salt, and mace; roll them tight, and lay them close into a dish; pour over them an equal quantity of vinegar and beer, with two or three bay leaves, and some whole black pepper; tie over the dish a sheet of buttered paper, and bake them an hour.

To Pot Trout or Grilse

MIX together the following quantity of finely-pounded spices: one ounce of cloves, half an ounce of Jamaica pepper, quarter of an ounce of black pepper, quarter of an ounce of cayenne, two nutmegs, a little mace, and two tea-spoonfuls of ginger; add the weight of the spices, and half as much again of salt, and mix all thoroughly. Clean the fish, and cut off the heads, fins, and tails; put a teaspoonful of the mixed spices into each fish, and lay them into a deep earthen jar, with the backs downwards; cover them with clarified butter, tie a paper over the mouth of the jar, and bake them slowly for eight hours. When the back bone is tender, the fish are done enough. Take them out of the jar, and put them into a milk-pan with the backs upwards; cover them with a board, and place upon it a heavy weight. When perfectly cold, remove the fish into fresh jars, smooth them with a knife, and cover them with clarified butter.

To Broil Fresh Sturgeon

CUT it into cutlets; rub them with the yolk of an egg beat up; strew them over with some parsley, minced very fine, and mixed with grated bread crumbs, pepper, and salt; put them into pieces of white paper buttered, and broil them gently. Sauces; – oyster, melted butter, and anchovy.

Sour Krout with Pike

WHEN the krout is boiled, clean a large pike, scrape and cut it into neat pieces, dip them into the beaten yolk of an egg, then into bread crumbs, and fry them of a nice brown; rub some butter upon a dish, and put into it a layer of krout, and some grated cheese, then a layer of pike, and a little sour cream; then krout, and so on till the dish be full. On the top put some bits of butter, and some good broth or gravy, strew crumbs of bread thickly over it, and bake it half an hour.

To Boil Pike

WASH clean, and take out the gills; stuff them with the following forcemeat: Equal parts of chopped oysters, grated bread crumbs, beef suet, or butter, two anchovies, a little onion, pepper, salt, nutmeg, minced parsley, sweet marjoram, thyme, and savory; an egg to bind it. Stuff the insides and sew them up; put them on in boiling salt-and-water, with a glass of vinegar, and let them boil for half an hour. Sauces; – oyster, and melted butter.

They may also be broiled.

Baked Pike

SCRAPE the scales off a large pike, take out the gills, and clean it, without breaking the skin; stuff the fish with a forcemeat made of two handfuls of grated bread, one of finely minced suet, some chopped parsley, and a little fresh butter seasoned with pepper, salt, mace, grated lemon-peel and nutmeg, pounded all together in a mortar, with two whole eggs. Fasten the tail of the pike into its mouth with a skewer, and then dip it, first into a well-beaten egg, and then into grated bread, which repeat twice; baste it over with butter, and bake it in an oven.

If two of them are to be served, make one of them of a green colour, by mixing a quantity of finely minced parsley with the grated bread. When the fish is of a fine brown colour, cover it with paper until it is done. Serve with a Dutch sauce in a sauce-tureen.

Maids

THEY are the better for being hung up for a day, and may be fried like soles, or, if large, boil the middle part, and fry the fins to put round the dish. Serve with shrimp sauce.

To Broil Perch

SCRAPE, gut, and wash them; dry them in a cloth, dust them with flour, and broil them. Sauce; –melted butter. Or they may be broiled without gutting them.

When they are to be boiled, follow the directions for boiling haddocks at page 52. They may also be stewed as carp are done.

To Pot Perch

CLEAN the fish, take off the head and skin, and season them with a little pounded mace, and some salt; put them into a pan with some butter, and bake them two hours; drain off the butter, take out the back bone, and strew over the fish a little pounded cinnamon and grated nutmeg. Keep them in a pan, with clarified butter poured over them.

Red Mullet

SCRAPE and wash them, fold them in buttered paper, lay them into a dish, and bake them gently. The liquor that comes from them, boil with a piece of butter, dusted with flour, a tea-spoonful of soy, two of essence of anchovy, and a little white wine. Serve the sauce in a butter-tureen.

This fish is called the sea woodcock, from being dressed with the inside.

To Boil Eels

SMALL ones are preferable; clean them well, skin, wash, and cut off the heads. Curl and put them on in boiling salt-and-water, with a little vinegar. Garnish with parsley. Sauce; – parsley and butter.

To Fry Eels

CLEAN them as before directed, cut them into pieces of three or four inches long, and then score across in two or three places; season them with pepper and salt, and dust them with flour, or dip them into an egg beat up, and sprinkle them with finely-grated bread crumbs; fry them in fresh lard or dripping. Let them drain and dry upon the back of a sieve before the fire. Garnish with parsley. Sauce; – melted butter and lemon pickle.

If small, they may be curled and fried whole.

To Spitchcock Eels

CLEAN and skin the eels, – large ones are best for this purpose; cut them into pieces of three or four inches long, score and sprinkle them with pepper and salt, dip them into an egg beat up, and then into grated bread crumbs, mixed with chopped parsley, and seasoned with pepper, salt, and nutmeg; rub the gridiron with a bit of suet, and broil them over a clear fire; or they may be fried. Sauces; – lemon pickle and catsup, in melted butter, or parsley and butter.

To Collar Eels

CLEAN and skin them, take out the bones, and cut off the heads and tails; lay them flat, and strew over plenty of the following seasoning: grated nutmeg, grated lemon peel, some salt and pepper, minced parsley, sweet marjoram, a little thyme, savory, and a leaf or two of sage; roll them very tight, and bind them firmly with tape; boil the heads, tails and bones in two quarts of water, and one pint of vinegar or cider, with one onion, three bay leaves, some salt and pepper; when it boils, put in the collars, and when tender take them out, and boil the liquor a little longer; strain and skim it, and when cold put in the fish. If the fish is to be kept long, it will be necessary to boil up the liquor, occasionally adding a little fresh vinegar.

To Pot Eels

CLEAN, skin, and bone them; season them well upon both sides with pepper, salt, a little mace, and Jamaica pepper; let them lie for six hours, then cut them into small pieces, and pack them close into a dish; cover them with a coarse paste, and bake them. When quite cold, take off the paste, and pour over them clarified butter.

Stewed Eels

CLEAN and skin the eels, wipe them dry, and cut them into pieces about four inches long; take two onions, two shalots, a bunch of parsley, thyme, two bay leaves, a little mace, black and Jamaica pepper, a pint of good gravy; the same of port wine, and the same of vinegar, six anchovies bruised; let all boil together for ten minutes; take out the eels; boil the sauce till reduced to a quart; strain and thicken it with a table-spoonful of flour, mixed smooth in a little cold water. Put in the eels, and boil them till they are tender.

Eels may also be roasted, with a common stuffing.

Another way to Stew Eels

AFTER the eels are cleaned and skinned, cut them into pieces, season well two pounds and a half with salt and black pepper, put an ounce of butter into a stew-pan with a large handful of sorrel, three or four sage leaves, half an onion cut small, a little grated lemon-peel, and one anchovy chopped; put in the eels, and pour over half a pint of water, stew them gently for half an hour, shaking them occasionally; before serving, add a little grated nutmeg, and the juice of half a lemon.

To Stew Lampreys

CLEAN them well with salt and warm water, and remove the cartilage which runs down the back, season them with black and Jamaica pepper, grated nutmeg, two or three cloves, and some salt; stew them till tender in equal parts of port wine and water, with some horse-radish and an onion; strain and thicken the liquor with flour and butter, and add a table-spoonful of lemon pickle and one of mush-room catsup; heat it, and pour it hot over the lampreys.

Eels may be stewed in this way, keeping on the skins, curling and first frying them of a good brown.

Fish Soup Cake

PICK free from bones and skin any cold boiled white fish, weigh it, and add one third of grated bread crumbs, a little cold melted butter, a small onion minced very fine, some pepper and salt, and the whites of two eggs to bind it; mix it well to-gether, and make it up into the form of a thick cake the size of the dish it is to be sent to table in, and fry it on both sides a nice brown; then stew it in a gravy made of weak stock; and the fish bones boiled in it, with an onion, pepper, and salt; thicken the sauce with a little flour and water, and add a dessert-spoonful mush-room catsup, and one of soy.

Veal, beef, or mutton, dressed in this way, is very good.

Fish Rechauffé

AFTER pike, cod, skate, turbot, soles, or any other white fish, has been dressed, pick it from the bones into small bits; add to a pound of fish, or in the same proportion, half a pint of good cream, one table-spoonful of mustard, the same of anchovy essence, the same of catsup, and of Harvey sauce, a little flour, some salt, pepper, and butter; make it all hot in a sauce-pan, then put it into the dish in which it is to be served up, strew crumbs of bread over it, and baste it with butter till it is a little moist, then brown it with a salamander, or in a Dutch oven.

A wall of mashed potatoes round the dish is an improvement.

Another way to make Fish Rechauffé

PICK from the bone in large flakes about two pounds of cold salmon, cod fish, or soles; melt a quarter of a pound of butter, in half a pint of cream, with a little flour and salt; add the fish, and heat it thoroughly.

To Boil Lobsters

TIE the claws with a bit of twine, and put them on in boiling water, boil them for twenty minutes, or half an hour, according to the size; rub them over with a small bit of butter, and lay them upon their claws to drain till they become cold.

Crabs are boiled in the same manner.

Dressed Lobster

PICK out all the meat, and mince it finely with one anchovy, mix it with a large table-spoonful of grated bread, a little salt, cayenne, and Indian pickle vinegar; moisten it with melted butter, and heat it thoroughly; split the tail, and fill it, as also the body shell, and brown it with a salamander.

To Fricassee Lobster

BREAK the shells, and take out the meat carefully, cut it and the red part, or coral, into pieces, adding the spawn; thicken with flour and butter some white stock, with which the shells have been boiled; season it with white pepper, mace, and salt, put in the lobster and heat it up; just before serving, add a little lemon juice, or lemon pickle. The stock may be made with the shells only, boiled in a pint of water, with some white pepper, salt, and a little mace, thickened with cream, flour, and butter.

To Pot Lobster

Pick out all the meat with the red part, and the spawn; season it with pepper, mace, and salt; lay it in a dish, and put over it clarified butter. Tie a sheet of buttered paper over it, and bake it twenty minutes; when it is cold, pound it and the butter that was baked with it, pack it into potting jars, and pour upon the top a little more clarified butter. Allow to one lobster two ounces of butter in baking.

Lobster à la Braise

Pound the meat of a large lobster very fine with two ounces of butter, and season it with grated nutmeg, salt, and white pepper; add a little grated bread, beat up two eggs, reserve part to put over the meat, and with the rest make it up into the form of a lobster. Pound the spawn and red part, and spread it over it; bake it a quarter of an hour, and, just before serving, lay over it the tail and body shell, with the small claws put underneath to resemble a lobster.

To butter Lobsters or Crabs

Pick all the meat from the bodies of either, mince it small, put it into a saucepan with two or three table-spoonfuls of white wine, one of lemon pickle, and three or four of rich gravy, a bit of butter, some salt, pepper, and grated nutmeg; thicken it with the yolks of two eggs beat up, and when quite hot, put it into the large shells; garnish them with an edging of bread toasted.

Cutlets of Lobster, Crab, or Oyster

Pick out carefully all the meat of a large lobster, mince it, and add it to two ounces of butter, which has been browned with two table-spoonfuls of flour, and seasoned with a little white pepper, salt, and cayenne; add about half a pint of strong stock, stir it over the fire till it is quite hot; put it in separate table-spoonfuls upon a large dish. When cold, make them up into the form of mutton cutlets, brush over them the beaten yolks of eggs, dip them into grated bread, and fry them of a light brown colour in boiling clarified beef dripping. Stick into the narrow end of the cutlet a bit of a small claw, about an inch long; place the cutlets round the dish, one a little over the other, and lay fried parsley in the centre of the dish.

Instead of the claw, a bit of stick may be put into the end of the oyster cutlet.

Bradu Fagadu

Pick the meat out of a lobster, cut it into small bits, season it with two table-spoonfuls of currie powder, some salt, and a little cayenne. Well wash and pick a quantity of spinach sufficient for a dish, half stew it, closely covered, without any water; then strain off the liquor from it, and add the lobster to it, with a large piece of butter; cover the stew-pan, and let it stew a quarter of an hour.

Indian Fagadu

CLEAN and wash a quantity of spinach, put it into a sauce-pan without any water, and the meat of a lobster or a pint of shrimps, picked from the shells and cut small, an onion, and a clove of garlic minced fine, some salt, a few chilies, or cayenne; when nearly done, add some onions sliced, and fried brown; cover the stew-pan close for a short time, then keep stirring it till it becomes quite dry; sour it with lemon juice.

Lobster Salad

BROIL a boiled lobster, mince the meat with minced onions, pickled green apples, green capsicums, lemon juice, and salt.

Dressed Crabs

AFTER the crabs are boiled, break the claws, and pick out all the meat carefully from them, and the breast; taking the roe along with a little of the inside. Keep the shell whole; mince up the meat, season it with grated nutmeg, white pepper, salt, some white wine, and a little vinegar; mix in a few bread crumbs, and a good bit of butter; put it into a sauce-pan to heat, stirring it all the time; when thoroughly heated, fill the shells previously washed clean, with or without puff-paste round the edge, brown them in an oven.

Another way to prepare Dressed Crabs

PICK out the meat from the shell, mince it finely with a bit of butter, and season it high with pepper, salt, and nutmeg, a glass of port wine, and a dessert-spoonful of vinegar; mix it altogether, put it into the shell, and strew over it finely grated bread crumbs. Brown it in a Dutch oven, and serve it hot.

Dressed Cold Crabs or Lobsters

PICK the meat from the shells, and dress it with a sauce as for salad, adding a little pepper and cayenne.

To Pot Prawns, or Shrimps

AFTER they are boiled, pick them from the shells, season them with grated nutmeg, ditto lemon-peel, white pepper, and salt; pack them close into a jar, put over the top a thin bit of butter; tie paper over it, and bake them for eight or ten minutes. When cold, put over them clarified butter.

To Stew Prawns, Shrimps, or Cray Fish

PICK the meat from the shells, bruise the shells and put them into half a pint of white wine, the same quantity of water, and a spoonful of vinegar, seasoned with salt, pepper, and mace. Stew them for half an hour, strain them, and thicken the sauce with flour and butter; add a little grated nutmeg and the fish, heat them thoroughly; toast a slice of thin bread, cut off the crust, and cut it into six pieces, lay it on a dish, and pour over it the stewed prawns, shrimps, or cray fish.

To Keep and Fatten Oysters

PUT them into water, and wash and clean them with a birch broom; lay them with the deep shell downwards into a tub or broad platter, and then sprinkle them over with salt. The following day pour over them and fill the vessel with clean cold water, in which they must remain an hour, then pour it off again; sprinkle them with salt, and let this be repeated every day. This method will keep them good for a fortnight.

To Fry Oysters

MAKE a batter as for pancakes, seasoned with grated nutmeg, white pepper, and salt, and add some finely grated bread crumbs; dip in the oysters, and fry them of a light brown in beef dripping.

Another way to Fry Oysters

IS, to dip them into the white of an egg beat up, and roll them in finely grated bread crumbs, seasoned with grated nutmeg, pepper, and salt, and fry them as directed.

To Stew Oysters

STEW with a quart of oysters, and their liquor strained, a glass of white wine, one anchovy bruised, seasoned with white pepper, salt, a little mace, and a bunch of sweet herbs; let all stew gently a quarter of an hour. Pick out the bunch of herbs, and add a quarter of a pound of fresh butter kneaded in a large table-spoonful of flour, and stew them ten or twelve minutes. Serve them garnished with bread-sippets and cut lemon.

They may be stewed simply in their own liquor, seasoned with salt, pepper, and grated nutmeg, and thickened with cream, flour, and butter.

To Scallop Oysters

PUT them, with their liquor strained, two or three blades of mace, a few pepper-corns, a little cayenne, and a piece of butter the size of a walnut, kneaded with flour, into a stew-pan. Simmer them very gently for half an hour, by no means letting them boil; pick out the mace and pepper; have ready finely-grated bread crumbs, seasoned with pepper and salt; put into the scallop-shells, or into a dish, alternately a layer of bread crumbs, then one of oysters, and part of their liquor; and stick over the last layer of bread crumbs a few bits of butter, and brown them in a Dutch oven for fifteen or twenty minutes.

Another way to Scallop Oysters

TAKE off the beards, stew them in their liquor strained, with a little mace, white pepper, and salt. Fry in a stew-pan, with a bit of butter, some grated bread crumbs, till of a nice brown; put them alternately with the oysters into a dish.

To Pickle Oysters

OPEN them carefully, preserving all their liquor; put them into a sauce-pan over the fire, stirring them now and then, and when the liquor boils take them off, skim the surface, and put the oysters into a bowl; let the liquor settle, pour off the clear part, and put it on to boil, with spices, allowing for three hundred oysters, half an ounce of whole black pepper, a little mace and allspice; boil it ten minutes, then add the oysters, and let them boil two minutes; put them into a jar, and when they are cold, tie a paper over it.

Oyster Loaves

CUT off the top of some small French rolls, take out the crumb, and fry them brown and crisp with clarified butter, then fry some bread crumbs; stew the requisite quantity of oysters, bearded, and cut into two, in their liquor, with a little white wine, some gravy, and seasoned with grated lemon-peel, pounded mace, pepper, and salt; add a bit of butter; fill the rolls with the oysters, and serve them with the fried bread crumbs in the dish.

Oyster Attelets

CUT into small pieces a sweet bread and a slice or two of bacon, beard some large oysters, and season all highly with chopped parsley, shalot, a little thyme, pepper, and salt. Then fasten them alternately upon wire skewers; put sifted bread crumbs over them, and boil or fry them of a light brown colour. Take them off the skewers, and serve them with some rich gravy, to which add a little catsup, and lemon pickle.

To Pickle Mussels

SHELL and beard them, save their liquor, put them on with it and some whole black and Jamaica pepper, ginger, mace, and salt; boil them five minutes, and when cold, if they are required to be kept, add a little vinegar.

Another way to Pickle Mussels

WASH them clean, and put them into a saucepan over a quick fire, shake them, that all may be done equally; take them off as soon as the shells open, pick out the mussels and beard them, and keep the liquor separate; let it settle, strain it, and boil it with a little whole black and Jamaica pepper and salt; put in the mussels and boil them for three minutes.

Cockles are managed in the same manner, and both ought to be eaten quite fresh.

Imitation Anchovies

To a peck of perfectly fresh sprats just taken out of the water, and neither washed nor wiped, allow the following quantity of ingredients, all to be finely-pounded, and well mixed together: Two pounds of common salt, a quarter of a pound of bay salt, four ounces of saltpetre, two ounces of prunella salt, and a small portion of cochineal. Lay alternately in a stone pan till it be full, a layer of the sprats, and a layer of the prepared mixture; press the whole well down, and cover the pan closely. They will require to stand six months before they are used.

CHAPTER III
BEEF

The names of the various pieces, according to the English and Scotch method of dividing the carcass, are as follows: –

IN ENGLAND.

The hind quarter contains the Sirloin – Rump – Edgebone – Buttock – Mouse Buttock – Veiny-Piece – Thick Flank – Thin Flank – Leg – Fore Rib – Five Ribs.

The fore quarter contains the Middle Rib of four ribs – Chuck of three ribs – Shoulder, or Leg-of-Mutton piece, containing a part of the Blade-Bone – Brisket – Clod – Neck End, or Sticking Piece – Shin – Cheek.

IN SCOTLAND

The Middle Sirloin – top of the Rump and Hook-bone – Middle Hook-bone and Round – the Hough – the Spare Rib – the Flank and part of the Hough – the Fore Saye – the Breast and Nine-holes – the Lair – Neck and Sticking-Piece – the Knap – Cheek and Head.

Besides these are the Tongue and Palate. The Entrails consist of the Heart – Sweetbreads – Kidneys – Skirts – and three kinds of Tripe, the Double, the Roll, and the Red Tripe.

PREPARATORY REMARKS ON BEEF

Ox Beef is considered the best. The flesh should feel tender, be fine in the grain, and of a bright red colour nicely marbled or mixed with fat. The fat should be white, rather than of a yellow colour.

Heifer Beef is excellent when finely fed, and is most suitable for small families. The bone should be taken out of a round of beef before it is salted, and it must be washed, skewered, and bound round firmly before being boiled. Salt beef should be put on with plenty of cold water, and when it boils the scum removed. It is then kept simmering for some hours. A piece weighing fifteen pounds will require three hours and a half to boil. Carrots and turnips for garnishing should be put on to boil with the beef. If in the least tainted, a piece of charcoal may be boiled with it.

When beef is to be kept any length of time, it should be carefully wiped every day. In warm weather, wood vinegar is an excellent preservative: it is put all over the meat with a brush. To protect the meat from flies, it may be sprinkled over with pepper. Tainted meat may be restored by washing in cold water, afterwards in strong camomile tea, after which it may be sprinkled with salt, and used the following day, first washing it in cold water. Roughly pounded charcoal rubbed all over the meat also restores it when tainted. In summer, meat in Scotland is frequently kept a fortnight smothered in oatmeal, and carefully wiped every day; and if it should be a little tainted, it is soaked for some hours before it is used, in oatmeal and water.

These directions apply equally to all sorts of meat.

The sirloin is the prime joint for roasting. When to be used, it should be washed, then dried with a clean cloth, and the fat covered over with a piece of white paper tied on with thread. The spit should be kept at all times exceedingly clean: it must be wiped dry immediately after it is drawn from the meat, and washed and scoured every time it is used. Care should be taken to balance the roast properly upon the spit; but, if not exactly right, it is better to make it equal by fastening on a leaden-headed skewer than to pierce it again. The fire should be prepared by putting on plenty of coals at the back. When put down, it should be about ten inches from the fire, and gradually drawn nearer. It is first basted with a little butter or fresh dripping, and then well basted with its own fat all the time it is roasting. Ten minutes before serving, it should be sprinkled with a little salt, then dredged with flour, and basted till it is frothed. When it is drawn from the spit some gravy will run out, to which may be added a little boiling salt-and-water poured along the bone: the beef is then garnished with plenty of finely scraped horse-radish. A sirloin, weighing about fifteen pounds, should be roasted for three hours and a half. A thinner piece of the same weight requires only three hours. In cold weather meat requires longer roasting than in warm, and if newly killed than if it has been kept.

To Stew a Rump of Beef

Tie up the beef, and put it on to stew with nearly as much cold water as will cover it; add three pounds of fat bacon cut into slices, a handful of thyme, eight onions, four small carrots, two turnips, two or three bay leaves, some black pepper, a little allspice, mace, and three cloves, a pint of port wine, and one of sherry. Let it stew gently between seven and eight hours. Take out the beef, strain the liquor, and skim off all the fat; thicken it with a little flour rubbed down in cold water, boil it up, and pour it over the beef. Have ready carrots and turnips, cut according to fancy, and boiled tender in weak gravy, and put them round the beef before serving.

Another way to Stew a Rump of beef

Bind the beef tightly, stick into it four cloves, and put it into a sauce-pan with three quarts of water, a quarter of an ounce of black pepper half-beaten, some salt, a bunch of sweet herbs, and three anchovies; turn it often, and when half done take it out, pour off the liquor; put in the beef again, with a pint of port wine and half a pint of table-beer made scalding hot, and some of the liquor strained; stew it till tender, clear off the fat, and if the sauce is not strong enough, add well-seasoned beef gravy; thicken it with flour rubbed down in a little cold water. Dish the beef, and pour the gravy round it.

Another way to Stew a Rump of Beef

FRY a small rump, or fore rib of beef in butter till it is brown all over. Make a sauce with butter browned with flour, and some water in which two or three onions have been boiled; season with pepper, salt, and three table-spoonfuls of vinegar; put in the beef, turn it frequently, and stew it gently for three hours. A little before serving, add a tea-cupful of port wine. Carrots and turnips, cut into dice, may be stewed with it.

A Rump of Beef à la Braise

AFTER a rump of beef has hung for five or six days, bone, and lard it thickly, but so as not to appear upon the surface, with bits of bacon or ham cut about half an inch square, and rolled in the following seasoning well mixed: Finely minced onion, parsley, thyme, a little garlic, pepper, and salt. What is left over of the seasoning add to a pint of vinegar, one of port wine, and a tea-cupful of salad oil; steep the beef in this for one night; the following day paper it, and roast it in a cradle spit. Baste it well, and serve it with a thick brown gravy. A little lemon juice, and sliced pickled cucumbers may be added. Garnish with slices of boiled carrot and scraped horse-radish.

Stewed Beef

STEW in five quarts of water the middle part of a brisket of beef weighing ten pounds, add two onions stuck with two cloves, one head of celery, one large carrot, two turnips cut small, a handful of sorrel leaves, half an ounce of black pepper, and some salt. Stew it gently for six hours. Make a strong gravy with carrots and turnips, the turnips to be scraped and fried of a brown colour in butter; add pepper, salt, and a little cayenne; thicken it with flour and butter, and pour it over the beef, with the carrots and turnips.

Another way to Stew Beef

TAKE ten pounds of a brisket of beef, cut the short ribs; and put it into a well-buttered sauce-pan, with two large onions, stuck with three or four cloves, two or three carrots cut into quarters, a bunch of sweet herbs, a small lemon sliced, and five quarts of water; let it stew seven hours. Strain and clarify the gravy – thicken it with butter and flour. Chop the carrots with some capers, mushroom catsup, and cayenne. Any other pickle that is liked may be added.

Another way to Stew Beef

POUND and mix together two ounces of Jamaica pepper, half an ounce of black pepper, and a little ginger, and half a pound of bay salt; rub it well into a round or rump of beef weighing fourteen or sixteen pounds; let it lie five or six days, turning it daily. Put a flat plate at the bottom of a sauce-pan, put in the beef, cover it with water, and let it stew for five hours, keeping the pan perfectly close. If the water wastes, add more boiling hot. Before serving, take out about a quart of the gravy, skim, and add to it some grated nutmeg and pepper, and some cut pickles; heat and pour it over the beef. Garnish with cut pickles.

Hunting Beef

RUB well into a round of beef weighing about forty pounds, three ounces of saltpetre; let it stand five or six hours; pound three ounces of allspice, one of black pepper, and mix them with two pounds of salt and seven ounces of brown sugar. Rub the beef all over with the salt and spices, let it remain fourteen days, and every other day turn and rub it with the pickle; then wash off the spices, and put it into a deep pan. Cut small nearly six pounds of beef-suet, put some into the bottom of the pan, but the greater part upon the top of the beef. Cover it with a coarse paste, and bake it eight hours. When cold, take off the crust, and pour off the gravy. It will keep good for three months. Preserve the gravy, as a little of it improves the flavour of hashes, soups, or any made dishes.

Beef à la Braise

BONE a rump of beef; lard it very thickly with bacon seasoned with pepper, salt, cloves, mace, and allspice, and season the beef with pepper and salt; put some slices of bacon into the bottom of the pan, with some whole black pepper, a little allspice, one or two bay leaves, two onions, a clove of garlic, and a bunch of sweet herbs. Put in the beef, and lay over it some slices of bacon, two quarts of weak stock, and half a pint of white wine. Cover it closely, and let it stew between six and seven hours.

Sauce for the beef is made of part of the liquor it has been stewed in, strained, and thickened with a little flour and butter, adding some green onions cut small, and pickled mushrooms. It is poured hot over the beef.

Beef Olives

CUT the beef into long thin steaks; prepare a forcemeat made of bread crumbs, minced beef-suet, chopped parsley, a little grated lemon-peel, nutmeg, pepper, and salt; bind it with the yolks of eggs beaten; put a layer of it over each steak; roll and tie them with thread. Fry them lightly in beef dripping; put them in a stew-pan with some good brown gravy, a glass of white wine, and a little cayenne; thicken it with a little flour and butter; cover the pan closely, and let them stew gently an hour. Before serving, add a table-spoonful of mushroom catsup; garnish with cut pickles.

Dressed Beef Steaks

CUT thin steaks, longer than they are broad, off a rump; beat them with a rolling-pin; season them with pepper, salt, and finely-minced onions; roll and tie them with thread; cut them even at the ends; fry them brown with a little butter; make a sauce with a piece of butter browned with flour, some gravy or water, a minced onion, pepper, and salt. Boil it, and add the steaks, and let them stew an hour. Before serving, add some mushroom catsup, and take off the threads.

Beef Steaks with Potatoes

CUT some thin slices off a rump of beef, beat and season them with a little pepper and salt; dip them into a little melted butter, that the gravy may not drop out whilst they are broiling. When done, serve them with the following mixture laid underneath. Some finely chopped parsley, a little butter, pepper, salt, and lemon; and put, all round the dish, potatoes fried of a fine brown colour.

Beef Balls

MINCE very finely a piece of tender beef, fat and lean: mince an onion, with some boiled parsley; add grated bread crumbs, and season with pepper, salt, grated nutmeg, and lemon-peel; mix all together, and moisten it with a beaten egg; roll it into balls; flour and fry them in boiling fresh dripping. Serve them with fried bread crumbs, or with a thickened brown gravy.

Minced Collops

CUT two pounds of lean tender beef into thin slices – it is best taken from off the rump, or round; mince it very finely; brown two ounces of butter in a frying-pan, dredging it with a little flour, then add the minced meat, and keep beating it with a beater till of a nice brown colour. Have ready some highly-seasoned beef gravy, which, with the minced collops, put into a sauce-pan, and let it stew half an hour; and, just before serving, put a table-spoonful of mushroom catsup, and, if liked, some green pickles. Beef-suet is as often used as butter to fry the collops in.

Another way to Make Minced Collops

MINCE any piece of lean or tender beef very finely, with one or two onions previously cut small and parboiled; season with pepper and salt; brown in a saucepan a table-spoonful of butter; add the minced meat; beat it with a beater till it is of a light brown colour, then dust in a little flour, and add about half a pint of gravy or water, with half a table-spoonful of vinegar. Cover the sauce-pan closely, and let it stew gently for half an hour. A little before serving, add a table-spoonful of mushroom catsup. The gravy may be made with the parings and stringy parts of the beef. When the flavour of onions is disliked, boil some whole small onions, and garnish the dish with them. Minced collops may be kept some weeks packed closely into a jar, after being fried without any onions, and covered with clarified butter. When to be dressed, follow the above directions.

Short, or Spiced Beef

To be eaten cold.

HANG up ten or twelve pounds of the middle part of a brisket of beef for three or four days, then rub well into it three ounces of finely-powdered saltpetre, and if spice is approved of, one ounce of allspice, and half an ounce of black pepper; let it stand all night, then salt it with three pounds of well-pounded bay salt, and half a pound of treacle, in which let it remain ten days, rubbing it daily. When it is to be boiled, sew it closely in a cloth, let the water only simmer, upon no account allowing it to boil, for nine hours over a slow fire, or upon a stove. When taken out of the water, place two sticks across the pot, and let the beef stand over the steam for half an hour, turning it from side to side, then press it with a heavy weight. It must not be taken out of the cloth till perfectly cold.

To Salt Neats' Tongues

SALT two tongues, and turn them every day for four or five days; then rub them with two ounces of common salt, one of brown sugar, and half an ounce of saltpetre; turn them daily, and in a fortnight they may be used.

The best sort of vessel for salting them in is an earthenware pan, as wide at top as bottom, so that the tongues may lie in it long-ways.

To Salt Beef for immediate Use

SALT a round of beef moderately upon the top and sides, put it upon sticks, or the tongs of a cheese-tub, over a tub of cold water, and the salt will be drawn through it, so that it will be fit for boiling next day.

Another method

IS, to rub for half an hour into any piece of beef a good quantity of salt, and let it lie for three or four days without touching it, when it may be used.

Pickle for Beef

ALLOW to four gallons of water two pounds of brown sugar and six pounds of bay salt, boil it about twenty minutes, taking off the scum as it rises; the following day pour it over the meat which has been packed into the pickling-tub. Boil it up every two months, adding three ounces of brown sugar and half a pound of common salt. By this means it will keep good a year. The meat must be sprinkled with salt, and next day wiped dry, before pouring the pickle over it, with which it should always be completely covered. With the addition of two ounces of saltpetre and one pound of bay salt, this pickle answers for pickled pork, hams, and tongues. The tongues should be rubbed with common salt, to cleanse them, and afterwards with a little saltpetre, and allowed to lie for four or five days before they are put into the pickle. The meat will be ready for use in eight or ten days, and will keep for three months.

To Collar Beef

CUT off the end of a brisket of beef, and bone it; sprinkle it with salt and saltpetre, and let it lie a week; mix together some grated nutmeg, Jamaica and black pepper, some chopped lemon thyme, sweet marjoram, and parsley; strew it over the meat, roll it up hard, sew it in a cloth, put it into a large jar of water, tie it closely, and bake it in an oven; take it out of the jar, and press it with a heavy weight. When it is quite cold, take off the cloth, and keep it dry.

Hessian Stew

CUT the root of a tongue into large pieces, lay it into a deep pan, rub well into it a handful of salt, pour over it some hot water, and stir it round; when cool enough, scour it well with the hands, and wash it thoroughly in cold water; when perfectly clean, dust it with flour, fry it of a light brown, with a good quantity of small whole onions; put it into a digester, with a tea-cupful of strong beer; rinse out the pan with boiling water, put it to the meat, with three quarts more of hot water, a head or two of garlic, some sliced carrots and turnips; season with ground black, Jamaica, and cayenne pepper, three cloves, and some salt; let it stew three or four hours. Half an hour before serving, take out the meat and some of the soup for gravy, add more spices, and of mushroom catsup, soy, walnut-pickle, and corach, a table-spoonful each, and three of port wine; boil it all together, thicken the sauce with butter rolled in flour, and garnish with sippets of thin toasted bread cut into a three-cornered shape. The soup that is left may be strained, and served clear, or with vegetables that have been previously boiled.

Ox Tail à la Matelote

CUT an ox tail into pieces and blanch it in boiling water, put it into fresh water and parboil it, then make a sauce with a spoonful of flour and a bit of butter, moistening it with a little of the liquor in which the tail was boiled; cut into it the pieces of the tail, with a dozen whole onions from which the outer skin has been taken, add a glass of white wine, a bunch of parsley and cibol, a clove of garlic, a laurel leaf, and some basil and thyme, two cloves, salt, and pepper; let them stew gently till the meat and onions are done, taking care to skim well. Put into the sauce an anchovy cut, a tea-spoonful of whole capers; place the pieces of the tail in the middle of the dish, and put the onions round and over them; garnish with seven or eight bits of fried bread the size of a crown piece, and being ready to serve, pour the strained sauce over it.

To Stew Beef-Steaks

FRY the steaks in a little butter; take them out of the pan, and fry in it a minced onion; return the steaks, with a little boiling water or gravy, some pepper, salt and a table-spoonful of vinegar; stew them gently for two or three hours; thicken the sauce with butter rolled in flour; and serve with or without pickles.

Dutch Beef

RUB on a beef heart two ounces of common salt, half an ounce of saltpetre, an ounce and a half of coarse brown sugar, and a little bay salt; turn and rub it every day for nine days, then hang it in the kitchen to dry, when it will become quite hard. When required for use, cut off a small bit, boil, and when cold grate it. It may be served with curled butter over it.

Scots Collops

Cut any piece of tender lean beef into slices, beat them; brown some butter and flour in a sauce-pan; put in the beef, with some salt, pepper, and a finely-minced onion – half a minced apple is an improvement; add a little hot water; cover the pan closely, and let them stew till tender.

Another way to make Scots Collops

Cut some very thin slices of beef; rub with butter the bottom of an iron stew-pan that has a cover to fit quite closely; put in the meat, some pepper, and a little salt, a large onion, and an apple minced very small. Cover the stew-pan, and let it simmer till the meat is very tender. Serve it hot.

Beef Rissoles

Chop finely a pound of lean tender beef, and a quarter of a pound of beef-suet; pound them in a marble mortar; mix with it a quarter of a pound of grated bread, a little onion, and a head of garlic bruised; season with salt and pepper; bind it with three eggs well beaten; make it up into small cakes, fry them of a light brown, then stew them in gravy for fifteen or twenty minutes.

To Stew a Tongue

Wash it very clean, and rub it well with common salt and a little saltpetre; let it lie two or three days, and then boil it till the skin will pull off. Put it into a sauce-pan, with part of the liquor it has been boiled in, and a pint of good stock. Season with black and Jamaica pepper, and two or three pounded cloves; add a glass of white wine and a table-spoonful of mushroom catsup, and one of lemon pickle; thicken the sauce with butter rolled in flour, and pour it over the tongue.

Pickled Tongue Glazed and Bigarrée

Boil a large tongue till it be tender, skin and glaze it, and serve it with mashed turnips on one side, and mashed carrots, or carrots and spinach, on the other.

Beef Tongue to Roast

Put it to stew with some roots; a laurel leaf, some basil, onion, a bunch of cibol, parsley and thyme, pepper, salt, and a clove, and gravy sufficient to moisten the meat; when it has stewed slowly for three hours, take off the skin and lard it delicately, then roast it on a spit, and serve under it clear gravy, to which a little vinegar is added.

Beef à la Mode

TAKE the bone out of a small round of fine ox beef, cut some fat bacon in long strips, dip them into common and shalot vinegar mixed, and roll them in the following seasoning: Grated nutmeg, black and Jamaica pepper, one or two cloves, and some salt, parsley, chives, lemon thyme, knotted marjoram, and savory, shred quite small. Lard the beef very thickly, bind it firmly with tape, and rub the outside with the seasoning. Put it into a saucepan, with the rind of a lemon, four large onions, the red part of three or four carrots, and two turnips cut into dice; and a tea cupful of strong ale and one of vinegar; let it stew for six or eight hours, turning it two or three times. Half an hour before serving, take out the beef and vegetables, skim off the fat, strain the sauce, an thicken it with a little flour and water mixed smooth; add a teacupful of port wine, return it all into the pot, and let it boil.

Another Beef à la Mode

RUB well into a piece of the thick flank of ox beef, two or three ounces of saltpetre, and half a pound of brown sugar; let it lie for twenty-four hours, then salt it with common salt, and let it lie for ten days or a fortnight; wash the brine from it, and fillet it firmly. Prepare a stuffing of chopped parsley, anchovy, mace, black and Jamaica pepper, and a little butter; make holes every here and there with a large knife, and stuff them with the above mixture. Put it into a pan that will just hold it, and fill it up with cold water; add some whole black pepper, and cover it with a flour-and-water paste: bake it for some hours. When cold, take off the crust and all the fat, and keep the beef in the pan.

Baked Beef

MIX together three quarters of a pound of common salt, half an ounce of saltpetre, and two ounces of sugar; rub it well into ten pounds of a fore rib of beef; let it lie a fortnight, basting it daily; smoke it for three weeks in a chimney where saw-dust is burnt; wash it very clean; put it into a deep earthen-pan; cover it with a coarse flour-and-water paste, and bake it for three or four hours in an oven.

Hashed Beef

CUT the beef into small thin slices, free from fat and skin; put the trimmings, and part of the bones, into a sauce-pan, with two large onions sliced, a little vinegar, and about a pint of stock; let it simmer for an hour, strain it, and skim off the fat; put an ounce of butter into a sauce-pan, and when it melts, shake in a spoonful of flour; stir it for two or three minutes, then add the strained gravy; stir it till it boil, put in a little catsup, and add the beef; let it simmer to make it hot, but it must not be allowed to boil. If the bones are to be served with the hash, score, and season them with pepper and salt; put them into a tin pan, with a little bit of butter here and there; heat them in a Dutch oven, and then broil them on a gridiron to brown them well.

To Dress Cold Roast Beef

CUT into dice some under-done beef, dredge it with flour, and fry it for three or four minutes in butter, with an onion, a little parsley, and a sprig of lemon thyme minced; put it into a sauce-pan, with some well-seasoned gravy, a tea-spoonful of vinegar, and one of mushroom catsup; simmer it for half an hour. Serve it with poached eggs laid upon the top.

Fricandellans

MINCE about two pounds of tender lean beef, and three quarters of a pound of fresh suet; then pound it till it be as smooth as a paste, and carefully pick out all the threads and sinews; add four well-beaten eggs, half a pint of rich cream, and as much grated and sifted bread as will make it sufficiently consistent to form into rolls resembling corks, and season it with salt, black and Jamaica pepper. Boil the corks in some good stock, or in boiling water.

Beef Gobbets

CUT a piece of beef into small bits, season them with pepper, salt, grated lemon-peel, and nutmeg, some parsley and shalot finely chopped; fry them brown in butter, and stew them till tender in a rich brown gravy, adding a table-spoonful of vinegar and one of port wine. Put thickly over them grated bread, seasoned with pepper, salt, and a little butter, and brown them with a salamander.

To Dress the Inside of a Cold Sirloin of Beef

CUT off the meat, with a little of the fat, into strips three inches long and half an inch thick; season with pepper and salt, dredge them with flour, and fry them brown in butter; then simmer them in a rich brown gravy; add of mushroom catsup, onion, and shalot vinegar, a table-spoonful each. Garnish with fried parsley.

Another way to Dress the Inside of a Cold Sirloin of Beef

CUT off entire the inside of a large sirloin of beef, brown it all over in a stew-pan, then add a quart of water, half a pint of port wine, a tea-cupful of strong beer, two table-spoonfuls of vinegar, some pepper, salt, and a large onion, finely minced; cover the pan closely, and let it stew till the beef be very tender. Garnish with pickles.

To Roast Beef Heart

WASH it well, and clean all the blood carefully from the pipes; parboil it ten or fifteen minutes in boiling water; drip the water from it; put in a stuffing which has been made of bread crumbs, minced suet or butter, sweet marjoram, lemon thyme, and parsley, seasoned with salt, pepper, and nutmeg. Put it down to roast while hot, baste it well with butter, froth it up, and serve it with melted butter and vinegar; or with gravy in the dish, and currant jelly in a sauce-tureen. To hash it, follow the directions given for hare.

To Boil Tripe

CLEAN it extremely well, and take off the fat; let it lie a night in salt-and-water, again wash it well, and let it lie in milk-and-water for the same length of time; then cut it into small pieces, roll and tie them with thread; put them, with a clean washed marrow-bone, into a linen bag; tie it closely, and put it into a stew pan that has a cover to fit quite closely, fill it up with water, and let it boil gently for six hours. Take the tripe out of the bag, put it into a jar, and pour over it the liquor in which it was boiled. When to be dressed, boil some whole small onions in a part of the liquor, add a little salt, then put in the tripe, and heat it thoroughly.

Or it may be fried in butter; fricasseed, or stewed in a brown sauce.

Instead of being boiled in a bag, the tripe may be put, with some salt and whole pepper, into a stoneware jar, which must have a piece of linen tied over it, and a plate laid upon the top. The pot should always be kept full of boiling water, taking care that it do not boil into the jar.

To Roast Tripe

CUT the tripe into two oblong pieces, make a forcemeat of bread crumbs and chopped parsley, seasoned with pepper and salt; bind it with the yolks of two eggs; spread it upon the fat side of the tripe, and lay on the other fat side; then roll it very tightly, and tie it with packthread. Roast, and baste it with butter; it will take one hour, or one hour and a half. Serve it with melted butter, into which put a table-spoonful of catsup and one of lemon pickle.

To Fry Tripe

CUT it into bits three or four inches square; make a batter, thicker than for pan-cakes, of three eggs beaten up with flour and milk, a little salt, pepper, and nutmeg; dip in the tripe, and fry it in butter, or fresh dripping, of a light brown colour. Serve it garnished with parsley. Sauce; – melted butter with lemon pickle in it

To Boil Marrow Bones

SAW them even at the bottom; butter and flour some bits of linen, and tie a piece over the top of each bone; boil them for an hour or two, take off the linen, and serve them with thin slices of dry toast cut into square bits; at table the marrow should he put upon the toast, and a little pepper and salt sprinkled over it.

Mock Hare

CUT the lean meat from the inside of a sirloin of beef, soak it eight-and-forty hours in a tea-cupful of port wine and a glass of vinegar; cut it open, lard it, and make a stuffing as for hare, using the raw liver of a fowl; lay it on the meat, roll and tie it tightly, and roast it by a hanging jack. Baste it with the liquor in which it was soaked, adding a little more port wine and vinegar, and mixing with it nearly a tea-spoonful of pounded allspice. Serve it with some good gravy in the dish, and currant jelly in a sauce tureen.

A Fillet of Beef

BONE a middle rib of beef weighing about fifteen pounds; roll the meat tightly and firmly, and skewer it. Roast and garnish it in the same manner as a sirloin.

Burgess's Method of Boiling Hung Beef

HUNG beef for grating should be put on in boiling water, and, to preserve the colour, kept boiling as fast as possible. Allow for six pounds of beef one hour and a half. It will keep good for a length of time.

Scarlet Beef

MIX a little mace, cloves, allspice, black pepper, and saltpetre together, rub it well into two pounds of tender lean beef; let it lie six days, turning it daily, and rubbing it with the pickle; then roll and tie it firmly with tape; put it and the pickle into a small jar, with a slice or two of beef-suet under and over it; tie it closely, and bake it an hour. It is eaten cold, cut in thin slices, and garnished with parsley. If long kept, the colour fades.

Spring-Garden Beef

CUT a piece of lean tender beef into thick slices; lard and season them with pepper, salt, and sweet herbs; pour over them a little port wine, and stew them in weak stock, with one or two bay leaves, till tender; strain the sauce; thicken it with flour and butter. Heat it up, and pour it over the slices of beef.

Bubble and Squeak

CHOP small some boiled white cabbage; season it with pepper and salt, and fry it with a little butter; pepper and broil some slices of cold boiled salted beef; put the fried cabbage into a dish, and lay round it the slices of broiled beef and serve it very hot. The beef does best when underdone.

Salt Beef Pudding, or Debris Pudding

MASH a few boiled potatoes with a little salt, milk, and a good bit of butter; mince very finely the lean part of some cold boiled salted beef, mix it with the mashed potatoes, and brown it in a Dutch oven in the same way that a salt fish pudding is done.

This pudding may be made of the remains of a piece of boiled beef, allowing to one pound of the beef one pound and a quarter of potatoes.

To Cure Hung Beef

RUB a small quantity of salt on eight ribs of the thin part of the beef, and let it lie three days; pound two ounces of saltpetre, and two ounces of very brown sugar, and rub it well into the beef; turn it every day, and if it becomes slimy, strew over it a little common salt, but let it be very little; lay it upon a sloping board, that the brine may run off. Let it lie a fortnight, and hang it up to dry, but not too near the fire, nor in a warm kitchen, as it would then soon grow rancid.

Beef or Mutton Baked with Potatoes

BOIL some potatoes, peel, and pound them in a mortar, with one or two small onions; moisten them with milk and an egg beaten up; add a little salt and pepper. Season slices of beef, or mutton chops, with salt and pepper, and more onion, if the flavour is approved; rub the bottom of a pudding-dish with butter, and put a layer of the mashed potatoes, which should be as thick as a batter, and then a layer of meat, and so on alternately till the dish is filled, ending with potatoes. Bake it in an oven for one hour.

Olive Royals

BOIL one pound of potatoes, and when nearly cold, rub them perfectly smooth with four ounces of flour and one ounce of butter, and knead it together till it become a paste; roll it out about a quarter of an inch thick, cut it into rounds, and lay upon one side any sort of cold roasted meat cut into thin small bits, and seasoned with pepper and salt; put a very small bit of butter over it, wet the edges, and close the paste in the form of a half circle. Fry them in boiling fresh dripping of a light brown colour; lay them before the fire, on the back of a sieve, to drain. Serve them with or without gravy in the dish. For a change, mince the meat, and season it as before directed. The potatoes should be very mealy.

Beef and Oyster Sausages

SCALD three quarters of a pint of oysters in their own liquor; take them out and chop them finely; mince one pound of beef and mutton, and three quarters or a pound of beef suet; add the oysters, and season with salt, pepper, mace, and two cloves pounded; beat up two eggs, and mix them well with the other ingredients, and pack it closely into a jar. When to be used, roll it into the form of small sausages; dip them into the yolk of an egg beaten up; strew grated bread crumbs over them, or dust with flour, and fry them in fresh dripping. Serve them upon fried bread, hot.

Hamburg Beef

PUT on in cold water a brisket of beef; when it boils, skim it well; take out the beef, let it cool, and then rub it well with three handfuls of salt, and two tea-spoonfuls of saltpetre; beat it well with a rolling-pin for twenty or thirty minutes; put it into pickling-tub, strew over it a small handful of salt, let it lie four days, then turn it; put the same quantity of salt, and let it lie four days more; after which sew it into a piece of old linen, and let it hang twelve days in smoke.

To Boil Ox Cheek

WASH very clean half a head; let it lie in cold water all night; break the bone in two, taking care not to break the flesh. Put it on in a pot of boiling water, and let it boil from two to three hours; take out the bone. Serve it with boiled carrots and turnips, or savoys. The liquor the head has been boiled in may be strained and made into Scots barley broth, or Scots kale.

To stew ox cheek

Clean the head, as before directed, and parboil it; take out the bone; stew it in part of the liquor in which it was boiled, thickened with a piece of butter mixed with flour, and browned. Cut into dice, or into any fancy shape, carrots and turnips, as much, when cut, as will fill a pint basin. Mince two or three onions, add the vegetables, and season with salt, black and Jamaica pepper. Cover the pan closely, and stew it two hours. A little before serving, add a glass of port wine or ale.

Dressed Ox Cheek

Prepare it as directed for stewing. Cut the meat into square pieces; make a sauce with a quart of good gravy, thickened with butter mixed with flour; season with salt, black and Jamaica pepper, a little cayenne, and a table-spoonful of vinegar. Put in the head, and simmer it till quite tender. A few minutes before serving, add a little catsup or white wine. Forcemeat balls may be added.

Potted Ox Cheek

May be made of the meat that is left from any one of these dishes. It is cut into small bits, or minced and heated up with a little of the liquor in which the cheek was boiled, seasoned with black and Jamaica pepper, salt, nutmeg, and a little lemon juice or vinegar, then put into a mould, and turned out when required for use. It is used for supper or luncheon, and is eaten with mustard and vinegar.

Many excellent and economical dishes are made of an ox cheek, and it is particularly useful in large families.

To Dress Kidneys and Skirts

Wash the kidneys, cut them into slices; take the skin off the skirts, and cut them into small pieces; dust them with flour, and fry them brown in butter. Simmer them an hour in a pint of gravy, with an onion finely minced, some salt and pepper. A little before serving, add a table-spoonful of mushroom catsup. They may be broiled and eaten like a beef-steak.

To Dress Palates and Sweetbreads

Boil the palates till the black skin can be easily peeled off; parboil the sweetbreads with them; skin and cut the palates into pieces, and if the sweetbreads are large, cut them in two the long way; dust them with flour, and fry them of a light brown, in butter; then stew them in rather more than a pint of the liquor in which they were boiled. Brown a piece of butter with flour; add it, with a little cayenne, salt, pepper, grated lemon-peel, and nutmeg, and a glass of white wine. A little before serving, stir in a spoonful of vinegar, or the squeeze of a lemon.

Beef Palates

PARBOIL, skin, and cut the palates into stripes; fry an onion in butter, and add the palates and a bunch of sweet herbs; moisten them with some well-seasoned stock, and when sufficiently done, add a little mustard.

Blanquette of Palates of Beef

BOIL in weak broth or water, six or eight nicely cleaned beef palates, and when the black skin will easily peel off, they are done enough; then skin and cut them into pieces the size of a shilling, and stew them in a sauce tournée. Serve them in a casserole of rice, or a vol au vent.

To Broil Beef-Steaks

CUT the steaks off a rump or the ribs of a fore-quarter; beat them well with a rolling-pin. Have the gridiron perfectly clean and heated over a clear quick fire; lay on the steaks, and with meat tongs keep turning them constantly, till they are done enough; throw a little salt over them a little before taking them off the fire. Serve them as hot as possible, plain, or with a made gravy and sliced onion, or rub a bit of butter upon the steaks the moment of serving. The dish may be garnished with bits of fat, which should be done apart from the steaks, that the dripping of the grease may not smoke the meat. Mutton chops are broiled in the same manner.

Ox-Feet or Cow-Heel

WASH them well; boil them in plenty of water, till the hoofs come off, and the hair can be pulled off, and scraped clean; wash them well, and boil them in fresh water till all the bones can be easily taken out. To pot them, cut them into small pieces, add a little of the liquor, heat it, and season it with some salt and vinegar; put it into a mould, and when it becomes cold, turn it out. It is eaten with vinegar and mustard. They may be served without being cut small, either hot or cold; if hot, serve with thick parsley and butter.

Another Ox-Feet or Cow-Heel

CUT them into small bits; dip them into the yolk of an egg beaten up; roll them in bread crumbs, seasoned with pepper, salt, and minced parsley; fry them in butter. Cut into thin slices a good dish of onions, fry them in butter, and serve them hot, with the fried heel laid upon them. The liquor may be made into jelly, or used to enrich sauces and gravies.

Ox-Blood Puddings

LET the blood run into a deep pan, stir it all the time, and when it is nearly cold, throw in a little salt; rub it through a hair sieve; mix a pint of milk with two quarts of blood. Chop some suet, mix it with minced onion, pepper, salt, and two or three handfuls of oatmeal, then add the blood and milk. To clean the pudding skins, wash them thoroughly, and let them lie a night in salt-and-water. When they are to be filled, tie one end, and turn the inside out; half fill them, and tie them in rings, or in equal lengths. When the water boils, throw in a little cold, to put it off the boil, and put in the puddings. In five minutes, put them upon a dish, and prick them with a large needle; return them into the pot, and boil them half an hour. Hang them up in a dry cool place, to keep them. When they are to be used, put them on in hot water for ten or fifteen minutes, and then broil them.

Meal Puddings

SIFT a pound of oatmeal, chop three quarters of a pound of suet, mince some onions, and mix all together; season well with pepper and salt; half fill the skins, and boil and dress them as directed in the receipt for ox blood puddings. Some people think a little sugar an improvement.

Ox-Liver Puddings

BOIL the liver and grate it; mix, in equal quantities, grated liver, grated bread, and minced suet; season well with black and Jamaica pepper, a little grated nutmeg, salt, and a glass of rum. Half fill the skins, and manage them in the same way as the other puddings. Some persons use double the quantity of suet.

Apple Puddings in Skins

PARE, core, and mince a pound of apples; grate a pound of bread, or the same quantity of pounded biscuit; mince half a pound of suet; mix all together with half a pound of brown sugar, and a quarter of a pound of cleaned currants; season with half a grated nutmeg, four cloves pounded, a little grated lemon-peel, and four table-spoonfuls of white wine. Half fill the skins; boil them for fifteen minutes, taking care to prick them well. When they are to be used, boil them for a few minutes, and brown them in a Dutch oven.

Currant Puddings in Skins

CLEAN and dry half a pound of currants; stone and mince a quarter of a pound of raisins; of pounded beef suet, grated bread, and brown sugar, three quarters of a pound each. Mix all these ingredients well, season with grated nutmeg, lemon-peel, and two or three cloves pounded, and a little wine. Half fill the skins, and do them the same as the apple puddings.

Beef Ham

RUB a little common salt over a piece of beef of about twenty pounds weight; take out the bone, and in one or two days, rub well into the beef the following ingredients, finely pounded and well mixed: Two ounces of sal-prunella, four ounces of brown sugar, six ounces of bay salt, one ounce of white pepper, and of cloves and nutmeg, a quarter of an ounce each; then strew over it half a pound of common salt. Let it lie fifteen days, turning it daily. It is then hung up; or when taken out of the pickle, it may be boiled, and allowed to stand till cold in the water in which it was boiled; or it may be baked in a deep dish, covered with a coarse paste.

CHAPTER IV
MUTTON

The names of the various pieces are:

IN ENGLAND

Hind quarter: Leg – Loin, best end – Loin, chump end – Neck, best end. Fore quarter: Neck, scrag end – Shoulder – Breast.

IN SCOTLAND

The Leg – the Loin – the Fore quarter. The two loins joined together are called a Chine. A Saddle of Mutton is the two Necks joined together.

PREPARATORY REMARKS ON MUTTON

THE finest mutton is that of the mountain, or black-faced sheep of Scotland, and that of the South Downs and Welsh sheep. Sheep are in perfection from the age of four to five. In May and June, or just before shearing, mutton tastes strongly of the coat, or what is called woolly.

Wedder mutton, which is the best, may be known by a prominent lump of fat at the edge of the broadest part of the inside of the leg. That meat should be chosen which is fine in the grain, bright in the colour, and the fat firm and white. The flesh of the ewe is of a paler colour; that of the ram is strongly flavoured, is of a deep red colour, and the fat spungy.

For keeping mutton, the same directions may be observed as for keeping beef.

The haunch is the prime joint. It should be roasted at a good brisk fire, and basted as beef, the fat being first covered with a piece of white paper. Before serving, half a sheet of foolscap paper, folded and fringed, should be put round the shank bone.

The haunch, weighing fourteen pounds, will require two hours and a half to roast. Currant jelly sauce should be served with it.

When a leg of mutton is to be boiled, it should first be washed clean, then put on, in boiling water, and carefully scummed. If weighing eight or nine pounds, it should be boiled nearly three hours, and then served with caper sauce. A saddle or a chine, that is to say, two necks or two loins, a joint, generally called, indifferently, a saddle of mutton, being broad, requires a high and strong fire. The skin should be taken off, and skewered on again, or paper may be substituted for it, tied on with a buttered string. It should be well basted, and a quarter of au hour before serving, the skin or paper removed; it is then allowed to brown a little, is sprinkled with salt, basted, and dredged with flour, served with gravy in the dish, and currant jelly sauce.

A shoulder of mutton should be roasted an hour and a half, and served with onion sauce, in a sauce tureen.

A loin of mutton should be carefully jointed, roasted the same length of time as a shoulder, and is carved lengthwise.

The best end of a neck of mutton should be jointed, and roasted, the same as the loin; or it may be boiled. If boiled, the skin should be taken off before serving, and caper sauce poured over it.

A breast of mutton may be parboiled, grilled, and served with onion and caper sauce.

Many persons think that every kind of meat should be boiled in a floured cloth, and in the writer's opinion, this greatly improves its appearance. This, however, does not supersede the necessity of skimming, which, in boiling, should always be carefully attended to.

To Dress a Shoulder of Mutton

BONE a small shoulder of mutton; roll it, and put it into a cloth; put it on in boiling water. Have ready a nice white sauce; stir into it some thick cream, and add some chopped Indian pickle. Make it all hot, but take care not to let it boil, and pour it over the mutton.

French Mutton Steaks

CUT a neck of mutton into neat steaks; put them into a sauce-pan, with sufficient water to cover them; add a small bunch of sweet herbs, two or three onions, and some pepper. Let them boil two minutes; take them out, and stew the trimmings of the steaks with the herbs till the gravy is sufficiently strong, then strain it, and take off all the fat. Rub the steaks with a well beaten yolk of an egg, strew over them bread crumbs mixed with finely chopped sweet herbs, and fry them of a nice brown. Thicken the gravy with a little browned butter and flour, add a tablespoonful of vinegar, and when it is quite hot, pour it into the dish, and lay in the steaks.

Mutton Cutlets

CUT into cutlets a pound and half of the thick part of a leg of mutton, and beat them; mix with grated bread crumbs, some pepper, salt, and finely chopped parsley, lemon, thyme, and sweet marjoram. Rub the cutlets with melted butter; and cover them thickly with the prepared bread; fry them for ten minutes in butter, then put them into a sauce-pan, with some good gravy thickened with flour and butter, and simmer them for ten or fifteen minutes.

Mock Venison

HANG up a large fat loin of mutton for several days; then bone it, and take off all the kidney fat, and the skin from the upper fat; mix together two ounces of brown sugar, and one ounce of ground black pepper. Rub it well into the mutton; pour over it two or three wine-glasses of port wine; keep it covered with the skin; rub and turn it daily for five days. When it is to be roasted, cover it with the skin, and paper it the same way as venison is done. Serve it with made gravy, and the same sauces as for venison.

Maintenon Chops

CUT a neck of mutton into chops; beat them flat with a rolling-pin. Bruise the yolk of a hard-boiled egg, and mix with it chopped sweet herbs, grated bread, nutmeg, salt, and pepper. Cover the steaks with it, and put each into a piece of well-buttered paper; broil them over a clear fire, turning them often. Serve them in the paper, or with a browned gravy.

A Haricot of Mutton

TRIM the chops neatly, by shortening the bone; if the whole of the best end of the neck is to be used, put on the trimmings in half a pint of water, and let it simmer for fifteen minutes. Fry some sliced onions in a little butter; take them out; flour the chops, and fry them quickly, of a nice brown colour; put them into a sauce pan with the onions, and some carrots and turnips cut into dice; strain the gravy into the frying-pan, boil it up, and add to the chops and vegetables, with two or three cloves, a little allspice and pepper. It should simmer for two hours; and just before serving, clear off the scum, and thicken with a little flour rubbed down in cold water, and add a table-spoonful of mushroom catsup.

To Stew a Shoulder of Mutton

BONE a shoulder of mutton with a sharp knife, and fill the space with the following stuffing: Grated bread, minced suet, parsley, pepper, salt, and nutmeg; bind with the yolks of two well-beaten eggs. Sew or fasten it with small skewers; brown it in a frying-pan, with a bit of butter. Break the bone, put it into a sauce-pan, with some water, an onion, pepper, salt, and a bunch of parsley; let it stew till the strength be extracted; strain, and thicken it with butter rolled in flour; put it, with the mutton, and a glass of port wine into the sauce-pan; cover it closely, and let it stew gently for two hours. Before serving, add two table-spoonfuls of mushroom catsup. Garnish with pickles.

Another way to Stew a Shoulder of Mutton

BONE and flatten a shoulder of mutton, sprinkle over it pepper and salt, roll it up tightly, bind it with tape, and put it into a stew-pan that will just hold it, pour over it a well-seasoned gravy made with the bones, cover the pan closely, and let it stew till tender; before serving, take off the tape, thicken the gravy, and garnish with cut pickles.

To Stew a Fillet of Mutton, or a Breast of Beef

PUT a fillet of mutton or a piece of beef, weighing about seven pounds, into a stew-pan, with a carrot, a turnip, an onion stuck with two or three cloves, and a pint of water. Put round the edge of the stew-pan, a rim of coarse paste, that the cover may be kept very close, and let it stew gently three hours and a half, take out the meat, skim off the fat, strain and thicken the gravy, have ready some boiled carrots and turnips cut to fancy, add them to the gravy, make all hot, and serve with a garnish of sliced gherkins.

To Stew a Loin of Mutton

BONE and skin the loin; stew it in a pint of water, turning it frequently; when the liquor is half wasted, take out the loin and strain it, and when cold take off the fat; make a rich highly-seasoned gravy of the bones; strain and mix it with the liquor the loin was stewed in; add a teacupful of port wine, and some small mushrooms; thicken the sauce with butter rolled in flour; put in the mutton, and heat it thoroughly; garnish with pickles.

Kew Mince

CUT a pound of meat from a leg of cold roasted mutton, and mince it very finely, together with six ounces of suet, mix with it three or four table-spoonfuls of crumbs of bread, the beaten yolks of four eggs, one anchovy chopped, some pepper and salt, and half a pint of port wine; put it into a caul of veal, and bake it in a quick oven; turn it out into a dish, and pour some brown gravy over it; serve with it venison sauce. When a veal caul is not to be had, the mince may be done in a saucepan.

Irish Stew

CUT the best end of a neck of mutton into chops, put them into a sauce-pan with four or five pounds of potatoes, six minced onions, some pepper and salt, and a quart of cold water; keep the pan closely covered, and when it boils remove it to the side of the fire, that it may simmer with a gentle heat for two or three hours; before serving, add a table-spoonful or two of catsup.

To Haricot a Neck of Mutton

ROAST it till nearly done, then cut it into cutlets, and stew it in a well-seasoned gravy, adding, cut like straws an inch long, the red part of two or three carrots and some turnips.

Rolled Mutton

BONE a shoulder of mutton carefully, so as not to injure the skin, cut all the meat from the skin, mince it small, and season it highly with black and Jamaica pepper, nutmeg, and a clove, some parsley, lemon thyme, sweet marjoram chopped, and a pounded onion, all well mixed together with a well-beaten yolk of an egg; roll it up very tightly in the skin, tie it round, and bake it in an oven two or three hours, according to the size of the mutton. Make a gravy of the bones and parings, season with an onion, pepper, and salt, strain and thicken it with flour and butter; add of vinegar, mushroom catsup, soy, and lemon pickle, a table-spoonful each, and a tea-cupful of port wine; garnish with forcemeat balls, made of grated bread, and part of the mince.

Haggis

WASH and clean the heart and lights, parboil and mince them very small, add one pound of minced suet, two or three large onions minced, and two small handfuls of oatmeal; season highly with pepper and salt, and mix all well together; the bag being perfectly clean and sweet, put in the ingredients, press out the air, sew it up, and boil it for three hours.

To Broil a Cold Roasted Shoulder of Mutton

A cold shoulder of roast mutton, having only a little meat upon the blade bone, may be scored, sprinkled with pepper and salt, then broiled, and served with caper sauce poured over it, or melted butter, in which should be mixed of mushroom catsup, lemon pickle, and Harvey sauce, a table-spoonful each.

A Haunch of Mutton like Venison

TAKE a fat haunch of large fine mutton, let it hang a week, then pound one ounce of black, and one ounce of Jamaica pepper, and rub them over the mutton, pour a bottle of port wine over it, and let it remain in this five days, basting it frequently every day with the liquor, take it out and hang it up four or five days more, or as long as the weather favours its keeping; wipe it three or four times a day with a clean cloth. While it is roasting baste it with the liquor it was steeped in, adding a little more port wine; a quarter of an hour before taking it from the fire, baste it well with butter, and dredge flour over it to froth it up. Serve it with sauces as for venison.

Baked Mutton Chop

CUT a neck of mutton into neat chops, season them with salt and pepper, butter a dish, lay in the chops, and pour over them a batter made of a quart of milk, four eggs beaten up, four table-spoonfuls of flour, and a little salt. An hour will bake them.

To Dress Mutton Chops

PARE and rim the chops, dip them into hot melted butter, and cover them with grated bread mixed with chopped parsley, a little sweet marjoram, salt, and pepper, then dip the chops into the yolks of eggs beaten up, and cover them with the crumbs as before; fry them in butter and serve them with onions browned in butter and seasoned with salt and pepper, or with a thickened brown gravy.

Another way to Dress Mutton Chops

CUT the chops off a loin or the best end of a neck of mutton, pare off the fat, dip them into a beaten egg, and strew over them grated bread, seasoned with pepper, salt, and some finely minced parsley; fry them in a little butter, and lay them upon the back of a sieve to drain before the fire. Thicken about half a pint of gravy, add a table-spoonful of catsup, and one of port wine; put the gravy into the dish, and lay in the chops; garnish with fried parsley or cut lemon.

Hashed Mutton

CUT the meat into small thin bits, pare off the skin and sinews, leaving a little fat; thicken some well-seasoned gravy, add the meat, and let it simmer till it be hot, but do not allow it to boil. A little catsup, port wine, or vinegar may be put in just before serving. Garnish with sippets of bread or with cut pickles.

China Chilo

SKIN and chop the meat finely, and also part of the fat of a loin of mutton, and season it with a large spoonful of salt, and a tea-spoonful of ground pepper; add two large onions shred, half a pint of green peas, one lettuce cut small, four spoonfuls of water, and a quarter of a pound of clarified butter. Let all this stew in a pipkin for three hours and serve it in the middle of a pound of rice boiled dry.

Sheep's Liver

CUT it into slices; wash it well, and dry it in a cloth; flour, and season it with pepper and salt, and fry it in butter, with a good deal of minced parsley and an onion; add a sufficient quantity of gravy or hot water to make a sauce, and let it stew a few minutes. It may be fried quite plain, and when cut into slices, should be washed in milk-and-water.

Sheep's Mince

WASH the heart and lights very clean; boil them about half an hour; mince them finely; mix a piece of butter with flour, brown it in a stew-pan, and add some of the liquor the heart and lights were boiled in. Put in the mince with some chopped onion; season with salt and pepper, cover it closely, and let it stew half an hour. Before serving, add a table-spoonful of mushroom catsup.

To Collar a Breast of Mutton

BONE it and take out all the gristles, make a forcemeat with crumbs of bread, chopped parsley, a little lemon thyme, and one anchovy minced; season with salt and white pepper, rub the mutton over with an egg beaten up, cover it with the forcemeat, roll it firmly, tie it with tape, and put it on in boiling water. Make a good gravy of the bones, two onions, a bunch of parsley and lemon thyme, pepper and salt; strain and thicken it with a piece of butter mixed with flour. A little before serving, add a table-spoonful of vinegar and two of mushroom catsup. Garnish with cut lemon or pickles.

The Breasts of Mutton, à la Ste. Menoult

STEW them with carrots, onions, and spices in gravy, and when done, drain them and take out the bones, flatten the meat between two dishes, and when cold cut it into the form of cutlets or hearts; brush them with the beaten yolk of an egg, roll them in grated bread, then in clarified butter, and again in the grated bread. Bake them in an oven till of a fine brown colour, and serve them with a sauce Italienne, or any other sauce.

Leg of Mutton Stuffed

CAREFULLY bone and cut off all the fat of a leg of mutton, but keep the skin whole, take out the meat also, and mince it with one third of its quantity of fat bacon, and some parsley, season the whole well, stuff the skin with it, and sew it upon the under side; fasten it in a cloth, and put it into a stew pan, with some slices of veal, some carrots and onions, cut small, a bunch of parsley, and one of green onions, and cover the whole with thin slices of fat bacon; let it stew for about four hours, then drain the liquor through a silk sieve, reduce it to a glaze, and glaze the leg of mutton; serve it with haricot beans dressed as follows: Soak one quart of white haricot beans in water for three hours, and boil them in cold soft water with a little bit of fresh butter. Fry a very large white onion, finely minced, in two ounces of butter, when done, add a table-spoonful of flour, and moisten it with some good gravy, then add a few of the haricot beans, and rub it through a tammy or sieve, season it with pepper and salt. Drain the beans and add the sauce to them.

To Salt a Leg of Mutton

Rub it well with common salt, the next day wipe it dry, and put it into beef pickle for six or seven days when it will be ready for use, and should be plain boiled. Mashed turnips and brocoli, or greens, may be served with it.

To Stew Sheep's Tongues

Boil three tongues till the skin will come off; split, without separating them, put them into a sauce-pan with some good stock, adding two spoonfuls of cullis, or two spoonfuls of bread chippings boiled in a little stock, and passed through a tammy, a glass of white wine, some parsley, cibol, mushrooms, and a clove of garlic, all finely minced, a little bit of butter, pepper and salt, let it boil for half an hour, that the sauce may neither be too thin nor too thick, and serve it.

Sheep's Tails

Stew five or six tails for three or four hours in some stock, with roots, sweet herbs, pepper and salt, let them cool, dip them into the beaten yolks of eggs, then into bread crumbs, fry them of a fine colour, and serve them with fried parsley. Calves' tails may be done in the same way.

Boiled Neck of Mutton

Bone the best end of a neck of mutton, boil it for an hour, take off the skin, and serve it with turnips mashed with a little butter and cream.

Sheep's Kidneys Broiled

Wash and dry some nice kidneys, cut them in half, and with a small skewer keep them open in imitation of two shells, season them with salt and pepper, and dip them into a little fresh melted butter. Broil first the side that is cut, and be careful not to let the gravy drop in taking them off the gridiron. Serve them in a hot dish, with finely chopped parsley mixed with melted butter, the juice of a lemon, pepper and salt, putting a little upon each kidney.

This is an excellent breakfast for a sportsman.

Sheep's Trotters Fried

CLEAN some sheep's trotters nicely, scald and wash them in hot water; stew them in that sauce in which calf's head, plain, (p. 107,) is boiled, and bone them. Fry, but not till brown, in a little butter, some carrots, onions, a little parsley-roots, all cut small, thyme, a shalot, a small bay leaf, and a clove. When they begin to colour, moisten them with water and vinegar mixed in equal parts, and let it all stew till the vegetables are quite tender; season with pepper and salt, and strain it through a silk sieve over the sheep's trotters, then fry the trotters in this batter; put nearly four table-spoonfuls of flour into an earthen pan, with a little salt, a little olive oil, and as much good beer or water as will moisten the paste; when well mixed, add the beaten whites of two eggs, dip the trotters into this, and fry them instantly.

The marinade cuite, or pickle, into which the trotters are laid, and the paste in which they are fried, may be used for beef, and other meats. The same recipe may be followed exactly for calf's feet.

To Cure Mutton Ham

CUT a hind quarter of good mutton into the shape of a ham, pound one ounce of saltpetre, with one pound of coarse salt and a quarter of a pound of brown sugar, rub the ham well with this mixture, taking care to stuff the hole of the shank well with salt and sugar, and let it lie a fortnight, rubbing it well with the pickle every two or three days; then take it out, and press it with a weight for one day; smoke it with saw-dust for ten or fifteen days, or hang it to dry in the kitchen. If the ham is to be boiled soon after it has been smoked, soak it one hour, and if it has been smoked any length of time it will require to be soaked several hours. Put it on in cold water, and boil it gently two hours. It is eaten cold at breakfast, luncheon, or supper. A mutton ham is sometimes cured with the above quantity of salt and sugar, with the addition of half an ounce of white pepper, a quarter of an ounce of cloves, and one nutmeg.

CHAPTER V
LAMB

PREPARATORY REMARKS ON LAMB

THE fore quarter of lamb consists of the shoulder, the neck, and the breast together; the hind quarter is the leg and loin. There are also the head and pluck, the fry or sweetbreads, skirts, and liver.

In choosing the fore quarter, the vein in the neck should be ruddy, or of a bluish colour. In the hind quarter, the knuckle should feel stiff, the kidneys small, and perfectly fresh. To keep it, the joints should be carefully wiped every day, and, in warm weather, sprinkled with a little pepper. The fore quarter is the prime joint, and should be roasted and basted with butter; the gravy is made as for beef or mutton. Mint sauce is served in a sauce tureen, and half a lemon is sent to table with it, the juice of which is squeezed upon the ribs, after the shoulder is cut off, and they have been sprinkled with salt. If the joint weighs five pounds, it will require to be roasted one hour; if ten pounds, one hour and three quarters. The hind quarter may be roasted, or the leg of it boiled. The loin is then cut into steaks, fried, and served round it; the outside hones being covered with a fringe of fried parsley. A dish of spinach is generally served with lamb.

Lamb's Head and Mince

SCALD the head, and take off the hair; parboil it with the pluck; divide the head, and take out the brains; mince the heart and lights, also an onion; put it into a sauce-pan with a little gravy, thickened with butter and flour, add a little salt and pepper, cover the pan closely, and let it stew an hour. Rub the head with the yolk of an egg, beaten up, and strew over it finely grated bread, mixed with salt and pepper and boiled minced parsley; stick bits of butter here and there, and brown it in a Dutch oven. Cut the liver into slices, and fry it in butter; make the brains into cakes. Serve the head upon the mince, and garnish with the liver and brain cakes.

Lamb Dressed with Rice

HALF roast a small fore-quarter of lamb; cut it into steaks, season them with a little salt and pepper; lay them into a dish, and pour in a little water. Boil a pound of rice with a blade or two of mace; strain it, and stir in a good piece of fresh butter, and a little salt, add also the greater part of the yolks of four beaten eggs; cover the lamb with the rice, and with a feather put over it the remainder of the beaten eggs. Bake it in an oven till it has acquired a light brown colour.

Lamb Chops

CUT a neck or loin of lamb into chops; rub them over with the beaten yolk of an egg; dip them into grated bread, mixed with plenty of chopped parsley, and seasoned with lemon-peel, pepper, and salt; fry them a light brown in good dripping; make a sauce with the trimmings, and thicken the sauce with butter rolled in flour; add a little lemon pickle and mushroom catsup. Garnish with fried parsley. They may be served with or without the gravy.

To Dress Lamb's Feet

CLEAN, wash well, and blanch six lamb's feet; stew them, till they become tender, in some white stock, with a slice of lean ham, one onion, some parsley, thyme, two blades of mace, a little whole white pepper, and a few mushrooms. Before serving, strain the sauce; thicken it with flour and butter, and half a pint of cream; boil it a quarter of an hour, add the feet and the juice of half a small lemon. Garnish with sippets of thin toasted bread, cut into a three-cornered shape.

Lamb Chops Broiled

CUT a loin or best end of the neck into chops, flatten them, and cut off the fat and skin; rub the gridiron with a little fat, and broil them on a clear fire. Turn them with steak tongs, till quite done. Serve them hot.

Dressed Lamb Chops

CUT the chops off the best end of a neck of lamb, flatten them, and cut off the skin and fat; dip them into the beaten yolk of an egg, and then into bread crumbs, mixed with minced parsley, pepper, and salt. Fry them in boiling clarified beef suet, and drain them before the fire upon the back of a sieve. Thicken a little gravy with flour and butter; add a table-spoonful of white wine and one of catsup; make it quite hot, pour it into the dish, and lay in the chops. Garnish with fried parsley.

Lamb Cutlets

CUT the cutlets off the loin, into round bits; trim off the fat and skin; clip them into the beaten yolk of an egg, and then into bread crumbs, mixed with minced parsley, grated nutmeg, and lemon-peel, pepper, and salt. Fry them a light brown in clarified beef suet; drain them on the back of a sieve before the fire. Serve them with melted butter and a little lemon pickle in it, or a brown sauce thickened. Garnish with cut lemon.

To Dress a Breast of Lamb

CUT it into pieces, and stew it in weak stock, with a glass of white wine; add pepper and salt. When it is perfectly tender, thicken the sauce with butter and flour. Have cucumbers stewed in gravy ready to put over the lamb before serving.

A breast of mutton may be served up in the same way.

CHAPTER VI
VEAL

The names of the joints are as follows:

IN ENGLAND

Loin, best end – Loin, chump end – Fillet – Hind Knuckle – Fore Knuckle – Neck, best end – Neck, scrag end – Blade Bone – Breast, best end – Breast, brisket end.

IN SCOTLAND

The Loin, Fillet, and Knuckle – Back Ribs – breast, Neck, and Head.

In Scotland, the veal seldom exceeds four weeks old, therefore it is not cut into so many divisions as is the practice in England, where it is often eight weeks old. The entrails are named the pluck, which consists of the heart, liver, lights, nut, melt, and skirts, the throat, wind pipe, and sweetbreads.

PREPARATORY REMARKS ON VEAL

Veal should be fine in the grain, firm, white, and fat, and the leg bone small. The finest calves have the smallest kidney, and its being well covered with thick white fat, indicates good veal. The fillet of a cow calf is to be preferred, on account of the udder. The prime joints are the fillet, the loin, the chump end of the loin, and the best end of the neck. To keep it, the same directions may be followed, which are given for keeping beef.

When the fillet is to be roasted, it should be washed, well dried, and the bone taken out, the space filled with a fine stuffing, part of which should be put under the flap, then formed into a round, and firmly skewered. That the fire may be clear and strong, it should be made up some time before putting down the roast, which should at first be placed at some distance from it, and be frequently and well basted with butter. When about half roasted, a piece of white paper is tied over the fat; a little before serving, it is removed; the meat is then sprinkled with salt, dredged with flour, and well basted to froth it. When dished, finely melted butter is poured over it, with which may or may not be mixed some lemon pickle or brown gravy. It is garnished with cut lemon.

A fillet weighing ten or fourteen pounds requires four hours to roast. The loin will take about three hours to roast; and is basted, the fat covered with paper, and served like the fillet. A slice of thin toasted bread is also served with it, on which the carver should lay a part of the kidney fat, and sprinkle it with salt and pepper. A shoulder stuffed with forcemeat will take from two to three hours to roast.

The best end of the neck may be roasted or boiled; if boiled, melted butter, made thick with parsley, is poured over it. A knuckle of veal may be boiled and served in the same way.

Pickled pork, ham, bacon, tongue, or sausages, is the general accompaniment to roasted or boiled veal.

Veal Collared White

BONE a breast of veal; chop and strew over it some finely chopped sweet herbs; make a forcemeat of beef suet, grated bread, lemon-peel, a small onion pounded; season with white pepper, grated nutmeg, and salt; pound it in a marble mortar, and lay it thickly over the veal; roll it up firmly, sew it in a cloth, and boil it for three hours. The sweetbread is to be boiled, sliced, and laid round the dish. For gravy, boil the bones and parings of the veal with a bunch of parsley. Strain and season it with white pepper, salt, and mushroom powder; thicken it with butter and flour; and a little before serving, add three or four table-spoonfuls of cream.

Brown Rollklops of Veal

CUT off some thin slices from a fillet of veal, and beat them. Take part of the fat from the loin and kidney; mince it finely, with a small bit of veal, and six anchovies; season with salt, pounded ginger, and mace; put it over the slices of veal, and roll them up. Dip them into the beaten yolk of an egg, and then into grated bread; repeat this a second time, and fry them of a nice brown colour in clarified beef dripping, then stew them in some good gravy, adding a little walnut pickle and half a pint of white wine.

Veal Roll

BONE a small breast of veal, and spread over it a rich and highly-seasoned forcemeat. Cut four hard-boiled eggs the long way into four pieces, and lay them in rows, with green pickles between each row. Roll up the veal tightly, and sew it; then put it into a cloth, and bind it with tape. Lay a slice of ham over it, and put it into a sauce-pan, together with some strong stock, and a little whole pepper, and stew it for three hours. Make a rich gravy, and boil it up with a little white wine and lemon juice or lemon pickle; pour it over the veal; add some egg and forcemeat balls, and garnish with cut green pickles. This dish is very good when cold.

To Stew a Breast of Veal

HALF roast the veal till of a light brown, then stew it over a stove for two hours, in a rich gravy, with a shalot, three cloves, a blade of mace, a little walnut pickle, some oyster liquor, and a few small mushrooms. Half an hour before serving, add a little anchovy liquor. Garnish with cut lemon, and curled parsley.

Another way to Stew a Breast of Veal

CUT out the blade bone, and stuff the hole with a nice forcemeat; sew it up, half roast it, and make a quart of gravy of the bones and trimmings; season it with whole pepper, two blades of mace, a bit of lemon-peel, a large onion, some salt, and a bunch of parsley. Strain and thicken it with butter rolled in flour; put in the veal, and a table-spoonful of vinegar; let it stew nearly two hours. A little before serving, add a table-spoonful of lemon pickle, and a glass of white wine. Forcemeat balls may be served with it.

Another way to Stew a Breast of Veal

CUT off the short bones or gristles of a breast of veal; stew them in a little white stock, with a slice of ham, an onion, stuck with one or two cloves, some whole pepper, a bunch of parsley, and a little salt. When tender, take out the meat, strain the stock, and put it on with a pint and a half of green peas; boil them, and add the veal, and let them stew for twenty minutes. Serve the gristles in the middle, and the peas round them.

Another way to Stew a Breast of Veal, with Green Peas

MAKE a quart of gravy with the scrag end; strain it; cut the rest of the veal into small pieces of nearly an equal size; put it into a stew-pan, with the gravy, some pepper, salt, mace, half an ounce of butter, and a quart of green peas. Cover the pan closely, and let it stew nearly two hours; then put in a lettuce cut small, and let it stew half an hour longer. A little before serving, add half an ounce of browned butter, mixed with a little flour.

To Broil a Breast of Veal

HALF roast and then score it; season it with parsley, a few finely-minced sweet herbs, a little pepper and salt, and broil it. Make a sauce of some gravy seasoned with onion, grated nutmeg, mace, salt, and an anchovy; boil and strain it; thicken it with flour and butter. Add some minced capers and small mushrooms; pour it quite hot over the veal. Garnish with sliced lemon.

To Roast a Loin of Veal with Béchamel

CUT an oblong piece of skin from the most fleshy part of a loin of veal, leaving one long side attached to the meat; turn it back, take out all the meat, being careful not to let the knife go through the under side; mince it, put it into a basin, season it with cayenne pepper and grated nutmeg, and moisten it well with good cream. Wash and dry the loin, and put the meat into the space from which it was taken; sew the skin neatly round the three open sides. When put down to roast, cover the loin with a buttered paper, and baste the joint very frequently; take off the paper half an hour before it is taken up, to let the roast get a fine brown colour. Serve it with melted butter poured over it, and garnish it with cut lemon.

To Stew a Fillet of Veal

BONE, lard, and stuff a fillet of veal; half roast, and then stew it with two quarts of white stock, a tea-spoonful of lemon pickle and one of mushroom catsup. Before serving, strain the gravy, thicken it with butter rolled in flour, add a little cayenne, salt, and some pickled mushrooms; heat it, and pour it over the veal. Have ready two or three dozen of forcemeat balls to put round it and upon the top. Garnish with cut lemon.

Veal Cutlets

CUT a neck of veal into cutlets, or take them off a leg. Season two well-beaten eggs with pounded mace, nutmeg, salt, pepper, and finely chopped sweet marjoram, lemon thyme, and parsley; dip the cutlets into it, sift over them grated bread, and fry them in clarified butter. Serve with a white sauce, forcemeat balls, and small mushrooms. Garnish with fried parsley.

Another way to Dress Veal Cutlets

CUT a neck of veal into thin cutlets, and beat them; brown some butter with an onion and some parsley chopped small. Dip the cutlets into the butter, and then in finely grated bread, seasoned with pepper and salt; broil them of a brown colour; mince the peel of half a Seville orange pared very thin; add it and a grate of ginger to some good thickened gravy, and pour it hot upon the cutlets.

Another way to Dress Veal Cutlets

Cut them off a leg, or from the thick part of a loin of veal; beat them a little with a rolling-pin, and fry them in butter of a light brown. Take them out of the pan, pour off the butter, and strew over them grated bread, seasoned with minced parsley and lemon thyme, grated lemon-peel and nutmeg, white pepper, and salt. Put them into a stew pan with a piece of fresh butter, and let them fry slowly till of a good brown. Add a quarter of a pint of good gravy, and a small tea-cupful of thick cream; let all be made very hot, frequently shaking the pan. Serve it garnished with cut lemon or forcemeat balls, mushrooms, and false eggs. False eggs are made of the yolks of two hard-boiled eggs, which are rubbed smooth, and then made up with fresh butter into the form of small eggs.

Veal Cutlets à la Vénitienne

Cut into neat cutlets the best part of a neck of veal; trim and flatten them. Chop separately half a pint of mushrooms, a few shalots, and a little parsley; stew these over a slow fire, with a small bit of butter and a little rasped fat bacon. When done, put in the cutlets, and season them well with pepper and salt, and let them stew over a slow fire till quite tender; skim off the fat, and add a spoonful of sauce tournée, and the yolks of three eggs beaten with a little cream, then mix in the juice of a lemon and a little cayenne.

To Collar a Breast of Veal

Bone it, and lay over it a thick layer of forcemeat, made with bread crumbs, chopped oysters, parsley, and grated ham, seasoned with lemon-peel, salt, white pepper, and nutmeg, mixed with an egg beaten up. Roll and bind it with tape; boil it in a cloth, and put it on in boiling water; let it boil gently for three hours. Boil the bones with an onion, a bunch of sweet herbs, salt and white pepper; strain and thicken it with three table-spoonfuls of cream, the yolks of two eggs beaten up, and a bit of butter mixed with flour. Parboil and slice the sweetbread, dip it into an egg, and strew over it grated bread; fry it with forcemeat balls. Serve the veal with the sauce poured over it. Garnish with the sweetbread and forcemeat balls.

To Collar Veal

Bone a breast of veal, and beat it flat; cover the inside with a nice stuffing moistened with eggs; roll it very tightly, bind it, and bake it in an oven with some weak stock in the dish. Make a rich gravy; strain and thicken it, and pour it over the veal. Serve with or without forcemeat balls, and garnish with cut lemon.

It will keep for a long time, in a pickle made with bran and water, a little salt and vinegar, poured cold over it.

Neck of Veal à la Chreme

CUT the bones short of a small breast of veal, and skewer the flank underneath, and make the neck as square as possible. Lay it for two hours in oil, with chopped parsley, sliced shalots, pepper, salt, thyme, and bay leaves. Fold it in buttered paper, and fasten it upon the spit, so as to preserve the square form; roast it about an hour and a quarter; take off the paper, baste it with, and pour over it, a thick veloutée sauce.

Neck of Veal à la Barbarie

TRIM a neck of veal neatly; lard it in chequers, with black truffles cut into nails. Stew the neck the same way as a fricandeau, putting bacon over the top, that the colour of the veal and truffles may be preserved. When done, glaze it slightly, and serve it with a sauce Italienne, with truffles.

Croquets

POUND, in a marble mortar, cold veal and fowl, with a little suet, some chopped lemon-peel, lemon thyme, chives, and parsley. Season with nutmeg, and pepper and salt; mix all well together, and add the yolk of an egg well beaten; roll it into balls, and dip them into an egg beaten up, then sift bread crumbs over them, and fry them in butter.

Kidney Toasts

POUND, in a marble mortar, the kidney and the surrounding fat, season with pepper, salt, grated lemon-peel, and nutmeg; mix with it the yolk of an egg well beaten, lay it upon thin toasted bread, cut into square bits. Put a little butter in a dish, lay in the kidney toasts, and brown them in an oven. Serve them very hot.

Kidney Cakes

MIX, together with a beaten egg, equal quantities of grated bread, and the fat and lean part of a cold kidney of veal, very finely minced, and seasoned with pepper and salt; form it into small cakes, fry them in boiling lard or butter, drain them upon the back of a sieve before the fire, and serve them garnished with fried parsley. The lean part of the cold roasted veal may be substituted for the lean part of the kidney.

Fricandeau of Veal

CUT a piece of veal from the leg, the same in width and depth, and about eight inches in length. Make a hole in the under part, and fill it with forcemeat; sew it up, lard the top and sides, cover it with slices of fat bacon, and then with white paper. Put into a sauce-pan some slices of undressed mutton, three onions and one carrot sliced, a bunch of sweet herbs, and a quart of good stock; put in the veal, cover the pan closely, and let it stew for three hours. Take out the veal, strain the gravy, and take off all the fat; add a table-spoonful of lemon pickle, and three of white wine; boil it quick to a glaze; keep the fricandeau over hot water and covered, then glaze it, and serve with the rest of the glaze poured round it, and sorrel sauce in a sauce-tureen.

Another way to make a Fricandeau of Veal

CUT some slices of veal, lard them all through, and put them into a sauce-pan with some white stock, and a bit of ham, one onion, a little mace and pepper. Stew them gently an hour and a half; take them out, strain the gravy, and take off all the fat; boil it up quickly, lay in the fricandeau, and stew them till the liquor becomes like a brown jelly, take care they do not burn. Scald in boiling water three handfuls of sorrel, chop it, take out the meat, and make the sorrel hot in the sauce, and serve the fricandeau upon it.

Another way to make a Fricandeau of Veal

CHOP very finely one pound of the lean of a loin of veal, and half a pound of the kidney fat; season it with white pepper, salt, grated lemon-peel, the juice of one lemon, and a finely-shred anchovy. Soak, in boiling milk, two rusks, or biscuits, and mix it all well together; make it into balls, with a little flour. Fry them of a light brown, in butter, then stew them in some highly-seasoned gravy, dish them carefully, and strain the gravy over them. Garnish with cut lemon.

Another way to make a Fricandeau of Veal

CUT a slice of veal about an inch and a half thick, lard the top, and blanch it for a moment in boiling water; then stew it in stock, with a bunch of sweet herbs, and, when it is done enough, withdraw it from the sauce-pan, that the sauce may be well skimmed; strain it, put it into another sauce-pan, and reduce it on the fire till almost wasted; put in the veal, and glaze it, and when the larded side is well glazed, put it on the dish in which it is to be served. Add a little cullis to what is in the sauce-pan, and a very little stock, to detach it from the pan; put it in the dish with the fricandeau, and under it a sorrel sauce, made as follows: Put into a sauce-pan some sorrel, lettuce; chervil, parsley, cibol, and purslain, all well washed, minced, and pressed, with a good bit of butter; do it on a brisk fire, till no water remains; put in a pinch of flour moistened with cullis and gravy, adding pepper and salt, and stew it till done enough.

All fricandeaux may be done in the same way.

Veal Cake, to be eaten cold

POUND, in a mortar, as much cold roasted lean veal as will fill a small mould, together with a slice of ham, or bacon, a piece of the crumb of bread soaked in cold milk, two beaten eggs, a small bit of butter, the same of shalot, or onion; season with pepper and salt, and mix all well together; butter the mould, fill it, and bake it in an oven for about an hour; turn it out when cold, and cut it into slices. Garnish with pickled eggs and parsley.

Minced Fowl, with Veal

MINCE the white part of a cold roasted or boiled fowl; put it, and some thin slices of veal, into a sauce-pan, also some white stock, a squeeze of a lemon, a few drops of shalot vinegar, and a dust of sugar; simmer it for a short time, and serve it upon bread sippets, with the slices of veal laid on the mince.

Potted Calf's Feet

BOIL the feet as for jelly, pick all the meat from the bones, add to it half a pint of gravy, a little salt, pepper, and nutmeg, garlic, a shalot, and some shred ham; simmer it for half an hour, dip a mould into water, put in a layer of the meat, then some neatly-cut pickled beet-root, and some boiled minced parsley, then a layer of meat, and so on, till the mould be filled; when cold, turn it out. Garnish with pickled eggs, beet-root, and parsley.

Calf's Feet, Plain

SCALD, clean, and blanch some calves' feet, boil them till the bones will come out, then stew them in a blanch. See Calf's Head, plain, p. 107. When done, drain and serve them with parsley and butter.

Veal Olives

CUT thin slices off a fillet, and flatten them with a roller; season them highly with white pepper, mace, salt, and grated lemon-peel; put a bit of fat into each roll, and tie them with a thread. Fry them of a light brown, and stew them in some white stock, with two dozen of fried oysters, a glass of white wine, a table-spoonful of lemon pickle, and some small mushrooms. Stew them nearly an hour; take off the threads before serving.

Beef olives may be dressed in the same way.

Minuten Fleisch

CUT from off a leg of veal some slices as thin as the blade of a knife, and about four inches long; season them with pepper and salt, lay them into a deep dish, pour over them nearly half a pint of white wine, let it stand for three hours. Cover the bottom of a stew-pan with butter, dredge each slice of the veal on both sides with flour, add a little more wine, and as much good white stock as will cover it, and the juice of a lemon. Cover the pan closely, and let it simmer five minutes, and serve it instantly, otherwise it will become hard.

Minced Veal

CUT thin slices of lean cold veal; mince them very finely with a knife, and season with white pepper, salt, grated lemon-peel and nutmeg; put it into a sauce-pan, with a little white stock, or water, a table-spoonful of lemon pickle, and a little mushroom powder. Simmer, but do not let it boil; add a bit of butter rolled in flour, and a little milk, or cream; put all round the dish thin sippets of bread cut into a three-cornered shape; or, cover the mince thickly with grated bread, seasoned with white pepper, salt, and a little butter, and brown it with a salamander; or serve with poached eggs laid upon the top.

Calf's Head, Plain

CLEAN a calf's head nicely, and cut out the bone of the lower jaw, and of the nose, taking out the nose bone as close to the eyes as possible; wash the head well in warm water, and let it blanch in some clean water. Prepare a blanc, or sauce, as follows: One pound of beef suet, and one pound of fat bacon, cut small, half a pound of butter, a bunch of parsley, a little thyme, two or three bay leaves, one or two onions, and the juice of a lemon; season with salt, pepper, mace, cloves, and allspice; boil all this an hour in six pints of water, then tie up the head in a cloth, boil it in the sauce about three hours, and drain it; take out the tongue, skin, and replace it; serve quite hot, with the following sauce; – minced shalots, parsley, the brains minced, some vinegar, salt, and pepper.

Dressed Calf's Head

To take the hair off the head, first wash it clean, and put it on the fire with plenty of cold water; let it boil a little time, try if the hair will pull off easily, if not, boil it till it does, then lay it into cold water to blanch; take off the skin, and cut it into bits an inch and a half square, cut what meat is on the head into thin slices, pick out the black part of the eyes, and cut the remainder into rings ; cut the ears like small straws, skin the tongue, and cut it lengthwise, or leave it whole, put the brains carefully upon a plate. Make a sauce of a quart of good gravy, thicken it with butter and flour; season with half the peel of a lemon and the juice, two blades of mace, or grated nutmeg and cayenne; put in the head, and let it stew till tender, add forcemeat balls, fried brown, a few hardboiled yolks of eggs, and a glass of white wine. Garnish with brain-cakes, made as follows:

Beat up the brains with a knife, pick out all the skin and strings, mix with them two table-spoonfuls of flour, a grate of lemon-peel, a little white pepper and salt, two eggs, well beaten, and half a pint of milk; fry them in butter, dropping them in with a spoon, so as to make them the size of a crown piece. Lay them before the fire upon the back of a sieve, to drain and brown a little.

To make a simple white gravy, that answers very well, take the bones of the head, chopping away the nose, put them into a stew-pan with a quart of water, an onion, some whole pepper, and salt, a little winter savory, and lemon thyme; let it stew nearly two hours, strain it, put in the prepared head.

Another way to make Dressed Calf's Head

SCALD and clean a calf's head very nicely, and with a sharp knife cut all the meat entire from the bone, cut out the tongue, and carefully take out the brains; lay it all in cold water for two or three hours. Mince very small two pounds of lean veal, and one pound of beef suet, with the grated crumb of a penny loaf, some sweet herbs, grated lemon-peel, nutmeg, pepper, and salt; mix them well together, and bind it with the yolks of four eggs beaten up; reserve as much of the forcemeat as will make twenty small balls; wash the head clean, wipe it dry, and put the forcemeat into the inside; close it, and tie it firmly with tape; put it into a stew-pan with two quarts of gravy, half a pint of white wine, and a bunch of sweet herbs; cover it closely, and let it stew gently; boil the tongue, cut it into thin slices, mince the brains with a little parsley and a table-spoonful of flour, add some pepper, salt, grated lemon-peel, and nutmeg; beat two eggs and mix with the brains, drop it with a spoon in small cakes into a pan of boiling dripping, and fry them of a light-brown colour. Fry the forcemeat balls, and drain them, with the cakes, upon the back of a sieve before the fire; when the head has stewed till it be sufficiently tender, put it into a dish and take off the tape, strain the gravy, and thicken it with a table-spoonful of flour of rice, and a little bit of butter; if not well seasoned, add more salt and pepper, put in the tongue, make it all hot, and pour it over the head. Garnish with the brain-cakes, forcemeat balls, and cut lemon.

To Roast a Calf's Head

WASH and clean it well, parboil it, take out the bones, brains, and tongue; make forcemeat sufficient for the head and some balls with bread crumbs, minced suet, parsley, grated ham, and a little pounded veal, or cold fowl; season with pepper, salt, grated nutmeg, and lemon-peel; bind it with an egg, beaten up, fill the head with it, which must then be sewed up, or fastened with skewers, and tied. While roasting, baste it well with butter; beat up the brains with a little cream, the yolk of an egg, some minced parsley, a little pepper and salt; blanch the tongue, cut it into slices and fry it with the brains, forcemeat balls, and thin slices of bacon. Serve the head with white or brown thickened gravy, and place the tongue, forcemeat balls, and brains round it. Garnish with cut lemon. It will require one hour and a half to roast.

Calf's Head Bigarrée

CLEAN and blanch a calf's head, boil it till the bones will come out easily, then bone and press it between two dishes, so as to give it an oblong form; beat with the yolk of four eggs, a little melted butter, pepper, and salt. Divide the head when cold, and brush it all over with the beaten eggs, and strew over it grated bread; repeat this twice. With the grated bread, which is put over one half, a good quantity of finely-minced parsley should be mixed; place the head upon a dish, and bake it of a nice brown colour. Serve it with a sauce of parsley and butter, and with one of good gravy, mixed with the brains which have been previously boiled and chopped, and seasoned with a little cayenne and salt.

To Plain Boil a Calf's Head

SPLIT the head, and take out carefully the brains and tongue, wash the head well, and let it lie two or three hours in cold water. Boil it with the tongue and brains gently in plenty of water, till it be quite tender; take out the bones, and pour over the head parsley and butter made very thick; rub the brains through a sieve; add to them a little chopped parsley, some pepper, salt, flour, and butter; mix all well together, and put it round the tongue, which may be served as a corner dish, or it may be salted. When salted, the brains, with the addition of a little butter and chopped parsley, may be put over the head, or served in a sauce tureen.

Calf's Brains, with Fried Parsley

Blanch three or four brains, of nearly an equal size; parboil them, and take off the skin; then boil them in water, with a little salt, vinegar, and butter. Serve them with a sauce made of a little browned butter, a tablespoonful of vinegar, some salt and pepper, and some parsley fried very green.

To Dress Calves' Ears

Cut the ears of two calves deep at the bottom, and even, so that they may stand; clean and wash them well, and boil them till tender in milk-and-water; fill them with a nice forcemeat, tie them with thread, and stew them in a little of the liquor they were boiled in; season it with pepper, salt, mace, and a small onion minced. Before serving, thicken the sauce with the yolk of an egg beaten up in a little cream.

Boudin à la Reine

Cut the meat of cold roasted veal, or that of fowls, into dice; season, and heat it in a veloutée sauce. When cold, form it into rolls the length of the dish; dip them into beaten eggs, and then into grated bread; repeat this, and let them be completely covered with the grated bread; fry them of a fine brown colour, drain and serve them with fried parsley laid between each.

Veal en Blanquette

Cut some cold roasted veal into very little bits, without any fat; reduce and clarify two spoonfuls of white cullis, thicken it with the yolks of eggs and a good bit of fresh butter; add a pinch of minced parsley and the squeeze of a lemon; heat the veal in this, and serve it immediately.

Blanquettes of fowls may be made in the same way.

To Pot Veal

Cut slices off a leg of veal, and season them with white pepper, pounded mace, cloves, and salt. Lay thin slices of fresh butter between each layer of meat into a potting pan or jar; cover it closely, and bake it in a quick oven from one to two hours. When it is cold, pound the meat in a marble mortar, pack it closely into a jar, and pour clarified butter over it.

Veal Cones

MINCE small one pound and a half of cold veal, two ounces of butter, and a slice of lean ham; pound them in a mortar, and mix in five table-spoonfuls of cream, two tea-spoonfuls of white pepper, one of salt, and some grated lemon-peel. Make it up into cones about three inches high; rub them over with an egg beaten up, sift grated bread over them, and fry them of a light brown colour; put fried bread crumbs into the dish, and place the cones upon them, or serve them with a brown gravy instead of crumbs. Cold fowl, turkey, or rabbit, make good ones. Half the ingredients will be sufficient for a corner dish.

Pyramids of Rice

BOIL some whole rice, make it up into the form of pyramids about three inches high, or press it into small tin frames of that shape; take out part of the rice at the bottom, and fill the space with sausage, or rich forcemeat; place them in a dish, take off the frame, and pour round them some rich brown gravy.

Casserole of Rice

HAVING cleaned and drained about half a pound of rice, moisten it in a stew-pan, with some fat – that which gather on the top of liquor in which meat has been boiled; strain some broth or soup, add to it a large quantity of grease, some pieces of fat bacon, and a little salt, and mix it with the rice, to make it swell as much as possible; stir it frequently over a slow fire to keep it from sticking; when it is soft strain it through a cullender, and press it well with a wooden spoon. The mould being selected for the casserole, rinse it with the fat drained from the rice, taking care that every part of the inside of the mould be well greased, then cover it with rice, and place a piece of the crumb of bread in the middle, and cover it with rice also; press it in equally with a spoon, and let it cool. When the rice has become firm, dip the outside of the mould into boiling water; put a covering of paste made with flour and water; flatten it all round with a spoon, and make an opening in the top with a knife, then put it into the oven, which cannot be too hot for a casserole, baste it with the grease, and when it has become of a fine colour, take it out of the oven, remove the crust, and take out the bread carefully, so that the casserole may not be injured; next remove some of the rice from the inside, taking care to leave enough to resist the weight of whatever may be put inside of it. Fill it with minced meat, ragout, blanquette, fricassee of chickens, macaroni, or scallops of fish, that have been already served at table; return it to the oven, and when nicely browned, serve it.

Cassolettes of Rice

THE rice prepared as above may be put into smaller moulds, those called dariole moulds, and it should be quite cold before it is turned out, the mince or whatever is put inside being also cold; it must be put in carefully, that none of it may mix with the rice, otherwise the cassolettes would break in the process of frying; for the same reason, the dripping must be very hot. Frying is the best and quickest method of doing them, but they may also be browned in the oven as the casserole of rice.

Casserole of Potatoes

BOIL and peel some good mealy potatoes, pound, and mix with the mash some butter, cream, and a little salt, put it about an inch and a half high upon a flat dish, and leave an opening in the centre; bake the mash of a light brown colour, and take out as much from the centre as will admit of a ragout, fricassee, or macaroni, being put into it.

Rissoles

MINCE very finely some old roasted veal, and a small bit of bacon; season it with grated nutmeg and salt; moisten it with cream, and make it up into good-sized balls; dip them into the yolks of eggs beaten up, and then into finely grated bread. Bake them in an oven, or fry them of a light brown colour in fresh dripping. Before serving, drain them before the fire on the back of a sieve. Garnish with fried parsley.

Kebobbed Veal

CUT into thin bits the size of a crown-piece some lean veal; season them with turmeric, pepper, and salt. Slice onions very thinly, and some garlic; put the slices of veal and onion upon a skewer, together with thin bits of pickled pork. Fry them brown with butter, and garnish with fried parsley.

Cutcharee

BOIL a quarter of a pound of split peas till they be tender; drain them in a cullender. Wash very clean a pound of rice; chop the peas finely, mix them with the rice, and season with a little turmeric. Fry in an ounce and a half of butter, a minced onion, and of cloves, mace, cardamom, and black pepper, when pounded, half a tea-spoonful each; stir them constantly, to prevent their burning. Season a quart of veal stock with salt and pepper; put in the rice and the fried onion and spices;

cover the stew-pan closely, and let it simmer till the rice becomes tender and dry. Serve it with a cup of oiled butter.

Calf's Liver Larded and Roasted

Lard a fine calf's liver the same as a fricandeau, and let it lie for twenty-four hours in vinegar, with a sliced onion, some parsley, a little thyme, a bay leaf, some salt and pepper. Roast and baste it well with butter, then glaze it with a light glaze, and serve it with a poivrade, or any other sauce.

Scollops of Calf's Liver

Parboil and cut into slices a very fine calf's liver, and shape them into hearts. Stew some fine herbs, parsley, shalots, and mushrooms; then add the calf's liver, and let it stew over a slow fire; when done on one side, turn and season it with pepper and salt; take out the liver, dredge in a little flour over the herbs, and add some more gravy; let this boil for ten minutes, then heat the liver in the sauce before serving it. This may be eaten at breakfast.

Calf's Pluck

Wash it very clean, and, if liked, stuff the heart with a forcemeat, made of crumbs of bread, butter, and parsley, and seasoned with pepper, salt, and grated nutmeg. Fasten it firmly with the liver and lights, tying them to the skewers while roasting; baste it well with butter, and froth it the same way in which veal is done, and serve it with melted butter, mixed with a table-spoonful of lemon pickle, or vinegar poured over it.

Another way to Dress a Calf's Pluck

Stuff the heart with a rich forcemeat, enclose it in paste, rub it over with the beaten whites of eggs, lay over it vermicelli, which has been boiled, and bake it. Boil the liver and lights, mince part of them, stew it in some gravy, thicken it with butter rolled in flour, and add a little catsup. Slice and fry the remainder of the liver and lights with a little bacon; place the heart upon the mince, and garnish with the fry.

To Broil a Sweetbread

Parboil it, rub it with butter, and broil it over a slow fire; turn it frequently, and baste it now and then, by putting it upon a plate kept warm by the fire with butter in it.

To Roast Sweetbreads

WASH, and parboil them in milk-and-water; then dry and rub them over with the beaten yolk of an egg, and roll them in grated bread, repeat this twice; roast them of a nice brown colour, in a Dutch oven, and baste them now and then with butter. Sweetbreads dressed in this way may be served with brown gravy, or with bread sauce, so as nearly to cover them.

To Fricassee Sweetbreads with Brown Sauce

PARBOIL two or three fine sweetbreads, cut them in slices, and dip them into the beaten yolk of an egg which has been mixed with a little flour, salt, pepper, and grated nutmeg; fry them a nice brown; thicken some well seasoned gravy with a little flour, adding a tea-spoonful of lemon juice, two of catsup, and a table-spoonful of white wine; boil it well, and then stew in it the sweetbreads for a few minutes before serving.

Sweetbreads à la Dauphine

IF for a round dish, take four large and fine sweetbreads. If for a long dish, three will suffice. Pare off the fat and sinews, and blanch them in warm water; parboil them, and when cold, lard them. Rub a stew-pan with fresh butter, and put into it a few sliced carrots and onions, then a layer of slices of fat bacon, place the sweetbreads upon the bacon, sprinkle a little salt over them, and stew them with a great deal of fire on the top, and a very slow one beneath; when they are nicely browned, cover them with a piece of buttered paper, cut round, and lessen the fire upon the top. They will require to stew for three quarters of an hour, then drain and put them into a pan, with some glaze, and the bacon underneath. Leave them in the glaze till dinner time, drain them again, glaze them of a fine brown, and serve them with sorrel or endive.

Italian Attelets of Sweetbreads

BLANCH some nice sweetbreads, and stew them in a well-seasoned gravy, made of meat and vegetables; when cold, cut them into pieces of nearly an inch square, put them into a sauce d'attelets, and let them cool. With silver skewers, skewer the sweetbreads, and a bit of ready-dressed calf's udder alternately; make them all as much as possible of an equal size, and of square form. Moisten them with the sauce, and cover them with grated bread, then dip them into four well-beaten eggs, strew over them some more grated bread, and level it with a knife; fry them of a fine brown, and serve with an Italian sauce, white or brown. If the attelets are ready before they are required to be fried, strew grated bread over the cover of a stew-pan, and lay them upon it.

Small Cases of Scollops of Sweetbreads

BLANCH and parboil some fine sweetbreads, cut them into small scollops. Then chop separately, and finely, half a pint of mushrooms, a little parsley, and four or five shalots, add a little fat bacon rasped, and a piece of fresh butter; season the scollops with pepper, salt, and a little mace, stew it altogether over a slow fire; when done, drain off the fat, place the scollops in small paper cases, which have been fried in olive oil, cover them with plenty of finely-chopped herbs, and strew over them fried bread crumbs; lay the paper cases for a moment into the oven, and before serving, pour into each a little rich gravy, and a little lemon juice.

Croquets of Sweetbreads

MINCE some cold sweetbreads, which have been dressed, and boil them in a sauce veloutée; when quite cold, form them into balls, or into rolls about two inches long; fry and serve them with fried parsley in the middle. Or, make the croquet meat into a rissole. Roll out a piece of thin puff-paste, enclose the meat in it, brush it over with a beaten egg, and strew over it grated bread; fry it of a light-brown colour.

To Dress Cold Veal

MINCE finely the fat and lean of cold roast veal, season it with grated nutmeg, lemon-peel, white pepper, and salt; moisten it with a little rich white stock, and a beaten egg; butter a pudding shape, put in the mince, and press it firmly, cover it closely, and set it into a pan of boiling water; let it boil an hour or two. Serve it with a white gravy thickened, or when turned out of the shape, rub it over the top with the beaten yolk of an egg; sift bread crumbs thickly over, and brown it in a Dutch oven; baste it with a little melted butter. Garnish with fried parsley or cut lemon.

Italian Veal

BOIL with some bread-and-milk an onion, a bay leaf, a little cayenne and white pepper, and a beaten egg; take out the bay leaf, and add some pounded raw lean veal, with a little fat of veal which has been boiled and pounded; rub the mixture through a coarse sieve, and with a little flour form it into rolls; tie each roll in a bit of cloth first dipped into hot water, and dusted with flour; put them on in boiling water, and boil them ten or twelve minutes. Serve them with a white or brown gravy well-seasoned.

Calf's Chitterlings, or Fraise

CUT them open with scissors, wash and cleanse them thoroughly, lay them for a night into salt-and-water, then wash them well; parboil, and cut them into small pieces, dip them into a thick batter, seasoned with pepper, salt, and a little white wine. Fry them of a light-brown colour in beef dripping; serve with a fringe of fried parsley. Or,

After being parboiled, they may be roasted, when they must be constantly basted with butter, dredged with flour to froth them nicely; then served with melted butter, and lemon pickle poured over them. Or,

They may be baked – when, after being parboiled, they are rubbed over with butter, and put into the oven on an iron frame, which is placed in a deep dish. This oblong frame of white iron, about two inches high, will be found useful in baking every kind of meat.

Savoury Cabbage

POUND, in a marble mortar, about two pounds of veal, a large slice of ham, two shalots, and a quarter of a pound of fresh beef suet; season with white and cayenne pepper, nutmeg, lemon-peel, salt, and some parsley and lemon thyme finely minced; beat all well together till thoroughly mixed, and add the well-beaten yolks of three eggs. Wash and clean a large head of cabbage, take out the heart, and stuff it with the above ingredients; roll it in a cloth, and sew it tightly; boil it slowly for three hours, and serve it with a white sauce.

A Grenade

PUT alternately into a small potting pan or jar, a layer of each of the following ingredients: vermicelli, ham, hard-boiled yolks of eggs, veal, and highly-seasoned forcemeat, all finely pounded, excepting the vermicelli, which is merely boiled. Cover the pan, and bake it in an oven from one to two hours; when turned out, pour over it some rich brown gravy, and garnish with mushrooms, cut lemon, or truffles and morels.

Potato Patties

WASH and scrape off the rind of four or five large potatoes, cut off the top, and scrape out the inside; mix a part of it with a little pounded veal and ham; add a little cream, nutmeg, lemon-peel, salt, and pepper, and a little mushroom catsup. Put this mixture into the patties, put on the top, and place them upright in a pudding dish, with a little butter in the bottom of it; bake them in an oven; a little bit cut off the bottom of each will make them stand even.

Frogs

Having cut off the feet and the body, so as to have scarcely more than the legs, put them into boiling water, and let them boil a little; next, put them into fresh water, and then drain them; put them into a sauce-pan with some mushrooms, a bunch of parsley, cibol, a clove of garlic, two cloves and a bit of butter; give them two or three turns on the fire, and add a dust of flour, moisten them with a glass of white wine and a little gravy; season with salt and pepper; let them boil a quarter of an hour, and thicken the sauce with the yolks of three eggs, a little cream, and a pinch of finely minced parsley, let it thicken without boiling it.

This is given as a national dish.

CHAPTER VII
PORK

The names of the various pieces are:

IN ENGLAND

Fore quarter: Spare Rib – Hand – Belly, or Spring. Hind Quarter: Fore Loin – Hind Loin, which, if too long, a spare rib may be cut off – Leg.

IN SCOTLAND

Spare Rib – Breast and Shoulder – Sirloin – The Ham or Gigot.

The entrails are named the liver, crow, kidney, skirts, sometimes called the harslet, also the chitterlings or guts.

PREPARATORY REMARKS ON PORK

Dairy-fed pork is the best; the flesh should look white and smooth, and the fat be white and fine. In preparing a hog for bacon, the ribs are cut, with a very little flesh on them, from the side, which has the fore and hind leg attached to it; the hind leg is then called a gammon of bacon, but it is generally reserved for ham. On each side there is a large spare rib, which is usually divided into two, one called the sweet bone, the other the blade bone. There are also griskins, chine, or back bone.

Hog's lard is the inner fat of the bacon hog.

Porkers are not so old as hogs; they make excellent pickled pork, but are chosen more particularly for roasting. To roast a leg, a small onion is minced together with three sage leaves, seasoned with pepper and salt, and put under the skin at the knuckle bone; the skin is cut into strips nearly half an inch apart, and rubbed over with a bit of butter. If weighing seven or eight pounds, it will require nearly three hours to roast.

A spare rib should be roasted, is basted with butter, and has sage leaves, dried, rubbed to a powder, and mixed with salt and pepper, sprinkled over it.

Both a loin and neck are jointed, the skin scored in narrow strips, and rubbed with butter. If weighing six or seven pounds, it will require rather more than two hours to roast.

A griskin may be either broiled or roasted.

A chine is stuffed here and there with bread crumbs, mixed with a little butter, and seasoned with some finely-shred sage, parsley, and thyme, some pepper and salt. The skin is cut into strips, and rubbed with butter; it is then roasted, and served with apple sauce, as are also the preceding roasts.

A porker's head is stuffed like a sucking pig, sewed firmly, and hung on a string to roast. The shoulder may be roasted, but, being very fat, it is generally preferred pickled.

The breast may be made into pie, or broiled.

Westphalia Ham

Rub each ham well with an ounce and a half of pounded saltpetre, and an equal quantity of coarse brown sugar. The following day, boil, in a quart of strong stale beer or porter, a pound of bay salt, the same of common salt, half a pound of coarse brown sugar, of pounded black pepper and cloves an ounce each, and a small bit of sal prunella. Pour it boiling hot over the ham, and let it lie a fortnight, rubbing and turning it twice or thrice daily, when it should be smoked for a fortnight.

To Cure Hams

Sprinkle a ham weighing eighteen pounds or upwards with a little common salt, and let it lie a day; then rub it well with one ounce of ground black pepper, and one ounce of pounded saltpetre. Let it lie another day, then rub in a pound of bay, and a pound of common salt. In two hours, pour over it a pound of treacle, and let it lie for three weeks or a month, according to the size of the ham, turning and rubbing it daily. Let it lie in cold water for four-and-twenty hours, then hang it for a fortnight up a chimney where wood or turf is burnt.

Another way to Cure Hams

To each ham allow the following ingredients, finely pounded: one pound of bay, and half a pound of common salt, two ounces of saltpetre, and one ounce of black pepper. Rub the mixture well into the ham, turning it daily for four days, and then pour over it one pound and a half of treacle, and let it lie for four weeks, turning it daily, and basting it frequently with the pickle. Lay it for four-and-twenty hours into cold water. Smoke it for a fortnight, and bury it with malt dust in a box. It ought to be kept three or four months before it is used, and should not be soaked before boiling.

Another way to Cure Hams

For two hams weighing sixteen pounds each, allow one pound and a quarter of brown sugar, three ounces of powdered saltpetre, one pound of bay salt, the same of common salt, two or three heads of garlic pounded. Mix all together, and rub it into the hams; let them lie for three or four weeks, turning and rubbing them daily, when they may be dried in the kitchen, or smoked for a fortnight.

Another way to Cure Hams

Pound two ounces of saltpetre, one ounce of black pepper, and one pound of bay salt. Rub it over the ham, and let it lie four days, turning it daily, then pour over it a pound and a half of treacle. Baste it daily for a month, then put it in cold water for twenty-four hours. Wipe it dry, and sew it in a piece of old linen. Hang it up in a chimney where wood is burnt.

Another way to Cure Hams

For two hams, boil, in one quart of strong beer, one pound and a quarter of common salt, three ounces of saltpetre, one pound and a quarter of coarse brown sugar. When it is cold, pour it over the hams, rub them well daily, basting them more frequently. Let them remain for three weeks, and then smoke them. When hams which have been hung up are not keeping well, they must be returned to their pickle, and allowed to remain till required for use.

Ham with Madeira

SOAK in water for two hours a Bayonne or any other fine ham, boil it for two hours, trim it quickly, and then put it into a stew-pan, with thin slices of veal at the bottom; add some carrots and parsley, and season with spices. Pour over the ham a pint of rich stock and a bottle of madeira; let it boil for two hours, strain and skim the fat off the sauce, which, with the ham, must be served quite hot.

To Boil a Ham

WHEN the ham is not to be soaked, wash it well in warm water, and scrub it clean; pare off any rusty part, and trim it neatly. Put it on in a large pot, with plenty of lukewarm water, and let it simmer for four or five hours. Take off the skin as whole as possible; sift over the ham bread raspings and a very little pounded sugar, and set it before the fire for two or three minutes, and put a fringe of white paper round the knuckle. The skin may be laid over the ham, when cold, to keep it moist.

To Collar a Pig's Cheek

STREW over a pig's face, and a neat's or pig's tongue, a little salt and saltpetre; let it stand eight or nine days, then boil them with two cow-heels, till all be sufficiently tender to admit of the bones being taken out; lay upon a dish a piece of strong cloth, put the cheek upon it with the rind downwards; season it highly with black and Jamaica pepper, cloves, and a little salt; add the tongue and cow-heels, with more seasoning; roll and sew up firmly, put it into a jar and boil it for two hours, then press it with a heavy weight, and when cold take off the cloth. The cow-heel may be omitted, and both cheeks used.

To Pot Pig's Head

SPLIT the head of a small pig, take out the brains, cut off the ears, and let it lie in cold water for one day, then boil it till all the bones come out; take off the skin, keeping it as whole as possible. Chop the tongue and all the meat while it is hot; season it highly with pepper, salt, and nutmeg; place part of the skin at the bottom of a potting-pan or bowl, lay in the chopped meat, and put the rest of the skin over the top; press it down hard, place a small plate upon it, put on that a heavy weight, which must not be taken off till it be perfectly cold. Boil up part of the liquor with some vinegar and salt, and keep the head in this pickle. It may be served for breakfast or luncheon, and is eaten with vinegar and mustard.

To Make Sausages

Take a pound of the inward fat of the pig, and half a pound of lean pork; pick both clean from skin and sinews, mince them very finely, grate a large nutmeg, take its weight of pounded mace and cloves, the largest proportion mace, the weight of all of black pepper, and twice the weight of the spices of salt; chop finely a few sage leaves and a little lemon thyme; mix all well together with two large table-spoonfuls of grated bread and the yolk of an egg beaten. It may be put into skins, or packed into a jar and tied closely with bladder. When to be used, moisten it with the yolk of an egg beaten, make it up in the form of sausages, flour them, and fry them in butter.

Another way to make Sausages

Chop together two pounds of lean pork, and one and a half of the inward fat of the pig, the crumb of a penny loaf cut into slices and soaked in cold water; season with pepper, salt, grated nutmeg, lemon thyme, and a little sage. Mix all the ingredients well, and half fill the skins; boil them half an hour.

Spreadbury's Sausages

Cut from the leg or griskin one pound of nice lean pork, free from sinews and skin, mince it very finely; mince one pound of the best beef suet, mix it with the pork, and pound it as finely as possible in a marble mortar; add two large table-spoonfuls of stale bread rubbed through a sieve, also a good deal of black pepper, salt, and a little finely-chopped sage, mix all together with the yolks of two eggs beaten up. It will keep for some time, if put into an earthen jar and pressed closely down. When it is to be used, make it into rolls, and as thick as common sausages, and three or four inches long; dust them with a little flour; have ready a frying-pan made very hot, and fry them without anything but their own fat, till they are done quite through, taking care not to make them too dry. By breaking one of them, the cook will know whether they are sufficiently done. They may be fried in lard or fresh beef dripping.

To Cure Pig's Cheek

Strew salt over it, and let it lie for two or three days, then pour over it the following mixture when it is cold: half a pound of bay salt, half an ounce of saltpetre, a quarter of a pound of coarse brown sugar, one handful of common salt, and a pennyworth of cochineal, boiled in a pint of strong beer or porter; let it lie in the pickle a fortnight turning it daily, then hang it to smoke for a week. When to be dressed, put it into lukewarm water to soak for a night; and in dressing it, follow the directions given for boiling hams.

To Dress Pig's Kidneys and Skirts

CLEAN and wash them very nicely, cut the kidneys across, and the skirts into small square bits; fry them a light brown in beef drippings, brown a bit of butter the size of a walnut, with a little flour, and add as much boiling water as may be required of gravy, and an onion, minced small. Add the meat, a little pepper, salt, and mushroom catsup, and let it stew till tender.

To Collar a Small Roasting Pig

CUT off the feet, head, and tail; bone and wash it well and dry it in a cloth. Season it highly with a quantity of black pepper and salt; roll it up firmly, and bind it with a piece of linen; sew it tightly. Put it on in boiling water, with the bones, let it boil for an hour, then put it under a weight to press till it be cold, and take off the cloths

Ham Toasts

GRATE some lean ham, mix with it the beaten yolk of an egg, and some pepper; fry it in clarified butter; put it on square bits of toast, and brown it with a salamander.

Soused Pig's Head and Feet

CLEAN them extremely well, and boil them; take for sauce part of the liquor, and add vinegar, lime or lemon juice, salt, cayenne, black and Jamaica pepper; put in, either cut down or whole, the head and feet; boil all together for an hour, and pour it into a deep dish. It is eaten cold with mustard and vinegar.

To Roast a Sucking Pig

TO kill the pig, stick it just above the breast bone, running the knife into the heart; plunge it for a minute or two into cold water; rub it over with resin beaten exceedingly fine; it is sometimes tubbed with its blood before the resin is put on; dip it into a pail of scalding water, take it out and rub off all the hair as quickly as possible; if it should not all come off, repeat the scalding and rubbing with resin. When quite clean, wash it in warm, and frequently in cold water. Cut off the feet at the first joint; take out all the entrails; put the pettitoes, heart, liver, and lights together. Wash the pig well in cold water, and dry it thoroughly. Make a stuffing of grated bread, butter, a small onion, and three or four sage leaves minced; season with pepper and salt, put it inside and sew it up. The pig being made perfectly dry, put the well-beaten white of an egg all over it with a feather. Put it down to roast before a very quick fire, and under it a small basin to catch gravy. Do not flour it, and be sure to cover it well with the egg, which will crisp it nicely, and make it of a delicate light brown. It will take from one to two hours to roast. When done, cut off the head, part it and the body down the middle; mix with the chopped brains a little finely-minced boiled sage and some melted butter, add to it the gravy that has run from the pig, also mix with the stuffing some melted butter. Lay the pig on the dish, placing the shoulder of the one side to the hind quarter of the other. Observe in roasting the pig to skewer the legs back, so that the under part may be crisp. A pig prepared as above may be baked.

Ham and Eggs

Cut some ham into thin slices, and broil them on a gridiron. Fry some eggs in butter. Serve it, laying an egg on each slice of ham.

Pig's Harslet

Parboil the liver and lights, slice and fry them along with thin bits of bacon. Garnish with fried parsley.

Pickled Leg of Pork

Salt it eight or ten days, turn and rub it daily. Before being dressed, let it lie in cold water for half an hour; put it on in cold water; when it boils, take off the scum, and let it simmer till done. If weighing seven or eight pounds, it will take nearly three hours to boil. Serve with peas-pudding and boiled greens. About two or three pounds of pickled pork will require to be simmered for an hour and a half.

Pork Steaks

Cut them off a neck or loin, trim them neatly, and pepper them; broil them over a clear fire, turning them frequently; they will take twenty minutes. Sprinkle them with a little salt before serving.

Black Puddings

Throw a little salt into the blood while it is warm, and stir it till it become cold; boil in milk till quite tender two quarts of half grits. When nearly cold, put in the inward fat of the pig cut into pieces the size of a small nutmeg; season with pepper, salt, cloves, and mace; of herbs, parsley, sweet marjoram, winter savory, penny-royal, and leeks, all finely minced. Mix them with the grits and fat, and add a sufficiency of the blood to make it of a dark colour. The skins or guts must be very well washed, and when perfectly cleansed, laid into salt-and-water the night before. When they are to be filled, tie one end, and turn the inside out; half fill them, tie them of equal lengths or in rounds; put them into hot water, and when they have boiled five minutes, take them out, prick them with a large needle and then boil them half an hour. When they are cold, hang them up in a cool dry place.

Another way to make Black Puddings

PREPARE the blood as before directed, and to a pint and a half allow six ounces of rice boiled in a quart of milk till it be tender, the grated crumb of a half-quarter loaf. Season with black pepper, salt, cloves, and mace; of herbs, parsley, savory, pennyroyal, a little sage and onion, all finely minced; one pound of beef suet chopped very fine, a small quantity of the inward fat of the pig finely cut, and four eggs well beaten and strained. Mix all these ingredients together, and stir in the blood. Divide it into three puddings, and boil them in pudding cloths floured. When they are to be used, heat them whole in a Dutch oven, or cut them into slices, and broil them upon a gridiron, or they may be put into the skins.

To Dress the Blood of Pigs, Calves, or Lambs without Skins

CUT an onion in small dice, and put it into a sauce-pan on a stove, or on the fire, with a bit of butter or hog's lard; when it is done, put in the blood, season it with pepper and salt, and stir it gently on the fire as buttered eggs are done.

A Collar of Brawn

WASH, scrape, and clean very thoroughly a large pig's head, feet, and ears; lay them into salt-and-water, with a little saltpetre, for three hours. To make the collar larger, boil two ox-heels, with the head, feet, and ears, till all the bones can be taken out easily, then put the head round the mould, and the feet and small pieces into the middle; put it together while hot, and press it with a heavy weight till it become cold. Boil for half an hour, in as much of the liquor as will cover the brawn, one handful of salt, one ounce of pepper, black and white mixed, and one or two bay leaves. When cold, pour it over the brawn.

Mock Brawn

TAKE the blade bone out of the shoulder, and boil it gently two hours or more, according to the age of the boar. When it is cold, season it very highly with black pepper, cayenne, salt, a very little allspice, minced onion, and thyme. Let it lie a night in this seasoning; the following day, make a savoury forcemeat of pounded veal, ham, beef suet, minced parsley, thyme, and an onion, a little lemon-peel, salt, nutmeg, white pepper, and cayenne; bind it with an egg beaten, and stuff where the bone has been taken out. Put it into a deep pan with the brown side downwards, and lay under it twigs or small sticks, to keep it from sticking to the bottom; pour in a bottle of beer, and put it into the oven. When nearly done, take it out and clear off all the fat, add a bottle of madeira and the juice of a large lemon, return it to the oven, and bake it till it become as tender as a jelly, so that a straw will pierce it easily. If the boar is an old one, it will require to be baked six or seven hours. This dish is eaten hot.

To Stew Pig's Feet

CLEAN them well, and boil them till they are tender. Brown some butter with flour, and add it to a quantity of gravy or water sufficient to stew the feet in. Season with a minced onion, three sage leaves, salt and black and Jamaica pepper. Cut the feet into two, add them and cover the pan closely; let them stew half an hour. A little before serving, mix in half a table-spoonful of lemon pickle or vinegar, and pick out the sage leaves.

Pettitoes

PARBOIL them, with the liver, heart, and lights; mince the liver, heart, and lights small, simmer it in some gravy or a little of the water, with a bit of butter mixed with flour. Season with pepper, salt, and one or two sage leaves minced; and having split the feet into two, and them, and when they become tender, mix in a tea-spoonful of vinegar. Serve the mince with the pettitoes upon it, and garnish with sippets of bread.

Pork Cheese

CHOOSE the head of a small pig which may weigh about twelve pounds the quarter. Sprinkle over it and the tongues of four pigs, a little common salt and a very little saltpetre. Let them lie four days, wash them, and tie them in a clean cloth; boil them until the bones will come easily out of the head, take off the skin as whole as possible, place a bowl in hot water and put in the head, cutting it into small pieces. In the bottom of a round tin, shaped like a small cheese, lay two strips of cloth across each other – they must be long enough to fold over the top when the shape is full – place the skin round the tin, and nearly half fill it with the meat, which has been highly seasoned with black pepper, cayenne, and salt; put in some tongue cut into slices, then the rest of the meat and the remainder of the tongue, draw the cloth tightly across the top; put on it a board or a plate that will fit into the shape, and place on it a heavy weight, which must not be taken off till it be quite cold. It is eaten with vinegar and mustard, and served for luncheon or supper.

To Stew a Ham

SOAK the ham in lukewarm water for twelve hours, drain it and scrape the rind; put it into a stew-pan with some slices of fat bacon round the sides, four quarts of weak stock, a good deal of parsley, a bunch of sweet herbs, six large onions, four carrots, a little allspice and black pepper, a pint of madeira, and one of port wine over the ham with slices of fat bacon, and put over it a sheet of white paper; stew it eight hours, or ten if it be a very large ham. Before serving, take off the rind, strain the sauce, skim it well, and boil it till reduced to a glaze, and pour it round the ham, or serve it with any other sauce that may be preferred.

To Prepare the Fat of Bacon for Larding

CUT the fat from the pork, rub it with salt, allowing one pound of salt to every ten pounds of lard. Put it in a cellar on a board, laying one piece upon another, put a board on the top, and stones upon the board to firm the lard; when it has lain at least a fortnight in salt, hang it up in a dry place.

Bacon

FOR one side of a large pig allow one pound of coarse common salt, the same quantity of coarse brown sugar, two ounces of saltpetre, and two of rock salt finely pounded. Mix them well, and rub it on both sides of the pork, and when all is rubbed in, then lay it upon a wooden table placed slopingly, and put on it a board and weight. Place under it a vessel to catch the brine. Turn it once in two or three days, and baste it with the brine. Let it remain this way for three weeks, and then hang it up to smoke for twenty-four hours, which will be a sufficient length of time, if the smoke is powerful.

CHAPTER VIII
POULTRY

PREPARATORY REMARKS ON POULTRY

In choosing a turkey, the young cock bird is to be preferred; the best have black legs, and if young, the toes and bill are pliable and feel soft. A hen turkey is chosen by the same rules.

Fowls with black legs are the best; if fresh, the vent is close and dark; if young, the combs are bright in the colour, and the legs smooth – the spurs of a young cock are short.

A goose, if young and fine, is plump in the breast, the fat white and soft, the feet yellow, and but few hairs upon them.

Ducks may be chosen by the same rules, and are hard and thick on the breast and belly.

Pigeons should be quite fresh, the breast plump and fat, the feet elastic, and neither flabby nor discoloured at the vent.

To prepare a turkey for dressing, every plug is carefully picked out; and in drawing turkeys and fowls, care must be taken not to break the gall bag, nor the gut which joins the gizzard, as it is impossible to remove the bitterness of the one, or the grittiness of the other. The hairs are singed off with white paper; the leg-bone is broken close to the foot, and the sinews drawn out – a cloth is then put over the breast, and the bone flattened with a rolling pin, the liver and gizzard, made delicately clean, are fastened into each pinion. A stuffing made with sausage meat, adding some grated bread, and mixing it with the beaten yolks of two eggs, or a stuffing as for a fillet of veal, is then put into the breast, and the turkey, well rubbed over with flour, is put down to roast. It is basted constantly with butter, and when the steam draws towards the fire, it is nearly done; – it is then dredged with flour, and basted with more butter, served with gravy in the dish, and garnished with sausages, or with forcemeat balls (if veal stuffing is used), and bread sauce in a sauce tureen.

To boil a turkey. After being nicely cleaned, it is trussed with the legs drawn in under the skin, stuffed with a forcemeat, as for veal, adding a few chopped oysters; then boiled in a well-floured cloth, and served with oyster, white, or celery sauce, poured over it, and also some in a sauce tureen. Boiled ham, tongue, or pickled pork, is eaten with it. A large-sized turkey will require more than two hours to boil. Turkey, with celery sauce, is stuffed and trussed neatly, laid all over with slices of bacon, tied in a cloth, and boiled in water, with a little salt, butter, and lemon juice added. It is served thickly covered with celery sauce.

Turkey poults are stuffed and roasted in the same manner as a full-grown turkey. They will require rather more than an hour to roast. They are dressed with the heads twisted under the wing, as are also turkeys sometimes, but it seems an injudicious custom, as the side on which the head is cannot be nicely browned, and in carving, the blood from the neck is apt to mingle with the gravy.

To roast a fowl. It is picked, nicely cleaned, and singed; the neck is cut off close by the back; the fowl is then washed, and, if a large one, stuffed with forcemeat. It is trussed and dredged with flour; and when put down to roast, basted well with butter, and frothed up. When the steam is observed to draw towards the fire, it is sufficiently done; served with gravy in the dish, and bread sauce in a butter tureen. A good sized fowl will require above an hour to roast.

Chickens are roasted as the above, and served with gravy in the dish, which is garnished with fried eggs, and bread sauce in a sauce tureen; they will require from half an hour to three quarters to roast.

To boil a fowl. When nicely singed, washed, and trussed, it is well dredged with flour, and put on in boiling water, and if a large one, boiled nearly an hour. It is served with parsley and butter, white, or liver sauce.

Two boiled fowls, served with a tongue between them, make a handsome top dish.

Boiled chickens are improved by being stuffed, and will require nearly half an hour to boil.

To roast a goose. After being well cleaned, picked, and singed, it is washed, made perfectly dry, and stuffed with about four table-spoonfuls of grated bread, an onion finely minced, together with three sage leaves, seasoned with salt and pepper, and mixed with a well-beaten egg; or the stuffing is made of boiled mashed potatoes, seasoned in the same way as the other, and mixed with a beaten egg. If roasted on a spit, each end is tied on tightly; it is basted at first with a little bit of butter, after which the fat that drops from it is used. It is served with gravy in the dish, and apple sauce in a sauce tureen. A large goose will require an hour and a half to roast. At table, an opening is cut in the apron, and a glass of port wine, with which is mixed a large tea-spoonful of made mustard, is poured into the body of the goose. This is also an improvement to ducks. When a goose is too old for the spit, it may be made into a ham, preparing it as for boiling, and following the same rules as for pork hams.

A green goose, about two or three months old, is seasoned with pepper and salt only, and requires to be basted with butter. It requires about an hour to roast.

To roast ducks. They are nicely picked, cleaned, singed, and washed, seasoned with pepper and salt; or stuffed, and served with gravy, as directed in page 137. A duck may be boiled for nearly an hour, and served with onion sauce poured over it.

Forced Goose, or Duck

CUT the goose open at the back, and take out the bones carefully, excepting those of the legs and wings. Take out all the meat from the body, leaving the skin perfectly whole. With the meat pound three quarters of a pound of lean and tender beef, add three handfuls of grated bread, four well-beaten eggs, and half a pint of rich sweet cream; season with black and Jamaica pepper, mace, and salt; mix it all well together; let it stand for half an hour, and then put it into the goose, which sew up, and make it of as natural a form as possible; but take care that it be not too much stuffed. Boil it for half an hour in some good stock, and then put it into a flat tin baking-pan, with some fresh butter over and under it. Bake it in an oven another half hour, and serve it with the following sauce: Brown a table-spoonful of butter with flour, add about a pint of the stock in which the goose has been boiled, three grated onions, two table-spoonfuls of capers cut fine, a little lemon pickle, and a few small pickled onions; boil it about a quarter of an hour, and, just before pouring it over the goose, stir in gradually half a pint of rich cream.

When this dish is to be served cold, the fat being carefully removed from the goose, it may be ornamented or covered with cold jelly made as follows: boil for five hours in four quarts of water the bones of the goose, with three nicely-cleaned calf's feet; strain it, and when cold, take off all the fat, and boil the jelly with some whole black and Jamaica pepper, ginger, and salt; add two ounces of dissolved isinglas, the juice of two lemons, and the beaten whites of three or four eggs; stir it while it is upon the fire, and allow it to boil about ten minutes; then run it through a jelly-bag, and repeat this till it becomes quite clear.

To Roast Pigeons

PICK, clean, singe, and wash them well; truss them with the feet on, and put into them some pepper and salt. While roasting, baste them with butter. A little before serving, dust them with flour, and froth them with butter. Roast them for half an hour. Serve them with parsley and butter in the dish, or make a gravy of the giblets; some minced parsley, seasoned with pepper and salt. Thicken with a little flour and butter; pour it with the giblets into the dish, and then put in the pigeons.

Pigeons with Rice and Parmesan Cheese

PICK and wash clean half a dozen nice pigeons, cut them into quarters; brown some butter with flour, add to it a pint of good stock, with three grated onions, some pepper and salt, stew the pigeons in this till tender, take them out and mix in the juice of one lemon, boil and strain the sauce over the pigeons. Boil about three quarters of a pound of whole rice in a pint and a half of stock, with half a pound of fresh butter, some grated nutmeg and salt; when it is tender, add two handfuls of grated Parmesan cheese. Put more than half of the rice equally round the dish in which the pigeons are placed, and cover them with what remains, brush it over with a well-beaten egg, and then strew it thickly with more Parmesan; cover a flat baking-tin with salt, place the dish upon this, and bake it for nearly three quarters of an hour in a slow oven; it should be of a fine gold colour.

Pigeons en surprise

TRUSS five pigeons as for boiling, and blanch them for an instant in boiling water; after taking them out, put in five fine-headed lettuces, and boil them a quarter of an hour good; put them into fresh water, and then press out all the water; open them in two without detaching the leaves, put in a forcemeat made of the livers of the pigeons, parsley, cibol, five or six leaves of tarragon, a little chervil, two shalots, all finely minced, mixed with a bit of butter or lard, seasoned with salt and pepper, and bound with the beaten yolks of two eggs; then put a pigeon into each lettuce, so as to conceal it completely; tie it up, and stew all slowly for an hour in a fat broth, with parsley, cibol, two onions, a carrot, a parsnip, two cloves, some pepper and salt; then drain and untie them, and serve over them a fine veal cullis, or the sauce in which they were stewed, first straining, taking off the fat, reducing, and thickening it with flour kneaded with a bit of butter the size of a walnut, and the yolks of two eggs.

To Broil Pigeons

CLEAN them and split the backs, season them with pepper and salt; broil, and serve them with parsley and butter poured round them.

To Broil Pigeons Whole

CLEAN them well, cut off the wings and neck, leaving skin enough at the neck to tie; make a forcemeat with bread crumbs, three or four of the livers, one anchovy, some parsley minced, and a quarter of a pound of butter; season it with salt, pepper, and grated nutmeg, bind it with the yolk of an egg beaten up, and put into each pigeon a piece the size of a large walnut; tie the neck and rump, rub them with butter, and dust them with pepper, salt, and nutmeg mixed; broil them over a slow fire; to baste them, put them upon a plate, and with a feather brush them over with butter; broil them of a nice brown colour; serve them with melted butter and parsley, or a thickened brown gravy.

To Stew Pigeons

TRUSS six pigeons neatly, and season them within with pepper, nutmeg, and cloves; fry them in butter, then put them into a stew-pan with a quart of good gravy and a little cider; stew them till tender; a little before serving, add a glass of white wine, and thicken the gravy with butter rolled in flour.

Another way to Stew Pigeons

CLEAN them nicely, truss them as for boiling, put into their inside some pepper and salt; brown in a sauce-pan three ounces of butter with a table-spoonful of flour, add as much gravy or water as will nearly cover the pigeons, put them in with the livers, gizzards, and pinions, salt, and some minced parsley, spinach may also be added; let them stew for three quarters of an hour; add, a few minutes before serving, the yolks of four or six hard-boiled eggs.

Another way to Stew Pigeons

WASH and clean six pigeons, cut them into quarters and put all their giblets with them into a stew-pan, a piece of butter, a little water, a bit of lemon-peel, two blades of mace, some chopped parsley, salt, and pepper; cover the pan closely, and stew them till they be tender; thicken the sauce with the yolk of an egg beaten up with three table-spoonfuls of cream and a bit of butter dusted with flour; let them stew ten minutes longer before serving.

Fowl à la Condé

DRAW the sinews of the legs of two fine white fowls, and take out the breast bones, truss them, and put into each a little lemon juice, and salt, mixed with a piece of butter; place them in a stew-pan, and cover them with thin slices of fat bacon; pour over them the following sauce: Cut into dice a pound of veal, the same quantity of fat bacon, and a little fat of ham, fry all this white in half a pound of butter, adding a bunch of parsley, a little thyme, half a bay leaf, a clove, some salt and pepper, and some boiling water; when sufficiently stewed, strain it over the fowls, and let them stew for three quarters of an hour upon a slow fire, but have a pretty brisk one upon the cover of the stew-pan; drain, and serve them with a rich brown sauce, and a scarlet tongue placed between them in the dish.

To Stew a Fowl with Onions

WASH it clean, dry and truss it as for boiling, put a little pepper and salt into it, rub it with a bit of butter, as also the sauce-pan; put in with the fowl a pint of veal stock or water, a little pepper and salt, turn it now and then, and when it becomes quite tender, add twelve or sixteen small onions, and let them stew for half an hour; a young fowl will take one hour, and an old one three hours, to stew

Hashed Fowl

CUT a cold roasted fowl into pieces as for a fricassee, put the trimmings into a sauce-pan with two or three shalots, a little lemon-peel, a blade of mace, a quarter of a pound of lean ham, and a pint of stock; simmer it for half an hour, strain it, put a bit of butter into a sauce-pan, and when melted, dredge in as much flour as will dry it up, stirring it all the time; then add the gravy, let it boil a minute, and put in the fowl, also a little pepper, salt, and a dust of sugar. Before serving, squeeze in a little lemon juice.

To Pull a Chicken

HALF roast a chicken or fowl, skin and pull off in small flakes all the white meat and the meat of the legs, break the bones, and boil them in a little water till the strength be drawn out, strain it, and when it becomes cold, skim and put it into a sauce-pan with a little mace, white pepper, and salt; add a bit of butter mixed with flour, and rather more than a quarter of a pint of cream, then put in the meat, and a little mushroom powder; before serving, add the squeeze of a lemon.

Another way to Pull a Chicken

PICK all the white meat from the bones of a cold roasted fowl, cut off the legs, and keep the back and sides in one. Score, and season the legs and back with pepper and salt, and broil them; warm up the white meat in some sauce made of the bones boiled in a little water, and which has been strained and thickened with a piece of butter, mixed with flour, a little milk, and the yolk of an egg beaten up and seasoned with white pepper and salt; serve the broiled back upon the mince, and the legs at each end.

To Souse a Fowl

CUT into joints a hot roasted fowl, sprinkle over it of pepper and salt a dessert-spoonful each, and two or three onions cut small, pour on it nearly a pint of boiling water, cover it with another dish, and let it stand till cold; a cold fowl may be prepared in the same way, and put into a sauce-pan for a few minutes to heat.

Poulet à la Francaise

Cut a chicken up the back, fill it with thick slices of fat bacon, and put a slice of bread over the bacon, sew it up, and tie it round with a bit of packthread, and then roast it.

Chicken à la Creme

HALF roast a chicken; while it is hot, take out the entire breast, leaving perfectly whole the pinions, legs, and skin; boil in milk two ounces of bread crumbs and an ounce of bacon very finely chopped, and some chopped parsley; season the meat of the breast of the chicken with pepper, salt, nutmeg, and a little grated lemon-peel; pound it with the boiled bread crumbs, and add an egg beaten up; stuff it so as to represent a whole chicken, sift over it grated bread, and heat it thoroughly in the following sauce: A pint of new milk, one ounce of butter, kneaded in flour, a slice of bacon not very fat, two shalots, a little salt and white pepper; put the chicken into a dish, brown it with a salamander, and strain the sauce over it.

Capons à la Turque

PICK, and clean very nicely, two fine capons; wash the inside perfectly clean with warm water, and let them soak in warm water for a quarter of an hour; dry them well, and put into them some rice which has been boiled till soft in some rich well-seasoned stock, truss, and cover them with layers of bacon, wrap them in paper, and roast them for an hour by a hanging-jack; serve them, putting all around the dish a part of the rice which was prepared for the stuffing, and pour over the fowls a veloutée sauce.

One fine large fowl may be dressed in this manner.

A Fowl à la Holandaise

Make a forcemeat of grated bread, half its quantity of minced suet, an onion, or a few oysters and some boiled parsley, season with pepper, salt, and grated lemon-peel, and an egg beaten up to bind it. Bone the breast of a good-sized young fowl, put in the forcemeat; cover the fowl with a piece of white paper buttered, and roast it rather more than half an hour; have ready a thick batter made of flour, milk, and eggs, take off the paper, and pour some of the batter over the fowl; as soon as it becomes dry add more, and do this till it is all crusted over, and of a nice brown colour; serve it with melted butter and lemon pickle, or a thickened brown gravy.

Cold Chicken Fried

Cut the chicken in quarters, and take off the skin, rub it with an egg beaten up, and cover it with grated bread seasoned with pepper, salt, grated lemon-peel, and chopped parsley, fry it in butter, thicken a little brown gravy with flour and butter, add a little cayenne, lemon pickle, and mushroom catsup.

To make a Pillau

Wash very clean two pounds of rice, stew it till perfectly tender with a little water, half a pound of butter, some salt, whole white pepper, cloves, and mace, and keep the stew-pan closely covered; boil two fowls and one pound and a half of bacon, put the bacon in the middle, and the fowls on each side, cover them all over with the rice, and garnish with hard-boiled eggs and fried whole onions.

Chicken Baked in Rice

Cut a chicken into joints as for a fricassee, season it well with pepper and salt, lay it into a pudding dish lined with slices of ham or bacon, add a pint of veal gravy, and an onion finely minced; fill up the dish with boiled rice well pressed and piled as high as the dish will hold, cover it with a paste of flour and water; bake it one hour, and before serving take off the paste.

Chickens in Peas

Cut the chickens into joints, and put them into a sauce-pan with nearly a quart of young peas, a bit of butter, a cibol, and sprig of parsley; put them on the fire, dusting them with flour, moisten them with gravy, and boil them till the sauce is thick. Add a little salt just before serving, and, if liked, a little sugar.

To Fricassee a Chicken with White Sauce

CUT the chicken into joints, parboil it with the liver and gizzard, and take off the skin; thicken a little of the liquor with a bit of butter mixed with flour, heat it, and put in the chicken with a little white pepper, grated lemon-peel and nutmeg, a blade of mace, and some salt; boil it for about twenty minutes, take it off the fire, pick out the lemon-peel and mace, and stir in gradually half a pint of cream with the yolk of two well-beaten eggs, make it hot, but after adding the cream do not let it boil; the liver and gizzard may be dressed with it, or scored, seasoned with pepper, cayenne, and salt, broiled and served with the fricassee.

A cold chicken or fowl may be dressed in this way, with a little white stock for sauce; or they may be dressed with a little brown sauce, browning some butter and flour, adding with the liquor a minced onion, a little catsup, black pepper, nutmeg, salt, and a bit of lemon-peel which last take out before serving.

To Fricassee Chickens

WHEN well washed, cut the chickens into joints, scald, and take off the skin; put them into a stew-pan, with an onion, cut small, a bunch of parsley, a little thyme, lemon-peel, and grated nutmeg, a slice of ham, and a bit of butter the size of a walnut; let them stew a quarter of an hour, add some white stock thickened with flour and butter. Take out the parsley, ham, thyme, and lemon-peel; and a little before serving, beat up the yolks of three eggs in half a pint of cream, and stir it in gradually.

Another way to Fricassee Chickens

PUT into a stew-pan half a pint of water, three ounces of butter, a table-spoonful of flour, some salt, and white pepper; stir all together till it is hot, and add a chicken cut into joints and skinned, with one or two onions minced and a blade of mace. Stew it for an hour; and a little before serving, add the yolks of two eggs beaten up with two table-spoonfuls of cream; stir it in gradually, taking care it does not boil.

Broiled or Grilled Chickens

PICK and singe them nicely, wash them clean, and dry them in a cloth; cut them down the back, truss the legs and wings, as for boiling; flatten them, and put them upon a cold gridiron; when they become a little dry, put them upon a plate, baste them with butter, and strew a little salt and pepper over the inside, which part is laid first upon the gridiron; baste them frequently, and let them broil slowly for about half an hour. Serve them very hot, with melted butter poured over them, or plenty of stewed mushrooms. The livers and gizzards may be broiled with them, fastened into the wings, or well seasoned, broiled, and served with the chickens.

Boudin à la Richlieu

PUT the crumb of a good-sized stale roll into a basin, and cover it with milk, about as warm as when it comes from the cow; let it stand half an hour, then with a spoon take off all the milk, and put the bread into a sauce-pan, with a good bit of butter, one onion chopped very finely, a little parsley and herbs. Keep stirring it on the fire till it becomes quite stiff, then take it off, and add the yolk of an egg, which must be well beaten into it; let it then cool before adding the meat, which may be of chicken, veal, or lamb, that has been already dressed. Half a pound of any of these meats, pounded or grated very fine, is the quantity required. Beat two eggs, whisking up well both yolks and whites; add them to the meat and bread, and beat them altogether for some time; the more they are beaten, the lighter the boudin will be. Butter a shape, and fill it; tie the shape in a cloth, and put it on to boil for three hours. A rich sauce, thickened and seasoned, is to be poured over the boudin when it is dished.

Burdwan Stew

CUT into joints a cold fowl or duck, put it into a stew pan, with half a pint of gravy, a large wine-glass of ale, half a one of white wine, the juice of half a lemon, a tea-spoonful of soy and cayenne; of mushroom catsup, lemon pickle, cucumber vinegar, corach escavecke, a dessert-spoonful each. Heat all thoroughly before serving.

To Pot Chicken with Ham

POUND, in a marble mortar, the white meat of a cold fowl; season it with mace, white pepper, and a little salt; pound a piece of ham fat and lean, red beef or tongue; season it with pepper; put a layer alternately of each kind of meat into a jar, and press it closely; bake it an hour and a half, and when cold, cover it with clarified butter. Cold turkey, veal, venison, or hare, may be done in this manner.

To Boil a Duck

MAKE a paste, allowing half a pound of butter to a pound of flour. Truss a duck as for boiling; put into the inside a little pepper and salt, one or two sage leaves, and a little onion finely minced; enclose the duck in the paste, with a little jellied gravy. Boil it in a cloth, and serve it with brown gravy poured round it.

To Stew Duck

CUT one or two ducks into quarters; fry them a light brown in butter; put them into a sauce-pan, with a pint of gravy, a tea-cupful of port wine, four onions whole, black pepper, and some salt, a bunch of parsley, two sage leaves, a sprig of winter savory, and sweet-marjoram. Cover the pan closely, and stew them till tender; take out the herbs and pepper; skim it; if the sauce be not sufficiently thick, mix with two table-spoonfuls of it a little flour, and stir it into the sauce-pan; boil it up, and garnish the dish with the four onions.

Another way to Stew Duck

PUT into a duck some pepper, salt, a minced onion, and one leaf of sage also minced; half roast it; brown, with two ounces of butter, a table-spoonful of flour; add as much weak stock or water as will half cover the duck, and some pepper and salt; put in the duck, and a quart of green peas; let it stew for half an hour, stirring it now and then. For a variety, a dozen of middling-sized onions may be substituted for the peas, and stewed the same length of time.

Cold roasted duck may be dressed exactly in the same manner; and to hash it, cut it into joints, and heat it thoroughly in gravy, adding a little soy, and a glass of port wine.

To Stew Goose Giblets

CLEAN the giblets nicely, parboil them. Cut the necks into three, the gizzards into four, the livers, pinions, and heads into two; take the outer skin off the feet, stew them in one quart of good stock, with a bunch of sweet herbs, a few pepper-corns, two cloves, one anchovy, two large onions, and a table-spoonful of catsup. When the giblets are tender, take them out, and strain the sauce; thicken it with flour and butter, and a table-spoonful of white wine or cream. Add the giblets, and serve them quite hot; put sippets of thin toasted bread round the dish. Ox tail may be dressed in the same way as the above.

Another way to Stew Goose Giblets

PREPARE the giblets as before directed, parboil them; thicken a pint of gravy soup, or the liquor they have been parboiled in, with flour and butter, boil and skim it; add the giblets, with an onion cut small, some pepper and salt; let them stew till they become very tender. Before serving, add a tea-spoonful of vinegar, and a tablespoonful of white wine.

To make a giblet pie, prepare them in the same manner, and add with the gravy a glass of port or white wine.

Sandwiches

CUT some bread into thin slices, pare off the crust, and spread a little butter on them; cut them nicely into oblong pieces, put between each some bits of fowl, and then thin bits of ham, both nicely trimmed; add a little mustard and salt. Any cold roasted or potted meat may be used. Serve them for luncheon, garnished with curled parsley.

Devil

SCORE the leg of a roasted turkey, goose, or fowl; pepper and salt it well, broil it, and pour over it the following sauce made quite hot: Three table-spoonfuls of gravy, one of melted butter, and one of lemon juice; a large wine-glass of port wine; of mustard, chili vinegar, Harvey sauce, and mushroom catsup, a tea-spoonful each; a little cayenne and black pepper. The devil may be served without a sauce, and be more highly seasoned.

Eggs à la Tripe

CUT into thick round slices a dozen of hard-boiled eggs, and put them into the following sauce: Cut three large white onions into dice, fry them white in butter, and when nearly done, dust them with flour, and moisten them with some milk and a few spoonfuls of cream; keep stirring with a wooden spoon, to prevent their burning. When the sauce is done, grate in a little nutmeg, season with a little salt and pepper, and put in the eggs.

Glass Eggs

BUTTER a dish, and break into it a piece of butter nearly as large as an egg; add a tea-cupful of cream, and drop in four or five eggs; put upon each a little pepper and salt, set the dish upon a stove, and serve it when the eggs are firm, which may be in ten or fifteen minutes.

Poached Eggs

FILL a frying-pan with boiling water, break some eggs one by one into a tea-cup, and slip them one by one into the water. When the white part is sufficiently done, take them out with an egg slice, and lay them upon toasted bread cut into square bits, or upon spinach. To poach eggs nicely, they must be quite fresh.

Buttered Eggs.

BEAT and strain ten or twelve eggs; put a piece of butter into a sauce-pan, and keep turning it one way till melted; put in the beaten eggs, and stir them round with a silver spoon till they become quite thick. Serve them in a dish upon buttered toast. They may be eaten with fish, fowl, or sausages.

Fried Eggs.

EGGS boiled hard, cut into slices, and fried, may be served as a second course dish, to eat with roasted chickens. Or, make three little omelets, of three eggs each, seasoned with parsley, cibol, salt, and pepper; as they are done lay them out on the top of a sauce-pan, and roll them tight up; cut each omelet in two, so as to make six pieces in all; dip them into beaten eggs, then into bread crumbs, and fry them.

To Preserve Eggs.

POUR a gallon of water over a pound of unsliced lime, stir it well; the following day, pour off the clear water into a jar, and put in the eggs as they are laid. In this manner they will continue perfectly good for six month or more. To know when eggs are fresh, hold them to a light; if they are transparent and clear, it is a good sign; if they are pricked, they may be considered old; if they have a stain attached to the shell, they are good for nothing.

CHAPTER IX
CURRIES

Currie

CUT a fowl into small pieces, skin it, and let it blanch in cold water for two hours; mince an onion very small, and put it into a sauce-pan, with two ounces of butter, and a large table-spoonful of flour of rice stirred in by degrees; brown it well, and when just boiling, add a quart of cold water, with the pieces of fowl and a large table-spoonful of currie powder mixed in it. Let it boil till the fowl be quite tender, and just before serving, squeeze the juice of half a lemon over the blade of a hot knife into it. Vinegar will answer instead of the juice; and if it be required very fine, in place of rice, thicken it with an ounce of sweet almonds blanched and pounded.

Currie of Veal

Cut part of a neck of veal into cutlets, and make a gravy of the trimmings; season it with pepper, salt, and an onion; strain and thicken it with flour and butter, and add two spoonfuls of currie powder. Fry the cutlets with an onion minced very small, in butter, of a light brown colour, and then stew them in the prepared gravy till they become quite tender. Before serving, add the juice of half a lemon, and a little chili pepper.

A Dry Currie

Skin and cut a fowl into joints, or take off small cutlets from the best end of a neck of veal; fry in butter three or four minced onions, and drain them; then fry the fowl or veal, and dust it with three tea-spoonfuls of currie powder, and a quarter of a tea-spoonful of cayenne. Put the fried meat and onions into a stew-pan, with a little salt, half a pint of milk, and the same quantity of water keep the pan closely covered, and let it stew till perfectly tender, and ten minutes before serving, add two tea-spoonfuls of lemon juice.

Currie Pimento

Having skinned and cut a fowl into joints, and rubbed it well with currie powder, and a little cayenne, stew it gently, and till very tender, in some well-seasoned veal or mutton broth, to which some whole rice is added with the fowl; and before serving, mix in a little lemon juice and salt.

Kebobbed Currie

Cut into small bits, veal, or the meat of fowl, and pickled pork, and, with slices of onion, fasten them alternately upon small skewers, three or four inches long. Pound in a mortar a couple of onions, a small apple, a head of garlic, and a large table-spoonful of currie powder, with some gravy; press it through a sieve. Fry in butter a finely minced onion; dust the meat with turmeric, fry it, and add the strained liquor, with two bay leaves, a little salt and pepper. Let it stew till the liquor be nearly wasted, and the flavour be very rich. Before serving, squeeze in the juice of half a lemon, and take out the bay leaves.

Cuchon, a China Dish

Is dressed much in the same manner, without pork, and not put upon skewers, but cut into very small pieces.

A Fish Currie

After a cod-fish, haddock, or mackerel has lain some hours in salt, cut it into pieces, and stew it in water sufficient to cover it, into which a large table-spoonful of currie powder has been mixed. Fry, in a quarter of a pound of butter, a shalot and two or three onions minced, a little pepper and salt. When well browned, add it to the fish, and stew all together till it be quite tender. Sprats make a good currie, but should be stewed in less water.

Cold Fish Currie

Cut into round thick slices cold boiled salmon, soles, cod, or haddocks; fry them in butter. In as much vinegar as will cover the fish, boil a little salt, two or three cloves of garlic, a good deal of turmeric finely pounded, three cloves, a little nutmeg, ginger, and black pepper pounded, as much as will season it highly, and pour it hot over the fish. Cover it closely, and when it has stood twenty-four hours, it will be fit for use, and should be eaten cold with boiled rice.

Indian Currie

Stew in two ounces of butter, for ten minutes, a teaspoonful of cayenne, and one of Jamaica pepper, a dessert-spoonful of pounded coriander seed, six small onions, and two heads of garlic minced. Cut the fowl or rabbit into small pieces, and cover it over with the curd of sweet milk. Put the whole into a stew-pan, with as much boiling water as may be desired for sauce, and let it simmer till very tender.

Currie of Veal, Rabbit, or Fowl.

Fry sliced veal, rabbit, fowl, or sweetbreads, in a good deal of butter, dusting it with flour. Dust one side with currie powder; then turn and dust the other, strewing over it finely-minced onions, taking care not to burn them. When the meat is of a light brown, add some white stock, with a little salt; stew it till tender. Before serving, skim off the fat, and add a tea-spoonful of lemon juice or vinegar. Rabbit, fowl, and sweetbreads should be parboiled.

To Boil Rice

Wash the rice perfectly clean, and put on one pound in two quarts of cold water; let it boil twenty minutes, strain it through a sieve, and put it before the fire; shake it up with a fork every now and then, to separate the rains, and make it quite dry. Serve it hot.

Currie Powder

POUND extremely fine, in a mortar, six ounces of coriander seed, three ounces of black pepper, one ounce and a half of fennigreck seed, one ounce of cummin seed, three ounces of turmeric, and three quarters of an ounce of cayenne; sift it through muslin, and put it before the fire for four or five hours, stirring it every now and then. Keep it in a bottle with a glass stopper.

Another way to make Currie Powder

ONE pound of rice picked clean, eight ounces of coriander seed, four ounces of cummin seed, and four ounces of yellow mustard seed – put all these into a frying-pan, stir it constantly until it becomes quite hot, taking care it does not brown; then grind it in a peppermill, with six ounces of cayenne, and two ounces of turmeric. Sift it through muslin, and grind the coarser part, repeating this till it is all sufficiently fine, and keep it in bottles with glass stoppers.

Another way to make Currie Powder

DRY and finely pound the following ingredients: Half a pound of turmeric, two ounces of ginger, the same of black pepper; of cummin seed, fennigreck seed, and cayenne, half an ounce each. Mix them thoroughly, and dry it before the fire for some hours. Keep it in a wellcorked bottle.

Cooke's currie paste will be found an excellent preparation for all the varieties of currie. Directions for using it are given with each pot – 99, Hatton Garden.

CHAPTER X
GAME

PREPARATORY REMARKS ON GAME

IN choosing venison, the fat of that which is good is thick, clear, and bright; the cleft part smooth and close. When the venison is perfectly fresh, it is hung in a cool place, and carefully wiped dry every day. When extreme tenderness is required from long keeping, but without its having a high flavour, it is well rubbed over with powdered charcoal.

The haunch is the prime joint, and when it is required to be roasted, it is first well washed in lukewarm milk-and-water, and then made quite dry before it is spitted. It is then covered with a sheet of well-buttered white paper, over which is laid a coarse paste of flour-and-water, about a quarter of an inch thick; this is again covered with buttered white paper, and tied on with packthread. A substantial fire being made, the haunch is put down, and constantly basted with fresh beef dripping, till nearly done, when the paste is taken off, the meat well basted with butter, and lightly dredged with flour, till it froths and becomes of a fine light brown colour. It is served with its own gravy in the dish, if there be enough of it; also a sauce tureen of good brown gravy, and one of currant jelly sauce beat up, and melted with a little port wine and sugar.

A large haunch takes about four hours to roast.

A neck and shoulder, when roasted, is managed in the same way as the haunch, omitting the paste; but it is more frequently used for soups, pasties, and collops.

Hare. When fresh, the body is stiff; and if young, the claws are smooth and sharp, the ears tender and easily torn. Hares are kept from a week to a fortnight for roasting; but for soup, they cannot have been too recently killed.

Rabbits are chosen by the same rules as hares.

Wild fowl, in general, is chosen by the same rules as tame poultry. The birds should be plump and fat, and hard in the vent. If the skin comes off when rubbed hard with the finger, they are stale. Old birds improve by keeping for some time; young birds are best if dressed soon; and small birds, of all descriptions, should be immediately dressed. In warm weather, a stopper of charcoal should be put into the vent of all game, and a string tied tightly round the neck.

To roast pheasants and partridges, they are picked, cleaned, and nicely singed; a slit is made in the back part of the neck, and the craw taken out, leaving on the head, the feet twisted closely to the body, the claws cut off, and the head turned under the wing. Both sorts are roasted by the directions for roasting a turkey or a fowl. A pheasant is served with gravy in the dish; partridges, with a gravy, or laid upon buttered toast, and melted butter poured round them. Bread sauce is served with both. A pheasant will require nearly an hour to roast; partridges half an hour. Guinea and peafowl are roasted in the same way as pheasants.

To roast black-cock, follow the directions for roasting pheasants and partridges; it will require an hour, and is served with gravy in the dish, and bread sauce in a sauce tureen.

Moorfowl are roasted in the same manner, and require three quarters of an hour. They may be served upon buttered toast, or with gravy in the dish, and bread sauce in a sauce tureen. It improves moorfowl and partridges to put a bit of butter into them, when trussing them for roasting; and sometimes a bit of fresh undressed beef is substituted for the butter, which is taken out before serving.

To restore tainted game or poultry, pick it carefully clean, and wash it, then put into each bird a little newly made pounded charcoal, tied in a bit of muslin. Before serving, take out the bag, which will have a most offensive smell, while the bird will be left perfectly sweet.

To roast a wild-duck. It should be roasted by a quick fire, well basted with butter, and browned. It will require nearly three quarters of an hour, and when to be served, some beef gravy is poured through the duck into the dish, and in a sauce tureen some hot port wine is served. The carver makes four cuts along the breast, it is then sprinkled with salt and a little cayenne, the juice of half a lemon is squeezed over it, and the port wine is then poured over all.

To roast a wild-goose, the same directions are followed as for a wild-duck, allowing more time to roast it according to the size of the bird.

Widgeons and teal are dressed in the same manner as the wild-duck, and are roasted in ten minutes, and may be served upon fried bread crumbs.

Woodcocks and snipes are roasted without being drawn; a piece of toasted bread buttered is put under each bird, to catch the trail; they are well basted with butter, and served upon the hot toast over which they were roasted; a rich brown gravy, or melted butter, is poured round them. Woodcocks will require half an hour, snipes and quails fifteen or twenty minutes, to roast.

Ortolans and green plovers are not drawn, and are roasted and served in the same manner as woodcocks.

To roast larks, wheatears, and other small birds, they are nicely picked, gutted, cleaned, and trussed; brushed over with melted butter, and rolled in grated bread, then spitted on a bird spit, which is fastened upon a larger one. They are basted with butter, and sprinkled with some bread crumbs. They will require nearly fifteen minutes to roast, and are served upon fried bread crumbs, and brown gravy in a sauce tureen.

Wild pigeons may be roasted, or made into a pie.

Plovers' eggs are boiled hard, and served in a napkin, or with green moss put round each in the dish.

To Stew Moorfowl

TRUSS them, keeping on their heads, but draw the legs within the body; mix well some salt and pepper with flour and a piece of butter, and put a small bit into each bird; fry them all over of a nice brown in butter. Brown some butter and flour, and add to it some good gravy, seasoned with pepper, salt, mace, and two cloves pounded; boil up the sauce, put in the moorfowl, and let them stew very slowly till tender. A little before taking them off the fire, add a table-spoonful of mushroom catsup. If the birds are old, stew them for two hours; if young ones, half that time.

Cold roasted moorfowl are dressed exactly in the same way, only cut into joints, and stewed very gently nearly as long. Half an hour before serving, a small tea-cupful of port wine should be added.

To Stew a Hare

CUT a hare into pieces, put it into a sauce-pan, with half a pint of port wine, the same of good gravy, and a pint of cider, two or three small onions, a quarter of a pound of butter, some salt and pepper. Let it all stew till the hare be quite tender, and the liquor a good deal reduced.

Another way to Stew a Hare

BONE a hare; make a sauce with the bones and a little beef stock, adding sweet herbs, spices, and some port wine; thicken it with browned butter and flour. Stuff the hare with forcemeat, or with equal quantities of minced mutton and suet, well-seasoned; put it into the boiling sauce, and let it stew two hours. Place the hare on a dish, and strain the sauce over it.

To Roast and Stuff a Hare

WHEN the hare is skinned and cleaned, lay it into cold water for three or four hours, changing the water several times, then rub it well with a little salt, and wash it thoroughly; dry it well. Make a stuffing of the raw liver minced, by no means parboiled, grated bread crumbs, twice the quantity of chopped fat bacon, and a bit of butter; season with grated nutmeg, lemon thyme, lemon peel, pepper and salt; an anchovy may be added. Bind with a beaten egg, put it into the hare, sew it up, and truss it properly. Put into the dripping-pan warm salt-and-water, baste the hare well till all the blood be out of it, pour away the water, and put in a quart of milk, with which it must be constantly basted till it be nearly done; then baste and froth it with butter. Serve with gravy, and, in a butter tureen, currant jelly sauce.

Hashed Hare

CUT it into small pieces, heat it thoroughly in highly seasoned gravy, adding, with the stuffing, a tea-spoonful of vinegar, and a glass of port wine. The legs may be scored, seasoned with pepper and salt, rubbed with cold butter, and broiled. They may be served with the hash, or on a separate dish.

Stewed Hare

CUT off all the meat, in small pieces; make a strong gravy with the bones of the hare, a bunch of sweet herbs, and two onions; strain it, and put in the hare, with two table-spoonfuls of port wine, two or three thin bits of bacon, a little salt, mace, and a clove pounded. Cover it closely, and let it stew two hours, and if the gravy is much reduced, add a little more.

Florentine Hare

AFTER a hare has hung a week, prepare it as for roasting, and take out all the bones of the body, leaving the head whole; making a stuffing as before directed, lay it over the inside of the hare, roll it up, sew it, and fasten it with packthread; roll it into a cloth, and boil it in two quarts of water an hour and a half. When the liquor is reduced to a quart, add a pint of port wine, and of lemon pickle and mushroom catsup, a table-spoonful each, also a tea-spoonful of browning; thicken it with flour and butter, and stir it till reduced a little. Serve with forcemeat balls, morels, and mushrooms; make the ears lie back upon the roll, and garnish with barberries and curled parsley.

Hare and Venison Collops

THESE are dressed in the same manner as mince collops of beef, only that, in place of the seasoning of the collops of beef, they have a little Jamaica pepper, salt, and some port wine.

To Hash Venison

FOR a gravy, boil a part of the bone and trimmings of the cold haunch in a little water; season with a few peppercorns and some salt; strain and thicken it with a bit of butter. Rolled in flour, add a glass of port wine, and a table-spoonful of mushroom catsup, and one of currant jelly. When hot, add the venison cut into thin slices, heat it thoroughly, and serve with sippets of toasted bread.

To Stew Partridges

TRUSS the partridges as fowls are done for boiling; pound the livers with double the quantity of fat bacon and bread crumbs boiled in milk; add some chopped parsley, thyme, shalots, and mushrooms; season with pepper, salt, grated lemon-peel, and mace. Stuff the inside of the birds, tie them at both ends, and put them into a stew-pan lined with slices of bacon; add a quart of good stock, half a pint of white wine, two onions, a bunch of sweet herbs, and a few blades of mace; let them stew gently till tender; take them out, strain and thicken the sauce with flour and butter, make it hot, and pour it over the partridges.

To Stew Young Partridges

TRUSS them as for roasting, stuff the craws with forcemeat; lard down each side of the breast, roll a lump of butter in pepper, and salt, and beaten mace, put it into the inside of each bird, and sew it up; dredge them with flour, and fry them of a light brown in butter; put them into a stew-pan, with a quart of good gravy, half a tea-cupful of white wine or of table-beer, the same of mushroom catsup, a dessert spoonful of lemon pickle, half a tea-spoonful of mushroom powder. Cover the pan closely, and let them stew half an hour; take them out, and thicken the gravy with a little flour mixed in water; boil it up, and pour it upon the partridges. Garnish the dish with forcemeat balls and hard-boiled yolks of eggs.

Perdrix aux Choux

TRUSS the birds as for roasting, rub them slightly with garlic, put over each breast a piece of bacon, and into the inside a bit of butter the size of a walnut, dusted with flour, and seasoned with pepper, salt, and thyme; half roast, and then stew them with some good gravy, a bit of lean ham or bacon, one spoonful of white wine, the same of mushroom catsup and of lemon pickle, a little cayenne, one anchovy, and one shalot. Have ready boiled the hearts of some cabbages, put them into the stew-pan, and stew them altogether till the partridges be sufficiently tender. Before serving, take out the ham.

To Roast Rabbits

TRUSS them for roasting, and stuff them with the liver minced raw, grated bread, and ham, butter or suet, and chopped parsley, seasoned with a little lemon thyme, grated nutmeg, salt and pepper, and bound with an egg beaten. Sew them up, and roast them before a quick fire, and baste them with butter. Serve them with gravy, or melted butter with lemon pickle in it. Two will take an hour to roast. They may be larded with bacon.

They may also be fricasseed or fried, cut into joints, with plenty of fried parsley, and served with a sauce made of the liver and some parsley chopped, and mixed in melted butter, with a little pepper and salt; or made into a pie the same as chickens.

Rabbits Stewed with a Brown Sauce, or with a White Sauce

WASH and clean the rabbits well, let them lie for two or three hours in cold water, cut them into joints, wash and dry them in a cloth, dust them with flour, and fry them of a light brown with butter, and stew them in the following sauce: Brown three ounces of butter in a stew-pan, with a table-spoonful of flour, a minced onion, some pepper and salt; add a pint of gravy and the rabbits, stew them till they are tender, and a little before serving, stir in a table-spoonful of catsup.

When it is wished to dress them with a white sauce, the rabbits are not fried, but stewed in white stock, which is seasoned with white pepper and salt, and thickened with a piece of butter mixed with flour. A few minutes before serving, a little cream is added, and a table-spoonful of lemon pickle.

Rabbits Smothered in Onions

PREPARE them as before directed, and truss them; thicken a sufficient quantity of white stock, in which boil them with a piece of butter mixed with flour; season it with salt and pepper, and when it boils, put in the rabbits with plenty of onions cut in quarters. Let them stew till they are tender. Serve them with the onions put all over the rabbits.

Ragout of snipes

PICK six or eight snipes very nicely, but do not wash them; take out the inside. Roast the birds, and cut off all the meat from the breasts, in thin slices; pound the bones, legs, and backs in a mortar, and put them into a stew-pan, with the juice of a lemon, a little flour, and some well-seasoned gravy; boil it till it be thick, and well flavoured with the game, then strain it. Cut half a pound of ham into thin long slices, and heat it in a little butter, with two minced shalots; put it, with the breasts of the snipes, into the strained sauce, and let it boil. Pound the inside or trail, with a little salt, spread it over thin bits of toasted bread, and hold it over a hot salamander. Put the ragout upon this, and place the ham round it.

CHAPTER XI
GRAVIES, SAUCES, FORCEMEATS, AND OTHER THINGS

BROWNING for made dishes. Put into a sauce-pan one pound of good brown sugar, stir it constantly over a slow fire, boil it till it is as thick as treacle, and resembles it in colour; take the pan off the fire, stir it for a minute or two, and pour in very slowly a quart of boiling water, stirring constantly; put it again on the fire, and boil it for a little; pour it into a bowl, and when cold, bottle it. This browning will keep good for a year, and very little of it serves for colouring soups, gravies, or sauces.

To clarify butter. Put the butter cut into slices into a nicely-cleaned brass pan, stir it gently till dissolved; when it boils, draw the pan to the side of the fire, skim it, and let it boil gently a second time, and if any scum again rises, take it off; let it settle for two or three minutes, and strain it gently through a sieve which has a piece of muslin laid into it.

Fresh beef suet, picked free from skin and sinews, is dissolved in the same way; it is then strained through muslin into small jars, and when cold, covered with bladder, or it may be strained into cold water; and the cake when cold, wiped dry, folded in white paper, and kept in a linen bag.

Beef suet will keep fresh for some time if finely chopped and dredged well with flour, and kept in white paper bags in a cool place.

Beef and mutton drippings are clarified exactly in the manner butter is done, and each kept in a separate jar.

To melt hog's lard, put it into a jar placed in a pot of water, or water bath, strain it into clean bladders or small jars, and cover them with paper. Thus prepared, it will keep a good length of time, and is the best thing for frying fish in.

To fry parsley, wash it, pick it clean, and put it into fresh cold water; take it out, and then throw it into boiling lard or dripping, when it will instantly become crisp. It is then taken out with a slice.

White Roux, or White Thickening for Sauces and Made Dishes

Melt gradually, over a slow fire, a good piece of butter, and dredge in a sufficiency of flour to make it like a thin paste; keep stirring it for a quarter of an hour, and then put it into a small jar to be kept for use.

Brown Roux, or Thickening

Put into a nicely-tinned sauce-pan about a pound of fresh butter, melt it slowly, and dredge in flour till it be like a paste, carefully stirring it all the time, put it for a few minutes upon a quick fire and then return it to where there is less heat, and stir it till it assumes a light brown colour, when it may be put into a jar.

These thickenings keep for some time.

Gravy made from Bones

Break into small pieces a pound of beef, mutton, or veal bones, if mixed together so much the better; boil them in two quarts of water, and after it boils, let it simmer for nearly three hours; boil with it a couple of onions, a bunch of sweet herbs, some salt and pepper; strain, and keep it for making gravy or sauces. The bones of broiled or roasted meat being scraped, washed clean, and boiled in less water, answer equally well for this purpose.

To make Gravy

Cut down into slices four pounds of lean beef, rub the bottom of the pot with butter, and put in the meat; turn it frequently till it be well browned, and do it slowly, then add four quarts of cold water; when it has boiled two hours, put in a dessert-spoonful of whole black pepper, and the same of Jamaica pepper, one carrot, and three onions; let it stew gently for four hours longer, strain it, and when it is required for use, take off the fat. This gravy answers for all made dishes when brown gravy sauce is used.

Another way to make Gravy

Dip a beef liver into water, wipe it, and rub over it some salt and coarse brown sugar; let it lie seven or eight days, turning it frequently; boil, in as much water as will quite cover the liver, one ounce of saltpetre, and three of common salt; wipe the liver dry, and put it into the pickle; let it lie for six weeks, then hang it to dry. Boil for an hour and a half, in a pint of water, a slice of this nearly the size of three fingers, a carrot, an onion, and some pepper; strain, and use it for gravy.

To Clarify Gravy

Clarify gravy drawn from beef or veal, with the beaten whites of eggs, allowing one white to a quart. Gravies and soups which are to be clarified should be made very strong, and be highly seasoned.

To make Gravy without Meat

Slice three onions, and fry them brown in a little butter; add them to half a pint of water, and the same of beer, put in some peppercorns, salt, a little lemon-peel, three cloves, a little mace or Jamaica pepper, a spoonful of walnut pickle, and one of mushroom catsup, of soy and essence of anchovy a dessert-spoonful each, a small bunch of sweet herbs, and a quarter of a slice of bread toasted brown on both sides; simmer all together in a closely-covered sauce-pan for twenty minutes, then strain it for use, and when cold, take off the fat. It will taste exactly like a gravy made with meat.

Another way to make gravy without meat

KNEAD a good deal of flour into a piece of butter the size of an egg, fry it in a frying-pan over a clear fire, stir it constantly with a wooden spoon till it become a nice brown colour, taking particular care that it be made perfectly smooth; pour in some boiling water, add a little finely-minced onion, some whole black pepper, and a little salt, put it into a small sauce-pan, cover it closely, and simmer it for a short time; strain, and mix with it a little mushroom catsup, and port wine.

To make gravy for roast meat

WHEN the spit is taken from the meat, a good deal of gravy will run into the dish; pour in addition to this a little boiling water and salt over the under part of the bone of the beef, or over the shank-bone of a leg or shoulder of mutton, taking great care not to let it run over the meat.

Another way is:

ABOUT a quarter of an hour before the meat is taken from the fire, put a common dish with a tea-spoonful of salt in it under the meat; pour over it a small tea-cupful of boiling water; when it has all run into the dish, remove it, baste and froth the meat, and pour the gravy into the dish on which the roast is to be served.

To Draw Gravy

PUT a few pounds of gravy-beef sliced, and a little whole black pepper, into a jar with a cover to fit closely; set the jar into a pot of cold water, and when it boils, add as it wastes more hot water, and keep it boiling gently for six or seven hours, when the richest gravy imaginable will be obtained. It may be used in that state, or reduced with water.

To make a Pint of Rich Gravy

BROWN a quarter of a pound of butter, dredging in two table-spoonfuls of flour, and stirring it constantly; add a pound of gravy-beef cut into small bits, and two or three onions chopped. When it becomes brown, add some whole black pepper, one carrot, a bunch of sweet herbs, and three pints of water; let it boil gently till reduced to one, then strain it. This gravy may be served with roasted turkey or fowl.

Essence of Ham for Gravies

Pick off all the bits of meat from a ham-bone, pound it, break the bone, and put both into a sauce-pan, together with nearly half a pint of water, and a bunch of sweet herbs; simmer gently for some time, stirring it occasionally; then add a pint of good beef gravy, and some black pepper, and continue to simmer it till it be well flavoured with the herbs; strain, and keep it for improving rich gravies and sauces of all descriptions.

Lobster Catsup

Choose a lobster that is full of spawn, and weighing as nearly as possible three pounds; pick out all the meat, and pound the red part or coral in a marble mortar; when completely bruised, add the meat, pound and moisten it with a little sherry wine, mix with it a tea-spoonful of cayenne, add the rest of the bottle of sherry, and mix it thoroughly; put it into two wide-mouthed bottles, and on the top put a small table-spoonful of whole black pepper, cork the bottles tightly, and tie them over with leather. It will keep good a twelvemonth, and exactly resembles fresh lobster sauce. Four table-spoonfuls heated in melted butter are sufficient for a large sauce-tureen.

Oyster Sauce

Beard the oysters, and put them into a sauce-pan, with their liquor strained, a good bit of butter, a few black peppercorns, a little salt, cayenne, and a blade of mace. Simmer them gently for fifteen or twenty minutes, on no account allowing them to boil. Knead some flour into a bit of butter, and melt it, adding a little milk; pick out the peppercorns and mace from the oysters, and pour upon them the melted butter.

Another Oyster Sauce

Beard and scald the oysters, strain the liquor, and thicken it with a little flour and butter, squeeze in a little lemon juice, and add three table-spoonfuls of cream. Heat it well, but do not let it boil.

Another Oyster Sauce, for Boiled Fowl, or Turkey

Put into a stew-pan, with their liquor, two dozen of oysters, and a little water; when it boils, take out the oysters with a silver spoon, and drain them upon a hair sieve; let the liquor settle, and pour it off from the sediment; beard the oysters. Put into a stew-pan with one or two spoonfuls of fine flour, two ounces of fresh butter, and stir it till the flour is a little fried; add the liquor of the oysters, and a pint of cream; stir, and let this boil a quarter of an hour, then add two table-spoonfuls of bechamel, or a little highly-seasoned gravy, and the oysters, which must be made quite hot.

Mock Oyster Sauce

PUT into a sauce-pan two or three chopped anchovies, a quarter of a pint of water, a little mace, and one or two cloves; let them simmer till the anchovies be quite dissolved. Strain it, and when cool, add a tea-cupful of cream; thicken it with a piece of butter rolled in flour, and heat it up. It may be poured over boiled fowls or veal.

Chesnut Sauce, for a Roast Turkey

SCALD a pound of good chesnuts in hot water for five minutes, skin them, and stew them slowly for two hours in white stock, seasoned and thickened with butter and flour. Cut a pound of pork sausages into bits about an inch long, dust them with flour, and fry them a light brown; lay them into the dish on which the turkey is to be served, and pour the chesnuts and sauce over them.

Some people prefer the fried sausages stewed a little with the chesnuts; but this method makes the sauce of a darker colour.

White Sauce, for Fowls or Turkey

PUT on, in a quart of water, the necks of fowls, a piece of the scrag-end of a neck of mutton, two blades of mace, twelve black peppercorns, one anchovy, a small head of celery, a slice from off the end of a lemon, and a bunch of sweet herbs; cover it closely, and let it boil till reduced to nearly half a pint; strain, and put to it a quarter of a pound of butter dredged with flour; let it boil for five minutes, and then add two spoonfuls of pickled mushrooms. Mix with a tea-cupful of cream, the well-beaten yolks of two eggs, and some grated nutmeg; stir this in gradually, and shake the pan over the fire till it is all quite hot, but do not allow it to boil.

To make Bechamel, or White Sauce

CUT into small pieces half a pound of veal and a quarter of a pound of lean ham, put it into a sauce-pan, with eight white peppercorns, a shalot, two cloves, two blades of mace, a bay leaf, some parsley, and a quart of veal broth or water. Let it boil till it is strong and well flavoured; strain, and thicken it with a little flour rubbed smooth in cold water. Boil it up, and mix in very slowly a pint, or nearly so, of cream.

Sauce for Roast Beef

MIX well together a large table-spoonful of finely grated horse-radish, a dessert-spoonful of made mustard, and half a one of brown sugar, then add vinegar till it be as thick as made mustard. Serve in a sauce tureen.

Another Sauce for Roast Beef

PUT into a stone jar one gill of soy, two of vinegar, two of water, a good-sized stick of horse-radish, and two sliced onions. Cover the jar closely, and set it into a pan of cold water; when it boils, let it simmer for two or three hours.

To make a Quart Bottle of Fish or Meat Sauce

TO half a bottle of vinegar put one ounce of cayenne, two cloves of garlic, one table-spoonful of soy, two of walnut, and two of mushroom catsup. Let it stand six days, shaking it frequently, then add the remaining half of the bottle of vinegar; let it stand another week, strain, and put it into small bottles.

Pink Sauce, for Fish

PUT into a pan, or wide-mouthed jar, one quart of good vinegar, half a pint of port wine, half an ounce of cayenne, one large table-spoonful of walnut catsup, two ditto of anchovy liquor, a quarter of an ounce of cochineal, and six cloves of garlic. Let it remain forty hours, stirring it two or three times a day; run it through a flannel bag, and put it into half-pint bottles

Fish Sauce

MIX well with two ounces of melted butter, of mushroom catsup, essence of anchovies, and lemon pickle, a table-spoonful each, a teaspoonful of soy, and a little cayenne. Boil it before serving.

Escavecke Sauce, for Cold Game, Fowl, or Meat

BEAT, in a marble mortar, the following ingredients: Five cloves of garlic, six cloves of shalot, as much pounded ginger as will lie upon a sixpence, and the same of cayenne, a table-spoonful of coriander seed, and a little salt. Pour upon them, boiling hot, a pint of the best white wine vinegar; add the peel of a lemon, cut very thin. When cold, put the whole into a bottle, cork it tightly, and shake it well before using.

White Sauce

THICKEN half a pint of cream with a little flour and butter, four shalots minced, a little mace and lemon-peel; let it boil, and a little before serving, add a spoonful of white wine, the well-beaten yolk of an egg, the squeeze of a lemon, and a tea-spoonful of anchovy liquor. This sauce will answer for boiled fowls, or for a fricassee.

Liver Sauce

WASH the liver of a fowl perfectly clean, and boil it four minutes in a little water; bruise it, and rub it through a sieve, with a part of the water in which it was boiled; dust about two ounces of butter with flour, add a table-spoonful of cream, and melt it, shaking it round one way; when quite hot put in the liver, a little pepper, salt, and grated lemon-peel and nutmeg, heat it thoroughly, and pour it round the fowl. Serve parsley and butter in a sauce tureen.

Quin's Sauce

HALF a pint of mushroom pickle, the same of walnut pickle, three whole and three pounded cloves of garlic, six anchovies bruised, and a tea-spoonful of cayenne. Mix together in a large bottle, shake it daily for three weeks, then strain, and bottle it for use.

Another Quin's Sauce

ONE pint of port wine, one of mushroom catsup, one of walnut liquor, one of essence of anchovies, and a tea-spoonful of cayenne; mix all together, and boil it for a quarter of an hour. If essence of anchovies is not to be had, boil half a pound of anchovies in a quart of water till reduced to a pint. Strain, and use it.

Melted Butter

DUST a little flour over a quarter of a pound of butter, put it into a sauce-pan, with about a wine-glass of water; stir it one way constantly till it be melted, and let it just boil. A round wooden stick, called in Scotland a thevil, is the best thing to stir butter with in melting. If the butter is to be melted with cream, use the same proportion as of water, but no flour; stir it constantly, and heat it thoroughly, but do not let it boil.

To oil butter, cut about a quarter of a pound into slices, put it into a small jar, and place it in a pan of boiling water. When oiled, pour it off clear from the sediment.

French Melted Butter

MIX, in a stew-pan, with a quarter of a pound of fresh butter, a table-spoonful of flour, a little salt, half a gill of water, half a spoonful of white vinegar, and a little grated nutmeg. Put it on the fire, stir it, and let it thicken, but do not allow it to boil, lest it should taste of the flour.

Bread Sauce

BOIL, in a pint of water, the crumb of a French roll or of a slice of bread, a minced onion, and some whole white pepper. When the onion is tender, drain off the water, pick out the peppercorns, and rub the bread through a sieve; then put it into a sauce-pan, with a gill of cream, a bit of butter, and a little salt. Stir it till it boil, and serve it in a sauce-tureen.

Another Bread Sauce

MIX, in rather more than half a pint of milk or water, a slice of grated bread, a dessert-spoonful of potato flour, a small onion pounded, a bit of butter, the size of a walnut, a few whole peppercorns, a little mace, and salt. Boil it well, pick out the spices, and mix it smooth. Serve quite hot.

Fish Sauce

CHOP two dozen of whole anchovies, mix with them half a pint of anchovy liquor, two shalots, cut small, and three pints of port wine, one of vinegar, one lemon sliced, one handful of scraped horse-radish, and ten blades of mace, one nutmeg, twelve peppercorns, six cloves, all bruised, and one table-spoonful of flour of mustard. Boil these together about fifteen or twenty minutes; when cold, strain and bottle it, waxing the corks. It will keep good a year. A table-spoonful improves oyster sauce, and that quantity is sufficient for a sauce-tureen of melted butter.

Tomata Sauce

BAKE six tomatas in an oven till quite soft; take out the pulp with a tea-spoon, add salt, cayenne, and vinegar, till reduced to the consistence of thick cream.

Dutch Sauce

Beat up the yolks of six eggs, mix in a little flour, cream, salt, and lemon vinegar. Strain it through a sieve, add a small piece of fresh butter, two blades of pounded mace, and a little white pepper. Put it into a sauce-pan, and stir it till it is almost boiling.

Another Dutch Sauce, for fish, or Boiled Fowls

Mix, with two ounces of fresh butter, one tea-spoonful of flour, two table-spoonfuls of cold water, the same quantity of vinegar, and one well-beaten egg; put it into a sauce-pan, and stir it over the fire till it be quite hot, but do not allow it to boil.

Another Dutch Sauce

Put into a stew-pan a tea-spoonful of flour, four table-spoonfuls of elder vinegar, a quarter of a pound of fresh butter, the yolks of five eggs, and a little salt; keep stirring it over the fire, and work it well till thick. If it be not curdled, it will not require to be strained. Season with pepper.

Poivrade Sauce for Cold Meat

Chop finely six shalots and a handful of picked and washed parsley; mix with it a little vinegar, mustard, cayenne, oil, cold gravy, and salt.

Another Poivrade Sauce for Cold Meat

Bruise the yolk of a hard-boiled egg with a little salt; add mustard, oil, soy, chopped parsley, and chives, and pour it over slices of any cold meat.

Another Poivrade Sauce

Put into a sauce-pan a little butter, two onions sliced, carrots, and parsnips cut, a clove of garlic, two shalots, two cloves, thyme, basil, a laurel leaf, and a dust of flour; moisten with a glass of port wine, a glass of water, and a spoonful of vinegar; let it boil half an hour; season with pepper and salt, skim and strain it. In this sauce any cold roasted meat may be warmed up.

Sauce for Pike

With a pint of cream a table-spoonful of anchovy sauce, the same of soy, and two of catsup, a piece of butter rolled in flour; put it into a sauce-pan, and stir it one way till nearly boiling.

White Sauce for Pike

SIMMER, till half wasted, two table-spoonfuls of white wine, one of vinegar, half a small onion, and some grated nutmeg; add a piece of butter rolled in flour, then a small tea-cupful of cream; heat it thoroughly, stirring it all the time, and taking care that it do not boil.

Fish Sauce

A quart of port wine, half a pint of best vinegar, one pound of bruised anchovies, one ounce of mace and one of cloves, half an ounce of black pepper, one large onion, and the peel of one lemon; boil all these ingredients together over a slow fire till a pint is wasted; then strain, and bottle it, and keep it closely stopped.

Sauce for Boiled Beef

MINCE a large onion, parboil it, and drain off the water; put the onion into a sauce-pan, with a table-spoonful of finely-chopped parsley, some good gravy, and one ounce of butter dredged with a little flour. Let it boil nearly ten minutes, and add a spoonful of cut capers, which must be thoroughly heated before the sauce is served.

A Sauce for any Sort of Meat

BOIL and strain three table-spoonfuls of gravy, two of vinegar, a blade of mace, a little pepper, salt, and a large sliced onion.

Sauce Tournée

To a little white thickening add some stock drawn from the trimmings of veal, poultry, and ham; do not make it too thick. Boil it slowly with a few mushrooms, a bunch of parsley, and some green onions; strain and skim it well, and use it as required.

German sauce is made as the sauce tournée, adding the beaten yolks of two or more eggs, and is used for ragouts, fricassees, and any made dish which may require a rich white sauce.

Sauce d'Attelets

TAKE of finely-minced parsley, mushrooms, and shalots, a table-spoonful each; fry them with a little butter, and then dredge in a little flour; moisten the mixture with some good stock, season it with pepper and salt, and boil it till it begins to thicken; then take it off the fire, and add the well-beaten yolks of two or three eggs. Stir it well all the time it is making.

This sauce is generally used instead of butter, when crumbs of bread are to be put over any thing.

A Sauce

MIX together a pint of vinegar, two shalots or heads of garlic, a tea-spoonful of cayenne, three large tablespoonfuls of Indian soy or mushroom catsup, and two of walnut pickle. Let it stand a week, shaking it daily; strain, and bottle it for use.

Lobster Sauce

BRUISE the body, add it to some thick melted butter; pull the flesh into small bits, and mix all together with some rich beef gravy; boil it up, and before serving, add a little salt, and squeeze in a little lemon juice.

Another Lobster Sauce

POUND very finely the spawn of a lobster, rub it through a sieve, mix it with a quarter of a pound of melted butter, then add the meat of the lobster cut into small bits. Make it quite hot, but do not allow it to boil.

Sauce Robart, for Beef Steaks, or Mutton Chops

PUT into a sauce pan a little gravy, two ounces of butter dredged with flour, a small slice of raw ham, and two or three minced onions; when the onions are browned, dust in a little more flour, and add nearly a pint of gravy, a little salt and pepper, a tea-spoonful of mustard, and a table-spoonful of vinegar. Boil it for some minutes; strain and serve it.

A Sauce for Broiled Meat, Game, or Poultry

BRUISE the yolks of two hard-boiled eggs with a little water and salt; bone one anchovy, mince it, and a small onion, two shalots, a little parsley and tarragon, and a few capers; mix them with the egg, add a table-spoonful of fine oil, a little mustard, two table-spoonfuls of lemon, and one of tarragon vinegar; mix all exceedingly well together, put it into a sauce-tureen, and serve it with the broil; or it may be served with cold veal.

A Bunch of Sweet Herbs

IS made up of parsley, sweet marjoram, winter savory, orange and lemon thyme; the greatest proportion of parsley.

To Prepare Onions for Seasoning

PEEL and mince three or four onions, put them into a sauce-pan with a little cold water. Let them boil till quite tender, and then pulp them with the liquor through a hair sieve, when it may be mixed with any made dishes or sauces.

Celery Sauce

CLEAN nicely, and cut into small pieces, the white part of two or three heads of celery; boil it in a little white stock, season with white pepper, salt, and a little nutmeg. When it is tender, add a piece of butter rolled in flour, and three table-spoonfuls of cream; heat it, but do not let it boil. Pour it over boiled turkey or fowl.

Sauce Piquante

PUT a little chopped shalot and a few spoonfuls of gravy into a sauce-pan; let it boil till the gravy be nearly boiled away, but not burned to the bottom of the sauce-pan; add as much braise as may be required for the sauce, season with pepper and salt, boil it a few minutes, then add a little lemon juice, sugar, and a tea-spoonful of garlic vinegar.

N.B. Braise is an onion stuck with cloves, and boiled till tender in gravy and white wine.

White Italian sauce

PEEL some mushrooms, and throw them into a little water and lemon juice, to keep them white. Put into a stew-pan two-thirds of sauce tournée, and one-third of good veal stock, two table-spoonfuls of finely-chopped mushrooms, and half a table-spoonful of washed and chopped shalots; let it boil till well flavoured, and then serve it. The mushrooms should be as white as possible.

White Sharp Sauce

BOIL with a little tarragon, or tarragon vinegar, if the tarragon is not to be had, four table-spoonfuls of white wine vinegar, and about twenty peppercorns; reduce this to one-fourth, and add it to six table-spoonfuls of sauce tournée, and two of good stock; boil and strain it; put it again on the fire, and thicken it with the beaten yolks of two eggs, a small bit of butter, a little salt and cayenne. Just before serving, stir in a spoonful of cream

White Sauce for Fish

Four anchovies chopped, two glasses of white wine, a large one of vinegar, an onion stuck with three cloves, and cut into quarters; let all these simmer till the anchovies dissolve; strain it, and add a quarter of a pound of butter kneaded in a table-spoonful of flour. When it has melted, stir in gradually, one way, half a pint of cream, taking care that it do not boil. When thoroughly heated, serve in a sauce-tureen.

Parsley and Butter

Pick and wash clean a large bunch of parsley, tie it up, and boil it for a few minutes in water; drain and chop it very finely, add to it some melted butter, and make it quite hot. It is better to be made thick with parsley.

Onion Sauce

Boil twelve or more onions in water; when it boils, pour it off, add more hot water, and when the onions are tender, strain and mash them in a bowl, add a piece of butter, a little salt, and one or two spoonfuls of cream. Heat it before serving. An apple may be boiled with the onions.

Apple Sauce

Pare, core, and slice some apples; boil them in water, with a bit of lemon-peel; when tender, mash them; add to them a bit of butter the size of a walnut, and some brown sugar, heat, and serve in a sauce-tureen.

Egg Sauce

Boil three or four eggs about a quarter of an hour; put them into cold water, take off the shells, cut three of the whites and four yolks into small pieces, mix them with melted butter, and heat it well.

Shrimp Sauce

Pick some shrimps nicely from the shell, put them into melted butter, add a table-spoonful of lemon pickle and vinegar; heat it.

Mint Sauce

Pick and wash some green mint; add, when minced, a table-spoonful of the young leaves, to four of vinegar, and put it ln to a sauce-tureen, with a tea-spoonful of brown sugar.

Shalot Sauce

BOIL a few minced shalots in a little clear gravy and nearly as much vinegar, add a few peppercorns and a little salt. Strain, and serve it in a sauce-tureen.

Sorrel Sauce

PICK and wash some sorrel, put it into a stew-pan with a little water, stir it, to prevent its burning, and when it is tender, drain and mince it finely; fry it for half an hour in a stew-pan with a little butter, then dredge in a table-spoonful of flour, moisten it with boiling cream, and let it stew on a slow fire for an hour; add a little salt, and if too acid, a little sugar. Before serving, thicken with the beaten yolks of four eggs.

Maitre d'Hotel Maigre

PUT into some nicely-melted butter a little chopped parsley, salt, and lemon juice; one or two minced shalots may be added, and heat it all together.

The Veloutée

BOIL quickly about the same quantity of good stock, and of sauce tournée; when the sauce is thick, add some boiling cream, and let it boil up twice; season with a little salt, and strain it through a tammy.

Caper Sauce

CHOP some capers, and add them to melted butter, with a table-spoonful of lemon pickle; heat it well, taking care not to let it boil after the capers and lemon pickle are put in.

The Old Currant Sauce for Venison

BOIL in water for a few minutes an ounce of nicely cleaned currants, add three table-spoonfuls of grated bread, a piece of butter the size of a walnut, four cloves, add a glass of port wine; stir it till it boil, and serve it hot.

Horse-Radish Sauce, to eat with Hot or Cold Meat

MIX a tea-spoonful of mustard, a table-spoonful of vinegar, and three of cream; add a little salt, and as much finely-grated horse-radish as will make the sauce the consistence of onion sauce.

Sauce for Hashes and Made Dishes

A pint of port wine, twelve anchovies chopped, a quarter of a pint of vinegar, as much beaten pepper as will lie on half a crown, two or three cloves, a blade or two of mace, a nutmeg bruised, one small onion minced, two bay leaves, a little lemon thyme, marjoram, and parsley, and a piece of horse-radish about the length of a finger, split into quarters; put all into a sauce-pan, and let it simmer till the anchovies are dissolved; then strain it, and, when cold, bottle it for use.

Green Gooseberry Sauce

Boil some green gooseberries in water till soft, and sweeten them with brown sugar.

Pudding Sauce

Mix with half a pint of melted butter two wine glasses of sherry, and a table-spoonful of pounded loaf sugar; make it quite hot, and serve in a sauce-tureen, with grated nutmeg on the top.

Fish Sauce

A table-spoonful of anchovy juice, one of soy, and two of mushroom catsup, mixed in a quarter of a pound of melted butter.

Another Fish Sauce

Three anchovies and an onion chopped, and a small bit of horse-radish boiled in some stock, then strained, and thickened with a piece of butter rolled in flour.

Another Fish Sauce

Boil in half a pint of water one or two anchovies, two cloves, a blade of mace, a bit of lemon-peel, a few peppercorns, and two table-spoonfuls of port wine; strain and thicken it with a piece of butter rolled in flour.

Fish Catsup

A quart of port wine, half a pint of vinegar, three quarters of a pound of anchovies with their pickle, a quarter of an ounce of mace, twelve cloves, six races of white ginger, a table-spoonful of black pepper, a stick of horse-radish, half the peel of a lemon, three shalots, and a bunch of thyme; mix all together, stew them upon a stove for an hour; when cold, strain, bottle, and cork it tightly.

Coratch

Two heads of garlic cut, one ounce of cayenne, two spoonfuls of Indian soy, one spoonful of walnut catsup, half a drachm of cochineal pounded – mix these in a pint of the best wine vinegar, let them infuse for a fortnight, and then filter it through paper.

To Make Mustard

Mix very smoothly the best flour of mustard with cold water, add a little salt, and a very little sifted loaf sugar; it will keep good some time if put into a small jar and covered closely, or it may be mixed with milk instead of water, but in this way it will not keep so long.

Mushroom Sauce for Boiled Turkey or Fowl

Pick clean and wash a pint of small mushrooms, rub them with flannel, put them into a sauce-pan, with a blade of mace, a little salt, grated nutmeg, a piece of butter rolled in flour, and a pint of cream, keep stirring them till they boil, then pour them round the turkey, fowl, or chicken.

Poor Man's Sauce

Chop a few shalots very fine, and mix with them a little pepper, salt, vinegar, and water, and serve in a sauce-tureen. This sauce is generally served with young roasted turkeys.

White Sauce for Boiled Fowls

Melt in a tea-cupful of milk a large table-spoonful of butter kneaded in flour, beat up the yolk of an egg with a tea-spoonful of cream, stir it into the butter, and heat it over the fire, stirring it constantly; chopped parsley improves this sauce. It also may be made melting the butter with water, and mixing milk with the egg.

La Sauce Robert

Cut some onions small, fry them of a fine brown; moisten them with some veal gravy, skim it, put in a little pepper and salt, and just before serving, mix in a spoonful of mustard.

Salade Sauce

Bruise the yolk of a hard-boiled egg with a small, tea-spoonful of salt, then add a dessert-spoonful of mustard, and stir in gradually a large table-spoonful of olive oil, oiled butter, or cream, then by degrees mix in two or three table-spoonfuls of vinegar; serve it in a saucetureen, or mix it with the salad. Instead of the hard egg, some persons prefer the sauce made with the yolk raw.

Another Salad Sauce

RUB smooth a hard-boiled egg, beat well a raw egg, and mix them together with a little water, a tea-spoonful of salt, one of cayenne, one of black pepper, and one of mustard, a table-spoonful of vinegar, one of essence of anchovies, and five of rich cream.

The artist, as he styled himself, who invented this salad sauce, drove in his carriage to his employers, and charged them ten shillings and sixpence for each visit!

Forcemeat

MINCE very finely the following ingredients: three ounces of fresh beef suet, one of fat bacon, three of raw or dressed veal, two of grated bread, a little grated lemon-peel, nutmeg, white pepper, salt, and finely-minced parsley; mix all well together, and bind it with the beaten yolks of eggs; make it into balls the size of a large nutmeg, and fry them in clarified beef dripping; or use it for stuffing.

Forcemeat for Fish

PICK from the bones the meat of a large haddock, or any sort of white fish, mince it finely, and add the same proportions of minced suet and of grated bread, a few chopped oysters, and some boiled parsley chopped; season with a little pounded onion, Jamaica and cayenne pepper, salt, nutmeg, and lemon-peel; mix all well together, and bind it with the well-beaten yolks of eggs, roll it into small balls, and fry them of a light brown, in fresh beef drippings. Or,

It may be made with the meat of the tail, claws, and the soft part of the body, of a lobster; pound it and half an anchovy; mix with it an equal quantity of grated bread, a few chopped oysters, and some butter; season with grated nutmeg, lemon-peel, salt, Jamaica and cayenne pepper; bind it with the beaten yolks of eggs; make it into small balls, and fry them.

Stuffing without Meat

SEASON a quarter of a pound of finely-minced beef suet, and an equal quantity of grated bread, with grated nutmeg, lemon-peel, lemon thyme, and parsley, salt, and pepper; mix it well together, and bind with a well-beaten yolk of an egg, when it may be used for stuffing veal and fowl.

Stuffing for a Hare

PARBOIL the liver and mince it; add an equal quantity of grated bread, double the quantity of fat bacon chopped, a bit of butter the size of a walnut. Season with pepper, salt, nutmeg, chopped lemon thyme, and parsley; bind with a beaten egg. If quite fresh, the liver may be minced raw.

Forcemeat Balls

MAY be made of pounded veal or mutton, minced beef suet, or fat of veal, taking an equal quantity of meat, suet, and grated bread crumbs, adding a bit of fat bacon chopped, seasoning with salt, pepper, and grated nutmeg, and mixing all well together with a beaten yolk of an egg.

Stuffing for Turkey or Fowl

WASH a quart of oysters in their own liquor, strain it, and put into it the oysters, with a little mace, whole pepper, and lemon-peel; when parboiled, chop small a dozen and a half, add an equal weight of grated bread, twice the quantity of finely-minced beef suet, the yolk of three hard-boiled eggs, one anchovy, a little salt, pepper, nutmeg, lemon-peel, and some minced parsley; bind it with the beaten yolks of two eggs. For the sauce, boil with the liquor of the oysters a pint of white stock, half a pint of white wine, one anchovy, pepper, salt, and nutmeg; strain it, and add a quarter of a pound of butter rolled in flour, heat it up with the remainder of the oysters.

Stuffing for Fowls, Pheasants, or Turkeys

A little hog's lard, the liver of a fowl minced, a little parsley and cibol minced, and a very little salt; the mixture to be put inside the fowl, which is then sewed up.

Gravy and Stuffing for Ducks

BOIL all the giblets excepting the liver for an hour in a pint of water with a chopped onion, some salt, and pepper; strain, and add a very little browning, with a tea-spoonful of coratch, and one of mushroom catsup; for the stuffing, mince the raw liver with two sage leaves, a small onion, some pepper and salt, a bit of butter, and grated bread crumbs.

Forcemeat Onions

PEEL four or five large onions, scoop out the inside, fill them with forcemeat, and roast them in an oven. They may be served with roast turkey or fowl.

Kitchen Spice for White Sauce

POUND two ounces of white pepper, a quarter of an ounce of mace, grate one nutmeg, and the peel of one lemon; mix all together in a bottle.

Another Kitchen Spice for General Use

ONE ounce of black pepper, and of Jamaica pepper, cinnamon, nutmeg, and ginger, half an ounce each, and eight cloves; pound and mix altogether in a bottle. A little of each kind of spice should be well dried, pounded and kept separately in small bottles, which should be labelled.

Mushroom Powder

PICK, skin, and clean half a peck of mushrooms, throw them into cold water, drain, and put them into a saucepan, with two spoonfuls of white pepper, a quarter of an ounce of mace, and five cloves pounded, simmer and shake them till the liquor is wasted away, but be careful they do not burn; lay them upon dishes, and put them into a cool oven to dry, then beat them to a powder; put it into wide-mouthed bottles, and tie leather over the corks; keep them in a dry place. Or, skin and wipe with flannel some small fresh-gathered mushrooms, lay them upon a tin, and dry them in a moderate oven, or in a Dutch oven; put them into small paper bags, and hang them near the kitchen fire, and, when required for use, rub them to a powder.

Ragout Powder

TWO ounces of truffles, two of dried mushrooms, the peel of a lemon, and the same of a Seville orange grated, half a grated nutmeg, half an ounce of mace, the same of black pepper, and one drachm of cayenne, dry them all well before the fire, pound them to a fine powder, add one ounce of salt, sift the powder through a sieve, and keep it in a bottle for use.

Fried Bread Crumbs

PUT into a frying-pan or sauce-pan a piece of butter, oil, and skim it, pour it from the sediment, return it to the pan, throw in two or three spoonfuls of grated bread, keep stirring them constantly till of a beautiful yellow brown, and drain them before the fire.

Glaze, Brown and White

Brown glaze is made of stock clear and pale in the colour; should it not be sufficiently clear, it must be made so with the white of eggs, and run through a jelly bag; a little white wine is added, and it is then boiled until it hang to the spoon, when it may be put into a glaze kettle; this kettle is made similar to a milk kettle, and of the best block tin; when the glaze is wanted for use, the kettle is put into a stew-pan of water by the side of a stove; it should be of a beautiful clear yellow brown, and is put over ham, tongue, and many made dishes, with a brush. A white glaze is made in the same manner as the brown, substituting white for brown stock.

A Rich Cullis, or Gravy

Cut into slices some lean beef, veal, and mutton; cover the bottom of the sauce-pan with the veal, then put in a few slices of fat bacon, next a layer of beef, add a few onions sliced, and the red part of one or two carrots, a little mace, two or three cloves, some whole black and Jamaica pepper, and two or three bay leaves, above that the mutton; cover the pan closely, set it on a slow fire, and when the meat is a fine brown, mix quite smooth a small quantity of flour in water, stir it in, and then add as much boiling water as will cover the meat well, and a little salt; cover the pan closely, and let it stew an hour and a half; strain, and keep it for use; it will continue good for eight or ten days.

To Pot Mushrooms

Put into salt-and-water a peck of clean-picked button mushrooms, take them out immediately, and wipe them with a bit of flannel; dip them into the same water, and put them into a sauce-pan with a dessert-spoonful of salt, six blades of mace, and two cloves; let them stew till half the liquor is consumed, then add two pounds and a half of fresh butter, and stew them till no liquor is to be seen at the bottom of the pan; put them into pots, and when cold, tie a bladder closely over them.

CHAPTER XII
VEGETABLES

PREPARATORY REMARKS

Vegetables are always best when newly gathered, and should be brought in from the garden early in the morning; they will then have a fragrant freshness, which they lose by keeping.

They must be cleaned with the greatest care, the outside leaves of every description of greens removed, and they, and all other vegetables, more particularly when not recently gathered, should be laid for several hours in cold water, and well shaken to throw out the insects. A teaspoonful of salt should always be put into the water in which they are to be boiled, and if it is hard, a tea-spoonful of salt of tartar, or potash, may be added, to preserve the green colour of the vegetables.

All vegetables should be boiled quickly, and, with the exception of spinach, in an open vessel, skimming them carefully.

Kitchen greens should be kept in a cool and shady place. Potatoes, carrots, turnips, and beet-root should be stored up, without being cleaned from the earth adhering to them, in layers of sand, or laid in heaps, and covered with earth and straw. Parsnips and skirrets, not being injured by frost, are generally left in the ground, and taken up as wanted. Onions are stored in a warm, dry place, never in a cellar; they are sometimes strung in bunches, and suspended from the roof, and, more effectually to prevent their growing, some people select the finest bulbs, and singe the roots with a hot iron.

Herbs of all sorts should be gathered when in flower, and on a dry day, and being well cleaned from dust and dirt, they are tied up in small bunches, and dried before the fire in a Dutch oven. They may then be kept in paper bags labelled; or rubbed to a powder, sifted, and put into bottles.

To Boil Large White Cabbages

Wash and clean them thoroughly; if large, cut them into quarters or divide them; put them on in boiling water, and throw in a little salt; boil them for nearly two hours.

To Boil Young Green Cabbages

Wash and clean them well, put them on in boiling water with a little salt in it, and let them boil quickly from three quarters to nearly an hour; serve with melted butter.

To Boil Green Peas

After being shelled, wash them, drain them in a cullender, put them on in plenty of boiling water, with a teaspoonful of salt, and one of pounded loaf sugar; boil them till they become tender, which, if young, will be in less than half an hour; if old, they will require more than an hour; drain them in a cullender, and put them immediately into a dish with a slice of fresh butter in it; some people think it an improvement to boil a small bunch of mint with the peas; it is then minced finely, and laid in small heaps at the end or sides of the dish. If peas are allowed to stand in the water after being boiled, they lose their colour.

To Boil Carrots

SCRAPE, wash, and clean them; if large, cut them into two or four pieces, put them on in boiling water with some salt in it, and boil them from two to three hours. Very young carrots will require one hour.

To Boil Parsnips

SCRAPE and wash them nicely; when large, divide them; boil them in milk-and-water till quite tender; they will take nearly as long to boil as carrots. They may also be mashed like turnips.

To Boil Potatoes

WASH and pare them, throwing them into cold water, as they are pared; put them into a sauce-pan, cover them with cold water, and throw in a little salt; cover the sauce-pan closely, and let them boil quickly for half an hour, pour off the water immediately, and set the pan by the side of the fire to dry the potatoes.

Another way to Boil Potatoes

WASH them very clean, put them on in cold water, cover the sauce-pan, and let them boil quickly; as soon as the water boils, pour it off, and cover them with cold water, add a little salt, and when the water boils, pour it off instantly, when the potatoes will be sufficiently done; dry them, and take off the skins before serving. Some people prefer potatoes being steamed. New potatoes require much less boiling, and will be done enough in twenty minutes; if allowed to remain long upon the fire, they will become water-soaked. Before dressing, they are washed, and the skins rubbed or scraped off.

Mashed Potatoes

BOIL the potatoes, peel and mash them very smoothly; put for a large dish four ounces of butter, two eggs beat up in half a pint of good milk, and some salt; mix them well together, heap it upon the dish with a table-spoon to give it a rough and rocky appearance, or put it on the dish and score it with a knife, dip a brush or feather into melted butter, and brush over the top lightly; put it into a Dutch oven, and let it brown gradually for an hour or more.

To mash potatoes in a plain way, mix with them two ounces of butter, half a pint of milk, and a little salt. When mashed potatoes are not browned, it is a great improvement to add white pepper, salt, and one onion minced as finely as possible; heat the potatoes in a sauce-pan, and serve them hot.

To Broil Boiled Potatoes

AFTER boiling potatoes, not quite sufficiently to send to table, put them on a gridiron over a clear fire, and turn them frequently till they are of a nice brown colour all over; serve them hot; take care they do not become too hard, as that spoils the flavour.

To Brown Potatoes under Meat while Roasting

AFTER being boiled, lay them on a dish, and place it in the dripping-pan, baste them now and then with a little of the meat dripping, and when one side is browned, turn the other; they should all be of an equal colour.

Potato Ribands

WASH four or five large potatoes, scrape them, and cut them into thin strips round and round, keeping as nearly to one width as possible; throw them into cold water as they are cut, and then fry them of a light brown in boiling beef dripping; strew over them a little salt and pepper, and before serving, drain them upon a dish turned up before the fire.

Potato Eggs

MASH perfectly smooth six or seven boiled potatoes, add a piece of butter the size of a walnut, the beaten yolk of an egg, half an onion pounded, a little boiled minced parsley, some pepper and salt; make it into the form of small eggs or pears, roll them into a well-beaten egg, and then into grated bread seasoned with white pepper and salt; fry them in plenty of lard or dripping till they are of a fine brown colour, lay them before the fire to drain; serve them with a fringe of fried parsley.

To Fry Potatoes, Raw or Cold

WASH, peel, and put them into cold water for one or two hours, cut them into slices about half an inch thick, and fry them a light brown in boiling clarified beef suet. Cold boiled potatoes, cut into slices, may be done in the same manner.

To Roast Potatoes

WASH them very clean, put them into a Dutch oven, turn them frequently, and roast them for two hours; taking care not to let them burn; or, they may be parboiled, and then roasted.

To Boil Yellow or Large White Turnips

WASH, pare, and throw them into cold water; put them on in boiling water, with a little salt, and boil them from two hours to two and a half, drain them in a cullender, put them into a sauce-pan, and mixing in a bit of butter, with a beater mash them very smoothly, add half a pint of milk, mix it well with the turnips, and make them quite hot before serving. If they are to be served plain, dish them as soon as the water is drained off.

To Dress Young White Turnips

WASH, peel, and boil them till tender in water with a little salt; serve them with melted butter poured over them. Or,

They may be stewed in a pint of milk thickened with a bit of butter rolled in flour, and seasoned with salt and white pepper, and served with the sauce.

To Fry Turnips

PARBOIL some turnips, cut them into long slices, and fry them in a little butter, or clarified beef dripping.

To Boil Cauliflower

TRIM them neatly, and let them lie an hour or two in cold water, then rinse them in fresh cold water, and put them with a very little salt into boiling water; boil them twenty minutes, or half an hour if very large. They may be boiled in milk-and-water, and require to be skimmed with particular attention.

To Boil Spinach

PICK it very carefully, and wash it thoroughly two or three times in plenty of cold water, then put it on in boiling water, with a little salt; let it boil nearly twenty minutes, put it into a cullender, hold it under the water-cock, and let the water run on it for a minute; put it into a sauce-pan, beat it perfectly smooth with a beater or with a wooden spoon, add a bit of butter, and three table-spoonfuls of cream; mix it well together, and make it hot before serving. When dished, it is scored in squares with the back of a knife.

Another way to Boil Spinach

After being nicely picked and well washed, put it into a sauce-pan, with no more water than adheres to it; add a little salt; cover the pan closely, and boil it till tender, frequently shaking it; beat it quite smooth, adding butter and cream, and make it quite hot. Spinach may be served with poached eggs, or fried sausages laid on it. When the spinach is bitter, it is preferable to boil it in water.

To Dress Spinach

Pick the spinach with great care; strip the leaves from the stalks, and wash it in several waters, till perfectly clean; boil the spinach in salt-and-water; drain it well; pound it in a mortar, and put it into a stew-pan, with a little butter and broth, and let it stew over a slow fire for three quarters of an hour, till it be very dry; then add a quarter of a pound of fresh butter, with salt and grated nutmeg; work the spinach well, till it is thick, but take care the butter does not turn to oil. Garnish with fried toasts of bread, which may be cut like cock's combs, or in any other form.

To Boil Windsor Beans

Shell and wash them, put them on in boiling water with a little salt in it; boil them fifteen or twenty minutes. In Scotland, they are, when old, parboiled, the skins taken off, and then put on in boiling water, and boiled till tender. When there is neither pickled pork nor bacon at table, parsley and butter is served with them.

A Bean Pudding

Take off the skins, pound the beans in a mortar; season with salt and pepper; add a piece of butter; tie it lightly in a buttered and floured cloth. Put it on in boiling water, and boil it for half an hour; squeeze the water from the pudding-cloth, and if another shape is desired, put the cloth with the pudding into the shape, press it down, and let it stand a few minutes; then place the dish it is to be served in over the shape, and turn it out.

Another Bean Pudding

Boil half a pound of blanched beans, pound them in a mortar along with the crumbs of a new roll soaked in milk; add two ounces of butter, some salt and pepper, and mix it well with the beaten yolks of four eggs. Boil it in a basin, or bake it in a pudding-dish lined with puff paste. Carrots may be dressed in the same way.

To Boil French Beans

CUT off the stalk, and string them; if not very young, cut them in four, or into very thin slices; put them into water as they are done, and put them on in boiling water, with a little salt, and let them boil for half an hour. If they are old, they will require a longer time to boil. Melted butter in a sauce-tureen is served with them.

To Boil Asparagus

WASH them well, scrape, and tie them up in small bundles; cut them all even at the bottom, and, as they are done, put them into cold water. Put them on in boiling water, with a little salt, and let them boil twenty or twenty-five minutes. Take them up, lay them upon a slice of toasted bread cut in four, and the crusts pared off, with the tops meeting in the middle of the dish, and cut off the strings. Melted butter is served in a sauce-tureen.

Cardoons may be dressed in the same manner.

Asparagus à la Francaise

BOIL it, and chop small the heads and tender part of the stalks, together with a boiled onion; add a little salt and pepper, and the beaten yolk of an egg; heat it up. Serve it on sippets of toasted bread, and pour over it a little melted butter.

To Boil Brocoli

WASH it, cut off all the outside leaves and stalks, throw it into cold water as it is trimmed; put it on in boiling water, with a little salt, and boil it, for twenty minutes or half an hour. It is sometimes served upon bits of toasted bread, and a little melted butter poured round it.

To Boil Brussels Sprouts

TRIM and wash them perfectly clean, and let them lie an hour in cold water. Put them on in boiling water, with a little salt, and boil them till tender. Drain off the water, and serve them hot.

To Boil Sea Kale

LET it lie some time in cold water, then clean and trim it nicely, cutting off any part that may be at all green, and parting it as little as possible. Put it on in boiling water, with a little salt. Let it boil half an hour; drain off the water. Pare the crust off a slice of toasted bread, lay it in the dish, pour over it a little melted butter, and serve the kale upon it.

To Boil Artichokes

LET them lie for some hours in cold water; put them on in boiling water, with a little salt in it, cover the pan closely, and boil them an hour and a half. If they are old, and have not been fresh gathered, they will take a longer time to boil. Melted butter is served with them in a sauce-tureen.

To Dry and Pickle Artichoke Bottoms

HALF boil the artichokes, strip off the leaves, and pull out the choke; put the bottoms into small jars, and cover them with a cold boiled brine of salt and water; put melted mutton suet on the top to exclude the air, and tie a bladder over them. To dry them, they are boiled as for eating, the leaves and choke pulled out, and the bottoms dried upon dishes in an oven, and then kept in paper bags. When to be dressed, they must be laid into warm water, and soaked for two or three hours; they may then be plain boiled, and eaten with melted butter, or stewed in gravy, with a little mushroom catsup, pepper, and salt, and thickened with a bit of butter rolled in flour. They are a great improvement to all made dishes and meat pies.

To Fricassee Jerusalem Artichokes

WASH and scrape or pare them; boil them in milk-and-water till they are soft, which will be from a quarter to half an hour. Take them out and stew them a few minutes in the following sauce: Roll a bit of butter, the size of a walnut, in flour, mix it with half a pint of cream or milk; season it with white pepper, salt, and grated nutmeg.

They may be served plain boiled, with a little melted butter poured over them. Scorzonera is fricasseed in the same manner.

Onions Plain Boiled

PEEL them, and let them lie an hour in cold water. Put them on in boiling milk-and-water; boil them till tender, and serve them with melted butter poured over them.

To Stew Cucumbers

PARE eight or ten large cucumbers, and cut them into thick slices, flour them well, and fry them in butter; then put them into a sauce-pan with a tea-cupful of gravy; season it highly with cayenne, salt, mushroom catsup, and a little port wine. Let them stew for an hour, and serve them hot.

Another way to Stew Cucumbers

PARE the cucumbers, and let them lie in vinegar-and-water, with a little salt in it; drain them, and put them into a sauce-pan, with a pint of gravy, a slice of lean ham, an onion stuck with one or two cloves, a bunch of parsley and thyme; let them stew, closely covered, till tender. Take out the cucumbers, strain and thicken the gravy with a piece of butter rolled in flour. Boil it up, and pour it over the cucumbers.

Another way to Stew Cucumbers

PARE a number of cucumbers, slice them the long way, and put them for one hour into salt, vinegar, and water; drain them; slice three large onions, and put them with the cucumbers into a frying-pan, with a bit of butter, and some pepper. Fry them till they are of a nice light brown colour, stirring them frequently; cover them with a large plate, and let them stew gently over a slow fire till they are very tender, which will require a length of time. Cucumbers dressed in this manner are particularly good with roast mutton.

To Stew Mushrooms

CLEAN them as for pickling, and after washing them, put them into a sauce-pan, with an anchovy, two cloves, some nutmeg sliced, mace, whole pepper, and salt; let them stew in their own liquor till tender.

In this way they will keep for some time, and when required to be dressed, pick out the spice, and to a dish put two large table-spoonfuls of white wine; add part of their own liquor, and let them just boil, then stir in a bit of butter dredged with flour, and two table-spoonfuls of cream.

Another way to Stew Mushrooms

FOR a good-sized dish, take a pint of white stock, season it with salt, pepper, and a little lemon pickle, thicken it with a bit of butter rolled in flour; cleanse and peel the mushrooms, sprinkle them with a very little salt, boil them for three or four minutes, put them into the gravy when it is hot, and stew them for fifteen minutes.

Another way to Stew Mushrooms

PEEL off the skin, and cut away the stalks; brown a little butter and flour, then add some gravy seasoned with pepper and salt. Put in the mushrooms, and let them stew very gently for three quarters of an hour. If required to be done with a white sauce, follow the same method as with the onions, and when dished, serve them with sippets of bread.

To Stew Onions

TAKE a dozen of good-sized onions, peel, and put them on in the following sauce: A pint of veal stock, a bit of butter rolled in flour, a little white pepper, and salt. Stew them gently for an hour, and, just before serving, mix in three table-spoonfuls of cream. To stew them in a brown sauce, take the same quantity of good gravy. In a stew-pan, brown – of a light colour – a little butter and flour, add the gravy and onions, with a little pepper and salt, and stew them gently one hour.

Another way to Stew Onions

PEEL five or six large onions, put them into a Dutch oven or cheese-toaster to roast, turn them frequently, and when they are well browned, put them into a saucepan, with a bone of dressed or undressed meat, a slice of bacon, a little water, and some pepper. Cover the pan closely, and stew them till tender. Take out the bone and the bacon; thicken the sauce with a bit of butter rolled in flour.

To Roast Onions

ROAST them with the skins on in a Dutch oven that they may brown equally. They are eaten with cold fresh butter, pepper, and salt.

To Stew Red Cabbage

WASH a cabbage well, slice it as for pickling, and put it into a stew-pan, with half a tea-cupful of port wine, and a bit of butter kneaded in flour, a little salt and pepper; stir it till the butter is melted; cover the pan, and let it stew a little, but not to become too soft, as it heats better rather crisp; add a table-spoonful of vinegar, give it one boil, and serve it hot. The wine may be omitted.

A Stew of Vegetables

PICK and wash very clean as much spinach as will make a dish; mince finely three small onions, pick and chop two handfuls of parsley; put all into a sauce-pan, with rather more than half a pint of gravy, a bit of butter dusted with flour, a little salt and pepper. Cover the pan closely, stir it now and then, and when the spinach is tender, mash it smooth. Serve it with slices of broiled ham, or with sausage.

To Stew Old Peas

POUR into a sauce-pan a pint of weak stock, a slice of ham or bacon, and a quart or three pints of peas; and a tea-spoonful of pounded loaf sugar. Cover the pan closely, and stew them nearly an hour, or till they become tender. Take out the ham, and add a bit of butter rolled in flour. Serve them quite hot.

To Stew Beet Root

MIX half an ounce of butter with a little flour, melt it in rather more than half a pint of water, add some salt and pepper. Wash a middling-sized root, scrape and cut it into slices, put it into the sauce-pan, with the butter. Cover the pan closely, and stew it for an hour and ten minutes. Before serving, add a large table-spoonful of vinegar.

To Stew Celery

WASH and clean some heads of celery, cut them into pieces of two or three inches long, boil them in veal stock till tender. To half a pint of cream add the well-beaten yolks of two eggs, a bit of lemon-peel, grated nutmeg, and salt, also a bit of butter; make it hot, stirring it constantly; strain it upon the celery; heat it thoroughly, but do not let it boil.

To Stew Sorrel à la Francaise

STRIP the leaves from the stalks, wash them well, scald them in boiling water in a stew sauce-pan, or in an earthen pipkin; strain, and stew them in a little gravy till tender. Serve with hard-boiled eggs cut in quarters.

Endive with Gravy of Veal

WASH and clean thoroughly ten or twelve heads of fine endive, take off the outer leaves, and blanch the heads in hot water; throw them into cold water, and then squeeze them as dry as possible. Stew them in as much gravy as will cover them; add a tea-spoonful of pounded sugar, and a little salt. When perfectly tender, put in a little veloutée sauce, and serve quite hot.

To Stew Young Peas and Lettuce

WASH and make perfectly clean one or two heads of cabbage lettuce, pick off the outside leaves, and lay them for two hours in cold water, with a little salt in it; then slice them, and put them into a sauce-pan, with a quart or three pints of peas, three table-spoonfuls of gravy, a bit of butter dredged with flour, some pepper and salt, and a tea-spoonful of pounded loaf sugar. Let them stew, closely covered, till the peas are soft.

To Dress Dried French Beans

Boil for more than two hours, two quarts of water, a pound of the seeds or beans of scarlet runners; fill a pint basin with onions peeled and sliced, brown them in a sauce-pan, with rather more than a quarter of a pound of fresh butter; stir them constantly; strain the water from the beans, and mix them with the onions; add a teaspoonful of black pepper, some salt, and a little gravy. Let them stew for ten minutes, and stir in the beaten yolks of two eggs, and a table-spoonful of vinegar. Serve them hot.

To Dress Cardoons

Choose a few heads of nice white cardoons, cut the leaves into pieces of six inches long, rejecting those that are hollow; take off their prickles, and throw the thickest pieces into boiling water; after these have boiled a little, put in the more tender leaves and the stalks. When it is ascertained, by trying a little piece in cold water, that the surface slime will come off by rubbing, take them immediately off the fire, and mix in as much cold water as will admit of the hands being held in it; then rub off all the slime, and throw the cardoons into a stew-pan, with some good gravy, a little salt; and a little sugar. Boil them over a quick fire, skim them carefully, strain the sauce through a sieve, pour it over them, and serve them quite hot.

Skirrets

Wash and scrape them, put them on in boiling water, and boil them for ten minutes; dry them in a cullender, and fry them brown in a little butter. They are sometimes plain boiled, and a little melted butter poured over them.

Vegetable Marrow

Is fit for use when about the size of a turkey's egg. After being washed clean, it is put on in boiling water, with a little salt, and when tender it is drained from the water, cut into half, and served on toasted bread, over which some melted butter has been poured. Or, after being boiled in milk and water, they may be fricasseed as Jerusalem artichokes, or stewed like cucumbers.

Peas for a Second Course Dish, à la Francaise

PUT a quart of fine green peas, together with a bit of butter the size of a walnut, into as much warm water as will cover them, in which let them stand for eight or ten minutes. Strain off the water, put them into a saucepan, cover it, stir them frequently, and when a little tender, add a bunch of parsley, and a cibol or a young onion, nearly a dessert-spoonful of loaf sugar, and an ounce of butter mixed with a tea-spoonful of flour; keep stirring them now and then till the peas be tender, and add, if they become too thick, a table-spoonful of hot water. Before serving, take out the cibol and bunch of parsley.

A Summer Salad

WASH very clean one or two heads of fine lettuce, divide it, let it lie some time in cold water; drain and dry it in a napkin, and cut it small before serving. Mustard and cresses, sorrel and young onions, may be added, and the dish garnished with nasturtium flowers.

A Winter Salad

WASH very clean one or two heads of endive, some beads of celery, some mustard and cresses; cut them all small, add a little shredded red cabbage, some slices of boiled beet-root and onion, if the flavour is not disliked; mix them together with salad sauce. In spring, add radishes, and also garnish the dish with them.

Laver

IS dressed in a silver dish, over a lamp; a bit of fresh butter, and the juice of a Seville orange, are stirred into it till quite hot. It is sent to table in the dish over the lamp.

This plant grows upon rocks on the sea shore. It is much used in Wales, and is sent to London in jars prepared for dressing.

To Dress the Leaves of White Beet

PICK and wash them clean, put them on in boiling water with a little salt, cover the sauce-pan, and boil them longer than spinach; drain off the water, and beat them as spinach, with a bit of butter and a little salt.

To Dress French Beans

TRIM some nice young French beans, and boil them in salt-and-water; drain them quite dry, and pour over them the following sauce: Boil a little sauce tournée, and thicken it with the beaten yolks of two eggs and a little finely-chopped parsley, with a piece of fresh butter, a little pepper, salt, and the juice of a lemon added, and all stirred till hot. Or, put them into a stew-pan, and when quite hot, add a quarter of a pound of fresh butter, a little pepper, salt, and the juice of half a lemon; shake the stew-pan frequently, but do not use a spoon. If the butter does not mix well, add half a spoonful of sauce tournée.

To Fricassee French Beans

Boil the beans as for eating, and having strained off the water, put them into a sauce-pan, with half a pint of cream, dredge in a little flour and grated nutmeg. Make them hot before serving.

Peas Pudding

Put a quart of split peas to soak for two hours into warm water; boil them in soft water, with a bit of butter, till sufficiently tender to press through a sieve; pulp them, and add the beaten yolk of one egg, a little pepper and salt, and an ounce of butter. Tie it into a buttered and floured cloth, and put it on in boiling water; boil it nearly an hour.

To Preserve Green Peas for Winter Use

Fill wide-mouthed quart bottles to the neck with green peas, place them upon the fire in a pan of cold water, and when it boils, take them out, and immediately cork them tightly, and seal them. Keep them in a cold place.

Another way to Preserve Green Peas

Put into a sauce-pan of boiling water fresh-gathered and fresh-shelled peas, but not very young; as soon as they boil up, pour off the water, and put them upon a large dry cloth folded, and then upon another, that they may be perfectly dry without being bruised; let them lie some time before the fire, and then put them into small paper bags, each containing about a pint, and hang them up in the kitchen. Before using, soak them for two to three hours in water, and then boil them as directed for green peas, adding a little bit of butter, when they are put on to boil.

To Keep French Beans for Winter Use

Gather them when young, and on a dry day, put a layer of salt into a jar, and then one of about two inches thick of beans; do this till the jar be nearly full; place a small plate upon the top of them, and tie bladder closely over the jar; keep it in a cool dry place. When to be used, soak them a night in cold water, and change it on them repeatedly in the course of the day they are to be dressed. Cut them, and put them on in boiling water.

To Make Sour Krout

THE best cabbage for this purpose is the drum, or white Strasburg, and it should not be used till it has endured some severe frost; the stocks are then cut into halves, and shred down as fine as possible with a knife, or more properly with a plane made in the form of a cucumber slice. Burn a little juniper in a cask or tub which is perfectly sound and clean, and put a little leaven into the seam round the bottom, – flour and vinegar may be substituted for leaven; then put in three or four handfuls of cabbage, a good sprinkling of salt, and a teaspoonful of caraway seed, and press this hard with a wooden mallet; next add another layer of cabbage, with salt and caraway seed, as at first; and so on in the same manner until the cask be full, pressing down each layer firmly as you advance. A good deal of water will come to the top, of which a part may be taken off. The cask being full, put on the head so as to press upon the cabbage, and place it in a warm cellar to ferment; when it has worked well for three weeks, take off the scum which will have gathered on the top, and lay a clean cloth on the krout; replace the head, and put two or three heavy stones upon it. The juice should always stand upon the top. Thus, in a good cellar, it will keep for years.

When to be dressed, it is boiled for five or six hours in water, or stewed with a little gravy, and may be also substituted for a crust over a beef-steak pie, when cheese is grated over it.

CHAPTER XIII
PUDDINGS, PIES, AND TARTS

PREPARATORY REMARKS

GREAT nicety is to be observed in preparing every material used for boiled or baked puddings.

The eggs require to be well beaten, for which purpose, if many are to be done, a whisk is used; if few, a three-pronged fork. The flour is dried and sifted. The currants are carefully cleaned, by putting them into a cullender, and pouring warm water over them; if very dirty, this is to be repeated two or three times, and after being dried in a dish before the fire, they are rubbed in a clean coarse cloth, all the stalks and stones picked out, and then a little flour dredged over them. The raisins are stoned with a small sharp-pointed knife; it is cleansed in a basin of water, which also receives the seed. The pudding-cloth must be kept especially clean, or it will impart an unpleasant taste to anything that is boiled in it; and when taken off a pudding, it ought immediately to be laid into cold water, and afterwards well washed with soda or pearl-ashes in hot water. Just before being used for a rice, bread, or batter pudding, it should be dipped into hot water, wrung, shaken, and well dredged with flour; and for a plum, suet pudding or any sort of fruit pudding in paste, it must be buttered before being floured.

All puddings in paste are tied tightly, but other puddings loosely, in the cloth. When a pudding is to be boiled in a shape, a piece of buttered white paper is put upon the top of it before the floured cloth is tied on. The pan, dish, or shape, in which a pudding is to be either boiled or baked, must always be buttered before it is filled. It is an improvement to puddings in general to let them stand some time after being prepared either for boiling or baking. When a pudding is to be boiled, it must be put in a covered pot, in plenty of boiling water, and never for a moment be allowed to be off the boil until ready to be served. As the water wastes, more, and always boiling, must be added. A plum pudding is the better for being mixed the day before it is to be boiled. It may be useful to observe that this pudding will keep for months after it is dressed, if the cloth be allowed to remain upon it, and if, when cold, it be covered with a sheet of foolscap paper and then hung up in a cool place. When about to be used, it must be put into a clean cloth, and again boiled for an hour; or it may be cut into slices, and broiled as wanted. If in breaking eggs, a bad one should accidentally drop into the basin amongst the rest, the whole will be spoiled; and therefore they should be broken one by one into a tea-cup. When the whites only of eggs are required for jelly, or other things, the yolks, if not broken, will keep good for two or three days, if the basin they are in be covered.

A slab of marble, stone, or slate, is preferable to wood, for rolling out paste on. The rolling-pin, cutters, and every other implement used in these processes, must be kept particularly clean; they should always be washed immediately after being used, and then well dried. Before using butter for paste it is laid for some time into old water, which is changed once or twice. When salt butter is used, it is well worked in two or three waters. If it should not be convenient to make the paste immediately before it is baked, it will not suffer from standing, if made early in the morning, and the air excluded from it, by putting first a tin cover over the pie or tartlets, and above that a folded tablecloth. To ascertain if the oven be of a proper heat, a little bit of paste may be baked in it, before anything else be put in. Puff paste requires rather a brisk oven. If too hot, it binds the surface and prevents the steam from rising; and if too slow, it becomes sodden and flat. Raised crusts require a quick oven; puffs and tartlets, which are filled with preserved fruit, are sufficiently done when the paste is baked. When large pies have been in the oven for a few minutes, a paper is put over them to prevent their being burned.

Cheese cakes, queen cakes, spunge biscuits, and small spunge cakes, require a quick oven till they have risen; afterwards the heat should be more moderate. Plum, seed cakes, and all large kinds, must be well soaked, and therefore do not require a brisk oven. To preserve their colour, a sheet of white paper is put over them, and after they have risen and, become firm, they are turned round. To ascertain if a large cake be sufficiently done, a broad-bladed knife is plunged into the centre of it, and if dry and clean then drawn out, the cake is baked; but if any thing adheres to the blade, it must instantly be returned to the oven, and the door closed. When the oven is too hot, it is better to lessen the fire than to open the door.

Puff Paste

Weigh an equal quantity of flour and butter, rub rather more than the half of the flour into one-third of the butter, then add as much cold water as will make it into a stiff paste; work it until the butter be completely mixed with the flour, make it round, beat it with the rolling-pin, dust it, as also the rolling-pin, with flour, and roll it out towards the opposite side of the slab, or paste-board, making it of an equal thickness; then with the point of a knife put little bits of butter all over it, dust flour over and under it, fold in the sides and roll it up, dust it again with flour, beat it a little, and roll it out, always rubbing the rolling-pin with flour, and throwing some underneath the paste, to prevent its sticking to the board. If the butter is not all easily put in at the second time of rolling out the paste, the remainder may be put in at the third; it should be touched as little as possible with the hands.

Another Puff Paste

Make nearly all the flour into a stiff paste with cold water, knead it well, and divide it into two, roll out each piece rather more than a quarter of an inch thick; take the butter out of the water, and with the hands put it out into a cake or flat piece, flour one piece of the paste, lay on it the butter, which is then floured and covered with the other piece of paste; flatten it a little with the rolling-pin, and then roll it out, dusting the paste and the pin with flour before and after rolling, fold in the sides, roll it up, and repeat the rolling out, folding up, and dusting with flour, till the butter is incorporated thoroughly with the paste.

Puff paste, if good, will rise into blisters in the course of rolling it out; it may be made with three quarters of a pound of butter to one of flour; the flour should be dried, and is the better for being sifted. When the paste is rolled out for the last time, and made a quarter of an inch thick, place upon it the dish to be covered; and having dipped the paste-cutter into flour, run it round by the rim; the cover being thus cut, lay it aside, and cut a border for the rim of the dish; wet it with water and lay on the border, brush it over with a little water, and put on the cover; ornament it with the paste-cutter; notching it all round the edge; make a hole in the middle, take a small bit of paste, roll it out as thin as paper, dust it with flour, and fold it in four, pinch, or gather it round; wet it, and put it into the opening in the pie, which must also be wetted, cut it twice across, and with the knife turn out the folds to resemble leaves; this ornament is for meat pies; those of fruit have merely a small hole made in the centre.

Paste for Cheese Cakes

Rub equal quantities of flour and butter together, with a little pounded and sifted loaf sugar, make it into a paste with warm milk, roll it out, and line the pans with it.

Crisp Paste

Rub a quarter of a pound of butter into a pound of flour, add two table-spoonfuls of pounded loaf sugar, and the well-beaten yolks of two or three eggs, work it well with a horn-spoon, and roll it out very thin, touching it as little as possible with the hands; the moment before putting it into a quick oven, rub it over with the well-beaten white of an egg, and sift all over the tart finely-pounded sugar.

This crust may be used for any fruit tarts. .

Short Pie Crust

Rub into twelve ounces of dried and sifted flour, three ounces of pounded and sifted loaf sugar, and four ounces of fresh butter; add the beaten yolks of three, and the whites of two eggs; roll it out thin. With a feather; put a little of the beaten white of an egg over the top of the pie, just before it is put into the oven.

Rich Short Paste

WEIGH equal quantities of flour, of butter, and of pounded and sifted loaf sugar; rub the butter with the flour, then mix in the sugar, and rub it together till it will roll out; put it about half an inch thick over the tart, which may be of cherries, raspberries, or currants.

Another Rich Short Paste

RUB into three quarters of a pound of flour a quarter of a pound of lard and a spoonful of grated sugar. Make it into a paste with milk, roll it out, and add a quarter of a pound of butter. For a fruit tart it must be rolled out half an inch thick.

Fine Paste

DRY and sift a pound of flour, weigh half a pound of butter and two ounces of fresh hog's lard; mix with the flour two well-beaten whites of eggs, and add as much water as will make it into a stiff paste; work it well, roll it out, and put over it the butter and hog's lard; flour it, and fold in the sides, and roll it till the butter is well mixed with the paste.

Paste for a Common Dumpling

RUB into a pound of flour six ounces of butter, then work it into a paste with two well-beaten eggs and a little water. This paste may be baked, a large table-spoonful of pounded loaf sugar being added to it.

Tart Paste

RUB into half a pound of flour six ounces of butter and one table-spoonful of pounded loaf sugar, make it into a paste with hot water.

Sweet Paste

RUB into half a pound of flour three ounces of butter and the same of pounded loaf sugar, add one beaten egg, and as much warm water as will make it into a paste; roll it thin for any kind of fruit tart, rub it over with the beaten white of an egg, and sift sugar over it.

Rich Paste for Tarts and Cheese Cakes

POUND and sift six ounces of loaf sugar, and add it by degrees to eight ounces of fresh butter beaten to a cream; beat four eggs till very light, and add them, together with a little grated lemon-peel, some cinnamon or nutmeg. Stir in dried and sifted flour, to make it into a paste, but not very stiff.

Paste for Tarts

MIX one ounce of grated and sifted loaf sugar with one pound of flour, make it into a stiff paste with a gill of boiling cream; work well into it three ounces of butter, and roll it out very thin.

Rice Paste

MIX together half a pound of sifted ground rice and a quarter of a pound of fresh butter, work it into a paste with cold water, dredge flour over the paste-board and rolling-pin, roll out the paste, and put over it, in little bits, another quarter of a pound of butter; fold and roll it out three times, strewing each time a little flour over and under it, as also over the rolling-pin. Cover the tart, and glaze it before being baked.

This paste must be eaten the day it is baked.

Another Rice Paste

BOIL, in a pint of water, half a pound of good rice; drain off the water, and pound the rice in a mortar, with a small bit of butter, and an egg beaten; then roll it out to cover any fruit tart.

Potato Paste

MASH sixteen ounces of boiled potatoes, while they are warm, then rub them between the hands, together with twelve ounces of flour; when it is well mixed, and looks like flour, add half a tea-spoonful of salt, and, with a little cold water, make it into a stiff paste; beat and roll it out three or four times, making it very thin the last time. Lay over it black currant jam, raspberries, or any sort of preserve, rub the edges with water, roll it up like a bolster pudding, and boil it in a buttered and floured cloth for three or four hours. Serve it with a sweet sauce.

Suet Paste

RUB well with half a pound of fresh beef suet, chopped as finely as possible, three quarters of a pound of flour, and half a tea-spoonful of salt; make it into a stiff paste with cold water, work it well, beat it with the rolling-pin, and roll it out two or three times. This paste answers for any kind of boiled fruit pudding.

Another Suet Paste

CUT small three quarters of a pound of fresh beef suet, pound it very finely in a mortar with a little lukewarm milk, carefully picking out all the strings; make it up into a roll, and rub it into a pound and a half of flour; moisten it with milk, and roll it out three or four times.

Paste for Family Pies

RUB into one pound and a half of flour half a pound of butter, wet it with cold water sufficient to make it into a stiff paste; work it well, and roll it out two or three times

Beef Dripping Paste

RUB into one pound of flour half a pound of clarified beef dripping, till it all look like flour; work it to a stiff paste with cold water, and roll it out two or three times. This paste answers very well for common pies, but must be used when hot and fresh baked.

Raised Crust

MELT, in one pint of water, one pound of fresh lard; weigh four pounds of flour, put it into a basin, and when the water and lard is hot, with a horn spoon stir it by degrees amongst the flour. When well mixed, work it with the hands till it is a stiff paste, when it is fit for use.

Another Raised Crust

PUT in to a sauce-pan one pint and a half of water, four pounds of flour, and four ounces and a half of butter; stir it till it is a thick paste, take it out, and add the yolks of three or four beaten eggs; work it well together, roll it out rather more than half an inch thick; cut out the top and bottom, find a long piece of a proper depth for the sides. Brush round the bottom with well-beaten whites of eggs; set on the sides, keeping the paste rather within the edge of the bottom; pinch it all round, to make the pieces adhere, then fill the pie, and brush round the upper sides of the crust and the outer edges of the cover with egg; lay on the cover, pinch it round neatly, and ornament it according to fancy with leaves, festoons, or chains of rings made of the paste.

Fine Icing for Tarts and Puffs

POUND and sift four ounces of refined loaf sugar, beat up the white of an egg, and by degrees add to it the sugar, till it look white and is thick. When the tarts are baked, lay the icing over the top with a brush or feather, and then return them to the oven to harden, but take care that it do not become brown.

Vol-au-Vent

ROLL out puff paste about half an inch thick, lay upon it a small oval flat dish, and cut out, with a paste cutter, two pieces the same size. Butter the dish, and lay upon it one piece of the paste; brush over the edge to the width of the rim of the dish with water, and lay upon it the second piece of paste, and with a tin cutter, the size of the inner part of the dish, cut the paste nearly through, or cut it round with a knife. Bake it of a light brown colour. Cut off the central part, and fill it with pulled chicken or turkey, minced veal, stewed oysters, or any sort of fricassee. Put on the top, and serve it on a napkin.

Pheasant Pie

CUT off the heads of a brace of pheasants, and bone them carefully; make a forcemeat of grated bread, pounded veal, and fat bacon, in equal quantities, and half the quantity of one of these of minced beef suet, also a little grated lean ham; season it with truffles, nutmeg, mace, pepper, and salt; a very little garlic is an improvement; bind it with the beaten yolks of eggs. Put a part of it inside of the pheasants, and fry them for a few minutes. Put them into a standing crust, or a deep dish, lined with slices of fat bacon and some forcemeat laid at the bottom; add a glass of brandy, some truffles, and more of the forcemeat; then lay slices of fat bacon over the whole. If in a dish, cover it with a coarse paste, and bake it for four or five hours. When the pie is to be used, take off the coarse paste, and put over the dish a rich puff paste, and when this is sufficiently baked, it may be served.

Chickens, partridges, or grouse, may be substituted for pheasants, and mushrooms for truffles.

Partridge Pie

TRUSS half-a-dozen partridges in the same way in which chickens are done for boiling, and season them with pepper, salt, and mace. For a forcemeat, bake in an oven two pounds of lean veal, and half a pound of lean ham sliced, and seasoned with a shalot, parsley, and lemon thyme minced, white pepper, nutmeg, and salt;

and with half a pound of butter put over it. When the meat is perfectly tender, drain it, pound it in a mortar, and then mix with it the liquor. To a part of this forcemeat add grated bread and a little chopped fat bacon; put a bit of it, the size of a walnut, into each bird. Make a raised crust, and form it of an oblong shape; put into the bottom a layer of sliced bacon and one of veal, and some artichoke bottoms, cut small; lay in the partridges over them a layer of forcemeat an inch thick, and then slices of fat bacon; brush the edges of the top and sides with the beaten-up white of an egg, put on the top, and pinch it close. It will take three hours and a half to bake; and before serving, the outside should be brushed over with the white of an egg, and covered neatly with foolscap paper, cut into a fringe, round the top. This pie may be baked in a dish, and the forcemeat made of cold ham and roast veal pounded.

Goose Pie

PREPARE a very strong raised crust, and make the sides thick and stiff. Take the bones out of a goose, turkey, and fowl, cutting each down the back; season them highly with pepper, salt, mace, cloves, and nutmeg all finely pounded and well mixed. Lay the goose upon a dish, with the breast skin next to the dish; lay in the turkey, put some slices of boiled ham and tongue, and then the fowl; cover it with little bits of ham or bacon. Put it all into the pie, made of an oval form, and the sides to stand an inch and a half above the meat; put on the top, and make a hole in the centre of it. Brush the outside of the pie all over with the beaten whites of eggs, and bind it round with three folds of buttered paper; paste the top over in the same way, and when it comes out of the oven, take off the paper, and pour in at the top, through a funnel, a pound and a half of melted butter.

Sweetbread and Palate Pie

SCALD the sweetbreads, and when quite cold, fry them a nice brown; boil the palates tender, skin, and cut them into square pieces. Brown a bit of butter with flour, and a pint of good gravy seasoned highly with spice and salt; put in the sweetbreads and palates, and let them stew till nearly ready for eating. Lay them into the pie-dish, and break down in the sauce the yolks of two hard-boiled eggs, and add it. This pie is better to be prepared the day before it is required. Cover with a rich puff paste, and when the paste is sufficiently baked, the pie may be served.

Another Sweetbread Pie

PARBOIL five or six sweetbreads; cut them into two or three pieces, stew them ten or fifteen minutes in a little white stock, with some chopped shalot, a bit of butter rolled in flour, some salt, with white pepper, and a good many mushrooms. Put them into a pie-dish, with some asparagus tops, forcemeat balls, and hard-boiled yolks of eggs, and slices of fat bacon on the top; cover it, and bake it till the paste be done enough; or it may be put into a vol-au-vent, and served upon a napkin; or baked in a paté.

French Pie

MINCE some cold roast veal together with a little ham, season it highly with pepper, salt, mace, and lemon-peel; add a large table-spoonful of mushroom catsup, and a quarter of a hundred of oysters, with their liquor, and three or four table-spoonfuls of rich gravy. Line a dish with puff paste, put in the ingredients, cover the pie, and let it remain in the oven only long enough to bake the paste.

Beef Steak Pie

CUT the steaks off a rump, or any nice piece of beef, fat and lean together, about half an inch thick; beat them a little with a rolling-pin, put over them some pepper, salt, and parboiled onion minced; roll them up, and pack them neatly into the dish, or lay the beef in slices; add some spoonfuls of gravy, and a tea-spoonful of vinegar. Cover the pie with a puff paste, and bake it for an hour.

It is a common but mistaken opinion, that it is necessary to put stock or water into meat pies. Beef, mutton, veal, and pork, if not previously dressed, will be found to yield a sufficiency of gravy, and the pie will be better without any additional liquid.

Veal Pie

CUT a neck of veal into neat steaks, season them well with white pepper, salt, mace, and grated nutmeg mixed ; pack them closely into a dish, and put in half a pint of white stock; five hard-boiled yolks of eggs may be added; put puff paste on the edge of the dish, and cover with the same. Lamb's tails may be made into a pie, with lamb chops seasoned in the same manner as the above.

Another Veal Pie

CUT into steaks a loin or breast of veal, season them highly with white pepper, salt, grated nutmeg, mace, and a little lemon-peel mixed; lay them into the bottom of a dish, and then a few slices of sweetbreads seasoned with the spices; add some oysters, forcemeat balls, and the yolks of hard-boiled eggs, half a pint of white stock, a glass of white wine, and a table-spoonful of lemon pickle; put puff paste on the edge of the dish, and cover with the same; bake it for one hour.

Another Veal Pie

CHOP, but not very small, the meat of a cold loin of veal, season it with minced parsley, white pepper, salt, grated lemon-peel, and nutmeg; add rather more than half a pint of stock made with the bones, thickened with a bit of butter rolled in flour, and seasoned with a tea-spoonful of lemon pickle, and a table-spoonful of white wine; make a paste of the fat of the loin, and an equal quantity of flour, rub it together, and mix with it a little cold water, roll it out two or three times, line the sides of the dish, put in the meat, and cover it.

Solid Veal Pie

STEW in veal stock, till it be perfectly tender and like a jelly, a piece of a knuckle of veal, with the gristles adhering to it; let it cool, and then pull the meat and gristles into small bits; butter a pie-dish or shape, and lay at regular distances the yolks of the hard-boiled eggs and some of the white parts cut into rings or strips; then put over them some bits of the meat and gristle, and strew over it some white pepper, salt, and grated nutmeg mixed, and a little of the gravy, and then more eggs with small bits of beet-root, green pickles, and the red part of a carrot cut to fancy; add more meat-seasoning, and all the gravy; when the shape is full, put it into an oven for twenty minutes, and when quite cold, turn it out. If rightly done, it will have a glazed appearance, and the variety of colours looks well by candlelight.

Mutton Pie

CUT into neat steaks a loin or the best end of a neck of mutton, pare off the skin and fat, and season them highly with pepper and salt mixed, and a little finely minced onion. If the loin, divide the kidney in two, season it with pepper and salt, lay the steaks into a dish, and add a little stock made with the trimmings, three table-spoonfuls of port wine, and one of mushroom catsup; cover the dish with puff paste.

Pork Pies

WITH a raised crust make round shapes about the size of a small plate, and nearly three inches high; pare off the rind and pare off the fat, and cut into neat short steaks a loin or neck of pork, beat them with a rolling pin, season them highly with pepper and salt, pack them closely into the shapes, wet the edges, put on the top, and pinch it all round; make a small hole in the middle of the crust, and if to be eaten hot, pour in, before serving, some white gravy, with a little white wine, and a tea-spoonful of vinegar in it. They will keep good in cold water for a fortnight or three weeks, and may be served for breakfast or luncheon.

Venison Pasty

CUT a neck or breast into small steaks, rub them over with a seasoning of sweet herbs, grated nutmeg, pepper, and sat; fry them slightly in butter; line the sides and edges of a dish with puff paste, lay in the steaks, and add half a pint of rich gravy made with the trimmings of the venison; add a glass of port wine, and the juice of half a lemon, or a tea-spoonful of vinegar; cover the dish with puff paste, and bake it nearly two hours; some more gravy may be poured into the pie before serving it.

Another Venison Pasty

CUT into small pieces the meat of a breast or shoulder, fat and lean, season them highly with pepper, salt, and a little beaten mace; place them in a dish, and put some thin slices of butter over the top; wet the edges, and cover the dish with a paste half an inch thick, made of flour and water, and a small quantity of dripping; bake it for two hours; when cold, take off the crust, and cover the dish with a rich puff paste, and bake it nearly an hour. It will keep for some time if the coarse paste be not removed. In this manner most meat pies may be made when required to be kept.

Sheep's Head Pie

SCALD and clean nicely a sheep's head and feet; parboil them, and when cold, cut off all the meat in square bits; season with pepper, salt, and a little finely-minced onion. Pack the meat closely into a pudding dish or shape, adding some bits of butter; and fill up the dish with some rich highly-seasoned gravy, or with some of the liquor that the head and feet were boiled in. Cover the dish with a coarse paste, and bake the pie for one hour. When cold, and to be served, the paste is taken off, and the pie is cut into slices like potted meat, and garnished with culled parsley.

Moorfowl Pie

PICK clean, and wash very nicely, five or six moorfowl; truss them as chickens are done for boiling, season them highly with two or three pounded cloves, some salt, black and Jamaica pepper, all mixed; put into each blade a bit of butter rolled in the spices, lay them closely into a dish, and add half a pint of rich brown stock, and a wine glass of port wine; cover the dish with puff paste, and bake it one hour.

Hare Pie

CUT the hare into small joints, divide the back into five or six pieces, wash it extremely well, and let it lie some time in cold water; dry, and season it highly with two pounded cloves, some black and Jamaica pepper; lay it in a dish, with half a pint of brown stock, and two wine glasses of port wine; cover the dish with puff paste. For a family dinner, and when it is to be eaten hot, the paste may be made of lard or dripping.

Giblet Pie

SCALD two or three sets of goose-giblets, pick and singe them; take the outer skin off the feet, which, with the pinions, cut into two, the neck into three, the gizzard into four, and the liver and heart into two bits; wash them all clean, put them in a sauce-pan, cover them with water, add two onions, a little salt, and a tea-spoonful of whole black pepper; stew them till the gizzards be tender; take them out, and put them into the pie-dish, season them with more pepper and salt, strain the liquor, and add half a pint of it with a glass of port wine; when cold, put puff paste round the edge of the dish, and cover it with the same. A beef-steak, well-seasoned, may be laid in the bottom of the dish.

Another Giblet Pie

STEW the giblets in a little water, with an onion stuck with two or three cloves, a bunch of sweet herb, some salt, and whole black pepper; cut a fowl into joints; skin and wash it, season it with white pepper, salt, and half an onion finely minced. Take out the onion, herbs, and whole pepper; put the fowl, giblets, and gravy into a dish, add a glass of white wine, and two table-spoonfuls of mushroom catsup; cover the dish with puff paste, and bake it for an hour.

Chicken Pie

PICK clean and singe the chickens; if they are very young, keep them whole, and truss them as for boiling; if large, cut them into joints, and take off the skin, wash and dry them well, season them with salt, white pepper, grated nutmeg and mace mixed, and if whole, put in them a bit of butter rolled in flour, and a little of the mixed spices; lay them into a dish with the livers, gizzards, and hearts well-seasoned, add half a pint of white stock, a glass of white wine, a table-spoonful of lemon pickle, or some pickled mushrooms, and the yolks of five hard-boiled eggs; cover with a puff paste, and bake it for an hour.

Slices of cold ham and forcemeat balls may be added to this pie. Or wash in cold water two or three ounces of macaroni, break it into small bits, simmer it for nearly half an hour in milk and water, drain, and put it with the chickens into the dish, and also three quarters of an ounce of butter. Omit the lemon pickle, or pickled mushrooms, when macaroni is added.

Pigeon Pie

DRAW, pick, singe, and wash six or eight newly-killed pigeons; cut off the pinions, necks, and feet, truss them, put into each bird a bit of butter mixed with flour, and rolled in pepper, salt, and grated nutmeg mixed; rub the pigeons and giblets over with the seasoning, as also one or two slices of tender beef, which put into the bottom of the dish, and add the pigeons and giblets; strew over a good deal of the seasoning, and put in half a pint of rich brown stock, with a little port wine, and the yolks of five hard-boiled eggs; cover the dish with puff paste; stick into the paste four of the feet round the ornament of paste in the centre of the dish.

Italian Pie

MIX together some chopped thyme, parsley, and one or two sage leaves, some salt, white and cayenne pepper; lay into the bottom dish some thin slices of lean veal, sprinkle them with the seasoning, and add slices of ham, and a few forcemeat balls; put a layer of seasoned veal, and of ham and forcemeat balls, till the dish is full, and then add the yolks of five hard-boiled eggs, and some good white stock; cover the dish with a puff paste, and bake it for an hour. Before serving, pour in, through a funnel at the centre of the crust, a tea-cupful of rich cream.

Rook Pie

DRAW and skin six or eight rooks, let them lie in cold water one or two hours, cut out the back bones, wash the birds, season them highly with pepper and salt, and pack them closely into a pie-dish; add half a pint of gravy or water, and lay over them half a pound of fresh butter; cover the dish with a flour and water paste, and bake them for two hours. The following day take off the coarse, and cover with puff paste, and bake it till it be sufficiently done.

Fife Pie

SKIN a rabbit, cut it into bits, and let it lie for an hour in cold water; cut into small thin slices a pound of fat pickled pork, season the meat well with pepper, a little grated nutmeg, and salt. Make forcemeat balls with the liver minced, some grated bread, and chopped fat bacon, season with minced parsley, lemon thyme, grated nutmeg, pepper, and salt, bind with an egg, pack the meat and balls closely into a dish, and add a tea-cupful of good gravy, and three table-spoonfuls of white wine; cover it with a puff paste, and bake it for an hour.

Ham Pie

HALF boil a ham, skin it, and take out the bone, fill the space with a rich forcemeat, and season the ham with pepper, mace, cinnamon, and cloves, pounded and well mixed; put it into a raised crust made of an oval shape, and lay over it a few bay leaves, and some slices of fat bacon; close, and bake it four or five hours.

Devizes Pie

CUT into very thin slices, after being dressed, cold calf's head, with some of the brains, pickled tongue, sweetbreads, lamb, veal, a few slices of bacon, and hard-boiled eggs; put them in layers into a pie-dish, with plenty of seasoning between each, of cayenne, white pepper, allspice, and salt; fill up the dish with rich gravy; cover it with a flour-and-water paste; bake it in a slow oven, and when perfectly cold, take off the crust, and turn the pie out upon a dish; garnish it with parsley and pickled eggs cut into slices.

Vegetable Pie

OF a variety of vegetables, such as carrots, turnips, potatoes, artichoke bottoms, cauliflower, French beans, peas, and small button onions, equal quantities of each; half boil them in good broth for a short time, put them into a pie-dish, cover it with puff paste, and bake it in a slow oven; make a gravy of a bit of veal, a slice of ham, pepper, salt, a bay leaf, mushrooms, shalots, parsley, and an onion; when it has boiled thick, strain the liquor, and mix in three or four table-spoonfuls of cream, and pour it into the pie before being served. The cream may be omitted.

Tripe Pie

LAY into the bottom of a dish some thinly-sliced cold or raw ham, then put in a layer of tripe with the jelly adhering to it, season with pepper and salt, and add a bit of butter; fill the dish in this manner, and put in a few table-spoonfuls of brown stock; cover the dish with puff paste. A beef-steak may be substituted for the ham, laid into the bottom, and the dish filled up with tripe.

A Pie of Cold Beef, Veal, or Mutton

POUND in a mortar some boiled potatoes; boil a cupful of milk, and while hot, mix it with the potatoes, and beat them till they become like a light paste; roll it out, cut with a flat dish, the size of the pie-dish, so as it may be laid from off it upon the pie; cut the meat into slices, season it with pepper and salt, put half a pint of gravy, wet the edges of the dish, and put over it the paste, and bake it till the paste be sufficiently done.

Leicestershire Medley Pie

CUT some apples into quarters, take out the core, but do not peel them; cut thick slices of cold fat bacon, and any sort of cold roasted meat, season them with pounded ginger, pepper, and salt; put into the dish a layer of each, and pour over the top a large cupful of ale; cover the dish with a paste made with dipping or lard.

Sea Pie

SKIN and cut a large fowl into joints; wash and lay it into cold water for an hour; cut some salt beef into thin slices, and if it is very salt, soak it a short time in water; make a paste of flour and butter in the proportion of half a pound of butter to one of flour, cut it out into round pieces according to the size of the bottom of the pot in which the pie is to be stewed; rub the bottom of a round iron pot with butter, and lay in a layer of the beef, seasoned with pepper, and finely minced onion; then put a layer of the paste, and then the fowl, highly seasoned with pepper, onion, and a little salt, add another layer of paste, and pour in three pints of cold water; cover the pot closely, and let it stew gently for nearly four hours, taking care it does not burn, which, if neglected, it is apt to do. It is served in a pudding dish, and answers well for a family dinner.

Beef-Steak Pudding

MAKE a paste with suet or butter, roll it out large enough to line a quart basin; cut thin slices of tender beef, free from skin and sinews, beat them with a rolling pin, season them with pepper, salt, and a very little finely-minced onion; roll up each steak; rub the basin with butter, lay in the paste, and put in the steaks, wet the edges of the paste, and fold it over closely; dip into hot water a pudding-cloth, wring, shake, and dust it with flour, tie it over the rim of the basin, put into boiling water, and boil it for three hours.

Rabbit Pudding

WASH a rabbit in several waters, cut off the head, and cut the rest into small pieces; make a nice suet paste, allowing a quarter of a pound of fresh beef or veal suet, finely minced, to one pound of flour; season the rabbit with pepper, salt, and a little mushroom powder, put it all except the head into the paste, with a little flour and water; boil it in a cloth for two hours and a half; serve it with gravy in a sauce-tureen. One or two thin slices of pickled pork may be added.

A young hare may be made into a pudding in the same manner, and if an old one is used, cut off the bits of meat from the back and legs for the pudding, and make the rest into soup.

Lobster Pie

TAKE out, as whole as possible, the meat from the tail and claws of two or three boiled lobsters; cut them into slices, and season them with nutmeg, pepper, and salt. Make a forcemeat of the soft part of the bodies, together with grated bread, some parsley, and one anchovy minced, grated lemon-peel, mace, salt, and pepper, the yolks of two hard-boiled eggs bruised, and a bit of butter; mix it all together with the well-beaten yolk of an egg, and make it up into small balls. Put the lobster into the pie dish, and cover it with the forcemeat balls, and hard-boiled yolks of eggs; and add more than half a pint of rich white stock, a glass of white wine, and a table-spoonful of lemon juice or vinegar. Cover it with puff paste, and bake it only till the paste be done.

Another Lobster Pie

BOIL the lobsters, and cut the meat of the tail into four bits; take out the meat from the claws and bodies; pound it in a mortar, add the soft part of one lobster, and season with pepper, salt, and nutmeg, add three table-spoonfuls of vinegar; melt half a pound of butter, and mix it with the pounded meat and the crumb of a slice of bread, grated. Put puff paste round the edge and side of the dish; put in the tail of the lobster, then a layer of oysters with their liquor, and next the pounded meat; cover it with a puff paste, and bake it till the paste be done.

Before serving, pour in some rich gravy, made of a little weak stock in which the lobster shells have been boiled, with an onion, pepper, and salt, and which has been strained and thickened with a bit of butter rolled in flour.

Haddock Pie

CLEAN, skin, and wash the haddocks; take off the heads and tails, and cut the fish into two or three pieces; season them highly with finely-minced onion, parsley, some salt and pepper; make forcemeat balls with a small boiled haddock. Put into the bottom of a dish some bits of butter, add the fish and forcemeat balls, with rather more than half a pint of white stock, and a glass of white wine; put puff paste round the edge of the dish, and cover it with the same.

Eel Pie

CLEAN, skin, and wash them; take off the heads and tails, and cut the eels into pieces of two or three inches; season them highly with pepper, salt, and grated nutmeg. Put them into a dish, and add a quarter of a pint of white stock, or water, a glass of white wine, and a large table-spoonful of lemon pickle; put puff paste round the edge of the dish, and cover with the same.

Shrimp Pie

BOIL in salt-and-water three pints of shrimps or prawns, pick, and season them with a table-spoonful of essence of anchovies, one of lemon pickle, some pounded pepper and mace, and a little salt. Lay some bits of butter into the bottom of the dish, put in the shrimp, with a tea-cupful of rich gravy, and a glass of white wine; cover it with a puff paste, and bake it till the paste be done enough.

Oyster Pie

BEARD a quart of fine oysters, strain the liquor, and add them to it. Cut into thin slices the kidney fat of a loin of veal; season them with white pepper, salt, mace, and grated lemon-peel; lay them into the bottom of a pie-dish, put in the oysters and liquor, with a little more seasoning; put over them the marrow of two bones. Lay a border of puff paste round the edge of the dish; cover it with paste, and bake it nearly three quarters of an hour

Lobster Patties

PICK the meat and red berries out of a lobster, mince them finely, add grated bread, chopped parsley and butter; season with grated nutmeg, white pepper, and salt; add a little white stock, cream, and a table-spoonful of white wine, with a few chopped oysters; heat it all together. Line the patty-pans with puff paste; put into each a bit of crumb of bread about an inch square, wet the edge of the paste, and cover it with another bit; with the paste-cutter mark it all round the rim, and pare off the paste round the edge of the patty-pan. When baked, take off the top, and with a knife take out the bread and a little of the inside paste, put in the prepared lobster, lay on the top paste and serve them in a napkin.

Another way to prepare the paste. Roll it out nearly half an inch thick, and cut it into rounds with a tin cutter, and, with one two sizes less, mark it in the middle about half through. When they are baked, carefully cut out the inner top of the paste, and scoop out the inside, so as to make room for the mince, which put in and place on the top.

Veal Patties

MINCE some under-done veal with a little parsley, one or two sage leaves, a very little onion; season with grated lemon-peel, nutmeg, pepper, and salt; add some grated lean ham or tongue, moisten it with some good gravy, heat it up, and put it into the pattie.

Patties in Fried Bread

CUT the crumb of a loaf of bread into square or round pieces nearly three inches high, and cut bits the same width for tops; mark them neatly with a knife; fry the bread of a light brown colour in clarified beef dripping or fine lard. Scoop out the inside crumb, take care not to go too near to the bottom; fill them with minced meat, prepared as for patties, with stewed oysters, or with sausage meat; put on the tops, and serve them upon a napkin.

Vol-au-Vent

CUT some cold turkey or veal into small thin slices, season it with dried lemon-peel grated, white pepper, pounded mace, and salt; add one anchovy, some garlic and onion pounded, also a little good gravy, a table-spoonful of lemon pickle, one of white wine, half an ounce of butter rolled in flour; then make it quite hot, but do not allow it to boil, and serve it in the prepared vol-au-vent. Some gravy may be made with the bones, or a little cream, and the beaten yolk of an egg may be substituted for the cream.

Another way to make Vol-au-Vent

IN opening the oysters, separate them from the liquor; which must be strained; take off the beards, and add to them the liquor, together with some white stock a half of butter rolled in flour, two or three blades of mace, a bit of lemon peel, white pepper, and salt; simmer them for fifteen or twenty minutes, and a little before putting them into the vol-au-vent, pick out the mace and lemon peel, add a table-spoonful of white wine and three of good cream, and make it quite hot. To make oyster patties, when they are bearded, cut them into three or four bits, and prepare them in the same manner.

Rissoles

CUT puff paste with a round tin cutter, about three inches wide; have ready some cold fowl or veal, very finely minced, and seasoned with a little pounded garlic, grated lemon-peel, white pepper, salt, and mace, the juice of half a lemon, and moistened with a little good gravy. Put some of the mince upon one bit of the paste, wet the edges, and lay over it another bit; press it gently round the rim; brush them all over with a well-beaten egg, and strew over them sifted bread crumbs; fry them a light brown in boiling clarified beef dripping, and lay them upon the back of a sieve before the fire to drain. Serve them in a napkin. The paste may be cut of the size of a large breakfast plate, then the mince put into the middle of it, the edges wet all round, and gathered up into the form of a pear, brushed over with egg, and strewed over with bread crumbs. Served in a dish garnished with fried parsley.

Pancake Rissoles

MINCE finely some cold veal, season it with grated lemon-peel, nutmeg, white pepper, salt, and a little lemon pickle; warm it up with some good gravy, and a small bit of butter rolled in flour. Have ready a batter as for pancakes, seasoned with a little salt and grated nutmeg. Fry a thin pancake, turn it, and put into the middle two table-spoonfuls of the minced veal; fold it in at each side and at the ends in an oblong form, and fry them of a light brown colour; lay them upon the back of a sieve to drain before the fire. Four or six will make a dish. They are served as a corner or top dish.

Mince Pies

WEIGH equal quantities of fresh lemons, cleaned currants, stoned raisins, fresh beef suet minced, and good brown sugar. Cut the lemons in half, squeeze and strain the juice; put the skins into a sauce-pan of cold water, cover it closely, and boil them till perfectly tender; drain off the water, and pound them in a mortar. Grate a small nutmeg, and cut very small a little citron; mix all the ingredients thoroughly, adding the lemon juice last, and mixing it in well; then pack it into small jars, upon the top put a bit of white paper dipped into spirits, and tie the jars over with paper.

This will keep good for a twelvemonth, and when it is to be made into pies, dust the pans with flour, line them with puff paste, and put in the mincemeat; wet the edges of the paste, lay on the top, and cut it even round the edge; mark it all round neatly with a paste cutter, and pare off the loose paste with scissors. The mincemeat may be baked in a large patty-pan lined with puff paste.

Another way to Make Mince Pies

CAREFULLY stone and cut, but not too small, one pound and a half of bloom raisins; cut small half a pound of orange-peel, mince finely half-a-dozen of middlingsized good apples, a quarter of a pound of sweet almonds, pounded to a paste with a little white wine, half a nutmeg grated, a quarter of an ounce of Jamaica pepper, one head of clove, and a little cinnamon pounded; one pound and a half of fresh beef suet, minced finely, one pound of good brown sugar; mix all these ingredients extremely well, and add half a pint of white wine, and one glass of brandy. Pack it closely into small stone jars, and tie paper over them. When it is to be used, add a little more wine.

Another way to make Mince Pies

CUT the root off a neat's tongue, rub the tongue well with salt, let it lie four days, wash it perfectly clean, and boil it till it becomes tender; skin, and when cold, chop it very finely. Mince as small as possible two pounds of fresh beef suet from the sirloin, stone and cut small two pounds of bloom raisins, clean nicely two pounds of currants, pound and sift half an ounce of mace and a quarter of an ounce of cloves, grate a large nutmeg; mix all these ingredients thoroughly, together with one pound and a half of good brown sugar. Pack it in jars.

When it is to be used, allow, for the quantity sufficient to make twelve small mince pies, five finely minced apples, the grated rind and juice of a large lemon, and a wine glass and a half of brandy; put into each a few bits of citron and preserved orange-peel.

Three or four whole green lemons, preserved in good brown sugar, and cut into thin slices, may be added to the mincemeat.

Another way to make Mince Pies

Two pounds of fresh suet minced finely, two of wellcleaned currants, two of good apples minced, one pound of loaf sugar pounded, the peel of two lemons grated, and their juice; of mace, cinnamon, and cloves pounded, finely sifted, and dried before the fire, a quarter and half a quarter of an ounce each; half a nutmeg grated; a quarter of a pint of brandy, and the same of sweet wine. The materials must all be prepared, weighed, and then well mixed together, and packed in small jars.

Brandy Minced Pies

CLEAN a pound of currants, mince a pound of nonpareil apples, and one of fresh beef suet; pound a pound of loaf sugar; weigh each article after being prepared; the peel of two lemons grated, and the juice of one; a quarter of a pound of citron, the same of orange-peel minced. Mix all these ingredients well with a quart of brandy.

Lemon Minced Pies

WEIGH one pound of fine large lemons, cut them in half, squeeze out the juice, and pick the pulp from the skins; boil them in water till tender, and pound them in a mortar. Add half a pound of pounded loaf sugar, the same of nicely cleaned currants, and of fresh beef suet minced, a little grated nutmeg, and citron cut small. Mix all these ingredients well, and fill the patty-pans with rather more of the mince than is usually put.

Apple Pie

PARE, quarter, and core the apples; cut them into thin bits. Put into the bottom of a pie-dish a table-spoonful of brown sugar, with half a tea-spoonful of grated ginger and same of lemon peel, then a layer of apples and so on alternately, till the dish is piled as full as it will hold. The next day wet the rim of the dish, line it with puff or tart paste, brush it with water, and cover it with paste; press the edge all round, notch it with a paste cutter, and make a small hole with the point of a knife in the middle.

It may be seasoned with two table-spoonfuls of lemon or orange marmalade, pounded cinnamon, mace, and cloves, in addition to the ginger and lemon-peel.

Currant Tart

To a quart of red currants add one pint of red raspberries, strawberries, or cherries; sweeten them well with brown sugar; before putting in the fruit, line the side of the dish with tart paste, place in it a small tea-cup, put in the fruit, and cover it with paste. Four ounces of brown sugar are generally allowed to a quart fruit.

Cherry Tart

THE cherries may be stoned, and a few red currants added; sweeten with loaf or brown sugar, and put into the bottom of the dish a small teacup; cover it with paste.

Rhubarb Tart

STRIP off the peel, and if the rhubarb is large, cut it into two or three strips, and then into bits about an inch long; sweeten well with brown sugar, and cover the dish with paste.

Gooseberry Tart

GOOSEBERRIES, green-gage, magnum-bonum, and purple-egg plums, damsons, and cranberries, are sweetened with brown sugar, and made into tarts in the same manner as the preceding. The tops and tails must be taken off the gooseberries, and the plums may be scalded and skinned.

Cheshire Tart

LINE a tart-dish with puff paste, fill it with a rich custard; pare and take out the core of three or four apples, place them in the custard, and put upon each some orange marmalade, or any other preserve. Bake it in an oven.

Tartlets

RUB over patty-pans a little bit of butter, and line them with tart or puff paste; fill them with marmalade, preserved strawberries, raspberries, currants, or any sort of fruit. Take a small bit of the paste, and with the hand, roll it upon the paste board with flour till it be stiff, and will draw out in straws; hold it in one hand, and with the other draw it out. With these small strings cross the tartlets according to fancy; wet the edge, and lay on a narrow rim of paste cut with the paste-cutter.

Another way to make Tartlets

ROLL out the paste about a quarter of an inch thick; and lay upon it the top part of the patty-pan; cut it round with the paste-cutter. Rub the patty-pans with a little butter, and line them with the paste, and place in the middle a little bit of bread, which take out when they are baked. They may be filled with any preserved fruit, and a star or leaf of paste placed on the top. To make ornaments of paste, roll it quite thin, and as even as possible; cut it with tin stars, leaves, or any other form, and bake them a light brown colour, upon flat tins dusted with flour.

Preserved Fruit Tarts

Rub over with a little butter an oval dish, or tin shape, line it with paste, and fill it with any sort of preserved fruit. Roll out a bit of paste thin, and, with a paste-cutter, cut it into narrow strips; brush with water the rim of tile shape, and lay the bars of paste across and across, and then put round a border of paste, and mark it with the paste-cutter.

Puffs

Roll out puff paste nearly a quarter of an inch thick, and, with a small saucer, or tin cutter of that size, cut it into round pieces; place upon one side raspberry or strawberry jam, or any sort of preserved fruit, or stewed apples; wet the edges, fold over the other side, and press it round with the finger and thumb. Or cut the paste into the form of a diamond, lay on the fruit, and fold over the paste, so as to give it a triangular shape.

Pyramid of Paste

Make a rich puff paste, roll it out a quarter of an inch thick, and cut it into five or seven pieces with scolloped thin paste-cutters, which go one within another; leave the bottom and top piece entire, and cut a bit out of the centre of the others; bake them of a light brown, upon buttered paper placed upon tins. When served, build them into a pyramid, laying a different preserved fruit upon each piece of paste, and on the top a whole apricot, with a sprig of myrtle stuck into it, or three green-gages, ornamented with a branch of barberries.

Curd Cheese Cakes

Boil, in two quarts of cream, the well-beaten yolks of four, and the whites of five eggs; drain off the whey gently, and mix with the curd grated nutmeg, pounded cinnamon, three table-spoonfuls of best rose water, as much white wine, four ounces of pounded loaf sugar, the same quantity of butter beaten to a cream, and of pounded biscuit. Mix all these ingredients well together, and stir in a quarter of a pound of currants. Bake it in a large tin, or in patty-pans lined with paste; or it may be baked in a dish previously buttered.

Another way to make Curd Cheese Cakes

With a little rennet, turn two quarts of new milk; drain off the whey. Rub through a sieve the curd, and a quarter of a pound of fresh butter; mix with it half an ounce of sweet and four bitter almonds, blanched and pounded, three ounces of powdered loaf sugar, a little candied citron cut small, the grated peel of half a lemon, three well-beaten eggs, a glass of brandy, and three ounces of currants. Mix them all well together, and bake them in patty-pans lined with paste.

Potato Cheese Cakes

Boil and peel half a pound of good potatoes, bruise them in a mortar, and when nearly cold, drop in the yolk and white of an egg at intervals, until four have been added, beating the potatoes well all the time; then add a quarter of a pound of sifted bread crumbs, and put in two more eggs. Beat to a cream six ounces of fresh butter with the same quantity of pounded loaf sugar; put it into the mortar, with the grated peel of one lemon, and mix all thoroughly. Line the patty-pans with paste, fill them three parts full and bake them in a moderate oven.

Another way to make Potato Cheese Cakes

Pound in a mortar five ounces of potatoes, with four of fresh butter, and the same quantity of pounded loaf sugar, the grated peel and the juice of half a lemon, three well-beaten eggs, and a table-spoonful of brandy; mix all well together, and bake as before directed.

Lemon Cheese Cakes

Pound in a mortar with rose water half a pound of blanched sweet almonds, mix them with the grated peel of two lemons, half a pound of pounded loaf sugar, the same quantity of melted butter when nearly cold, and eight well-beaten yolks and four whites of eggs; beat all the ingredients well together, and bake in patty-pans lined with paste.

Orange cheese cakes are made in the same manner; or orange marmalade may be used.

Almond Cheese Cakes

Blanch and pound, with a little orange-flower water, half a pound of sweet and ten bitter almonds; beat, with eight yolks and four whites of eggs, three quarters of a pound of pounded loaf sugar; add one pound of melted butter. When nearly cold, also one nutmeg, and the peel of one lemon grated, a wine glass of orange-flower water, and one of ratafia, or of brandy; mix all the ingredients well, and bake in patty-pans lined with paste.

Rice Cheese Cakes

FOUR ounces of sifted ground rice, the same quantity of pounded loaf sugar and of melted butter, the wellbeaten yolks of six eggs and the whites of three, a glass of brandy, and the grated peel of a lemon; mix all well together, and bake in patty-pans lined with paste.

Maids of Honour

BEAT with the yolks of seven eggs half a pound of pounded loaf sugar; pound, not too finely, the same quantity of blanched sweet almonds, with a few bitter ones, and two table-spoonfuls of orange-flower water, mix in the almonds the last thing, and bake in patty-pans lined with paste.

Cheese Cakes

TAKE one pound of pounded leaf sugar, six yolks, and four whites of eggs beaten, the juice of three fine lemons, the grated rind of two, and a quarter of a pound of fresh butter; put these ingredients into a sauce-pan, and stir the mixture gently over a slow fire till it be of the consistency of honey; pour it into small jars, and when cold put paper dipped in brandy over them. It will keep good for a year.

Cheese Cake Pudding

BOIL in a quart of milk a laurel leaf, and a stick of cinnamon, strain it, and when nearly cold, add six unbeaten eggs, and two more eggs with which two table-spoonfuls of flour have been beaten; put it into a saucepan, and stir it over the fire till it be as thick as a custard cream; take it off, and mix in a quarter of a pound of fresh butter; six ounces of sugar, and the same quantity of nicely cleaned currants, half a grated nutmeg; add a small glassful of brandy, and bake it in a dish lined with puff paste. It may be served in a napkin.

Apple Pudding

PARE and core twelve large apples, put them into a sauce-pan, with water sufficient to cover them, stew them till soft, and then beat them smooth, and mix in three quarters of a pound of pounded loaf sugar, a quarter of a pound of fresh butter, the juice and grated peel of two lemons, and the well-beaten yolks of eight eggs; line a dish with puff paste, put in the pudding, and bake it for nearly three quarters of an hour; before serving, grate loaf sugar all over the top till it looks white.

Another way to make Apple Pudding

PARE and core ten or twelve good-sized apples, stew them with sugar, a bit of cinnamon, and the peel of a lemon, and when quite soft, rub them through a hair sieve. Beat the yolks of seven, and the whites of five eggs together, with half a pint of sweet cream, and a dessert-spoonful of sifted ground rice; stir it over the fire till it boil, and then mix it well with the apples, and bake the pudding in a dish lined with puff paste.

Another way to make Apple Pudding

PEEL and core six very large apples, stew them in six table-spoonfuls of water, with the rind of a lemon; when soft, beat them to a pulp, add six ounces of melted fresh butter, the same of good brown sugar, six well-beaten eggs, half a wine glass of brandy, and a tea-spoonful of lemon-juice; line a dish with puff paste, and when baked, stick all over the top thin chips of candied citron and lemon peel.

Orange Pudding

BEAT separately, till perfectly light, the yolks of eight and the whites of four eggs; beat with the yolks four ounces of grated loaf sugar; pound one ounce and a half of sugar biscuit, and with two table-spoonfuls of orange marmalade, mix all well together; beat before the fire with a horn spoon four ounces of butter; line a dish with puff paste, and just before putting the pudding into the oven, stir in the butter. Bake it for fifteen or twenty minutes.

Another way to make Orange Pudding

THE yolks of six, and the whites of three eggs, well beaten; three table-spoonfuls of orange marmalade, a quarter of a pound of loaf sugar pounded, the same of melted butter; three table-spoonfuls of grated bread, and a quarter of a pint of cream; mix all well together, and bake them in a dish lined with puff paste.

Another way to make Orange Pudding

CUT in half three large Seville oranges, squeeze and strain the juice; boil the skins till quite soft in a good deal of water, pound them in a mortar, and mix them with the yolks of nine, and the whites of four well-beaten eggs, nearly a pound of pounded loaf sugar, the juice of the oranges, and half a pound of melted butter. Bake it in a dish lined with puff paste for half an hour.

Another way to make Orange Pudding

STEEP in cold water for two days, changing the water twice a day, six large Seville oranges; put them on in cold water to boil in a closely covered sauce-pan; when a straw will pierce them, take them out, and weigh equal quantities of pounded loaf sugar and of oranges; cut and pick out the seeds of the oranges, pound them with the sugar in a mortar till they are like a paste; take out all the white and stringy parts, and when quite smooth, pack it into jars, and tie them closely over with paper. It will keep for a year, and when it is to be made into a pudding, mix with two table-spoonfuls of it five well-beaten yolks of eggs, two ounces and a half of sugar, the same of melted butter, three table-spoonfuls of white wine, and two of rose water; beat the ingredients together for nearly half an hour; bake it in a dish lined with puff paste.

Lemon Pudding

BOIL in water, in a closely covered sauce-pan, two large lemons till quite tender; take out the seeds, and pound the lemons to a paste; add a quarter of a pound of pounded loaf sugar, the same of fresh butter beaten to a cream, and the yolks of three well-beaten eggs; mix all together, and bake it in a tin lined with puff paste; take it out, strew over the top grated loaf sugar, and serve it upon a napkin.

Another way to make Lemon Pudding

CUT in half three lemons, squeeze the juice, and boil the rinds in a good deal of water; change it twice, putting each time hot water upon them; when quite tender, cut them into thin parings, about half an inch long; mix them with six ounces of loaf sugar pounded, and four table-spoonfuls of water; bake it in a tin lined with puff paste.

Another way to make Lemon Pudding

BEAT the yolks of seven, and the whites of five eggs, grate the rind of three lemons, squeeze and strain the juice, pound three quarters of a pound of loaf sugar, and melt six ounces of butter; beat all these ingredients together for fifteen minutes; bake it in a dish lined with puff paste, turn it out, and serve it upon a napkin.

Raspberry Pudding

MIX with three ounces of raspberry jam, a gill of cream, the beaten yolks of eight eggs, some sugar, and half a pound of clarified butter; beat all well together, and bake it in a dish lined with puff paste.

A Sweet Pasty

PARE, core, and mince six apples; blanch six ounces of sweet almonds, cut them very small; cut finely a quarter of a pound of citron and orange-peel; cut very finely three quarters of a pound of fresh marrow; pound a quarter of a pound of loaf sugar or use good brown sugar, and a tea-spoonful of cinnamon; mix well with these ingredients a glass of brandy; line and cover the top of the dish with puff paste, and when baked, take it out, and serve it upon a napkin.

Fresh suet may be substituted for the marrow, and when there is not a sufficient quantity of the marrow, the weight may be made up with suet. Each article must be very finely minced.

Bread Pudding

CUT two or three slices of bread rather thin, and without the crust, put them into a dish, and pour over them half a pint of boiling milk; let it stand till cold, and then mash the bread; lay into the bottom of a pudding-dish a layer of preserved gooseberries, then add the bread; sweeten well a pint of good milk, and mix with it three well-beaten eggs, with two table-spoonfuls of rose water; pour it over the bread, and bake it for half an hour. Before serving nutmeg may be grated over the top.

Another way to make Bread Pudding

POUR a pint of boiling milk over four ounces of bread crumbs, and two of fresh butter; cover it till cold, and mix with it three well-beaten eggs, a table-spoonful of sugar, and half the peel of a grated lemon, or a little pounded cinnamon; bake it in a butter dish, and serve with a sweet sauce.

Indian Meal, or Maize, Pudding

BOIL in a quart of good milk a tea-cupful of Indian meal, stir it constantly till thick, sweeten it with treacle or brown sugar, and stir in two well-beaten eggs, and an ounce of butter; bake it in a Dutch oven for half an hour. Half a grated nutmeg may be added, and it may be made without eggs.

A boiled Indian meal pudding is made in the same way, and after being mixed with or without eggs in it, it is tied in a buttered and floured cloth, and boiled for two hours. It is eaten with cold or melted butter.

Cheese Pudding

BEAT the yolks of ten, and the whites of two eggs, till quite light; mix well with them a pound of good cheese grated, then add a quarter of a pound of fresh butter beaten to a cream, and half a pint of cream; bake it half an hour in a dish rubbed over with butter, and lined or not with puff paste. Before serving, grate Parmesan cheese over the top.

Another way to make cheese pudding

GRATE one pound of mild Cheshire cheese; beat well four eggs, boil one ounce of butter; mix these ingredients together with one gill of cream, and two table-spoonfuls of grated and sifted bread, and bake it in a dish or tin lined with puff paste.

Another way to make cheese pudding

GRATE a quarter of a pound of good cheese, put it into a sauce-pan, with half a pint of new milk, and nearly two ounces of grated bread, and one beaten egg; stir it till the cheese be dissolved; put it into a buttered dish, and brown it in a Dutch oven. Serve it quite hot.

Egg Pudding

MELT a quarter of a pound of butter, and when nearly cold, mix well with it the following ingredients: the well-beaten yolks of ten, and the whites of two eggs, half a pint of rich cream, half a pound of good brown sugar, two table-spoonfuls of flour, a grated nutmeg, and a glass of brandy; bake it with or without a lining of puff paste.

A Pudding

BEAT separately the yolks and whites of six eggs; pound half a pound of loaf sugar, melt half a pound of fresh butter, blanch three ounces of sweet almonds, and pound them with a little rose water; mince four ounces of marmalade; mix all these ingredients well, and bake it in a dish lined with puff paste; turn it out, and serve it upon a napkin. It may be eaten cold.

Bread and Butter Pudding

CUT thin slices of bread and butter, without the crust, lay some in the bottom of a dish, and then put a layer of well-cleaned currants, or any preserved fruit; then more bread and butter and so on, till the dish is nearly filled; mix with a quart of milk four well-beaten eggs, three table-spoonfuls of orange-flower or rose water; sweeten it well with brown sugar, and pour it over the bread and butter, and let it soak for two or three hours before being baked. It will take nearly an hour. Serve with a sauce, in a sauce-tureen, made with a tea-cupful of currant wine, a table spoonful of brown sugar, three of water, and a bit of butter the size of a walnut, stirred till boiling hot.

Jelly Pudding

BEAT to a light cream ten ounces of fresh butter, then add by degrees the well-beaten yolks of six eggs, and half a pound of loaf sugar pounded; stir in two or three table-spoonfuls of orange-flower or rose water; beat to a stiff froth the whites of six eggs, mix them in lightly; bake it five-and-twenty minutes in a dish lined with puff paste.

Sago Pudding

BOIL five table-spoonfuls of sago, well picked and washed, in a quart of water, also half the peel of a lemon and a stick of cinnamon; when it is rather thick, add half a pint of white wine, and sweeten it with good brown sugar; beat the yolks of six, and the whites of three eggs, pick out the lemon-peel and cinnamon, mix all well together, and bake it in a dish with or without puff paste.

Millet Pudding

WASH four table-spoonfuls of the seed, boil it in a quart of milk with grated nutmeg and lemon-peel, and stir in, when a little cooled, an ounce of fresh butter; sweeten with brown sugar, and add the well-beaten yolks of four, and the whites of two eggs, and a glass of wine or spirits. Bake it in a buttered dish.

Another way to make Millet Pudding

WASH a quarter of a pound of millet, mix it with a quart of new milk, three ounces of brown sugar, a quarter of a pound of butter, broken into small bits, and a teaspoonful of grated nutmeg. Put it into a well-buttered dish, and bake it for an hour and a half.

Tapioca Pudding

WASH two large table-spoonfuls of tapioca, and soak it for an hour in a little warm water; strain off the water, and mix it with the well-beaten yolks of four, and the whites of two eggs, a quart of good milk, half a tea-spoonful of grated nutmeg, a small tea-cupful of white wine, and sweeten it with brown sugar. Bake it in a dish, with or without puff paste round the edges.

Camp Puddings

PUT into a sauce-pan half a pint of water, a quarter of a pound of butter, a table-spoonful of brown sugar, and the peel of half a lemon, or orange. Let it just come to a boil, take it off, and stir in a quarter of a pound of sifted flour: mix it perfectly smooth, and when cold, beat in four well-beaten eggs. Half fill twelve yellow tea-cups, and bake them in a quick oven. Serve them with a sauce of wine, sugar, and butter, in a sauce-tureen.

Prune Loaf

BOIL a pound of prunes, with half a pint of port wine, nearly as much water, and a table-spoonful of brown sugar; stone the prunes, cut some thin bits of bread into round forms, the size of half-a-crown, or into strips about an inch wide; soak them in clarified butter, and line a shape with them, and then add the prunes and a little marmalade; put over this a layer of bread, and tie a piece of buttered paper over the shape, and bake the loaf for one hour in a moderate oven.

Carrot Pudding

POUND in a mortar the red part of two large boiled carrots; and a slice of grated bread, or a pounded biscuit, two ounces of melted butter, the same quantity of sugar, a table-spoonful of marmalade, or a bit of orange-peel minced; half a tea-spoonful of grated nutmeg, and four well-beaten eggs; mix all well together; bake it in a dish lined with puff paste.

Another way to make Carrot Pudding

THE red part of two pounds of carrots grated, half a pound of grated bread, five well-beaten eggs, half a pound of fresh butter beaten to a cream, a quarter of a pound of sugar, half a pint of cream, a glass of brandy or white wine, two table-spoonfuls of orange-flower water; mix all these ingredients well together, and bake it in a dish lined with puff paste; turn it out to serve, and strew pounded sugar over the top.

Gooseberry Pudding

SCALD a quart of gooseberries, and when tender, rub them through a sieve, sweeten them well with brown sugar, melt six ounces of butter in a quarter of a pint of cream, beat the yolks of eight and the whites of four eggs, grate half the peel of a lemon; mix all well together, adding one spoonful of orange-flower water, and bake it in a dish lined with puff paste. Put grated sugar over it before serving.

A Pudding

SWEETEN a pint and a half of cream, and boil it with the peel of a small lemon; cut the crumb of a twopenny roll, and put it into the cream, and boil it for eight minutes, stirring constantly; when thick, add a quarter of a pound of fresh butter beaten to a cream, a tea-spoonful of grated nutmeg, and four well-beaten eggs; beat it all well together for some minutes. It may be baked or boiled.

A Voldron

MELT eleven ounces of fresh butter in a brass pan, and when quite hot, add the same quantity of pounded loaf sugar, and eight well-beaten eggs; stir constantly for six or eight minutes, and put it into a dish; the following day mix with it a wine glass of orange-flower water; of citron, orange, and lemon-peel, cut fine, half a pound; butter a pudding dish, and lay into the bottom a sheet of white paper buttered, then put in the voldron, and bake it for twenty minutes; turn it out, ornament it with cut citron and orange-peel, and serve it in a silver or glass dish.

Transparent Pudding

PUT into a sauce-pan half a pound of fresh butter, the same quantity of pounded loaf sugar, and eight well-beaten eggs; stir it over the fire till of the thickness of buttered eggs, put it into a basin to cool, and mix with it a tea-spoonful of grated nutmeg; bake it in a dish lined with puff paste. Before serving, grate loaf sugar over the top.

German Puffs

MIX very well with two large table-spoonfuls of flour; a quarter of a pint of cream, two well-beaten eggs, half a tea-spoonful of grated nutmeg, a very little salt, and one ounce of butter beaten to a cream; bake it in buttered cups for twenty or thirty minutes; turn them out upon a dish, and serve them instantly; pour a sweet sauce round them.

Another way to make German Puffs

BEAT to a cream a quarter of a pound of fresh butter, blanch and pound one ounce of sweet almonds with a little rose water, beat the yolks of five, and the whites of three eggs; mix all together with two large table-spoonfuls of flour, and sweeten it with pounded loaf sugar; bake it in buttered cups, and serve them with a sweet sauce.

Irish Puffs

ADD to the well-beaten yolks of five, and the whites of two eggs, a large table-spoonful of flour, not quite an ounce of melted butter, and half a tea-spoonful of salt; beat it all well for ten minutes, and add half a pint of cream; bake it in buttered tea-cups, turn them out, and serve them with a sweet sauce.

Citron Pudding

MIX together one pint of cream, one large spoonful of flour, four ounces of pounded loaf sugar, half a grated nutmeg, the beaten yolks of four eggs, and three ounces of citron cut very small; bake it in a dish lined with puff paste.

Rich Ground-Rice Pudding

STIR into a quarter of a pound of ground rice, a pint and a half of new milk; put it into a sauce-pan, and keep stirring it till it boils; then add three ounces of melted butter, the same quantity of sugar, half a grated nutmeg, and a tea-spoonful of grated lemon-peel; mix it very well, and when cold, add the well-beaten yolks of four, and the white of one egg, with a glass of ratafia, and half a one of orange-flower or rose water; bake it in a dish lined with puff paste, for three quarters of an hour. Before serving, strew over the top grated loaf sugar.

Another way to make Ground-Rice Pudding

MIX till quite smooth, with a small tea-cupful of ground rice, a quart of good milk, stir it over the fire till it boils, and let it boil for three minutes; put it into a basin, and when nearly cold, add the well-beaten yolks of six, and the whites of two eggs, with a tea-cupful of sweet wine, or a glass of spirits; put it into a buttered dish, and bake it for three quarters of an hour, or for one hour, in a Dutch oven, in the same way as the marrow pudding is done. (See below.) Any sort of preserve may be put into the bottom of the dish, and a sweet sauce may be served with it.

Rich Pudding

PUT into a sauce-pan four ounces of fresh butter, six ounces of pounded loaf sugar, six of marmalade, and six ounces of eggs, well beaten; stir all one way till it be thoroughly warmed; it must not be allowed to boil. Bake it in a dish lined with puff paste.

Butter-Milk Pudding

TURN two quarts of new milk with one of butter-milk; drain off the whey, and mix with the curd the grated crumb of a twopenny roll, the grated peel of a lemon, nearly a whole nutmeg grated, half a pint of rich cream, six ounces of clarified butter, and the beaten yolks of nine, and the whites of four eggs; sweeten it well, and bake it, with or without a puff paste, for three quarters of an hour. It may be boiled.

Marrow Pudding

PUT into a mug the crumb of a twopenny loaf, and pour over it a pint and a half of boiling milk; cover it closely for an hour; cut into small bits half a pound of marrow, stone and cut a quarter of a pound of raisins, take the same quantity of nicely-cleaned currants, beat well six eggs, a tea-spoonful of grated lemon-peel, and the same of nutmeg; mix all thoroughly with the bread and milk, sweeten it well with brown sugar, and bake it, with or without a border of puff paste round the dish, three quarters of an hour. It may be baked in a Dutch oven, and after baking it for three quarters of an hour, put a tin cover over the top, and place the dish upon a gridiron, over a slow fire, and let it remain for fifteen minutes.

Ratafia Pudding

POUND, with a little rose water, two ounces of blanched sweet almonds, and half a quarter of a pound of ratafia cakes, add the well-beaten yolks of six, and the whites of two eggs, a pint of thick cream, two glasses of white wine, and one ounce of pounded loaf sugar. Bake it in a dish, lined with puff paste, for three quarters of an hour.

Whole Rice Pudding

BOIL, in one pint and a half of water, till it be swelled, twelve dessert-spoonfuls of whole rice, with two table-spoonful of minced suet, and four of cleaned currants; then add two table-spoonfuls of grated bread, six of brown sugar, two well-beaten eggs, a quart of warm milk, a tea-spoonful of grated nutmeg, and one of ginger. Bake it in a buttered dish.

It may be baked in a Dutch oven. Half the quantity will make a pudding for a small family.

Whole Rice Pudding without Eggs

WEIGH six ounces of rice, six of brown sugar, and three and a half of fresh butter; break the butter into small bits ; wash the rice in several waters; put all into a pudding dish, and fill it up with good milk; let it soak some hours. Bake it in a moderate oven for nearly two hours, and as the milk wastes, fill up the dish with more, till they be swelled and soft; then let it brown.

Baked Hasty Pudding

BOIL two ounces of flour in a pint of milk, stir it till it be thick and stiff; put it into a basin, and add half an ounce of butter and a little nutmeg, with sugar sufficient to sweeten it. When cold mix in three well-beaten eggs; line a dish with thin paste, and in the bottom of it put a layer of orange marmalade, or any other preserve, and bake the pudding in a moderate oven for half an hour. It is very good without the paste, and may be baked in a Dutch oven.

Nassau Pudding

PUT into a sauce-pan the whole yolks of eight and the whites of four eggs, half a pound of pounded loaf sugar, and one pound of fresh butter; stir it over a slow fire for nearly half an hour; line a dish with thin puff paste, lay over the bottom a thick layer of orange marmalade, and then put in the pudding. Bake it for fifteen or twenty minutes.

Macaroni Pudding

BOIL a quarter of a pound of macaroni in a pint of good milk; when quite tender sweeten it with brown sugar, and add two well-beaten eggs, and three table-spoonfuls more of milk. Put it into a pudding-dish, and bake it in a Dutch oven for half an hour.

Potato or Carrot Pudding

WEIGH half a pound of boiled potatoes, or of boiled carrots, and pound them in a mortar; blanch one ounce of sweet almonds; pound them, but not finely, with a little orange-flower water; add the well-beaten whites of two, and the yolks of four eggs, a little salt, grated nutmeg, and one or two table-spoonfuls of brown sugar; mix all well together. Line the dish with puff paste, and just before putting the pudding into the oven, stir in half a pound of melted butter. Bake it for twenty minutes.

Potato Pudding

Boil and peel half a pound of potatoes, pound them in a mortar, with six ounces of fresh butter, then add the well-beaten yolks of six, and the whites of three eggs, six ounces of pounded loaf sugar, half a tea-spoonful of grated nutmeg, the same of pounded cinnamon, and a glass of spirits. Bake it in a buttered dish; turn it out before serving, and strew over it grated loaf sugar. A sweet sauce may be served with it.

Another way to make Potato Pudding

Boil three large mealy potatoes, mash them very smoothly, with one ounce of butter, and two or three table-spoonfuls of thick cream; add three well-beaten eggs, a little salt, grated nutmeg, and a table-spoonful of brown sugar. Beat all well together, and bake it, in a buttered dish, for half an hour in an oven, and three quarters in a Dutch oven. A few currants may be added to the pudding.

Tansy Pudding

Pour a quart of boiling milk over a thick slice of the crumb of bread; cover it till cold. Beat the yolks of six, and the whites of two eggs. Pound some tansy with two or three leaves of spinach; squeeze the juice, and put as much of it as will make the pudding a good green colour, a glass of brandy, half a grated nutmeg, and four ounces of fresh butter; mix all the ingredients, sweeten and put it into a sauce-pan, and stir it over the fire till it be hot. Bake it in a buttered dish for half an hour. Before serving, strew grated loaf sugar over the top.

Charlotte des Pommes

Pare, core, and mince fourteen or fifteen French rennet apples; put them into a frying-pan, with some pounded loaf sugar, a little pounded cinnamon, grated lemon-peel, and two ounces and a half of fresh butter; fry them a quarter of an hour over a quick fire, stirring them constantly. Butter a shape of the size the charlotte is intended to be; cut strips of bread about the width of two fingers, and long enough to reach from the bottom to the rim of the shape, so that the whole be lined with bread; dip each bit into melted butter, and then put a layer of the fried apples, and one of apricot jam or marmalade and then one of bread dipped into butter; begin and finish with it. Bake it in an oven for nearly an hour; turn it out to serve it. It may be boiled, and served with a sweet sauce.

Speaker's Pudding

STONE and weigh three quarters of a pound of raisins. Rub with butter a plain oval mould, and stick upon it some of the raisins, in strips or circles. Cut some thin slices of bread without the crust, dry them a while before the fire, butter, and cut them into strips about an inch and a quarter wide; line the mould with part of the bread, then put a layer of raisins, and strew over them a table-spoonful of pounded loaf sugar; add a layer of the bread and butter; then raisins, and so on till the shape be nearly full, putting bread and butter on the top. Mix with a pint of good milk, the well-beaten yolks of four eggs, a table-spoonful of sugar, one and a half of rose water, and a glass of brandy; pour this over the pudding, and let it soak one or two hours. Bake it three quarters of an hour. It may be boiled by steam for an hour and a half.

Almond Pudding

BLANCH eight bitter, and half a pound of sweet almonds; pound them in a mortar, with a glass of orange-flower water, and one of brandy. Soak, in a pint and a half of rich cream, four ounces of pounded biscuit; melt four ounces of butter; beat, till very light, the yolks of seven eggs, with half a pound of pounded loaf sugar, and a tea-spoonful of grated lemon-peel. Mix all well together, and stir it over the fire till it be thoroughly heated, but not allowed to boil. Bake it in a dish lined with puff paste for half an hour.

Another way to make Almond Pudding

POUND with orange-flower or rose water, half a pound of blanched sweet almonds; add a small tea-cupful of white wine, a quarter of a pound of melted butter, the same of pounded loaf sugar, four well-beaten eggs, a pint of cream, a tea-spoonful of grated lemon-peel and nutmeg, and two table-spoonfuls of grated bread. Mix all well, and bake it in a dish lined with puff paste.

Custard Pudding

MIX, with one table-spoonful of flour, a pint of cream or new milk, the well-beaten yolks of six eggs, a spoonful of rose water, one of brandy, one ounce of fresh butter broken into small bits; sweeten with pounded loaf sugar, and add a little grated nutmeg. Bake it in a dish lined with puff paste, for half an hour. Before serving, strew over it pounded loaf sugar, and stick over it thin cut bits of citron.

Light Puddings

MIX, with two ounces of flour, half a pint of cream, four well-beaten eggs, and two ounces of clarified butter; half fill buttered cups, and bake them nearly half an hour. Serve them turned out upon a dish, with a sweet sauce poured into it.

Vermicelli Pudding

WASH three ounces of vermicelli; boil it for fifteen minutes in a pint of milk, with a bit of cinnamon and lemon-peel. When nearly cold pick out the cinnamon and peel, sweeten it, and add the well-beaten yolks of six, and the whites of two eggs. Mix it well, and bake it in a buttered dish for half an hour.

It may be boiled for one hour and a half, and served with a sweet sauce.

Chous

STIR into a pint of boiling water half a pound of butter, and add by degrees the same quantity of flour; stir it constantly till quite smooth, and then add eight eggs unbeaten, with half a tea-spoonful of salt, and a wine-glass of orange-flower water; take it off the fire, and beat it for a few minutes, then with a spoon form it into small balls; place them in rows upon a floured tin, and bake them in a moderate oven for a quarter of an hour. Serve them with grated loaf sugar sifted over them.

Arrow-Root Pudding

FROM a quart of new milk take a small tea-cupful, and mix it with two large spoonfuls of arrow-root. Boil the remainder of the milk, and stir it amongst the arrow-root; add, when nearly cold, the well-beaten yolks of four eggs, with two ounces of pounded loaf sugar, and the same quantity of fresh butter broken into small bits; season with grated nutmeg. Mix it well together, and bake it in a butter dish fifteen or twenty minutes.

Scotch Pudding

THE yolks of eight, and the whites of three well-beaten eggs, half a pound of pounded loaf sugar, a quarter of a pound of melted butter, two table-spoonfuls of sifted ground rice, the grated peel and juice of one lemon; mix all together, and bake it in a dish lined with puff paste; turn it out to serve, and strew over the top grated loaf sugar.

Potato-Flour Pudding.

Boil some cinnamon, lemon-peel, and sugar, in a quart of milk; strain, and stir it with three table-spoonfuls of potato flour previously mixed smooth with a little cold milk; stir it till it be nearly cold; add four well-beaten eggs, a glass of sweet wine, or two table-spoonfuls of spirits, and a little marmalade. Bake it in a Dutch oven.

Potato Flour, or Starch

Wash some large mealy potatoes, peel, and throw them into a deep pan of cold water, in which grate them down upon a bread grater; then strain the mass through a hair sieve, let it settle for ten or fifteen minutes; pour off the water, put on fresh, stir it up, and again let it settle for half an hour or longer; repeat this until the water be perfectly clear, and the powder blanched of a pure white. Lay a linen cloth upon a riddle, put the flour upon it, and dry it in the sun or before the fire; turn, and stir it frequently; or it may be dried upon large flat dishes. Put it into jars, and tie paper over them. The potato which has a yellow tint yields the best flour, and most abundantly in October and March.

Plum Pudding

Take one pound of fresh beef suet, very finely minced, one pound of good raisins stoned and chopped, one pound of currants nicely cleaned and dried, one pound of flour, the grated peel of one lemon, and half a large nutmeg, six well-beaten eggs, one ounce of candied orange, and half a one of candied lemon-peel minced, half a pound of brown sugar, one glass of brandy, and a tea-cupful of cream. Mix all the ingredients well with the flour. Boil it in a cloth, put it on in a copper of boiling water, and keep it boiling for seven hours. Before serving, strew grated loaf sugar over it. Sauces: – Half a pint of white wine, three table-spoonfuls of water, three or four of pounded loaf sugar, and one ounce of butter, stirred till boiling hot; and plain melted butter, sweetened with sugar. Brown sugar and currant wine may be used for the sauce.

Another way to make Plum Pudding

One pound of the best raisins stoned, half a pound of currants well cleaned, one pound of fresh beef suet finely minced, five table-spoonfuls of grated bread, three of flour, two of brown sugar, one tea-spoonful of pounded ginger, one of cinnamon, and one of salt, six well-beaten eggs, and three wine-glasses of rum, all to be mixed thoroughly together the day before it is to be boiled. Boil it in a cloth or mould for four or five hours. Serve with melted butter or the following sauce: – Heat two or three table-spoonfuls of sweet cream, and mix it gradually with the well-beaten yolks of two eggs; add three table-spoonfuls of white wine, brandy, or rum, and a table-spoonful of sugar; season with grated nutmeg, and stir it over the fire till quite hot; but do not allow it to boil.

Another way to make Plum Pudding

HALF a pound of raisins stoned, the same of currants cleaned, six ounces of minced suet, three table-spoonfuls of flour, the same of grated bread, five ounces of brown sugar, eight well-beaten eggs, three cloves pounded, half a tea-spoonful of Jamaica pepper ground, a small grated nutmeg, a little salt, and a glass of brandy; mix it all extremely well, and boil it for three or four hours. Serve with wine and sugar sauce.

Another way to make Plum Pudding

ONE pound of fresh beef suet, finely minced, one pound of raisins stoned, five table-spoonfuls of flour, five of brown sugar, the yolks of five, and the whites of three well-beaten eggs, a tea-spoonful of salt; mix all the ingredients thoroughly, and boil it in a cloth for four or five hours. Serve with grated loaf sugar, and melted butter poured over it.

Another way to make Plum Pudding

FOUR ounces of apples finely minced, the same quantity of currants cleaned and dried, and of grated bread, two ounces of raisins, stoned and minced, two of pounded loaf sugar, half a nutmeg grated, a little candied orange or lemon peel, four well-beaten eggs, one ounce and a half of melted butter just warm; mix all the ingredients well together, and boil it in a buttered shape for four hours. If the pudding does not fill the shape, add a slice of the crumb of bread at the bottom. Serve with a sweet sauce.

Plum Pudding without Eggs

HALF a pound of grated bread, a quarter of a pound of finely-minced suet, a table-spoonful of flour, half a pound of currants cleaned, rather more than two ounces of brown sugar, and a glass of brandy; mix all together with a sufficient quantity of milk to make it into a stiff batter; boil it in a cloth for four hours. It may be baked, adding half a pound of stoned raisins, and a little candied orange and lemon peel.

Treacle Pudding

HALF a pound of flour, the same of finely-minced suet, of raisins stoned, and cut small, and well-cleaned currants, a quarter of a pound each, three table-spoonfuls of treacle; and half a pint of water; mix it all well together; boil it in a cloth for four hours, and serve it with a sweet sauce.

Jeneton Pudding

BUTTER a mould, and ornament it with raisins in festoons, or in any other form; line it with spunge biscuit, and fill it up with a mixture of ratafia and spunge biscuit, then pour a rich custard over the whole, and let it stand for two hours, adding more custard as it soaks into the biscuit. The mould being quite full, tie a cloth over it, and boil it for about an hour.

Batter Pudding

BEAT seven eggs for fifteen or twenty minutes; mix with six large table-spoonfuls of flour a quart of new milk, and add the eggs, with a little salt; stir it well together, and let it stand an hour or two; lay a buttered and floured pudding-cloth into a basin, pour in the batter, tie it tightly, and boil it for an hour and a half.

It may be boiled in a mould. Serve it with the following sauce: – Dredge a large table-spoonful of butter in with flour; melt it with a little water, add a large tea-cupful of currant wine, well sweetened with brown sugar, and the well-beaten yolks of two eggs; stir it constantly till it be thoroughly heated, but take care it does not boil; pounded cinnamon, or grated nutmeg, may be added.

Another way to make Batter Pudding

BEAT the yolks of four, and the whites of three eggs, for a quarter of an hour; mix gradually with five table-spoonfuls of flour, a pint of good milk, and half a tea-spoonful of salt, add the eggs, and beat it well; boil it in a cloth for one hour. Serve it with the following sweet sauce: – Two glasses of white or sweet wine, one of water, three table-spoonfuls of sugar, and a bit of butter the size of a large walnut; stir it till it boil.

Muffin Pudding

PARE off the crust of two muffins, split and halve them; put into a tin shape a layer of any sort of preserves, – apricot is the best, – then a layer of muffin, next one of fruit, and then the remainder of the muffin, and pour over it a pint of warm milk, in which four well-beaten eggs have been mixed. Cover the shape, and place it in a sauce-pan with a small quantity of boiling water. Keep on the cover, and let it boil twenty minutes; turn it out, and serve it with pudding sauce.

Light white bread cut thin may be substituted for the muffins. The pudding will be better if prepared three or four hours before it is boiled.

Ardovie Pudding

MIX two table-spoonfuls of ground rice with a quart of milk; stir it over the fire till it boils, and then add five well-beaten eggs and a little salt; pour the mixture into a basin rubbed with butter; place it in a steam sauce-pan, or in a cullender; if in the cullender, cover it with the lid of a sauce-pan, and put it into a sauce-pan of boiling water, and let it steam two hours; then put the basin into a Dutch oven, and let it stand a quarter of an hour to firm the pudding, but it must not be browned: turn it out, and pour over it the following sauce: add half a pint of cream to the beaten yolk of an egg; stir it over the fire till it thickens; take it off for a little, then mix in a quarter of a pint of white wine and three ounces of sugar; stir it again over the fire.

Ground-Rice Pudding

BOIL in a pint of milk a quarter of a pound of flour of rice, with two table-spoonfuls of rose water, and half the peel of a lemon, stir it till thick, take it off, and mix in a quarter of a pound of butter, half a grated nutmeg, the well-beaten yolks of four, and the whites of three eggs; sweeten it with brown sugar, pick out the lemon-peel, and boil it in a buttered basin, which must be completely filled. Serve with a sauce made with a glass of white wine, boiled in melted butter, and sweetened with brown sugar.

Another way to make Ground-Rice Pudding

STIR into a quart of boiling milk a breakfast-cupful of ground rice, and a few pounded bitter almonds; when quite thick, take it off, and add eight well-beaten eggs, sweeten it, and again stir it over the fire till it boil, and then put it into an earthenware mould, and let it stand before the fire a few minutes before turning it out. Serve it with pounded cinnamon strewed over it, and a sauce of melted butter, wine, and sugar, poured round it.

Wiltshire Pudding

MIX, with three well-beaten eggs, a pint of milk, as much flour as will make it a thick batter, and a little salt; beat it for some minutes, stir in gently a large tea-cupful of picked red currants, and half that quantity of red raspberries; boil it in a cloth for two hours, turn it out upon the dish it is to be served in, cut it into slices about three quarters of an inch thick, but do not separate them; put between each a thin slice of butter, and some brown sugar, and serve it hot, with pudding sauce in a sauce tureen. It is very good without the raspberries.

Tealing Pudding

WHISK together for ten minutes eight eggs, some sugar, nutmeg, ginger, and the grated peel of a lemon; stir in three spoonfuls of flour, and a quart of milk which has been allowed just to boil; dip a cloth into boiling water, dust it with flour, tie the mixture into it, and boil it for an hour. Serve with pudding sauce.

Middleton Pudding

BEAT together ten eggs, five spoonfuls of flour, a pint of new milk, a table-spoonful of brown sugar, a little nutmeg, and a pinch of salt; tie it loosely in a cloth, and boil for two hours. Serve it with pudding sauce.

Bread Pudding

BOIL the grated peel of a Seville orange in a pint of milk, and pour it over the sliced crumb of a twopenny toll, cover it closely for an hour, beat the yolks of three, and the whites of two eggs, mix them with the bread and milk, and beat it for ten minutes; sweeten and boil it in a buttered basin for an hour. Serve with a sauce of melted butter and sugar.

Family Pudding

MIX with a pound of flour half a pound of raisins stoned and chopped, the same quantity of minced suet, a little salt, and milk or water sufficient to make it into a stiff batter; boil it for five hours. Serve it with melted butter poured over it. Two well-beaten eggs may be added.

Half-Hour Dumplings

MINCE finely half a pound of suet, mix it with the same proportion of grated bread, and a table-spoonful of flour, a quarter of a pound of currants, some sugar, a little grated lemon-peel, nutmeg, and three well-beaten eggs; roll the mixture into round balls, tie them in bits of linen, and boil them for half an hour. Serve with melted butter and sugar poured over them.

Shropshire Pudding

OF fresh beef suet finely minced, of brown bread grated, and of brown sugar, one pound each, one nutmeg grated, a tea-cupful of brandy, the well-beaten yolks of eight, and the whites of four eggs; mix all well together; and boil it in a cloth or mould for four hours. Serve it with a sauce of melted butter, sugar, and two table-spoonfuls of brandy.

Apple Pudding

WEIGH one pound and three quarters of apples, pare, core, and cut them into thin bits; weigh also ten ounces of brown sugar; make a suet paste, rolled thinner towards the edges than in the middle, and sufficiently large to lay into a two-quart basin, previously buttered; put in the apples and sugar alternately, wet the edges of the paste, and fold it closely over; dredge it with flour, and tie a pudding-cloth over the top of the basin; boil it for three hours.

A light paste may be made with flour, half its quantity in bulk of grated bread and suet, mixing it with milk or water, and, instead of apples, currants, damsons, or any other fruit, may be enclosed in it.

West Country Pudding

MIX, with four well-beaten eggs, half a pound of apples, finely minced, the same quantity of grated bread and of well-cleaned currants, a quarter of a pound of brown sugar, and half a tea-spoonful of grated nutmeg. This pudding may be either boiled or baked, and, instead of grated bread, four ounces of whole rice may be used, which must be boiled in milk, strained, and allowed to be cold before being mixed with the other ingredients. This pudding is done in one hour and a half, and served with a sweet sauce.

Prune Pudding

STEW a pound of prunes with half a pint of port wine, a quarter of a pint of water, and a large table-spoonful of brown sugar; break the stones, and put the kernels with the fruit; spread it over a sheet of puff paste, wet the edges, and roll it into the form of a bolster; tie it firmly in a buttered and floured cloth, and boil it between two and three hours. Serve with a sweet wine sauce.

Damson Pudding

MAKE a batter with three well-beaten eggs, a pint of milk, and of flour and brown sugar four table-spoonfuls each; stone a pint of damsons, and mix them with the batter; boil it in a buttered basin for an hour and a half.

Apple Dumplings

PARE and scoop out the core of six large baking apples, put part of a clove, and a little grated lemon-peel, inside of each, and enclose them in pieces of puff paste; boil them in nets for the purpose, or bits of linen, for an hour. Before serving, cut off a small bit from the top of each, and put in a tea-spoonful of sugar, and a bit of fresh butter; replace the bit of paste, and strew over them pounded loaf sugar.

Potato-Flour Pudding

BOIL half a pint of milk, and the same quantity of cream, with a stick of cinnamon, and the peel of a lemon; strain it, and stir in gradually three table-spoonfuls of potato flour; mix it very smoothly, and add six well-beaten eggs; sweeten with pounded loaf sugar; stick all round a buttered tin mould, dried cherries, or stoned raisins, put in the pudding, and put a bit of buttered linen over the top, and then the cover of the mould; place in a sauce-pan of boiling water, boil it for an hour and half; take care the water does not boil over the mould. Serve with a sweet sauce.

Potato Pudding

BOIL a pound of potatoes, peel and pound them in a mortar, and mix them well with half a pound of melted butter, the same of pounded loaf sugar, two ounces of blanched sweet almonds pounded, with two spoonfuls of rose water, eight well-beaten eggs, and half a nutmeg grated; boil it in a cloth, or buttered basin. Serve with a sweet sauce of wine, sugar, butter, and grated nutmeg.

Rice Pudding

BOIL a quarter of a pound of rice in water till it is soft, then drain it in a sieve, and pound it in a mortar; add five well-beaten yolks of eggs, a quarter of a pound of butter, the same proportion of sugar, a small nutmeg, and half the rind of a lemon grated; work them well together for twenty minutes, and add a pound of cleaned currants; mix it all well, and boil it in a pudding-cloth for an hour and a half. Serve with wine sauce.

Whole Rice Pudding

BOIL, in water sufficient to cover it, eight table-spoonfuls of rice till quite swelled, put it into a basin, stir in about two ounces of butter, of grated bread and brown sugar, two table-spoonfuls each, two well-beaten eggs, a tea-spoonful of grated nutmeg, half a one of pounded ginger, and enough of milk to make the whole fill a quart basin, which may be about a pint; the basin must be buttered, and a piece of buttered paper put under the cloth. Boil it for an hour, and serve with a sweet sauce. Half this quantity may be used.

Another way to make Whole Rice Pudding

WASH in several waters a quarter of a pound of rice, put it into a sauce-pan with one ounce of fresh butter, and a sufficiency of water to cover it; stir it frequently till it becomes thick, add six well-beaten eggs, a few pounded bitter almonds, a tea-spoonful of pounded cinnamon, and a glass of rum; sweeten and boil it in a cloth for one hour to serve it with a sweet sauce.

American Snow Balls

BOIL some rice in milk till it be swelled and soft; pare and carefully scoop out the core of five or six good-sized apples, put into each a little grated lemon-peel and cinnamon; place as much of the rice upon a bit of linen as will entirely cover an apple, and tie each closely. Boil them two hours, and serve them with melted butter, sweetened with sugar.

Aunt Mary's Pudding

OF bloom raisins stoned, currants nicely cleaned, suet finely minced, bread grated, apples minced, and brown sugar, a quarter of a pound of each; four well-beaten eggs, a tea-spoonful of pounded ginger, half a one of salt, half a nutmeg grated, and one glass of brandy; mix all the ingredients well, and boil it in a cloth for two hours. Serve with a sauce of melted butter, a glass of wine, and some sugar.

Custard Pudding

MIX with a pint of cream or milk six well-beaten eggs, two table-spoonfuls of flour, half a small nutmeg grated, or an equal quantity of pounded cinnamon, a table-spoonful of pounded loaf sugar, and a little salt; boil it in a cloth, or buttered basin that will exactly hold it, for half an hour. Or, boil in a quart of milk a bit of cinnamon, lemon-peel, and grated nutmeg; when nearly cold, strain and mix it with the beaten yolks of six, and the whites of four eggs, and boil it half an hour. Serve with wine sauce.

Suet Pudding

MIX six table-spoonfuls of grated bread with a pound of finely-minced fresh beef suet, or that of a loin of mutton, one pound of flour, two tea-spoonfuls of salt, six well-beaten eggs, and nearly a pint of milk. Boil it in a cloth, four or five hours. Serve it plain, or with a sweet sauce

Irish Black Pudding

Blanch and pound to a paste, with a glass of rose water, a quarter of a pound of sweet almonds; grate half a pound of the crumb of bread; mince one pound of fresh suet, add half a pound of cleaned currants, a tea-spoonful of pounded cinnamon, nutmeg, and cloves, a pint of cream, the well-beaten yolks of four, and whites of two eggs, a glass of brandy, and some candied lemon-peel.

Mix all the ingredients well together; sweeten with pounded loaf sugar, and boil it in a cloth, and when cold, cut it into thick slices; heat it in a Dutch oven, or broil it upon a gridiron.

A Pudding

Eight ounces of grated bread, three of finely-minced suet, four of pounded loaf sugar, the juice and grated peel of two lemons, and one well-beaten egg. Mix all together, and boil it in a cloth or buttered basin for one hour. Serve with a sweet sauce.

White Pudding

Boil in a quart of milk two table-spoonfuls of orange flower or rose water; add to two well-beaten eggs, three table-spoonfuls of flour, and a little salt; stir it into the milk, and if not thick, dredge in a little more flour; just before it is taken off the fire, put in a bit of fresh butter the size of a walnut. Serve it with red currant jelly upon the top of it.

Calf's-Feet Pudding

Pick all the meat off three well-boiled calf's feet; chop it finely, as also half a pound of fresh beef suet; grate the crumb of a penny loaf; cut like straws an ounce of orange-peel, and the same of citron; beat well six eggs, and grate a small nutmeg; mix all these ingredients well together, with a glass of brandy or rum, and boil it in a cloth nearly three hours. Serve with a sweet sauce.

Suet Apple Pudding

Of finely-minced fresh mutton suet, grated apples, flour, and brown sugar, six ounces each, half a grated nutmeg, a tea-spoonful of salt, and four well-beaten eggs, all well mixed together; boiled for two hours, and served with a sweet sauce.

Fruit Suet Pudding

Of finely-minced suet, flour, grated bread, and cleaned currants, a quarter of a pound each; a tea-spoonful of pounded ginger, one of salt, two ounces of brown sugar, and a tea-cupful of milk; mix all the ingredients well together, and boil it in a cloth for two hours. Serve with a sweet sauce.

Regent's Pudding

Rub an earthenware mould with butter, and cover the bottom with bloom raisins stoned; cut thin slices of the crumbs of bread, butter, and lay one or two over the raisins; upon that put a layer of ratafia cakes, then one of bread and butter, and raisins; do this till the mould is nearly full, and pour over it the following mixture: A pint of cream well sweetened with pounded loaf sugar, and mixed with four well-beaten yolks of eggs, a glass of brandy, and two table-spoonfuls of rose water; let it soak one or two hours; put over the top a piece of writing paper buttered, and tie over it a cloth. Boil it for one hour and a half and serve it with wine sauce.

Stirred-in Gooseberry Pudding

Rub into six ounces of flour a quarter of a pound of finely-minced mutton suet; put it into a basin with half a tea-spoonful of salt, four or five table-spoonfuls of brown sugar, two well-beaten eggs, and a gill of milk; stir in a pint, or a pint and a half of gooseberries; butter a basin, that will exactly contain it, and boil it for two hours. Serve with a sauce of butter melted with milk, and well sweetened with brown sugar.

Oxford Pudding

Wash in four or five waters half a pound of good rice; tie it into a pudding cloth, not too tightly; put it on in a pot of cold water, and when it boils, let it boil for two hours. It may be eaten with cold butter and sugar, or treacle. A quarter of a pound of nicely-cleaned currants may be boiled with the rice.

Oatmeal Porridge

Boil some water in a sauce-pan with a little salt, and stir oatmeal into it with a thevil; when of a proper thickness, let it boil for four or five minutes, stirring it all the time; then pour it into a dish, and serve it with cream or milk, it is sometimes eaten with porter and sugar, or ale and sugar.

If made with milk instead of water, less meal is requisite, and it is then eaten with cold milk.

Sowens

HALF-FILL a tub, large jar, or any other vessel, with oatmeal seeds, and fill it up with milk-warm water. Let it stand till it get a little sour, which in warm weather may be in three or four days; then strain it through a cheese drainer, squeezing the seeds, and adding to them a little cold water to obtain all the substance from them; the liquid is allowed to stand a little, till the thick matter falls to the bottom, the thin is then poured off, and fresh cold water added, stirring it well. The sowens, being thus prepared for boiling, will keep a week or more in cold weather; and when too sour for use, a little may be mixed with the next making, by which means it will be sooner ready. When to be dressed, pour off some of the water from the top, stir it up from the bottom, and boil the portion required, adding a little salt, and stirring it all the time it is upon the fire; it will take from ten to twenty minutes to thicken, when it is poured into a deep dish, and milk served with it.

Ale Berry

STIR into a bottle of cold beer a handful of oatmeal; put it on the fire, and stir it till it thickens like porridge, which may be in five minutes after it boils. It is served in a deep dish, and eaten with sugar. This, and the preceding preparations of oatmeal, may be found useful for children, and an acceptable variety to those for whom a low diet is described.

Bread and Butter Pudding

BUTTER a mould; lay into the bottom thin-cut bread and butter, with the crust pared off; strew over it a layer of currants and stoned raisins, mixed; half fill the shape, and add half a pint of brandy or rum, or currant wine may be used; in an hour, pour over it a quart of good milk, mixed with six well-beaten eggs, half a nutmeg grated, and some brown sugar; boil it for one hour and a half, and serve it with melted butter, currant wine, and sugar.

Yorkshire Pudding

MIX, with five table-spoonfuls of flour, a tea-spoonful of salt, one pint of good milk, and three well-beaten eggs; butter a square tin pan, put in the batter, and set the tin upon a gridiron for a few minutes, and then place it under beef that is roasting. Serve it cut into small oblong pieces.

New College Puddings

HALF a pound of fresh beef suet, finely minced, the same of currants, a quarter of a pound of grated bread, and of pounded sweet biscuit, half a tea-spoonful of salt, a small nutmeg grated, an ounce of candied orange-peel minced; mix all together with two or three well-beaten eggs, and fry them in butter till of a light brown; shake the pan, and turn them frequently till done enough. Serve with pounded loaf sugar strewed thickly over them,

Croquettes de Pommes de Terre

WHEN boiled and peeled, allow four large, mealy potatoes, half their weight of butter, and of pounded loaf sugar, two eggs beaten, half the grated peel of a lemon, and a little salt; pound the potatoes in a mortar with the other ingredients; beat the yolks of four eggs; roll up the croquettes; dip them into the beaten eggs, and roll them in sifted bread crumbs; in an hour, roll them again as before, and fry them in butter; put them upon the back of a sieve before the fire to drain.

Cottage Puddings

SIX ounces of currants, half a pound of minced suet and the same quantity of grated bread, half a grated nutmeg, a table-spoonful of white wine, or rose water; mix all well together, with the beaten yolks of five eggs, to a stiff paste, and with floured hands roll it into twelve or thirteen small puddings in the form of sausages; fry them gently in butter till of a nice brown; roll them well in the frying-pan. Serve with pounded loaf sugar strewed over them, and with a sweet sauce. They may be boiled.

Pudding in Haste

BEAT separately the yolks and whites of four eggs, and with the yolks a little brown sugar, a tea-cupful of good milk, two table-spoonfuls of flour, one of rum or sweet wine; and when they are well mixed, add the beaten whites. Fry it in butter in a broad sauce-pan; brown the upper side before the fire. Serve with pounded loaf sugar strewed over, and sweet sauce.

Oxford Puddings

HALF a pound of sifted bread crumbs, the same quantity of suet and of currants finely minced, a tea-spoonful of grated nutmeg, some brown sugar and a little salt, a table-spoonful of rose water, one of brandy or rum; make it into a stiff paste with cream, and the beaten yolks of two eggs; roll it into balls, and fry.

Point de Jour Fritters

MIX with two handfuls of flour a glass of sweet wine, a table-spoonful of brandy, and warm milk, sufficient to make it into a paste; add the well-beaten whites of four eggs, a little minced citron, candied orange-peel or currants; beat it well together, and drop it through a wide tin funnel, into boiling lard. Serve with pounded loaf sugar strewed over them.

Sweetmeat Fritters

CUT small any sort of candied fruit, and heat it with a bit of fresh butter, some good milk, and a little grated lemon-peel; when quite hot, stir in enough of flour to make it into a stiff paste, take it off the fire, and work in eight or ten eggs, two at a time; when cold, form the fritters, and fry, and serve them with pounded loaf sugar strewed over them.

Apple Fritters

STEW some apples cut small, together with a little water, sugar, lemon-peel, and cinnamon; when soft, add a little white wine; the juice of half a lemon, and a bit of fresh butter; when cold, mix them with a batter as for Tunbridge puffs (page 235), or enclose them in rounds of puff paste. Fry, and serve them with sifted loaf sugar over them.

Another way to make Apple Fritters

FOUR well-beaten eggs, half a pint of cream, two table-spoonfuls of yeast, three of white wine, and two of rose water; half a tea-spoonful of grated nutmeg, and of salt; make it into a thick batter with flour, peel and core two or three apples, cut them into thin bits, and mix them with the butter; cover it over, let it stand, placed near the fire, about an hour; drop it into boiling lard, and serve them in a napkin with sugar strewed over them. Gooseberries previously stewed may be done in the same way.

French Fritters

BREAK three eggs into two handfuls of flour, work it well with a little milk, and half a tea-spoonful of salt, and, when well worked, add a tea-spoonful of pounded cinnamon, the grated peel of a lemon, and a little minced citron; rub a sauce-pan with butter, put in the paste, and when it becomes firm, take it out and cut it into bits of three or four inches long, and one wide; notch each bit at the ends; fry, and serve them with sifted loaf sugar over them.

Almond Fritters

BLANCH three quarters of a pound of sweet almonds. Pour over them three table-spoonfuls of rose water, and in a quarter of an hour a pint of cream; let them stand two or three hours, then pound them in a mortar till they become quite a paste; add the beaten yolks of six eggs, two or three pounded Naples biscuit; sweeten with pounded loaf sugar, and mix all well together; melt a quarter of a pound of fresh butter in a frying-pan, and when hot, pour in the mixture, and stir it constantly till thick, and of a light brown colour. Serve it with sifted loaf sugar over the top.

Currant Fritters without Eggs

STIR into half a pint of mild ale, as much flour as will make it into a thick batter; add a little sugar and a few currants; beat it up quickly, and with a spoon drop it into boiling lard.

Potato Fritters

PEEL, and pound in a mortar, six mealy potatoes, with a little salt, a glass of white wine, some pounded sugar, cinnamon, and an ounce of butter; roll it out with a little flour, cut them the size of a wine glass, and fry them in boiling clarified dripping. Serve them with sifted loaf sugar over them.

Fried Toasts

CUT the crumb of a twopenny loaf into round or oblong pieces, nearly an inch thick, and soak them for four or five hours in a pint of cream, mixed with three well-beaten eggs, half a pint of white wine, a little grated nutmeg, and sweetened with pounded loaf sugar. Fry them in butter till of a light brown colour, and serve with wine and sugar sauce.

Bonnets

BOIL in half a pint of water, for ten minutes, a bit of cinnamon, and of lemon-peel; strain, and mix it with three table-spoonfuls of flour, and stir it over the fire for two or three minutes; add a bit of butter the size of a walnut; when cold, mix in the beaten yolks of two eggs, a little salt and pepper; beat it well, drop a dessert-spoonful of the mixture into boiling lard, then drain them upon the back of a sieve, and when served, throw over pounded loaf sugar.

Instead of the salt and pepper, a little preserve may be dropped upon each, before the sugar is thrown over.

Puffs

PUT into a sauce-pan a pint of milk, boil it slowly, and stir in flour till it be very thick, like paste; when cold, mix with it six well-beaten eggs, a table-spoonful of sugar, half a nutmeg, and the peel of a small lemon grated, and a table-spoonful of brandy; beat it well together for fifteen minutes, and when quite light, drop it from a dessert-spoon into a pan of boiling clarified suet or lard. Serve with pounded loaf sugar strewed over them.

Tunbridge Puffs

PUT into a nicely-tinned sauce-pan a pint of milk, and when it boils, stir in it as much flour as will make it a thick batter; add three well-beaten eggs, and two or three drops of oil of cinnamon, or any other seasoning; dust a large flat plate with flour, with a spoon throw on it the batter, in the form of balls or fritters, and drop them into boiling clarified dripping or lard. Serve them with pounded loaf sugar strewed over.

The batter may be made into a pudding, adding with the eggs an ounce of salt butter. Boil, and serve it with a sweet sauce.

Spanish Puffs

PUT into a sauce-pan half a pint of water and a quarter of a pound of butter; stir it till it boils, and mix in four table-spoonful of flour; stir it well together, and add six yolks and four whites of eggs, two at a time; let it cool, and, with a dessert-spoon, drop it into boiling clarified dripping or lard.

To make ginger puffs, a tea-spoonful of pounded ginger may be added.

Snowballs Boiled in Butter

MIX with six well-beaten eggs one pint and a half of sour cream, and add by degrees as much flour as will make the batter thick enough for the spoon to stand in it; sweeten it with brown sugar, and put in a few cardamoms; stir into this mixture half a pint of beer, beat it all well together, and drop it with a dessert-spoon into some boiling lard, or butter. Drain them upon a towel before the fire, and serve them in a napkin, with sugar sifted over them.

Deer Horns

BEAT one white, and six yolks of eggs; mix them with five table-spoonfuls of pounded and sifted loaf sugar, the same quantity of sweet cream, ten sweet almonds, blanched and pounded, the grated peel of one lemon, and as much flour as will make the whole into a paste sufficiently thick to roll out. Then cut it with tins for the purpose, into the form of horns, branches, or any other shape, and throw them into boiling lard.

Nuns

ROLL puff paste about a quarter of an inch thick, cut it into rounds, or any other shape; lay upon one bit a small tea-spoonful of any sort of preserved fruit, wet the edges, and put over it another bit of paste; fry them in boiling clarified beef suet, or fresh lard; drain them upon the back of a sieve. Serve them in a napkin, and strew pounded loaf sugar over them.

Nun's Beads

POUND in a mortar four ounces of good cheese, with a little salt, the beaten yolks of three eggs, and some crumbs of bread; roll them as large as walnuts, cover them with puff paste, and fry them in butter a light brown colour. Serve them in a napkin.

Fine Pancakes

To three table-spoonfuls of flour add six well-beaten eggs, three table-spoonfuls of white wine, four ounces of melted butter, nearly cold, the same quantity of pounded loaf sugar, half a grated nutmeg, and a pint of cream; mix it well, beating the batter for some time, and pour it thin over the pan.

Scotch Pancakes

MIX with six table-spoonfuls of flour a little cream, add the beaten yolks of six eggs, and then mix in a pint of cream, the grated peel of a small lemon, a table-spoonful of pounded sugar, and a little ratafia; when the batter is very well beaten, and just before using, mix in the whites of the eggs, beaten with a knife to a stiff froth. Put a little butter or lard into the frying-pan, make it hot, pour it out, and wipe the pan with a clean cloth; put in some more butter or lard, and when hot, pour in a tea-cupful of the batter; shake it, and when firm, prick it a little with a fork, but do not turn it; hold it before the fire a minute to brown. Serve them with pounded loaf sugar strewed over them.

French Pancakes

BEAT separately the yolks and whites of seven eggs; beat with the yolks four table-spoonfuls of pounded loaf sugar, the same quantity of flour, one pint of cream or milk, the grated peel and juice of one lemon, and two table-spoonfuls of rose water; add the beaten whites the last thing. Allow three table-spoonfuls to each pancake.

Common Pancakes

WITH nearly half a pound of flour, mix five well-beaten eggs, and then add, by degrees, a quart of good milk; fry them in fresh lard, and serve them with pounded loaf sugar strewed between each.

A Thick Pancake

BEAT separately the yolks and whites of two eggs; mix with the yolks a table-spoonful and a half of flour, a little sugar and white wine, half a pint of cream or good milk; add the whites, and fry it in a broad sauce-pan, with butter or clarified suet; brown the upper side before the fire; warm any sort of preserve, spread it upon one half, and turn the other over it, and strew upon it pounded loaf sugar.

Indian Pancake

ADD to three well-beaten eggs a pint of new milk, three table-spoonfuls of boiled rice, some sugar, and a little pounded cinnamon; mix it all well together, and fry it in butter; brown the upper side for a minute before the fire; serve it, cut into four, with pounded sugar strewed over it.

Apples in Pancakes

CUT some apples very small, stew them with a little white wine, grated lemon-peel, pounded cinnamon, and brown sugar; mash them, and spread it over pancakes; roll them up, and serve with sifted loaf sugar over them.

Leipzeger Pancakes

BEAT well the whites of four, and the yolks of eight fresh eggs, and add, by degrees, half a pound of pounded loaf sugar, a pint and a half of sweet cream just warmed, half a pound of clarified fresh butter, two table-spoonfuls of fresh yeast, and a wine-glass full of spirits of wine; then mix in as much sifted flour as will make it into a thick batter; let it rise for half an hour; roll it out thin; cut it into rounds or oblong pieces, and lay on them jam or marmalade; double them, and let them stand again to rise, and fry them in boiling fresh lard or butter.

Aberdeen Crulla

BEAT to a cream a quarter of a pound of fresh butter, and mix with it the same quantity of pounded and sifted loaf sugar, and four well-beaten eggs; add flour till thick enough to roll out; cut the paste into oblong pieces about four or five inches in length; with a paste-cutter, divide the centre into three or four strips, wet the edges, and plait one bar over the other, so as to meet in the centre; throw them into boiling lard, or clarified suet; when fried of a light brown, drain them before the fire, and serve them in a napkin, with or without grated loaf sugar strewed over them.

French Supper Dish

PARE off the crust, and cut one or two slices of bread into bits of two or three inches square; fry them in butter; put them upon a hot dish, and lay upon each bit some warmed preserve; or stew for a few minutes, in sweet wine and a little sugar, some stoned bloom raisins, and put them upon and round the toast.

The preserves may be heated by placing the jars in hot water by the side of the fire.

Fondeux

BEAT separately the yolks and whites of four eggs; add to the yolks a pint of cream, and half a pound of grated Parmesan cheese; mix in the whites of the eggs just before putting it into paper cases; or bake it in a round tin about three inches high, and before serving it, which should be instantly when taken out of the oven, put round it a sheet of white paper folded, and cut so as to form a fringe at the top. Any mild, dry cheese may be used, and butter beaten to a cream substituted for cream.

Another way to make Fondeux

MIX by degrees, with a quarter of a pound of flour, half a pint of cream, and half an ounce of butter; put it into a sauce-pan, and stir it over the fire till quite thick; add five yolks of eggs, well beaten, with half a pint of new milk, and two ounces of grated Parmesan cheese; stir it together in a basin, and mix in lightly the whites of eggs beaten to a thick froth; bake it in a tin, lined with puff paste, for half an hour; turn it out instantly to serve.

A soufflet pudding may be made exactly in this way; substituting sugar for the cheese.

Omelet Soufflet

Beat, with the yolks of ten eggs, four table-spoonfuls of pounded sugar, and half the peel of a grated lemon; add, the instant before putting into the pan, the well-beaten whites of the eggs; fry it in a quarter of a pound of fresh butter; shake it to prevent its adhering to the pan; when firm, sift grated sugar over the top, and brown it with a salamander, or hot shovel; serve it immediately when done.

Another way to make Omelet Soufflet

Beat six yolks of eggs with two table-spoonfuls of sugar, one of flour, a little salt, half a wine glass of orangeflower water, or the grated peel of half a lemon; mix in the well- beaten whites the last thing; fry, and serve it with grated sugar over the top.

Apple Soufflet

Prepare apples as for baking in a pudding, put them into a deep dish, and lay upon the top, about a inch and a half thick, rice boiled in new milk with sugar; beat to a stiff froth the whites of two or three eggs, with a little sifted loaf sugar, lay it upon the rice, and bake it in an oven a light brown. Serve it instantly when done.

Rich Soufflet

Soak in white wine and a little brandy, sweetened with sugar, some slices of spunge-cake; put them into a deep dish, and pour over them a rich custard; beat to a stiff froth the whites of three or four eggs, and with a table-spoon lay it over the top in heaps to look rough; brown it in a Dutch oven, and serve quickly.

Rice Soufflet

Soak in half a pint of milk, for an hour, one ounce of rice, and the peel of a lemon cut thin; put it into a sauce-pan, with a little salt, and add by degrees a pint of new milk, and a bit of butter the size of a walnut; stir it till it boil, and for five minutes after, when cool, add the yolks of six eggs, beaten with two table-spoonfuls of pounded loaf sugar, and stir in the well-beaten whites of the eggs, and dress the soufflet in the dish like a pyramid. Bake it in an oven.

It may be made with two table-spoonfuls of potato flour, which mix with a little milk, and a little salt, and then thicken it over the fire with more milk; put a little orange-flower water, or any other perfume; whilst in the oven, it may be glazed with sifted loaf sugar.

Orange Soufflet

MIX with a table-spoonful of flour a pint of cream, put it into a sauce-pan, with two spoonfuls of rose water, a little cinnamon and orange-peel; stir it till it boil; strain and sweeten it, and when cold, mix in two table-spoonfuls of orange marmalade; beat well six eggs with a glass of brandy; mix all together; put it in a buttered shape; place it in a sauce-pan of boiling water, over a stove; let it boil one hour and a quarter without a cloth or cover over it.

Omelet

BEAT up eight eggs extremely well, strain and season them with pepper, salt, nutmeg, minced parsley, and shalot, some grated lean ham, and a little good gravy; fry it lightly in a quarter of a pound of butter; hold a salamander, or a hot shovel, over the top, to take off the raw appearance of the eggs; serve with a rich thick brown gravy, or without it, if it be preferred dry. In frying the omelet, raise it frequently, as it begins to fasten, with a knife, from the bottom of the pan, so that the butter may get under it.

Another way to make Omelet

BEAT eight eggs till they are very light; add a tea-cupful of rich cream, two middling-sized onions pounded, and some boiled parsley minced, half a tea-spoonful of salt, and a little pepper; mix all well together, and fry it of a light brown, in three or four ounces of butter; before serving, let it stand a few minutes before the fire. If onions are disliked, finely-minced sweet herbs may be substituted.

Another way to make Omelet

BEARD and parboil twelve or sixteen oysters, seasoning them with a few white peppercorns, strain and chop them; beat well six eggs; parboil and mince a little parsley; mix all together, and season with a little nutmeg, salt, and a table-spoonful of mushroom catsup; fry it lightly in three ounces of butter, and hold it for a minute or two before the fire.

Another way to make Omelet

BEAT well and strain six eggs; add them to three ounces of butter made hot; mix in some grated ham, pepper, salt, and nutmeg, some chopped chives and parsley. Fry it of a light brown colour. Salt herring grilled and minced may be substituted for the ham.

Omelet with Kidney of Veal

To eight well-beaten eggs, add a little salt, and part of a cold roasted kidney of veal, finely minced; season with pepper, and a little more salt; melt in a frying-pan one ounce and a half of butter, and pour in the omelet; fry it gently, and keep the middle part moist; when done roll it equally upon knife, and serve it very hot.

Macaroni

Break the macaroni into small bits; wash it, and simmer half a pound in a quart of good veal stock, and when quite tender, add some grated Parmesan cheese, and make it quite hot; put grated cheese into the bottom of a dish, and put over it the boiled macaroni; strew some cheese upon the top, and put small bits of butter here and there; brown it with a salamander, or in an oven. A border of puff paste may be put round the dish, when it is baked, and the cheese ought not to be previously heated with the macaroni.

The macaroni may be dressed without the cheese.

Another way to dress Macaroni

Simmer the macaroni in milk, and when quite tender, mix with it two ounces of salt butter, put grated cheese into the bottom of the dish, and then a layer of macaroni; begin and end with the cheese, and over the top strew sifted bread; put on it small bits of butter, and brown it in a Dutch oven, or with a salamander.

Another way to dress Macaroni

Simmer the macaroni with a little salt, gravy, and water, half and half; when tender, strain, and put it into a sauce-pan with a quarter of a pound of butter, a finely-minced onion, and a tea-cupful of cream; grate half a pound of cheese, and heat the half of it with the macaroni; dish it, and strew over the top the remainder of the cheese; brown it with a salamander.

Another way to dress Macaroni

Pour the macaroni into boiling milk-and-water, with a little salt, and about an ounce of fresh butter; let it simmer till tender, drain off the water, and mix with it a cupful of thick cream; make it quite hot, and if approved, add some grated nutmeg.

Another way, Plain dressed

Throw a little salt into a sauce-pan of boiling water, put in half a pound of macaroni, let it simmer three quarters of an hour, stir it occasionally, strain off the water; have ready a breakfast-plateful of grated Dutch cheese, put little bits of butter in the bottom of the dish, then some macaroni, and a layer of cheese: Put them alternately, mix all together, and serve it hot.

To make Macaroni

BEAT four eggs for eight or ten minutes, strain them, and stir in flour till stiff enough to work into a paste upon a marble or stone slab; add flour till it be a stiff paste, and work it well; cut off a small bit at a time, roll it out as thin as paper, and cut it with a paste-cutter or knife into very narrow strips; twist, and lay them upon a clean cloth, in a dry, warm place; in a few hours it will be perfectly hard; put it into a box, with white paper under and over it. It maybe cut into small stars, or circles, to be used for soup, and does not require so much boiling as the Italian macaroni.

Fromage Cuit

CUT half a pound of Cheshire cheese into thin bits, and pound it in a mortar; add by degrees the well-beaten yolks of two, and the white of one egg, and half a pint of cream; mix it well together, and bake it for ten or fifteen minutes.

Ramakins

THE well-beaten yolks of four eggs, half a pound of grated cheese, a gill of cream, one ounce of oiled butter; mix all together, and bake it in small paper cases in a Dutch oven. To oil the butter, put it into a tea-cup, and set it in a basin of boiling water.

To Toast Cheese

CUT some double or single Gloucester cheese into small shavings, and put it with a bit of butter into a cheese toaster; place it before the fire till the cheese dissolves, stirring it now and then. Serve with a slice of toasted bread, divided into four, and the crust pared off. It is generally eaten with mustard, salt, and pepper.

Another way to Toast Cheese

MIX, with four ounces of grated and sifted bread crumbs, two ounces and a half of fresh butter, three ounces of good cheese finely grated, the well-beaten yolks of two eggs, a table-spoonful of cream, a tea-spoonful of mustard, a little salt and pepper; put it into a sauce-pan, and stir it till it be heated, and then lay it thick upon small bits of toasted bread, and brown it with a salamander or hot shovel, or lay the paste upon the bits of toast; put them, covered with a dish, into a Dutch oven till hot through, and let the cheese just brown. Serve as hot as possible.

Welsh Rabbit

PARE the crust off a slice of bread, toast it nicely, divide it in two, butter it, and lay upon each half a thin slice of cheese which has been toasted in a Dutch oven; if, when put upon the toast, it is not sufficiently browned, hold a salamander, or hot shovel, over the top. Serve it very hot.

To Stew Cheese

MELT three quarters of an ounce of butter in a teacupful of cream, mix with it a quarter of a pound of good cheese finely grated, beat it well together; put a slice of untoasted bread into a dish, and pour the mixture over it, and brown it with a salamander.

Boiled Cheese

GRATE a quarter of a pound of good cheese, put it into a sauce-pan, with a bit of butter the size of a nutmeg, and half a tea-cupful of milk, stir it over the fire till it boil, and then add a well-beaten egg; mix it all together, put it into a small dish, and brown it before the fire; or serve it without being browned.

To Pot Cheshire Cheese

SCRAPE down three pounds of fine Cheshire or Gloucester cheese. With half a pound of fresh butter, pound it to a paste in a marble mortar, adding a large wine glass of malmsey madeira, or of sherry, and a quarter of an ounce of pounded and sifted mace; when beaten to a paste, press it into a deep pot, and cover it with clarified butter. A thick slice may be served in a napkin to resemble cream cheese.

Anchovy Toast

PARE the crust off a slice of bread, cut it into six or eight bits, fry them in clarified butter, and when cold, spread upon them two or three anchovies, boned, washed, and pounded to a paste, together with a little fresh butter.

Another way to make Anchovy Toast

BONE and roll up two or three anchovies, place them upon pieces of dry toast, and garnish with curled parsley.

Butter of Anchovies

WASH from the pickle some fine young anchovies. Bone, and take off the heads, then pound them in a mortar with fresh butter till quite smooth, and rub it through a sieve.

CHAPTER XIV
CREAMS, CUSTARDS, JELLIES, AND OTHER SWEET DISHES

Red Currant, or Pink Cream

PICK the currants from the stalks, put them into a jar closely covered, and set it in a pan of cold water; let it boil for two hours, strain the juice through a sieve, and sweeten it well with pounded loaf sugar. When cold, add a quart of cream to a pint of juice, and beat it with a whisk till thick. Serve in a deep glass dish.

Another Red Currant, or Pink Cream

SQUEEZE three quarters of a pint of juice from red currants when full ripe, add to it rather more than a quarter of a pound of pounded loaf sugar, and the juice of one lemon; stir it into a pint and a half of cream, and whisk it till quite thick. Serve it in a glass dish, or in jelly glasses. It may be made with currant jelly, which mix with the lemon juice and sugar.

Custard Cream

BOIL, in half a pint of milk, a stick of cinnamon, the peel of a lemon cut thin, two or three laurel leaves, or a few bitter almonds bruised; strain, and add it to three pints of cream; stir into it the well-beaten yolks of eight eggs, sweeten with pounded loaf sugar, put it into a sauce-pan, and stir it constantly till it thickens, which it will do before it comes to a boil; pour it into a deep dish, and stir it now and then till cold. Serve in a glass dish, or custard cups.

Raspberry Cream

GATHER the fruit upon a dry day, mash, and drip it through a jelly-bag; to every pint of juice add a pound of pounded loaf sugar, and when it is completely dissolved, bottle it in pint and half-pint bottles, filling them only to the neck. When to be used, mix it with rich cream, add more sugar, and whisk it till thick. It may be made the day before it is required.

Another way to make Raspberry Cream

Mix a little pounded loaf sugar with a pint and a half of good cream, about a tea-cupful of raspberry jelly, the grated rind of one, and the juice of half a lemon; beat it well together, and, with a syllabub, mill it slowly for half an hour, or till it be thick and solid. Put it into a glass dish, or serve it in custard glasses.

Another way to make Raspberry Cream

Put six ounces of raspberry jam to a quart of cream, pulp it through a lawn sieve, mix it with the juice of a lemon and a little sugar, and whisk it till thick. Serve it in a dish or glasses.

Strawberry cream may be made in the same way. For common use, substitute good milk for the cream.

Whipt Cream

Sweeten, with pounded loaf sugar, a quart of cream, and add to it a lump of sugar which has been rubbed upon the peel of two fine lemons or bitter oranges; or flavour it with orange-flower water, a little essence of roses, the juice of ripe strawberries, or of any other fruit. Whisk the cream well in a large pan, and, as the froth rises, take it off, and lay it upon a sieve placed over another pan, and return the cream which drains from the froth, till all is whisked, then heap it upon a dish, or put it into glasses. Garnish with thinly-pared citron, or cedraty, cut into small leaves, or into any fanciful shape.

To colour the rose cream, or to heighten that of strawberry, a little carmine or lake may be mixed with the cream, which may be iced when made.

Spanish Cream

Boil, in half a pint of water, half an ounce of isinglass, till dissolved; strain, and mix it with a quart of cream or good milk; if cream, not so much isinglass; stir it over the fire till it comes to a boil; when a little cooled, add gradually the beaten yolks of six eggs, and a glass of white wine. Pour it into a deep dish, sweeten with pounded loaf sugar, stir it till cold, and then put it into a shape.

Honeycomb Cream

Mix in a glass or china dish the strained juice of three lemons with half a pound of pounded and sifted loaf sugar. Put about a quart of good cream into a tea-pot, place the dish upon the floor, and pour the cream very slowly over the sugar and lemon juice, holding the teapot as high as possible, so as to froth the cream. At table it should be well stirred before it is helped.

Coffee Cream

PUT two handfuls of fresh-burnt coffee, while hot, into a quart of boiling new milk; cover it closely for three or four hours, strain, sweeten it with pounded loaf sugar, and add the well-beaten yolks of eight eggs; strain it again, and put it into custard-cups, which place in a sauce-pan of boiling water, to remain till they become firm.

Another way to make Coffee Cream

DISSOLVE half an ounce of isinglass, boil it with a quart of cream, and mix with it about a pint of very strong coffee, sweeten it well with pounded white sugar-candy; whisk it for a few minutes, and serve it in custard cups. It may be perfumed with a tea-spoonful of the essence of the cedrat fruit.

Solid Cream

SQUEEZE the juice of a large lemon upon three or four table-spoonfuls of pounded loaf sugar, add two table-spoonfuls of brandy, and one pint of cream; pour it from one cup into another, till it be sufficiently thick.

Italian Cream

MIX, with the well-beaten yolks of four eggs, a table-spoonful of flour, a little salt, half the grated peel of a lemon, and a pint of milk; sweeten with pounded loaf sugar, beat it quite smooth, put it into a sauce-pan, and stir it constantly till it thickens; then put some into the bottom of a dish, and put in a layer of sponge-cake dipped in white wine, and another layer of the cream, till all is in the dish; cover the top with a thick snow froth, and brown it with a hot shovel.

The snow froth is made with the white of a new-laid egg well beaten, with a little sifted loaf sugar.

Another way to make Italian Cream

SWEETEN a pint of cream with pounded loaf sugar; boil it with the thinly-pared rind of a lemon, and a bit of cinnamon; strain, and mix it with half an ounce of dissolved isinglass; add it, while boiling hot, to the well-beaten yolks of six eggs, stir it till quite cold, and put it into a shape or mould.

Burnt Cream

BOIL a pint of cream with the peel of a lemon, sweeten it with pounded loaf sugar; beat, with the yolks of six, and whites of four eggs, one table-spoonful of flour, the same of orange-flower water and of ratafia; strain the cream, and when nearly cold, mix it with the eggs and other things; stir it over the fire till it be as thick as a custard; put it into a silver dish, strew sifted loaf sugar over the top, and brown it with a salamander. Serve it cold.

Another way to make Burnt Cream

Beat, with the yolks of four eggs, a table-spoonful of flour, the grated peel of half a lemon, and three pounded bitter almonds; sweeten it with pounded loaf sugar, and stir it over the fire till it becomes as thick as a custard; put it into the dish it is to be served in. Boil with a little water some pounded loaf sugar, till it turn brown, but do not stir it till taken off the fire; by degrees pour it in figures over the top of the cream. It may be eaten hot or cold.

White Lemon Cream

Rub, with some lumps of loaf sugar, the rinds of six lemons, and grate off the remainder; squeeze and strain the juice, and add the grated peel and sugar, with three-quarters of a pound of pounded loaf sugar; put to this a quart of rich cream, and whisk it till very thick. The following day, soak five or six spunge biscuits in white wine, and put over them the cream.

Another way to make White Lemon Cream

Boil the thin peel of two lemons in a pint of cream; strain, and thicken it with the well-beaten yolks of three and whites of four eggs; sweeten it with pounded loaf sugar, stir it till nearly cold, and put it into glasses.

Stone Cream

Pour three table-spoonfuls of lemon juice, and the grated peel of one, some preserved apricots, or any other sweetmeat, into a glass or china dish. Boil a quarter of an ounce of isinglass in a little water, till dissolved; add it to a pint of cream, sweetened well with pounded loaf sugar; boil it, and stir it all the time; pour it into a jug, stir it now and then till milk-warm, then pour it over the sweetmeat round and round. It may be made the day before being served.

Apple Cream

Boil twelve large apples in water till soft, take off the peel, and press the pulp through a hair sieve upon half a pound of pounded loaf sugar; whip the whites of two eggs, add them to the apples, and beat all together till it becomes very stiff, and looks quite white. Serve it heaped up on a dish.

Another way to make Apple Cream

PEEL and core five large apples; boil them in a little water, till soft enough to press through a sieve; sweeten, and beat with them the whisked whites of five eggs. Serve it with cream poured round it.

Swiss Cream

BOIL the grated peel of a large lemon, and three quarters of a pound of pounded loaf sugar, in a pint of cream; squeeze the juice of the lemon upon a table-spoonful of flour, work it well together, and gradually add to it the boiling cream, and heat it all over the fire; pour it into a basin, and when nearly cold, put it into a glass or china dish, and garnish it with candied orange- peel, and citron cut into straws. This dish requires to be constantly stirred till it is put into the one in which it is to be served.

Another way to make Swiss Cream

WHISK, upon a hot plate, the yolks of eight eggs, half a pound of finely-pounded sugar, the grated rind of a lemon, and half a pint of light French or Rhenish white wine, and send it warm to table.

Lemon Cream

STEEP the thinly-pared rinds of four large lemons in a pint of water for twelve hours; strain, and dissolve in it three quarters of a pound of fine loaf sugar, add the juice of the lemons strained, and the well-beaten whites of seven, and the yolk of one egg. Boil it over a slow fire, stirring it constantly one way, till it is like a thick cream; pour it into a glass or china dish.

Another way to make Lemon Cream

STEEP the peel of a large lemon in half a pint of water for twelve hours; strain, and add to the water a quarter of a pound of loaf sugar, the juice of two lemons, and the well-beaten yolks of three, and whites of two, eggs; stir it constantly one way over the fire till thick. Serve in custard-cups.

It may be perfumed with orange-flower water, ambergris, or musk.

Cream Roseat

BEAT to a stiff froth the whites of four eggs; sweeten and boil a pint of good milk, drop about three table-spoonfuls of the froth into it, turn it over once or twice with the spoon, take it out, and put it upon the back of a lawn sieve placed over a large plate; repeat this till it is all done; add to the milk another half pint, with a little more sugar, and mix it with the beaten yolks of the eggs; stir it over the fire till thick; put it into a basin, and stir it now and then till nearly cold; add a table-spoonful of rose water, and one of brandy. Serve it in a glass dish, and lay the whites of the eggs over the top at equal distances. Cut citron and candied orange-peel into straws, and put them over the whites of the eggs, or strew over them coloured comfits.

Cream for Fruit Tarts

BOIL a stick of cinnamon, two or three peach leaves, or a few bruised bitter almonds, in a quart of milk; strain, sweeten, and mix it, when cool, with three or four well-beaten eggs; stir it constantly over the fire till it thickens. It may be eaten with stewed apples, prunes, damsons, or any other fruit.

Arrow-Root Cream

MIX a table-spoonful of arrow-root with a tea-cupful of cold water; let it settle, and pour the water off. Sweeten and boil a quart of milk with the peel of a lemon and some cinnamon; pick them out, and pour it boiling upon the arrow-root, stirring it well and frequently till it be cold. Serve it in a glass or china dish, with or without grated nutmeg on the top. It may be eaten with any preserved fruit, or fruit tarts.

Orange Cream

SQUEEZE and strain the juice of eleven oranges, sweeten it well with pounded loaf sugar, stir it over a slow fire till the sugar be dissolved, and take off the scum as it rises; when cold, mix it with the well-beaten yolks of twelve eggs, to which a pint of cream has been added; stir it again over the fire till thick. Serve in a glass dish or custard-cups.

Another way to make Orange Cream

BOIL three quarters of an ounce of isinglass in half a pint of water, till half reduced; sweeten well, with pound and sifted loaf sugar, the strained juice of four oranges and one lemon; mix in the isinglass when nearly cold, and immediately stir in a pint of cream previously beaten to a froth; stir it occasionally till it begin to stiffen, and then put it into a mould. The juice of any sort of fruit may be managed in the same way, always adding the juice of a lemon.

Another way to make Orange Cream

SWEETEN, with pounded loaf sugar, a quart of good cream; mix with it a small wine-glass of orange-flower water, the grated rind and the juice of a Seville orange; whisk it till quite thick; soak some macaroons in white wine, and pile them in the middle of a glass or china dish, and heap the whipt cream over them as high as possible. Some hours after, ornament it with slices of green citron cut into straws, and stuck into the cream.

Caledonian Cream

MINCE a table-spoonful of orange marmalade; add it, with a glass of brandy, some pounded loaf sugar, and the juice of a lemon, to a quart of cream; whisk it for half an hour, and pour it into a shape with holes in it, or put it into a small hair sieve, with a bit of thin muslin laid into it.

Imperial Cream

SQUEEZE and strain the juice of three lemons, grate the rinds of two, mix them with two glasses of brandy, and sweeten well with pounded loaf sugar; add a quart of cream made hot, and also sweetened; pour it through a tea-pot. The dish must stand upon the floor, and the person who pours in the cream upon a table, carrying the stream up by degrees as high as possible. When cold, garnish the dish with lemon-peel.

Another way to make Imperial Cream

ADD a table-spoonful of orange-flower water to the juice of three lemons, and stir in pounded loaf sugar till as thick as a sirup; boil a pint of milk, with half the peel of a lemon, and a little sugar; stir it till milk-warm, and put it all into a tea-pot, from which pour it into a dish placed upon the floor.

Ratafia Cream

IN a tea-cupful of thin cream boil two or three large laurel, or young peach leaves; when it has boiled three or four minutes, strain, and mix with it a pint of rich sweet cream; add three well-beaten whites of eggs, and sweeten it with pounded loaf sugar. Put it into a sauce-pan, and stir it gently one way over a slow fire till it be thick; pour it into a china dish, and when quite cold, ornament it with sweetmeats cut out like flowers; or strew over the top harlequin comfits.

Curds and Cream

WITH about half a table-spoonful of rennet, turn two quarts of milk just from the cow; drain off the whey and fill a mould with the curd; when it has stood an hour or two, turn it out. Strew coloured comfits over it, sweeten some cream, mix grated nutmeg with it, and pour it round the curd.

Curds and Cream, as in Scotland

PUT two quarts of new milk into the dish in which it is to be served, and turn it with a tea-spoonful of rennet; when the curd has come, serve it with cream in a separate dish.

Naples Curd

PUT into a quart of new milk a stick of cinnamon, boil it a few minutes, take out the cinnamon, and stir in eight well-beaten eggs, and a table-spoonful of white wine; when it boils again, strain it through a sieve; beat the curd in a basin, together with about half an ounce of butter, two table-spoonfuls of orange-flower water, and pounded sugar sufficient to sweeten it. Put it into a mould for two hours before it is sent to table.

White wine, sugar, and cream, may be mixed together, and poured round the curd, or served in a sauce tureen.

Kerry Buttermilk

PUT six quarts of buttermilk into a cheese-cloth and hang it in a cool place, and let the whey drip from it for two or three days; when it is rather thick, put it into a basin, sweeten it with pounded loaf sugar, and add a glass of brandy, or of sweet wine, and as much raspberry jam, or sirup, as will colour and give it an agreeable flavour. Whisk it well together, and serve it in a glass dish.

Hattered Kit

MAKE two quarts of new milk scalding hot, and pour it quickly upon four quarts of fresh-made buttermilk, after which it must not be stirred; let it remain till cold and firm, then take off the top part, drain it in a hair-sieve, and put it into a shape for half an hour. It is eaten with cream, served in a separate dish.

Another way to make Hattered Kit

PUT into the dish it is to be served in one-third of cream with two-thirds of buttermilk, add a little pounded loaf sugar, and beat it well together, strew over it a little pounded cinnamon, and let it stand for three or four hours.

Almond Cream

Blanch and pound to a paste, with rose water, six ounces of almonds, mix them with a pint and a half of cream which has been boiled with the peel of a small lemon; add two well-beaten eggs, and stir the whole over the fire till it be thick, taking care not to allow it to boil; sweeten it, and when nearly cold, stir in a table-spoonful of orange-flower or rose water.

Raspberry Iced Cream

Mix a table-spoonful of pounded loaf sugar, a large wooden-spoonful of raspberry jelly, and a little cochineal, to heighten the colour, with the juice of a large lemon; strain, and put it into the freezing-pot; cover it closely, and place it in a bucket which has a small hole near the bottom, and a spigot to let the water run off, and which has in it plenty of ice broken small, and mixed with three or four handfuls of coarse salt; press the ice closely round the freezing-pot, turn it round and round for about ten minutes, take off the cover, and remove the frozen cream to the centre with a spoon, cover it again, and turn it till all be equally iced. Serve it in china ice pails, or put it into moulds, cover them tightly with wet bladder, and place them in a bucket with ice, as before, for an hour or more; dip the moulds into cold water before turning out, and serve them immediately. Water ices are made in this way, substituting water for cream.

Apricot Iced Cream

Mix table-spoonful of pounded loaf sugar with a large one of apricot jam, the juice of a lemon, and half an ounce of blanched bitter almonds pounded with a little rose water; add a pint of cream, and stir it all well together before putting it into the freezing pot.

Mille Fruit Iced Cream

Strain the juice of three lemons, grate the peel of one. Mince finely, of orange marmalade, dried cherries, and preserved angelica, a dessert-spoonful each; add to these half a pint of sirup, and mix the whole with a pint and a half of cream, or a pint of water, and then drop in here and there a few drops of the prepared cochineal. Put it into a mould, and freeze it.

Orange Water Iced

Mix with a pint of water the strained juice of three china oranges, and that of one lemon, also the grated peel of one orange; sweeten it well with sirup.

The Juice of Fresh-Gathered Fruit Iced

PRESS through a sieve the juice of a pint of picked currants or raspberries, add to it four or five ounces of pounded loaf sugar, a little lemon juice, and a pint of cream. It may be whisked previous to freezing, and a mixture of the juice may be used.

Blancmange

BOIL till dissolved, in a large tea-cupful of water, three quarters of an ounce of isinglass; when milk-warm, add it to a quart of rich cream, with a stick of cinnamon, the peel of a lemon, two or three laurel leaves, or a few bitter almonds; sweeten with pounded loaf sugar; stir it over the fire, and let it boil for two or three minutes; strain it through a bit of muslin into a deep dish, and stir it till nearly cold, then pour it into an earthenware mould or shape; the following day, dip the mould into warm water for a minute or so, clap it with the hand to loosen the edge, place the glass or china dish over the mould, and turn it out quickly upon the dish. As much cow-heel stock as will half fill the shape may be substituted for the isinglass.

Another way to make Blancmange

BLANCH and pound, with a little ratafia or rose water, two ounces of sweet, and six bitter almonds; dissolve three quarters of an ounce of isinglass; add it, when milk-warm, to a quart of good cream; half milk half cream may be used; mix in the almonds, the peel of a small lemon, and a bit of cinnamon; sweeten it with pounded loaf sugar, let it stand for two or three hours, put it into a sauce-pan, stir it constantly, and let it boil for six or eight minutes; strain it through a lawn sieve, and stir it till nearly cold, then pour it into a mould.

Another way to make Blancmange

BLANCH and pound one ounce of sweet almonds with a glass of sherry, and a table-spoonful of pounded loaf sugar; add it to three quarters of an ounce of isinglass dissolved in half a pint of water, and boil it till the flavour of the almond be extracted, stirring it all the time; strain it through a bit of thin muslin, and mix with it a quart of good cream; stir it till quite cold, and pour it into a shape.

Blancmange Eggs

MAKE a small hole at the end of four or five large eggs, and let out all the egg carefully; wash the shells, drain, and fill them with blancmange; place them in a deep dish filled with rice or barley to keep them steady, and when quite cold, gently break and peel off the shell. Cut the peel of a lemon into delicately fine shreds, lay them into a glass dish, and put in the eggs; or serve them in a glass dish with a pink cream round them.

American Blancmange

MIX half a pint of cold water with two ounces of arrow-root, let it settle for fifteen minutes, pour off the water, and add a table-spoonful of laurel water, and a little sugar; sweeten a quart of new milk, boil it with a little cinnamon, and half the peel of a lemon; pick out the cinnamon and lemon, and pour the boiling milk upon the arrow-root, stirring it all the time. Put it to a mould, and turn it out the following day.

Dutch Blancmange

WASH one ounce and a half of isinglass, pour a pint and a half of boiling water over it, let it stand for an hour, and then boil it for twenty minutes; strain, and when it is nearly cold, add the beaten yolks of six eggs, a pint of Lisbon wine, the peel of one, and juice of two lemons, with a stick of cinnamon, and sweeten with pounded loaf sugar; stir it over the fire till it begin to simmer, but do not allow it to boil; pick out the peel and cinnamon, pour it into a basin, stir it till nearly cold, and put it into a shape.

Custard

SWEETEN a quart of thin cream, or good milk, with pounded loaf sugar; boil it with a bit of cinnamon, and half the peel of a lemon; strain it, and when a little cooled, mix it gradually with the well-beaten yolks of ten eggs; stir it over a slow fire till it be pretty thick, pour it into a basin, and add a table-spoonful of rose water, and one of brandy; keep stirring it every now and then till cold, and then put it into glasses, cups, or a dish. It may be made the day before it is used.

Almond Custard

BLANCH and pound with two table-spoonfuls of orange-flower water a quarter of a pound of almonds, add rather more than a pint of cream, and the well-beaten yolks of six eggs; sweeten with pounded loaf sugar, and stir it over a slow fire till it thickens; but do not allow it to boil. Serve it in a glass dish, or cups, and put over the top sifted loaf sugar.

Another way to make Almond Custard

WITH a quart of thin cream, mix four ounces of pounded loaf sugar, two ounces of sweet, and one of butter almonds finely pounded, and a stick of cinnamon; stir till it boils, and then till nearly cold; pick out the cinnamon, and add the beaten yolks of eight eggs, and of rose water and of brandy two table-spoonfuls each; stir it again over the fire till it thickens, but do not allow it to boil. Serve in custard glasses.

Lemon Custard

BOIL two glasses of white wine, half a pint of water, and two table-spoonfuls of brandy; when nearly cold, add the grated peel and juice of two lemons, with half a pound of pounded loaf sugar, and the well-beaten yolks of six eggs; stir it over a slow fire till it thickens, pour it into a basin, and stir now and then till cold; put it into a dish, or cups, with sifted loaf sugar over the top.

Another way to make Lemon Custard

PUT the juice of four lemons, with three ounces of pounded loaf sugar, into a deep dish; boil the grated peel of one lemon and two ounces of pounded loaf sugar in a quart of cream, and pour it over the juice and sugar. It will keep for four days.

Turning out Custard

MIX with the well-beaten yolks of four eggs a pint of new milk, half an ounce of isinglass dissolved, or enough of calf's-feet stock to stiffen it, and two laurel leaves; sweeten with pounded loaf sugar, and stir it over a slow fire till it thickens; pour it into a basin, and stir it till a little cooled, then pour it into cups to turn out when quite cold. Beat the yolks of two eggs with a little cream; add it to nearly half a pound of brown sugar burnt; strain it through a sieve, and when cold, pour it round the custards.

Orange Custard

SWEETEN the strained juice of ten oranges with pounded loaf sugar, stir it over the fire till hot, take off the scum, and when nearly cold, add to it the beaten yolks of twelve eggs, and a pint of cream; put it into a sauce-pan, and stir it over a slow fire till it thickens. Serve in cups or a dish.

Durham Custard

To a pint of cream add the well-beaten yolks of two eggs, and about a third of a pint of mild strong ale; sweeten, and stir it over the fire till it nearly boils, then pour it into a dish, in the bottom of which is laid thin toasted bread, cut into square bits.

Rice Custard

Mix a pint of milk, half a pint of cream, one ounce of sifted ground rice, five or six bitter almonds, blanched and pounded with two table-spoonfuls of rose water; sweeten with loaf sugar, and stir it altogether till it nearly boils; add the well-beaten yolks of three eggs; stir, and let it simmer for about a minute; pour it into a dish, or serve it in cups, with sifted loaf sugar over the top.

Common Custard

Boil a pint of milk with a bit of cinnamon and two or three laurel leaves; mix with one table-spoonful of flour, or potato flour, two and a half of cold milk, put it into a lawn sieve, and pour the boiling milk upon it; let it run into a basin, mix in by degrees the well-beaten yolks of three eggs; sweeten, and stir it over the fire for a few minutes to thicken.

To Ornament Custards or Creams

Whisk for one hour the whites of two eggs, together with two table-spoonfuls of raspberry, or red currant sirup or jelly; lay it in any form upon a custard or cream, piled up to imitate rock. It may be served in a dish with cream round it.

Calf's-Feet Jelly Cake

Scald, take off the hair, and clean two dozen of calf's feet; put them on in cold water, allowing the proportion of two quarts to four feet; boil them slowly for eight or nine hours; take out the bones, and strain the liquor through a hair sieve. The following day remove carefully every particle of fat, and the sediment at the bottom, then put the jelly into a nicely-cleaned brass pan; let it boil over a stove, or slow fire, till it becomes very thick, and appears almost black in the pan; then put a little of it over the bottom of small plates to dry, and when cool, turn it; the next day lay it upon tins, or sheets of paper, and place them at a little distance from the fire, that it may dry gradually; when clear and hard, put it up in paper bags. Four ounces of this jelly, dissolved in three pints of water, and boiled to a quart, is sufficient to make what will fill two middling-sized moulds. Ox feet may he substituted for calf's feet; the jelly made from them is equally good, but not so delicate in colour.

Jelly

To a quart of the stock jelly put half a pound of loaf sugar pounded, a stick or two of cinnamon broken into small bits, the peel of a lemon, a pint of currant wine, and one of sherry or teneriffe, and the beaten whites of five eggs; put it all into a nicely cleaned sauce-pan, stir it gently till it boils, and boil it for three or four minutes. Pour it into a jelly-bag, with a basin or mug placed underneath; run it immediately through the bag again into another basin, and repeat this till it begins to drop. It will then be as transparent a possible, and may be put into moulds or glasses. When all has apparently dripped, pour about a pint of boiling water into the bag, which will produce a little thin jelly fit to drink; the stand with the jelly-bag should be placed near to the fire; sherry alone, or teneriffe, may be used. The jelly may be put into quart bottles, corked tightly, which will make it keep good for some weeks; place the bottle in warm water when it is required for use.

Fresh Calf's-Feet Stock

Scald, take off the hair, and wash very clean four feet; put them into a sauce-pan with two quarts of cold water, and when it comes to a boil, let them simmer for six or seven hours; take out the feet, and strain the liquor into a deep dish. The following day remove the fat carefully from the top, and give it another boil, which will reduce it to one quart of stiff stock or jelly.

Ale or Porter Jelly

For a large shape, put to the prepared stock or jelly more than half a bottle of strong ale or porter, a pound of loaf sugar, the peel of one, and the juice of four large lemons, a stick of cinnamon, and the beaten whites of eight eggs; put it all into a sauce-pan, stir it gently; let it boil for fifteen minutes, and pour it into a jelly-bag till it runs perfectly clear.

Ox-Feet Jelly

Pour a little hot water over the top of the stock, pour it off, and wipe it dry with a clean cloth; put a quart of it into a sauce-pan with the beaten whites of five or six eggs, the juice of five lemons made very sweet with good brown sugar, a clove or two, and a little cinnamon pounded; let it boil twenty minutes, stirring it all the time; take it off the fire, and add a pint, or half a pint, of white wine, and run it through a jelly-bag till clear.

Hartshorn Jelly

BOIL ten ounces of hartshorn shavings in four quarts of water till reduced to three pints; strain it; when cold, add to it a pint of white wine, one pound of loaf sugar, and the peel of two lemons; set it over the fire, stir it till the jelly is melted, and pour in the strained juice of eight lemons, and the beaten whites of twelve eggs: stir it, and let it boil quietly a few minutes; pour it into a jelly-bag till it looks perfectly clear.

Another way to make Hartshorn Jelly

BOIL half a pound of hartshorn shavings for three hours and a half in four pints and a half of water; strain it through a bit of muslin, and stir into it three ounces of dissolved isinglass; if large, the peel of one, if small, of two lemons, and their juice, half the peel of an orange, three parts of a tea-cupful of brandy, and one of white wine; sweeten with pounded loaf sugar, and when lukewarm, put it into a sauce-pan with the beaten whites of six eggs; stir it, and let it boil for two minutes; strain it through a jelly-bag two or three times till perfectly clear.

Apple Jelly

PARE and cut small thirteen good-sized acid baking apples; as they are cut, throw them into two quarts of cold water; boil them in this till the substance is extracted and nearly half the liquid wasted; drain them through a hair sieve, and with the back of a spoon press out all the juice, run it through a jelly-bag, and to a pint of the liquid allow half or three quarters of a pound of pounded loaf sugar. Put it on the fire with the peel of a lemon, stir it till the sugar is melted; when it boils take off the scum, add the juice of the lemon; let it boil for twelve or fifteen minutes; try a little of it in a saucer, and when it jellies, take out the peel and pour it into a mould. This jelly will keep good for some weeks.

Jaune Mange

BOIL, till dissolved, in a pint of water, two ounces of isinglass, and the thinly-pared peel of one lemon and a half; strain, and add to it a pint of white wine, the juice of three Seville oranges or lemons, and the beaten yolks of eight eggs; sweeten it with pounded loaf sugar, put it into a sauce-pan, and stir it over the fire till it thicken; pour it into a mould, and turn it out when cold.

Arrow-Root Jelly

Steep for some hours, in two table spoonfuls of water, the peel of a lemon, and three or four bitter almonds pounded; strain, and mix it with three table-spoonfuls of arrow-root, the same quantity of lemon juice, and one of brandy; sweeten, and stir it over the fire till quite thick, and when quite cold, put it into jelly glasses.

Rum Jelly

Clarify, and boil to a sirup, a pound of loaf sugar; dissolve one ounce of isinglass in half a pint of water, strain it through a sieve in the sirup when it is half warm, and when nearly cold, stir in a quart of white wine; mix it well, and add one or two table-spoonfuls of old Jamaica rum, stir it for a few minutes, and pour it into a mould, or into glasses.

Punch Jelly

Dissolve one ounce of isinglass in five or six tea-cupfuls of water; strain, and add to it, when boiling hot, one tea-cupful and a half of brandy, the same of rum, and one of lemon juice, with half a pound of pounded loaf sugar; stir till the sugar is dissolved, and pour it into a shape.

Orange Jelly

Squeeze the juice of eight oranges and six lemons, grate the peel of half the fruit, and steep it in a pint of cold water; mix it with the juice, three quarters of a pound of loaf sugar, one ounce and a quarter of isinglass, and the beaten whites of seven eggs; put it into a sauce-pan, and stir it till it boils; let it boil for a few minutes, strain it through a jelly-bag till clear; put it into a mould or glasses.

Another way to make Orange Jelly

Dissolve three quarters of an ounce of isinglass in half a pint of water; add it to a quart of cream, and the strained juice of three sweet or bitter oranges, and six ounces of loaf sugar, part of which has been previously rubbed upon the rind of the oranges; stir it in a sauce-pan over the fire till it boils, put it into a basin, stir it till nearly cold, and then pour it into a mould.

Another way to make Orange Jelly

Dissolve two ounces of isinglass in boiling water, add it to the strained juice of twelve oranges and one lemon; sweeten with pounded loaf sugar; boil, and strain it. The oranges may be cut into half, and the pulp taken out, the skins placed in a dish to keep them steady, and filled with the jelly. It will be firm in three or four hours; or it may be served in a mould.

Another way to make Orange Jelly

Dissolve one ounce of isinglass in a pint of water; when nearly cold, mix with it the strained juice of eight or nine oranges; sweeten with pounded loaf sugar, and stir it till it be dissolved; strain it through a lawn sieve, and pour it into a shape.

Pomona Jelly

Peel, core, and cut into quarters six large, green, acid apples, throw them into cold water, as they are done; take them out, and adding about five ounces of pounded loaf sugar, stew them till quite soft; rub them through a sieve, and add three quarters of an ounce of isinglass, which has been boiled till dissolved in less than half a pint of water. Rub two lumps of sugar upon the peel of lemon to extract the flavour, add it to the jelly, with a little more sugar if not sufficiently sweet; stir it over the fire till quite hot, and then put it into a mould. Turn it out the next day.

Strawberry Jelly

Put some freshly gathered strawberries into an earthen pan, bruise them with a wooden spoon, add a little cold water, and some finely-pounded loaf sugar. In an hour or two, strain it through a jelly-bag, and to a quart of the juice add one ounce of isinglass, which has been dissolved in half a pint of water, well skimmed, strained, and allowed to cool; mix all well, and pour it into an earthen mould.

Raspberry jelly, red currant jelly, and red currants mixed with raspberries, may be made exactly in the same manner; and the bright red colour may be improved by mixing in a little carmine or lake. When this kind of jelly is to be made with cherries, the fruit should be boiled a few minutes in clarified sugar, and when cold, the juice of one or two lemons may be added with the isinglass.

A little lemon juice may be added to any of the other jellies in proportion to the acidity of the fruit.

They may be iced by covering and surrounding the mould with ice, without any salt.

Floating Island

Boil, with a pint of milk, a bit of cinnamon, and half the peel of a lemon; when almost cold, strain it, and mix with it the beaten white of one, and the yolks of three eggs; stir it over the fire till thick, pour it into a dish, and stir it now and then till cold. Whisk the whites of two eggs, and half a pint of guava quince or red currant jelly, till it be a very stiff froth, and heap it upon the custard.

Another way to make Floating Island

THREE spoonfuls of raspberry or currant jelly, and the whites of as many eggs; beat them together one way till the spoon will stand erect; pile it upon cream beaten up with wine and sugar, and a little grated lemon peel; or upon apple jelly.

Un Turban de Ris, et de Pommes

BOIL, in milk, some fine whole rice, with half the peel of a lemon. Pare and core some apples, and cut them into quarters; stew them in a sirup of sugar and water, with a little orange marmalade, taking care to keep them quite whole. Make a rich custard as follows: Sweeten a quart of thin cream or good milk, and boil it with lemon-peel and cinnamon; strain the cream, and let it cool. Beat up the yolks of ten eggs, and mix the cream gradually with them; put it over a slow fire, and keep stirring constantly till it is pretty thick; pour it into a dish, and stir in a table-spoonful of rose water or brandy, but both will enrich the flavour; keep stirring it occasionally till nearly cold. Place the rice round a dish in the form of a wall, put the custard into it, and build the apples all round the outside, so as to hide the rice. It may be sent to table quite cold, or in some degree warm

Orange Fool

MIX the strained juice of three Seville oranges with six well-beaten eggs, a pint of cream, some grated nutmeg and lemon-peel; sweeten with pounded loaf sugar, and stir it over a slow fire till it is as thick as a custard, but do not allow it to boil; pour it, when a little cool, into a glass dish or custard-cups; put sifted loaf sugar over the top.

Gooseberry Fool

SCALD a quart of gooseberries with half a pint of water; when quite soft, rub the pulp through a sieve. Boil half a pint of milk, and the same quantity of cream, with half the peel of a lemon, and a stick of cinnamon; strain it when nearly cold, and mix it with the pulped fruit, and sweeten with good brown sugar. Serve in glasses or custard-cups. It may be made with three beaten yolks of eggs, and a pint of milk sweetened, and which is to be stirred over the fire till a little thick, and when cold, mixed with the gooseberries.

Apple Fool

PARE, core, and cut into thin bits, some good stewing apples; stew them till tender, with a little water, two cloves, a bit of cinnamon, and the peel of half a lemon; pulp half a pound through a sieve, and add the same weight of brown sugar, the juice of a lemon, and the whites of two eggs; beat them all together for an hour. Serve it upon rich cream, or a boiled custard, in a glass dish. It may be made in the same way as the gooseberry fool, as may also stewed rhubarb.

Stewed Pears

SLICE a small beet root, and boil it in a quart of water; strain, and boil in the eight pears peeled and cut into half, three quarters of a pound of loaf sugar, and the peel of one lemon; cover the sauce-pan closely, and stew them till quite tender. A little before they are taken off the fire, add the juice of a lemon.

Another way to stew pears

PARE, cut into quarters, and take out the core of some good baking pears; throw them as they are done into cold water. To a pound of fruit allow a quarter of a pound of brown sugar, and three cloves; put them into a sauce-pan, cover them with cold water, keep the pan closely covered, and stew them gently till red and tender; add, just before serving, a glass of port wine. They may be eaten hot or cold, with cream, after dinner or at supper.

Dutch Flummery

BOIL, with a pint of white wine, some sugar, the juice of two, and the peel of one lemon, a stick of cinnamon, and half an ounce of dissolved isinglass; strain and mix it with the well-beaten yolks of seven eggs, stir it over the fire till it simmer, but do not allow it to boil; stir it till quite cold, and put it into a shape.

Another way to make Dutch Flummery

BOIL for ten minutes, in half a pint of white wine, and the same proportion of water, the juice of three, and the peel of two lemons, rather more than a quarter of a pound of loaf sugar, and an ounce of isinglass dissolved; strain, and mix it gradually with the beaten yolks of five eggs; put it again over the fire, and stir it for five minutes; stir it till cold, and put it into a shape.

Mock Ice

Of preserved strawberries, raspberries, and red currant jelly, a table-spoonful each; rub it through a sieve, with as much cream as will fill a shape; dissolve three quarters of an ounce of isinglass in half a pint of water; when almost cold, mix it well with the cream, put it into a shape, set it in a cool place, and turn it out the following day.

Another way to make Mock Ice

Dissolve one ounce of isinglass in half a pint of water; strain, and when nearly cold, mix it with a quart of cream; simmer it over the fire, and stir it all the time; add some raspberry juice and sugar. Whisk it till almost cold, and put it into a shape.

Clear Apples

Boil half a pound of loaf sugar in a pint of water; take off the scum, and put in some large apples, pared, cored, and cut into quarters, with the peel and juice of a lemon; let them boil till clear, without a cover upon the sauce-pan.

To Stew Apples in Halves

Pare the apples, cut them in half, and take out the core; to eight good-sized baking apples allow a pint of water and a quarter of a pound of loaf sugar, the peel of a lemon, and half the peel of an orange cut into thin parings; stew them in a covered sauce-pan till they are soft; serve them with the parings and sirup poured over them.

To Bake Apples

Pare the apples, cut them in quarters, or keep them whole; put them into a jar, with a glass of port wine, three ounces of brown sugar, and a few cloves, to each pound of apples. Cover the jar closely, and bake them in a quick oven for an hour.

Family Luncheon, or supper dish

Wash seven or nine good-sized baking apples, put them in a sauce-pan, with cold water, and boil them till they are soft; drain the water from them, and serve them quite hot, placed upon a dish, with the stalks upwards. They are eaten with sugar. When to be eaten with cream, the apples may be peeled before being boiled.

Italian Cheese

MIX with nearly half a pound of pounded loaf sugar, the juice of three lemons, two table-spoonfuls of white wine, and a quart of cream; beat it with a whisk till quite thick, which may be in half an hour; put a bit of muslin into a hair sieve, and pour in the cream. In twelve hours turn it out, and garnish it with flowers. It may be put into a tin shape with holes in it.

Dutch Cream Cheese

BEAT the yolks of eight, and the whites of three eggs, and mix them with a pint of butter-milk; add this to three quarts of boiling milk just from the cow; let it boil up once, take it off the fire, cover it, and let it stand a little that the curd may form; then put it into a small hair sieve, and press it with a weight for twenty-four hours, when it may be turned out. It is eaten with cream and sugar.

Snow Cheese

SWEETEN, with pounded loaf sugar, a quart of thick cream; add the strained juice of three lemons, and one ounce and a half of blanched sweet almonds pounded, with two table-spoonfuls of rose water, and one of ratafia. Beat it with a whisk till thick, and put it into a shape or sieve, with a bit of muslin laid into it, and in twelve hours turn it out.

Claret Puffs

MIX together, and sweeten with pounded loaf sugar, a pint of claret, and rather more than one of rich cream; let it stand a night, and then whisk it to a froth, which take off as it rises, and put upon the back of a sieve to drain; heap it upon a dish, sweeten some rich cream, and pour it round the froth to make it float.

Fairy Butter

WASH a quarter of a pound of fresh butter in orange-flower water, and beat it with the pounded yolks of five or six hard-boiled eggs; blanch, and pound to a paste with a little orange-flower water, two ounces of sweet almonds; add a little grated lemon-peel, and pounded and sifted loaf sugar; mix all together, and with a wooden spoon, work it through a stone cullender. Soak some Naples biscuit in white wine, and put over them the fairy butter, in heaps high as it can be raised.

Whim Wham

SWEETEN a quart of cream, and mix with it a tea-cupful of white wine, and the grated peel of a lemon; whisk it to a froth, which drain upon the back of a sieve, and put part into a deep glass dish; cut some Naples biscuit as thin as possible, and put a layer lightly over the froth, and one of red currant jelly, then a layer of the froth, and one of the biscuit and jelly; finish with the froth, and pour the remainder of the cream into the dish, and garnish with citron and candied orange-peel cut into straws.

Devonshire Junket

TURN some new milk, as for cheesecakes, in a wide shallow dish; when cold, pour over the top a pint of rich cream mixed with pounded loaf sugar, six dessert-spoonfuls of brandy, and some grated nutmeg.

Another way to make Devonshire Junket

TURN some new milk from the cow with a little rennet; sweeten some thick cream, add a little pounded cinnamon, make it scalding hot, and when cold pour it over the curd, and put a little wine and sugar into the bottom of the dish.

Irish Rock

BLANCH a pound of sweet and an ounce of bitter almonds, pick out a few of the sweet almonds, and cut them like straws, and blanch them in rose water; pound the rest in a mortar with a table-spoonful of brandy, four ounces of pounded and sifted loaf sugar, and half a pound of salt butter well washed; pound them till the mass looks very white, and set it in a cool place to stiffen; then dip two table-spoons into cold water, and with them form the paste, as much like an egg as possible; place in the bottom of a glass dish a small plate or saucer turned, and lay the rock high up; stick over it the cut almonds with green sweetmeats, and ornament with a sprig of myrtle.

Rice Cake, a sweet Dish

WASH well and drain a quarter of a pound of rice, boil with a quart of fresh cream the peel of one lemon, and when nearly cold, take it out, and put in the rice; place the sauce-pan over a slow fire, and when the rice has swollen, add a little salt, and sweeten with pounded loaf sugar; when the rice is quite tender, add the yolks of eight eggs, and mix in gradually the beaten whites, with a good bit of fresh butter; clarify a quarter of a pound of fresh butter, and pour it into a mould; turn this round, that the butter may equally cover every part of it, then pour out the butter, and strew over the inside a layer of grated bread; with a paste brush or a slip of paper, sprinkle all over it some of the clarified butter, add more grated bread, pour in the rice, and bake it in a moderate oven for an hour. Turn it out upon a dish, and serve it with or without a garnishing of preserved raspberries, cherries, or currants.

Croquettes with Marmalade

PREPARE the rice as in the receipt for a rice-cake, a sweet dish; when it is cold form it into rolls of the size of a cork, and with the handle of a wooden spoon make an opening in the centre of them, fill it with marmalade, and close it with some rice; roll them into a beaten egg, and strew some grated bread over them; repeat this once or twice, and then fry them of a light brown colour.

These croquettes may be fried without the marmalade.

Apples and Rice

SCOOP the pulp from some roasted apples; sweeten it with brown sugar, and add a little grated lemon-peel; wash two ounces of whole rice, and, with a stick of cinnamon, boil it in a pint of milk; when quite soft, and nearly dry, pick out the cinnamon, and mix in the well-beaten yolks of two eggs; sweeten it with sugar, and pour it over the apples, previously put into a dish; let it bake in a Dutch oven till it be thoroughly heated, and brown it with a salamander.

Rice Flummery

BOIL in a quart of milk five ounces of sifted ground rice, half an ounce of bitter almonds, blanched and pounded with two table-spoonfuls of rose water; sweeten, and stir it till very thick, so that the bottom of the sauce-pan is seen, and then put it into a mould; when quite cold, turn it out, stick over it sweet almonds, cut it into straws, and pour round it some thick cream, and a little white wine and sugar mixed with it.

Raspberry Flummery.

MIX with half a pint of white vine vinegar one pound of raspberries, or one pound of preserved raspberries, let it boil for three or four minutes, stirring it constantly; strain it through a hair sieve; dissolve one ounce of isinglass in half a pint of water; mix with it three quarters of a pound of pounded sugar, add it to the strained raspberries, stir it all well together; boil, and strain it through a bit of muslin, and put it into a shape. Turn it out when cold.

Whole Rice in a Shape

WASH a large tea-cupful of rice in several waters, put it into a sauce-pan with cold water to cover it, and when it boils, add two cupfuls of rich milk, and boil it till it become dry; put it into a shape, and press it in well. When cold, turn it out, and serve with preserved black currants, raspberries, or any sort of fruit round it.

Rice Cups

SWEETEN a pint of milk with pounded loaf sugar, and boil it with a stick of cinnamon; stir in sifted ground rice till thick; take it off the fire, and add the well-beaten whites of three eggs; stir it again over the fire for two or three minutes, then put it into tea-cups previously dipped in cold water; turn them out when cold, and pour round them a custard cream made with the yolks of the eggs; place upon the rice a little red-currant jelly or raspberry jam. This dish may be served warm or cold; if cold, raspberry cream or custard may be poured round it.

Gooseberry Paste

GATHER, when quite ripe, the rough red gooseberries; top and tail them; put them into a jar, tie it over with bladder, and boil it in a pot of water till the fruit be perfectly soft; pour off the thin juice, and with a wooden spoon rub the gooseberries through a fine hair sieve; allow rather more than half the weight of the pulp of pounded loaf sugar, mix it together, and boil it till it will jelly, which will take almost two hours; stir, and skim it, then put it into a dish, and serve it when cold, to be eaten with cream.

The thin juice may be boiled with its weight of good brown sugar, and used as gooseberry jelly.

Gooseberries, Currants, Cherries, Apples, and other Fruits

To stew any of these fruits, put them into a wide-mouthed jar, with a sufficiency of brown sugar to sweeten them; cover it very closely, and set it into a pot of water to boil till the fruit becomes tender. By this method the flavour of the fruit is better preserved than by any other.

Apricots in White Jelly

PUT a few preserved apricots into a shape, fill it up with white currant jelly, and when cold and firm turn it out.

Cassile

MIX two table-spoonfuls of potato-flour with two or three of cream or good milk; boil for a few minutes, with a quart of cream or milk, the peel of a lemon and a bit of cinnamon; stir it with the flour and cream; sweeten and stir it again over the fire for three or four minutes; pour it into a mould; turn it out when cold.

Egg Marmalade

BLANCH and pound with a little rose water two ounces of sweet almonds, the same of orange marmalade, and four of citron; add two spoonfuls of brandy, and when quite smooth, the beaten yolks of six, and the whites of two eggs, with a little pounded loaf sugar; put it into a sauce-pan, and stir it till it becomes thick, then pour it into a shape. When quite cold, serve it, turned out and garnished with flowers.

Gateau de Pommes

BOIL in a pint of water one pound and a half of loaf sugar till it become a rich sirup; weigh two pounds of apples after they have been peeled, cored, and cut small; boil them in the sirup with the grated peel and juice of a large lemon till they are reduced to a pulp; put it into a mould. The following day serve it, turned out in a glass dish, with a rich custard.

Stewed Seville Oranges

FOR three large Seville oranges make a sirup with one pound of sugar; grate off the outer rind of the oranges, and boil them in water till tender; carefully scoop out the seeds, and stew them in the prepared sirup.

Meringues

BEAT one pound of pounded and sifted double-refined sugar with the whites of three eggs till quite light; when nearly so, add the juice of a lemon; whisk, till very light, five whites of eggs, and mix all together; drop it with a spoon upon white paper in the form of small oval cakes, dust them with a little sifted sugar, and bake them in a very slow oven. When they become lightly coloured upon the top, which may be in ten or twelve minutes, take them out; carefully take off a little of the top, fill them with whipt cream or strawberry jam, and put them together so as to resemble a whole egg, and serve them in a napkin.

Sugar Ruffs

A pound of pounded and sifted loaf sugar beaten well with the whites of three eggs, and flavoured with oil of cinnamon, lemons, or orange flower water, and baked in the same way as the meringues, served in a napkin, or used to garnish dishes of preserves.

Potato Biscuit

Beat separately the yolks and whites of fifteen eggs, and with the yolks beat a pound of pounded and sifted loaf sugar, and the grated peel of a lemon; when very light, add the whites, and sift in through a silk sieve half a pound of flour of potatoes; mix all lightly together, half fill paper cases, and strew over them roughly pounded sugar; put a piece of paper upon a board, place the paper cases upon it, and bake them in a moderate oven to ornament them, put here and there upon the top a little red-currant jelly, and serve them.

Tipsy Bread

Pare off the crust, and cut into thin round slices of four or five inches, the crumb of a twopenny or threepenny roll; spread over each bit raspberry or strawberry jam, and place the slices one over the other pretty high in a glass dish, and pour over them as much sherry, sweetened with sugar, as the bread will soak in; stick round the sides, and over the top, blanched sweet almonds; cut like straws, and pour a custard round it. It may be made the day before, or two or three hours before dinner, and with the crumb of loaf bread.

Tipsy Cake

Pour over a spunge cake, made in the form of a porcupine, as much white wine as it will absorb, and stick it all over with blanched sweet almonds, cut like straws; or pour wine in the same manner over a thick slice of spunge cake, cover the top of it with preserved strawberries or raspberries, and stick cut almonds all round it.

Lemon Spunge

Boil half an ounce of isinglass in a pint of water till dissolved; strain it, and the following day add the juice of two lemons, and the grated peel of one; rub through a hair sieve into the isinglass a good quantity of raspberry jam, that has stood before the fire some time, and whisk it altogether, till like a spunge; put it into an earthen mould, set it in a cold place for some hours, and turn it out. Any other sort of preserve may be used, and if made with only orange or lemon juice, sweeten it with sugar, or make it with orange jelly which may have been left the day before.

Another Lemon Spunge

Boil an ounce of isinglass in a pint and a half of water, and when it is half wasted, strain it, and let it stand till quite cold; then mix with it the juice of three lemons, the whites of three eggs, and pounded sugar to sweeten it. Whisk it about twenty minutes, when it may be put into a shape; and if required, will be ready to be turned out in an hour or two. The white of one egg only may be used.

Raspberry Spunge

Dissolve in a little water three quarters of an ounce of isinglass, add to it three quarters of a pint of cream, and the same proportion of new milk, nearly half a pint of raspberry jelly, and the juice of a lemon. Whisk it well one way till it becomes thick, and looks like spunge, then put it into an earthenware mould, and turn it out the next day.

Cake Sandwiches

Cut a spunge cake, a few days old, as for bread sandwiches, and spread strawberry jam or currant jelly over them.

A Trifle

Add to a pint of rich cream a tea-cupful of white wine sweetened with pounded loaf sugar, whisk it well, and as the froth rises, lay it upon a sieve placed over a deep dish; as it drains, pour the cream into the pan in which it is whisked till all is done; dip some spunge biscuit, ratafia cakes, or Savoy biscuit, into sweet wine and a little brandy; pour over them a rich boiled custard, and when quite cold, lay on the whipt cream, piled as high as possible. Coloured confits may be strewed over the top.

Another way to make Trifle

Mix three table-spoonfuls of white wine, and one of sugar, with a pint and a half of thick cream; whisk it, and take off as much froth as will heap upon the dish, into which lay some pieces of spunge cake, or one spunge biscuit, soaked with sweet wine, and covered with preserved strawberries, or any other fruit; pile the froth upon this, and pour the remainder of the cream into the bottom of the dish; garnish with flowers.

A Large Syllabub

ONE pound of ratafia cakes pounded and steeped in two bottles of port wine, one of claret, and one of brandy, the grated peel and juice of two lemons, one large nutmeg grated, and two ounces of sweet almonds, blanched and pounded with a little rose water, and pounded sugar sufficient to make it sweet – Put all these ingredients, well mixed, into a large china bowl, or bowls of an equal size, and let the milk of a good cow be milked upon them; add a little rich cream and sifted loaf sugar, and cover it to keep it warn. It may be served out into glasses with a silver ladle.

Another way to make Large Syllabub

A large glass of madeira, one of rich sweet wine, and half a one of ratafia, half a pound of pounded loaf sugar, the grated peel of a large lemon, the juice of two, and a little pounded cinnamon; stir it altogether till the sugar be dissolved, and add a quart of rich cream; whisk it well; lay some macaroons into the bottom of a dish, and pile the frothed syllabub high upon it. It may be kept nine or ten days, and is better the third and fourth than when first made.

Solid Syllabub

A quarter of a pint of mountain, the same of white wine, the grated peel of two, and juice of one lemon; sweeten, and add it to a quart of rich cream; whisk it for an hour, and put it into glasses. It will keep a week in cold weather.

Whipt Syllabub

MIX together half a glass of brandy, a little lemon juice, and grated peel, with sugar enough to sweeten the whole; stir it into a pint of thick cream, and add the well-beaten whites of six eggs; whisk it for an hour, and put the froth, as it rises, upon a sieve to drain; put a little port and sweet wine into glasses, and fill them up with the froth.

Common Syllabub

HALF a pint of currant, the same of port or white wine, half a grated nutmeg, and the peel of a lemon; sweeten well with pounded loaf or good brown sugar, and mix it together in a china bowl, and when the sugar dissolves, milk upon it three or four pints of milk. Serve it when cold.

To Preserve Lemons for Eight or Ten Months

THE lemons must be perfectly fresh and sound, and free from every blemish. Put into a box a layer of earth, previously sifted, and made sufficiently damp for corn to spring in; strew over it a little barley, and place the lemons on it so as not to touch each other, and again put a layer of earth and barley; do this till all the lemons are packed, and taking care they be entirely covered with the earth. The box must be kept in a cellar, or some damp place, to prevent the earth becoming too dry.

To Preserve Lemon Juice

SQUEEZE, and strain a pint of lemon juice; put into a china basin one pound of double-refined sugar finely pounded and sifted, add the lemon juice, and stir it with a silver spoon till the sugar be perfectly dissolved. Bottle it, and cork it tightly; seal the cork, or tie bladder over it, and keep it in a dry cool place.

To Purify Lemon Juice

To one quart of strained lemon juice, add one ounce of well-burned and finely-pounded charcoal; in twelve hours filter it through filtering paper, and put it into small phials, which cork tightly, and keep in a cool place; a thick crust will form beneath the cork, and the mucilage will fall to the bottom. Hang up the peels, and when dried, keep them in a paper bag.

Colouring for Jellies, Creams, Ices, and Cakes

BOIL very slowly in a gill of water, till reduced to one half, twenty grains of cochineal, the same quantity of alum and of cream of tartar finely pounded; strain, and keep it in a small phial.

For yellow, use an infusion of saffron.

For green, wash well, and pull into small bits, a handful of spinach leaves; put them into a closely-covered sauce-pan; let them boil for a few minutes, and then express the juice.

CHAPTER XV
CAKES, BISCUITS, AND BREAD

PREPARATORY REMARKS

THE currants and raisins should be prepared as directed under the preparatory remarks on Puddings, Pies, and Tarts (page 182); and the flour dried before the fire on a large sheet of white paper, then sifted and weighed. Almonds should be blanched by pouring hot water over them, and, after standing some minutes, taking off the skin, then throwing them into rose or cold water. When not pounded, they should be cut lengthwise into thin bits.

Sugar should be roughly pounded, rolled with a bottle upon white paper, and then sifted. All spices, after being well dried at the fire, should be finely pounded and sifted. Lemon and orange peel must be pared very thin, and pounded with a little sugar.

The butter, after being weighed, should be laid into cold water, or washed in rose water, and if salt, be well washed in several waters.

The yolks and whites of eggs should be separately and long beaten, then strained; two whisks should be kept exclusively for that purpose, as the whites especially require to be managed with the greatest care. A horn spoon should be used for mixing those cakes which are not directed to be beaten with the hand.

To make cakes light, sal volatile, or smelling salts, may be added immediately before putting them into the oven, allowing, to a spunge cake, made of one pound of flour, one tea-spoonful; and two or three to a large plum cake.

Plum Cake

Two pounds of sifted and dried flour, one pound and a half of pounded and sifted loaf sugar, two pounds of nicely-cleaned and dried currants, half a pound of stoned and chopped raisins, half a pound of sweetmeats, one nutmeg grated, the weight of it in pounded cinnamon and mace, half a pound of almonds blanched and cut small, fourteen eggs, the whites and yolks beaten separately, the yolks with three table-spoonfuls of rose or orange-flower water. These ingredients being prepared, with the hand beat to a cream two pounds of fresh butter; add the sugar by degrees, and then the yolks of the eggs, the whites, the flour, the spice, the almonds, the fruit, and sweetmeats, and lastly, mix in a glass of brandy; beat it all well together; butter the hoop or frame, and pour in the cake, and put it into a moderate oven. It will take between three and four hours to bake.

Frost, or Icing, for Cakes

BEAT till very light the whites of four eggs, and add gradually three quarters of a pound of double-refined sugar, pounded and sifted through a lawn sieve; mix in the juice of half a lemon; beat it till very light and white; place the cake before the fire, pour over it the icing, and smooth over the top and sides with the back of a spoon.

Pound Cake

TAKE one pound of dried and sifted flour, the same quantity of sifted loaf sugar, and of fresh butter washed in rose water; the well-beaten yolks of twelve, and the whites of six eggs; then with the hand beat the butter to a cream, by degrees add the sugar, then the eggs and the flour; beat it all well together for an hour. Bake it in a tin pan buttered, or in small ones in a quick oven.

Another way to make Pound Cake

TAKE of dried and sifted flour, sifted loaf sugar, fresh butter, cleaned and dried currants, one pound each, and twelve eggs; then whisk the yolks and whites of the eggs separately, while another person with the hand beats the butter to a cream; and as the froth rises upon the eggs add it to the butter, and continue so doing till it is all beaten in; mix the flour and sugar together, and add them by degrees; the last thing, mix in the currants, together with a glass of brandy. It will require to be beaten during a whole hour. Bake it in a buttered tin.

Spunge Cake.

TAKE sixteen ounces of finely-pounded loaf sugar, the same quantity of eggs, and twelve ounces of dried and sifted flour; then whisk the eggs, yolks and whites, nearly half an hour; beat in the sugar with a horn spoon, and, just before it is to be put into a buttered tin, stir in the flour lightly, adding a few caraway seeds. Bake it for one hour.

Another way to make Spunge Cake

TAKE the juice and grated rind of a lemon, twelve eggs, twelve ounces of finely-pounded loaf sugar, the same of dried and sifted flour; then with a horn spoon beat the yolks of ten of the eggs, add the sugar by degrees, and beat it till it will stand when dropped from the spoon; put in at separate times the two other eggs, yolks and whites; whisk the ten whites for eight minutes, and mix in the lemon juice; and when quite stiff, take as much as the whisk will lift, and put it upon the yolks and sugar, which must be beaten all the time; mix in lightly the flour and grated peel, and pour it all gradually over the whites; stir it together, and bake it in a buttered tin, or in small tins; do not more than half fill them.

Another way to make Spunge Cake

THREE quarters of a pound of loaf sugar, a quarter of a pint of water, boil the sugar and water, skim it well; six well-beaten eggs, pour in the sugar boiling hot, whisk it till cold; seven ounces of flour well dried, mixed in gradually with the grated peel of a lemon. The above should be put into a cake tin, well buttered and lined with buttered paper. It must be immediately put into a moderate oven, and baked three quarters of an hour. This spunge cake will keep moist and good for weeks.

Another way to make Spunge Cake

TAKE one pound of dried flour, three quarters of a pound of finely-pounded loaf sugar, seven eggs, the yolks and whites beaten separately, the grated peel and juice of a lemon, a table-spoonful of rose water, and one of brandy, and half an ounce of caraway seeds dried and pounded; beat all for an hour with the hand; butter a tin, line it with paper also buttered, put in the cake, and sift pounded sugar over the top. Bake it for an hour. Potato flour may be substituted for wheat flour in this, and the other spunge cakes.

Scots Seed Cake

TAKE one pound and a half of dried and sifted flour, the same quantity of fresh butter washed in rose water, and of finely-pounded loaf sugar; six ounces of blanched sweet almonds, three quarters of a pound of candied orange-peel, half a pound of citron, all cut into thin narrow strips; one nutmeg grated, and a tea-spoonful of pounded caraway seeds, fifteen eggs, the yolks and whites separately beaten; then with the hand beat the butter to a cream, add the sugar, and then the eggs gradually; mix in the flour a little at a time, and then the sweetmeats, almonds, and spice, and lastly, stir in a glass of brandy; butter the hoop or tin pan, and pour in the cake so as nearly to fill it; smooth it over the top, and strew over it caraway comfits. Bake it in a moderate oven; it must not be moved or turned till nearly done, as shaking it will occasion the sweetmeats to sink to the bottom.

A Cake

TAKE two pounds and a half of dried and sifted flour; the same of well-cleaned and dried currants, two pounds of fresh butter, two of finely-pounded and sifted loaf sugar, a nutmeg grated, a tea-spoonful of pounded cinnamon, one ounce of citron and candied orange-peel, cut small, the yolks of sixteen, and the whites of ten eggs, beaten separately; then with the hand beat the butter to a cream, and add the sugar, then the eggs by degrees, and the flour in the same way, and then the currants, sweetmeats, and spice, one glass of orange-flower water, and one of brandy. Butter a tin pan, line it with white paper buttered, put in the cake, and bake it in a moderate oven four hours.

Tunbridge Cakes

RUB two ounces of butter into half a pound of dried flour; add a few caraway seeds, and a quarter of a pound of pounded loaf sugar; mix it to a stiff paste with a little water, roll it out very thin, cut it into round cakes with a glass or the top of a dredging box, prick them with a fork, and bake them upon floured tins.

Brighton Cakes

WITH one pound of dried and sifted flour, mix half a pound of sifted loaf sugar, three ounces of sweet, and one ounce of bitter almonds pounded with a little rose water, and, if approved, four ounces of cleaned currants. Stir in to this half a pound of fresh butter, beaten to a cream, mix it well together. The cakes may be baked in very small tins, or chopped in rough knobs upon floured tins.

Spunge Biscuits

BEAT together for half an hour, four well-beaten eggs, and half a pound of finely-pounded loaf sugar; then mix in lightly six ounces of dried and sifted flour, and the grated peel of a lemon, or a tea-spoonful of essence of lemon, with a table-spoonful of rose water. Flour the pans, fill them half full, and sift pounded sugar over them. Bake them in a quick oven. Potato flour may be substituted for wheat flour.

Tea Cakes

WITH a pound of flour rub half a pound of butter; add the beaten yolks of two, and the white of one egg, a quarter of a pound of pounded loaf sugar, and a few caraway seeds; mix it to a paste with a little warm milk, cover it with a cloth, and let it stand before the fire for nearly an hour; roll out the paste, and cut it into round cakes with the top of a glass, and bake them upon floured tins.

Simple Cakes

RUB lightly into half a pound of dried flour a quarter of a pound of fresh butter, and a quarter of a pound of sifted loaf sugar; make it into a paste with a beaten egg, roll it out thin, cut it into round cakes, and bake them upon tins. They may be baked upon a girdle, putting the cakes upon white paper, and a tin cover over them.

Madelon Cakes

TAKE three quarters of a pound of dried and sifted flour, one pound of eggs, and one of pounded and sifted sugar; then beat the eggs well, add the, sugar, flour, and grated peel of two lemons, two table-spoonfuls of brandy, and one pound of oiled butter stirred in, the last thing; with a spoon, nearly fill small tins dusted with flour.

French Biscuit

WEIGH five egg, and their weight in dried and sifted flour, and in finely pounded loaf sugar; beat the whites of the eggs to stiff froth, and by degrees beat in the sugar and the flour, and then add the beaten yolks; with a spoon, half fill yellow tea-cups, previously rubbed with butter, and sift loaf sugar over the top. Bake them in a quick oven. Or, drop the biscuit in a round form upon sheets of white paper buttered; sift sugar over them.

Sugar Biscuits

THE weight of eight eggs in finely-pounded loaf sugar, and of four in dried flour; beat separately the whites and yolks; with the yolks beat the sugar for half an hour, then add the whites and the flour, and a little grated nutmeg, lemon-peel, or pounded cinnamon. Bake them in yellow tea-cups, or drop them upon paper, as the French biscuits.

Scots Christmas Bun

TAKE four pounds of raisins stoned, two and a half of currants well cleaned and dried, half a pound of almonds blanched, of candied orange and lemon-peel a quarter of a pound each, cut small; of pounded cloves, Jamaica pepper, and ginger, half an ounce each, four pounds of flour, and twenty-two ounces of butter. Then rub the butter with the flour, till well mixed together; add a little warm water, and a quarter of a pint of fresh good yeast, and work it into a light smooth paste; cut off nearly one-third of the paste, to form the sheet or case, and lay it aside; with the rest work up the fruit, sweetmeats, and spices; make it into a round form like a thick cheese. Roll out the sheet of paste, lay the bun in the centre, and gather it all round, closing it at the bottom, by wetting the edges of the paste, and cutting it so as to lie quite flat. Turn it up, and run a wire or small skewer through from the top to the bottom every here and there, and prick the top with a fork, double and flour a sheet of grey paper, and lay the bun upon it; bind a piece round the sides, also doubled and floured, to keep the bun in a proper shape. Bake it in a moderate oven.

Sugar Cakes

TAKE half a pound of dried flour, the same quantity of fresh butter washed in rose water, and a quarter of a pound of sifted loaf sugar; then mix together the flour and sugar; rub in the butter, and add the yolk of an egg beaten with a table-spoonful of cream; make it into a paste, roll, and cut it into small round cakes, which bake upon a floured tin.

Honey Cakes

ONE pound and a half of dried and sifted flour, three quarters of a pound of honey, half a pound of finely pounded loaf sugar, a quarter of a pound of citron, and half an ounce of orange-peel cut small, pounded ginger and cinnamon, three quarters of an ounce. Melt the sugar with the honey, and mix in the other ingredients; roll out the paste, and cut it into small cakes of any form.

Rice Cakes

TAKE the weight of four eggs in sifted rice flour and finely-pounded loaf sugar, half that weight of fresh butter, washed in rose water, and beaten to a cream; whisk the eggs, add to them the sugar, and beat these for twenty minutes; then mix in the butter and the rice flour, along with a few pounded bitter almonds, or the grated peel of a lemon, and beat all together for ten minutes. Butter small tins, half fill, and bake them in a quick oven.

Another way to make Rice Cakes

BEAT, till extremely light, the yolks of nine eggs; add half a pound of sifted loaf sugar, and the same quantity of sifted rice flour; melt half a pound of fresh butter, and mix it with the eggs, sugar, and flour, along with a few pounded bitter almonds; half fill small tins buttered with the mixture, and bake in a quick oven.

Currant Cakes

TAKE half a pound of cleaned and dried currants, the same quantity of dried and sifted flour, a quarter of a pound of pounded sugar, a quarter of a pound of fresh butter, four yolks, and three whites of eggs, both well beaten, and a little grated nutmeg or pounded cinnamon; then beat the butter to a cream; add the sugar, and then the eggs and the flour; beat these well for twenty minutes, mix in the currants and the grated nutmeg. Drop the cakes in a round form upon buttered paper, or bake them in small tins in a quick oven.

Another way to make Currant Cakes

TAKE six ounces of currants, the same quantity of pounded loaf sugar, a little grated nutmeg, half a pound of butter, and three quarters of a pound of dried and sifted flour; rub the butter with the flour till they be well mixed, then add the other ingredients, and bind them with three beaten yolks of eggs, and two or three spoonfuls of rose or orange-flower water; roll it out, and cut it into round cakes with the top of a wine glass or a tin.

Wafers

MIX, with six table-spoonfuls of dried and sifted flour, nearly a pint of thick cream, the well-beaten yolks of four eggs, three table-spoonfuls of sifted loaf sugar, and one of orange-flower water; beat all these well together. Heat the wafer-irons, and put into them a table-spoonful of the batter; turn the irons, that the cake may be baked equally, and while hot, roll them round a stick. When cold, they will be very crisp.

Rich Cake

To two pounds and a half of dried and sifted flour allow the same quantity of fresh butter washed with rose water, two pounds of finely-pounded loaf sugar, three pounds of cleaned and dried currants, one nutmeg grated, half a pound of sweetmeats cut small, a quarter of a pound of blanched almonds pounded with a little rose water, and twenty eggs, the yolks and whites beaten separately. The butter must be beaten with the hand till it become like cream; then add the sugar, and by degrees the eggs, after these, the rest of the ingredients, mixing in at the last the currants, with a tea-cupful of brandy, and nearly as much orange-flower water. This mixture must be beaten together rather more than an hour, then put into a cake-pan, which has previously been buttered and lined with buttered paper; fill it rather more than three parts full. It should be baked in a moderate oven for three hours, and then cooled gradually by at first letting it stand some time at the mouth of the oven.

Almond Cake

BLANCH half a pound of sweet, and three ounces of bitter almonds; pound them to a paste in a mortar with orange-flower water; add half a pound of sifted loaf sugar, and a little brandy; whisk separately, for half an hour, the whites and yolks of twenty eggs, add the yolks to the almonds and sugar, and then stir in the whites, and beat them all well together. Butter a tin pan, sift bread raspings over it, put the cake into it, over the top of which strew sifted loaf sugar. Bake in a quick oven for half or three quarters of an hour.

Water Cakes

MIX together three quarters of a pound of sifted loaf sugar, and one pound of dried and sifted flour, and some caraway seeds; make it into a stiff paste, with the white of an egg beaten with a little water; roll it out very thin, cut the cakes round with the top of a glass or tin, prick them with a fork, and bake them upon buttered tins.

Caraway Cakes

MIX half a pound of sifted loaf sugar with a pound of flour and a quarter of a pound of butter, add some caraway seeds; make it into a stiff paste, with three well-beaten eggs, and a little rose water; roll it out thin, cut it into round cakes, prick them with a fork, and bake them upon floured tins in a quick oven.

Another way to make Caraway Cakes.

THREE quarters of a pound of flour, half a pound of butter well rubbed into it, a quarter of a pound of sifted loaf sugar, and some caraway seeds; make these into stiff paste with a little cold water, roll it out two or three times, cut it into round cakes, prick them, and bake them upon floured tins. For a change, currants may be substituted for the caraway seeds.

Banbury Cakes

STREW some nicely-cleaned currants over a piece of puff paste, roll it out, cut it into round cakes with the top of a dredging box; bake them upon floured tins, and the moment they are taken out of the oven, sift sugar over them, and put them upon a dish to cool. After making pies, they may be made with the remainder of the paste.

Rout Cakes

RUB into one pound of flour half a pound of fresh butter washed in rose water; of brown sifted loaf sugar, sweetmeats cut small, and well-cleaned currants, a quarter of a pound each; mix all the ingredients with three well-beaten eggs, and add one or two table-spoonfuls of brandy. Drop it in rough knobs upon floured tins, and bake them in a quick oven.

Rich Currant Cake

HAVE ready three pounds of dried and sifted flour, two pounds and a half of fresh butter, one pound of sifted loaf sugar, one pound of citron and lemon-peel cut small, three quarters of a pound of blanched sweet almonds cut into thin bits, and steeped in rose water, five pounds of well-cleaned currants, one nutmeg grated, half an ounce of pounded mace, the yolks of fifteen, and the whites of seven eggs beaten separately, half a pint of fresh yeast, a pint and a half of cream, an eighth of a pint of orange-flower water; then mix the spice with the flour; melt the butter and cream together, and when cold, stir them into the flour; add the yeast to the beaten eggs, and strain them into the flour, then mix in the rest of the ingredients, and beat them well together. Butter a cake-pan, line it with buttered paper, pour in the cake, and put it immediately into the oven. As soon as it rises, and is a little coloured, cover the top with paper. It will take nearly three hours to bake.

Macaroons

BEAT to a froth the whites of eight eggs, then add two pounds of finely-pounded and sifted loaf sugar, one pound of blanched sweet almonds, which must be pounded to a paste with rose water. Beat all these together till they become a thick paste, then drop it from a spoon upon wafer paper or tins, and bake them in a slow oven.

Small Almond Cakes

ONE pound of butter beaten to a cream, half a pound of finely-pounded and sifted loaf sugar, half a pound of dried and sifted flour, and the same quantity of blanched sweet almonds cut into thin small bits, one well-beaten egg, and a little rose water, must be mixed well together, and with a spoon dropped upon wafer paper or tins, and then baked.

The Queen's Tea Cakes

MIX together half a pound of dried and sifted flour, the same quantity of pounded and sifted loaf sugar, the weight of two eggs in fresh butter, the grated peel of a lemon, and a little salt; beat the two eggs with a little rose water, and with them make the ingredients into a paste; roll it out, cut it into round cakes, and bake them upon floured tins.

Potato-Flour Cake

MIX half a pound of potato-flour, very much dried, with three quarters of a pound of pounded and sifted leaf sugar; roll it with a bottle. Beat separately the yolks and whites of eight new-laid eggs, and then mix them together; whisk all the ingredients till quite light. Heat the tin shape well, butter it, as also the paper, put in the cake, and bake it in a moderate oven for half an hour. If properly done, it will rise high and be light.

Common Cake

TAKE two quarts of flour; mix with it three quarters of a pound of butter, a tea-cupful of fresh yeast, one pint of milk, nine well-beaten eggs, two pounds of well-cleaned currants, one pound and a half of good brown sugar, the grated peel of a lemon, and one nutmeg; a glass of brandy must be stirred in just before it be put into a buttered tin. Bake it for two hours or more.

Another way to make a Common Cake

RUB into one pound of flour a quarter of a pound of fresh butter; mix, with two well-beaten eggs, and a table-spoonful of fresh yeast, as much warm milk as will make the flour into a very thick batter. Let this remain near the fire, covered with a cloth, for an hour, then mix into it six ounces of good brown sugar, and nine ounces of well-cleaned and dried currants; let it stand again for half an hour, and bake it in a buttered tin for an hour.

Another way to make a Common Cake

WITH the hand beat three quarters of a pound of fresh butter to a cream, and mix it with as much dough as would make a half-quartern loaf; add eight ounces of finely-pounded loaf, or good brown sugar, and the same quantity of well-cleaned currants, a little pounded cinnamon, or grated nutmeg; beat all well together, and bake it in a buttered tin.

French Cake

TWELVE eggs, the yolks and whites beaten well and separately, one pound of pounded and sifted loaf sugar, the grated peel of a large lemon, half a pound of sifted and dried flour, the same weight of sifted and dried ground rice, four ounces of sweet, and one of bitter almonds, pounded in a mortar together with a table-spoonful of orange-flower water. Mix all these ingredients gradually, and beat them well. Paper the pan, and bake the cake for one hour.

Bourbon Cake

BEAT well and separately the yolks of ten, and the whites of five eggs; grate and sift a pound of loaf sugar, grate the peel of two bitter oranges, blanch and pound, with a little rose water, half a pound of sweet almonds; whisk all these ingredients together for half an hour; and lastly, mix in half a pound of dried and sifted flour; lay it about three inches deep into a hoop, and bake it in a moderate oven for one hour and a quarter. Immediately upon taking the cake out of the frame, ice it over the top and sides.

Irish Seed Cake

BEAT to a cream eight ounces of fresh butter, and a quarter of a pint of rose water, putting in a table-spoonful of rose water at a time; by degrees, mix into it a pound of sifted loaf sugar, and then nine well-beaten eggs; add twelve ounces of flour, and three of flour of rice dried and sifted, a quarter of a pound of blanched and pounded sweet or bitter almonds, a tea-spoonful of essence of lemon, and one ounce of caraway seeds; beat all these well together; bake it in a cake tin, which must be buttered, and lined with paper also buttered. It will require about one hour and a half to bake in a quick oven. It may be made without the almonds or the essence of lemon.

Bairn Brack

To three pounds of dried flour allow one pound of fresh butter, one pound of good brown sugar, two ounces of caraway seeds, eight well-beaten eggs, three tablespoonfuls of fresh yeast, and some grated nutmeg; dissolve the butter in a pint of milk, so as to make the whole into a dough, not very stiff; work it well; cover it with a cloth, and set it before the fire to rise; when well risen, bake it in a buttered tin. When it becomes dry, it may be toasted and eaten with butter.

Short Bread

For two pounds of sifted flour allow one pound of butter, salt or fresh; a quarter of a pound of candied orange and lemon-peel, of pounded loaf sugar, blanched sweet almonds, and caraway comfits, a quarter of a pound each; cut the lemon, the orange-peel, and almonds, into small thin bits, and mix them with a pound and a half of the flour, a few of the caraway comfits, and the sugar; melt the butter, and when cool, pour it clear from the sediment into the flour, at the same time mixing it quickly. With the hands, form it into a large round of nearly an inch thick, using the remainder of the flour to make it up with; cut it into four, and with the finger and thumb pinch each bit neatly all round the edge; prick them with a fork, and strew the rest of the caraway comfits over the top. Put the pieces upon white paper dusted with flour, and then upon tins. Bake them in a moderate oven

Plain Short Bread

The same proportions of flour and butter must be used as in the above receipt for short bread; this must be mixed together, rolled out, but not made quite so thick as in the rich kind; but in the same form, pricked with a fork, and pinched all round. A little sugar may be added

Queen Cakes

Prepare eight ounces of fresh butter beaten to a cream, six ounces of pounded and sifted loaf sugar, half a pound of dried and sifted flour, the same quantity of cleaned and dried currants, four well-beaten eggs, a little grated nutmeg, pounded cinnamon, and a few pounded bitter almonds; then add the sugar to the butter, put in the eggs by degrees, after that the flour and the other ingredients; beat all well together for half an hour, and put it into small buttered tins, nearly filling them, and strew over the top finely-pounded loaf sugar. Bake them in a pretty brisk oven.

Shrewsbury Cakes

Mix with half a pound of fresh butter washed in rose water, and beaten to a cream, the same quantity of dried and sifted flour, seven ounces of pounded and sifted loaf sugar, half an ounce of caraway seeds, and two well-beaten eggs; make them into a paste; roll it thin; cut it into round cakes; prick them, and bake them upon floured tins.

Another way to make Shrewsbury Cakes

Rub into a pound of dried and sifted flour half a pound of fresh butter, seven ounces of sifted loaf sugar, and the same quantity of cleaned and dried currants, and a little grated nutmeg; make it into a paste with a little water, two table-spoonfuls of rose or orange-flower water; roll it out, and cut it into round cakes; prick them, and bake them upon tins dusted with flour.

Montrose Cakes

Of dried and sifted flour, pounded and sifted loaf sugar, and of fresh butter, one pound each will be required, also twelve well-beaten eggs, three quarters of a pound of cleaned and dried currants; beat the butter to a cream with the sugar; add the eggs by degrees, and then the flour and currants, with two table-spoonfuls of brandy, one of rose water, and half a grated nutmeg; beat all well together for twenty or thirty minutes, when it is to be put into small buttered tins, half filling them, and baking them in a quick oven. The currants may be omitted.

Rice Cake

Whisk ten eggs for half an hour, add to them half a pound of flour rice, half a pound of pounded and sifted loaf sugar, and the grated peel of two lemons; mix this into half a pound of fresh butter, previously beaten to a cream. Bake the cake in a buttered tin.

Little Rice Cakes

Whisk well six yolks and two whites of eggs; then with a horn spoon beat in six ounces of finely-pounded loaf sugar, add eight ounces of sifted ground rice, and two table-spoonfuls of orange-flower or rose water, or the grated peel of a lemon, and just before the mixture is to be put into the tins, stir into it six ounces of fresh butter melted; dust the patty-pans with flour, or rub them with butter; let them be half filled, and bake the cakes in a quick oven.

White Cake

TAKE of dried and sifted flour, of fresh butter, and of finely-pounded loaf sugar, one pound each; five well-beaten eggs, a quarter of a pint of cream, of candied orange, and lemon peel, cut small, three quarters of an ounce each; one ounce of caraway seeds, half a grated nutmeg; a glass of brandy, and a little rose water; then beat the butter to a cream, and add all the other ingredients to it, and at the last mix in one table-spoonful of fresh yeast; let the cake rise before the fire for half an hour. Bake it in a buttered tin. Instantly upon taking it out of the oven, with a feather brush the top all over with the beaten white of an egg, and then sift loaf sugar upon it. Let it stand at the mouth of the oven to harden.

Rich Cakes

MIX together one pound of flour, half a pound of pounded loaf sugar, and half a pound of melted butter; add a quarter of a pound of currants, and a glass of brandy, or of raisin wine; roll out the paste, cut the cakes with a small round tin, and bake them upon a floured tin.

Cheshire Cake

BEAT for half au hour the yolks of eight, and the whites of five eggs; add half a pound of pounded and sifted loaf sugar, a quarter of a pound of dried and sifted flour, and the grated peel of a small lemon; beat all together, and bake it in a floured tin.

Little Cakes

BEAT a pound of fresh butter to a cream, and add to it one pound of pounded loaf sugar, a little pounded cinnamon and nutmeg, the grated peel of a lemon, three well-beaten eggs, one pound of currants, one pound of flour, and a little sweet wine. Work it altogether, roll it out, cut it into little cakes; brush some sweet wine over them with a feather, sift grated sugar over them, and bake them upon tins. These cakes will keep good a year.

Little Almond Cakes

BEAT, with a three-pronged fork, the whites of two eggs to a stiff froth. Blanch and pound with a little sugar, two ounces of sweet, and one ounce of bitter almonds, mix them with six ounces of pounded and sifted loaf sugar, and rub it through a cullender; then beat it with the eggs, and add two ounces of dried and sifted ground rice; beat all well together, and when very light, drop it from a spoon in small round cakes upon a sheet of tin, and bake them in a slow oven.

Little Cinnamon and Clove Cakes

To the well-beaten white of an egg, add dried, pounded, and sifted loaf sugar, till it be thick enough to cut into cakes, with small tin shapes. Flavour the beaten egg and sugar with two or three drops of essential oil of cinnamon, or of cloves, and bake the cakes upon tins in a slow oven.

Flemish Wafers

PUT into a deep pan half a pound of flour; strain and mix with it half a pint of warmed milk, and two tablespoonfuls of fresh yeast; work the paste till it be soft and smooth, and place it in a stove, or close to the fire, to rise; then add the beaten yolks of six eggs, half a pound of fresh butter beaten to a cream, and a lump of sugar which has been rubbed upon the peel of a lemon, and then pounded; last of all, beat in lightly the well-whisked whites of the egg; again place the pan in a warm place, and it will rise to nearly double its bulk. Heat and rub the irons, which should be square, with a little butter; fill one side with the mixture, and close them; when one side is done, turn the other, and when of a fine colour, take out the wafers; put them upon a plate, and whilst hot, sift over this quantity a quarter of a pound of grated loaf sugar.

Spanish Cakes

RUB, till quite fine and smooth, one, pound of butter with two pounds of flour, then add a pound of good brown sugar, rolled fine; mix all together with four well-beaten eggs; break the paste into small bits or knobs, and bake them upon floured tins.

Small Rout Cakes

RUB into one pound of dried and sifted flour, half a pound of butter, six ounces of pounded and sifted loaf sugar, and the yolks of two well-beaten eggs; mix them all into a paste with a little rose water; divide the quantity, put a few dried currants or caraway seeds into one half; roll out the paste, cut it into small round cakes, and bake them upon buttered tins.

Sugar Biscuits

MIX together one pound of dried and sifted flour, the same quantity of pounded and sifted loaf sugar, ten well-beaten eggs, and a few pounded cloves. Drop this upon floured tins, and bake it.

Handsch Kirchen, or Glove Cake

WITH flour make into a paste thick enough to roll out, the beaten yolks of ten eggs, five table-spoonfuls of rich sweet cream, a little sugar, and some cardamoms; cut into fanciful forms with small tins, and throw them into fresh boiling lard or butter; when of a light brown colour, drain them before the fire. If fried in butter, add a little water to the butter, and make it boiling hot.

Cake without Butter

TAKE the weight of three eggs in sugar, and the weight of two in flour; when the five eggs are well beaten, gradually add the sugar, and then the flour, with a little grated lemon-peel, or a few caraway seed so bake it in a tin mould, in rather a quick oven.

Common Cake

ONE pound and a half of flour, one pound of good brown sugar, eight well-beaten eggs, and one ounce of caraway seeds, are to be mixed together; then add of fresh yeast, milk, and of water, one table-spoonful each. Let it stand a little time, and bake it in a floured tin.

Plum Cake

TO one pound of dried and sifted flour, allow three quarters of a pound of sifted loaf sugar, eight eggs, the yolks and whites separately beaten; three quarters of a pound of butter beaten to a cream, three pounded cloves, half a grated nutmeg, half a pound of cleaned and dried currants; add the sugar to the butter, and next the eggs by degrees, then the flour and spices. Beat all well together for nearly an hour, mix in the currants with the grated peel of a lemon, half a glass of white wine, and the same quantity of brandy; put it into a cake-pan lined with buttered paper; bake it in a moderate oven.

Gateau à la Dauphine

BEAT separately the whites and yolks of twenty eggs; to the yolks add a pound of pounded and sifted loaf sugar, the grated peel of one lemon, and two or three table-spoonfuls of orange-flower water; then stir in the whites, and lightly mix in half a pound of dried and sifted flour. Bake in a buttered tin, in a moderate oven.

Gingerbread Cake

TAKE two pounds of treacle, two and a quarter of flour, of brown sugar and fresh butter three quarters of a pound each, four ounces of caraway seeds, the same quantity of candied orange-peel cut small, three ounces of finely-pounded ginger, four well-beaten eggs, and half an ounce of pearl ashes; beat the butter to a cream, and mix it with the rest of the ingredients. The next day work it well up, and bake it in a buttered tin.

Gingerbread Nuts

TAKE one pound of dried and sifted flour, one pound of treacle, three ounces of brown sugar, four ounces of fresh butter, one ounce and a half of pounded and sifted ginger, of candied orange-peel and citron, cut small, three quarters of an ounce each; melt the butter with the treacle, and when it is about milk-warm, add it to the flour and other ingredients, and then mix all well together; with a spoon drop the nuts upon buttered tins, and bake them.

Another way to make Gingerbread Nuts

DISSOLVE a quarter of a pound of butter in three quarters of a pound of treacle, put it into a pan large enough to contain the rest of the ingredients, and when almost cold, stir in one pound of dried and sifted flour, half a pound of coarse brown sugar, half an ounce of caraway seeds, three quarters of an ounce of pounded ginger, and the grated peel of a lemon; mix all these well together, and let it stand till it be stiff, or till the following day; then make it into nuts, by pinching it into pieces with the finger and thumb. Bake them upon buttered tins in a quick oven. Half an ounce of coriander seeds may be added.

Another way to make Gingerbread Nuts

RUB half a pound of butter into two pounds of flour; add one pound of coarse sugar, and one ounce of pounded ginger; mix all well together with one pound and two ounces of treacle; form it into nuts, or roll it out, and cut it into round cakes; bake them upon tins.

American Ginger Bread

TAKE half a pound of fresh butter melted, one pound and a half of dried and sifted flour, the same quantity of brown sugar, a quarter of a pound of pounded ginger, nine eggs, the yolks and whites beaten separately, one glass of rose water, and one of white wine; mix all these well together, and beat it for an hour; then with a spoon spread it over flat tin pans, about the thickness of a penny-piece; bake it of a light brown, and while warm, cut it into oblong pieces, and place them on end till cool, when they will be very crisp.

Rich Gingerbread Cakes

To one pound of dried and sifted flour, allow half a pound of pounded loaf sugar, three quarters of a pound of fresh butter washed in rose water, one pound of treacle, one nutmeg grated, the weight of a nutmeg of pounded mace, and as much of pounded cinnamon, one ounce of pounded ginger, one and a half of candied orange and lemon peel, cut small, half an ounce of blanched sweet almonds, cut into long thin bits, and two well-beaten eggs. Melt the butter with the treacle, and when nearly cold stir in the eggs and the rest of the ingredients; mix all well together, make it into round cakes, and bake them upon tins.

Indian Gingerbread

TAKE twelve ounces of pounded loaf sugar, a quarter of a pound of fresh butter, one pound of dried flour, two ounces of pounded ginger, and of cloves and cinnamon a quarter of an ounce each. Mix the ginger and spice with the flour; put the sugar and a small tea-cupful of water into a sauce-pan; when it is dissolved, add the butter, and as soon as it is melted mix it with the flour and other things; work it up, and form the paste into cakes or nuts, and bake them upon tins.

Honeycomb Gingerbread

HALF a pound of flour, half a pound of the coarsest brown sugar, a quarter of a pound of butter, one dessert-spoonful of allspice, and double that quantity of ginger, half the peel of a lemon grated, and the whole of the juice. Mix all these ingredients together, adding about half a pound of treacle, so as to make a paste sufficiently thin to spread upon sheet tins. Beat it well, butter the tins, and spread the paste very thinly over them. Bake it in rather a slow oven, and watch it till it is done; withdraw the tins, cut it in squares with a knife, the usual size of wafer biscuits, and roll each round the fingers as it is raised from the tin. This paste, put into a jar, and covered closely, will keep for a month; but the biscuits will be found best when newly baked.

Breakfast, or Tea Cakes

TAKE one pound of flour, and mix it with half a pound of butter dissolved, together with a little cream, milk, or water, and half a tea-spoonful of salt; work it well, and roll it into round balls. Have wafer-irons ready heated, put into them a ball of the paste, press them, and hold the irons upon the fire for a minute or two.

Slim Cakes for Breakfast or Tea

To one pound of flour, allow two beaten eggs, one ounce of butter, half a tea-spoonful of salt, and as much warmed milk as will make the whole into a pretty stiff paste; work it well, cover it over, and let it remain before the fire for half an hour; roll it out, and cut it into round cakes, with a small saucer or the top of a tumbler; do them in a nicely-cleaned frying-pan; dust them with a little flour. They may be baked upon a plate of iron, or what in Scotland is called a girdle.

Another way to make Cakes for Breakfast or Tea

To one pound of flour allow two beaten eggs, one table-spoonful of fresh yeast, and as much cream as will make them into a light dough; cover it over for an hour; make it into cakes, and bake them upon tins in a moderate oven.

Another way to make Cakes for Breakfast or Tea

Dissolve, in half a pint of warm water, one ounce of fresh butter, mix it with two pounds of dried and sifted flour, and stir in lightly two large spoonfuls of fine fresh yeast; cover it with a cloth, and let it stand to rise; then make it up into rolls, place them upon floured tins, let them again stand to rise, and bake them in a quick oven.

Short Cakes

Dissolve half a pound of fresh butter in as much milk as will make a pound and a half of flour into a paste, roll it out about a quarter of an inch thick, and cut it into large round cakes. Do them in a frying-pan, and serve them hot. They are eaten with butter.

Parkin, or Leeds Gingerbread

Sift four pounds of oatmeal, and mix with it four pounds of treacle, half a pound of brown sugar, the same quantity of melted butter, and three quarters of an ounce of powdered ginger. Work it all well together, let it remain for twenty four hours, and then make it into cakes.

Parliament Cakes

PUT into a sauce-pan two pounds of treacle, and when it boils, add a quarter of a pound of butter, and pour it upon two pounds of flour; add a little alum, and a bit of pearl ash about the size of a nut, and an ounce of ginger. Work it well with the hand till quite smooth; let it stand a day and a night, then roll it out very thin, and cut it into oblong cakes.

Oatmeal Cakes

ONE should only be made at a time, as the mixture dries quickly. Put two or three handfuls of meal into a bowl, and moisten it with water merely sufficient to form it into a cake; knead it out round and round with the hands upon the paste-board, strewing meal under and over it; it may be made as thin as a wafer, or thicker, according to taste, and put it on a hot iron plate, called a girdle. Bake it till it be a little brown on the under side then take it off, and toast that side before the fire, which was uppermost on the girdle. The toaster is such as is commonly used for heating smoothing irons, having a back to support the cake. To make these cakes soft, they must not be toasted before the fire, but both sides done quickly on the girdle.

Girdle Cakes

RUB three ounces of fresh butter into one pound of flour, with half a tea-spoonful of salt; moisten with a sufficiency of sweet buttermilk to make it into a paste; roll it out, and cut it into cakes with a cup or tumbler, and bake them upon a girdle.

Bath Buns

To four pounds of dried and sifted flour allow one pound of fresh butter, three quarters of a pound of caraway comfits, the well-beaten yolks of four, and the whites of two eggs, six table-spoonfuls of cream, and the same quantity of fresh yeast. Melt the butter, mix it with flour, and add the eggs, cream, and yeast, previously beaten together; cover it, and let it rise for twenty or thirty minutes, then shake in the caraway comfits, keeping a few to strew over the tops; form the buns, and bake them upon buttered tins.

Biscuit

MAKE as stiff a paste as possible of the finest flour, mixing it with cold water, and adding a little salt; beat it out with a rolling pin, cut it into pieces, lay them one over the other, and again beat it out; roll it very thin, cut it into biscuits, and prick them well with a fork. To make the Prince of Wales biscuit, roll the paste into small balls, and press it with a stamp.

Another way to make Biscuit

Rub seven ounces of fresh butter into two pounds of flour, mix with it two large spoonfuls of yeast, cover it with a cloth, and let it stand an hour; then add as much warmed new milk as will make it into a paste as stiff as pie-crust; form it into biscuits of about an ounce and a half each; bake them in a quick oven. The following day, after bread has been baked, put them again into the oven, and let them remain for nearly three hours.

Sweet Biscuit

One pound of flour, half a pound of butter; the same quantity of finely-pounded sugar, and two eggs, without being beaten; make it all into a very stiff paste with cold water, roll it out, and to form the biscuits, roll a bit of the paste into a ball about the size of the yolk of an egg, flatten it a little, and place them upon tins to bake.

Another way to make Sweet Biscuit

To one pound of flour allow half a pound of sugar, two beaten eggs, a tea-spoonful of caraway seeds, and a quarter of a pound of melted butter; mix all well together, roll it out thin, and cut it into round biscuits; prick them, and bake them upon tins.

Oliver's Biscuit

Melt a quarter of a pound of fresh butter in half a pint of new milk; add a table-spoonful of fresh yeast, and stir it into one pound and a half of flour; knead it well, then wrap it in warm flannel, to remain for fifteen minutes; roll it out several times, and the last time about the thickness of a penny-piece: cut it into small biscuits, prick them well with a fork, and bake them in a slow oven till of a pale brown colour.

Biscuits

Dissolve half a pound of butter in half a pint of milk, and make it into a stiff paste with four pounds of flour; beat and work it perfectly smooth, roll it out very thin, stamp out the biscuit, prick them well with a fork, and bake them upon tins in a quick oven.

Leman's Biscuit

SIFT and dry a pound of fine flour; rub into it a quarter of a pound of butter, two ounces of pounded and sifted loaf sugar, and a bit of volatile salt about the size of a nut; mix in it as much new milk warmed as will make it into a stiff paste; work it well together, and let it remain for two or three hours, and then roll it out, and make it into small square biscuits, and into round balls a little flattened; prick them with a fork, and bake them upon tins in a quick oven. Take care they do not become brown.

Cold Harbour Balls

DISSOLVE one ounce of butter in as much milk warmed as will make four pounds of flour into a stiff paste; about two pints may be required; add half a tea-spoonful of salt, one egg beaten together with a table-spoonful of yeast; mix it all well, cover it with a cloth, and let it remain before the fire for half an hour; then make it into small round balls, and bake them upon tins in a quick oven.

Rusks

To three pounds and a half of flour allow half a pound of butter, the same quantity of pounded loaf sugar, and five spoonfuls of yeast; mix the flour and sugar together; melt the butter in two pints and a half of milk, and mix it with the flour, and then add the yeast and one beaten egg; work it well together; cover it, and let it stand for five or six hours; take it out of the pan, and form it into little rolls; place them upon tins, and let them rise for about an hour; bake them in a quick oven, and when they become brown, cut them through the middle or into three slices; put them again into the oven to brown and crisp.

Muffins

MAKE two quarts of milk rather warmer than when it comes from the cow; then, with a horn or wooden spoon, mix with it about a tea-cupful of good fresh yeast; stir flour into it till it be as thick as a batter; cover it, and let it remain to rise for an hour, then take it out by spoonfuls, and drop it amongst flour, and let it remain fifteen minutes; take them up, flatten them a little, and bake them upon a metal plate; when one side is a little brown, turn them. When to be eaten, toast them, and with a knife cut them a little all round, then pull them open and butter them.

Sally Luns, or Bath Breakfast Cakes

Rub into two pounds of flour half a pound of butter, and mix with it one pint of milk a little warmed, a quarter of a pint of fresh yeast, four well-beaten eggs, and a tea-spoonful of salt; cover it, and let it stand before the fire to rise for three quarters of an hour; make it into thick cakes about the size of the inside of a dinner plate; bake them in a quick oven, then cut them into three, that the middle slice, as also the top and bottom, may be well buttered. Serve them hot.

To make Bread

To thirteen pounds of sifted flour allow four quarts of lukewarm milk or water, – in winter it must be warmer, but not scalding hot even in the coldest weather; put the milk into a wooden trough or large earthen pan; add a large table-spoonful of coarse salt; stir in a few handfuls of flour, and three quarters of a pint of beer yeast, or more if not very thick; then stir in flour till it be like a thick batter; throw some flour on the top, and set it before the fire. If the yeast be good, the mixture will rise in ten minutes to the top of the pan; then stir in some more flour, and replace it before the fire. When it has risen a second time, take out as much dough as will make the rolls, knead it about five minutes, form the rolls, prick them with a fork, and put them on a tin; place them before the fire to rise for ten minutes, and bake them in a pretty quick oven. The dough for the loaves must be kneaded for twenty minutes or half an hour. Form the loaves, and put them into tin pans, which may be rather more than half filled; prick them, and place them before the fire; when they have risen nearly to the top of the pans, they may be put into the oven and baked one hour. If a metal oven is used, it must be made moderately hot, that the bread may be well raised without being scorched.

The addition of an ounce of potato, to a pound of wheaten flour, will be found a great improvement to bread. When it is to be used, moisten it with a little cold water or milk, then pour into it a portion of the water, or milk, to be used for the baking, made nearly boiling hot; add the remainder of the liquid required, which should be milk-warm and, when the whole is a proper heat, mix with it the yeast and flour; and proceed as before directed.

Another way to make Bread

Mix into six pounds of sifted flour one ounce of salt, nearly half a pint of fresh sweet yeast as it comes from the brewery, and a sufficient quantity of warmed milk to make the whole into a stiff dough; work and knead it well upon a paste-board, on which a little flour has been strewed, for fifteen or twenty minutes, then put it into a deep pan, cover it with a warmed towel, set it before the fire, and let it rise for an hour and a half, or perhaps two hours; cut off a piece of this spunge or dough; knead it well for eight or ten minutes, together with flour merely sufficient to keep it from adhering to the board; put it into small tins, filling them three parts full; dent the rolls all round with a knife, and let them stand a few minutes before putting them into the oven. The remainder of the dough must then be worked up for loaves, and baked either in or out of a shape.

Brown Bread

EITHER of the above receipts may he followed, allowing a little more yeast, less liquid, and kneading the dough for a longer time. It may be made of oatmeal, or of a mixture of wheat, barley, and rye flour, the proportion of wheat flour being doubled; but the finest brown bread is made of wheat ground over head.

Stale Bread

MAY be made nearly as good as when newly baked, by putting it into a cool oven for nearly an hour.

French Bread

WITH one pound of flour rub two ounces of fresh butter. Mix with three or four table-spoonfuls of lukewarm milk, one of fresh beer yeast, and a beaten egg; work this with the flour, and set it to rise before the fire for about an hour, then knead it like bread; make it into two cakes, and place them upon buttered tins; let them stand before the fire an hour and a half, and bake them in a quick oven for fifteen minutes. A little sugar and a few caraway seeds may be added for a change. These cakes may be eaten hot.

Rolls

DISSOLVE two ounces of butter in one pint of new milk, and stir it into four pounds of flour, as also three table-spoonfuls of yeast, a tea-spoonful of salt, and the well-beaten whites of two eggs; cover the pan with a warmed towel, and set it before the fire to rise for half an hour, then work it one way for fifteen minutes; form it into rolls, place them upon tins, and let them rise for ten minutes before putting them into an oven.

French Rolls

MIX rather more than an ounce of coarse salt with eight pounds of sifted flour; make a hole in the middle, and pour in about half a pint of good yeast, the well-beaten whites of four eggs, and as much new milk warmed as will mix it to a middling stiffness; clap and work it down one way with the hands for half an hour, but do not knead it; cover it with a warmed towel, and let it rise before the fire for half an hour; take off the surface, which soon becomes hard, and put it aside to be made into a roll; work and clap the dough, form it into rolls, place them upon tins, and let them rise for ten minutes; bake them in a quick oven.

Yeast

BEER yeast, which is the best for bread, should be strained through a hair sieve, and two or three quarts of cold spring water poured over it; when it has stood for twenty-four hours, the water should be poured off, the yeast will then be found at the bottom of the vessel, quite thick. To preserve that which may be left over the baking, it should be put into a bottle, corked tightly, and kept in a cool place. In cold weather it will continue good for a fortnight, but fresh yeast is always preferable. When it does not appear sufficiently strong, honey or brown sugar may be mixed with it, in the proportion of a tea-spoonful to half a pint.

Bran Yeast

BOIL for ten minutes, in two quarts of water, one pint of bran, and a small handful of good hops; strain it through a sieve, and, when milk-warm, add three or four table-spoonfuls of beer yeast, and two of brown sugar or treacle; put it into a wooden stoup or jug; cover it, and place it before the fire to ferment. It may be bottled, tightly corked, and kept in a cool place.

Potato Yeast

BOIL some good mealy potatoes; peel and weigh them; while hot, bruise them finely, and mix them quickly with boiling water, allowing one quart to each pound; rub it through a hair sieve, then add honey or brown sugar, in the proportion of one ounce to each quart of water; boil it to the consistency of batter, and when nearly cold, add a large table-spoonful of good yeast to every quart of water; cover it with a cloth to rise, and the following day it will be ready for use; keep a bottle of it, which may be used instead of beer yeast for the next making, first pouring off the thin liquid that is on the top. It must be made with fresh beer yeast every two or three months. Double the quantity of this, as of beer yeast, is required to make bread light.

A Baker's Yeast

BOIL two ounces of hops in four quarts of water one hour, adding more water as it decreases, carefully stirring it all the time, and taking care that it do not boil over; strain the liquor, and mix well with it two pound of malt; cover, and let it stand for eight hours, or until it be milk-warm, then stir in half a pint of good yeast; when mixed well together, let it work for ten hours, and then strain it through a hair sieve.

CHAPTER XVI
PRESERVES

PREPARATORY REMARKS ON SWEETMEATS

ALL sweetmeats should be preserved in a brass pan, which must be well scoured with sand and vinegar, washed with hot water, and wiped perfectly dry before it is used.

An iron plate or a stove is preferable to a fire for preserving on; and by boiling the fruit quickly, the form, colour, and flavour, will be better preserved, and there will be less waste, than in slow boiling. A round wooden stick, smaller at the one end than the other, in Scotland called a thevil, is better adapted for stirring sugar or preserves with than a silver spoon, which last is only used for skimming. That there may be no waste in taking off the scum, it is put through a fine silk sieve, or through a hair sieve, with a bit of muslin laid into it; the clear part will run into the vessel placed below, and may be returned to the preserving pan.

A silver soup ladle is used for putting preserves into the jars, which should be of brown stone, or of white wedgewood ware. After the jellies or preserves are put in, they must not be moved till quite cold, when they are covered with a piece of white paper, cut so as to fit into the jar, and dipped into brandy or rum. They are then stored in a cool dry place, and should be looked at occasionally. If in a few weeks they be observed to ferment, the sirup should be first strained from the fruit, then boiled till it is thick, and again poured over the fruit, previously put into clean jars.

Sugar, low in price, and consequently coarse in quality, is far from being cheapest in the end; while that which is most refined is always the best. White sugars should be chosen as shining and as close in texture as possible.

The best sort of brown sugar has a bright and gravelly appearance.

A jelly-bag is made of half a square of flannel folded by the corners, and one side sewed up; the top bound with tape, and four loops also of tape sewed on, so as to hang upon a stand made of four bars of wood, each thirty-six inches in height, fastened with four bars at the top, each measuring ten inches, with hooks upon the corners. Twelve inches from the bottom four more bars are placed. A pan or basin is put underneath to receive the juice or jelly as it drops through the bag.

To Clarify Sugar

To every three pounds of loaf sugar, allow the beaten white of one egg, and a pint and a half of water; break the sugar small, put it into a nicely-cleaned brass pan, and pour the water over it; let it stand some time before it be put upon the fire; then add the beaten whites of the eggs; stir it till the sugar be entirely dissolved, and when it boils up, pour in a quarter of a pint of cold water; let it boil up a second time; take it off the fire, and let it settle for fifteen minutes; carefully take off all the scum; put it on the fire, and boil it till sufficiently thick, or, if required, till candy high, in order to ascertain which, drop a little from a spoon into small jar of cold water, and if it become quite hard, it is then sufficiently done; or dip the thevil into the sugar, plunge it into cold water, draw off the sugar which adheres to the stick, and if it be hard and snaps, the fruit to be preserved must be instantly put in and boiled.

To Boil Sugar

To every pound of sugar allow half a pint of water; stir it over the fire till the sugar be entirely dissolved; when it first boils up, pour in a little cold water and when it boils a second time, take it off the fire; let it settle ten minutes, carefully scum it, and boil it for half an hour or a little longer, and then put in the fruit.

Orange Marmalade

Allow equal weight of bitter oranges and fine loaf sugar; wash the oranges, wipe them dry, and grate off any discoloured part; cut the rind in half, and with a dessert-spoon loosen it all round to take off each of the halves entire; take the core and seeds clean from the oranges, leaving the juice with the pulp; put the skin into a sauce-pan with plenty of cold water, and cover it closely with a cloth underneath the cover; let them boil for some hours, till so tender that the head of a pin will easily pierce them; drain off the water, and while they are hot, with a silver spoon scoop out all the soft part, leaving the skins quite thin; cut them into thin parings half an inch long; clarify and boil the sugar candy high; put in the parings, and in ten minutes add the juice and pulp, and boil all together till transparent. Part of the peel may be grated to heighten the colour, and a pound and a half of sugar to the pound of oranges may be used.

Another way to make Orange Marmalade

To three pounds of fruit allow five of sugar; pare the oranges; cut the peel into thin chips, and put them into cold water; clear the pulp from the seeds and inside skin, and strew over it pounded loaf sugar; next day drain the chips, put them into a linen bag, and boil them for three hours in plenty of cold water; they are again drained and boiled, together with the pulp, for ten minutes, or till it jelly in the sugar, which has been clarified and boiled candy high. In making minced marmalade, the skins must be boiled, and then finely minced with a knife. The juice of a pound of lemons is sometimes added, but in other respects the process is the same.

Another way to make Orange Marmalade

WASH the oranges, and grate off any defective part; to three pounds of fruit allow five of fine loaf sugar; put the oranges into a sauce-pan with plenty of cold water; cover it closely, and let them boil till a straw or the head of a pin will easily pierce them; take them out, cut them into four, pick out the seeds, and slice them, skin and all, as thin as possible; break the sugar small, and to each pound allow a quarter of a pint of water; stir it till the sugar be dissolved, and when it has boiled a few minutes, take it off the fire; pour in a quarter of a pint of cold water, which will throw up all the refuse; scum it off; put it again on the fire, and if any more scum rises, remove it; add the sliced oranges, and boil for fifteen minutes.

Lemon Marmalade

ALLOW to a pound of lemons eighteen ounces of fine loaf sugar; grate the rind of a few; cut them into half; squeeze and strain the juice; boil the skins in the same way as those of the orange are done; scoop out the pulp and white part; cut half into thin chips or parings, and put the other half in a mortar; pound the sugar, and pour over it the juice; stir, and let it boil for five minutes; take it off the fire; skim it; put in the parings and the pounded skins; boil it for five minutes, then add the grated peel, and let it boil for five minutes more; take it off, and stir it till half cold, before putting it into jars.

Orange Jelly for Breakfast

WASH the oranges, grate off the outer rind, cut them in half, and after squeezing out the juice, put them into a pan with water in the proportion of one quart to every pound of oranges; boil them gently for an hour, or till the water is reduced to rather less than half; strain it and the juice through a sieve; to every pint of the liquor add one pound of loaf sugar; boil them together till they jelly, which may be in twenty minutes, skimming it well.

Red Currant Jelly

GATHER the currants upon a dry day, pick them clean, pound them in a mortar, and drip them through a tammy, or flannel bag; to every pint of juice allow a pound of fine loaf sugar; it may be broken small, and boiled with the juice; but to make the jelly beautifully clear, clarify and boil the sugar candy high; add the juice, and boil it six minutes.

A pint of white currants to every quart of red improves the colour.

Another way to make Red Currant Jelly

CLARIFY and boil, till candy high, fourteen pounds of sugar; add three pounds of nicely-picked raspberries, boil them quickly for three minutes, and then put in twelve pounds of clean-picked currants, and boil them for three or four minutes; and strain it through a fine sieve.

The currants may be made into a rolled pudding.

Another way to make Red Currant Jelly

GATHER the currants with the stalks, put them into a tub of cold water; take them out gently, put them into a sieve, and then lay them out for half an hour upon a table-cloth. Put them into a preserving pan, adding one pint of raspberries to four of currants; and as much water as to prevent their burning; allow them to become quite hot, but not to boil; shake the pan to prevent the fruit adhering to the bottom or sides; strain it through a jellybag. To every pint of juice allow one pound of pounded loaf sugar, and when it comes to a boil, boil it one minute. Only remove the scum when the pan is taken off the fire.

Wash and prepare black currants as the red are directed to be done; put them into a preserving pan, adding a pint of water to a quart of fruit; let it be so hot as merely to admit of its being squeezed though a thin linen cloth with the hand. To a pint of juice allow a pound of loaf sugar, and when it boils, boil it three minutes. Skim it when taken off the fire.

Magnum Bonum Plums

Gather the plums with stalks, scald them in boiling water, and take off the skins, leaving on the stalks. If not quite ripe, they will require to be simmered a few minutes over a stove; to every pound of fruit, allow one of fine loaf sugar; clarify it, and when nearly boiled candy high, put in the plums, and boil them fifteen minutes; with a spoon carefully put them into a basin, and let them stand a day or two; then boil them ten minutes, or till perfectly transparent; put them into the jars; strain the sirup through a sieve, and pour it equally over them.

White Currant Jelly

Gather the fruit upon a dry day, and pick it from the stalks; pound it in a mortar, and drip the juice through a flannel bag. To every pint allow a pound of fine loaf sugar; break it small, and with the juice, put it into a preserving pan; stir it till it boils; skim, and let it boil exactly six minutes; or the juice may be boiled the same length of time in sugar previously clarified and boiled candy high.

To Preserve Yellow White Gooseberries, called The Sulphur

Gather them upon a dry day, and before they are very ripe; take equal weight of finely-pounded sugar and gooseberries; top and tail, and prick them with a large needle; as they are done, strew over them a little sugar. To each pound of gooseberries, allow half a pint of white currant juice, and half a pound of pounded sugar. Put the sugar, gooseberries, and juice alternately into the preserving pan, set it over the fire, and shake it every now and then, till the sugar be dissolved, and then carefully remove the fruit from the sides of the pan. When it boils, skim it, and let it boil exactly twenty-four minutes. The large rough red gooseberries are preserved precisely in the same way, and when they come to a boil, must be allowed to boil for twenty minutes.

Another way to Preserve Gooseberries

The tops and tails being removed from the gooseberries, allow an equal quantity of finely-pounded loaf sugar, and put a layer of each alternately into a large deep jar; pour into it as much dripped currant juice, either red or white, as will dissolve the sugar, adding its weight in sugar; the following day, put all into a preserving pan, and, boil it.

To Preserve Yellow or Green Gooseberries

THE tops and tails being removed from the gooseberries, slit them up the sides, and with a silver knife, or the top of a tea-spoon, take out the seeds, and put them, with the pulp which adheres to them, into a sieve; the juice which drains from them boil with the sugar, previously weighed in equal quantities with the fruit; then add the gooseberry skins, and boil them till perfectly clear.

Gooseberry Jam for Puddings

ALLOW equal weight of the red rough gooseberries, and of good brown sugar; gather the fruit upon a dry day; top and tail them, and put a layer alternately of gooseberries and of sugar into a preserving pan; shake it frequently, skim it well, and boil it till the sirup jellies, which may be ascertained by cooling a little in a saucer. Black and red currants may be done in this way for common use.

Black Currant Jelly

GATHER the fruit upon a dry day, pick it clean from the stalks; put into a preserving pan eight pounds, and one pint of water; bruise the currants till they get a scald; pour them into a hair sieve, and with the hands press out all the juice, which strain through a piece of muslin; and to each pint, allow one pound of fine loaf sugar; break it small, and with the juice put it into a preserving pan; stir it till it boils; let it boil for three minutes, and skim it.

Raspberries Preserved Whole

GATHER the raspberries upon a dry day, and when the sun is not upon them; weigh equal quantities of finely-pounded loaf sugar and of fruit; put a layer of each alternately into a preserving pan, shake it constantly till it boils, carefully take off the scum, and boil it for fifteen minutes; or the sugar may be clarified, boiled candy high, and the fruit added.

White Raspberries Preserved Whole

GATHER the raspberries upon a dry day, and to each pound allow one of sugar; clarify and boil till candy high all but one pound, which pound and sift; put the raspberries into the clarified sugar, and boil it for five minutes; take it off, and strew over the pound of sifted sugar; when almost cold, to every pound of fruit, add half a pint of dripped white currant juice, and half a pound of finely pounded sugar; boil and skim it till the fruit be transparent.

To Preserve Raspberries

Gather the fruit upon a dry day; to each pound of raspberries, allow half a pint of red currant juice, and a pound and a half of finely-pounded loaf sugar; put each alternately into a preserving pan, shake it frequently till the sugar be dissolved; carefully remove the fruit from the sides of the pan, and stir it round gently with a thevil or a silver spoon; when it boils, skim it, and let it boil twenty-five minutes; or the sugar may be clarified, boiled candy high, and the fruit and currant juice added to it.

Raspberry Jam

Weigh equal proportions of pounded loaf sugar and of raspberries; put the fruit into a preserving pan, and with a silver spoon, bruise and mash it well; let it boil six minutes; add the sugar, and stir it well with the fruit; when it boils, skim it, and boil it for fifteen minutes.

Raspberry Jelly

Put into a jar raspberries and white currants in equal quantities; let them be thoroughly heated on the fire in a water bath, then run them through a jelly-bag, and to every pint of juice add a pound of pounded sugar; let it just boil, take it off the fire, and skim it; repeat this two or three times till it is quite clear, when it will be sufficiently done.

To Preserve Black Currants

Gather the currants upon a dry day; to every pound allow half a pint of red currant juice, and a pound and a half of finely-pounded loaf sugar. With scissors clip off the heads and stalks; put the juice, sugar, and currants into a preserving pan; shake it frequently till it boils; carefully remove the fruit from the sides of the pan, and take off the scum as it rises; let it boil for ten or fifteen minutes. This preserve may be eaten with cream, or made into tarts.

Black Currant Jam

Allow equal weight of clipt currants and of pounded loaf sugar; bruise and mash the fruit in a preserving pan over the fire; add the sugar; stir it frequently; when it boils, skim, and let it boil for ten minutes.

White or Red Currant Jam

Pick the fruit very nicely, and allow an equal quantity of finely-pounded loaf sugar; put a layer of each alternately into a preserving pan, and boil for ten minutes; or they may be boiled the same length of time in sugar previously clarified, and boiled candy high.

To Preserve Strawberries

Weigh a large deep dish or milk pan, into which put the finest rose strawberries, gathered when perfectly dry; then weigh them, and to each pound allow one of fine loaf sugar, which clarify and boil candy high; pour it over the strawberries; wash out the preserving pan; return the fruit and sugar into it, and boil the strawberries for five minutes; strain them through a large sieve, and boil the sirup for twenty minutes; then with a silver spoon carefully add the strawberries to it, and, if approved, half a pint of dripped red currant juice, and half a pound of sugar, to each pound of strawberries, and boil all together for ten minutes; carefully scum it.

The Large Bath, or Hautboy Strawberries

May be preserved with an equal quantity of fine loaf sugar; the sugar must be scummed and boiled for half an hour; then, the fruit being added, it is boiled for half an hour or three quarters, and carefully scummed. Or the sugar may be finely pounded, and boiled with the fruit. In this last manner any kind of strawberry may be preserved.

Another way to Preserve Strawberries

Gather the strawberries in the middle of a dry day, taking care that they are quite ripe, sound, and good; the best kinds are the rose, and large scarlet pine; in gathering, pick them carefully from the stalks. Pound fine loaf sugar, and allow equal weight of each; lay the strawberries into one or two large dishes, and cover them completely over with the sugar. On the following day, put them into a preserving-pan, and place them over the fire till they are heated through; do the same the next day, and on the third boil them up very fast, allowing them fifteen minutes after they come to boil all over; take them off the fire, and have ready some aired silver paper to put upon them, to take off the scum, instead of using a silver spoon, which is apt to break them.

This preserve may be eaten with cream.

The process of boiling may be completed in one day, if begun at an early hour.

Strawberry Jam

ALLOW equal weight of pounded loaf sugar and of the scarlet pine or rose strawberries; mash them in the preserving-pan, and mix the sugar well with it; stir, scum, and boil it for twenty minutes.

Pounded Strawberries, for Strawberry Cream

TAKE equal weight of sugar and strawberries; pound and sift the sugar, add it to the strawberries, and pound them in a marble mortar till perfectly smooth. Put it into jars, and tie them over closely with paper. It will keep good for several months.

Imitation West Indian Ginger

PEEL off the outer coat of the tender stems of lettuce that is shot, cut it into bits one or two inches long, and throw it into cold water; to each pound put in a teaspoonful of cayenne, and a little salt; let it stand one or two days; allow an equal proportion of fine loaf sugar, which clarify. Soak some good ginger in hot water, slice it, and add it to the sugar, allowing one ounce and a half to the pound, and boil it for fifteen minutes; strain off the water from the lettuce, and pour over it the sirup, keeping back the ginger, with which the sirup must be boiled three times, and poured over the lettuce, two or three days intervening between each boiling; and at the last add the strained juice of one or two lemons.

Ripe Melon, to Resemble West Indian Ginger

PARE off the rind, scoop out the seeds, and cut it into small bits; put them into salt-and-water for ten days; then put them into fresh water for four or five days, changing the water daily, morning and evening; scrape off the outside of some best white ginger, and put it into a thin sirup, which pour boiling hot upon the cut melon; repeat this for five or six days. Boil up the sirup pretty thick, and boil the melon in it for ten minutes. To every pint of sirup put the rind of a lemon, pared very thin, and cut into straws. This sweetmeat ought to be kept for a year before it is eaten. A melon of six pounds weight will require four pounds of refined sugar, and half a pound of ginger.

To Preserve Red Pears

PARBOIL a dozen of pound pears in water; peel them. Clarify the same weight of fine loaf sugar that there is of pears; add a pint of port wine, the juice and rind of one lemon, with a little cochineal, a few cloves, and a stick of cinnamon; boil the pears in this till they become clear and red; take them out, boil up the sirup, strain, and put it over the pears.

To Preserve Large Smooth Green Gooseberries

WEIGH equal proportions of sugar and of fruit; with a penknife, slit the gooseberries on one side, and take out all the seeds; put them into a preserving-pan with cold water, scald them; pour off the water when cold; put over and under them vine leaves, with more cold water; set them over the fire to green. Clarify the sugar; put the gooseberries into a deep jar, and pour the boiling sirup over them; in two days pour it off, boil, and put it over the fruit; repeat this till the sirup becomes thick, then put them into small jars.

To Preserve the same before they are Ripe

GATHER the largest sized gooseberries, and allow an equal quantity of pounded loaf sugar; cut the gooseberries in half, and take out the seeds; wet the sugar with a little water, and put altogether into a preserving-pan; carefully stir and scum them, and boil them till the sirup is clear and the fruit soft.

Preserved Apples

WEIGH equal quantities of good brown sugar, and of apples; peel, core, and mince them small. Boil the sugar, allowing to every three pounds a pint of water; skim it well, and boil it pretty thick; then add the apples, the grated peel of one or two lemons, and two or three pieces of white ginger; boil till the apples fall, and look clear and yellow.

This preserve will keep for years.

Preserved Cherries

To a pound of cherries allow three quarters of a pound of pounded loaf sugar; stone them carefully, and as they are done, strew part of the sugar over them; boil them fast, with the remainder of the sugar, till the fruit is clear and the sirup thick; take off the scum as it rises. Or they may be boiled ten minutes in an equal quantity of sugar, which has been previously clarified and boiled candy high. Part of the kernels may be added; or they may be preserved with the stones and part of the stalks. Should the sirup be desired particularly rich and thick, they may be done as strawberries, first receipt, p. 305, omitting the currant juice.

Cherry Jam

STONE six pounds of cherries; bruise them as they boil, and when the juice is a little wasted, add three pounds of pounded loaf sugar; stir, and take off the scum; boil till it will jelly.

To Preserve Apricots

WEIGH equal quantities of fine apricots and of loaf sugar. Pare the fruit with a silver knife, and take out the stones carefully; as they are done, strew a little pounded sugar over them. Boil the sugar as directed under that head (p. 299); put in the apricots, and let them just simmer; take off the pan, put over it a piece of white paper, and let it stand till nearly cold; put it again on the fire, let them simmer as before, and again cool them; repeat this three or four times, and the last time let them boil till quite transparent, which they will probably be in a quarter of an hour; remove the scum carefully, and a few minutes before taking them off the fire, blanch the kernels, and add them; or the kernels, after being blanched, may be put into a small jar, covered with spirits of wine, and allowed to stand till the jars are tied up, when a few may be put upon the top of each.

If the stones cannot be easily extracted, the apricots may be divided into halves; or they may be preserved without being stoned. The Moor Park apricot, the best for eating, and excellent for jam, cannot be preserved so whole as the common apricot.

Apricot Jam

WEIGH equal quantities of pounded loaf sugar and of apricots; pare and cut them quite small; as they are done, strew over them half of the sugar. The following day, boil the remainder, and add the apricots; stir it till it boils, take off the scum, and when perfectly clear, which may be in twenty minutes, add part of the kernels blanched, and boil it two or three minutes.

Another way to make Apricot Jam

ALLOW equal proportions of pounded loaf sugar and of apricots; pare, and cut them small; as they are done, strew part of the sugar over them, and put the parings into cold water. Break the stones, blanch and pound the kernels, which, with the shells and parings, boil till half the quantity of water is reduced, and there is a sufficiency of the liquor, when strained, to allow three or four table-spoonfuls to a pound of apricots; put it, with the sugar and fruit, into a preserving-pan; mash, and take off the scum; boil it quickly, till transparent.

Apricots in Brandy

WEIGH equal quantities of loaf sugar and of apricot; scald them, and take off the skin. Clarify and boil the sugar, put the fruit into it and let it remain for two or three days; put the apricots into glasses. Mix with the sirup the best pale brandy half and half, and pour it over the apricots and keep them closely covered.

Peaches and nectarines may be done in the same way.

To Dry Apricots

PARE the apricots, and carefully take out the stones; blanch the kernels, and put them into the apricots; strew over a pound of fruit the same quantity of finely-pounded loaf sugar, and let them stand till the sugar has extracted the juice, then boil all together gently; when the fruit is tender, take it out with care, and boil the sirup till very rich; pour it over the fruit, and in three days put it upon dishes, and dry them in the sun under garden glasses, turning them once or twice a day to keep the shape as round as possible.

Any inferior apricots may be cut down and boiled in the sirup for tarts.

To Candy Angelica

CUT the stalks when thick and tender, put them on in boiling water, and, when very tender, drain it off, and throw them into cold water; peel off the skin, and scald them in a thin sirup, made with the same proportion of sugar that there is of fruit; heat it twice a day till the sirup is almost dried in, and then dry them under garden glasses, or in a stove, and turn them twice a day.

To Preserve Quinces

PARE the quinces, and at the end scoop out the core. Put them into a preserving-pan with water; and closely covered; let them boil till soft and of a fine red; when they are cold, put them into a sirup made with the same proportion of sugar as of quinces. The following day, boil them two or three times till clear, and the last time for twelve minutes. Cut some small quinces into quarters, put them into a sauce-pan, with as much water as will cover them, boil it fast, till strongly flavoured of the quinces; strain it through a flannel bag, and boil a pint of the liquor with a pound of sugar till it be a rich sirup, and when cold, pour it over the quinces.

To Preserve Cucumbers

LAY, in a strong brine of salt-and-water, some large, smooth, green cucumbers; put vine or cabbage leaves over them, cover the jar or pan, and keep them near the fire till they turn yellow, which may be in three or four days; take them out, wash them, and put them into a pan, with leaves under and over, and a little salt in the water; let them simmer, but not boil; when cold, if not sufficiently greened, again put them into fresh water, with fresh leaves. Take them out when cold, divide them into four, scoop out the seeds and soft part, lay them into cold water, which change frequently through the day, till it be quite clear and tasteless. Clarify the same weight of sugar as of cucumbers; soak in boiling water some white ginger, scrape it, and put one ounce to a pound of sugar, and the thinly-pared rind of a lemon. Boil them with the sirup, and when cold, put in the cucumbers, and boil them slowly for half an hour; put them into jars, and in five days, boil them again for ten minutes; carefully take out the cucumbers, boil up the sirup, and when cold, put it over them.

Another way to Preserve Cucumbers

WEIGH equal quantities of sugar and the large smooth green cucumbers. Split them down the middle, and take out all the seeds; cover four large cucumbers, cut in this way, with cold water, mixed with a dessert-spoonful of salt; let them stand by the fireside, or in a warm place, for three or four days. Boil the sugar with as much water as will dissolve it, and as long as any scum rises; then put in the cucumbers, and simmer them for a little time. Repeat this till they are clear and green, and, the last time of boiling, add some white ginger soaked in hot water and scraped, a few grains of allspice, and the peel of a lemon cut very thin. Put the cucumbers into jars, cover them completely with the sirup, and the following day tie them over with bladder. Look at them in a week or ten days, and if the sirup be wasted, boil more, and add it when cold.

To Preserve Small Cucumbers

WEIGH equal proportions of small green cucumbers and of fine loaf sugar; clarify it; rub the cucumbers with a cloth, scald them in hot water, and, when cold, put them into the sirup, with some white ginger and the peel of a lemon; boil them gently for ten minutes. The following day just let them boil, and repeat this three times, and the last, boil them till tender and clear.

To Preserve Oranges

TAKE six large high-coloured and smooth-skinned bitter oranges; with a penknife cut the rinds up and down, or into the form of leaves; cut a hole in the top to admit the end of a tea-spoon, with which carefully scoop out the inside; put the rinds into cold water, mixed with half a pound of salt. After standing two days and nights, change them into fresh cold water, and change it frequently through the day; then boil them with plenty of cold water in a closely-covered sauce-pan, till the head of a pin will easily pierce them; clarify the sugar, allowing a pound to each orange; place the skins in a potting can or flat vessel, and pour the sirup into and over them. The following day pour it off, boil it up, and repeat this four times, and, at the last, add the strained juice of four bitter oranges and the prepared rinds, and boil them about eight minutes; carefully take them out, one by one, and put them into jars, and pour over the sirup so as entirely to cover them. They may be served with a rich custard put into them.

To Preserve Sliced Oranges

WEIGH a pound of oranges, add one pound and a half of loaf sugar; grate a little of the rind off each orange, put them into a pan of water, cover it closely, and boil them till the head of a pin will easily pierce the rind; cut them into slices, take out the seeds, and boil the fruit in clarified sugar till perfectly clear, which may be in twenty minutes.

Damson Cheese

PUT sound fresh-gathered damsons into an earthen jar, tie it closely with a bladder, and put it into a pot of cold water; let it boil for three or four hours; add more boiling water as it wastes. Strain the juice through a sieve, and to each pint allow sixteen ounces of pounded loaf sugar; boil and stir it over a clear fire till it will jelly, which may be three quarters of an hour; pour it into shapes, small saucers, or flat plates, to dry. Keep it in a box, with sheets of white paper between each layer. Apricot cheese may be made in this way.

To Preserve Siberian Crabs

BOIL, in half a pint of water, a little cinnamon, sliced ginger, and a few cloves, till the flavour be extracted; strain, and boil it with one pound of pounded loaf sugar; skim and boil it ten minutes; let it stand till cold, and then add a pint of fine Siberian crabs, which make scalding hot in the sirup; take them off the fire till nearly cold; heat them in the same manner three times. If the under ones look clear, take them out carefully, and put them into a jar, and let the rest boil till quite clear.

To Preserve Jargonelle Pears

GATHER pears with stalks before they are quite ripe; allow equal quantities of fine loaf sugar and of fruit. Pare the pears as thinly as possible, keeping on the stalks; cut out the black top carefully; as they are peeled, put them into cold water. Put cabbage leaves into the bottom of a preserving-pan; lay in the pears, cover them with cold water, and one or two cabbage leaves upon the top; boil them thirty minutes, and lay them upon a dish. To six pounds of sugar allow a quart of water, boil and skim it; then add one ounce of white ginger, previously soaked in hot water, and scraped clean, and the juice and thinly-pared rind of two lemons. Boil the sirup ten minutes, put in the pears, and let them boil twenty minutes; take them out, put them into a bowl or deep dish; boil the sirup eight minutes, and when cold pour it over the pears; cover them with paper; in four days pour off the sirup, boil it eight minutes, and pour it over the pears when cold. In four days repeat this process, and do it a third time; then stick a clove into each pear, where the black top was cut out. Put them into jars, divide the ginger and lemon-peel, and pour on the sirup when cold.

Peach Jam

GATHER the peaches when quite ripe, peel, and stone them, put them into a preserving-pan, and mash them over the fire till hot; rub them through a sieve, and add to a pound of pulp the same weight of pounded loaf sugar, and half an ounce of bitter almonds, blanched and pounded; let it boil ten or twelve minutes, stir and skim it well.

To Preserve Figs

ALLOW equal weight of loaf sugar and of small green figs; wipe and cut them across the top; lay them into a strong brine of salt-and-water for ten days. Boil them in water till the head of a pin will easily pierce them, and then lay them into cold water for four days, changing it daily.

Clarify the sugar, and put in the figs while hot; heat them in the sirup three times, and the last, boil them till they look green and clear.

To Preserve Apples

PARE, core, and quarter six pounds of good hard baking apples; finely pound four pounds of loaf sugar; put a layer of each alternately, with half a pound of the best white ginger, into a jar; let it remain eight-and-forty hours; infuse, for half that time, in a little boiling water, half a quarter of a pound of bruised white ginger; strain and boil the liquor with the apples till they look clear, and the sirup rich and thick, which may be in about an hour. Take off the scum as it rises. When to be eaten, pick out the whole ginger.

To Preserve Green Gages

GATHER the largest green gage plums with stalks; allow an equal proportion of loaf sugar; put vine or cabbage leaves into the bottom of a pan, lay in the fruit, cover with leaves, and fill up with cold water. When the plums rise to the top, take them off, and carefully pare off the skin, and put them upon a sieve. Drain the water from the leaves; with fresh ones again heat the plums in it, and closely cover the pan; they must be done very slowly, and will take some hours to become green. Take them out and drain them upon a sieve. Clarify the sugar, boil it for eight minutes, put in the plums, boil them gently till transparent, and carefully put them into jars. Boil the sirup a few minutes, and pour it over them when cold. In three or four days pour off the sirup, boil it up, and, when cold, put it over the fruit.

Another way to Preserve Green Gages

PUT the plums into boiling water, pare off the skin, and divide them; take an equal quantity of pounded loaf sugar, strew half of it over the fruit; let it remain some hours, and, with the remainder of the sugar, put it into a preserving-pan; boil till the plums look quite clear, take off the scum as it rises, and, a few minutes before taking them off the fire, add the kernels.

Apple Jelly

PARE and cut into slices eighteen large acid apples; boil them in as much water as will cover them; when quite soft, dip a coarse cloth into hot water, wring it dry, and strain the apples through it; to each pint of juice allow fourteen ounces of fine loaf sugar, clarify it, and add, with the apple juice, the peel of a large lemon; boil it till it jellies, which may be in twenty minutes; pick out the lemon-peel, and immediately put it into jars.

Another way to make Apple Jelly

PARE and mince three dozen of juicy acid apples, put them into a pan, cover them with water, and boil them till very soft; strain them through a thin cloth or flannel bag; allow a pound of loaf sugar to a pint of juice; clarify and boil it; add the apple juice with the grated peel and juice of six lemons; boil it for twenty minutes; take off the scum as it rises.

Gooseberry Cheese

TOP and tail some red gooseberries, put them into a jar, tie it over, and boil it in a pan of water, till the fruit will easily pulp through a fine hair sieve; allow a quarter of a pound of loaf sugar to a pint of the juice, stir, boil, and skim it for twenty minutes, put it into saucers or small plates, dry it before the fire, and when dry, keep it between folds of white paper.

To keep Currants for Tarts

GATHER the fruit perfectly dry, and before it be too ripe, pick it from the stalks, and put it into clean, dry, wide-mouthed bottles; if the flavour of raspberries is approved, some may be added with the currants; tie tightly over each bottle a piece of sound bladder previously soaked in water; set them into a pan of cold water, with a little straw at the bottom, and a little between the bottles; put them on the fire, and when they begin to simmer, keep them in that state about three quarters of an hour, but they must not be allowed to boil; take the pan off the fire; the bladders will be raised, but will fall soon after, and sink into the mouth of the bottles; in an hour, take them out, and tie strong paper over each, and set them in a dry cool place.

The bottles may be placed in a bottle-rack, with the neck downwards.

Damsons, cherries, and gooseberries may be done in this way; any sort will keep for a year. Cut off the stalks of the cherries, and top and tail the gooseberries.

To keep Green Gooseberries

GATHER the gooseberries when quite formed, but not the least soft; top and tail them; fill them into wide-mouthed bottles up to the neck, and cork them slightly; place them in a copper, with sawdust or straw in the bottom, and pour in cold water to reach to the necks of the bottles; light the fire, and when the water boils up, instantly take out the bottles, and fill them up from a tea-kettle with boiling water; cork them again slightly, and when cold, put them in tightly; lay the bottles upon their sides in a dry cool place, and turn them every other day for a month. When to be used, the liquor and fruit are put into a dish, and sweetened with brown sugar.

To save Sugar in Preserving Cherries, Green Gages, Damsons, Currants, and Raspberries

GATHER the fruit perfectly dry, and to a pound allow five ounces of finely-pounded loaf sugar; put a layer of fruit into a wide-mouthed bottle or jar, and then one of sugar, till the vessel is full; tie tightly over it two folds of sound bladder, and put them into a copper or pan, with straw in the bottom, and water as high as the necks, and let them simmer for three hours. When the water cools, take out the bottles, and keep them in a cool dry place.

Damsons for Winter use

GATHER the damsons when just ripe, and perfectly sound; fill a two-gallon brandy keg, and pour over two pounds of treacle; close the keg firmly, and turn it every day.

To Preserve Damsons

To every pound of damsons allow three quarters of a pound of pounded loaf sugar; put into jars alternately a layer of damsons, and one of sugar; tie them over with bladder or strong paper, and put them into an oven after the bread is withdrawn, and let them remain till the oven is cold. The following day strain off the sirup, and boil it till thick. When cold, put the damsons one by one into small jars, and pour over them the sirup, which must cover them. Tie them over with wet bladder.

Another way to Preserve Damsons

PRICK them with a needle, and boil them with sugar in the same proportion as in the receipt to preserve damsons, till the sirup will jelly. Carefully take off all the scum.

To Preserve the Purple Plum

PUT into a stone jar a layer of fruit, and one of brown sugar, allowing one pound to a pound of the fruit; cover the jar with linen or bladder, and bake it in an oven for one or two hours. In a few weeks pour off the sirup, and boil it a short time; skim it, and when cold, pour it over the fruit.

It may be eaten with cream, or made into tarts or puddings.

Gooseberry and Raspberry Cakes

GATHER the gooseberries upon a dry day, and before they are quite ripe; top and tail them; scald them, or put them into an earthen jar; tie it closely over with bladder, and place it in a pan of water; let it boil till the fruit is sufficiently tender to pulp through a sieve. To a pound of the pulp add one pound of pounded and sifted loaf sugar, and the well-beaten white of one egg; mix all together, and whisk it for three hours; drop the cakes upon writing paper, and dry them in the sun, or upon a stove. The pulp of damsons may be done in the same way.

For the raspberry cakes, allow a pound of sugar to a pint of the fruit, measured before it is scalded, or pulped through a sieve; allow one white of an egg to each pound, and for each sort of cakes dry the sugar well, and use it while it is warm. Keep them in a tin box, with folds of white paper between each layer.

The whites of two eggs being added to each pound of sugar, half the beating will be found sufficient.

Quince Cakes

BOIL the quinces till quite soft, rub them through a sieve, and to a pint of juice add three quarters of a pound of pounded loaf sugar; mix all well together, and make it scalding hot, but do not allow it to boil; drop it upon tins in the form of small cakes, and dry them in a cool oven, and before the fire.

Seville Orange Cakes

DIVIDE the oranges in half, take out the seeds, and put the pulp and juice into a basin; boil the rinds in a sauce-pan of water, closely covered; when very tender take them out, and dry them upon a cloth; allow to a pound of orange rinds, two of pounded loaf sugar; pound the rinds in a mortar; add by degrees the sugar, and then the juice and pulp; mix it thoroughly till thick and yellow; drop it upon tins in small cakes, and dry them under garden glasses, or in a cool oven. If it be too thick to drop, let it stand a night.

To Dry Cherries

GATHER the cherries perfectly dry, and to every six pounds allow one and a half of finely-pounded loaf sugar; strew it over the cherries in a deep dish, and let them remain twelve hours; put them into a preserving-pan; make them scalding hot; put them into a bowl; the next day again heat them; take them out of the sirup, and lay them upon sieves under garden glasses, to dry in the sun; turn them daily upon clean sieves, till quite dry; spread them upon sheets of white paper, and keep them in a box.

The sirup may be boiled till thick, and kept as a jelly, or with currants made into a tart.

To Dry Barberries in Bunches

GATHER the barberries when ripe; tie the finest into bunches; bruise some of the inferior ones, and boil them in water; strain, and boil in a pint of it one pound and a half of loaf sugar to every three pounds of barberries; skim and boil the sugar fifteen minutes; put in the bunches of fruit, and simmer them for six minutes; let them stand in a china bowl till the following day, and boil them gently till clear. When cold, take them out of the sirup and dry them under garden glasses; turn them daily.

To Candy Currants, Barberries, and other Fruit

BOIL the fruit in clarified sugar as for preserving; take it out of the sirup and drain it upon sieves; sift over it, through a lawn sieve, till quite white, pounded loaf sugar. Place them in a cool oven, and turn and dust them with sugar till dry.

Raspberry Vinegar

BRUISE a quart of fresh-gathered raspberries in a china basin; pour over it a pint of good vinegar, cover it closely; let it stand three days, and stir it daily; strain it through a flannel bag; let it drip as long as anything will come from it, but do not press it; to a pint of the liquor put one pound of pounded loaf sugar, boil it ten minutes, and take of the scum as it rises. When cold, bottle and cork it tightly.

A glass of brandy may be added to a quart of raspberry vinegar.

Another way to make Raspberry Vinegar

FILL a dry clean bottle with raspberries, and put as much vinegar as the bottle will contain; stop it closely, and let it stand for a month; then strain it, and to a pint of the liquor put a pound of loaf sugar; boil it for half an hour; skim it. When cold, bottle and cork it tightly.

Sirup of Currants, Raspberries, or Mulberries

PICK the fruit from the stalks; squeeze the juice, and let it stand ten days or a fortnight, or till the fermentation ceases, which may be known by the scum cracking; carefully take off the scum, and pour the juice gently into a fresh vessel; let it stand twenty-four hours, and again pour it off; to one pound of pounded loaf sugar allow thirteen ounces of the juice, put it into a preserving-pan, and when it begins to boil, strain it through a jelly-bag, and bottle it when cold.

Burie pears boiled in a little of the sirup are beautiful.

Black Currant Lozenges

PUT six quarts of clean-picked black currants into a preserving-pan; with the hand bruise them as long as the heat will admit; squeeze them through a sieve, and to every pint of juice put four ounces of good brown sugar; boil and stir it for three quarters of an hour, and then pour it thinly over sauces or small plates, and dry it for three successive days before the fire; cut it into small dice, or with a turnip-scoop; lay them upon white paper in a box. Or the cakes may be cut into lozenges as they are required. A little dissolved isinglass may be added while the juice is boiling.

Elder Rob

Gather the elderberries when quite ripe, put them into a stone jar, tie a bladder or paper over the top, and place the jar in a pan of water; let it boil till the berries are very soft; strain them through a coarse cloth, and to every pint of juice allow half a pound of good brown sugar; put it into a preserving-pan, stir it, and when it boils, take off the scum, and let it boil for one hour.

Cinnamon Tablet

To a pound of loaf sugar, clarified and boiled till it can be blown through the holes of a skimmer, allow half an ounce of pounded and sifted cinnamon, or a tea-spoonful of the oil of cinnamon; stir it well with the sugar, and press it with a spoon to the sides of the pan, to make it perfectly smooth; rub some plates over with fresh butter, and pour in the tablet. When cold, cut it into square bits. Ginger tablet may be made in this way, allowing a quarter of an ounce of ginger to a pound of sugar.

Lemon Drops

Squeeze and strain the juice of six good-sized lemons; mix with it pounded and sifted loaf sugar, till so thick that it is stirred with difficulty; put it into a preserving-pan, and, with a wooden spoon, stir it constantly, and let it boil five or six minutes; then drop it from the point of a knife, upon writing paper, in drops as large as a shilling. When cold, they will readily come off.

Barley Sugar Drops

Clarify and boil the sugar to that degree, that upon dipping in a wooden stick, and plunging it into cold water, the sugar becomes crisp, and will snap; boil with it the thinly-pared rind of one or two lemons; drop the sugar upon a stone or marble slab in round drops; when quite cold, roll them in sifted loaf sugar, and lay them between layers of white paper, or fold them in little bits of square paper, and twist it at the end.

Barley Sugar

Boil the sugar as for the drops, and flavour it with lemon juice, or oil of lemons; rub a little fresh butter over a stone or marble slab, and pour the sugar along it in narrow strips; twist it while warm, and when cold, with a knife mark it across, and it will break into any lengths.

CHAPTER XVII
VINEGARS

A CASK which has not contained vinegar before, should have a quart of boiling hot vinegar poured into it, shaken till cold, and allowed to stand for some hours.

Sugar Vinegar

To five gallons of water put eight pounds of coarse brown sugar; let it boil as long as any scum rises, which must be carefully removed; then pour it into a cask, and when it is about milk-warm, or from 60 to 65 degrees Fahrenheit, cut off the crust, and toast a quarter of a slice of bread, and cover it over with fresh yeast; put it into the cask, leave it open for four or five days, and then paste over the bung-hole a piece of paper, and pierce it here and there with a pin. It should be kept in a warm, dry place, without being moved; and if made in March or April, it may be drawn off and bottled in September, when it may be boiled a quarter of a minute to prevent the mother from forming in the bottles, and it will keep good for years, though it should not be kept from the contact of the air, or in vessels entirely filled.

The vinegar cask, as soon as emptied, should be again filled in the same manner.

Gooseberry Vinegar

GATHER yellow gooseberries when quite ripe, crush and mash them well in a tub with a large wooden pestle; to every two gallons of gooseberries, after being mashed, put two of water; mix them well together; let it work for three weeks, stirring the mass two or three times each day; then strain the liquor through a hair sieve, and put to every gallon one pound of brown sugar, one pound of treacle, and a table-spoonful of fresh yeast; let it work for three or four days in the same tub, which has been well washed; then rub it into iron-hooped casks. Let it stand twelve months, and bottle it for use as this is a very strong vinegar.

Another way to make Gooseberry Vinegar

BRUISE to a mash any kind of gooseberries, when quite ripe, and mix thoroughly with a gallon of the mash three of cold boiled water; let it stand twenty-four hours, strain it through a cloth, and to each gallon of the liquor, put one pound of brown sugar; mix it well, and when quite dissolved, put it into a cask. It must stand nine or ten months before being bottled.

Currants, or any other fruit of which wine is made, may be substituted for gooseberries.

American Vinegar

Boil six gallons of water, and add, while it is hot, four quarts of molasses; put it into a tub to cool; when milk-warm, stir in a pint of fresh yeast; put it into the cask, and set it by the fire for twenty-four hours; then put it in the sun, with a bottle in the bung-hole. Bottle it three months afterwards.

Cucumber Vinegar

Pare ten large cucumbers, cut them into thin slices; pour over them a quart of vinegar; add a clove of garlic, and one or two shalots, a tea-spoonful of ground white pepper, and one of salt; let it stand for ten or twelve days; strain and bottle it; put a little whole pepper into the mouth of each bottle, and cork it tightly. The flavour of the cucumbers may be very well preserved, by simply steeping them in vinegar.

Garlic Vinegar

Cut small one ounce and a half of garlic, bruise one nutmeg and three cloves, steep them in a quart of vinegar for a week, shaking it daily; then strain and bottle it.

Shalot vinegar is made in the same manner.

Harvey's, or Camp Vinegar

Put the following ingredients into two quarts of strong vinegar, three table-spoonfuls of Indian soy, and the same quantity of mushroom catsup, six anchovies, two heads of garlic, a quarter of an ounce of cayenne, and as much cochineal as will colour it; shake it two or three times a day for a fortnight, then filter, and bottle it for use. Two tea-spoonfuls of this vinegar improves salad sauce, fish sauce also, and is good in most made dishes.

Elder Flower, and Tarragon Vinegar

Fill a quart bottle with the flowers of elder, or the leaves of tarragon, when it is in flower; pour vinegar upon them, and let them infuse for a fortnight; then strain it through a flannel bag, and put it into small bottles. By the same means, vinegar may be flavoured with the fresh gathered leaves of any sweet herb.

Vinegar from the refuse of Raisin Wine

On the raisins from which ten gallons of wine has been made, five gallons of nearly boiling water is poured, the dregs or lees, and stalks, are added; it is then covered up, and stirred occasionally. When the taste is completely extracted from the fruit, it is squeezed, and the vinegar strained and put into a cask, in which it should remain nine or ten months.

Vinegar from Honey

HALF a pound of honey must be put to a pint of water, and the honey well dissolved. This mixture is then exposed to the greatest heat of the sun, without closing wholly the bung-hole of the cask, which must be merely covered with coarse linen, to prevent the admission of insects. In about six weeks, the liquor becomes acid, and changes to a very strong vinegar, and of excellent quality.

PICKLES

PREPARATORY REMARKS ON PICKLES

PICKLES ought to be stored in a dry place, and the vessels most approved of for keeping them in, are wide-mouthed glass bottles, or strong stoneware jars, having corks or bungs, which must be fitted in with linen, and covered with bladder or leather; and for taking the pickles out and returning them to the jar, a small wooden spoon is kept. The strongest vinegar is used for pickling; that of white wine is more particularly recommended, but sugar vinegar will generally be found sufficiently strong.

It is essential to the excellence and beauty of pickles, that they be always completely covered with vinegar.

To Pickle Gherkins

GATHER, upon a dry day, some small cucumbers or gherkins; lay them into cold salt-and-water for four days, with a cabbage leaf laid over to keep them down; drain them, and put them into a perfectly clean brass pan, with vine or cabbage leaves in the bottom, and cover them with vinegar and water half and half, strewing a little pounded alum, and putting more leaves over them; let the water get scalding hot; take off the pan; when nearly cold, make it again hot, and repeat this as frequently as possible through the day. With fresh leaves, and the same liquor, put them into a basin to stand all night; the next morning, with fresh leaves under and over, and the same liquor, heat them twice, and then drain them; and if for six or eight dozen, put them into the pan with half a pint of vinegar, and water sufficient to cover them, and some salt; scald them as before, and put them off and on the fire till they are a good green; drain, and pour over them boiling water; let them lie a short time in this, and put them into wide-mouthed bottles or stone jars; have ready vinegar boiled up. With bruised nutmeg half an ounce, of ginger, black peppercorns, and whole allspice, one ounce each to a quart; pour it upon the gherkins while hot; cover them till cold, and tie them down with bladders. French beans done in this way are beautiful, and answer well pickled with the gherkins, and kept together. Nasturtium buds or imitation capers may be done after this receipt.

There is no method adopted which produces so fine a green in pickles, as the use of a brass pan; but where it is objected to, they may be done by the following receipts.

Gherkins

MAKE a pickle of salt-and-water strong enough to bear an egg, carefully skimming it while boiling; when cold, put in gherkins or French beans, or whatever is to be pickled, and let them stand at the side of the fire for three days; pour off the brine, wipe them dry, and put them into a stone jar. In another stone jar, boil, upon a hot plate, or in a water bath, as much strong vinegar as will cover the pickles; pour it over them, and cover them with fresh-gathered vine or cabbage leaves; place a cloth or plate over the jar, and let it stand by the side of the fire.

Next day pour off the vinegar, boil it as before, and pour it over the pickle, and cover them with fresh leaves; and if they are not a good green colour, repeat the same process a third time. Then put them into wide-mouthed glass bottles, or into strong stoneware jars; boil vinegar, together with spices, in the following proportions: Bruised nutmeg half an ounce, black peppercorns, whole allspice, and ginger, one ounce each to a quart; pour it hot over the pickles, cover them, and when cold, close the bottles or jars with a bung, and tie over them bladder or leather.

Cucumber Mangoes

CUT a long narrow piece out of the sides of large turkey cucumbers, scoop out the seeds, and with a part of them mix some mustard seed, shred garlic, and grated horse-radish; stuff the space as full as it will admit of, and replace the piece which was cut off; bind them with a thread; put over them hot vinegar three successive days, and boil with it the last time black pepper, flour of mustard, and some salt; put them into jars, and pour over them the boiling vinegar, and when cold, cover them closely.

Sliced Cucumbers and Onions

CUT full-grown cucumbers into slices about a quarter of an inch thick, and slice some onions thin; then lay them into a dish together, and strew salt over them; cover them with another dish, and let them remain for twenty-four hours. Put them into a cullender to drain, then into a large jar, and pour over them boiled vinegar three successive days; the last time of boiling the vinegar, add white pepper and ginger, pour it over them hot, and closely cover them when cold.

Walnuts

GATHER them for pickling when the head of a pin will pierce them easily; run a large needle through them here and there, or score them on one side with a knife; lay them into a brine of salt-and-water for twelve days, changing the brine twice in that time; strain, and put them into a jar, and sprinkle a little salt over them. Boil four quarts of vinegar for a hundred walnuts, allowing to each quart one ounce of whole black pepper, and one of ginger, half an ounce each of sliced nutmeg and whole allspice, a table-spoonful of mustard seed, and one of scraped horse-radish, one head of garlic, or a small onion; pour it boiling hot over the walnuts, and put a plate on the jar; when cold, tie it closely down. After the walnuts are used, the liquor may be boiled, strained, and bottled, to use as a pickle.

Another way to Pickle Walnuts

GATHER the nuts before the inside shell is hard, which may be known by trying them with a pin; lay them into salt-and-water nine days, changing the liquor every three days; then take them out, and dry them in the air on a sieve or mat; they should not touch each other, and they should be turned, that every side may become black alike; then put them into a jar. When half the nuts are in, put in an onion, with about thirty cloves stuck into it, and add the rest of the nuts. To one hundred walnuts allow half a pint of mustard seed, a quarter of an ounce of mace, half an ounce of black peppercorns, and six bay leaves; boil all the spice in some good common vinegar, and pour it boiling upon the nuts, observing that they are entirely covered; stop the mouth of the jar with a cloth, and when cold, cover it with bladder or leather. In about six weeks they will be fit for use, when they should be examined, and if they have absorbed the vinegar so much as to leave any of the nuts dry, more should be added, but it need not be boiled.

Walnut Catsup

WHEN green walnuts are fit for pickling, take a quart of the expressed juice, to which add one pint of vinegar; let it stand four days, then mix with it two large table-spoonfuls of salt; boil it till nearly half wasted; tie in a piece of muslin the following ingredients: The peel of a bitter orange, a small head of garlic separated, a quarter of an ounce each of finely-beaten mace, nutmeg, and cloves; put it into the bottom of a jar, and pour upon it the boiling liquor. Cover it closely, let it stand for a month, then strain and bottle it.

Another way to make Walnut Catsup

SLICE a hundred full-grown walnuts without shelling them, then beat them in a mortar; put them into a jar, with half a pound of shalots sliced, two heads of garlic, one pound of salt, and two quarts of vinegar; let it stand a week, stirring two or three times each day. Strain, and put the liquor into a sauce-pan, with a pint of port wine, two ounces of anchovies, and two of black pepper, half an ounce of cloves, and the same of mace; let it boil for half an hour, skim it well, run it through a jelly-bag, and when quite cold, put it into small bottles; cork them closely, and seal them; keep them in a dry place. It will keep for years, and is used as a fish sauce. It may be made without the wine.

Mushroom Catsup

CUT off the stalks from the broad flat mushrooms; peel, and break them into small bits; strew salt equally over them, allowing a large table-spoonful to every quart of the pulp. Let them stand twenty-four hours; put all into a sauce-pan, and let it boil gently for three quarters of an hour; strain, and let it stand to settle. The next day pour off the clear part, and to every pint of the liquor add half the quantity of port wine or old strong beer, a few blades of mace, twelve black peppercorns, and the same of allspice, a piece of ginger bruised, and eight cloves. Simmer it for nearly twenty minutes, pour it out, and when cold, bottle it with the spices equally divided.

Another way to make Mushroom Catsup

HAVING cut out the stalks, and the worm-eaten parts, of the mushrooms, break them small, and strew over them some salt; let them stand twenty-four hours. Strain off the liquor, and to a quart put the well-beaten whites of two or three eggs; boil it, and run it through a flannel bag; then boil it for about ten minutes with a little salt, three quarters of an ounce of black, and a quarter of an ounce of Jamaica pepper. When cold, bottle it with the spices, and seal the corks.

Tomata Catsup

WHEN tomatas are very ripe, slice them and put a layer into a jar, sprinkle salt over it, and lay in another layer; do this till the jar is full; stir them now and then for three days, and let the jar stand in a warm place; they must then remain for twelve days without being stirred, and a thick scum having gathered over them, squeeze the juice from the tomatas, and boil it with the same proportion of spice that is allowed for mushroom catsup; when cold, bottle it, and seal the corks. In three months strain and boil it again with fresh spice. It will then keep good a twelvemonth.

Oyster Catsup

BOIL one hundred oysters with their liquor, till the strength be extracted from them; strain them well, and add to the liquor an equal quantity of wine, one half port and the other sherry, also a quarter of an ounce of mace, the same of white pepper and of allspice, a drachm or tea-spoonful of ginger, and six anchovies; boil all together about fifteen minutes. Put into a jar twelve shalots, the peel of a lemon, and a piece of horse-radish cut small; pour upon them the boiling liquor, and when cold, bottle it, together with the spices.

Prince of Wales's Catsup

STRIP and fill a jar with ripe elderberries; add as much vinegar as the jar will contain, put it into a cool oven, and let it stand all night. Run the liquor through a jelly-bag, and to every pint put two ounces of anchovies, one of shalots; of cloves, mace, nutmeg, and ginger, a drachm or tea-spoonful each; boil it till the anchovies are dissolved. When cold, strain and bottle it.

Lemon Pickle

CUT into quarters, and pick out all the seeds of six middling-sized lemons; put them into a jar, strew over them two ounces of well-beaten bay salt; cover the jar with a cloth and plate, and let it stand three days; then put to them six cloves, and a quarter of an ounce of mace, beaten fine, one ounce of garlic or shalot, two of mustard-seed bruised, and one nutmeg sliced. Make a quart of vinegar boiling hot, and pour it over the ingredients; cover the jar, and in three or four days close it with a bung, and tie leather over it. It will be fit for use in a week, and is an improvement to most sauces, and particularly to fish sauce.

Another way to make Lemon Pickle

GRATE off a little of the outer rind of two dozen of lemons, divide them into four rather more than half way down, leaving the bottom part whole; rub on them equally half a pound of finely-beaten bay salt, spread them upon a large dish, and put them into a cool oven. When the juice has dried up, put them into a stone jar, with an ounce of cloves and one of mace finely beaten, one ounce of nutmeg cut into thin slices, a quarter of an ounce of cayenne, and four ounces of garlic peeled, also half a pint of white mustard-seed bruised and tied in a bit of muslin. Pour over the whole two quarts of boiling vinegar, stop the jar closely, and let it stand for three months; then strain it through a hair sieve, pressing it well through; let it stand till the next day, pour off the clear, and put it into small bottles. Let the dregs stand covered some days, when it will become fine. It will keep good for years. When the lemons are to be used as a pickle, no straining is necessary.

Another way to make Lemon Pickle

CUT into slices nine lemons, and put over them one pound of salt, two ounces of horse-radish sliced thin, the same of flour of mustard, half an ounce of white pepper; of cloves, nutmeg, mace, and cayenne, a quarter of an ounce each; pound the spices, add three quarts of vinegar, and boil the whole twenty minutes; put it into a jar, and let it stand three weeks, stirring it daily; then strain it through a sieve, and keep it for use in small bottles.

Yellow Pickle

CUT neatly into small pieces one large head of cauliflower, two of cabbage, six good-sized carrots, and a quart of French beans; put salt over them, and let them stand for twenty-four hours; drain them upon sieves for the same length of time, and lay them upon cloths to dry for twelve days in the sun, or near the fire; then mix with them a quart of small onions, and a quarter of a pound of garlic, and allow them all to dry for two days longer. Put the whole into a large jar, with of white mustard seed and turmeric two ounces each, one ounce of white ginger, and two table-spoonfuls of currie-powder; fill up the jar with boiling vinegar, cover it closely, and let it stand near the fire, or in a warm place, for a few days, when the pickle will be ready for use. If it be too thick, add more boiling vinegar.

To Pickle Eggs

Boil twelve eggs for twelve minutes, dip them into cold water, and take off the shells; boil a quart of vinegar for a quarter of an hour, with half an ounce each of black and Jamaica pepper, and ginger, also some slices of beet-root; put in the eggs to boil for eight or ten minutes, then put them into a jar with a slice of beet-root laid on each, and cover them with the vinegar and spices. They will be fit for use in four days, and are served in the following manner: – Place two or three in a dish, and put round them one or two cut into slices, then garnish with curled parsley.

To Pickle Mushrooms

Cut off the stalks, and wash clean, in cold water, some small button mushrooms; rub them with a bit of flannel, then throw them into fresh water, and when perfectly clean, put them into a sauce-pan with fresh cold water, and let them boil eight or ten minutes; strain off the water, lay them into the folds of a cloth. Boil, in a quart of vinegar, a quarter of an ounce of white pepper, the same of allspice, and two or three blades of mace, and a tea-spoonful of salt; put the mushrooms into a jar, and when the vinegar is cold, pour it, with the spices, over them.

Another way to Pickle Mushrooms

Clean them nicely, put them into a jar, cover them with vinegar, add a little salt, white pepper, and allspice; boil them in a water bath, or upon a hot plate, till the mushrooms are tender. Before bottling, put in a few shallots; cover them closely when cold.

To Pickle Beet-Root

Wash it perfectly clean, but do not cut off any of the fibres; put it on in plenty of boiling water with a little salt, and boil it for half an hour; if the skin will come off easily, it is done enough. Lay it upon a cloth, and with a coarse one rub off the skin. Cut it into slices, put it into a jar, and pour over it vinegar which has become cold, after having been boiled in the proportion of half an ounce of whole black pepper and a trace of ginger to a quart. Cover the jar closely when cold.

To Pickle Onions

Take off the outer skin of some small white onions, let them lie in salt-and-water for a week, changing it daily; then put them into a jar, and pour over them boiling salt-and-water; cover them closely, drain off the pickle when cold. Put the onions into wide-mouthed bottles, and fill them up with strong vinegar, putting in a little sliced ginger; cork the bottles closely.

To Pickle Young Onions

CHOOSE some of the small silver onion, put them on in cold water, and when it is scalding hot, take them out with an egg slice; peel off the skins till they look white and clear; lay them into the folds of a cloth. Boil, in a quart of vinegar, half an ounce of white pepper, a quarter of an ounce of allspice, the same of garlic, and one sliced nutmeg; put the onions into a jar, and pour over them the boiling vinegar and spices. When cold, tie leather over the jar.

Another way to Pickle Young Onions

PEEL some small onions, and steep them in salt-and-water for two days, changing the water two or three times; then drain them, and, when perfectly dry, put them into small jars, and pour over them, when cold, white wine vinegar which has been boiled with some whole black pepper and a few cloves.

Hot Pickle

BOIL, in two quarts of vinegar, a quarter of a pound of salt, two ounces of shalots or garlic, and two of ginger, one ounce of white pepper, one of yellow mustard seed, and a quarter of an ounce of cayenne; put into a jar that will hold four quarts, two ounces of allspice, and pour on it the hot pickle. When cold, put in any fresh gathered vegetables or fruit, such as asparagus, cauliflower, French beans, radish pods, unripe apples, gooseberries, currants, which may be added as the opportunity offers; and, as the pickle wastes, it should be replenished with the same mixture.

To Pickle Red Cabbage

CHOOSE two middling-sized, well-coloured, and firm red cabbages, shred them very finely, first pulling off the outside leaves; mix with them nearly half a pound of salt, tie it up in a thin cloth, and let it hang for twelve hours; then put it into small jars, and pour over it cold vinegar that has been boiled with a few barberries in it; tie the jar over closely with bladder; or boil, in a quart of vinegar, three bits of ginger, half an ounce of black and Jamaica pepper, and a quarter of an ounce of cloves. When cold, pour it over the red cabbage.

To Pickle Barberries

Boil the bruised berries of a few bunches in salt-and-water; strain, and put a gill of the liquor to a quart of vinegar, with an ounce of salt, a quarter of a pound of loaf sugar, a quarter of an ounce of pounded ginger, and a little sliced horse-radish; boil and strain it, then pour it hot over the barberries, the finest bunches having been previously selected and placed in jars; when cold, cover them closely with bladder. They may also be kept in a jar, with a strong brine of salt-and-water poured over them. When any scum is observed upon the surface, the brine must be poured off, and some fresh added. They are kept closely covered.

To Pickle Green or Red Capsicums

Place the capsicums in a jar, boil a dessert-spoonful of salt in a quart of vinegar, and pour it, while hot, upon the peppers; when cold, place a plate on the jar, and tie over it bladder or leather. They will be fit for use in a few weeks.

Indian Pickle

Scrape and wash a pound of white ginger; cut it into thin slices, and put it into salt-and-water for one night; then lay it upon a dish, strew salt over it, and let it stand till the rest of the ingredients are ready. Cut into bits a pound of garlic, let it lie for three days in salt; wash, drain, and dry it upon a sieve before the fire, or in the sun; boil, for a quarter of an hour, in some salt-and-water, some summer cabbages, cut them into quarters, drain them, and strew on them some finely-minced fresh beef suet; let them lie for twelve hours, then pull them into small bits, and dry them under glasses in the sun, so that no dust can get at them; turn them constantly for three days, and if not quite dry, put them before the fire; they should be like parchment. Boil, in salt-and-water, cauliflower, celery, French beans, and shred horse-radish; pull the cauliflower into bits, and cut the celery into pieces an inch long; dry them in the sun, or by the fire. Finely bruise a quarter of a pound of mustard-seed and an ounce of turmeric; add with it a quarter of a pound of long pepper, and the same of allspice, to a quart of the strongest vinegar; boil it, and add three quarts of common vinegar; pour it, when boiling hot, upon all the dried vegetables placed in a jar. In three weeks, if the vinegar be much wasted, fill it up with more. The jar may be added to, every year; and the pickles keep good any length of time.

To Pickle Artichoke Bottoms

Boil the artichokes till the leaves can be pulled off without breaking the bottoms; leave on the part called the choke, set them aside till cold, then put them into wide-mouthed bottles. Boil, in vinegar, some salt, white pepper, mace, and sliced nutmeg, and, when cold, pour it over the artichokes; tie bladder over the bottles.

Walnut Pickle

Put any quantity of the outside shells or green rinds of ripe walnuts into a tub in which there is a tap-hole; sprinkle them with water, raise the tub on one side, that it may stand in a sloping direction, place another vessel under it to receive the juice as it drops from the tap-hole; this it will soon begin to do; and, when a sufficient quantity has been obtained, to one gallon of this black liquor add two large table-spoonfuls of salt, one large onion, a stick of horse-radish, a bunch of sweet herbs, two bay leaves, a quarter of an ounce of black pepper, the same of allspice and of bruised ginger. Boil it slowly for twenty minutes; strain it, and, when cold, stir it and bottle it for use, putting the spice into the bottles.

CHAPTER XVIII
WINES

PREPARATORY REMARKS UPON DOMESTIC WINES

All wines are reducible to four general divisions, of dry and strong; sweet; light and flavoured; and brisk. When a dry wine is desired, the liquor is suffered to remain in the vat for three, four, or more days, according to circumstances; and a cask is provided for it sufficiently large to prevent the yeast from escaping at the bung-hole. To make a sweet wine, the fermentation must be discouraged by speedily removing it from the vat to the cask, which is carefully filled as the fluid subsides, and by frequent racking or sulphuring, or by both. To produce a light flavoured wine, similar to burgundy, the fluid is allowed to remain from six to twenty hours in the vat; and, for wines to resemble champagne, it is necessary the juice should remain in the vat but a few hours. Where small quantities are operated upon, the fermentation may be begun in the cask, the mask or mash being previously strained; for in no case should solid matter be introduced into the cask. The wine is strongest when the fermentation has been partially carried on in close vessels; and the flavour is also better preserved. To have a wine resembling champagne, a partially close ode of fermentation is adopted. For rich and strong sweet wines, the whole fermentation may be carried on openly; but, in all cases, it seems a useful practice to cover the vat with boards and blankets. The fermentation is much sooner completed in a large than in a small vessel. The sweeter and thicker juices require to be treated on a larger scale than the thinner ones. It is easy to make lemon wine in a cask of two gallons; but it is a very difficult task to operate on so small a quantity of thick and sweet raisin wine. The most favourable temperature for fermentation is about 54 degrees of Fahrenheit. When it languishes from cold, a portion of the fluid may be heated to a high degree of temperature, and mixed with the mass. The sweetest wines are most durable, and are improved by keeping; the thinnest and briskest ought to be drunk comparatively new. Boiling the fruit tends to make the wine sweet; and white sugar should always be used in preference to brown. The introduction of brandy neither prevents wine from turning sour, nor does it add to its durability, while it increases the expense, and diminishes its salubrity; but, for those who cannot overcome their prejudice in favour of established practices, it may be observed, that brandy will be least injurious when added before the fermentation is completed, in the proportion of a quart to every ten gallons.

The necessity of making the vats and casks clean requires to be particularly inculcated on the makers of domestic wines. The taste communicated by new casks is not usually thought unpleasant; where it is so, first rinsing with hot salt-and-water, and afterwards with more hot water, will remove it. Old and musty casks should be unheaded and scraped, then cleaned as before directed; and lastly, rinsed with a portion of the fermenting liquor made boiling hot. In removing the wine from the vat to the casks, it is requisite that the vat should be tapped at such a distance from the bottom, as to allow the wine to flow clear off the sediment which may have collected at the lower part of the vessel, by which means the scum may be easily prevented from running into the receiver. If the wine is not disengaged from the solid matters, straining will be further necessary. The skins are sometimes fermented with the juice in the vat, but they must in no case be introduced into the cask. To clarify the wine completely, prepared fining* may be used in the proportion of a wine-glassful to every five gallons of liquor; also isinglass or whites of eggs; half an ounce of isinglass, or nine eggs, is sufficient for fifty gallons of wine:

* Sold by James Edwards, Crutched Friars, London.

whichever of these is employed, it is first diluted in a portion of the wine, and then strongly agitated with the whole. In about ten days, when the wine has become clear, it is again drawn off. Instead of the common method of sulphuring, the sulphate of pot ash is to preferred, which may be used in the proportion of a drachm to a pipe of liquor, or the oxymuriate of potash, which is more easily procured. Dry, cold weather ought to be selected for racking.

Various kinds of wine, not to be distinguished from those of foreign growth, can in this country be made from grapes, and at a moderate expense; their being ripe is not a necessary circumstance; they may be used in any state, however immature, the quantity of sugar being proportionally increased. Where the vine is largely cultivated the thinnings may be used, as various kinds of grapes, and of different degrees of ripeness, may be mixed together. In situations where the vine may not produce even unripe fruit, the tendrils and leaves may be used, as they possess properties similar to the green fruit; the leaves of the claret vine produce wine of a delicate red colour.

Yeast should never be employed in making wine from native fruits. The deficiency of tartar in them, which in the grape promotes fermentation, may be supplied by the addition of cream of tartar, or, what is still better, crude tartar. Should the fermentation be slow, or appear as if it would not occur at all, no impatience need be felt on the subject; it will not finally be less effectual, because it has been more tedious. Attention to the temperature will commonly be sufficient. The cask may also be frequently stirred, or the filling up of the cask omitted, so that the scum, or head, may be compelled to remain in the liquor.

Gooseberry Wine to Resemble Champagne

THE fruit must be selected when about full grown, but before it has shown the least tendency to ripen; those gooseberries which have the least flavour when ripe are to be preferred, and perhaps the green bath are the best; the smallest should be separated by a sieve, the unsound or bruised fruit rejected, and the remains of the blossoms and fruit-stalks rubbed off, or otherwise removed. For a cask of ten gallons, forty pounds of such fruit are to be put into a tub that has been carefully cleaned, and that will hold fifteen or twenty gallons; it is to be bruised in successive proportions, by a pressure sufficient to burst the berries without breaking the seeds, or materially compressing the skins. Four gallons of water are then to be poured into the vessel, and the contents are to be carefully stirred, and squeezed in the hand, until the whole of the juice and pulp are separated from the seeds and skins; the materials are then to remain at rest from six to twenty-four hours, when they are to be strained through a coarse bag by as much force as can conveniently be applied to them; one gallon of fresh water may afterwards be passed through the mesh.

Thirty pounds of loaf sugar are now to be dissolved in the juice thus procured, and water added, to make the whole eleven gallons in quantity; this, together with three ounces of tartar in its crude state, being put into tub, a blanket is thrown over it, which is again covered with a board, and the vessel placed in a temperature varying from 55° to 60° of Fahrenheit; here it may remain for twenty-four hours, or two days, as the fermentation may be more or less rapid; from this tub it is to be drawn off into the cask in which it is to ferment; and, as the fermentation proceeds, the superfluous portion of juice made for the purpose, must be poured in, so as to keep the liquor still near the bung-hole for ten or twelve days, or until the fermentation becomes a little languid, as may be known by the diminution of the hissing noise; the bung is to be driven in, and a hole bored by its side, into which a wooden peg is to be fitted; it may be loosened every two or three days, for the space of eight or ten days, to give the air vent, so as to prevent the cask from bursting. When there appears no longer any danger, the spike may be permanently tightened.

The wine thus made may remain over the winter in a cool cellar. If the operator is not inclined to bestow any farther labour or expense upon it, it may be examined in some clear cold day towards the end of February or beginning of March, when, if fine, as it will sometimes be, it may be bottled without farther precaution. To ensure its fineness, however, it is a better practice to rack it, towards the end of December, into a fresh cask, so as to clear it from its first lees; or should it then prove too sweet, instead of racking it, the fermentation may be renewed by stirring up the lees, or by rolling the cask. At whatever time it is racked, it should be fined in the usual way with isinglass. Sometimes it is found expedient to rack it a second time, and to repeat the fining; and, in any case, bottle it during the month of March.

If it is wished to have a very sweet wine, as well as a brisk wine, the quantity of sugar may be increased to forty pounds; and to ensure briskness, without excessive sweetness, the proportion of fruit may be fifty pounds when the sugar is thirty. If there should appear any danger of the sweetness vanishing altogether from wine thus formed, the fermentation may be checked by racking and fining, when it will be speedily fit for use.

Wine from Unripe Currants

THIS fruit is perhaps better calculated for brisk wines than the gooseberry; greater care must be taken in separating the stalks, but otherwise the mash is more easily managed. By working the juice and solid matter together in the vat along with the sugar, the wine will prove stronger, and less sweet, but it will acquire more flavour. When the skins are not to be fermented with the liquid, it may be introduced at once into the cask, without being previously fermented in the vat, and in all cases strained before it is put into the cask. The same proportions are allowed for this wine as for gooseberry wine, and the same rules may be followed.

Sweet Wine from Ripe Currants

THE fruit is gathered when quite ripe, and the stalks being carefully picked out, it is bruised in the hands, and then strained through a canvass bag; to a ten-gallon cask, forty pounds of fruit, thirty of sugar, and a quarter of a pound of tartar are allowed; the material having remained some hours in the tub in which it was mixed, it is removed to the cask, the bung-hole covered with a tile, and the cask is stirred every other day, for ten days, and filled up every day as the fluid wastes. The fermentation may continue from three to six weeks; when it has subsided, the wine is racked into a cask in which matches, dipped in sulphur, have been burned, or in which a little of the sulphate of potash, or of oxymuriate of potash, has been put. It should be again racked and fined in March, when the wine is completed, and may be bottled, or allowed to remain in the cask.

Ripe Gooseberry Wine

MAY be made by the same rule, excluding carefully from it all the husks.

Black Currant Wine

THE same variety of proportions are allowed in this as in the others already mentioned. The fruit being picked, it is brought to the boiling point in as much water as to avoid any risk of burning; it may then be strained and put into the cask, or the liquid and skins may, with the other ingredients, be first fermented in the vat or tub, by which the wine will acquire a higher colour and flavour.

Strawberries and Raspberries

FROM either of these fruits agreeable wine may be obtained, by following the rules given for making currant wine; but it will be found a cheaper and a better method, to add a little sirup or juice of the fruit to any flavourless currant wine;

when the fermentation begins to decline, currant wine may also be flavoured with odoriferous flowers, such as cowslip, elder, or mignionette. The quality of roughness is communicated by catechu and keno, chips of oak and of beech, and also the sloe; a small quantity of these, or of the flowers, is put into the cask when the first fermentation is over, and as soon as the wine has acquired the desired flavour, it is racked and fined. The flavouring articles, such as orris-root, cloves, ginger, sweet and bitter almonds, are put into a muslin bag, and hung in the cask for a few days, during the stage of insensible fermentation, that is, after the first fermentation has ceased, care being taken to taste the liquor frequently, so that the flavouring matter may be withdrawn as soon as it has produced the desired effect.

Elderberries

CAN be made to produce excellent wine, allowing to a ten-gallon cask forty pounds of fruit, forty pounds of sugar, and a quarter of a pound of tartar. When elderberry wine is desired for a warm cordial, it is made in the following manner: – Twenty-five pounds of fruit are to be boiled for an hour, in eleven gallons of water, and along with it, tied in a piece of linen, one ounce of allspice, and two of ginger; forty pounds of sugar being put into a tub, the boiling liquor is strained over it, pressing the fruit quite dry; a quarter of a pound of crude tartar, or cream of tartar, is then added to the liquid. When it has stood two days in the tub, it may be removed to the cask, treated, as for sweet wine, in the usual manner, and bottled in March following. When to be drunk, a portion of it is heated with some sugar, two or three cloves, and a little nutmeg.

Wine from Mixed Fruit

THE three varieties of currant may be used in the largest proportion, and being nicely picked from the stalks they are allowed just to boil in as much water as to prevent their burning; of raspberries, strawberries, and cherries – black-heart are the best – equal quantities may be allowed; they are masked with a little water; gooseberries may be used to advantage, but must be prepared separately by more powerful bruising, in an equal quantity of water, and straining through a canvass bag, the other fruits being also strained; to each gallon of juice thus obtained, four pounds of loaf sugar, and half an ounce of crude tartar, are allowed; when the material has stood some hours in the tub in which it was mixed, it is removed to the cask, and managed as currant wine.

Wine from Unripe Grapes

THE proportions and treatment are exactly the same as those laid down for the gooseberry, only that the husks may always be fermented in the vat with the fluid, and also the stems when young; with the exception of the seeds, there is no objection to bruising the solid matters.

Wine from Vine Leaves

THE leaves are best when young; at farthest they should not be full grown, and must be plucked with their stems; the tendrils are equally useful; they may be taken from vines from which no fruit is expected, or from the summer prunings; when tainted with soot, they must be carefully washed. Forty or fifty pounds of such leaves being put into a tub, seven or eight gallons of boiling water are to be poured on them, in which they are to infuse for twenty-four hours; the liquor being poured off, the leaves must be pressed in a press of considerable power; and being then washed with an additional gallon of water, they are again to be pressed. Thirty pounds of sugar, and a quarter of a pound of tartar, are now to be added to the mixed liquor, and the quantity being made up to seven gallons, the process recommended in the case of gooseberries is to be followed; or that for ripe currants, if a sweet wine is desired.

Raisin Wine

TO every gallon of water, eight pounds of good raisins, and half an ounce of tartar, are allowed; the raisins being picked, they are to be put, together with the tartar, into a tub, which should be covered; the mash must be stirred every day till the sweetness has gone off, and the fruit has fallen a little, which may be in a month or six weeks; it is then to be strained, the raisins pressed to dryness, and the liquid put into the cask; no filling up is necessary, and the bung-hole is only to be so covered as to keep out the dust. When the wine has given over hissing, it is to be bunged down till the spring; when it is to be carefully fined and racked into a sulphured cask, and bottled, after being once more carefully fined.

Another way to make Raisin Wine

FOR a ten-gallon cask, fifty pounds of Malaga, and twenty-five of Smyrna raisins, ten pounds of loaf sugar, and a quarter of a pound of crude tartar, are allowed. The raisins being separated from each other, and the strong stalks picked out, they are to be put, together with the other ingredients, into a vat, and thirteen gallons of cold spring water are to be poured over them; the whole is then to be well stirred, and the vat covered; it must be stirred twice a day during the first fortnight, and afterwards once a day. When the fermentation has become very strong, and the liquor acquires a vinous smell and taste, which may be in three or four weeks, it is to be prepared for the cask in the following manner: – A sieve or a drainer, such as is used for sowens in Scotland, is to be put over a tub; in this the raisins are to be squeezed very hard with the hand; all the liquor is then to be run through a hair sieve, and put into the cask, and the remainder into bottles, from which the cask must be filled up twice a day for a week; then once a day, and less frequently as the fermentation begins to decline; when it is completed, the cask is to be bunged up, and allowed to stand for four months. Excellent vinegar may be made from the refuse.

Another way to make Raisin Wine

To twenty-eight gallons of water, one hundred and twelve pounds of Malaga, and twenty-eight pounds of Smyrna raisins, are allowed; the stalks being picked out, they are to be chopped very small, and with the water, and one pound of crude tartar, put into a tub, in which they are allowed to remain for a fortnight. The raisins are then to be squeezed to dryness, and the liquor strained, put into a cask, and treated as wine from ripe currants..

Orange Wine

For a ten-gallon cask, ninety bitter oranges are to be pared very thin, and the juice squeezed from them, which, with six gallons of water and twenty-eight pounds of sugar, is put into the cask; half the peel may be steeped in two gallons of water for twelve hours, and the water poured into the cask; they are again to be steeped in the remaining quantity of water, with which the cask is to be filled up; it must be stirred every day till the sugar is dissolved, and bunged up when the fermentation ceases. In two months it may be racked and fined, and in three months more bottled.

Those who think brandy necessary, may add a bottle at the end of the first two months. The wine will be more generally agreeable if the peel be altogether omitted.

Lemon Wine

To every gallon of water, four pounds of sugar, and the juice of ten lemons, are allowed; the lemons are to be pared very thin, and half the peel being put into a tub, the sugar and water are boiled and poured over it; when cold, the juice is added; if the fermentation does not begin in the course of a few days, it is to be promoted by the addition of a toast of bread covered with yeast; the peel is then taken out, and the liquor put into the cask, which must be bunged up when the fermentation ceases.

In this, as in orange wine, the peel may be omitted.

Malt Wine

THIRTY pounds of sugar are to be boiled half an hour with ten gallons of water, and well skimmed; when milk-warm, five gallons of new ale, from the vat, are added to it, and it is allowed to ferment two days in a tub; it is then put into the cask, with one pound of sugarcandy pounded, and four pounds of raisins of the sun chopped. When the fermentation ceases, it is racked and fined.

It may be bottled at the end of six or twelve months.

Parsnip Wine

To five gallons of water, eight pounds of parsnips, and fifteen pounds of sugar, are allowed; the parsnips, being well cleaned, and cut into slices, are to be boiled in the whole or in a portion of the water; when quite soft, they are to be taken out and mashed, then returned to the water they were boiled in, and being well stirred, are put through a hair sieve; the sugar is then to be added to the strained liquor, and the quantity made up with boiled water; when nearly cold, it is to be put into the cask with two spoonfuls of yeast, and three ounces of crude tartar, and stirred every day till the fermentation subsides, which may be in ten days or a fortnight; it is then bunged up, and may be racked and fined in three or six months, and bottled in six months more.

Birch Wine

To every gallon of juice from the birch-tree, three pounds of sugar, one pound of raisins, half an ounce of crude tartar, and one ounce of almonds, are allowed; the juice, sugar, and raisins, are to be boiled twenty minutes, and then put into a tub, together with the tartar; and when it has fermented some days, it is to be strained, and put into the cask, and also the almonds, which must be tied in a muslin bag. The fermentation having ceased, the almonds are to be withdrawn, and the cask bunged up, to stand about five months, when it may be fined and bottled.

Ginger Wine

To eight gallons of water, twelve, pounds of sugar, three pounds of bitter oranges, five pounds of lemons, and thirteen ounces of ginger, are allowed; the sugar and the ginger, bruised, are to be boiled with the water half an hour, and allowed to stand till next day; the fruit is to be pared very thin, and the strained juice, and half the peel, put into a cask with two gallons and a half of good whisky, or other spirit; when it has stood a night, the clear part of the boiled liquid is to be poured over it, the sediment being kept back; it does not ferment, and therefore it is not necessary that the cask should be full; it is immediately bunged up, and in a fortnight it must be fined and in another fortnight it may be bottled. To improve the colour, a table-spoonful of burnt sugar may be added when the cask is filled up, first diluting it with a portion of the liquor.

Another way to make Ginger Wine

Sixteen pounds of brown sugar, and the well-beaten whites of six eggs, are to be stirred into six gallons of water, and put on the fire to boil; the scum having well risen, it is to be taken clear off, and six ounces of the best white ginger, cut small, are to be added; it is then to be boiled for three quarters of an hour, and well scummed. When it has become milk-warm, it is to be put into a wooden vessel, together with a tea-cupful of fresh yeast, and also the juice of six lemons, and the same of Seville oranges, made into a sirup. When it has fermented for three days, it is to be put into the cask, with two bottles of brandy or four of whisky; the fermentation being over, it is bunged up, but not very tight at first. It may be fined in eight or ten weeks, and bottled, or allowed to stand in the cask nine or ten months.

Another way to make Ginger Wine

For a ten-gallon cask, three gallons of spirits, whisky, or rum, one gallon of the juice of Seville oranges, half a gallon of lemon juice, twenty pounds of loaf sugar, one pound and a half of best white ginger bruised, and half an ounce of isinglass, are allowed; the cask is to be filled up with cold boiled water, and in six weeks it maybe bottled.

Another way to make Ginger Wine

To ten gallons of water, fourteen pounds of brown sugar, a pound and a half of ginger, three gallons of whisky, the juice of three dozen lemons, and three dozen bitter oranges, and six rinds of each fruit, are allowed; the sugar and water is to be boiled, stirring it frequently, and skimming it; the ginger is to be boiled separately, in a small quantity of water, and strained; the rinds are to be steeped in the spirits all night, and the boiled liquid being cold, the whole is to be put into the cask, together with two drops of isinglass. In six weeks it may be bottled.

Vinous Mead

TO one gallon of water allow three pounds of honey; boil the mixture for a quarter of an hour; skim it, and when nearly cold, pour it gently into a cask, in which crude tartar has been put in the proportion of an ounce to the gallon.

As the fermentation may be long continued, a large portion of the liquid must be reserved for filling up the cask; it is put into bottles, which are closed with muslin or coarse linen to excite fermentation, expose the cask to the influence of the sun, or put it into the corner of a chimney in which a constant fire is kept. In about seven or eight days, the liquor emits a thick and dirty froth; the barrel must then be filled up from the bottles, and when the fermentation ceases, the cask must be bunged up, and placed in the cellar. It may be bottled in twelve months. It is sometimes flavoured with flowers, or with the juice of fruits.

Another way to make Mead

FOR a ten-gallon cask allow twenty pounds of honey, and fourteen gallons of water; boil and skim it; then add one ounce of cinnamon, one ounce of cardamoms, one and a half ounce of Jamaica pepper, two ounces of ginger, a quarter of an ounce of coriander seed, two large pieces of orris-root, and a few shavings of isinglass; boil these ingredients for about half an hour, and when the mixture has cooled, stir in a wine-glassful of yeast; next day pour it through a cloth into the cask, and allow it to ferment for about ten days; in a fortnight more it may be bottled, and the corks sealed. A variety of this mead may be made by adding a gallon of cranberry juice to the boiled honey and water, and substituting two ounces of cloves for the coriander and the cardamom seeds.

Simple Mead

ONE part of honey is dissolved in three parts of water and boiled over a moderate fire till it is reduced to two- thirds of the quantity. It is then skimmed, and put into a barrel, which must be quite full; it is allowed to subside for three or four days, and then drawn off for use.

To make it from the combs from which honey has been drained, they are to be beaten in warm water, and after the liquor has subsided, it is to be strained.

The cottagers in Scotland make an excellent beer by adding a little yeast to the strained liquor, and allowing it to ferment for a few days in a cask, and then bottling it.

Orgeat

A quarter of a pound of sweet, and one ounce and a half of bitter almonds, are to be blanched, and thrown into cold water, then beaten in a marble mortar, and moistened occasionally with a spoonful of milk, to prevent their oiling; three pints of milk are then to be mixed gradually with them, and after being sweetened, boiled, stirred till cold, and strained, a glass of wine or brandy is to be added.

Another way to make Orgeat

ONE pound of Jordan almonds are to be finely pounded, together with a little orange-flower water; two quarts of spring water being added by degrees, it is to be sweetened with double-refined sugar, strained through a napkin, and put into quart bottles, which should be iced. It must be made the day on which it is to be used.

Cherry Brandy

THE proportions are three quarts of the best brandy, six pounds of morella cherries, and a pound and a half of finely-pounded white or brown sugarcandy; the cherries and sugar are to be put in layers into a large-mouthed bottle or jar, which, when nearly full, is to be filled up with brandy, and closely corked.

Another way to make Cherry Brandy

TWELVE pounds of morella, and six pounds of common cherries, are to be baked, the juice pressed out, and the stones pounded in a marble mortar; the whole to be again mixed and sweetened with two pounds of sugarcandy, six quarts of brandy being added, which, with the fruit, will make three gallons; it is to be put into a large glass bottle, and shaken frequently in the course of three months. After which, it may be strained through a jelly-bag, and bottled for use.

Brandy Cherries

THE stalks are to be cut short, the cherries pricked with a needle, and some sugar strewed over them. A sufficient quantity of sirup to cover them being made, they are to be scalded in it on the fire, and put away till next day, when they are again to be scalded, and put into a jar; the sirup is then to be boiled till very thick, and if the quantity is not sufficient, more sugar may be added; when boiled enough, it is to be poured into the jar, with an equal quantity of brandy.

Shrub

ONE measure of lemon juice is allowed to five of rum and to every gallon of the mixture, six pounds of loaf sugar, which is to be melted in water, and the whole strained through flannel.

Another way to make Shrub

To one part of lemon juice, three of Seville orange are allowed, and to every pint of juice, a pound and a half of very finely pounded loaf sugar; these being well mixed, it is put into a cask, and one quart of the best rum added to each pint of the juice; the whole to be shaken three times a day for a fortnight, or longer, if the cask be large. It is then allowed to stand to fine for a month, or till it be sufficiently clear to bottle.

The dregs may be made into excellent milk punch, by pouring warm, but not boiling, milk on them, allowing three parts of milk to one of dregs; after being well mixed, it is allowed to stand for three days, when the clear part may be drawn off, and the thick run through a jelly-bag.

Lemon or Orange Shrub

THE rind of the lemons or oranges being grated off, they are to be squeezed, and two pounds of finely-pounded loaf sugar are to be added to every pint of the strained juice; when the sugar is quite dissolved, two pints of rum are allowed to every pint of sirup; the whole is to be well mixed in a cask, and allowed to stand five or six weeks, and then drawn off.

White Currant Shrub

THE currants are to be bruised and put into a bag to drip; three quarters of a pound of loaf sugar are to be dissolved in two quarts of juice, and a quart of rum being added, it is to be bottled for use.

Lemon Brandy

THREE quarts of brandy being put into an earthen jar that is fitted with a cover, a pound and three quarters of fine loaf sugar, the thin parings of six lemons, and the juice of twelve, are to be added; one quart of boiling milk is to be poured over the mixture, which must be stirred daily for eight days; it is then to be run through a jelly-bag, and bottled.

Lemonade

EIGHT lemons and eighty-four Seville oranges being selected, the two clearest lemons are to be rubbed over with loaf sugar, and the rinds scraped off into a gallon of spring water; the fruit is then to be squeezed into a sieve placed over the vessel containing the water, the liquid sweetened with double-refined sugar and run through a jelly-bag. It is then to be put into bottles, which may be cooled, by laying ice on the necks.

Transparent Lemonade

THE peel of fourteen lemons having been soaked in two quarts of water for two hours, their juice, one pound and a half of sugar, and a quart of white wine, are to be added; a quart of new milk, made boiling hot, is then to be mixed with it, and when it has stood an hour, it is to be strained through a jelly-bag till it runs clear.

A Receipt for Juice

THE proportion of oranges should be double that of lemons; the fruit being selected free from decay, and wiped dry, they are to be squeezed, and the juice strained through a sieve into an earthen pan; to each pint, according to the acidity of the fruit, a pound and a half or a pound and three quarters, of double-refined sugar, broken small, is to be added. It must be stirred and skimmed daily, till the sugar is well incorporated, or as long as the scum rises; and when it has been a month in the pan, it may be bottled.

The Duke of Norfolk's Punch

THE thin parings of six lemons, and of six oranges, are to be steeped in a gallon of brandy for twenty-four hours, the vessel containing it being closely covered; three pounds of single-refined sugar are to be clarified with the white of an egg, in a gallon of spring water, and boiled for a quarter of an hour, skimmed, and allowed to stand till cold. The brandy is then to be strained from the parings, and with the strained juice of eighteen oranges and eighteen lemons, added to the boiled sirup, and put into a vessel sufficiently large to contain the whole. It must be closely covered, and when it has stood six weeks, it may be bottled.

Milk Punch

THE rinds of nine lemons are to be steeped, for eighteen hours, in two quarts of brandy, then mixed with the strained juice of the lemons, one and a half pound of sugar, five pints of water, and one grated nutmeg; one quart of new milk, made boiling hot, being added, it is to be strained through a jelly-bag.

Another way to make Milk Punch

IN twenty quarts of brandy, the peel of thirty Seville oranges, and thirty-six lemons, are to be infused for twelve hours; thirty quarts of water and fifteen pounds of double-refined sugar are to be boiled, and when cold, the strained juice of the oranges and lemons is to be added to it; it is then to be put into a cask, together with the brandy, strained from the peel; a quart of boiling milk being poured into the cask, it is to be bunged up, and allowed to stand till it become fine, before being bottled. It will be the better for remaining a year in the cask.

Another way to make Milk Punch

EIGHT pounds of refined sugar are to be dissolved in the strained juice of three dozen lemons, and, when quite settled, two gallons of brandy, and two gallons and a half of cold water, are to be added, and also the lemon-peel; one gallon of boiling milk being then poured over the ingredients, they are to stand closely covered for twenty-four hours; when, being skimmed, and run through a very thick jelly-bag, it may be quickly bottled, and will be fit for immediate use; but it improves by keeping.

Ratafia

ONE gallon of brandy, three hundred kernels of apricots, the juice and very thin parings of eight lemons, and half an ounce of saffron; when these ingredients have stood a fortnight, they are to be strained, and one pound of white sugarcandy, dissolved in half a pint of water, added to the liquor.

Another way to make Ratafia

FIVE hundred peach kernels are to be steeped in one gallon of pale brandy, together with two quarts of frontignac, one pint of orange-flower water, and one pound and three quarters of double-refined sugar. It must be shaken daily for six weeks, and then put through a jelly-bag till clear.

Orange Liqueur

To each orange, one quart of strong spirits, and one pound and a quarter of loaf sugar are allowed; six or eight cloves are to be stuck into each orange, which, with the spirits and sugar, is to be put into a jar. It must be closely covered, and stirred occasionally in the course of two months; it is then to be filtered through blotting paper, and bottled for use.

Lemon liqueur is made in the same way, substituting lemons for oranges. Instead of mixing the sugar with the other materials in the jar, it may be made into a sirup, and added to the strained or filtered spirits. This, though more troublesome, will be found a better method.

Noyau

THE rinds of three large lemons, half a pound of pounded loaf sugar, one ounce of bitter almonds, blanched and pounded, are to be mixed into a quart of the best Hollands, three table-spoonfuls of boiling milk being added. It is to be put into a bottle or jar, and shaken every day for three weeks, and then filtered through chamois leather or blotting paper, when it will be fit for use.

Another way to make Noyau

PEACHES and nectarines, in equal quantities, are to be bruised, the stones broken, and the kernels blanched and bruised; they are then to be put into a jar in layers, one of fruit, one of kernels, and one of pounded loaf sugar, and so on until the jar is full; as much white brandy is then to be added as the jar will hold; and when it has stood for five or six months, it is to be filtered, and bottled for use.

Another way to make Noyau

ONE pound of bitter almonds, blanched, is to be steeped three months in four quarts of large-still proof whisky, or pale brandy; four pounds of loaf sugar are then to be clarified, and added to the strained or filtered spirits, together with half a pint of pure honey.

It is sometimes coloured with a little cochineal; and may also be made, allowing three parts of sweet, and one of bitter almonds.

Capillaire

THE best capillaire is that of North America. Put one ounce of it into a small quantity of boiling water, to infuse like tea; add a pound of sugar to the infusion; clarify it with the white of an egg, and boil it to a thick sirup; strain it through a cloth, and when cold, put in a little orange-flower water, and bottle it. That which is commonly sold as capillaire in England is simply sirup flavoured with orange-flower water.

Hawthorn Liqueur

THE full blossoms of the white thorn are to be picked dry and clean from the leaves and stalks, and as much put into a large bottle as it will hold lightly without pressing it down; it is then to be filled up with French brandy, and allowed to stand two or three months, when it must be decanted off, and sweetened with clarified sugar or with capillaire. Without the sweetening, it is an excellent seasoning for puddings and custards.

Caledonian Liqueur

AN ounce of oil of cinnamon is to be dropped on two pounds and a half of bruised loaf sugar; one gallon of the best whisky being added, and the sugar being dissolved, it is to be filtered and bottled.

A liqueur may be made with any other essential oil, such as caraway.

Imperial

TO one ounce of cream of tartar, two ounces of ginger, one lemon cut into slices, and two pounds of loaf sugar, two gallons of boiling water are added; when almost cold, two table-spoonfuls of yeast are stirred in. It may be bottled next day, and will be fit for drinking the day after it is bottled.

Another way to make Imperial

TWO ounces of cream of tartar, the juice and parings of two lemons, and a few cloves, are put in to a jar, and six quarts of boiling water added; it is sweetened with loaf sugar, covered, and allowed to stand till the following day, when a quart of rum is added; it is then strained, bottled, and tightly corked.

Bishop

ROAST four good-sized bitter oranges till they are of a pale brown colour; lay them in a tureen, and put over them half a pound of pounded loaf sugar, and three glasses of claret; place the cover on the tureen, and let it stand till next day. When required for use, put the tureen into a pan of boiling water, press the oranges with a spoon, and run the juice through a sieve; then boil the remainder of the bottle of claret, taking care that it do not burn; add it to the strained juice, and serve it warm in glasses.

Turkish Sherbet

WASH a small fore-quarter of veal, put it on the fire with nine pints of water; skim it well, and let it boil till reduced to two pints; run it through a sieve, and when cold, add to it a pint and a half of clear lemon juice, and two pounds of loaf sugar which has been made into a sirup with a pint and a half of water, and cleared with the white of an egg. It is served in glass mugs, for a dessert table, or offered at any other time as a refreshment.

Balm Beer

ELEVEN gallons of water and ten pounds of brown sugar are to be clarified with the whites of twelve eggs, carefully skimmed, and boiled till nearly reduced to ten gallons; two pounds and a half of the yellow flower of lemon balm being put into a cask, the liquor, when milk-warm, is to be poured over it, and four or five table-spoonfuls of thick yeast added. The cask must be filled up morning and evening with what works over it, and bunged up when the fermentation ceases; in a month the beer may be bottled, and in two or three months it will be fit for drinking. Half the quantity of the flower of lemon balm will probably be found to communicate a flavour sufficiently strong, if added when the fermentation is nearly over.

Medicinal Imperial, a favourite Spring Drink

ONE ounce of cream of tartar, one ounce of Epsom salts, twelve ounces of loaf sugar, the juice of two lemons, and the peel of one – put the whole into a large jug, and pour over it three pints of boiling water; cover it till cold; skim it, and pour the clear part into a decanter; and take two large wine-glassfuls every day.

Soda Water

TARTARIC acid, half an ounce, arated soda, half an ounce. Have two tumblers about one-third full of water, put thirty grains of soda into one glass, and twenty-five grains of the acid into the other; when dissolved, mix them together, and drink it immediately. The two sorts of salts must be kept in separate bottles, and should be bought ready powdered.

Another way to make Soda Water

CARBONATE of soda, forty-five grains, tartaric acid, thirty grains; put each powder with a quarter of a pint of cold water into separate tumblers, and mix them well; then pour the one containing the soda into that which has the acid in it, and drink it while it effervesces. Some persons prefer the citric to the tartaric acid, and a smaller quantity of it will suffice. For those who are delicate, or in very cold weather, a small quantity of brandy, or of white wine, may be added; and the water may be used in a tepid state. As a tonic, the carbonate of soda may be taken first, and the acid mixture instantaneously afterwards, by which means a powerful and salutary effervescence is produced in the stomach.

Spruce Beer

WHEN ten gallons of water, six pounds of treacle, and three ounces of bruised ginger, have boiled together for half an hour, two pounds of the outer sprigs of the spruce fir are to be added, and boiled for five minutes; the whole is then to be strained through a hair sieve, and when milk-warm, put into the cask, and a tea-cupful of good yeast stirred well into it. When it has fermented a day or two, it is to be bunged up, and the following day bottled. It will be fit for use in a week.

The ginger is sometimes omitted, and instead of the spruce fir, three ounces of the essence may be used, which is to be well whisked, together with the treacle, and a gallon or two of warm water; then put into the cask, which is to be filled up with water, and the yeast added.

Another way to make Spruce Beer

THE proportions are ten gallons of water, three quarts of treacle, a tea-cupful of ginger, the same of allspice, three ounces of hops, three ounces and a half of the essence of spruce, and half a pint of good yeast. The hops, ginger, and allspice, must be boiled together till the hops fall to the bottom; the treacle and spruce are then to be dissolved in a bucketful of the liquor, the whole strained into a cask, and the yeast well stirred in; when the fermentation ceases, the cask is to be bunged up.

Welsh Nectar

TWO gallons of water being boiled, and allowed to cool; one pound of raisins, two pounds of loaf sugar, the juice of three lemons, and their peel cut thin, are added; after being stirred daily for four days, it is run through a jelly-bag and bottled; in ten days, or a fortnight more, it will be fit for use, and will be found excellent in warm weather. The corks should be tied down.

Ginger Beer

FOR a ten-gallon cask, eleven gallons of water, fourteen pounds of sugar, the juice of eighteen lemons, and one pound of ginger, are allowed; the sugar and water are boiled with the whites of eight eggs, and well skimmed; just before coming to the boiling point, the ginger, which must be bruised, is then added, and boiled for twenty minutes; when cold, the clear part is put into the cask, together with the lemon juice and two spoonfuls of yeast; when it has fermented for three or four days, it is fined, bunged up, and in a fortnight bottled. It may be made without the fruit.

Another Ginger Beer Quickly Made

A gallon of boiling water is poured over three quarters of a pound of loaf sugar, one ounce and a quarter of sliced ginger, and the peel of one lemon; when milk-warm, the juice of the lemon and a spoonful of yeast are added. It should be made in the evening, and bottled next morning in half-pint stone bottles, and the cork tied down with twine.

CHAPTER XIX
MISCELLANY

Permanent Ink

RUB down, in a small mortar, five scruples of lunar caustic, with one drachm of gumarabic, one scruple of sap green, and one ounce of rain water.

Liquid Pounce

ONE ounce of sal-soda is to be mixed with two ounces of boiling water, and a little gumarabic; shake the bottle, wet the linen with the mixture, dry and iron it before using the ink, and again put the iron on it after it is marked.

Almond Paste

POUND and mix thoroughly the following ingredients: One pound of raisins stoned; two pounds of bitter almonds blanched; sixpence-worth of camphor; a wine-glass of brandy; one of honey; two beaten eggs, and a little fine sand sifted.

Another way to make Almond Paste

FINELY pound, and well mix, with a sufficient quantity of orange-flower or rose water, half a pound of bitter, one pound of sweet almonds blanched, and one pound of honey; put it into small pots, and pour over it a little orange-flower or rose water; tie them over closely with paper.

Lavender Water

PUT into a large bottle, eight ounces of the best rectified spirit of wine, three drachms of oil of lavender, one drachm of essence of ambergris, and threepence-worth of musk; cork it tightly, and shake it well every day, for a fortnight or three weeks.

To Make Ink

To four ounces of bruised galls, allow two of copperas, and two of gumarabic; put the galls into a large bottle, with three pints of rain water, and in three or four days dissolve the gum in hot water, and add it with the copperas; shake the bottle frequently for some days. A few cloves may be put into the bottle to prevent the ink from moulding.

To take out Iron Moulds

POUND two ounces of cream of tartar, and mix thoroughly with it one ounce of salt of sorrel; keep it in a bottle closely corked. Fill a metal water-plate with boiling water; wet the iron mould; place it upon the plate, and rub it with a little of the powder till it disappears; then rinse it in water. Or mix in a tea-cup one tea-spoonful of oil of vitriol, and two of common salt; place it in warm ashes; hold the stained part over it, and the stain will soon disappear; then wash the part in cold water.

Neats' Foot Oil

BOIL the feet for several hours, as for making stock for jelly; skim off the oily matter from time to time as it rises, and when it ceases to come up, pour off the water; next day take off the cake of fat and oil which will be found on the top; boil it and the oil before obtained, together with a little cold water; let it cool; pour off the water, and bottle the oil for use. This oil, being perfectly pure, and free from smell, may be used with the French lights in a sick room.

To Discharge all Stains which are not Metallic

MIX two tea-spoonfuls of water with one of spirit of salt; let the stain lie in it for one or two minutes; then rinse the article in cold water. This will be found particularly useful in removing stains from white doilys. Or, to remove port wine stains, cover them thickly, while wet, with salt, and instantly immerse the article in boiling water; repeat the process if the stains do not disappear at first.

To Wash Paint

BRUSH off the dust with a small long-haired brush; mix finely-powdered whitening and bullock's gall, till of the consistence of a batter; with a flannel rub it on the walls up and down, and then wash it off with a clean flannel and plenty of cold water, and when nearly dry, rub it hard with a clean linen cloth; the unpleasant smell from the gall will go off almost immediately. If the paint is not very much soiled, it may be washed merely with the whitening mixed with cold water, first wetting below the hand.

To Wash Imitation Wainscot

WASH first with cold water and a clean flannel, and then with sour porter; after which it is not to be wiped. Or wash with whitening mixed with cold water; wash off with clean water; dry it well, and then rub hard with linseed oil.

To Clean Papered Rooms

BLOW off the dust with a pair of bellows; cut the upper crust off a stale loaf of bread; hold the crust in the hand, and rub gently downwards, about half a yard at each stroke. The next time of going round, commence a little above where the last stroke ended, and take care not to cross the paper, or go up again. The process may be repeated; and, if carefully done, the paper will look nearly as well as new.

To Clean Polished Grates and Irons

MAKE into a paste, with cold water, four pounds of putty-powder, and one of finely-powdered whitening; dip a duster into the mixture; rub off carefully all the spots, and with a well-aired clean duster, rub the grate or irons one way till bright and clear. Plain dry whitening will keep it highly polished, if well attended to every day. The putty mixture should be used only to remove spots. To remove rust from the poker, tongs, and shovel, boil one pound of middling-sized emery powder with half a pound of soft soap, till it is as thick as paste; when cold, rub the irons with it; rub it off with a dry cloth, and polish with finely-powdered and sifted brick dust, or whitening.

To keep steel grates, fenders, and fire-irons from rusting, rub them over with fresh mutton suet, melted, and then dust them with unslaked lime, tied up in a bit of coarse muslin.

To Clean Brass and Copper

Rub it over slightly with a bit of flannel dipped in sweet oil; next, rub it hard with another bit dipped in finely-powdered rotten-stone; then make it clean with a soft linen cloth; and finish by polishing it with a plate-leather.

Another way to Clean Brass and Copper

Put one pennyworth of powdered rotten-stone into a dry clean quart bottle; nearly fill it up with cold soft water; shake it well, and add one pennyworth of vitriol. Rub it on with a rag, and dry it with a clean soft cloth, and then polish it with a plate-leather. This mixture will keep for a long time, and becomes better the longer it is kept. But the first method gives the most lasting polish, as well as the finest colour.

For Scouring Floors

Dry some fuller's earth, and with boiling water make it into a thick paste; mix it with one-third of its quantity of very fine sand, sifted; sprinkle this mixture over the floor, and with a scrubbing-brush and cold water, scrub the boards up and down, but not across, and finish by scrubbing with plenty of cold water. Very fine sand and cold water may be used in general; and to extract grease, mix some pearl ashes in hot water, and use it with fine sand. Equal proportions of spirits of salt, and of vinegar, mixed, will extract all stains out of floors.

To Wash Stone Stairs and Halls

Wash them first with hot water and a clean flannel, and then wash them over with pipe-clay mixed in water. When dry, rub them with a coarse flannel.

To Take Oil and Grease out of Floors and Stone Halls

Make a strong infusion of potash with boiling water; add to it as much quick-lime as will make it of the consistence of thick cream; let it stand a night, then pour off the clear part, which is to be bottled for use. When wanted, warm a little of it; pour it upon the spots, and after it as been on them for a few minutes, scour it off with warm water and soap, as it is apt to discolour the boards when left too long on them. When put upon stone, it is best to let it remain all night; and if the stain be a very bad one, a little powdered hot lime may be put upon it before the infusion is poured on.

To Clean Floor Cloths

SWEEP them clean, and wash off any dirty spots with a spunge and cold water, then rub them with a coarse flannel, and polish with a clean one.

To Prevent Creaking Hinges

RUB them with soft soap, or a feather dipped in sweet oil.

To Destroy Bugs

MIX one ounce of corrosive sublimate with a pint of spirits of wine; shake it well, and, with a feather, rub it over the joints and posts of the bedsteads. Repeat the application if the first is not successful. Or well wash with a strong infusion of tobacco leaves, steeped in boiling water.

To Sweep Carpets

SPRINKLE tea-leaves over them, and sweep them with a hair broom; a whisk should very seldom be used; and fine carpets should be done with a clothes brush. Dry snow is preferable to tea-leaves, and should be used in the same way.

To Wash and Clean a Carpet

SHAKE and beat it well; lay it upon the floor, and tack it firmly; then with a clean flannel wash it over with one quart of bullock's gall, mixed with three quarts of soft cold water, and rub it off with a clean flannel or house cloth. Any particularly dirty spot should be rubbed with pure gall.

To Take Stains out of Marble Chimney-Pieces and Hearths

MIX, with one quart of strong soap-lees, one pound of pearl ashes, and as much fine whitening as will make it into a paste; lay this all over the marble, and let it remain for some weeks; then wash it off with a flannel, and cold water and soap. Polish it with a dry flannel.

To Clean Feathers

ALLOW, to every gallon of water, half a pound of quick lime; stir the mixture well, and let it stand a night; then pour off for use the lime water that is perfectly clear; put the feathers to be cleaned into a deep tub, and pour as much lime water on them as will cover them; stir them well with a stick, and let them stand two or three days, stirring them frequently; then put them into a bag, and wash them thoroughly in cold water; then turn them out on sieves, and wring the water from them by squeezing them in small portions with the hands; after which, they may be separated, the hard quills picked out, and the down stripped from the large feathers. When they are thus carefully cleaned, lay them on a floor where air can be freely admitted; turn and shake them frequently, and when dry, put them into bags, and beat them on a knocking-stone with a knocker.

To Wash Silk Stockings, White and Black

CUT in thin bits some white soap, and boil it in soft water; pour a little of it amongst cold soft water, and wash the stockings, first upon the inner side; repeat the washing with fresh suds and water, till they are washed quite clean; turn the outside the last time of washing, and if the feet be very dirty, rub a little of the boiled soap upon them, but not upon the legs. If to be coloured, mix the dye with a little clean suds, and dip in the white stockings; draw them out smooth, and lay them upon a sheet on a bed, with the window open, and when almost dry, lay them upon a piece of flannel, and with another bit rolled up, rub them hard and quick one way, till they look glossy and are dry. They may be mangled, turned upon the inner side, and must always be folded straight upon the instep.

To Wash Lace

PLACE the lace in folds, and baste it on each side; lay it in cold water for a night, and wash it in cold water with the best white soap; gently rub and squeeze it; wash it in three or four waters with the soap and after that rinse it well in clean water; then put it into thin starch or rice water; take out the basting thread, and spread it on a blanket upon a bed to dry; when it is nearly so, pick it out; lay it in folds, and when quite dry, lay it in an old cambric handkerchief, and then in the folds of a towel; put it upon the rug, or upon a blanket laid upon a stone, and with a heavy wooden pestle, or rolling pin, beat it hard till the lace looks quite smooth. A scarf or veil, after being starched, should be pinned out tight upon a cloth on the floor, and when dry, beaten in the same manner.

To Wash Head and Clothes Brushes

IN a pint of hot water, put a dessert-spoonful of pearl ashes, and shake the brush about in it till it be perfectly clean; then pour some clean hot water over it; shake, and dry it before the fire.

To Wash Flannels and Worsted Things, to prevent their shrinking, and to keep them of a good Colour

TAKE half the weight of soda that there is of soap; boil them with water, allowing a gallon to every pound of soap, and use it when perfectly cold. Wet the flannels in cold water, then wash them in fresh cold water, with some of the boiled mixture amongst it; wash them in this, changing the water till they become perfectly clean; then rinse them well in cold water, and dry them in the shade. Worsted stockings, washed in this manner, will be made quite clean; but particular care must be taken to wet them in clean cold water, previous to washing them in the cold suds. Blankets should be washed in this way also, and when nearly dry, frequently shaken to raise the pile, and to make them soft.

All dirty clothes should be laid in cold water the night before being washed.

To Wash Cotton Stockings

LAY them in cold water at night; next day boil them in a copper with some soda and soap; stir them well about, and they will become quite clean without any rubbing; rinse them well in cold water, and bleach them; when nearly dry, draw them smooth, folding them straight over the instep. Place them under a heavy weight, or iron them.

To Wash Coloured Dresses

TURN the inner side out, and wash them in cold water, in which a little boiled soap is well mixed; rinse them well in clean cold water, and the last time with a little salt in the water, and dry them in the shade. They should be washed and dried with as much expedition as possible.

To Clean Gold Chains, Earrings, &c

MAKE a lather of soap and water; boil the chain in it for a few minutes, and immediately on taking it out, lay it in magnesia powder which has been heated by the fire; when dry, rub it with flannel; if embossed, use a brush. Or wash a gold chain in soap and water, put it whilst wet, into a bag filled with box-wood sawdust; shake it well, and take it out in a little, when it will be found perfectly clean. The bag must be about eight inches long and three broad; and if box-wood sawdust cannot be obtained, fresh clean bran may be substituted.

To Clean Glasses

GLASSES should be washed in a wooden vessel, in which put a sufficiency of cold water to cover them, and rinse them in fresh cold water; wipe off the wet with one cloth, and finish them with another.

To Clean Decanters

BOIL up, in small pieces, some coarse brown paper or blotting-paper; wet and soap them, and put them into the decanter, with a little pearl ashes; fill in some lukewarm water, shake it well for a few minutes, or, if very dirty, let them stand some hours; then rinse the decanters with clean cold water. If this does not remove the crust of wine which may be at the bottom, use stable litter, with which nearly half fill the decanter, adding some cold water, and let it remain for several hours; shake it well, and rinse with clean cold water till perfectly clean. The stable litter will also be found an effectual cleanser for bottles of any kind, however dirty; but it will be the less required, and much trouble will be spared, if all the bottles used throughout the day be rinsed at night with cold water before being put away.

To clean cut crystal, rub it well with a damp spunge, dipped in whitening; then take a clean brush and brush it off; afterwards wash the vessel in cold water.

To loosen glass stoppers. – When glass stoppers cannot easily be taken out, drop on them a little olive oil; place the decanter or bottle before the fire, and in a few minutes they will become loose.

To Clean Looking-Glasses

TAKE a bit of soft spunge, well washed, and cleaned from every thing gritty; just dip it into water, and squeeze it out again, and then dip it into spirits of wine, or any other spirits; rub it over the glass, then dust it over with some powder-blue, or whitening, sifted through muslin; rub it lightly and quickly off again, with a soft cloth; then take a clean cloth, and rub it well again, and finish by rubbing it with a silk handkerchief. If the frames be varnished, great care must be taken not to touch them with the spunge, or with any thing damp. To clean the frames, take a little cotton wool, and rub them with it.

Pictures should be rubbed lightly with cotton wool, or brushed with a feather brush.

To Clean Hats

WHEN a hat gets wet, wipe it as dry as may be with a cloth or silk handkerchief, then brush it with a soft brush; when it gets nearly dry, use a harder brush; and if the fur still sticks, damp it with a spunge dipped in beer or vinegar; then brush it with a hard brush till it is dry.

To Remove Spots of Grease out of Cloth

MOISTEN them with a few drops of concentrated solution of subcarbonate of potash; rub the spots between the fingers, and then wash the spot with a little warm water.

To remove oil-paint, or grease, rub the part with a bit of flannel dipped in spirits of wine or turpentine.

Furniture Oil

MIX with one pint of cold-drawn linseed oil, one ounce of spirits of white lavender, half an ounce of powdered gumarabic, dissolved in a little hot oil. This being thoroughly mixed, rub it over the tables with a little wool, and rub it off with clean linen cloths. A brush must never be used. If the furniture is desired of a very dark colour, add to this mixture three ounces of alkanet root, and two ounces of rose pink.

For giving a Bright and Beautiful Polish to Furniture

MIX well with an ox-gall one pint of cold-drawn linseed oil, then stir in two glasses of whisky, and when thoroughly mixed, add half an ounce of aquafortis, and stir it altogether for ten or fifteen minutes; bottle it, and when to be used, shake it well; rub it on with piece of flannel, and then rub very hard with a linen cloth.

To Clean Chairs

SCRAPE down one or two ounces of bees-wax, put it into a jar, and pour as much spirit of turpentine over it as will cover it; let it stand till dissolved. Put a little upon a flannel or bit of green baize, rub it upon the chairs, and polish them with a brush. A very small portion of finely-powdered white rosin may be mixed with the turpentine and wax.

To Clean Plate

CUT a yard of coarse calico into four, and boil it in a quart of water, together with two ounces of calcined, powdered, and sifted hartshorn, till all the liquid be absorbed. The plate being washed clean, rub it with a piece of the cloth.

All plate powder which is mixed with mercury is pernicious. Fine colcothar of vitriol, such as painters use, is an excellent plate powder; that, or whitening, may be used, dry, or wet with water, spirits, or oil. The last gives the brightest polish, but is the most troublesome; it should be put upon the plate with a piece of flannel, the powder then shaken over it, and rubbed off with a leather, or with the hand, if the article is plain; for the rough parts, it will be necessary to have brushes of various sizes, hard and soft; a small tooth-brush will be found useful amongst them. The spunge and leather used for washing plate should be soft, and a linen cloth must be used to wipe the plate before it is put upon the table. Plated articles should be cleaned with soft brushes, and not too often, and never with any thing but plate powder, wet with spirits or water, as above directed.

To remove wax or grease from plate or candlesticks; pour boiling water on them, and wipe them dry directly with an old cloth.

Japanned Candlesticks and Tea-Trays

To remove grease from candlesticks, just let the water be warm enough to melt it; then wipe them with a cloth, and if they look smeared, sprinkle a little flour upon them, and wipe it clean off. Wax candles should not be burned in them, as the wax cannot be taken off without injuring the varnish.

Wax Candles

Should they get dirty or yellow, wet them with a piece of flannel dipped in spirits of wine.

Shoe-Blacking

To four ounces of ivory-black, allow three ounces of loaf sugar, one table-spoonful of salad oil, one ounce of oil of vitriol, and one pint of vinegar; dissolve the sugar in a little vinegar, put it on the fire together with the oil, and stir it well; when moderately heated, add the pint of vinegar, and ivory-black; and, when cold, stir in the vitriol; put it into a quart bottle, shake it well, and fill it up with vinegar.

Another way to make Shoe-Blacking

Mix, in one quart of sour porter, the following ingredients: – Three ounces of ivory-black, the same quantity of treacle, two table-spoonfuls of sweet oil, and, lastly, one ounce of vitriol; bottle, and shake it well.

Blacking for Carriage Harness, and Leather

Boil, in one quart of vinegar, or sour ale, for twenty minutes, the following ingredients: – Four ounces of fine glue, three ounces of soft soap, half an ounce of isinglass, two ounces of logwood chips, half an ounce of black sealing wax, and three drachms of indigo; strain it while hot.

To clean Boot-Tops White

Mix, in a quart bottle of soft water, one ounce of oxalic acid, two ounces of finely-pounded pumice-stone, and two tea-spoonfuls of salt of lemon. Cork it tightly.

To clean Boot-Tops Brown

Mix, in the same quantity of water, one ounce of oxalic acid, half an ounce of muriatic acid, a small phial of spirit of lavender, and two tea-spoonfuls of salt of lemon. Each bottle should be carefully labelled, and marked – "Poison."

Directions for Using the Liquid

For the white tops: to be scrubbed well on with a clean hard brush, then spunged well with cold water, all one way, and allowed to dry gradually in the sun, or by the fire. Brown tops are not to be scrubbed with a brush, but spunged all over with the mixture, till all stains be removed; then spunged well with cold water, and rubbed with flannel till they be highly polished.

To render Boots and Shoes Water-proof

Mix carefully over a slow fire, a pint of drying oil, two ounces of turpentine, two ounces of yellow wax, and half an ounce of burgundy pitch. Lay the mixture, whilst hot, on the boots and shoes with a spunge, soft brush, or bit of flannel, and when dry, lay it on again; repeat the operation until the leather becomes quite saturated. Let them be put away, and not worn, till they become perfectly elastic, when they will be found not only impervious to wet, but soft, pliable, and more durable.

To take Ink out of Mahogany

Mix, in a tea-spoonful of cold water, a few drops of oil of vitriol; touch the spot with a feather dipped in it; and, when it disappears, wash the part that has been stained, with cold water.

To Clean Stone Kitchens

They should not be often washed, but dry-rubbed with a blue or grey stone, then wiped with a coarse flannel, and swept; thus all greasy spots will be removed. A common brick may be used instead of the stone.

To prevent the Smoking of a Lamp

SOAK the wick in strong vinegar, and dry it well before it is used.

Potpourri

GATHER, when perfectly dry, a peck of roses; pick off the leaves, and strew over them three quarters of a pound of common salt; let them remain two or three days, and if any fresh flowers are added, some more salt should be sprinkled over them. Mix with the roses half a pound of finely-pounded bay salt, the same quantity of allspice, of cloves, and of brown sugar, a quarter of a pound of gum-benjamin, and two ounces of orris-root; add a glass of brandy, and any sort of fragrant flower, such as orange and lemon flowers, rosemary, and a great quantity of lavender flowers – also white lilies; a green orange stuck with cloves may be added. All the flowers must be gathered perfectly dry.

To make Coffee when much is required

IN the morning, pour upon a quarter of a pound of fresh-ground coffee about two quarts of boiling water; stir it for three or four minutes; cover it closely, and let it remain till the evening; pour it off quite clear, and boil it up for use.

Another way to make Coffee

BEAT an egg, shell and all; mix it with a quarter of a pound of coffee, then pour two quarts of boiling water on it, and boil it for five minutes; let it settle a little that it may be fine; or, instead of clearing it with an egg, pour a little cold water into the coffee-pot before taking it off the fire. It may be made in this way in a large quantity, the clear part poured off, bottled, and corked. Thus prepared, kept in a cool place, it will continue good for ten or fifteen days.

Milk Coffee for Breakfast

BOIL one ounce of good coffee for fifteen minutes in a pint and a half of water. The next day pour off the clear liquor, and add to it one pint of new milk; make it quite hot, but do not allow it to boil. Sweeten it with pounded sugarcandy, or brown sugar.

Cocoa

PUT into a sauce-pan one ounce of patent cocoa, and one quart of water; cover it, and when it boils, set it by the side of the fire to simmer for two hours. It is sometimes made in a larger quantity, poured from the sediment, and boiled up as it is required.

Chocolate

SCRAPE down one square of chocolate, and mix it with one pint of boiling milk, or milk-and- water; then mill or stir it well, and serve it with the froth.

Oatmeal Gruel

MIX in a basin two table-spoonfuls of oatmeal with a little cold water, then pour on it about a quart of boiling water; stir it well, and let it settle for a few minutes; pour off the water into a sauce-pan, and boil it for ten or fifteen minutes, stirring it, and taking off the scum as it rises.

Barley Water

WASH two ounces of pearl-barley in water, boil it for a few minutes in a little fresh water; pour that off, and add a quart more; when it boils, let it simmer for nearly an hour, and then strain it. It may be sweetened with sugar, and seasoned with a little of the peel and juice of a lemon.

Apple Water

CUT three or four large apples into slices, put them into a jug, and pour a quart of boiling water over them; cover the jug. When quite cold, strain and sweeten it, and add a little lemon juice.

Cooling Drink

A palatable and cooling drink may be made by pouring hot water over slices of lemon; when cold, to be strained and sweetened.

Beef Tea

CUT a piece of lean beef into small thin bits; boil it with a quart of water in a closely-covered sauce-pan; let it simmer for an hour, then strain, and serve it with salt.

White Wine Whey

BOIL a pint of milk, and when it rises in the pan, pour in one glass of sherry and one of currant wine; let it again boil up, take it off the fire, and when it has stood a few minutes, remove the curd, pour on and sweeten it.

Irish, or Two Milk Whey

ONE-THIRD of fresh buttermilk is allowed to two-thirds of sweet milk; put the milk into a sauce-pan, make it boiling hot, and then pour in the buttermilk, and gently stir it round the edges of the pan; let it come to a boil, take it off the fire, let it settle, and strain off the whey. Sour milk may be substituted for buttermilk. An excellent drink in fever.

Toast and Water

PARE the crust off a thin slice of stale bread, toast it brown upon both sides, doing it equally and slowly, that it may harden without being burnt; put it into a jug, and pour upon it boiling water; cover the jug with a saucer, and set in a cool place.

Arrow-Root Water

BOIL the peel of half a lemon in a quart of water; pour it over a table-spoonful of arrow-root which has been mixed with a little cold water, and that poured off; stir it well; sweeten it with loaf sugar, and again stir it over the fire till it boil; before drinking it, squeeze in a little lemon juice. This is a grateful drink to a sick person.

Bread Jelly for an Invalid

CUT the crumb of a penny roll into thin slices, and toast them equally of a pale brown; boil them gently in a quart of water till it will jelly, which may be known by putting a little in a spoon to cool; strain it upon a bit of lemon-peel, and sweeten it with sugar. A little wine may be added.

Luncheon for an Invalid

PUT bread crumbs and red currant, or any other jelly, alternately into a tumbler, and when nearly half full, fill it up with milk.

Sago

CLEANSE it by first soaking it an hour in cold water, and then washing it in fresh water. To a tea-cupful add a quart of water and a bit of lemon-peel, simmer it till the berries are clear, season with wine and spice, and boil it all up together. The sago may be boiled with milk instead of water, till reduced to one-half, and served without seasoning.

Mulled Wine

PUT into a pint of port wine two or three cloves and a bit of cinnamon; boil it for a few minutes; take out the spice, sweeten it with loaf sugar, and grate in a little nutmeg. Serve with a slice of toasted bread, the crust pared off, and cut into oblong pieces. The port wine is sometimes boiled with a third of its quantity of water.

Gloucester Jelly

Boil, in two quarts of water, till reduced to one quart, the following ingredients:– Hartshorn shavings, isinglass, ivory shavings, barley, and rice, one ounce of each.

When this jelly, which is light, and very nourishing, is to be taken, a few table-spoonfuls of it must be dissolved in a little milk, together with a bit of cinnamon, lemon-peel, and sugar. It will be very good without the seasoning.

To make Arrow-Root

Mix with two or three table-spoonfuls of arrow-root half a pint of cold water; let it stand for nearly a quarter of an hour, pour off the water, and stir in some pounded sugar; boil a pint of milk, and pour it gradually upon the arrow-root, stirring it one way all the time. Or it may be made with water in which lemon-peel has been boiled, and then a glass of port or white wine and a little nutmeg stirred into it.

Cream of Tartar

When to be taken, either medicinally or as a cooling drink, may be mixed, in the proportion of a heaped teaspoonful to a pint of water, which has, when hot, been poured upon the thin peel of half a lemon, and allowed to stand till quite cold. Sweeten with honey or sugar.

Suet Milk

Cut into very small shavings one ounce of fresh mutton suet; dissolve it slowly over the fire in one pint of milk, together with a bit of lemon-peel and cinnamon; sweeten it with pounded loaf sugar.

Saline Draught

Salt of wormwood, twenty grains, lemon juice, a table-spoonful, water, two table-spoonfuls, magnesia, twenty grains; mix it in a tumbler, together with a little pounded sugar, and take two or three of these in the day.

For a Cough

Two ounces of squilled vinegar, two ounces of clarified honey, two drachms of tincture of tolu, sixty drops of laudanum; two teaspoonfuls to be taken morning and evening by a grown person, one by a child.

Sage Gargle

Boil quickly in a pint of water, a large handful of sage leaves; cover the pan closely, and when reduced to one-half, strain it; when cold, mix it with the same quantity of port wine and of vinegar; sweeten it with honey, or with brown sugar. The decoction of sage may be used alone as a gargle, or with vinegar and honey, without the port wine. Or gargle with vinegar and water.

Bitters

Put into a quart of sherry one ounce of best pounded aloes, the same of rhubarb and of liquorice root, also one tea-spoonful of powdered ginger; keep it in the sun, or by the fire, for eight or ten days, shaking it frequently; let it settle for twenty-four hours; strain it through flannel. Two or three tea-spoonfuls relieve headaches and weakness of the stomach.

Lip Salve

One ounce and a half of white wax, two ounces of fresh suet, one ounce of oil of sweet almonds, half an ounce of spermaceti, two drachms of alkanet root, two drachms of balsam of Peru, one ounce of finely-pounded double-refined sugar, and six raisins sliced; simmer all these ingredients together for ten minutes, and strain it through muslin. Or chapped lips may be washed frequently with an equal quantity of loaf sugar and salt dissolved in hot water.

Cold Cream

Cut one cake of white wax into thin shavings, and dissolve it in one pint of oil of sweet almonds, together with a table-spoonful of powdered spermaceti, and one of fresh lard; when melted, throw it into a large basin of cold water, and, with a silver spoon, beat it about briskly for half an hour; pour off the water, add as much fresh water, and beat it again for the same length of time; then pour off the water, and add a quart of rose water, and beat it briskly for half an hour. Put it into small pots, filling them not quite full, and pour a little fresh rose water on the top; cover them closely with bladder and paper.

Red Lavender Drops

Fill a quart bottle with the blossoms of lavender, and pour on it as much brandy as it will contain; let it stand ten days, then strain it, and add, of nutmeg bruised, cloves, mace, and cochineal, a quarter of an ounce each, and bottle it for use. In nervous cases, a little may be taken dropped on a bit of sugar; and in the beginning of a bowel complaint, a tea-spoonful, taken in half a glass of peppermint water, will often prove efficacious.

For the Ear-Ache

DIP a little cotton wool into a mixture of oil of sweet almonds and laudanum, and put it into the ear; or apply a small poultice, in which is put a raw chopped clove of garlic.

Burns

APPLY to, or wrap round, the burnt part some folds of cotton wool, bought in sheets, or as it comes from the West Indies; however severe the pain may be, it will abate in a few hours. Should blisters rise, they may next day be carefully pricked with a needle, so as to break the skin as little as possible; and the cotton kept on till the cure is effected.

To Stop Violent Bleeding from a Cut

MAKE a paste, by mixing fine flower with vinegar, and lay it on the cut.

Harvest Bugs

MIX equal parts of oil of cloves, laudanum, and spirits of hartshorn, and apply it to the part affected.

Tooth Powder

MIX hartshorn shavings, calcined and pulverized, three-fifths; myrrh, pulverized, two-fifths.

Paste

RUB two table-spoonfuls of flour quite smooth in one pint of water; put it on the fire, and stir it constantly till it become clear, which it may be after boiling for about ten minutes. A stronger and more delicate paste may be made of starch, by boiling it for a few minutes after it has been prepared as for starching muslin.

La Tire, or London Candy

RUB some fresh butter over the bottom and sides of a brass-pan, and boil in it two quarts of good treacle, with a tea-spoonful of cinnamon, and a dessert-spoonful of ginger, the grated peel and juice of one or two lemons; a glass of rum may be added; stir it all the time it is boiling; in ten minutes or so drop a little upon a buttered plate, and if it harden, pour it from the pan over the bottom of buttered plates; as soon as it cools sufficiently to be handled safely, pull it out with a machine made for the purpose, or rub the hands with butter, and draw it out at arm's-length, then fold it, touching it as lightly as possible with the fingers; and so continue to work it till it hardens, and becomes of a light colour; it is then pulled out as quickly as possible into small sticks, which must be cut with a buttered knife on a table or board dusted with flour: narrow strips of whity-brown paper should be prepared to twist round the sticks as they are cut. The plates should also be buttered before the boiling commences, and every thing had in readiness; as no time is to be lost after the treacle is boiled.

Captain Hall's Sandwiches for Travellers

SPREAD butter, very thinly, upon the upper part of a stale loaf of bread cut very smooth, and then cut off the slice; now cut off another thin slice, but spread it with butter on the under side, without which precaution the two slices of bread will not fit one another. Next take some cold beef, or ham, and cut it into very minute particles. Sprinkle these thickly over the butter, and, having added a little mustard, put the slices face to face, and press them together. Lastly, cut the whole into four equal portions, each of which is to be wrapped in a separate piece of paper.

CHAPTER XX
POULTRY

MANAGEMENT OF POULTRY

WARM, dry, and shingly soil, like the sea beach, is best adapted for the rearing of poultry; and such may be artificially formed, where it is not afforded by nature. A yard or court being pitched upon, the foundation should be laid with chalk or bricklayers' rubbish, the surface to consist of sandy gravel; and considerable spots of it may be sown with common trefoil or wild clover, with a mixture of burnet, spurry, or star-grass, which last species is particularly salubrious to poultry. The surface must be sloped and drained, so as to avoid all stagnant moisture, and the whole enclosed with a fence, lofty, and so secured at the bottom that the smallest chicken may not find passage through.

The poultry houses within the court should have a southern aspect, and if the number of the stock be large the houses had far better be small and detached; and should they abut upon a stable, brew-house, or any conductor of warmth, it will be a farther advantage. The floors should consist of well-rammed chalk or earth, so that they may be easily swept clean. In the roof, which must be lofty, there should be only one long and level range of perches; and if in the wall steps be so placed that the poultry may jump from the one to the other, the ascent will be rendered easy to the perches, and also to the nests, for which boxes are the most convenient, when properly constructed. A few railed doors may be provided, to bang before the entrance of those in which hens are sitting. Nests for breeders are generally preferred upon the ground, on account of the danger of chickens falling from those which are placed above. In making the nest, soft and short straw should be chosen. Various beds, or heaps, of sifted ashes or very dry sand, should be placed in the yard, in which the fowls may have the comfort and benefit of rolling and bathing themselves; and a place of refuge should be provided for such hens or chickens as the cock has taken a dislike to.

The feeding-room, at once warm and airy, and large enough to accommodate twenty or thirty fowls, should have perches in it for those birds that are inclined to perch, which they will not be after they have become heavy. The floor may be slightly littered down; the litter often changed. The greatest cleanliness should be observed, and sandy gravel placed in several layers, and often changed. A sufficient number of troughs, for both water and food, should be placed around, that the stock may feed with as little interruption as possible from each other. This description of feeding room is well adapted for the feeding of young chickens; and it will be found most advantageous to put them up immediately on their being quitted by the hen, more particularly young cocks, and all those which stand high upon the legs.

Under a regular system, it would be preferable to separate entirely the aquatic from the other poultry, the aquatic to have their houses ranged along the banks of a piece of water, with a fence, and sufficiently capacious walks in front; access to the water by doors, to be closed at will.

The White Dorking

Is one of the largest of our fowls, and is a plentiful layer; the polanders are similar, but generally black; they are very ornamental, and one of the most useful varieties – they are sometimes called everlasting layers, and being least inclined to sit of any other breed, their eggs are frequently set under other hens. The flesh of the game fowl is superior to all other breeds of domestic fowls for richness and delicacy of flavour; but from their disposition to fight, they are difficult to be reared. Yellow-legged fowls are often of a tender constitution, and always inferior in the quality of their flesh. A young and healthy fowl may be known by the fresh and florid colour of the comb, the dryness of the eye, and the nostrils being free from any discharge, and the plumage glossy. The indications of old age are, paleness of the comb and gills, fulness of colour, and a sort of downy stiffness in the feathers, length and size of talons, the scales upon the legs becoming large and prominent. Delicate white hens do not lay so many eggs in a cold season as the more hardy coloured varieties. Cordial horse-ball is good to promote laying in cold weather, and also toast and ale.

A hen desirous of sitting should not be prevented by any violent means; allowing her to sit will probably not deter her so long from laying as harsh treatment. Those above the common size of their respective varieties are not preferable as layers or sitters. They are in their prime at three years, and decline after five. The number of hens to one cock from four to six. When a cock is moulting it should be withdrawn, and one that is known to and familiar with the hens substituted. When a turkey-hen becomes sick, it is found beneficial to pull out the feathers of the tail. It should be a general rule to breed from young stock. A two-years-old cock, and pullets in their second year, provided they have the best food, accommodation, and attendance, may be allowed to sit so early as January. Eggs for sitting should never exceed the age of a month; the newest laid to be preferred, and as nearly of a size as possible; those which have the circular flaw, indicating the double yolk, should be avoided. The number of eggs may be from nine to fifteen, according to the size of the fowl; an odd number should be chosen, that they may lie the closer, and they may be marked with a pen and ink, so that any new laid ones may be removed. An egg being broken in the nest, it should be cleared away, and the remainder washed with warm water. It is proper to place corn and water occasionally beside the sitting hen, withdrawing them as soon as she is satisfied. Hens sit twenty days.

The chickens first hatched should be taken from the nest, and secured in a basket of wool or soft hay, and kept, if the weather be cold, near the fire. They will require no food for some hours, even for twenty-four. The whole brood being hatched, the hen is to be placed for some days under coop, upon a dry place, and, if possible, not within reach of another hen, nor near numbers of young fowls. The first food split grits, afterwards tail corn. All watery food, soaked bread, or potatoes, improper as first food; hard-boiled eggs, and curd chopped small, is much approved; their water should be pure, and often renewed. There are pans made in such forms, that the chickens may drink without getting into the water; a basin turned down in the middle of a pan of water, will answer the end, the water running round it. They must not be let out early in the morning, or whilst the dew remains upon the ground, far less be suffered to range over the wet grass; and they should be cautiously guarded against sudden changes of the weather, or exposure to rain.

When the hen begins to roost, the chickens may be associated with the young poultry as nearly of their own age as possible, or put up to feed. In choosing full-sized fowls for feeding, the short-legged and early hatched always deserve a preference. There are various modes of feeding, but whether for domestic use or sale the best method is constant high keep from the beginning; their flesh will in consequence be more juicy and finer flavoured, and they will be always ready for the table, except in the moulting season, which is during the autumn for the old, and the spring for the young poultry. The pullets which have been hatched in March, if high fed from the beginning, will lay plentifully through the following autumn, and in February may be used for the table; about which period their laying will be finished. The fowls will be finest that have the run of the farm-yard; but they will be little inferior if accommodated and attended to as before directed, and allowed abundance and variety of wholesome food. Barley is the best grain for poultry, but they will thrive well on oats and tail wheat; heavy wheat is generally considered injurious; any light grain ground, together with peas, and made into brose, will be found excellent food; as also potatoes, when boiled, peeled, and made into thick brose with meal, that is, boiling water stirred into the mixture. A cock and two hens, having as much food as they choose to eat, will consume a quarter of a peck of the best barley in a week.

Turkeys

THE true black Norfolk turkey is esteemed superior to all others. One turkey cock is sufficient for six hens. The hen will cover, according to her size, from nine to fifteen eggs. Her term of sitting is thirty days, during which period constant attendance, with both food and water, is necessary. The chicks must be withdrawn from the nest as soon as hatched, and kept very warm. The hen and brood should be housed during a month or six weeks, and fed with barley or oatmeal, which may be mixed with young nettles chopped, or garden cresses, and kneaded with water as dry as possible. Their food should be often renewed, as also their drink, which should be water only. In case of the chicks appearing sickly, and the feathers ruffled, indicating a chill from severity or change of weather, half-ground malt may be mixed with the barleymeal, and by way of medicine, powdered caraway seeds; also artificial worms, that is, boiled meat pulled into strings, in running after which the chicks have a salutary exercise. This diet is beneficial for every species of chicks. All slop victuals should be avoided; and their being kept dry, warm, and clean, is of the utmost consequence. A fresh turf of short sweet grass daily, cleared from snails and slugs, which will scour young chicks, is very pleasing to them, and promotes their health. After a month or six weeks' confinement within doors, the hens may be cooped for another fortnight; when full grown, they will, in a good range, provide themselves throughout the day, requiring only to be fed at their outletting in the morning, and on their return at even. Sodden barley, or barley and wheat meal mixed, is the proper food for fattening turkeys. The flesh of the young cocks, intended for the table, will become more delicate if the fleshy substance which grows immediately above the bill be taken off when it is about a quarter of an inch long; a worsted thread tied round it will bring it off in a few weeks.

The Bustard

WILL probably thrive well on the same food as the turkey. It is seldom reared; but as its flesh has ever been considered most delicious, it appears particularly worthy of the attention of those who aim at variety and novelty.

Guinea and Pea Fowls

ARE in season when game is going out, namely, from February to June. The guinea fowl assimilates perfectly with the common species in habits and in kinds of food. They are very prolific, and their eggs nourishing and good. The peacock is not only ornamental, but useful for the destruction of all kinds of reptiles; but some are apt to tear to pieces young chickens and ducklings. They are also destructive in gardens. The cock requires from two to four hens. They are granivorous, like other domestic fowls, preferring barley.

The Duck

THE Rhone ducks are of a darker flesh, and more savoury, than the English duck, but somewhat coarse. The white variety of the English duck is never so high-flavoured as the darker colours. The Muscovy and other foreign varieties are kept more for curiosity than use. The white Aylesbury are a beautiful stock. The canvass-backed ducks of America are said to be the finest in the world; they have probably not yet been imported into Europe. The duck will cover from eleven to fifteen eggs, and she sits thirty days. One drake to five ducks is allowed. The duck, when sitting, requires a secret and safe place; but no farther attendance is necessary till the whole brood is hatched, when a coop should be prepared upon the short grass, if the weather is fine, or under shelter, if otherwise; a wide and flat dish of water, often to be renewed, standing at hand; barley, or any meal, the first food. In rainy weather particularly, it is useful to clip the tails of the ducklings, and the surrounding down underneath, that they may not draggle and weaken themselves. The duck should be cooped at a distance from any other; their confinement to the coop need seldom extend to a fortnight. Oats whole or bruised are the standard fattening material for ducks and geese, to which may be added peasemeal, as it may be required; and if they are confined, the house-wash may be mixed with their food. They are very fond of acorns, and will get fat on them alone.

The Goose

THE best geese in England are probably to be found on the borders of Suffolk and Norfolk, and in Berkshire. The foreign varieties are kept only for ornament. Their treatment is similar to that of ducks. Some cooling greens, clivers, or the like, may be mixed with their first food, namely, barleymeal, bruised oats, or fine pollards. Hemlock, or deadly nightshade, should be removed from the range of young geese; and both old and young are often killed by swallowing slips of yew after they are able to frequent the pond. The young geese will obtain their living, and few people favourably situated allow them any thing more excepting the vegetable produce of the garden; but to have fine geese, a little solid corn or pulse may be given morning and evening. Equal quantities of the meal of rye and pulse, mixed with skimmed-milk, form an excellent feeding article for geese and ducks.

Pigeons

THE proper place for the pigeon-house, or cot, is the poultry yard; it should have a south-west aspect. The common barred dovecot is well adapted to every situation, and pigeons do well near dwellings, stables, bakehouses, or such offices. Its situation will necessarily depend on convenience. One general rule must, however, be observed, that every pair of pigeons have two holes or rooms to nest in. Cleanliness is one of the first and most important considerations. They will thrive the better if cleaned daily and thoroughly once a-week – the floor covered with sifted gravel often renewed. They are exceedingly fond of water, and when confined in a room should have a pan of water, often renewed, as a bath; and to take their attention from the garden, and to prevent their picking the mortar from buildings, they should be provided with a salt cat, which is a dish of the following composition: – Loam, sand, mortar, fresh lime, bay salt, cummin, coriander, caraway seed, and allspice, moistened with beer, heaped up in the dish, and a piece of board placed upon the summit to prevent the birds from dunging upon it.

It is always injudicious to purchase old pigeons for stocking, as even cutting their wings will not insure their remaining. Squeakers, or such as have not yet flown, will become perfectly domesticated if confined for a short time. In justice to the farmer, the proprietor of pigeons ought to feed them regularly, more particularly in seedtime, and towards harvest, and also when the ground is bound by frost, or covered with snow. Tares, and the smallest kind of horse-bean, commonly called pigeon-beans, are both the best and cheapest food, and the pulse is better to be of the previous year.

CHAPTER XXI
THE DAIRY

A DAIRY-HOUSE ought to be well aired, free from damp, and situated so that a proper temperature may be preserved, – from 50° to 55° Fahrenheit. A milk dairy requires two apartments; one for the milk, the other for scalding and cleaning the different utensils. To secure a proper degree of heat for common purposes, a vacuity of eight or ten inches, left betwixt the wall and the lath and plaster, will be sufficient. The roof should be of thatch, three feet thick at the least, and should project completely over the walls on each side. To afford shade and a beneficial degree of coolness to the whole building, the outer doors may be made to open under a penthouse, or lean-to shed. It would be advantageous to have an icehouse attached to the dairy, as a small quantity of ice, placed when necessary in the milk-room, would soon lower the temperature to any degree that might be wanted. If the cold in winter should become too great, a barrel of hot water, close stopped, or a few hot bricks, placed on the floor or table of the milk-room, would readily counteract its effects; a chafing-dish with burning coals should never be used. The utensils required for a dairy of twenty cows, may, in most cases, be provided for L.20 or L.30. Wood has in general been employed in their construction, and is, upon the whole, the most eligible material; lead, brass, and copper, are altogether inadmissible; the least objectionable of all the metallic milk-dishes are probably those which have been lately invented by Mr Braid, of the Shotts iron-works in Linlithgowshire.

A proper choice of cows is of the greatest importance. Of the black cattle of the island, the short-horned, or Dutch, and the long-horned, or Lancashire, are in general preferred; the first yields the greatest quantity of milk; that of the second is not so abundant, but richer; the polled, or Galloway cows, are excellent milkers, and the Suffolk duns are much esteemed, as are also the Ayrshire cows. For the management of cows, it is of the greatest consequence to keep them easy, clean, and well aired; when they are turned out to pasture, they must not be over driven, or have so far to travel as to induce fatigue. Their food in winter may be of two kinds, either dry or green; of dry food, hay and straw are almost the only kinds used; the most profitable kinds of green food are parsnips, carrots, cabbages, and turnips; from one or two hundred pounds a-day of cabbages or turnips will be consumed by a middle-sized cow. By means of stall-feeding, with green crops, a cow can be kept in milk not only for a month longer in autumn than by the common modes but even through the whole winter season. When green succulent food cannot be procured, it will be judicious to give them their preserved fodder either boiled, or steeped in warm water. It is found to be beneficial to them to vary their food from time to time, and for a few weeks before calving, they should have every night a little hay, or a somewhat greater allowance of green food.

On the day of calving, they should be kept in; and immediately after, it is useful to give them a handful or two of meal, mixed with lukewarm water. For a fortnight after calving, they should have, with their green food, a little hay, or chopped straw, with some ground or crushed oats. This food ought to be put into their stalls in small quantities at a time, and a little salt given with it improves the quality, and increases the quantity of milk. The land necessary to maintain a cow, may, at an average, be stated from two to three English acres, if there be taken into account, the corn, hay, straw, and every thing else the animal consumes.

One dairy-maid may manage a dozen or fifteen cows, having assistance in the milking of them. Cows should be milked in the house rather than in the field; three times a-day, at least, in summer: early in the morning, at noon, and just before nightfall. It is of the utmost consequence, that the whole milk secreted be at each milking drawn away. It may be laid down as a pretty general rule, that eighteen pounds of milk will yield one pound of butter, and that this is the produce of a single cow per day; some, however, will furnish twice or even thrice this quantity. The best age for a milk cow is betwixt four and ten. When old, she will give more milk, but of an inferior quality.

Of the Prevention and Cure of Diseases Incident to Black Cattle

REGULAR watering, as well as sound food, prevents many diseases; and cattle ought to be carefully kept from smelling carrion, or chewing bones.

The diseases of cattle may be divided into three classes. The first proceeds from feeding too greedily on clover or common grass, particularly in the fall of the year. The remedy usually employed is the probang, a flexible instrument, which being passed into the stomach, the confined air rushes out; when this is not at hand, three small canes, each six feet long, are bound together with waxed packthread, and a smooth ball of wood, about the size of a pigeon's egg, fixed at the end; in order to pass it down the throat, an assistant must lay hold of the nostrils, and keep out the head as nearly as possible in a line with the throat. The food that is in consequence thrown up, must be removed from the mouth; after which, the animal should be turned out into bare pasture, or get twice a-day, for three days, half a pint of mild ale, with one race of ginger grated into it. But in the first stage of the complaint, a table-spoonful of hartshorn, mixed with a pint of train-oil, will generally effect a cure.

The diseases of the second class proceed from derangement of the digestive system and occur chiefly late in winter or in spring. They are moor-ill, yellows, red-water, flatulent colic, scouring, tail-rot, joint-fallen, &c., for which the following opening medicine is administered: – Mix, for one drench, of common salt four ounces, Barbadoes aloes half an ounce, ginger one drachm, water one quart, and anodyne carminative tincture two ounces, or a glass of gin.

Having administered in the morning the opening medicine, for scouring or for tail-rot, the following cordial may be given in the evening; – Take of powdered catechu two drachms, fresh powdered allspice two drachms, fresh powdered caraways half an ounce, good strong beer or ale half a pint, table-beer or water half a pint; let the ingredients be simmered for a few minutes in the table-beer or water, and let the strong beer be added at the time the drench is given.

The third class depends on repletion of the blood vessels, and prevails most in summer; the symptoms of fever are, quick breathing, hot horns and ears, &c. The remedies to be employed are copious bleeding, that is, till the animal becomes faint, (a young and healthy cow will generally bear the loss of two gallons of blood,) opening medicine, and putting the animal on short or bare pasture.

The only application necessary for swollen udder, or swollen joints, is neat's feet oil, or olive oil; when the swelling is considerable, fomentation, with hot water having a little grease in it, may be of use. The best remedy for sore teats is rubbing them with hog's lard.

When a cow chokes upon a turnip, pour down its throat salt and water; if that will not do, use a hornful of salt and melted grease, such as hog's lard, or any kind of common grease; warm oil and salt would probably have the same effect.

When a calf seems indisposed and loose in the bowels, a little powdered chalk may be added to its milk; or boil a large table-spoonful of potato flour in each meal of milk, to bring it to the consistence of middling cream. When costive, the following laxative may be given; and when it scours, the following cordial will be found effectual: –

Laxative

OF common salt, from half an ounce to one ounce, aloes one drachm, soda one drachm, ginger half a drachm, water half a pint, and gin a table-spoonful, well mixed together.

Cordial

CARAWAY seeds, recently powdered, half an ounce, ginger half a drachm, carbonate of soda one drachm, water eight ounces, and brandy or gin one ounce, mixed well.

Calves

SHOULD, be taken from the cow immediately, and whether to be reared or fatted, are best fed entirely on milk; but if it be scarce, they may get milk-porridge, or turnips boiled to a mash, and mixed with two pints of milk at each meal, which should be given three times a-day the first month, twice the second, and once the third. When the calf is to be fed for the table, it should have as much milk, warm from the cow, (the last-drawn, to have extremely fine veal,) as it will take three times a-day. When it is five weeks old, it should be bled, and again a week after; in a few days more, it may be killed. Some persons consider bleeding unnecessary.

Butter

IN the production of good butter, more depends on management than on the quality of the cow, or the richness of its food. When dairying is conducted on a great scale, the horizontal, commonly called the barrel-churn, is the best; and on a small scale the patent box-churn will be found most eligible; the vertical, or pump-churn, is well adapted to the operation of making butter from the produce of a few cows only. Milk is not at the best till about four months after the cow has calved; and the degree of heat most favourable to the production of cream from milk, is from 50° to 55° Fahrenheit. In summer, the milk should be allowed to stand half an hour before it be put into the pans, which should not exceed two inches in depth. In winter, it should be set as soon as possible. From the last-drawn half of the milk, if allowed to stand till it tastes perceptibly sourish, cream of a superior quality will be obtained, and its quantity not considerably less than if the whole were set apart for the production of cream. Sweet cream requires four times as much churning as that which has become sour by standing. From twelve to twenty hours in summer, and about twice as long in winter, should be permitted to elapse before the milk is skimmed – after it is put into the pans, during the hot summer months, this should always be done in the morning before the dairy becomes warm. The cream should then be deposited in a jar, placed in the coolest part of the dairy, stirred often, and shifted every morning, into a clean and well-scalded jar, or other vessel. In hot weather, churning should be performed, if possible, every other day, and never less frequently than twice a-week. The operation ought to be moderate, equable, and uninterrupted. In summer, the churn ought to be chilled with cold water before the cream be put into it; and during the process of churning, it should be immersed in cold water, to the depth of a foot or so, provided a pump-churn be used; to a barrel-churn, wet cloths may be applied. In winter, heat must be cautiously employed. It is better to steep the churn for some time in warm water, than to pour water into it before churning; it may be placed in the warmest part of the house, but not close to the fire.

The cows should not be fed with turnips till after they are milked, otherwise the milk and butter will have an unpleasant taste; late in the season, when the turnips are not so good, this precaution may be insufficient. To counteract the effects of the turnip, or any other green food, boil two ounces of saltpetre, or the same quantity of cream of tartar, in a quart of water; and, when cold, add a table-spoonful, or more, if necessary, of the liquid, every other day to the collected cream.

Method of Making up Butter

WHEN the butter is sufficiently gathered in the churn, which is known by the largeness of the lumps and the cleanness of the dashers, it is taken out, kneaded in a bowl, or other shallow vessel, to let out the buttermilk, spread thin over the inside of the bowl, and clean cold water poured over it; kneaded, broken, and re-spread in the water; the water poured off; the butter beaten in large lumps, or handfuls, of three or four pounds, against the sides of the bowl, respread, salted, the salt worked in, rewashed, and rebeaten until the water comes off unsullied, which it will do after two or three washings. It is then broken, into pound lumps, rebeaten against the bowl, and printed, or otherwise made up.

There is a finishing operation which is sometimes given in the neighbourhood of London. It is thus performed: – The bowl or tray being wetted, to prevent the butter from sticking to it, and a cheese-cloth, strainer, or other cloth being washed in clean cold water, and wrung as dry as possible, a pound lump of butter is placed in the bowl, and with a stroke of the hand, proportioned to the stiffness of the butter, is beaten with the cloth; as the pat of butter becomes flat and thin, it is rolled up with the cloth, by a kind of dexterity which can only be acquired by practice, and again beaten flat; the dairy-woman, every three or four strokes, rolling up either one side or the other of the pat, and moving it about in the bowl, to prevent its sticking. As soon as the cloth fills with moisture, which it extracts from the butter, and imbibes in the manner of a spunge, it is wrung, and rewashed in clean cold water. Each pound of butter requires, in cool weather, four or five minutes to be beaten thoroughly, but two minutes are at any time of essential service. Before the dairy-woman begins to take the butter out of the churn, she first scalds, and then plunges immediately into cold water, every vessel and thing which she is about to make use of, in order to prevent the butter from sticking to them. In summer, when the butter is very soft, it is sometimes necessary to rub them, after scalding, with salt, which greatly assists the wood in retaining the moisture. She also puts her own hands into the hottest water she can bear them in, rubs them with salt, and immediately plunges them into cold water. This she repeats as often as she finds the butter stick to them.

The practice of washing butter in cold water is so general, that it seems necessary to describe it; but those who can divest themselves of prejudice, will find, on trial, that the butter may be made better, and perfectly free from milk, by beating and kneading, without pouring any water on it. When formed into pats, it may be put into a dish, and that floated in water till required; or it may be salted in the usual manner.

The best season for curing butter is from the beginning of August until the end of September; but if the pasture be rank, whether through soil, manure, or herbage, it is generally injudicious to put down butter from it. Care must be taken that the firkin be well seasoned before butter be put into it. The readiest method is by the use of unslaked lime, or a large quantity of salt-and-water well boiled, with which it should be scrubbed, and afterwards thrown into cold water, to remain three or four days, till wanted; and before receiving the butter, scrubbed and rubbed with salt.

To Put down Butter

After being worked up with salt, in the proportion of half an ounce to the pound and half of butter, and having lain in pound lumps twenty-four hours, the dairywoman takes two or three of the lumps, joins them together, and kneads them in the manner in which paste is kneaded. This brings out a considerable quantity of watery brine, which being poured out of the bowl, the butter is beaten with a cloth as before. The jar having been previously boiled, or otherwise thoroughly cleaned, and having stood to be perfectly cool and dry, the butter is thrown into it, and kneaded down, as firm and close as possible, with the knuckles and the cloth alternately; being careful not to have any hollow cell or vacuity for the air to lodge in, more particularly round the outsides, between the butter and the jar; for this purpose, she repeatedly draws her finger round the sides of the jar, pressing the butter hard, and thereby uniting intimately the jar and the butter. It is fortunate when the jar can be filled at one churning; but when this cannot be done conveniently, the top is left level, and when the next churning of butter is to be added, the surface is raised into inequalities, and the two churnings mixed into one mass. The jar being filled to within two or three inches of the top, it is filled up with brine, made by boiling salt and water, in the proportion of a handful to a pint, ten minutes or a quarter of an hour, straining it into a cooling vessel, and when perfectly cold, putting it upon the butter, about one and a half or two inches deep. If a wooden bung be put upon this, a bladder laid over it, and the jar kept in a dry place, the butter thus preserved will remain perfectly sweet for almost any length of time. The jar should be wider at the bottom than at the top, resembling the upright churn, the top of it being sufficiently wide to admit of its being filled conveniently, but not wider.

Another method of Preparing Butter

MIX one part of saltpetre, one of common salt, and two of sugar. This, thoroughly wrought into the butter, will keep it for a very long time, and communicates to it no salt nor disagreeable taste.

Scotch method of Salting Butter

WASH the butter thoroughly in cold water, pressing it strongly and frequently with the hands or broad pieces of wood, and changing the water till it comes off clear; then spread it out in thin layers, sprinkle it with salt, in the proportion of one ounce to every three pounds of butter, and work it well. In this manner each churning is prepared, till the quantity required to fill the kit is obtained. Make a pickle of salt-and-water strong enough to bear an egg, and boil it with two ounces of loaf sugar. Take each making separately, press all the watery brine from it, and work it in a little of the prepared pickle; if it should not come off clear, repeat the washing in fresh pickle. The kit having been well scoured, rubbed with dry salt, and rinsed out with a little of the pickle, pack into it separately each making of butter to within two inches of the top; put some pickle on it, and a clean linen tag; the head of the vessel is then put on, and should always be kept close upon it.

Method of Preserving Butter with Honey

THE butter being cleaned from the milk, it is put into jars, and melted on a stove, or in a water bath on the fire; just before it boils, it is put in a cool place to settle, and must never be stirred. When a little stiff, the froth is taken off the top, and the dregs removed, it is then worked up with honey, in the proportion of an ounce to each pound of butter. Preserved in this way, and potted, it will keep as long as salted butter; will be found more suitable for the table when to be eaten with sweetmeats, and, in many respects, better adapted for kitchen use.

To make Salt Butter Fresh

PUT four pounds of salt butter into a churn with four quarts of new milk, and a little arnatto; churn them together, and in about an hour take out the butter, and treat it exactly as fresh butter, washing it in water, and adding the customary quantity of salt.

Cheese

IN cheese-making, it is of the utmost consequence to have good rennet, which may be obtained from the stomachs of calves, hares, or poultry; that from the maw or stomach of calves is most commonly used, and the following Scotch method of preparing it seems to be the simplest and best:– When the stomach or bags, usually termed the yirning, in dairy language, is taken from the calf's body, straw, or any other impurity found in it, ought to be removed from the curdled milk, which, with the chyle, must be carefully preserved; a handful of salt is put inside; it is then rolled up, and put into a basin or jar, and a handful of salt strewed over it; after standing closely covered for eight or ten days, it is taken out and tied up in a piece of white paper, and hung up near a fire to dry, like bacon, and will be the better for hanging a year before it is infused. When rennet is wanted, the bag with its contents is cut small, and put into a jar or can, with a handful or two of salt; new whey, or boiled water, cooled to 65°, is put upon it. If the stomach is from a newly-dropped calf, about three pints of liquor may be employed. If the calf has been fed for four or five weeks, which will yield more rennet than that of one twice that age, eight pints or more of liquid may be put to the bag in mash. After the infusion has remained in the jar from one to three days, the liquid is drawn off, and about a pint more of whey or water put on the bag; when it has stood a day or two, it is also drawn off, strained with the first liquid and bottled for use as rennet. Some people put a dramglassful of whisky to each quart or choppin of the rennet. Thus prepared, it may be used immediately, or kept for months. One table-spoonful of it will coagulate, in ten or fifteen minutes, thirty gallons, or sixty Scotch pints, of milk, which will yield more than 24 lbs. avoirdupois of cheese. In England, the curdled milk is generally washed from the stomach, and in consequence, the rennet is so much weaker than that made in Scotland, that double the quantity is used, and it requires from one to sometimes three hours to form the milk into curd. The milk ought to be set, that is, the rennet put to it, at 85° or 90° of Fahrenheit, when the heat of the air is at 70°; but as the season gets colder, the heat of the milk should be increased, and covered till it coagulates.

Cheese-racks save labour in turning. The plate-rack, with four or five tier, one above another, seems to be the best form. If the cheeses be of different sizes, it ought to be much narrower at the top than at the bottom; and to preserve the cheeses from vermin, it ought to stand on legs about two feet high, with a broad base board projecting over the legs.

A One-Meal Cheese

WHEN the milk has been brought in warm from the cow, it is put into the cheese-tub, and the rennet added to it; the quantity must depend on its strength. As soon as coagulation has taken place, the curd is broken and gathered. A cheese-knife is employed to cut the curd in various directions; and this being allowed to subside for a short time, is again cut by the knife more freely than before, and the operation continued till the whole be reduced to small uniform particles. This business may occupy about the space of twenty minutes, after which the cheese-tub is again covered with a cloth, and allowed to remain nearly the same length of time. When the particles have subsided, the whey is laded off, the curd properly pressed by the bottom of the skimming dish, the hands, or a semicircular board and weight adapted to the size of the tub. The cheese-knife is now employed, as before, to cut the curd, thereby promoting the free separation of the whey; and pressure is again applied, till it be all drained off. The curd is then put into two or three separate vessels, and the dairy-woman breaks it with her hands as small as possible. During this part of the process salt is scattered over the curd, and intimately mixed with it; the proportion is generally regulated by taste – a handful of salt for every six gallons of milk, or about half an ounce to the pound, may be allowed.

Having made choice of a vat, commonly made of elm, with holes in the lower part of it, proportioned to the quantity of curd, a cloth is spread over it, and the curd put in by little and little, breaking it all the while; and having filled the vat, heaped up, and rounded above its top, the cloth is folded over it, a board of an inch thick is laid on the vat, and the whole put into the press, the power of which ought to be applied gradually, beginning with about half a hundred-weight. When it has been an hour or two in the press, it is taken out, the cheese placed in a vessel of hot whey or water, to stand for an hour or two, to harden the skin. It is then wiped dry, covered with a clean dry cloth; again placed in the vat, which is also wiped dry, and put under the press, to remain for six or eight hours. At this period of the process, if any of the edges happen to project, they are pared off, and the cheese is pricked all over with a small bodkin an inch or two deep. It is then wrapped in a clean dry cloth, and replaced in the vat, twice a-day, at least during two days, when it is finally removed, and put into the cheese-rack, or on a dry board, and turned every day for about a week. A small quantity of dry moss may be put under it.

When two meals of milk are used, unless the weather be very hot, a portion of the creamed milk of the first meal, as a half, or third, being placed in a brass pan, over a furnace, or in a vessel of hot water, is made scalding hot. Half of it is then poured into the pan in which the cream of this milk had been placed. The hot milk and cream, being now intimately mixed, are poured into the cheese-tub, and the warm milk added that had just come in from the cow.

In making cheeses of the inferior kind, as from skimmed milk, where, from its tendency to acidity, there is a risk that it will break, or curdle, while over the fire, the whole is brought to a proper temperature by the addition of hot water.

The cooler the milk, the more tender and delicate the curd becomes; on the contrary, if the milk be too hot, the curd proves tough and hard. The principal thing in skim-milk cheese operations is cleanliness, which is indeed the life and soul of dairy management. Wooden vessels in which milk has soured, ought to be washed with water into which some potash or lime has been thrown, then filled with water, which should be changed every hour in the course of a day or so, and afterwards scalded and well dried, before milk be again put into them.

The colouring matter arnatto adds nothing to the goodness of the cheese, but is perfectly harmless. An ounce of it is sufficient to colour a hundred-weight of cheese. When it is to be used, tie up as much of the substance as is required, in a linen bag, and put it into half a pint of warm water, to stand over night. The whole of this infusion is in the morning mixed with the milk in the cheese-tub, and the rag dipped in the milk rubbed on the palm of the hand, as long as any of the colouring matter can be made to come away.

To produce the Blue Coat, or Blue Mould, in Cheese

As soon as the cheese has become firm enough to be handled with safety, it may be brushed with a hard brush, frequently dipped in whey, and when nearly dry, rubbed over with a cloth on which fresh butter had been spread; this operation of washing, rubbing, and turning, to be repeated once every day, for some weeks, or till the cheese has acquired a rich golden polish, and the blue coat begins to appear.

Stilton Cheese

Take fifteen gallons of milk, warm from the cow; put twelve pints of sweet cream in a small tub, and pour on it a kettleful of boiling water; stir it till it be well mixed, and then put it into the cheese-tub, with the milk; when it is at 90° Fahrenheit, add the rennet, when it has coagulated, break the curd a little; put a thin cloth over it, and take the whey off through it; when as much has been taken off as will come easily, put the curd into a bag or net, and let it hang till it give over dripping, then cut the curd in pieces, and lay it in as much cold water as will covert it; let it lie an hour, and as the pieces are taken out, strew a little salt upon them, and put them into the vat, first breaking the top a little, to make it join with the next piece; then lay a small weight upon it, so as not to occasion the whey to come off white. It must be turned every three hours the first day, and three times a-day for three days, changing the cloth every time it is turned in the vat, and keeping it under a moderate pressure; it is then taken out of the vat, swathed tight till it begin to dry the bandage, which must be changed every twenty-four hours; it ought to be rubbed with a little salt before it is bandaged, and, for a considerable time, wiped and turned every day. The best season for making this cheese is from July to October.

Another way to make Stilton Cheese

The rennet being added to fifteen gallons of milk, it is allowed to stand an hour, when the whey is taken off slowly, breaking the curd as little as possible; this operation will occupy about the space of an hour and a half; cold water is then poured over the curd, so as to cover it, and when it has stood twenty minutes, the water is drained off, and the curd is broken, and salt added; a pound of newly-churned butter, or a quart of fresh cream, is then rubbed thoroughly into it, and it is put into the vat, and placed under a pressure of about twenty-two ounces; the cloth is changed every six or seven hours for some days, and in five or six days, it may be taken out of the vat.

Auchtertyre Stilton Cheese

To fifteen gallons of mid-day milk, add the cream taken from the same quantity of morning milk, put to it the rennet, and when it has coagulated, break the curd very much, and let it stand a little, that the whey may rise to the top; take it completely off, and work into it from six ounces to half a pound of salt, according to its strength. Place the vat or hoop (which should be long and narrow, made open at both ends, and without holes in the sides – thirteen inches by twelve is a good proportion for this quantity of milk) in a wooden milk cooler, pack the curd into it without any cloth under it, and then put on the top a round board made to fit closely into the vat; place a weight of four or five pounds upon it, and next evening shake the cheese carefully from the vat; bind a cloth round it, and change it for a dry one every day, till the cheese become firm and dry in the skin.

Bath Cream Cheese

THREE gallons of new milk, one of hot water, and one pint of cream, are mixed together, and a larger proportion of rennet added than for milk alone; when the curd is come, it is broken a little, and the whey dripped from it; a gallon of cold water is then poured over it, and it is again broken and dripped: the same process being repeated a third time, the curd is put into two quarts of boiling water, and the most of the whey squeezed out; it is then drained, put into the vat, and pressed for three hours; turned, and pressed for three hours more, which is sufficient. No salt nor colouring is necessary.

A Day Cheese

ONE pint of cream being mixed with twelve pints of noon-day milk, warm from the cow, a little rennet is added, and when the curd is come, the whey is pressed out gently, so as to break the curd as little as possible; it is then laid in a cloth, and put into a small sieve; the cloth is changed every hour during the day, and in twenty-four hours it will be fit for use. It may be served on a breakfast plate, with vine leaves under it, and will keep perfectly good only one day.

New Cheese

To six quarts of new milk from the cow, a little hot water, and rennet to turn it, are added; when the curd is come, it is cut twice across with a cheese-knife or spoon; then put into a cheese-cloth, and hung up; in half an hour it is again divided with the cheese-knife, hung up, and allowed to remain till night, when it is put into the press; the following day it is taken out, and each side well rubbed with a little salt. It will be fit for use in two days.

CHAPTER XXII
BREWING

PREPARATORY REMARKS

THE utensils must be large in proportion to the extent of the brewing to be carried on; in most families that point is determined by the size of the washing copper. For two kinds of beer, namely, nine gallons of one sort, (ale,) and nine gallons of another sort, (table beer,) the capacity of the copper should not be less than thirteen gallons. The size of the tub must be adapted to the mode of brewing to be pursued. If it is proposed to mash only twice, its capacity should be eighteen gallons: it ought to be narrower at top than at bottom. Two-third parts of any broad-bottomed cask will do very well for carrying out the operations of mashing in the small way. A metal cock is preferable to a wooden.

For coolers, common washing-tubs will do tolerably well. For each firkin (nine gallons) of liquor to be brewed, (containing ale and beer together,) let these tubs contain on the whole fourteen gallons; if the number can be conveniently increased, it will expedite the cooling process. For a brewing of eighteen gallons, whether of the same or different liquors, one sixteen and one twelve gallon tub are required, the larger tub being intended to serve in the threefold capacity of receiver, cooler, and gyle-tun. The tub intended to serve as underback, of receiver of the running wort from the mash-tub, ought to have its capacity divided into gallons; it may be done by notches cut in the surface, or small nails driven into the wood. A few pails should also be ready at hand. A gyle-tun ought properly to be narrow in proportion to its depth; but a cask of any shape, simply deprived of its head, allowing fifteen gallons capacity for every nine gallons of liquor intended to be suffered to ferment in it, will do very well. A common thermometer, with a metal scale, enclosed in a tin case, should be provided to ascertain the temperature of the water; but if there should not be one at hand, heat 220 measures, gallons or quarts, of water, according to the quantity required, and, when it boils, add 200 similar measures of cold water.

Barrels of eighteen gallons capacity are most convenient and economical for strong beer.

Cleanliness cannot be too much attended to in the brewing process. Some days before brewing, all the casks and tubs should be filled with water, to render them tight; and, after the brewing utensils are made use of, they should be thoroughly washed out; during the summer, the vessels may be scoured with lime water; and the copper ought to be kept especially clean. The moment a cask is empty, fasten down the vent peg, and stop the tap-hole with a cork well fitted and hammered into its place.

PALE-COLOURED malt is preferable to amber-coloured malt; if it be new, it should be left exposed to the open air one or two days after grinding, before it be used; if old, it should be ground the one day and used the next. When it is ground too finely, it clogs the mash, and impedes the draining of the wort; but every grain should be bruised. When economy is an object, a quantity of molasses or muscovado sugar may be substituted for a portion of the malt; 12 lbs. of molasses, or 10 lbs. of sugar, are equal to one bushel of malt; when used, it may be dissolved in the water employed for the second and third mashing. Farnham hops are esteemed the best; Nottinghamshire, termed Northclay hops, have a rank flavour in beer newly brewed, and should therefore only be used for strong keeping beers. Worcester hops have a flavour peculiarly mild and delicate.

Yeast produced from the fermentation of strong ale or porter is the best.

Quantity of ale or table-beer to be brewed from a given quantity of malt and hops: –

From a quarter of malt may be brewed 72 gallons of ale, or 144 of table-beer; or 27 of ale, and 90 of table beer. In mashing, the quantity of water employed must exceed the beer required in the proportion of six gallons to every bushel; three will be left in the goods, and the other three evaporated in the boiling, cooling, and working. The wort may be all mixed together in the gyle-tun; or, if strong ale be required, the first and second may be fermented separately from the third, which will be small beer. If the strong ale be desired particularly fine, the second and third may be fermented together, or each mashing may be kept separate; the first for strong ale, the second for keeping beer, and the third small beer for immediate use.

If the beer be not intended for keeping, one bushel of malt and ten ounces of hops will produce 12 gallons of common or table-ale; and ale brewers allow one measure of such ale to be equal to two of small beer. From one bushel of malt, therefore may be brewed 24 gallons of table-beer, without any table-ale; or nine gallons of ale, and six of table-beer; or six of ale, and twelve of table-beer. This is the smallest quantity of malt that should be employed for brewing twelve gallons of table-ale. If the ale be intended for keeping, it is advisable to allow six bushels (a boll) of pale malt to brew a hogshead (541 gallons) of good ale. The quantity of hops must be suited to the taste of the consumers; for those who do not like the strong flavour of the hop, two pounds in winter and three in summer may be allowed to the boll.

The mashing is done by two, three, and sometimes four infusions of hot water. The degree of heat depends on the combination of so many circumstances, that it cannot be fixed by any certain rule. When too hot, it forms the malt into a pulp or paste, so that it will not run out of the mash-turn, and the liquor will neither produce wort of good quality, nor in any considerable quantity. This is more particularly the case when the malt is low ground, that is, fine. When the water is of too low a heat, the beer will be spiritless, and liable to turn sour. A large quantity is mashed at a lower heat than a small; and when beer is intended for keeping, the water should be of a higher temperature. Well-made malt may be mashed at the highest heat; the extremes may be stated at 145° and 190° of Fahrenheit.

The first mash stands longer, and is taken at a lower heat, than the second, which again bears the same relation to the third. If the goods be glutinous, a longer time will be required for spending the tap, as the drawing off the wort is called. After it is drawn off, it should be boiled as soon as possible.

When the process of mashing commences, pour into the mash-tun four gallons of boiling water for every peck of malt to be employed; if the copper is not sufficiently capacious, boil the remaining quantity of water as quickly as possible, and add it to the mash. When the water has cooled down to the temperature of, say 170°, let one person gradually pour the malt into the tun, while another stirs and mixes it well with the water, which will occupy half an hour at least; then cover up the tun with blankets, carpets, or whatever else is ready at hand. The usual mode of covering with a cap of grist is a waste of malt. When the mash has stood one hour and a half in winter, and one hour in summer, let the wort run off into the vessel destined to receive it, returning the first gallon, which may be thick, to the .mash. While this mash is preparing, let the copper be again filled with water for the second mash, for which two gallons of water may be employed for every piece.

Let it be poured on the malt by one person, while another plies the oar for half an hour; after it has stood an hour, draw it off; if it be intended to brew only one kind of liquor, the second wort may run into the receiver containing the first wort. The third mash should be made with the remaining quantity of water, and may stand three quarters of an hour. The grist may be mashed in two operations; but it is always preferable to make three mashes.

To boil the wort. – Put along with the first ale wort (supposing it to have been kept separate for the purpose of brewing ale) the whole quantity of hops into the copper, boil the mixture till the liquor breaks, or becomes clouded with large fleecy flakes. This will take place probably when the wort has been boiled about an hour and a half: the breaking or curdling is best observed by taking a basinful of the wort out of the copper, and suffering it to cool, when the flakes will be distinctly seen in the wort. The tubs having been raised on a support from the floor, and arranged for the cooling process, strain the boiled liquor into them through a riddle or flour sieve; put the hops back into the copper, and boil them again with the second and third wort. The cooling of the boiled wort should be effected with the utmost expedition; in summer it should not, if possible, be laid at a greater depth than three inches; in winter five; and the coolers so disposed that the temperature of the whole may be the same. When it has become milk-warm, or from 62° to 65° Fahrenheit, strain it through a sieve which has a cloth laid over it, pour the whole into the gyle-tun, (for which the mash-tun may be used, after being cleared out and rinsed with water,) add the yeast, and, having covered up the vessel, let it stand in a moderately warm place. When the heat of the atmosphere is more than 60°, the cool of the night must be chosen to put the beer to work. In lower degrees of the atmosphere, the wort must be set at a greater heat than that of the air; when the air is at 50°, the beer may be set to work at 50°. It should rather be set at too low than too high a temperature. A greater proportion of yeast is required in winter than in summer; and beer intended to be kept ten or twelve months will not require so much as that which is to be used immediately. The extract of one quarter of malt will require, if for keeping, six pints when the atmosphere is at 40°, five at 60°, and three at 80°; but, for those who are not disposed to study all these particulars, the proportion is one quart of good stiff yeast to about forty gallons of good strong beer or ale wort, and one pint and a half to the same quantity of small beer wort.

As soon as the yeast is added to the wort, the mixture should be stirred for two or three minutes; it is a good practice to set the yeast to ferment before it is wanted, by diluting it with a portion of lukewarm wort, adding more wort as the fermentation proceeds.

If the fermentation in the gyle-tun be languid and feeble, one or two large stone bottles, filled with hot water, closely corked, may be let down into the tub. The fermentation in the gyle-tun is completed when the head of yeast begins to decline in the middle; or, observe when the head of yeast has well risen, skim it off, and repeat the skimming till no more can be separated. The fermentation of a small quantity of beer is usually completed in two days; after the collected yeast has stood a day, the beer that has separated from it may be returned to the skimmed liquor. When the fermentation has been apparently completed, draw off the fermented liquor from the thick sediment in the fermenting vessel, into clean casks, previously rinsed with boiling water, place them with the bung-holes inclined a little to one side. A slow fermentation will go on, and the same liquor which overflows from the casks may again (having been received in a vessel placed underneath the casks for that purpose) be used for filling up the barrels, along with any kind of beer that is ready at hand; it is of great consequence to keep the casks constantly filled. The fermentation ceases spontaneously in a few days, (more or less, in proportion to the heat of the atmosphere,) when the casks must be bunged up. If the brewing has been properly conducted, the beer will be clear in fourteen days at farthest; if it be intended to mantle in the glass, it must be bottled off before the insensible fermentation in the cask has ceased, or, at all events, immediately when it has become bright. In warm weather particularly, the casks should be occasionally examined; if a hissing noise is audible at the bung-hole, the spile may be left in loosely till the liquor has become quiet; or, which is better, check the fermentation by repeatedly mopping the cask all over with cold water. The beer being well prepared, remove it to the place where it is to remain for use; when placed in the cellar, the bung must be drawn, and the casks filled up quite full with fine beer, skimming off the head from time to time. After being attended in this manner for a day or two, the casks should be bunged tight, and a hole bored with a gimlet near the bung for the vent peg, which should be left rather slack for a day or two. If it be absolutely necessary to fine the beer by artificial means, it may be done by dissolving a small quantity of isinglass in stale sour beer. Beer, when once in a fit state for use, should not be again agitated. It is only requisite that the cask should be tapped at such a distance from the bottom as to allow the beer, particularly if it be strong beer, to flow clear of that sediment which may have collected at the lower part of the vessel. Strong beer requires to be six weeks in the cask if the quantity be small; half a hogshead, three or four months, before it be bottled; keeping beer about a fortnight, and small beer a week.

The best seasons for brewing are October and March.

Ale and porter should be perfectly transparent before they are bottled. Let the bottles be dry, and leave them, when filled, open for six or eight hours; then cork them perfectly air-tight, with good sound corks. The bottles should be strait-necked, smooth, and even in the mouth, narrowing a very little about the neck where the middle of the cork comes; one inch and a half of empty space should be left between the liquor and the lower surface of the cork in the bottle.

Mangel-Wurzel Beer

FOR a ten-gallon cask, boil in fourteen gallons of water sixty pounds of mangel-wurzel, which has been well washed and sliced across, putting some kind of weight on the roots to keep them under water; having boiled an hour and a half, they may be taken out, well broken, and all the liquor pressed from the roots; put it, and that in which they were boiled, on again to boil, with four ounces of hops; let them boil about an hour and a half, then cool the liquor, as quickly as possible, to 70° Fahrenheit; strain it through a thick cloth laid over a sieve or drainer; put it into the vat with about six ounces of good yeast, stir it well, cover it, and let it stand twenty-four hours; if the yeast has then well risen, skim it off, and barrel the beer, keeping back the thick sediment. While the fermentation goes on in the cask, it may be filled up with the beer left over, or any other kind at hand; when the fermentation ceases, which may be in two or three days, the cask must be bunged up, and in a few days more, the beer may be used from the cask, or bottled.

These small proportions are here given to suit the convenience of the humblest labourer; but the beer will be better made in larger quantities; and its strength may be increased by adding a greater proportion of mangel-wurzel. By this receipt, good keeping table-beer will be obtained.

Another Cheap Beer

FOR a ten-gallon cask allow three ounces hops, ten pounds bran, two ounces bruised ginger, four pounds treacle, four ounces good yeast. Boil the hops and ginger in fifteen gallons of water for an hour and a quarter, add the bran, and boil twenty minutes longer; strain the liquor on the treacle; stir the mixture well, and let it stand till it becomes milk-warm, or from 60° to 70° Fahrenheit; then strain it through a thick cloth laid over a riddle or sieve, add four or five ounces of yeast, stir it well, and when cold, put it into the cask; keep filling up the cask till it has done working, which may be in two days. It must then be bunged up, and will be fit for drinking in two days. It will keep good in the cask for ten days or a fortnight – or it may be bottled.

This beer will not be so strong nor so cheap as the mangel-wurzel beer; but being scarcely more than one halfpenny per bottle, and as good as the brewer's harvest beer, it may be found well worthy the attention of the farmer at a season when mangel-wurzel cannot be procured. The yeast which it affords will be found excellent for baking.

CHAPTER XXIII
KITCHEN GARDEN

In the following directions for the culture of kitchen vegetables, none are included which, in the climate of Britain, require the aid of artificial heat to bring them to maturity; as it is presumed, that when such are desired, an educated professional gardener will be employed, to whom the instructions here submitted, as they must necessarily be of a limited nature, might possibly be of little use. But it is confidently anticipated, that the directions which are given, if closely followed, will be found sufficient, in ordinary cases, to produce the desired result.

In choosing the situation most suitable for a kitchen garden, it will be necessary to regard the aspect, or exposure, of the ground; a southern exposure being always considered much better than any other; and a gentle declivity in that direction being very desirable. It should be screened to the north and west by a plantation of forest trees; and, on these sides, the trees may be less than a hundred yards from the garden; but to the south and east, there should be no tall trees, at least within a considerable distance. It is necessary, also, that there should be a sufficient supply of water within reach; and standing, or soft water, is always to be preferred to that taken immediately from a spring or well. The best general soil for a garden is a loam of a middling quality, partaking more of the sandy than the clayey nature. If a strong and a light soil can both be had, it will be so much the better, as the different plants may thus have the ground best adapted to their respective kinds.

Cabbages

The best soil for cabbages is a rich mould, rather clayey than sandy; and it can scarcely be too much manured, as they are an exhausting crop. The kinds generally preferred for summer use are, the small early dwarf, large curly Yorkshire, early dwarf Yorkshire, early Battersea, and early sugar-loaf. These are ready for use from April or May to July; for autumn and winter, the imperial, large sugar-loaf, hollow sugar-loaf, and the long or large-sided. The large Drum, white Strasburg, the Scots, and the American cabbage, resist the severity of winter, and grow to a very large size; but they are coarse kinds. The time of sowing for the summer crop is the beginning of the August of the preceding year. An open spot of rich light earth must be chosen, and the seeds of this, and of all the kale tribe, require a covering of no more than an eighth, or a quarter of an inch, in thickness of mould. In about six or eight weeks after the sowing, or when the plants have got several leaves, they are thinned; and those plants taken out of the seedbed are pricked into other beds, at three inches' distance every way. By these means, they have room to grow firm and shapely. In October and November, part of this crop is finally planted out, the remainder early in the following spring; and the plants are set in rows between two and three feet wide, and two feet asunder in the rows. As the cabbages advance, the earth in the rows must be stirred, and drawn round the plants; indeed the oftener the earth is stirred, the better will be the crop. In the end of April or beginning of May, the early cabbages begin to turn in their leaves, and to harden in the centre, when, if the leaves be bound close with willow twigs, or strands of bass-matting, they will be fit for use a fortnight the earlier. If the roots and stems of a portion of this crop be allowed to remain after the tops are cut off, and the ground dewed, and perhaps manured in autumn, very fine cabbages will be produced in the January and February following. For autumn and winter use, the seeds of cabbages are sown in the end of February or beginning of March, pricked out into shady borders in May, and allowed to remain there for some weeks. In June, they are finally transplanted, at the same distance as the early kinds. These cabbages come to be fit for use in the autumn months, and continue good, in sheltered situations, and in ordinary seasons, till February or March. Of the red cabbages, the dwarf dark-red kind is considered the best; it may be sown about the end of August, and planted out in the beginning of April. The white Strasburg is the variety of which the Germans chiefly make their sour krout. The long or large-sided cabbage, being rather tender, should not be sown till May, or planted out till July.

Savoys

The principal sorts are the yellow and the green; the green being considered the hardiest. They are sown about the middle of April, and planted out in June, considerably closer than the common cabbage. If savoys be wanted before winter, the seed must be sown in February, or even in the autumn before: in the last case, fine large plants will be ready for the table in September or October. The later crop affords a supply till February or March. Savoys are reckoned better when somewhat pinched by the frost. If cabbages be planted, year after year, in the same ground, they will become sickly and stunted; it is therefore advisable to change the cabbage ground every year.

Open Kale

YOUNG plants of the common cabbage are now generally used as coleworts; for this purpose, either the sugar-loaf or the large York is sown about the middle or end of June, and planted out in the end of July, or beginning of August, to be ready for use in winter.

Scots Kale

IS sown in the beginning of July; and in the course of the month of August, the young plants are set out in rows a root and a half wide, and ten inches' distance in the rows. This green will not be tender until it have endured some sharp frosts. When kale is planted out, it will be necessary to give water to the roots, should the weather be dry; no other attention is requisite, except that of drawing the earth to the stems before winter.

Brussels Sprouts

ARE sown in March or April; the seedlings planted out in June preferring showery weather, or watering carefully at the root: they are earthed up in October, and are ready for use by midwinter. As they grow upright, they may be planted closer than other kinds of greens.

Cauliflower

THE seed of the early crop of cauliflower is sown about the 20th of the August of the preceding year in beds. In September the seedlings are pricked into a dry border, near a wall, where they may be hooped over, and defended with bass mats, during the severe frosts of winter. In the month of March they are finally planted out, giving water liberally now and afterwards, should the weather be dry. They are planted in rows about two feet and a half asunder, and two feet apart in the rows; but they must not be set deep in the ground. After this they must have repeated hoeings, and the earth must be drawn close up to the roots and stems. To diversify the time of forming heads, some of the early cauliflowers are planted out on different successive occasions. Cauliflower will thrive the better that it have liberal supplies of the cleanings of the stable and cow-house.

Brocoli

THERE are many varieties of brocoli; but the most useful kinds are the dwarf sulphur-coloured, and the kind called green brocoli. For an autumn crop, the seed is sown in April, and planted out in the beginning of June. For a spring crop in the following year, the seed is sown late in May, or even in June; the seedlings are afterwards placed in nursery beds, where they remain till the middle or end of July, when they are finally transplanted in lines, two feet asunder, and a foot and a half apart in the lines. Water is given in dry weather; and they are hoed and earthed up like cauliflower. The heads of winter brocoli generally appear early in January, and continue till April. A light and deep, but rich soil, in an open situation, is to be preferred for them. Sea-weed is a useful manure for brocoli, and will prevent the grubs infesting its roots.

Kohl-rabbi

OF the khol-rabbi, or turnip-rooted cabbage, there are two varieties; the one having the stem swelling above ground; the other having this turnip-like protuberance in it. This plant may be cultivated in the same manner as brocoli: it is very hardy.

Turnip

MOST sorts of turnip like a sandy soil not recently manured; but the yellow Dutch turnip does best in a good soil. For a spring crop the early Dutch is usually preferred; it may be sown, broadcast, in the month of April, mixing a little fine earth with the seed to make it divide more equally. A small sowing of this kind may be made every month from April to August, in order to have them throughout the summer in a young state for the table. For a winter crop, the yellow Dutch turnip is considered superior to any other kind; it is sown thickly about the middle of July; and, if rain do not occur, frequent watering will be necessary. When the root leaves are about an inch broad, the young plants are thinned to within six or eight inches' distance from each other. To prevent the ravages of the turnip-fly, it is advisable to dust quick-lime lightly over the crop while it is in the seed-leef. Should the young plants threaten to run to flower, they may be trodden down, by gently placing the foot on the centre of the plant. If turnips be allowed to remain in the ground throughout the winter, the top leaves form excellent greens early in spring. The Swedish, the stone, and the yellow, are all likewise good winter turnips.

Carrot

CARROTS thrive best in a light soil, with a mixture of sand; it should be delved very deep, or even trenched, and, at the same time, well broken with the spade. Pigeon's dung added to the carrot ground promotes their health, by preventing the attacks of insects; when any other manure is used, it should be buried deep, that the roots may not touch it. In general, it is best to make the carrots the second crop after manuring. For the principal crop, the orange carrot, or the red or field carrot, is preferred; it is sown in March or April – in light soils not till the end of April or beginning of May. The seeds must be rubbed between the hands with some dry sand to separate them; and, as they are very light, a calm day must be chosen; they should be trodden in before raking. When the plants come up, several successive hoeings are given; at first with a three-inch, and latterly with a six-inch hoe. The plants are thinned either by drawing young plants for use, or by hoeing, till they are within eight or ten inches of each other, if broadcast; but if in drills, which should be a foot apart, till they are six or seven inches separate. If the hoeing is not done in showery weather, a regular watering must be given after the operation. For an early crop, the early horn-carrot is used; it is sown before the first of February, in a warm border, which must be hooped over, and covered with mats during frost. A bed of the late horn-carrot may be sown in June or July, to afford young roots in the autumn months. Carrots are taken up at the first approach of winter, cleaned, and stored up with sand in a place that will exclude the frost.

Parsnip

THIS plant requires a stronger soil than the carrot; it prefers a light loam; but any soil will do, provided it be pretty deep. The seed, which should never be more than a year old, is sown in March; the plants are afterwards thinned out to about eight or ten inches asunder, and are kept clear of weeds. When the leaves begin to decay, the roots are fit for use. They may be stored as carrots; or, as frost will not injure them, they may be allowed to remain in the ground till the beginning of February; but not longer, as then the flower-stalks begin to form, when the roots would become stringy.

Scorzonera

THE seeds of scorzonera are sown in the middle of April, in a cool deep soil, in drills about a foot separate. Afterwards the plants are thinned out to within four inches apart. The roots may be either lifted in November and stored as carrots, or they may remain in the ground all winter.

Salsify

SALSIFY is sown in April, and afterwards thinned to within six or eight inches apart. A mellow and deep soil affords the best plants. The roots may remain in the ground, and be taken up as wanted throughout the winter.

Skirret

A light deep soil is most suitable for the skirret, and should it be naturally moist, so much the better. In dry soils, or in long-continued droughts, watering is advisable. The seeds are sown in April, and repeated thinning and hoeing are necessary. When the leaves begin to decay in autumn, the roots are fit for use; they will not be injured by frost, and may therefore remain in the ground till wanted.

Red Beet

RED beet requires a light, but rich soil, of considerable depth, that has not been recently manured. The ground should be trenched, or very deeply delved, and broken small with the spade. The seed is sown in April, in drills an inch deep, and fifteen inches asunder. In autumn, beet-root is generally stored amongst sand in a cellar, or some place that will completely exclude the frost. In lifting it, great care must he taken that the roots be not anywise injured or broken, as they bleed much; for the same reason, the leaves must be cut off at least an inch above the top of the root.

White Beet

THIS kind of beet is cultivated only for its leaves, which are used as spinach. The seeds are sown in the beginning of March, in an open spot of ground. When the plants have put out four leaves, they are hoed, and thinned out to at least four inches asunder. A month afterwards a second hoeing is given, leaving the plants about eight inches separate. The outer leaves being first picked off for use, a succession is afforded for the whole season.

Jerusalem Artichoke

THIS plant is propagated by means of the tubers, which are cut in the manner of potato-sets, and planted in any light soil and open situation, in the end of March. They are placed in rows three feet asunder, and a foot or fifteen inches apart in the rows. In September they are fit for use, and may be left in the ground, and dug up as wanted throughout the winter, being best when newly raised.

Potato

THE varieties of the potato are very numerous; and as no particular kind will continue in perfection much more than fourteen years, new kinds are continually succeeding those that have worn out. At present, for a summer crop, the ash-leaved, early dwarf, and champion, are esteemed; and, for the winter crop, the American, large and small, and the kidney, are excellent. They will thrive in any light soil, in a free airy situation; and if quantity of produce be particularly desired, too much manure can hardly be given; but they will be of a more delicate flavour from ground not recently enriched. The potato is propagated by cuts of the tubers, leaving one or two eyes or buds to each cut, and eradicating all clustered eyes. The best shaped and cleanest potatoes are selected for this purpose; and the cuts are the better for being allowed to dry for a day or two before planting. They are planted in drills, and covered to the depth of three or four inches; and for the early crop, which may be planted in a light warm border, about the beginning or middle of March, sixteen inches between the lines and seven or eight inches between each plant, is sufficient; but, for the principal crop, which must be planted about the middle or end of April, two feet is allowed between the rows, and from ten to fifteen inches between the plants. The only attention the crop requires is hoeing, and drawing the earth to the stems, the oftener this last operation is performed, the greater will be the produce. The early planted potatoes will be fit for use in June and July. Only a few of them should be taken up at a time, as they will not keep good beyond a day or two. In autumn the principal crop will be known to be ripe, when the tops of the plants change to a yellow colour; they should then be taken up, and stored in as clean and dry a state as possible. The best way of keeping them is in heaps on the ground, covering well with straw and earth, so as completely to exclude the frost.

Peas

IF peas be sown in newly-enriched ground, they will be apt to run to haums; they are therefore seldom sown till the second year after manuring. Some of the early kinds, such as the Charleton, golden, and Reading, are generally sown towards the end of October, in front of a south wall; and, if slightly protected by means of branches of evergreens, or old peas-haum, the crop will survive the winter, and produce young peas by the end of May. In January and February, more of the early sorts are sown for a succession; and in March and April, full crops of the later peas must be sown. Some of the smaller late kinds, as the blue Prussian, dwarf marrowfat, Spanish dwarf, and Leadman's dwarf, if well earthed up, and the rows not too near each other, may do without sticking. Of the large and late kinds, the tall marrowfat, green marrowfat, grey rounceval, and the sugar pea, have long retained their character. The large kinds require nearly four feet distance between the rows. The young plants are frequently hoed; when they are three or four inches high, the earth is drawn to the rows; and when about eight or ten inches high, they must be sticked; the smallest kinds may have sticks three feet, the early sorts and dwarf marrowfat five feet, and the larger sorts seven or eight feet high. When branches for sticking cannot be procured, two lines of strong packthread, on each side of the rows, may be substituted. To prevent the attacks of mice, it is necessary to be careful, in sowing peas, that none be left exposed on the surface of the ground.

Beans

THE early sorts, such as the Mazagon and Lisbon, are sown in the end of October, in front of a wall or hedge. The plants are earthed up in November, as they advance; but, in earthing up beans, it is necessary to be very careful that the earth do not fall on the centre of the plant. In severe frost some haum or fern is laid over them. In March and April, as they begin to show flower, they are kept close to the fence by means of packthread; and, in order to forward the production of pods, when the lower blossoms begin to fade, the tops of the stems are pinched off. In February and March, full crops of the late and large beans, as the Windsor, Sandwich, and long podded, are planted in drills two inches deep, allowing two and a half or three feet between the rows.

Kidney, or French Bean

THE dwarf kidney-bean requires no support from sticks, but, as it is tender, must be sown before the middle or end of April; it may then be sown in drills, from two to three feet asunder, and about three inches separate in the lines, covering with something less than two inches of soil. As the plants advance, they are hoed and cleared of weeds, a little earth being, at the same time, drawn to the stems. The most esteemed kinds are, the speckled dwarf, early black or negro, and early white dwarf. The scarlet runner, being more tender than the dwarf kinds, must not be sown till about the middle of May; and, as tall slight stakes must be placed for it to climb upon, the distance between the rows is generally four feet. The kidney-beans like a good, light, rich soil.

Spinach

THERE are two kinds of spinach; the prickly-seeded, for winter, and the smooth-seeded, for summer use. The winter crop is sown, either in drills, or broadcast, in the beginning of August, when rains may be expected. A light, dry, but rich soil, in a sheltered situation, is desirable. When the plants show four leaves, the ground around them is hoed, and the spinach moderately thinned; the hoeing is repeated as the weeds grow. In February, when a few dry days may occur, the surface of the ground is stirred, the plants cleaned, and again thinned out. With this mode of treatment, and with due attention, the winter spinach should afford successive gatherings from November, and, in mild weather, throughout the winter, till April or May. The first sowing of the summer spinach is made in a sheltered border in January. If sown broadcast, it is first thinned out to three inches, and, at subsequent hoeings, to eight or ten inches apart. Successive sowings are made in February, March, and April; and these are at once thinned out to six or eight inches apart.

Asparagus

ASPARAGUS is of two kinds; the red-topped, which produces the larger shoots, and the green-topped, which are considered of the more delicate flavour. The best way of propagating asparagus is by means of seed. In the month of March it is sown in shallow drills, six inches asunder, and earthed in from half an inch to an inch deep. The young plants are kept as free of weeds as possible during the summer; and in the end of October, some litter is spread over the surface of the ground to protect them from frost. In the following spring, about April, the seedlings are transplanted to the quarter in which they are to remain. The soil of this quarter must not be less than two and a half feet deep; it should be light, but rich; damp ground, or a wet subsoil, would be very unsuitable; nothing is better than a sandy loam, well mixed with rotten dung, or sea-weed; and before planting a bed, it should be well trenched over to the depth of the soil, burying abundance of manure in the bottom. The seedling plants are cautiously raised with a narrow-pronged fork; and when they are taken up, the roots are kept in a little earth till replanted: they being very apt to be injured by exposure to the air. A trench, about six inches deep, being prepared, the roots are carefully laid in, a foot distant from each other, the buds or crowns being kept upright, and about two inches below the surface. A foot between each ordinary trench is reckoned sufficient, but between every four rows a double distance is left for an alley. In dry weather the new-planted beds should be carefully watered. Several hoeings, generally three, are given in the course of the summer. In the end of September, the haum decays, and is cut away; and small stable-dung or sea-weed is spread on the bed, previously stirring the surface with a fork. In spring, just before the buds begin to appear, the intervals of the beds are slightly delved over with the narrow-pronged fork, raking afterwards, with great delicacy of hand. The same practice, both for autumn and spring, is observed for the second year, it being only in the third year after planting out, or the fourth from the time of sowing, that cutting for the table is begun. In April a few shoots may generally be cut; in May and June they will be plentiful. In the first productive season only the large shoots are taken, but in subsequent years all the shoots are gathered as they advance till the end of the month of June. Shoots, two inches under ground, and three or four above, are the best for the table; and, in cutting them, some of the earth is first removed, in order to avoid the succeeding buds below. An asparagus quarter should not contain less than a fall of ground, as it often takes that quantity to furnish a good dish at one time.

Sea-Kale

THE best mode of propagating sea-kale is by sowing it. The soil intended for it should be sandy and light, but mixed with fine rich mould; and of all manures for this crop, drift-ware or sea-weed is the best. The ground must be trenched at least two feet deep, and in March the seed is sown, about two inches deep; they may be set in a triangular form, six inches apart, leaving a space of two feet between the triangles. To ensure a produce, it may be as well to drop in two or more seeds into each hole, and to thin out afterwards the superfluous plants. For the first summer no attention will be required in the culture, except that of keeping the plants clear of weeds. In November the whole bed is covered with rotten stable-litter, as is done with asparagus. During the second year the same plan is followed. In the third year most of the plants will be strong enough to be blanched for use; this is done by placing blanching covers over the plants as soon as the leaves are decayed in the end of autumn, and then covering up the whole bed with stable-dung, packing it closely between the pots, and heaping it over the tops of them to the depth of six inches or more. By this mode the sea-kale will be fit for cutting in January and February. If the heat of the litter at any time decline, which may be easily ascertained by introducing a thermometer into several of the blanching pots, some new stable-dung must be mixed with it. The blanching pots, mentioned above, are made for the purpose; they have movable covers that fit down closely, and they are nearly as wide at top as at bottom, in order to give room for cutting such shoots as may be ready, without breaking the others. It is necessary to have from thirty to fifty of such covers. A less expensive mode of blanching is, by covering the sea-kale beds to the depth of a foot and a half with leaves as they fall from the trees in autumn, adding, over all, a very slight layer of long stable-litter to prevent the leaves being blown about. In this manner the shoots will be very sweet and tender; but they will not be produced so early as by the former method.

Onions

THE soil for onions should be light, and not recently manured; it should be well delved and broken fine, and exactly levelled. There are several varieties in use, but the Strasburg may be mentioned as being as good as any. For the principal crop, the seed is sown in February or the beginning of March; but, should the land be heavy, it is better to defer the sowing till the end of March or beginning of April. The seed is sown broadcast; a very slight covering of earth is given, and the ground is merely smoothed over with the rake. A first hoeing is given when the plants have advanced three or four inches in growth, and they are then thinned out with the hand to about four inches apart. Another hoeing is given about a month or six weeks afterwards, when the plants are singled out to about six inches square. After this the hoe must never be used, but any large weeds must be drawn out with the hand. If the weather be dry at the time of thinning, a plentiful watering must immediately afterwards be given. About the end of August the crop will be known to be ripe by the leaves falling down. The onions are then drawn, and laid out on a gravel walk in some dry spot, and occasionally turned. In a fortnight they are generally found to be firm enough for keeping, and must be stored in a dry garret or loft, excluding them as much as may be from the air. The crop of winter onions is sown in August or beginning of September; they are thinned in the usual way, and weeds must be carefully kept down. In the spring, when the keeping onions fail, part of these may be drawn for use, the remainder will be ready in the early part of summer about the month of May, any of the stalks which appear to be pushing a flower-stem must be thrown out, and, to check this tendency, the rest of this crop should be laid down, which is done by passing the handle of a rake horizontally along the bed, so as to strike the stems an inch or two above the bulb, and bend them flat down. Winter onions thus managed may be taken up about the end of June, and are generally firm, and keep long. For pickling, the small silver-skinned variety is best; they should be sown pretty thickly about the middle of April, in light and very poor land, as they are not required of a large size for this purpose; they need not be thinned, unless when they rise absolutely in clusters. The will be fit for use in August.

Leek

LEEKS are raised much in the same way as onions. There are three varieties of them; the narrow-leaved or Flanders, the broad-leaved or tall London, and the Scotch or flag-leek; this last is by much the most hardy. They are, about the beginning of March, sown closely in beds, and in June or July are planted out in rows, first trimming off the tips of the leaves and the points of the fibrous roots. A good way is, to make a deep hole with a dibble, and merely lay in the leek plant up to the leaves, without closing the earth about it; this encourages the stem to swell and lengthen, while at the same time it blanches it. But this plan may be adopted only in moist weather, or the plants must be well watered, to ensure their taking root. If the leaves be topped two or three times during the summer, the leeks will grow to a larger size. They are ready for use in autumn and winter.

Cibol

CIBOLS are raised from seeds, which are sown in July. The seedling plants soon appear; but, in the course of the month of October, the leaves go off, and the ground seems quite bare. In January, however, they again begin to shoot, and by March they are fit for use.

Chives

CHIVES are readily propagated by parting the roots, either in autumn or spring, and they will grow in any soil or situation. They should be repeatedly cut during the summer, the successive leaves produced in this way being more tender. A small bed or border thus managed will afford a sufficient supply; it will continue productive for three or four years, when a new plantation should be made.

Garlic

GARLIC has a bulbous root, made up of a dozen or fifteen smaller bulbs, called cloves; it is propagated by detaching the cloves, and planting them. The soil should be light and dry, well dewed, and broken fine. The sets are placed four inches distant from each other in every direction, and between two and three inches deep. The smaller the cloves, the more healthy and productive will be the plants. They are put in in February or March; about the middle of June the leaves are tied in knots, to prevent the stronger plants from running to flower. The crop is taken up in August, when the leaves begin to wither. The roots are tied in bunches, and hung in a dry room for use.

Shalot

THE culture of the shalot is very similar to that of garlic. They are planted about the middle of October, the ground having been previously manured with old well-rotted dung, mixed with house-ashes. The crop is taken up in the end of summer, when the leaves become discoloured, and the bulbs are hung up in nets, in a cool airy place, for use.

Artichoke

ARTICHOKES may be planted in any open situation. They are propagated by means of rooted slips, or suckers, taken off at the time of the spring dressing, in the beginning of April. They like a light loam, cool, but dry, and which is at the same time rich and deep. In preparing for this crop, the soil should be trenched to the depth of three feet, and manure should be liberally supplied at the bottom of the trench. The plants may be placed four feet apart every way; and at the end of the first season after planting, a small and late crop of artichokes may generally be cut in October. In the second year they will be plentiful; and in autumn, as soon as all the heads are gathered, the whole stalks are broken down close to the ground. In November a portion of earth is drawn towards each plant, and some long dung, peas-haum, or the like is laid around, but kept at some distance from the stems and leaves of the plants. In March or April, the litter and earth are removed, the stocks are examined, and two or three of the strongest and best shoots being selected for growing up, the rest are detached. Every season, at the winter dressing, some small rotted dung or fresh sea-weed should be dug into the ground. It is advisable to renew the artichoke plantation every six years.

Cardoon

THE best soil for cardoons is one that is light, and not too rich; but it ought to be deep. The seed is sown in the middle or end of May, in small hollows, about three inches deep, and four feet distant from each other every way. Two or three seeds are placed in each hollow to ensure a crop, but only the strongest plant is allowed to remain. The cardoon requires a good deal of water, and in very dry weather, this should be copiously supplied. In September, when the leaves will be large, they are tied up with hay or straw bands for blanching, leaving only the top free, but a dry day must be selected for the purpose; at the same time a hillock of earth is formed around each plant to the height of a foot or eighteen inches, and this is smoothed on the surface that the rain may run off, and not fall into the centre of the plants. As they advance in growth, additional bands of straw are added, and the earth is raised higher. They will be ready for use in two months after the commencement of the blanching. In severe frost, the tops are covered with haum or long litter.

Lettuce

Of each of the two kinds of lettuce, the coss, also called the Roman and ice, and the cabbage lettuce, there are many varieties. Of the coss lettuces, the Egyptian green, the white coss or Versailles, and the royal cape lettuce, are esteemed; of the cabbage lettuces, the imperial and grand admiral, or admiral. The large Roman and the Cilicia lettuces are those chiefly used in soups. The seed is sown broadcast, and merely raked into the ground. A small sowing may be made in January, the seedlings being transplanted in March. A considerable crop is sown in the end of February, and the principal sowing is in March and April. A part of each crop should be regularly transplanted, to come in season immediately after those left in the seed-bed; they are fittest for transplanting when they have four or six leaves; and they are placed from ten to fifteen inches apart, according to the size they are likely to attain. To forward the cabbaging of coss lettuce, the leaves may be tied together in the manner practised with endive. If the winter be not very severe, lettuces will stand without much injury, close by the foot of a south wall, and be fit for use in January, February, and March.

Endive

The green curled-leaved and the white curled-leaved are the best kinds; the green curled-leaved, being the most hardy, is used for the latest crops. The seed, which must be scattered thinly, is sown some time between the middle of May and middle of June; another sowing is made in July. When the seedlings are three or four inches high; they are transplanted into a well-prepared bed of rich soil, in rows a foot asunder, at the distance of ten inches from each other in the row. In dry weather, watering is necessary. The blanching must next be commenced; it is accomplished, when the plants are perfectly dry, by tying up the heads with strands of bass-mat; some nicety is requisite in gathering the leaves together in regular order, so as not to cross each other, and in rejecting such leaves as are unhealthy. The plants are, at first, tied two inches below the top, afterwards about the middle of the plant. In three weeks or a month they will be found to be sufficiently blanched; but as they will continue in this state fit for use only a fortnight, a few plants must be tied up every week in order to their being ready for use in succession. After October, the mode adopted is, to make some trenches, and to sink the plants in them nearly to the head, where they will become sufficiently blanched in four or five weeks. Additional plants may be sunk in the trenches every fortnight when the weather happens to be so mild and dry as to permit it. Endive thus blanched in the earth must be dug out with the spade.

Celery

THERE are two varieties, one with hollow, the other with solid stalks; the solid stalk is generally preferred; another variety, with large red stalks, is also esteemed. Celery must be sown at several different times, in order to ensure a succession of plants fit for transplanting at various seasons. The first sowing is commonly made about the end of March or beginning of April, in a sheltered border; the next about the beginning of May, on a moist border. About the end of April, the plants of the first sowing will be ready for pricking into nursery beds of rich earth, in which they may stand three or four inches separate. Water is given, and the plants are shaded from the sun for a few days. A quantity of every successive sowing should be thus pricked out, in order to strengthen them. Towards the end of May, the most forward plants may be transplanted into trenches for blanching. In dry weather, at this season, water is given freely both to the transplanted plants and those left in the seed-bed. The usual mode of transplanting and blanching is the following: – Trenches are formed at the distance of three or four feet from each other, a foot and a half wide, and about a foot in depth. The soil in the bottom of this trench is delved and worked fine, and a little rotten dung is mixed with it. The soil for celery should be deep and rich; somewhat moist, yet of a light nature. The earth taken from the trench is laid in ridges on each side, ready to be drawn in as wanted. The plants, having the tops of the long leaves cut off, and any side-shoots removed, are placed in the bottom of the trenches, at the distance of four or five inches from each other; as they advance in growth, the earth is drawn in towards them, perhaps once in ten days, taking care to do this in dry weather, and not to cover the centre of the plants with soil. When the plants rise considerably above the surface of the ground, the earth laid in ridges will be exhausted; a new trench must, therefore, now be opened between each row, for a supply of soil to continue the earthing up till the leaf stalks of the celery be blanched to the length of from eight to fourteen inches. The last sowing is destined to stand the winter; and the soil into which this is finally transplanted, should be as dry as possible. In severe weather, peas-haum or loose litter is thrown over the beds. In lifting the plants for use, it is proper to dig deep, that the main root may not be injured.

Garden Cress and Mustard

THESE may be sown, thickly, in close drills, on a warm border, at the bottom of a south wall, about the middle of March. Throughout the summer they should be sown once a fortnight, as they are used only while quite young and tender. Besides the plain sort of garden cress, there is a variety with curled leaves, which, being the more hardy of the two, may be sown later in the season. This kind requires to be thinned out to half an inch asunder. The white mustard is the best kind for sowing along with the garden cress, and for using in salad.

French and Common Sorrel

THE French sorrel thrives best in a light sandy soil. It is easily propagated by means of offsets, or by seeds; if in the first way, the plants are placed a foot apart, the only attention the crop requires is that of cutting off the flower stems in the month of July. The plants should be renewed every four or five years. Common sorrel thrives best in a shady border. It is easily raised from seed sown early in spring.

Radish

THERE are the spindle-rooted and turnip-rooted radishes; of the turnip-rooted variety, there is a white and a red kind. The short-topped purple or the pink radish, both spindle-rooted, may be sown for the earliest crop in the beginning of November, in a sheltered border; and they will be ready for drawing early in March. More seed is sown in December and January, and sowings are continued once a fortnight until April, in order to secure a succession of young roots. Any sort of soil will suit this plant. In the end of March, should the weather happen to be very dry, the crops must be regularly watered; a slight covering of fern is useful early in spring, when sharp frosts occur; it may be raked off in the day time, and restored at night. If radishes are to be drawn small, they may stand at two inches apart; but if it be intended that the roots should grow large, they must be allowed twice that distance. The turnip-rooted radish is sown in February or March, and thinned out with a small hoe to within six inches apart.

Indian Cress, or Nasturtium

A fresh, but poor soil, is better for this plant than a rich one. The seeds may be sown in April, in drills about two inches deep. The plants must have a support, as the stalks will grow to the height of six or eight feet. The seeds will be ready for use in August or September. There is also a dwarfish variety, which may be allowed to spread on the ground.

Burnet

A few plants only of this are sufficient. It may be raised from seeds sown in autumn, or by parting the roots. The stems should be two or three times cut over in summer.

Horse-Radish

THE soil for horse-radish should be rich and deep. It is propagated by cuttings of the knotty parts of the root, provided these be furnished with one or two eyes. They are planted in February or March, in lines, leaving a foot and a half between each line. The sets are placed at the depth of at least a foot. The roots are not used till the second year, and then they are raised only as they are wanted. The bed will last for four or five years, care being taken, in digging the roots, to leave the original set, or stock, untouched.

Parsley

THE curled parsley is the preferable variety. It may be raised in drills on the edge of a border. The seeds, which lie for a month or six weeks in the ground before springing, may be sown in February or early in March. In order to have fresh parsley leaves throughout the winter, some larch or beech branches may be laid over the parsley borders; and in hard weather, above these are spread dry bean-haum, fern, or reeds.

Angelica

ANGELICA is easily raised from seed, which should be sown soon after it is gathered. It grows best in a moist soil, and thrives exceedingly well by the side of a ditch. Though a biennial plant, it may be made to continue for several years, by cutting down the flower stems before it ripen to seed.

Rhubarb

THE kind cultivated for the table is called monk's rhubarb. It is propagated by means of offsets, which should be planted any time between November and February, in good soil, at the distance of three feet from each other. If the rhubarb plants be covered in November with a good deal of stable-litter, the leaves will shoot up very early in spring, and their stalks will be improved by the blanching they will in this way receive.

HERBS

Sage

THE red kind is preferred for kitchen use; and the lighter and poorer the soil is, the better will the sage plants stand the winter. It is propagated in the spring by slips, and in the summer by cuttings. The cuttings should be five or six inches long, stripped of all the lower leaves and plunged nearly to the top in the earth, being at the same time well watered. The plants should be removed every three or four years.

Clary

CLARY is propagated by seeds sown in spring, transplanting the seedlings, in the summer months, to fifteen inches apart.

Mints

SPEARMINT is the kind required for culinary purposes, peppermint being little used, except for distilling. These mints like a moist soil, and are readily propagated by slips in spring, by parting the roots in autumn, and by means of cuttings in summer. In the latter end of summer, when the spearmint is coming into flower, it may be gathered, dried gradually in the shade, and kept for winter use. As mint plants are sometimes destroyed in very severe frost, it is advisable to cover them slightly with peas-haum or fern before winter.

Thyme

THYME grows best in a light dry soil that has not been recently manured; it is propagated by parting the roots, planting slips, or by sowing the seed in spring.

Marjoram

SWEET-MARJORAM, or knotted-marjoram, is propagated by seed, a little of which should be sown every spring. Pot-marjoram is easily propagated by slips or cuttings, and is sufficiently hardy to withstand our winters. Winter sweet-marjoram requires a sheltered border and a dry soil. It is a perennial plant, and is propagated by parting the roots in autumn. For winter use, both the kinds of sweet-marjoram should be dried slowly in the shade, and afterwards hung up in a dry place.

Savory

WINTER savory is propagated by slips, or by cuttings of the young roots, and also by seeds. It is hardy, and continues good for several years, especially in poor soils. Summer savory must be sown every spring, in shallow drills, thinly; the drills being eight or nine inches apart.

Tarragon

IN a dry loamy soil, tarragon proves quite a hardy plant; but it is apt to perish in a wet situation. It is easily propagated by parting the roots, or by planting in the spring young shoots with only two or three fibres.

Tansy

TANSY is extremely hardy, and will grow in any soil. It is easily propagated at any season by parting the roots.

Hyssop

A poor dry soil is most suitable to hyssop. It may be propagated in the spring months by seeds, by rooted slips, and by cuttings.

Costmary

COSTMARY does best in a dry soil. It is propagated by parting the roots in autumn.

Rosemary

ROSEMARY is easily propagated by slips or cuttings in spring. It should be planted in a dry soil, in a sheltered situation; but if its roots enter the crevices at the base of an old wall, the plant will not be injured by the severest frosts.

Lavender

LAVENDER is propagated by cuttings, in young slips, any time in the spring months. It should be planted in a dry, gravelly, or poor soil.

Balm

BALM is readily propagated by parting the roots, preserving two or three buds to each piece; or by slips, either autumn or spring. In order to have young leaves all the summer, some of the stalks should be cut down every month. The balm plantation need not be renewed oftener than every third or fourth year.

Coriander

THE seeds of coriander should be sown in autumn, and the plants afterwards thinned out to five or six inches asunder.

Caraway

THE caraway is a biennial plant, and should be sown soon after the seed is ripe, in autumn, thinning out the plants the next spring, to within four or six inches apart. A moist soil suits the caraway the best.

Samphire

SAMPHIRE is not easily cultivated; it seems to succeed best in a rich light soil, having sand and gravel mixed with it. It must be in a well-sheltered situation, and requires to be freely watered in dry weather, till the roots have struck deep among the soil. If a few plants can be induced to take root in an old wall, or on an artificial rock-work, they will have a good chance of remaining.

CHAPTER XXIV
ON BEES

The Apiary

SHOULD be situated so that the hives may have as much sun, and shelter from the wind, as possible. A few low trees or shrubs may be planted in the vicinity, to arrest the flight of the swarms, but all rubbish and noxious weeds must be carefully removed. The hives should be placed on pedestals, about two feet from the ground, and never less than five or six yards from each other. Of whatever form they be made, the material best suited for their construction is straw. When a hive is to be purchased, let it be chosen in the middle of the day; that which has the greatest number of bees going in with yellow pellets attached to their legs may be selected for farther examination. The interior should be crowded with bees, the comb of a yellow hue, and the side ones filled; if there be many queen cells, which are like small inverted acorns attached to the sides of the combs, or if the wings of the bees should be ragged or torn, the hive is certainly old, and ought to be rejected. If a hive is to be purchased in spring, its weight should not be less than fifteen pounds; if in autumn, not less than thirty; and if it is a stock hive, the weight should not be less than forty pounds. A good hive having been selected, it may be removed in the evening, and placed on its single pedestal; but it should not be plastered to the stool. The stand on which the hive is placed should be cleaned four times in the year, and sprinkled with salt. Dampness is very injurious to bees; in winter; therefore, the snow must be carefully brushed off the hives, and while it continues upon the ground, the bees must be confined. Should they at this season become unhealthy, a renovation of air may be beneficial, and were the hives to remain an hour turned up, it would be rather an advantage than otherwise. Where there is not a little running stream in the neighbourhood of the apiary, troughs with water should be placed near the hives. They may be made of stone or wood, the wood well pitched, of eight or ten inches in depth, and sunk in the earth. A few inches of mould may be put in the bottom, and some water-cresses planted therein, to preserve the purity of the water, with which they should be constantly supplied; or, put one or two pieces of wood in a basin of water, and place it near the hive.

Spring and autumn are the seasons for feeding the weak hives, beginning in February if the weather be fine. The food most approved of for them is a sirup composed of sugar or treacle, ale, and salt, in the proportion of two pints of ale to a pound of sugar, and about half an ounce of salt, the whole to be boiled a quarter of an hour, and carefully skimmed; when cold, it should be bottled, corked, and, to prevent its candying, kept for use in a warm place. In the beginning of the season, a little port wine incorporated with the food, may prevent dysentery. When the bees to be fed are in a plain cottage hive, an eek must be provided, of the same diameter as the hive. When the sun is set, and the bees all returned from the fields, let the hives be gently raised, and the eek placed on the stool; fill an empty comb with the food, place it in the cell, and replace the hive upon it; the bees will be less disturbed, if a slip of the eek be made to open, large enough to admit the piece of comb. It should be removed on the following morning, if the cold has not prevented their taking their usual supply in the night. Should that be the case, shut them up for a day or two, to prevent the mischief which would occur from strange bees entering the hive while it is feeding, or remove the weak hive to a considerable distance. A well-peopled hive will require about two pounds of sirup in the month. A new swarm ought always to be put into a new hive, which should be provided in April. Sticks in the inside are unnecessary, but the projecting straws must be singed off. Should any hive in May seem wholly destitute of drones – in Scotland they do not appear till the end of May or beginning of June – watch at the entrance of that hive which appears to have the greatest number of them, and catch forty or fifty, confine them in a box till the evening, when they may be easily introduced, and will be most thankfully received by the hive that appears to be without them. To supply a hive with a queen, cut out from some of the other hives that can be got at most easily, a piece of comb that has eggs in it; turn up the queenless hive, and with the left hand, shed two of the combs a little asunder, then with the right hand put in the piece of comb between them, observing that the cells be put in the hive in the same order as in their native hive; that is, the cells that were uppermost to be so still; then let the hand be removed, and the hive replaced. In England, a swarm may be expected in May, but not till June in Scotland; preceding the swarming, may be observed, amongst other signs, small drops of perspiration at the entrance, and when the bees cluster on the outside of the hive, the bee-master must be constantly on the watch. In general, they will swarm with the first sunshine; but if they continue to lie out when the weather is favourable, a little water may be squirted on them. The swarm once on the wing, it should never be lost sight of. Ringing of bells, and other noises, are more likely to do harm than good. It is unnecessary to prepare the hive with any thing sweet or odoriferous; but if the swarm does not remain in one hive, give them another. The easiest situation for hiving a swarm is that in which the hive can he held under the swarm, and the bees shaken into it. In all cases, a goose wing will be found of essential service to brush the bees off the post into the hive; but great care must be taken that none of the knots of bees which may contain the queen bee, drop upon the ground. The hive, when the bees have been all shaken or brushed into it, should be placed on the board, and left near the place of the swarm's first settling, until the evening, when it should be carefully removed and placed on a pedestal, at some distance from the parent hive. A second swarm may generally be looked for on the eighth or tenth day after the first; sometimes sooner, but never later than the twelfth day after. The day before the departure of the second swarm, the call of the queen bees may be distinctly heard; the note of the one is loud and clear, that of the other, the young queen, is lower, but equally distinct, and totally different from the hum of the other bees. As they give no other signal of their second swarming, it is necessary to keep a vigilant watch over the hives, to ascertain from which the swarm departs. It is generally necessary to return the second swarm to the parent hive immediately. They are seldom or never worth preserving as a separate colony, except when two fly off together, in which case they become, by a union, of little inferior value to a first swarm. Supposing the two swarms to have alighted upon separate branches, proceed to shake one of them into the empty hive, and then immediately shake the other into the same, leaving it to the bees to kill the superfluous queen bee, that is, if the proprietor has not the skill or courage to do it.

To join two swarms from different hives, it will be necessary to drench both with a mixture of beer, sugar, and water, made lukewam, or, with the fumigating bellows, give them a little smoke from lime leaves or tobacco. When a second swarm is to be returned to the parent hive, turn down a chair, and place the back parallel with the entrance of the hive, over which a sheet or tablecloth may be spread; then holding the hive containing the second swarm over it, give it a few sharp knocks on the top, and the bees will fall immediately on the cloth; proceed then, either with the finger or a stick, to guide a few of the bees to the entrance of the parent hive, and they will instantly crowd into it: those who are acquainted with the person of the queen, should take this opportunity of catching her. In regard to a third swarm, it would be folly to keep it. When the weather proves unfavourable after the hiving of a swarm, some food should be administered to the bees at night. When they lie out in clusters, and no more swarms are desired, an eek should be placed on the hive. If the heat be very great, it would be advisable to shade the hives, in addition to the common covering of straw, with which they ought always to be provided, as the best protection from the cold in winter, and the heat in summer. A particular value should always be put on those hives that kill their drones the earliest. It sometimes happens that their numbers deter the bees from attempting any violence against them; therefore, when the other stocks kill their drones, let the bee-master place himself quietly by the side of the hive, in the middle of a fine day, and crush every drone with his finger or a stick, as it passes out or in. Every hive will be the better for a little assistance in this massacre, which may be looked for in the end of July or beginning of August.

Instead of following the general plan of suffocating the bees in August, the hives should be removed to the vicinity of a heath, and there allowed to remain from four to six weeks. July is the best season for depriving the hives of a part of their store. When a hive is to be robbed of its honey, remove it from the stool to some distance, procure an empty hive, invert it on that from which you wish to dislodge the bees, either to take the honey, or to unite them with another hive. Stop up the entrance, and then strike gently the under hive on the side opposite to that to which the combs are fixed; in a few minutes, when the anger of the bees may be appeased, a piece of wood should be introduced to keep the two hives about an inch apart on one side; for the purpose of preventing the bees, after being driven up on the one side, descending, which they might do, by the other, to the hive from whence they were dislodged, the knocking on the under hive must be continued, till the bees, terrified by the noise, take refuge in the upper hive; then, with the fumigating bellows, or common tobacco pipe, blow into the hive a little smoke from lime leaves, or tobacco. The same operation having been performed on the other hive, that is, the hive destined to receive the new colony, the dislodged bees are emptied into it, and swept with a brush of feathers into the interstices between the combs; the board being then put upon the hive, it is instantly reverted, and placed upon the stand. When a hive is merely to be deprived of a part of its store, the hive with the bees in it may be placed upon the pedestal from which the full one was removed, and the hive from which the bees have been driven must then be taken into the house. A few bees will be found still straggling about the combs, but they will be too frightened to use their sting. When the requisite quantity of comb is cut out, breaking it as little as possible, the hive should be cleared of every noxious matter, and returned to its former position; but first invert the hive containing the bees, and place the deprived hive over it; leave them in this situation till the morning, when the bees will be found to have taken possession of their native home. At any season of the year, a weak hive may be strengthened from a strong one, by the following method: Take a strong hive from its pedestal, and place on it that which has few bees in it; then turning up the strong one, give it several raps on its sides, when many of the bees will fly to their old station; then place the strong hive where the weak one stood, or the other at a considerable distance.

The bee-master, in approaching a hive, should avoid breathing on the bees; and, if his manner be soft, calm, and gentle, he will in general need no protection from being stung; but when swarms are to be united, or hives deprived of a part of their store, the operator should be provided with thick worsted gloves, and a gauze, or piece of thin cloth, such, as milk is usually strained through, for the head; this last must be large enough to go over a man's hat, and around the neck, so as to tie before with a string running through a tape or loop holes; that part which comes next the face must be cut out, and a piece of very open gauze, catgut, or net-work, sewed therein. So protected, the most timid may proceed fearlessly; but every one who undertakes the management of the bee, is more or less subject to its sting. No time should be lost in extracting it. Rub the wound briskly with a piece of woollen cloth till it ceases to smart, and apply goulard-water, laudanum, or vinegar and spirits, as may be soonest attained; or wash with spirit of ammonia, and wrap a piece of linen about the part, steeped in spirits of wine. If the pain continue six hours, put on a hot poultice of bread and milk, and change it every four hours.

A List of Plants from which the Bees extract the greatest quantity of Honey

MIGNONETTE, heath, furze, white clover, thyme, particularly lemon thyme, rosemary, balm, beans, and every species of pulse, all resinous trees, borage, wild mustard, and golden rod; this last begins to blow when all other flowers have faded, and continues to blow till the middle of November; it will grow in the worst soil, and should be particularly cultivated in the vicinity of an apiary.

The Huish Hive

Is made of straw, in the form of a flower-pot inverted, but open at both ends, and having a band of straw projecting from the inside about two inches from the top; upon this band are placed seven bars of well-seasoned wood, about one and a half inch broad, and a quarter of an inch thick; they are slightly fastened down with small nails, then covered with thin gauze or net-work, and again with a circular board, in which small holes are made, to permit the steam to escape from the body of the hive. The whole to have a convex cover of straw, manufactured as the hive, and made to fit in like the cover of a sauce-pan. At any time or season of the year, when some honey-comb is required, or at the end of the season, when the bees are to be deprived of their superfluous store, remove the top and other coverings, and take the side bars out, from which having cut the honey-comb, replace them as before; the operation is facilitated by having some vacant bars ready to supply the places of the full ones. When the bees, by lying out in clusters, indicate that they stand in need of room, instead of an addition at the bottom, as in the common hive, this hive need only be deprived of a part of the comb attached to one or more of the bars. In time of snow, or when robbery is threatened, the centre should be closed by a tin wicket, or by a piece of lead with holes made in it to admit air.

Another Hive

The hive is formed as the common cottage-hive, being made to separate towards the middle. On the lower division, which may be made the largest, a board is placed, in which one large or some smaller holes are made, to admit of the bees ascending. When the upper part, or top, is filled with honey, it may be removed, and replaced by another prepared for the purpose. Those who wish to see the bees at work, may place a glass top under the straw one, or invert tumblers, or long glasses made for the purpose, over each hole, one or more of which may be removed as they are filled.

To Extract the Honey from the Combs

To obtain the primary honey, heat, celerity, and cleanliness, are necessary. Where a few hives only are kept, it will be sufficient to have two or three earthen pans, with a frame of wire adapted to their size, each wire being about one inch distant from another – a corn riddle or flour sieve placed over a tub answers the purpose very well – two horse-hair sieves, a bag of a conical form, that is, wide at top, and tapering to a point at the bottom, made of such canvass as is used in a dairy, and some jars for the reception of the honey, and in which it is to be preserved. The hives should be brought into a warm room, where no bees nor wasps can enter; the combs are then loosened from the hive by a long thin knife; those parts of the comb which are empty should be cut off first, and those that are black and drossy drained by themselves; as also those in which there is any farina. Should there be any brood, care must be taken not to rush it, as the juice will communicate a bad flavour to the honey; and those pieces of the comb which contain it, may be placed under any stock that most wants strengthening. If there be any bees upon the combs when taken out, they should be brushèd or blown off, and if besmeared with honey, washed in water made a little warm; then being laid on a sieve, and placed in the sunshine, they will revive, and fly to their respective homes. The pure combs should be cut in small pieces, sliced twice in a horizontal direction, that is, at the top and at the bottom, and laid on the wire frames to drain; in two or three hours they may be turned. When all the primary honey is extracted, it must be run through the bag, whereby it will be entirely freed from every particle of wax. This, the first drawn, should be preserved by itself; the next in value is that which drains from the combs indiscriminately; a third sort may be obtained by wringing the combs in a cloth, or by placing them in a lukewarm oven. They may be afterwards steeped for mead or vinegar, and the water in which the utensils and the hands of the operator have been washed, may be kept likewise for the same purpose. As soon as the jars in which the honey is to be preserved are full, they should be corked down, and deposited in a dry place. Liquid honey should never be put into a vessel containing honey which has acquired any consistency; this mixture will make it ferment and turn sour. A hundred pounds of honey-comb will not in general yield more than four pounds of wax.

To Melt and Purify Wax

WHERE six or eight stocks of bees are kept, it will be most profitable and convenient to have a tin vessel made to fit a due proportioned kettle or pot, the sides of which should be quite straight, so that, when it slides down, there may be no vacancy for the farina or bee-bread to rise up between. The holes in the tin separater should be as numerous and small as possible in the bottom, and about two inches up the sides; the bottom should be quite flat, without a rim, like that of a quart tin pot, that it may press the dregs the closer down when near the bottom. Set the pot on the fire, with about five or six inches depth of water therein, in which is to be mixed single aquafortis, in the proportion of half an ounce for each quart of water. In this put as many combs as will conveniently boil, when melted. As soon as they begin to melt, they should be frequently stirred, until all be thoroughly melted; let it then boil without stirring, that the wax may rise clear. It should be made to boil briskly during the whole process. As soon as the yellow froth rises, put in the separater, and press it down in the liquor, until it be about full; with a wooden spoon, or what is better, a tin ladle, first dipped in cold water, lightly skim off the wax as it rises upon the surface, and put it in a narrow-bottomed pan, previously rinsed in cold water, set as near as may be to the pot on the fire, and continue skimming the wax off as long as it rises, depressing the separater in proportion as the liquor rises. When the liquor in the pan is nearly cold, the wax is to be taken out, and what dross adheres to it scraped off. The wax is then to be reboiled in a small quantity of water, and about a fourth part as much aquafortis as before to a quart; as soon as it boils, take it off and let it stand until cold. The wax will concrete at the top, and the remaining dross, being scraped off, may be further purified with other combs.

Another and less expensive method is, to put the combs loosely into a canvass, or rather a fine hair bag, tied up close at the end, and put into a kettle, with a due proportion of aquafortis and water; a leaden or iron weight is to be laid on the bag, to keep it down to the bottom. It must be made to boil, so as to throw up the froth briskly, which is to be taken off with a ladle; a thick board with a handle in the middle is then to be put in, to press out what wax may be still adhering; it is afterwards to be re-melted, as in the first method. It should be carefully observed, that in these processes of skimming off the froth, what rises of a clear yellow should be reserved by itself, as often requiring no further purification. The more forcibly the froth is thrown up, the purer it will be, and the operation the sooner finished. The very old brood combs are not worth melting; but such refuse as has been pressed, may be kept in a close tub or vessel for five or six weeks, in which time the impurities will ferment and decay, and the wax will be in a better state for melting.

CHAPTER XXV
ON PIGS

Pigs may be considered of primary importance to the farmer, and to every other householder, as to them the refuse of the fields, the dairy, and the kitchen, is a feast. Though that food should be gross and dirty, they will not reject it; and they are often reared in cold and filthy habitations; but it is only by order and cleanliness that successful feeding can be ensured. Where a large stock is kept, their feeding-bouse should be thirty feet by fifteen; it may be divided into four rooms, the two in the middle to be adapted for eating, and the others for sleeping apartments; each should have an outside door, and also an inner communication, that the keeper may get their eating-rooms swept out, their mangers cleaned, and their food put in, while the pigs are at rest. Each of the above-mentioned eating and sleeping rooms, in case of being required for sows and young pigs, may be divided into two by partitions, made to remove at pleasure. The sleeping apartments ought to be dark; and the house, as also the square, or yard, formed by the huts or other buildings for sows, should be paved, and well littered; and water should be within reach of the pigs. The manger, or trough, must be always washed out before putting in their victuals; and that which remains in it after the pigs are satisfied, should be given to some of the young stock.

From the different varieties having become so much intermixed and blended together, (this is especially the case in Scotland,) it is difficult to describe any particular breed of swine. The Berkshire is allowed to be a good kind. They are generally of a brown, or rather a reddish colour, with black spots, the ears bending forward, but not hanging down so much as those of the large Cumberland kind; – they are short-legged and small-boned; their flesh is fine; and they are well disposed to fatten on common fare. The large spotted Woburn breed is well formed, prolific, hardy, and kindly disposed to fatten. – The Chinese black, or pot-bellied breed, are small in size, their necks thick, and legs short. They are one of the most profitable sorts in this island, as their flesh is delicate, and they fatten on very indifferent food, and more readily than any other small breed; indeed they may be said to be always ready for killing; they are excellent for bacon, and are well adapted for being used as pork. When young, that is, when about four months old, they are very mischievous when not well ringed.* And for those who do not

* The usual method of ringing swine is now superseded by an improved method adopted by Mr Tubb, which is to pare off, with a sharp penknife, the gristle on the tops of the noses of young pigs.

like very fat pork, the small breeds before mentioned will be preferable, their flesh being equally delicate. – There is another small breed, which is by far the best for the farmer, but it cannot be classified; they will feed in a shorter period, and will thrive upon articles that would starve the larger-sized animals. The kind in view will feed upon common fare, to seven or eight stones Amsterdam, when eleven or twelve months old, or to nine or ten stones when put up in the house to receive better food.

For a large establishment, a boar and two good sows, of a proper age, should constantly be kept; and one young sow annually reared, in order to supply the others, when they pass maturity, that is, when they arrive at three years of age. Their time of farrowing should be so arranged that they may produce two litters in the year; one about March, and the other towards the beginning of August. A sow, when with young, ought not to be entirely confined to a hut, but allowed to walk about at pleasure in the swine-yard, or court, belonging to the farm; nor should she be allowed to sleep with a number of swine. A sow goes with young 112 days, or sixteen weeks, not above a day over or under that time; a few hours previous to her farrowing, she will be observed carrying straws in her mouth, to make a bed with. When she is bringing forth her young, she ought not to have much litter or long straw in her apartment, nor for a few days after, lest the young pigs should be hid by it from their dam. She ought to be well fed when giving suck; if she is once allowed to get poor, it will take double the quantity of food and of time to restore her to her former state. If the pigs should be numerous, they, as also the sow, should be fed two or three times a-day with milk, and wheat bran, or meal. Should the milk be scarce, a little water, slightly warm, may be mixed with it, taking care that the mixture be not too thick, that is, more of the nature of a drink than of any thing else; and while the pigs are feeding on this, the sow should be turned out for an hour or two, that her milk may gather a little. She and her pigs should lie dry and warm. If they are well fed, the pigs will be ready for the spit in three weeks; and may be sold in six weeks. When the pigs are taken from the sow and weaned, whether with the breeder or purchaser, they must be regularly fed three times a-day with a little wheat bran, barley dust, or meal of some description or other, mixed with water, made milk-warm; in a few weeks after, they may have some potatoes, turnips, or any kind of grain; and after the harvest is concluded, they may be allowed to range at large among the fields, to pick up any left corn, beans, or peas. Before going out in the morning, they may receive a feeding of offal grain; and in the evening, an allowance of yams or turnips. They may also get the refuse from the garden, kitchen, and dairy; milk and whey is the finest of all fattening. When the pigs are put up to close feeding, they should have three meals a-day of potatoes, which have been strained, mixed with barley or any other meal, moistened with milk, whey, or water, and seasoned with a little salt; it should be given regularly, and only in such quantities as will be consumed with a relish. This will be found the best and most economical food; but where the trouble attending the preparation of it is considered too great, the next best method is to mix oats with barley, in the proportion of one part to four of barley, which will prevent the pigs from eating it too quickly; the oats being husky, require a longer time to be chewed. Buck-wheat is a quick and good fattening, somewhat similar to barley, not so good as peas; but peas are sometimes put amongst buck, for the same purpose that oats are mixed with barley. Pigs that are fed from the refuse of breweries are liable to eruptive diseases. Whenever grains are used for feeding, they should be fresh, and given in moderate quantities, and should only form a part of their diet; they will also feed well on the spent hops of the breweries. Sweet whey, unless given in very moderate quantities, is injurious to pigs; but when it becomes sourish, it proves very wholesome food. It is too general a practice to pay no attention to feeding pigs until they are put up, perhaps in November or December, when, with a little pains, they might be as fat, and weigh nearly as much, at the time they begin to feed, as at the period when they are fed, which may be about four or five weeks after they are put up. For pork, they are usually fattened from six to nine months old; for bacon and hams, from nine months to a year and half.

Pigs are subject to inflammatory and eruptive diseases, both of which require bleeding, purgatives, and cool air in an open field. The most easy way of bleeding pigs is by cutting off the tail, or part of the ear.

Purgative powder for pigs, jalap one drachm. Should this be found insufficient, eleven or twelve grains of scamony may be added, or ten grains of calomel; but it is better to try the jalap alone first.

When pigs are to be made into bacon hams, they should be allowed to fast twenty-four hours before the time of killing, and in killing them great attention ought to be had to prevent the knife from striking against the bone at the bottom of the gullet, by which a morbid state of the flesh in the fore-quarter will be avoided. After the pig has been killed and dressed, it should hang up till the next day, when it must be sawn down the back bone from the tail to the point of the snout; then all the seam or tallow should be removed, with the feet, tail, and ears, and such trifling pieces as may appear offensive to the eye. The side being laid upon a table, with the skin side uppermost, salt should be taken in indefinite quantities, and rubbed in well, particularly upon the shoulders and hams, for at least half an hour; the side weighing about six stones. In turning the side, four ounces of saltpetre, ground very fine, should be sprinkled very uniformly over the inside and ends of the shanks, above which ought to be laid a covering of salt, about an inch thick over the whole inside, and gently clapped down by the hand into every crevice, but by no means rubbed in on that side. The side may then be placed upon boards, on a floor where no frost can affect it. If more than one side is cured, they may be laid one above another to any depth, provided the back and belly parts be laid alternately and the skin side always down most. The whole should be covered with a cloth, and some, though not a very heavy weight, put upon the top.

After lying in this state for ten days, they are to be taken up, and rubbed again upon the skin side with salt, for about a quarter of an hour, and covering again the inside with salt, without rubbing, and without any more saltpetre. After the second rubbing, the sides are again put into their former position, and allowed to remain there for other ten days, when they may be taken up, and wholly covered over with barley meal, and hung up with cords by the shanks, which may be pierced with wooden pins to allow the cord a better hold, to the roof of the kitchen. After hanging there in the heat for two months, they may be hung up in any cool, but dry apartment. As the family require them, the pieces may be cut out to any size that may be found most convenient.

From the middle of September to the middle of April is the proper curing season. These approved directions for curing, are given here to make the chapter complete. Various other receipts on the subject will be found under the head of Pork.

Appendix

A Rule by which any gentleman may be enabled to establish a practical system of domestic economy, according to his income, to detect any error that may have arisen in the management, and to discover at once what part or parts he may best alter, in order to increase or diminish the expense of any other part that may be desired.

Rule

Divide the whole annual income, be it what it may into 100 equal parts, which may be appropriated to the several branches of the establishment in the following proportions, viz.

36 per cent for provisions and other articles of household expense.
22 per cent for servants, horses, and carriages.
12 per cent for clothing, haberdashery, and other incidental expenses of that nature.
8 per cent for education, pocket, private, and other extra expenses.
12 per cent for rents, taxes, and repairs of house and furniture.
10 per cent to be reserved for future contingencies.

100 Total.

From these premises is deduced the following table, by means of which this rule may be adapted to any amount of income, viz.

Annual Income	House expenses 36 per cent	Servants, &c. 22 per cent	Clothes, &c. 12 per cent	Rent, &c. 12 per cent	Extras 8 per cent	Reserve 10 per cent
£1000	£360	£220	£120	£120	£80	£100
1500	540	330	180	180	120	150
2000	720	440	240	240	160	200
3000	1080	660	360	360	240	300
4000	1440	880	480	480	320	400
5000	1800	1100	600	600	400	500
10000	3600	2200	1200	1200	800	1000

N.B. – L.10 is one per cent on L.1000. L.20 is one per cent on L.2000. L.300 is one per cent on L3000, and so on.

ESTIMATE of EXPENSES for a Family of Five persons living in town: a gentleman, lady and three children, having two maid-servants, and a man-servant out of the house.

Income of L.500 per annum.

Provisions and other articles of household expenses

	Weekly.			Annually.		
Bread and flour for 7 persons, 1s. each	£0	7	0	£18	4	0
Butter, ¾ lbs. each, 5 1/4lbs. at 1s., each 9d.	0	5	3	13	13	0
Cheese, 3lbs. at 10d. per lb.	0	2	6	6	10	0
Milk and eggs, 4d. each	0	2	4	6	1	4
Tea. Coffee. &c. 2 ½ oz. tea, at 8s. per lb.	0	3	3	8	9	0
Sugar, &c. 6 lbs. at 8 per lb. on an average	0	4	0	10	8	0
Other grocery of all kinds, including condiments, &c. 8d. each	0	4	8	12	2	8
Butcher-meat, 28 lbs. at 7d. per lb. £0 16 4 } 3s.6d.a-day Fish, &c. 1s.2d.per day }	1	4	6	63	14	0
Vegetables, garden fruits, &c. 8d. each	0	4	8	12	2	8

Beer, spirituous liquors, &c. 1s 9d. a day	0	12	3	31	17	0
Coals, coke, and wood; say 5 ¾ chaldrons coals at 48s, L.13, 16s. and wood 23s.	0	5	9	14	19	0
Candles, oil &c.; about 15 doz. candles a year, half stores and half moulds, average 6d. per lb. say 3 ½ lbs a week, 4d. a day	0	2	4	6	1	4
Soap, starch, &c. for washing; soap about 3 ¼ lbs. at 7d., and starch, 4d. a day.	0	2	4	6	1	4
Sundries for cleaning, scouring, &c.	0	1	0	2	12	0
Total for regular household expenses	4	1	10	212	15	4
Extra for entertainments, medicine, and other incidents				14	4	2
Total for household expenses				L226	19	6
Clothes and haberdashery – gentleman, L.24; lady, L. 21; children, L.18; sundries, L.2				65	0	0
Rent, taxes, &c.				50	0	0
Education, extra and private expenses				25	0	0
Two maid-servants, L.16 and L.12				28	0	0
Man-servant (out of the house) and duty				31	4	0
Horse, as per table				32	0	0
Total expense				L.458	3	6
Reserve one twelfth, or difference				41	16	6
Amount of income				L.500	0	0

Annual expense of one Horse

Oats, 3 quarterns per day, or 5 ½ pecks per week, at 26s. per quarter	L.0	4	6
Hay, about 1 ½ truss, at 3s. per truss, or L.4, 4s. per load	0	4	6
Straw, 1 truss per week	0	1	6
Food per week	L.0	10	6

46 weeks in the stable, at 10s. 6d.	L.24	3	0
6 weeks' grass in the spring, at 5s.	1	10	0
Food per annum	25	13	0
Shoeing, farriery, and incidental expenses	1	18	3
Duty (for one horse)	1	8	9
Annual loss, or wear and tear of the horse, at 10 per cent its value, say L. 30	3	3	0
	L32	0	0

N.B. – The stable rent may be compensated by the sale of the dung.

NOTE

ON FISH, MEAT, POULTRY, GAME, AND VEGETABLES TO SHOW THE TIME THEY ARE IN SEASON.

Fish

SALMON are in the highest perfection in April, May, and June; and are only quite out of season in September, October, and November.

Cod fish are in season from June to January.

Herring are in season from July to February.

Mackerel are in season from April to July.

The large lobsters are in their best season from the middle of October till the beginning of May. Many of the small ones, and some of the larger sort, are good all the summer.

Oysters are in season from September to April.

Haddocks are in season from May to February; in December and January they are in perfection.

Whiting are in season from January to March; but may be obtained during the greater part of the year.

Skate are best from January to June, and are only out of season in September.

Sprats are in season from the middle of November to February.

Smelts are in season from January to June, and are to be had in October and November.

Trout are in season from May to July.

Tench are in season from July to September.

Perch are in season in June and July, and till November.

Eels are in season from September to June.

Plaice, brill, and flounders are in season from January to March, and from July to September.

Turbot and soles are in perfection about midsummer, and are in the market almost all the year.

Pike are in season from July to November.

Mullets are in season in August and September.

Carp are always in season.

Sturgeon are in season from January to February.

Crabs are in season from August to May, as are also prawns, shrimps, and other small shell-fish.

Halibut are in season in the spring months only.

Meat

Beef is in the highest perfection from November to January; but is always in season.

Mutton is in the highest perfection from June to November; but, like beef, is always in season.

Veal is in season from February till October, and may be had in the other months.

Lamb: grass lamb is in season from April to August, and house lamb may be had in the other months; it is most esteemed in December and January.

Pork is the most plentiful from November to March, but may be had throughout the year. – Roasting pigs are always in season.

Poultry

Fowls are in season except when they are moulting, which is during the autumn for the old, and in spring for the young. Chickens may be had all the year, except sometimes in January.

Turkeys are in season from September to February; and turkey poults are in season from June to November.

Guinea and pea fowl are in season from February to June.

Geese are in season from September to February; and green geese are in season from April to September.

Ducks are in season from August to February; and ducklings from April to June.

Pigeons are in season from February to November.

Game

Venison: buck venison is in the highest perfection from June to September; and doe venison from October to December.

Hares are in season from September to February, and leverets during the other months.

Rabbits are in season throughout the year.

Pheasants are in season from October to December.

Partridges are in season from September to January.

Woodcock and snipes may generally be had from November to March.

Grouse and blackcock are in season from August to December.

Wild-ducks and wild-geese are in season from September to February, as are also teal and widgeons.

Wheatears are in season in July and August.

Plovers are in season from July to September.

Vegetables

Cabbages: early cabbages are in season from April to July, and other cabbages till February.

Scots kale is in season from November to April.

Brussels sprouts are in season from December to March.

Cauliflower is in season from May to November.

Brocoli is in season from December to April.

Turnips begin in May, and are used all the other months.

Carrots – the same may be observed as of turnips.

Parsnips are in season from October to April.

Scorzonera, salsify, skirret, and red beet, the same.

White beet: the leaves are in season from June to October.

Jerusalem artichokes are in season from September to March.

Potatoes begin in June, and continue all the year.

Peas are in season from June to November.

Beans are in season from June to September.

Kidney or French beans are in season from the end of June to September.

Spinach: the winter spinach is in season from November to May, and the summer spinach during the other months.

Asparagus is in season from April to July.

Sea kale is in season from December to April.

Onions begin in March, and continue all the year round.

Leeks are in season from October to May.

Chives and cibols are fit for use in March.

Shalots and garlic begin in August.

Artichokes are in season from June to October.

Cardoons are in season from November to February.

Lettuce, taking it in its varieties, is always in season.

Celery is in season from September to March.

Garden cress, mustard, and sorrel, throughout the year.

Radishes are in season from March to May.

Indian cress: the flower will be ready in May, the seeds in September.

Horse-radish is always in season; parsley is the same.

Rhubarb is in season from March to the middle of May.

Cucumbers are in season from June to September.

N.B.

THE WEIGHTS AND MEASURES IN THIS BOOK ARE,

16 ounces to a pound.
4 quarts to a gallon.
Two Scots pints to make one English gallon.
One choppin a quart.
One mutchkin a pint.

The End.

Recipes Modernized by Elizabeth Baird

SOUPS

Mullagatawny, or Currie Broth: Page 15

Original Recipe

Make about two quarts of strong veal broth, seasoned with two onions, a bunch of parsley, salt and pepper; strain it, and have ready a chicken, cut in joints and skinned; put it into the broth, with a table-spoonful of currie-powder; boil the chicken till quite tender, and a little before serving, add the juice of a lemon, and stir in a tea-cupful of cream. Serve boiled rice to eat with this broth.

Modern Version

The main modification to this delicious soup is the substitution of boneless skinless chicken breasts or thighs for the whole chicken, "cut in joints and skinned." It's easier for the cook as well as for the diners since there's no need to wrestle with a knife and fork to enjoy the broth and bite-size chunks of tender chicken.

8 cups (2 L) veal or chicken broth
2 onions, diced
10 stalks fresh parsley, tied together
½ tsp (2 mL) each salt and pepper
4 tsp (20 mL) curry powder (see Currie Powder, page 448)
2 lb (1 kg) boneless skinless chicken breasts or thighs
¼ cup (60 mL) freshly squeezed lemon juice
½ cup (125 mL) whipping (35%) cream
2 cups (500 mL) hot cooked rice (see To Boil Rice, page 447)

In a large saucepan, bring the broth, onions, parsley, salt, and pepper to a boil. Reduce the heat and simmer, uncovered, for 20 minutes. Remove the parsley. Strain the broth, if desired. Stir in the curry powder.

Trim any fat from the chicken parts. Simmer the chicken in the seasoned broth until tender, turning 2 or 3 times to cook evenly, for about 20 minutes for breasts (or until no longer pink inside) and a little longer for thighs (until juices run clear). Remove the chicken; cut into bite-size chunks.

Return the chicken pieces to the broth; heat through. Stir in the lemon juice, then the cream. Taste and adjust the seasoning.

Spoon the rice into the bottom of a warmed tureen or divide among individual warmed soup bowls. Ladle in the soup.

Makes 6 to 8 servings.

Soup Cressy: Page 18

Original Recipe

Slice twelve large onions, and fry them pretty brown in a quarter of a pound of fresh butter; scrape and clean two dozen of good red carrots, boil them in four quarts of water till quite soft; pound them in a marble mortar, mix them with the onions, and add the liquor in which the carrots were boiled, a bunch of sweet herbs, pepper, salt, a blade of mace, and two or three cloves; let them all boil about an hour, then rub them through a hair sieve; put it on again to boil rather quickly, till it be as thick as rich cream. Pour a little dry boiled rice in the tureen, and pour the soup over it. If the carrots are large, one dozen will be found sufficient.

Modern Version

Mrs Dalgairns describes "sweet herbs" as "parsley, sweet marjoram, winter savory, orange and lemon thyme; the greatest proportion of parsley." Use this list as a starting point for the soup, even if you don't have exactly this combination. In the modern version, regular thyme plus grated lemon and orange peel are substituted for the lemon and orange thyme.

¼ cup (60 mL) butter
3 large onions, chopped
6 large carrots, chopped
3 tbsp (45 mL) coarsely chopped fresh parsley
2 tsp (10 mL) each chopped fresh marjoram and thyme
1 tsp (5 mL) chopped fresh savory
½ tsp (2 mL) each salt and pepper
¼ tsp (1 mL) each finely grated lemon and orange peel

¼ tsp (1 mL) ground mace
Pinch ground cloves
2 cups (500 mL) hot cooked rice (see To Boil Rice, page 447)

In a large skillet, melt the butter over medium-low heat; fry the onions, stirring often, until golden, about 20 minutes. Set aside.

Meanwhile, in a large covered saucepan, bring 6 cups (1.5 L) water to a boil; add the carrots and simmer until tender, about 15 minutes. Scrape the onion mixture into the carrots; stir in the parsley, marjoram, thyme, savory, salt, pepper, lemon and orange peel, mace, and cloves. Return to a boil; reduce the heat and simmer, covered, for 20 minutes.

Press through the fine disc of a food mill or purée with an immersion blender or stand blender until silky smooth. Return the soup to a clean saucepan. Bring to a boil over medium heat, stirring. If the soup is too thick, add water so that it is, according to Mrs Dalgairns, "as thick as rich cream." Taste and adjust the seasoning.

Spoon the rice into the bottom of a warmed soup tureen or evenly divide among individual warmed soup bowls. Ladle in the soup.

Makes 6 to 8 servings.

Kitchen Notes:

A generous splash of fresh lemon juice adds a pleasing freshness to the soup.

There have been many colours of carrots; for example, purple, yellow, and red. In the seventeenth century, Dutch growers launched orange carrots, and that version dominated for a long time. Recently, there have been changes as new gourmet carrots come not in orange, but in the vibrant colours of their past, and more.

A Simple Soup: Page 34

Original Recipe

Cut small one pound of carrots, one pound of turnips, half a pound of onions, one lettuce, a little celery, and a handful of parsley; stew them for twenty minutes with a quarter of a pound of butter, some salt and pepper; then put them into three quarts of stock, made with two pounds of veal, and add one quart of green peas, and let it stew for three hours. Press it through a sieve, and boil it up before sending it to table.

Modern Version

Veal broth may not be a staple in every kitchen, nor the knuckles of veal necessary to simmer up the broth. Chicken broth is a mild-tasting substitute for the veal version. Choose lower-sodium stocks and broth.

¼ cup (60 mL) butter
2½ cups (625 mL) chopped carrots
2½ cups (625 mL) chopped white turnips
2 cups (500 mL) shredded romaine lettuce
1½ cups (375 mL) chopped celery
1 large onion, chopped
½ cup (125 mL) coarsely chopped fresh parsley
½ tsp (2 mL) each salt and pepper
6 cups (1.5 L) veal or chicken broth, approximate
1½ cups (375 mL) fresh or frozen peas

In a large saucepan, melt the butter over medium-low heat; add the carrots, turnips, lettuce, celery, onion, parsley, salt, and pepper. Cover and cook, stirring occasionally, until the vegetables are bright coloured, about 25 minutes.

Stir in the broth; bring to a boil. Cover, reduce the heat and simmer until the vegetables are softened, about 25 minutes. Add the peas; simmer for about 8 minutes if fresh or about 4 minutes if frozen. Let cool slightly. Pass the vegetables through the fine disc of a food mill or purée them with a hand-held or stand blender until silky. Add more broth for a thinner soup. Taste and adjust the seasoning.

(Make-ahead: Let cool. Refrigerate in an airtight container for up to 2 days. Reheat to serve.)

Makes 8 servings

FISH – CHAPTER II

Caveach Salmon: Page 44

Original Recipe

Boil in two quarts of vinegar three heads of shalots, half an ounce of whole black pepper, three cloves, two blades of mace, and a little salt. Cut the fish in slices, and fry them of a light-brown colour in fine oil, or clarified dripping; put them, when cold, into a pan, pour over them the vinegar and spices, and put on the top eight or ten spoonfuls of oil.

Soles may be done in this way, only lay over them sliced onions instead of shalots.

Modern Version

Caveach, from the Spanish "escabeche," is the name for a method of cooking and pickling raw fish in an acid – vinegar or limes. Here, slices of salmon are already cooked, then gently spiced with cloves, mace, and pepper. This adaptation is smaller than the original, calling for a 1-lb (500 g) salmon fillet rather than a whole fish.

1 cup (250 mL) white wine vinegar
½ cup (125 mL) diced shallots
1 tsp (5 mL) black peppercorns
½ tsp (2 mL) salt
1 whole clove or pinch ground cloves
1 blade mace or pinch ground mace
1 lb (500 g) salmon fillet
2 tbsp (30 mL) olive oil

In a saucepan, bring the vinegar, shallots, peppercorns, salt, cloves, and mace to a boil. Reduce the heat; cover and simmer gently until the shallots are translucent, about 5 minutes. Let cool.

Meanwhile, cut the salmon crosswise into scant 1-inch (2.5 cm) slices. Heat the oil in a large non-stick frying pan over medium heat; fry the slices, turning once, until golden on both sides and the fish almost flakes when gently probed. Using a long spatula, transfer to a shallow serving dish that is big enough to accommodate the slices in 1 layer. Pour the spiced vinegar over top. Cover and refrigerate for 1 hour, occasionally spooning the spiced vinegar over the salmon. (Make-ahead: Refrigerate for up to 1 day.)

Makes 4 servings.

Bradu Fagadu: Page 64

Original Recipe

Pick the meat out of a lobster, cut it into small bits, season it with two table-spoonfuls of currie powder, some salt, and a little cayenne. Wash well and pick a quantity of spinach sufficient for a dish, half stew it, closely covered, without any water; then strain off the liquor from it, and add the lobster to it, with a large piece of butter; cover the stew-pan, and let it stew a quarter of an hour.

Modern Version

This recipe is an excellent example of Mrs Dalgairns's interest in Indian cookery.

3 cups (750 mL) chopped cooked lobster meat
2 tbsp (30 mL) curry powder (see Currie Powder, page 448)
¼ tsp (1 mL) salt
Pinch cayenne, optional
8 cups (2 L) packed spinach, 9-oz (270 g) bunch
¼ cup (60 mL) butter, cubed

In a bowl, toss the lobster meat with the curry powder, salt, and cayenne (if using).

Wash and trim the spinach, reserving the tender stems. Place in a saucepan with only the water clinging to the leaves; cover and cook over medium heat until limp, about 5 minutes. Transfer to a sieve and press firmly to release as much liquid as possible. Loosen with a fork.

In a clean saucepan or skillet, melt half of the butter over medium heat. Add the lobster and spinach; toss to coat. Sprinkle with the remaining butter; cover and cook just until heated through, about 4 minutes.

Makes 4 modest servings.

BEEF — CHAPTER III

Beef: Spit Roasted Sirloin (Preparatory Remarks), page 70

Original Recipe

The sirloin is the prime joint for roasting. When to be used, it should be washed, then dried with a clean cloth, and the fat covered over with a piece of white paper tied on with thread. The spit should be kept at all times exceedingly clean: it must be wiped dry immediately after it is drawn from the meat, and washed and scoured every time it is used. Care should be taken to balance the roast properly upon the spit; but, if not exactly right, it is better to make it equal by fastening on a leaden-headed skewer than to pierce it again. The fire should be prepared by putting on plenty of coals at the back. When put down, it should be about ten inches from the fire, and gradually drawn nearer.

It is first basted with a little butter or fresh dripping, and then well basted with its own fat all the time it is roasting. Ten minutes before serving, it should be sprinkled with a little salt, then dredged with flour, and basted till it is frothed. When it is drawn from the spit some gravy will run out, to which may be added a little boiling salt-and-water poured along the bone: the beef is then garnished with plenty of finely grated horse-radish.

Modern Version

Roasting on a spit was one of the glories of the Georgian kitchen, here recreated by using an electric barbecue rotisserie.

4½ lb (2.1 kg) beef top sirloin roast
¼ cup (60 mL) butter, melted
½ tsp (2 mL) each salt and pepper
4 tsp (20 mL) all-purpose flour

Prepare the rotisserie equipment for spit roasting. Remove the racks and place a foil drip pan on bars under one side of a two-burner barbecue, or in the centre of a three-burner barbecue. Heat remaining burner(s) to medium heat, 350°F (180°C).

Pat the roast dry. Wet a sturdy butcher's string that is long enough to encircle the roast twice; tie firmly around the meat to hold it together. In a small bowl, combine the butter, salt, and pepper; set aside.

Attach one of the prongs to the spit and press the prong into one end of the roast; push the spit through to the opposite side. Centre the roast on the spit and press in the second prong. Secure the prongs. Brush the roast with about half of the butter mixture and set in place over the drip pan. Close the lid and grill over indirect medium heat, brushing occasionally with some of the remaining butter mixture, then drippings, until an instant-read thermometer reaches about 125°F (50°C). Dust the roast all over with the flour and brush again with the drippings so that the roast will "froth." Roast to medium-rare, 140°F (60°C), for a total rotisserie time of about 2 hours. The temperature will rise to 145°F (63°C), still medium-rare. Transfer to a cutting board and cover loosely with foil. Let stand for 10 to 15 minutes before carving across the grain into thin slices. Serve with any pan juices from the drip pan and carving board.

Makes 8 to 10 servings.

Kitchen Notes:

To barbecue without a spit, set up the burners and drip pan as directed above. Place the roast on a greased grill over indirect heat at the same temperature as for spit roasting. Cook for 1½ to 2 hours, turning occasionally.

For oven roasting, set the roast on a rack in a shallow roasting pan and roast at 350°F (180°C) for 1½ to 2 hours. For all roasts, insert a meat thermometer into the thickest part of the meat and check regularly.

Beef à la Braise: Page 72

Original Recipe

Bone a rump of beef; lard it very thickly with bacon seasoned with pepper, salt, cloves, mace, and allspice, and season the beef with pepper and salt; put some slices of bacon into the bottom of the pan, with some whole black pepper, a little allspice, one or two bay leaves, two onions, a clove of garlic, and a bunch of sweet herbs. Put in the beef, and lay over it some slices of bacon, two quarts of weak stock, and half a pint of white wine. Cover it closely, and let it stew between six and seven hours.

Sauce for the beef is made of part of the liquor it has been stewed in, strained, and thickened with a little flour and butter, adding some green onions cut small, and pickled mushrooms. It is poured hot over the beef.

Modern Version

Mrs Dalgairns's choice for this braised recipe is a rump roast; instructions follow below. Because a rump roast is so lean, it should be larded, and that requires a larding needle – a gadget not found in many kitchens – and more prep time. So that this delicious roast can be enjoyed without larding, the cut of choice is a boneless blade roast, a pot roast that's more tender and better marbled. It has all the flavours of the original but is a little easier for the cook to prepare. See also the larded version that follows.

1 beef pot roast, such as boneless blade, 3½ lb (1.6 kg)
¾ tsp (4 mL) salt
½ tsp (2 mL) each pepper and ground mace
¼ tsp (1 mL) each ground allspice and cloves
8 slices thick bacon, ½ lb (250 g), divided
2 large onions, diced
2 bay leaves
1 large clove garlic, minced
Sweet Herbs (see below)
2 cups (500 mL) beef broth
1 cup (250 mL) white wine
2 tbsp (30 mL) all-purpose flour
2 tbsp (30 mL) butter, softened
3 green onions, thinly sliced
1 cup (250 mL) sliced pickled mushrooms (see Pickled Mushrooms, page 478)

Set out a Dutch oven or a 6-quart (6 L) heavy-bottomed saucepan with a tight-fitting lid. Position an oven rack in the bottom third of the oven; heat to 350°F (180°C).

Pat the roast dry. In a large bowl, combine the salt, pepper, mace, allspice and cloves; add the roast, turning to coat it all over and rubbing in the spices.

Spread 4 of the bacon slices over the bottom of the Dutch oven. Place the spice-covered roast in the Dutch oven and top with the remaining bacon. Arrange the onions, bay leaves, garlic and sweet herbs around the beef. Pour in the broth and wine. Cover and roast, turning the beef once or twice during roasting, until very fork-tender, about 2 hours. Remove the bay leaves.

Set the roast on a cutting board; cover loosely with foil and let rest for 10 to 15 minutes. Skim the fat off the juices in the pan. Strain the juices into a smaller saucepan, pressing to extract as much of the liquid as possible. (Some cooks might like to omit the straining and enjoy the onions in the sauce.) Bring to a boil.

Meanwhile, in a small bowl, mash together the flour and butter; whisk into the juices and continue whisking until smooth and hot. Taste the gravy and adjust the seasoning.

To serve, shred the meat into chunks, cutting out the fat as desired, or slice across the grain. Garnish with green onions and pickled mushrooms.

Makes 8 servings.

Larded Beef à la Braise

Choose a top round roast of about the same weight. Combine all the spices and herbs. Cut the bacon in half crosswise, then cut one-quarter of the slices into strips about ¼ inch (5 mm) wide. Coat the strips lightly with the spice and herb mixture. Clamp 1 strip into the larding needle and press through the leanest part of the roast. Repeat, 1 strip a time, spacing evenly. Rub the remaining spice and herb mixture over the roast and place it in the Dutch oven. Proceed with roasting, about 3½ hours. Make the gravy and slice and garnish the roast as described in Beef à la Braise.

Kitchen Note:

For the Sweet Herbs in this recipe, combine 3 tbsp (45 mL) coarsely chopped fresh parsley, 2 tsp (10 mL) each chopped fresh marjoram and thyme, 1 tsp (5 mL) chopped fresh savory and ¼ tsp (1 mL) each finely grated lemon and orange peel. Or combine a generous ¼ cup (60 mL) chopped fresh herbs of a similar nature.

LAMB – CHAPTER V

Lamb Chops: Page 97

Original Recipe

Cut a neck or loin of lamb into chops; rub them over with the beaten yolk of an egg; dip them into grated bread, mixed with plenty of chopped parsley, and seasoned with lemon peel, pepper and salt; fry them a light brown in good dripping; make a sauce with the trimmings, and thicken the sauce with butter rolled in flour; add a little lemon pickle and mushroom catsup. Garnish with fried parsley. They may be served with or without the gravy.

Modern Version

While a sauce is generally much appreciated as an accompaniment to lamb, these crunchy chops don't need it. This parsley and lemon combination is one of Mrs Dalgairns's favourites.

1 lb (500 g) rack of lamb chops, about 9, trimmed
2 egg yolks
1 cup (250 mL) fine breadcrumbs
2 tbsp (30 mL) minced fresh parsley
1 tbsp (15 mL) finely grated lemon peel
½ tsp (2 mL) salt and pepper
2 tbsp (30 mL) vegetable oil

Pat the chops dry; place on a waxed paper-lined baking sheet. In a shallow bowl, beat the egg yolks until smooth. In a large pie plate or deep plate, mix together the breadcrumbs, parsley, lemon peel, salt and pepper.

Brush one of the chops with some of the egg yolk and press both sides into the crumb mixture; place on the baking sheet. Repeat with the other chops. (Make-ahead: Refrigerate for up to 1 hour.)

Heat the oil in a large skillet over medium-high heat; fry the chops until golden, about 4 minutes per side. Drain well and serve with fried parsley (see Kebbobed Veal, page 441).

Makes 4 servings.

Kitchen Note

For thicker loin chops, usually 5 chops to 1 lb (500 g) , coat with 1 egg yolk and ½ cup (125 mL) breadcrumbs, 1 tbsp (15 mL) minced parsley, 2 tsp (10 mL) grated lemon peel and ½ tsp (2 mL) each salt and pepper.

VEAL – CHAPTER VI

Kebobbed Veal: Page 112

Original Recipe

Cut into thin bits the size of a crown-piece some lean veal; season them with turmeric, pepper, and salt. Slice onions very thinly, and some garlic: put the slices of veal and onion upon a skewer, together with thin bits of pickled pork. Fry them brown with butter, and garnish with plenty of fried parsley.

Modern Version

The surprise here is that Mrs Dalgairns fries these mini kabobs in butter in a frying pan.

½ lb (250 g) pink grain-fed veal shoulder, in large chunks
2 cloves garlic, minced
¾ tsp (4 mL) turmeric
½ tsp (2 mL) each salt and pepper
1 small onion
3 oz (90 g) peameal bacon (3 slices) or unsmoked bacon such as pancetta
2 tbsp (30 mL) butter
Fresh parsley
Vegetable oil

Soak 1 dozen 4-inch (10 cm) skewers in water for 30 minutes.

Cut the veal into slices that are a scant ¼ inch (5 mm) thick and about the size of a large coin. (You should have about 30 slices.) In a bowl, combine the garlic, turmeric, salt, and pepper. Add the veal and toss to coat thoroughly. Cover and let mellow in the refrigerator for up to 1 hour.

Meanwhile, cut the onion crosswise in half, saving the top half for another recipe. Cut the bottom half into wedges; separate the pieces. Cut the bacon crosswise into strips about ½ inch (1 cm) wide. Assemble the kabobs: start by folding a slice of veal and threading it onto a skewer, then add a piece of onion and a strip of bacon folded like the veal. Repeat 2 to 3 times for each skewer. Make sure the layers of veal, onion, and bacon are not jammed together. (Make-ahead: Cover and refrigerate the kabobs for up to 8 hours.)

Melt the butter in a large skillet over medium heat. Add the kabobs and fry, adjusting the heat as necessary and turning the skewers from time to time, until glossy and golden brown on the outside and cooked through but still moist inside, 10 to 15 minutes.

Meanwhile, thoroughly pat dry the parsley. Choose stalks about 3 inches (8 cm) long. Place a deep skillet over medium-high heat; pour in enough oil to come 1 inch (2.5 cm) up the side. Fry the parsley, without crowding the pieces, until crisp, about 30 seconds. Let drain on a paper towel.

Serve the kabobs hot, brushed with pan juices and garnished with the fried parsley.

Makes 4 servings.

Kitchen Notes:

You can grill these kabobs on a greased grill over medium heat, brushing them with the melted butter.

This recipe works very well with pork tenderloin instead of the veal.

For another variation, replace the turmeric with Currie Powder, page 448, and increase the Currie Powder to 1½ tsp (7 mL).

PORK – CHAPTER VII

Roasted Spareribs, from Preparatory Remarks: Page 118

Original Recipe

A spare rib should be roasted, is basted with butter, and has sage leaves, dried, rubbed to a powder, and mixed with salt and pepper, sprinkled over it.

Modern Version

What to choose? Side or spare ribs are meatier, flatter, have better marbling and are somewhat cheaper than back, a.k.a. baby back ribs. More expensive back ribs are noted for their tenderness. Both are special-occasion cuts, whether roasted slow and long in the oven or outside on the barbecue. Mrs Dalgairns has chosen a simple rub of butter, sage, salt, and pepper to complement the pork so as not to overwhelm it with loud spices and sticky sauces.

6 lb (2.7 kg) side or back ribs, 2 to 3 racks
¼ cup (60 mL), butter softened
2 tbsp (30 mL) finely crumbled dried sage
2 tsp (10 mL) salt
1½ tsp (7 mL) pepper

Check to see if the ribs have a membrane covering the underside. If so, ease a small knife underneath the membrane at one corner to get a grip on it and pull it off.

Pat the ribs dry. In a small bowl, mash together the butter, sage, salt, and pepper; brush the mixture over the ribs.

To Roast in the Oven: Position an oven rack in the bottom third of the oven; heat to 275°F (135°C). Place a rack in the bottom of a large shallow roasting pan; place the ribs on the rack, meaty side up. (Cut the ribs if necessary to fit them in the pan.) Roast, turning meaty side down halfway through, until the meat is tender and pulling away from the ends of the bones, 1½ to 2 hours.

To Roast on the Barbecue: Place a foil drip pan (or pans, as needed) on bars under one side of a two-burner barbecue or in the centre of a three-burner barbecue. Turn the remaining burner(s) to low heat, 275°F (135°C). Brush the grill over the unheated burner with oil. Place the ribs, meaty side up, over the unlit burner; close the lid and grill, turning meaty side down halfway through, until the meat is tender and pulling away from the ends of the bones, 1¾ to 2 hours.

Makes 6 generous servings, 8 for more modest appetites.

Kitchen Note:

Back ribs, often called baby back ribs, weigh less than spare or side ribs. It may be necessary to opt for 3 racks.

To Make Sausages: Page 121

Original Recipe

Take a pound of the inward fat of the pig, and half a pound of lean pork; pick both clean from skin and sinews, mince them very finely, grate a large nutmeg, take its weight of pounded mace and cloves, the largest proportion mace, the weight of all of black pepper, and twice the weight of the spices of salt; chop finely a few sage leaves and a little lemon thyme; mix all well together with two large table-spoonfuls of grated bread and the yolk of an egg beaten. It may be put into skins, or packed into a jar and tied closely with bladder. When to be used, moisten it with the yolk of an egg beaten, make it up in the form of sausages, flour them, and fry them in butter.

Modern Version

Even for homey dishes such as sausages, Mrs Dalgairns brings a fine balance of spices. Note the frequency with which she calls for nutmeg and for mace, the aril that forms around the nutmeg itself. Both were popular spices in cooking of the era. Mrs Dalgairns suggests serving the sausages heaped over a popular three-season vegetable – spinach.

1 tsp (5 mL) grated nutmeg
½ tsp (2 mL) ground mace
¼ tsp (1 mL) ground cloves
1 tsp (5 mL) each salt and pepper
1 tbsp (15 mL) minced fresh sage leaves
2 tsp (10 mL) minced fresh lemon thyme leaves
2 large egg yolks or 1 large egg
¼ cup (60 mL) dry breadcrumbs
1½ lb (750 g) lean ground pork
3 tbsp (45 mL) all-purpose flour
Butter, softened

In a large bowl, mix together the nutmeg, mace, cloves, salt, and pepper; stir in the sage and thyme. Beat in the egg yolks and breadcrumbs. Add the pork and mix until well combined.

Divide the mixture into 10 balls, each about ⅓ cup (75 mL). Form the balls into sausage shapes, each about 3 inches (8 cm) long, or shape them into patties about ½ inch (1 cm) thick. (Make-ahead: Refrigerate, covered, for up to 1 day or layer between waxed paper in an airtight container and freeze for up to 2 weeks. Let thaw in the refrigerator before frying.) Spread the flour in a deep plate; lightly press the sausages into the flour.

Brush a little butter over the bottom of a large skillet over medium heat; fry the sausages or patties, in batches if necessary and turning often, until crispy and cooked through, 18 to 20 minutes for the sausages, 15 minutes for the patties. Test for doneness with an instant-read thermometer inserted sideways into patties or sausages; it should read 160°F (71°C).

Makes 10 sausages or patties, 5 to 6 servings.

POULTRY – CHAPTER VIII

To Fricassee Chickens: Page 135

Original Recipe

When well washed, cut the chickens into joints, scald, and take off the skin; put them into a stew-pan, with an onion, cut small, a bunch of parsley, a little thyme, lemon-peel, and grated nutmeg, a slice of ham, and a bit of butter the size of a walnut; let them stew a quarter of an hour, add some white stock thickened with flour and butter. Take out the parsley, ham, thyme, and lemon-peel; and a little before serving, beat up the yolks of three eggs in half a pint of cream, and stir it in gradually.

Modern Version

In the original version above, the chicken is cut into joints and skinned. The alternative of pot-ready boneless skinless breasts and thighs does cut prep time. However, for authenticity, you can use a 3 lb (1.5 kg) chicken, cut into pieces, instead of the 1½ lb (750 g) boneless skinless chicken pieces. Ham is used to enrich the flavour of the fricassee. If it seems wasteful to pull it out of the dish before serving along with the parsley, another approach is to dice the ham into small pieces and make it part of the dish from beginning to end.

1 ½ lb (750 g) boneless skinless chicken breasts or thighs
1 tbsp (15 mL) butter
1 large onion, diced
1 thick slice ham, or about 1 cup (250 mL) diced
10 stalks fresh parsley, tied together
1 sprig fresh thyme or 1 tsp (5 mL) dried thyme
2 strips lemon peel
¾ tsp (4 mL) grated nutmeg

Sauce:
2 tsp (10 mL) butter
1 tsp (5 mL) all-purpose flour
1 ½ cups (375 mL) chicken broth
2 egg yolks
½ cup (250 mL) whipping (35%) cream

Trim any fat from the chicken. In a large saucepan over medium heat, melt the butter; stir in the onion, ham, parsley, thyme, lemon peel, and nutmeg. Nestle the chicken into the onion mixture; let stew over medium heat, turning a few times and reducing the heat as needed, until the chicken is light golden and its juices run clear, 20 to 25 minutes. Remove the parsley, thyme, lemon, and ham (if using the slice).

Sauce: Mash together the butter and flour; using a wooden spoon, work the butter mixture around the chicken. Pour in the broth; bring to a boil, stirring often and turning the chicken occasionally. Reduce the heat and simmer until the ingredients form a sauce around the chicken.

In a bowl, whisk together the egg yolks and cream. Stir in a generous spoonful of the hot sauce; gradually whisk the mixture back into the saucepan and gently heat through, whisking, without boiling. Remove from the heat; taste and adjust seasoning.

Makes 4 to 5 servings.

Kitchen Note:

This pairing of cream and egg yolks, a favourite thickening/finishing element in Mrs Dalgairns's recipes, adds an indulgent touch. But be sure to cook on low, to stir some of the hot sauce into the eggs and cream (known as tempering) and to keep the sauce moving. Using a flat whisk helps reduce the risk of curdling the sauce.

CURRIES – CHAPTER IX

To Boil Rice: Page 141

Original Recipe

Wash the rice perfectly clean, and put on one pound in two quarts of cold water; let it boil twenty minutes, strain it through a sieve, and put it before the fire; shake it up with a fork every now and then, to separate the grains, and make it quite dry. Serve it hot.

Modern Version

This method of boiling rice is more like boiling pasta – in a generous amount of water. While most contemporary kitchens don't have a "fire" in front of which to dry the rice, an oven at a low temperature, and preferably with convection heat, works just fine. This recipe makes half of the original batch of the rice.

1 cup (250 mL) long-grain white rice
4 cups (1 L) cold water

Measure the rice into a sieve; immerse in a bowl of cold water and swish around to release the starch. Repeat with fresh water, rinsing until the water is clear.

In a medium saucepan, combine the rice and 4 cups (1 L) cold water; bring to a boil. Reduce the heat and simmer, uncovered, until the grains are tender but slightly firm in the centre, 12 to 18 minutes.

Meanwhile, position an oven rack in the centre of the oven; heat to 275°F (135°C).

Drain the rice. Using a fork, spread the rice on a shallow rimmed baking sheet. Warm in the oven, tossing occasionally with a fork, until grains are separate and dry, about 10 minutes.

Makes about 3 cups (750 mL).

Currie Powder: Page 142

Original Recipe

Pound extremely fine, in a mortar, six ounces of coriander seed, three ounces of black pepper, one ounce and a half of fennigreck seed, one ounce of cummin seed, three ounces of turmeric, and three quarters of an ounce of cayenne; sift it through muslin, and put it before the fire for four or five hours, stirring it every now and then. Keep it in a bottle with a glass stopper.

Modern Version

This version makes a smaller batch than Mrs Dalgairns prepared. The secret to keeping spices full of flavour is to buy them whole – seeds, bark, fruit, rhizome, or root – and to grind or grate as needed. The additional toasting step by the fire, described by Mrs Dalgairns in her recipe, takes away the raw taste and can be done on a smaller scale in a dry skillet over gentle heat – again, as needed.

1 ¼ cups (300 mL) coriander seeds
5 tbsp (75 mL) black peppercorns
2 tbsp (30 mL) fenugreek seeds
2 tbsp (30 mL) cumin seeds
1 piece dried turmeric rhizome, about 2 inches (5 cm)
4 tsp (20 mL) cayenne (see Kitchen Note, below)

In a spice grinder or clean coffee grinder, separately grind the coriander seeds, peppercorns, and fenugreek and cumin seeds until fine. Pound the turmeric into bean-sized chunks. Finely grind the turmeric.

Set a fine sieve over a bowl and pass each ground spice and the cayenne through the sieve. Toss to blend the spices; pass them through the sieve again. Store in a jar with a tight-fitting lid in a dark, cool place.

Before using the Currie Powder in a recipe, heat the required amount in an ungreased shallow skillet over medium-low heat, stirring, until fragrant. Immediately scrape out of the pan.

Makes about 2 cups (500 mL) Currie Powder.

Kitchen Note:

You can replace the dried turmeric rhizome with ¼ cup (60 mL) already ground turmeric. Reduce the quantity of cayenne as desired.

GAME – CHAPTER X

Rabbits Stewed with a Brown Sauce, or with a White Sauce: Page 148

Original Recipe

Wash and clean the rabbits well, let them lie for two or three hours in cold water, cut them into joints, wash and dry them in a cloth, dust them with flour, and fry them a light brown with butter, and stew them in the following sauce: Brown three ounces of butter in a stew-pan, with a table-spoonful of flour, a minced onion, some pepper and salt; add a pint of gravy and the rabbits, stew them till they are tender, and a little before serving, stir in a table-spoonful of catsup.

When it is wished to dress them with a white sauce, the rabbits are not fried, but stewed in white stock, which is seasoned with white pepper and salt, and thickened with a piece of butter mixed with flour. A few minutes before serving, a little cream is added, and a table-spoonful of lemon pickle.

Modern Version

A whole rabbit makes 8 pieces – 2 each legs and shoulders, and 4 pieces of the saddle. While it's not difficult to separate a whole rabbit into these parts, there are many supermarkets and butcher shops that sell already cut-up parts or employ a butcher who will prepare the pieces neatly.

1 rabbit, cut into parts, 3 lb (1.5 kg)
¼ cup (60 mL) all-purpose flour, divided
1/3 cup (75 mL) butter, divided
1 onion, minced
½ tsp (2 mL) each salt and pepper
2 cups (500 mL) chicken broth
1 tbsp (15 mL) Mushroom Catsup (see page 477)

Coat the rabbit parts lightly with about half of the flour. Melt 2 tbsp (30 mL) of the butter in a large saucepan over medium heat. Add the rabbit and brown gently on both sides, being careful not to let the butter burn. Remove and set aside. Add the remaining butter to the saucepan. Stir in the onion, salt, pepper, and remaining flour; cook, stirring almost constantly, until the onions are softened and golden.

Stir in the broth, working it into the onion mixture. Nestle the rabbit in the sauce; bring to a simmer. Cover and simmer, turning the rabbit pieces once or twice, until the juices run clear when the leg is pierced, about 20 minutes. Stir in the Mushroom Catsup; simmer for 2 minutes. Taste and adjust the seasoning.

Makes 4 to 5 servings.

GRAVIES, SAUCES, FORCEMEATS, AND OTHER THINGS – CHAPTER XI

Sauce for Roast Beef: Page 154

Original Recipe

Mix well together a large table-spoonful of finely-grated horse-radish, a dessert-spoonful of made mustard, and half a one of brown sugar, then add vinegar till it be as thick as made mustard. Serve in a sauce tureen.

Modern Version

This is a very potent sauce. For less potency, make the mustard (see page 451) a few days beforehand.

2 tbsp (30 mL) prepared horseradish
1 tbsp (15 mL) prepared mustard, such as Dijon or (see To Make Mustard, page 451)
2 tsp (10 mL) packed brown sugar
2 tsp (10 mL) white wine vinegar, approximate

In a bowl, stir together the horseradish, mustard, sugar, and vinegar, adding more vinegar as needed to make the sauce as thick as prepared mustard.

Makes about ¼ cup (60 mL).

Kitchen Notes:

Double or triple the recipe as desired.

It is certainly possible to make this sauce with freshly grated horseradish, but work with the windows open; as with onions, grating horseradish can cause serious sneezing and tearing up.

Horse-Radish Sauce, to eat with Hot or Cold Meat: Page 162

Original Recipe

Mix a tea-spoonful of mustard, a table-spoonful of vinegar, and three of cream; add a little salt, and as much finely-grated horse-radish as will make the sauce the consistence of onion sauce. (See page 161 for Onion Sauce.)

Modern Version

1/3 cup (75 mL) whipping (35%) cream
2 tbsp (30 mL) white wine vinegar
4 tsp (20 mL) prepared horseradish
2 tsp (10 mL) dry mustard powder
¼ tsp (1 mL) salt

In a small bowl, stir together the mustard, cream, vinegar, horseradish, mustard, and salt. Cover and let mellow in the refrigerator for 2 hours. (Make-ahead: Refrigerate for up to 3 days.)

Makes about ½ cup (125 mL).

To Make Mustard: Page 164

Original Recipe

Mix very smoothly the best flour of mustard with cold water, add a little salt, and a very little sifted loaf-sugar; it will keep good some time if put into a small jar and covered closely, or it may be mixed with milk instead of water, but in this way it will not keep so long.

Modern Version

Mixing powdered mustard with cold water produces a very hot spread that is a fine accompaniment for meats, even in sandwiches (see Sandwiches, page 138, and Captain Hall's Sandwiches for Travellers, page 366). For a milder mustard, such as is favoured in salad dressings, simply make it ahead – up to 2 weeks – to allow the heat to subside.

¼ cup (60 mL) mustard powder
¼ tsp (1 mL) salt
Pinch granulated sugar
¼ cup (60 mL) cold water

In a bowl, mix together the mustard, salt, and sugar; stir in the water to make a smooth, spreadable paste. Scrape into a small jar and store in the refrigerator for up to 4 weeks.

Makes a generous ¼ cup (60 mL).

Salad Sauce: Page 164

Original Recipe

Bruise the yolk of a hard-boiled egg with a small tea-spoonful of salt, then add a dessert-spoonful of mustard, and stir in gradually a large table-spoonful of olive oil, oiled butter, or cream, then by degrees mix in two or three table-spoonfuls of vinegar; serve it in a sauce-tureen, or mix it with the salad. Instead of the hard egg, some persons prefer the sauce made with the yolk raw.

Modern Version

You can ease the tartness of this dressing by adding more oil and a pinch of sugar.

1 hard-cooked egg yolk
1 tbsp (15 mL) prepared mustard, such as Dijon
¼ tsp (1 mL) salt

¼ cup (60 mL) white wine vinegar
2 tbsp (30 mL) olive oil

In a bowl, mash the egg yolk until smooth. Mash in the mustard and salt; stir in the vinegar and oil until combined. Taste and adjust the pairing of vinegar and oil as well as the seasoning. (Make-ahead: Scrape into an airtight plastic or glass container and refrigerate for up to 4 days. Stir well before serving in a tureen or mixing with salad ingredients.)

Makes about ½ cup (125 mL).

VEGETABLES – CHAPTER XII

Mashed Potatoes: Page 170

Original Recipe

Boil the potatoes, peel and mash them very smoothly; put for a large dish four ounces of butter, two eggs beat up in half a pint of good milk, and some salt; mix them well together, heap it upon the dish with a table-spoon to give it a rough and rocky appearance, or put it on the dish and score it with a knife, dip a brush or feather into melted butter, and brush over the top lightly; put it into a Dutch oven, and let it brown gradually for an hour or more.

To mash potatoes in a plain way, mix with them two ounces of butter, half a pint of milk, and a little salt. When mashed potatoes are not browned, it is a great improvement to add white pepper, salt and one onion minced as finely as possible; heat the potatoes in a sauce-pan, and serve them hot.

Modern Version

Floury potatoes such as large oval Russets make the best mashed potatoes. They are high in starch, low in moisture, break up readily and, because they are so absorbent, soak up enhancing ingredients such as milk or cream, and butter. An all-purpose potato such as Yukon Gold is also a good candidate for mashing.

9 medium Russet potatoes, 3 lb (1.5 kg)
1 large egg
1 cup (250 mL) whole milk
1 ¼ tsp (6 mL) salt
1/3 cup (75 mL) melted butter

Set out a 13- x 9-inch (2.5 L) ovenproof baking dish. Just before mashing the potatoes, position an oven rack in the centre of the oven; heat to 400°F (200°C).

Peel and cut the potatoes into chunks; cover and cook in a saucepan of boiling water until tender, 10 to 15 minutes. Drain and return to the saucepan to dry over low heat for 1 to 2 minutes. Remove from the heat. Mash until smooth.

Meanwhile, whisk the egg with the milk and salt. Mash into the potatoes. Reserving 1 tbsp (15 mL) of the butter, mash the remaining butter into the potatoes. Scoop into the baking dish, using a spoon to press the potatoes into a "rough and rocky appearance." Brush with the remaining butter. (Make-ahead: Let cool. Cover and refrigerate for up to 4 hours. Increase baking time by about 5 minutes.)

Bake until piping hot inside and golden on top, about 15 minutes.

Makes 8 generous servings.

Kitchen Note:

Use a ricer to achieve the most evenly puréed potatoes. Washing the parts of a ricer is more bothersome than washing a masher but worth the effort.

To Stew Young Peas and Lettuce: Page 178

Original Recipe

Wash and make perfectly clean one or two heads of cabbage lettuce, pick off the outside leaves, and lay them for two hours in cold water, with a little salt in it; then slice them, and put them into a sauce-pan, with a quart or three pints of peas, three table-spoonfuls of gravy, a bit of butter dredged with flour, some pepper and salt, and a tea-spoonful of pounded loaf sugar. Let them stew, closely covered, till the peas are soft.

Modern Version

In this recipe, Mrs Dalgairns calls for "cabbage lettuce." In her Kitchen Garden chapter, page 403, she says that "of the two kinds of lettuce, the coss, also called the Roman and ice, and the cabbage lettuce, there are many varieties."

2 cups (500 mL) thinly sliced romaine lettuce
4 cups (1 L) tender young peas
¼ cup (60 mL) chicken or vegetable broth
1 tsp (5 mL) granulated sugar
¼ tsp (2 mL) each salt and pepper
1 tsp (5 mL) all-purpose flour
1 tsp (5 mL) butter, softened

Place the lettuce in a medium saucepan along with the peas. Add the broth, sugar, salt, and pepper; cover and bring to a boil over medium-high heat. Immediately reduce the heat and simmer, stirring once or twice, until the peas are tender, about 8 minutes.

Mash together the flour and butter; stir into the pea mixture. Simmer, stirring often, until the juices thicken slightly, about 2 minutes.

Makes 6 servings.

Kitchen Note:

Freshly shelled small green peas have no equal, but if you must make a choice between older, larger shelled peas and frozen peas, opt for frozen. They are already blanched, which cuts the cooking time to 4 to 6 minutes.

A Summer Salad: Page 180

Original Recipe

Wash very clean one or two heads of fine lettuce, divide it, let it lie some time in cold water; drain and dry it in a napkin, and cut it small before serving. Mustard and cresses, sorrel and young onions, may be added, and the dish garnished with nasturtium flowers.

Modern Version

In chapter XXIII, Kitchen Garden, Mrs Dalgairns demonstrates her love of vegetables and her vast knowledge of how to grow them. From choosing seeds and the most suitable soil, to knowing when to add manure, to harvesting and storing techniques, she shares all. As for her selection of vegetables, consider skirret, scorzonera, and salsify along with more familiar beets, kale, and lettuce.

Prepare the salad ingredients according to Mrs Dalgairns's choices and preparation: combine 10 cups (2.5 L) fresh spring lettuces, cresses, sorrel, green onions, and nasturtiums, all washed and patted dry. More of these leafy greens are needed than the 8 cups (2 L) of denser ingredients in the Winter Salad. Dress with Salad Sauce, page 452.

Makes 6 to 8 servings.

A Winter Salad: Page 180

Original Recipe

Wash very clean one or two heads of endive, some heads of celery, some mustard and cresses; cut them all small, add a little shredded red cabbage, some slices of boiled beet-root and onion, if the flavour is not disliked; mix them together with salad sauce. In the spring, add radishes, and also garnish the dish with them.

Modern Version

The quantity of greens has been reduced to serve six to eight. For that number, you will need 8 cups (2 L) prepared salad ingredients. Vary them according to your favourites, the freshest-looking choices in the produce department and what you have in your winter crisper, such as thinly sliced fennel, Brussels sprouts, cauliflower, Belgian endive, kale, shredded carrots, and broccoli.

1 heart of curly endive, torn
1 cup (250 mL) thinly sliced celery heart
1 cup (250 mL) finely shredded red cabbage
1 cooked beet, peeled and thinly sliced or diced
½ cup (125 mL) thinly sliced mild onion or shallot, optional

2 cups (500 mL) watercress, coarse stems removed
1 cup (250 mL) thinly sliced radishes
½ cup (125 mL) Salad Sauce (see page 452)

In a shallow salad bowl, arrange the endive, celery, cabbage, beet and onion (if using); top with the watercress and radish slices. (Make-ahead: Cover and refrigerate for up to 2 hours.)

Drizzle the vegetables with Salad Sauce and bring to the table. Toss when guests have commented on the handsome salad.

Makes 6 to 8 servings.

PUDDINGS, PIES, AND TARTS – CHAPTER XIII

Tart Paste: Page 186

Original Recipe

Rub into half a pound of flour six ounces of butter and one table-spoonful of pounded loaf sugar, make it into a paste with hot water.

Modern Version

Salted or unsalted butter? It was customary to salt freshly churned butter in order to preserve it. For fine pastry making, the butter was often kneaded and washed, sometimes in rose water, to remove the salt.

1¾ cups (425 mL) all-purpose flour, preferably unbleached
1 tbsp (15 mL) granulated sugar
¾ cup (175 mL) cold unsalted butter, cubed
2 tbsp (30 mL) hot water, approximate

In a large bowl or a food processor, combine the flour and sugar. Work in the butter using fingertips or pulse in the food processor until evenly crumbly. Drizzle water over the surface; toss or pulse until a moist ragged dough forms, adding a very little more water if necessary. Turn out onto a floured work surface and press into a disc. (Make-ahead: Wrap and refrigerate for up to 2 days. Let come to room temperature before rolling out.)

Makes enough pastry for 24 tartlets or to fit a 9-inch (2.5 L) square metal cake pan or a 9- or 10-inch (23 or 25 cm) pie plate.

Kitchen Note:

To make this pastry with cold water, increase the amount to about ¼ cup (60 mL).

Apple Pie: Page 203

Original Recipe

Pare, quarter, and core the apples; cut them into thin bits. Put into the bottom of a pie-dish a table-spoonful of brown sugar, with half a tea-spoonful of grated ginger and same of lemon-peel, then a layer of apples, and so on alternately, till the dish is piled as full as it will hold. The next day wet the rim of the dish, line it with puff or tart paste, brush it with water and cover it with paste; press the edge all round, notch it with a pastry cutter, and make a small hole with the point of a knife in the middle.

It may be seasoned with two table-spoonfuls of lemon or orange marmalade, pounded cinnamon, mace, and cloves, in addition to the ginger and lemon-peel.

Modern Version

Ginger and lemon bring a whole new taste to apple pie. Choose Northern Spy apples if possible, or Cortland, Golden Delicious, or any other tart apple that keeps its shape when baked.

Tart Paste (see page 457)
½ cup (125 mL) packed brown sugar
2 tsp (10 mL) ground ginger
2 tsp (10 mL) grated lemon peel
10 cups (2.5 L) sliced apples, about 10 apples, 3 lb (1.5 kg)

Set out a 9-inch (2 L) square metal cake pan or a 10-inch (25 cm) pie plate. Position an oven rack in the lowest position in the oven; preheat to 425°F (220°C).

Sprinkle one-third of the sugar, ginger, and lemon peel over the bottom of the pan. Top with one-third of the apples. Repeat the layers, ending with the apples; arrange the top layer into a somewhat smooth dome.

Between 2 sheets of parchment paper, roll out ½ cup (125 mL) of the Tart Paste to an 1/8-inch (3 mm) thickness. Brush water over the rim of the pan or pie plate. Cut strips of pastry about ½ inch (1 cm) wide and arrange over the rim, pressing them down lightly on the rim. Roll out the remaining pastry, again between sheets of parchment paper, into a 10-inch (25 cm) square or an 11-inch (28 cm) circle. Brush the pastry rim with water. Roll the pastry square or circle around the rolling pin and unroll over the apples. Fold the overlapping pastry under. Gently press the 2 layers of pastry to the rim and flute.

Bake for 15 minutes; reduce the heat to 350°F (180°C). Loosely cover the top of the pie with foil. Bake until the pastry is golden, the apples are tender and the filling is bubbling, about 50 minutes.

Let cool on a rack. (Make-ahead: Cover and store at cool room temperature for up to 1 day. To serve, reheat in a 325°F/160°C oven to crisp the crust and revive the juicy filling, about 20 minutes.)

Makes 8 servings.

Tartlets: Page 204

Original Recipe

Rub over patty-pans a little bit of butter, and line them with tart or puff paste; fill them with marmalade, preserved strawberries, raspberries, currants, or any sort of fruit. Take a small bit of the paste, and with the hand, roll it upon the paste board with flour till it be stiff, and will draw out in straws; hold it in one hand, and with the other, draw it out. With these small strings cross the tartlets according to fancy; wet the edge, and lay on a narrow rim of paste cut with the paste-cutter.

Modern Version

This is an ideal recipe to showcase summer jams and winter marmalades.

Tart Paste (see page 457)
1 cup (250 mL) raspberry jam or orange marmalade (see Another way to make Orange Marmalade, page 474)
1 tsp (5 mL) all-purpose flour

Position an oven rack in the bottom third of the oven. A few minutes before finishing the tartlet assembly, preheat the oven to 375°F (190°C).

Set out 2 patty pans (sometimes called bun pans or tins) or shallow tart pans that measure 2½ inches (6 cm) in diameter and about 5/8 inch (1.5 cm) deep. Lightly butter 20 of the patty pan cups; set aside.

Divide the pastry into quarters: three of the quarters are for lining the patty pans and the fourth is for the decorative topping and the circles of pastry to be placed on the rim of each tartlet.

Between 2 sheets of parchment paper, roll out one-quarter of the pastry at a time to a 1/8-inch (3 mm) thickness. Using a 2¾-inch (7 cm) round cookie cutter, cut out 20 rounds, rerolling and cutting out the scraps. Gently press the pastry rounds into the greased pans. Fill each with 2 tsp (10 mL) of the jam.

Remove 2 tbsp (30 mL) of the remaining pastry and mash it with the flour; divide it into 6 pieces. On a work surface, roll each piece into thin strings; arrange the strings, "according to fancy," over the jam. (Or roll out the pastry until thin; cut into strips and arrange over the jam.)

Brush the rim of each tartlet with water. Roll out the remaining pastry. Using 2 round cookie cutters, one 2½ inches (6 cm) and the other 2 inches (5 cm), cut out bracelet-like rings of pastry (or cut strips). Arrange the rings on the moistened rims.

Bake until the jam is bubbling and the pastry is golden brown, 12 to 15 minutes. Remove from the pans and let cool on a rack. (Make-ahead: Store in an airtight container at room temperature for up to 2 days or freeze for up to 2 weeks.)

Makes 20 tartlets.

Kitchen Note:

For an easier way to make the tartlets, omit the extra round of pastry on the rim. Simply cut out 24 rounds of pastry, fill with jam, and decorate with the strings or strips.

To Pot Cheshire Cheese: Page 243

Original Recipe

Scrape down three pounds of fine Cheshire or Gloucester cheese. With half a pound of fresh butter, pound it to a paste in a marble mortar, adding a large wine glass of malmsey madeira, or of sherry, and a quarter of an ounce of pounded and sifted mace; when beaten to a paste, press it into a deep pot, and cover it with clarified butter. A thick slice may be served in a napkin to resemble cream cheese.

Modern Version

This cheese is excellent atop Oliver's Biscuit (see pages 471).

12 oz (375 g) Cheshire cheese
½ cup (125 mL) unsalted butter, divided
2 tbsp (30 mL) dry sherry
¼ tsp (1 mL) ground mace

Set out a small crock or deep serving dish that holds about 2 cups (500 mL) or, if making well ahead, an airtight container with tight-fitting lid; set aside.

Cube the cheese and half of the butter. Place in a food processor along with the sherry and mace. Whirl, scraping down the side of the bowl a few times, until blended and smooth. Press into the serving dish; smooth the top.

Melt the remaining butter over low heat. Skim the clarified butter off the milky liquid; spoon the clarified butter evenly over the cheese mixture. Let cool. Cover and refrigerate for up to 2 weeks. Let soften at room temperature until spreadable, about 30 minutes.

Makes about 2 cups (500 mL).

Kitchen Note:

If Cheshire or Gloucester cheeses are hard to find, substitute old Cheddar. Add an extra spoonful of sherry for a softer spread.

CREAMS, CUSTARDS, JELLIES, AND OTHER SWEET DISHES – CHAPTER XIV

Raspberry Iced Cream: Page 252

Original Recipe

Mix a table-spoonful of pounded loaf sugar, a large wooden-spoonful of raspberry jelly, and a little cochineal, to heighten the colour, with the juice of a large lemon; strain, and put it into the freezing-pot; cover it closely; and place it in a bucket which has a small hole near the bottom, and a spigot to let the water run off, and which has in it plenty of ice broken small, and mixed with three or four handfuls of coarse salt; press the ice closely round the freezing-pot, turn it round and round for about ten minutes, take off the cover, and remove the frozen cream to the centre with a spoon, cover it again, and turn it till all be equally iced. Serve it in China ice pails, or put it into moulds, cover them tightly with wet bladder, and place them in a bucket with ice, as before, for an hour or more; dip the moulds into cold water before turning out, and serve them immediately. Water ices are made in this way, substituting water for cream.

Kitchen Note:

In a subsequent edition of Mrs Dalgairns's book, the lack of cream in this iced cream was corrected with the addition of 1½ pints (3 cups) cream.

Modern Version

China ice pails are exquisite three-part porcelain containers: the bottom third was filled with salted ice, the next compartment contained ice cream, and the lid with projecting rim held another layer of salted ice. With salted ice underneath and above, the ice cream was guaranteed not to melt on the journey from kitchen to dining room.

1 cup (250 mL) raspberry jelly or seedless jam
¼ cup (60 mL) freshly squeezed lemon juice
2 tbsp (30 mL) granulated sugar
¼ tsp (1 mL) red food colouring, optional

3 cups (750 mL) whipping (35%) cream, or 2 cups (500 mL) whipping cream plus 1 cup (250 mL) light (5,10 or 18%) cream

To make ice cream without a machine, set out a 13- x 9-inch (3.5 L) metal cake pan. (Or set out an old-fashioned ice-and-salt maker, either a hand-crank or electric model, or an ice cream maker with a pre-frozen bucket or an internal compressor.)

In a heatproof bowl set over a saucepan of warm (not hot) water, mix together the jelly, lemon juice, sugar, and food colouring (if using). Stir until the sugar is dissolved and the jelly is melted. Let cool. Whisk in the cream. Cover and chill in the refrigerator.

Pour the cream mixture into the metal pan; cover and freeze until almost solid, 4 to 6 hours. Break the frozen mixture into chunks and purée in a food processor until smooth. Pack into a 4-cup (1 L) container or 2 smaller containers and return to the freezer to firm up, about 4 hours. (Or freeze according to manufacturer's instructions.)

Makes 4 cups (1 L).

Orange Water Iced: Page 252

Original Recipe

Mix with a pint of water the strained juice of three China oranges, and that of one lemon, also the grated peel of one orange; sweeten it well with syrup.

Modern Version

China oranges, or sweet oranges, became available in Europe in the sixteenth century and were named for their country of origin. Prior to their arrival, bitter Seville oranges were the only type available. They were used mostly for preserving, cooking, and baking (see Tartlets, page 204, and Puddings, page 182).

1½ cups (375 mL) water, divided
½ cup (125 mL) granulated sugar
3 large sweet oranges, such as navel oranges
1 lemon

To make the Orange Water Iced without a machine, set out a 13- x 9-inch (3.5 L) metal cake pan. (Or set out an old-fashioned ice-and-salt maker, either a hand-crank or electric model, or an ice cream maker with a pre-frozen bucket or an internal compressor.)

In a saucepan, bring ½ cup (125 mL) of the water and the sugar to a boil; boil for 1 minute. Let cool. (Make-ahead: Refrigerate the syrup in a clean airtight container for up to several months.)

Grate the peel from 1 of the oranges; halve the oranges and lemon. Squeeze and strain the juice of the oranges and lemon into a bowl. Stir in the grated orange peel, sugar syrup, and remaining water.

Pour the mixture into the metal pan; cover and freeze until almost solid, 4 to 6 hours. Break the frozen mixture into chunks and purée in a food processor until smooth. Pack into a 4-cup (1 L) container, or two smaller containers and return to the freezer to firm up, about 4 hours. (Or freeze according to manufacturer's instructions.)

Makes 4 cups (1 L) Orange Water Iced.

Kitchen Note:

In frozen desserts, it is preferable to use syrup rather than granulated sugar as it makes a smoother treat.

Floating Island: Page 260

Original Recipe

Boil, with a pint of milk, a bit of cinnamon, and half the peel of a lemon; when almost cold, strain it, and mix with it the beaten white of one, and the yolks of three eggs; stir it over the fire till thick, pour it into a dish, and stir it now and then till cold. Whisk the whites of two eggs, and half a pint of Guava quince or red currant jelly, till it be a very stiff froth, and heap it upon the custard.

Modern Version

Usually Floating Island is a sweet custard topped with sugary meringues. Mrs Dalgairns has cut through all the sweetness by leaving the custard unsugared and replacing the granulated sugar in the meringue island with redcurrant jelly. Yes, they are still sweet from the jelly, but well balanced by the tart redcurrants.

1 small cinnamon stick
2 strips lemon peel
2 cups (500 mL) whole milk
3 medium eggs, at room temperature
1 cup (250 mL) redcurrant jelly, at room temperature

Set out a shallow serving dish with a 6-cup (1.5 L) capacity.

Break the cinnamon stick into 3 or 4 shards. Drop the shards into a medium saucepan with the lemon peel; pour in the milk and heat slowly over low heat until steaming. Set aside to cool. Remove the cinnamon shards and lemon peel.

Separate the eggs, placing 1 of the whites in a medium bowl and 2 of the whites in a large bowl. Drop the yolks into a small bowl.

Beat the 1 egg white to firm peaks; whisk into the flavoured milk along with the 3 yolks. Heat over low heat, stirring constantly with a wooden spoon, until smooth and thick enough to coat the back of the spoon. Pour through a strainer into the serving bowl. Cover with plastic wrap; let cool and refrigerate until cold. (Make-ahead: Refrigerate the custard for up to 1 day. Refrigerate the remaining egg whites in an airtight container; let come to room temperature before using.)

Beat the remaining egg whites to soft peaks. Beat in the redcurrant jelly, 1 heaping tbsp (15 mL) at a time, beating until the egg white mixture stands in firm pink peaks. Gently "heap it upon the custard."

Makes 4 to 6 servings.

Kitchen Notes:

The meringue uses raw egg whites. If there are concerns, replace them with pasteurized egg whites.

This recipe makes an unbelievable amount of meringue for the topping, and Mrs Dalgairns was right in her choice of verb – "heap." With a modern hand mixer, it is possible to make a superb meringue with 1 medium egg white and ½ cup (125 mL) redcurrant jelly. Try it.

Whim Wham: Page 265

Original Recipe

Sweeten a quart of cream, and mix it with a tea-cupful of white wine, and the grated peel of a lemon; whisk it to a froth, which drain upon the back of a sieve, and put part into a deep glass dish; cut some Naples biscuit as thin as possible, and put a layer lightly over the froth, and one of red currant jelly, then a layer of the froth, and one of the biscuit and jelly; finish with the froth, and pour the remainder of the cream into the dish and garnish with citron and candied orange-peel cut into straws.

Modern Version

According to Collins English Dictionary, a whim wham is "something fanciful: a trifle." In the culinary world, that translates into "special occasion," a light-as-air combination of whipped cream, white wine, ladyfingers, and redcurrant jelly.

2 cups (500 mL) whipping (35%) cream
¼ cup (60 mL) white wine
2 tbsp (30 mL) superfine sugar
2 tsp (10 mL) grated lemon peel
¾ cup (175 mL) redcurrant jelly
20 Naples biscuits (6 oz/175 g), also known as ladyfingers or Savoy biscuits
2 tbsp (30 mL) strips or finely diced pieces candied citrus fruit

Set out a glass bowl with a capacity of 6 cups (1.5 L).

Beat the cream and wine to firm peaks; mix in the sugar and lemon peel. Using a table knife, break up the redcurrant jelly into bits the size of jellybeans. If the biscuits are thin enough to cut into slices, do so.

Spoon one-third of the whipped cream mixture into the bowl; smooth the top. Cover with about half of the biscuits, then half of the redcurrant jelly. Repeat the layers, finishing with the whipped cream mixture. Cover and refrigerate for at least 8 hours or for up to 1 day. Garnish the top with the candied fruit to serve.

Makes 8 servings.

CAKES, BISCUITS, AND BREAD – CHAPTER XV

Plum Cake: Page 273

Original Recipe

Two pounds of sifted and dried flour, one pound and a half of pounded and sifted loaf sugar, two pounds of nicely-cleaned and dried currants, half a pound of stoned and chopped raisins, half a pound of sweetmeats, one nutmeg grated, the weight of it in pounded cinnamon and mace, half a pound of almonds blanched and cut small, fourteen eggs, the whites and yolks beaten separately, the yolks with three table-spoonfuls of rose or orange- flower water. These ingredients being prepared, with the hand beat to a cream two pounds of fresh butter; add the sugar by degrees, and then the yolks of the eggs, the whites, the flour, the spice, the almonds, the fruit and sweetmeats, and lastly, mix in a glass of brandy; beat it all well together; butter the hoop or frame, and pour in the cake, and put it into a moderate oven. It will take between three and four hours to bake.

Modern Version

Plum cake is an example of a celebratory cake, large and richly studded with currants, raisins, and sweet meats – candied citrus fruit. Large indeed. The modern version below is half of the original recipe, still plenty for Christmas and holiday events.

3 cups (750 mL) currants
3½ cups (875 mL) all-purpose flour, preferably unbleached
2 tsp (10 mL) grated nutmeg
1½ tsp (7 mL) each ground cinnamon and mace
1½ cups (375 mL) seeded raisins such as Muscat or Lexia, roughly chopped
1 cup (250 mL) finely chopped candied citrus fruit, such as lemons, oranges, and citron
1 cup (250 mL) finely chopped blanched almonds
7 medium eggs, separated
4 tsp (15 mL) orange flower water or rose water
2 cups (500 mL) unsalted butter, softened
1¾ cups (425 mL) granulated sugar
¾ cup (175 mL) brandy

Line a 12-inch (30 cm) springform pan or a 13- x 9-inch (3.5 L) metal cake pan with a double layer of parchment paper; set aside. When the ingredients are prepared and ready to combine, position an oven rack in the centre of the oven. Set a pan of hot water on the lower rack and heat to 325°F (160°C).

Discard bits of stem from the currants. In a bowl, combine the currants and enough boiling water to cover them; let stand for 10 minutes. Drain and spread out on a clean kitchen towel to dry, tossing occasionally, about 1 hour.

In a large bowl, whisk together the flour, nutmeg, cinnamon, and mace. Add the currants, raisins, candied citrus peel, and almonds; stir well to coat the fruit and almonds evenly. Set aside.

In another large bowl, beat the egg whites to firm but not stiff peaks; set aside. In a separate bowl, beat the egg yolks with the orange flower water until thick and light coloured. In a very large bowl, beat the butter vigorously until cream coloured. Beat in the sugar, ¼ cup (60 mL) at a time; beat in the yolk mixture.

Using a wooden spoon, stir in one-third of the flour mixture, then half of the brandy. Repeat these additions and finish with the remaining flour mixture. Stir in one-third of the egg whites; fold in the remainder. Scrape into the prepared pan, smoothing the top; tap the pan lightly on the work surface. (Note: The rectangular pan will be almost full.) Lay a piece of foil lightly over the pan.

Bake until a tester inserted into the centre of the cake comes out clean, 1½ to 2 hours. Let cool on a rack. Turn out, top side up. A neat way to cut the round cake before wrapping and storing is to use a sharp knife to cut it into quarters. For the rectangular cake, cut the cake crosswise into 6 even logs, each about 2 inches (5 cm) wide, wiping the knife blade between cuts.

The cake can be wrapped well and stored in the refrigerator for up to 2 weeks. Or wrap it in a double layer of foil or plastic wrap and freeze in an airtight container or large resealable freezer bag for up to 1 month.

The cake slices best when cold from the refrigerator (or from the freezer after sitting for a few minutes at room temperature). To serve, cut the quarters into generous ½-inch (1 cm) slices, then into generous 1-inch (2.5 m) fingers. Cut the logs crosswise into slices just under ½ inch (1 cm) thick.

Makes about 96 slices or fingers.

Kitchen Note:

Even after halving the ingredients, this recipe makes a large amount of cake. To make one-quarter of the original Plum Cake, which fits neatly into a 9-inch (2.5 L) square metal cake pan, use these quantities: 1½ cups (375 mL) currants: 1¾ cups (425 mL) all-purpose flour, preferably unbleached; 1 tsp (5 mL) grated nutmeg; ¾ tsp (4 mL) each ground cinnamon and mace; ¾ cup (175 mL) raisins, roughly chopped; ½ cup (125 mL) each finely chopped candied fruit and almonds; 1 cup (250 mL) unsalted butter, softened; ¾ cup (175 mL) granulated sugar; 4 medium or 3 large eggs; 2 tsp (20 mL) orange flower water; and ½ cup (125 mL) brandy. Follow the method in the recipe but reduce baking time to 1 hour and 20 minutes.

Macaroons: Page 281

Original Recipe

Beat to a froth the whites of eight eggs, then add two pounds of finely-pounded and sifted loaf sugar, one pound of blanched sweet almonds, which must be pounded to a paste with rose water. Beat all these together till they become a thick paste, then drop it from a spoon upon wafer paper or tins, and bake them in a slow oven.

Modern Version

Half a batch of macaroons makes plenty to have on hand, especially to accompany the Orange Water Iced (page 463) or the Raspberry Iced Cream (page 462). Almost every cookbook of the Georgian era includes a recipe for almond macaroons. Mrs Dalgairns's is a classic.

2½ cups (625 mL) blanched almonds
4 egg whites, at room temperature
2 cups (575 mL) superfine sugar
1 tbsp (15 mL) rose water

Line 2 rimless baking sheets with parchment paper. Position oven racks in the top and bottom thirds of the oven; heat to 300°F (150°C).

In a food processor, chop the almonds, scraping down the sides of the bowl as needed, until they have the consistency of coarse sand. Set aside.

In a large bowl, beat the egg whites to soft peaks. Add the sugar, 2 tbsp (30 mL) at a time, beating until stiff glossy peaks form. Beat in the rose water. Fold in the almonds.

Working quickly, drop the almond mixture by rounded teaspoonfuls (7 mL) onto the prepared baking sheets, about 1 inch (2.5 cm) apart. Bake, rotating and switching the pans halfway through, until the macaroons feel dry to the touch and lift easily off the parchment paper but are still white, about 25 minutes.

Transfer the pans to a rack and let cool. (Make-ahead: Layer the macaroons between waxed paper in airtight containers and store at cool room temperature for several weeks or freeze for up to 1 month.)

Makes about 80 macaroons.

American Gingerbread: Page 289

Original Recipe

Take half a pound of fresh butter melted, one pound and a half of dried and sifted flour, the same quantity of brown sugar, a quarter of a pound of pounded ginger, nine eggs, the yolk and whites beaten separately, one glass of rose water, and one of white wine; mix all these well together, and beat it for an hour; then with a spoon spread it over flat tin pans, about the thickness of a penny-piece; bake it of a light brown, and while warm, cut it into oblong pieces, and place them on end till cool, when they will be very crisp.

Modern Version

Unlike most rolled or dropped gingerbread, this is very gingery, very grown up, and very crisp. The method is unusual for a cookie: spread the dough thinly on a baking sheet, bake it, and, as soon as it comes out of the oven, cut it into rectangles. They do crisp up immediately, as Mrs Dalgairns promises, and they stay crisp for weeks.

4 medium eggs, separated, plus 1 medium yolk
½ cup (125 mL) butter, melted
1¾ cups (425 mL) packed brown sugar
½ cup (125 mL) ground ginger
2½ cups (625 mL) all-purpose flour, preferably unbleached
¼ cup (60 mL) rose water
¼ cup (60 mL) dry white wine

Line two large rimmed baking sheets with parchment paper. Position the rack in the centre of the oven; preheat to 325°F (160°C).

In a large bowl, beat the egg whites to firm but not stiff peaks; set aside. In a medium bowl, beat the yolks until light and thick; set aside.

In another large bowl, beat the butter and sugar. Beat in the egg yolks, then the ginger. With a wooden spoon, stir in one-third of the flour, the rose water, another third of the flour, the wine, and the remaining flour. Stir in one-third of the egg whites; fold in the remainder.

Working with 1 prepared baking sheet at a time and using an offset spatula, spread the parchment paper with about 1 cup (250 mL) of the batter as evenly and as thinly as possible, about ⅛ of an inch (3 mm) thick. Bake until light brown, 15 to 20 minutes.

Slide the gingerbread onto a cutting board; using a pizza cutter, cut into pieces about the size of playing cards. Let cool on a rack. Repeat to make more batches until the batter is used up. (Make-ahead: Layer between waxed paper in an airtight container and store at room temperature for several weeks or freeze for up to 1 month.)

Kitchen Note

In some recipes, especially when baking, medium eggs are called for as they are closer to the size of eggs in Mrs Dalgairns's period. Where it doesn't matter and the ingredient is simply "egg," use large or medium. Keep in mind that a medium egg weighs 1¾ oz (50 g) and a large one 2¼ oz (65 g); you may need fewer large eggs than medium.

Oliver's Biscuit: Page 293

Original Recipe

Melt a quarter of a pound of fresh butter in half a pint of new milk; add a tablespoonful of fresh yeast, and stir it into one pound and a half of flour; knead it well, then wrap it in warm flannel, to remain for fifteen minutes; roll it out several times, and the last time about the thickness of a penny piece; cut it into small biscuits, prick them well with a fork, and bake them in a slow oven till of a pale brown colour.

Modern Version

Oliver's Biscuit is named for its eighteenth-century creator, William Oliver of Bath, England. This yeast-raised cracker, made with just flour, milk, yeast, and butter, is rather plain, but that's appropriate for its role as a base for cheeses, some of them quite nippy.

2 tsp (10 mL) instant dry yeast
1 tsp (5 mL) granulated sugar
½ cup (125 mL) lukewarm water
½ cup (125 mL) whole milk
¼ cup (60 mL) butter, cubed
2¾ cups (675 mL) all-purpose flour, approximate

Line 2 rimless baking sheets with parchment paper. Before cutting out the biscuits, position oven racks in the top and bottom thirds of the oven; heat to 300°F (150°C).

In a large bowl, stir together the yeast, sugar, and water. Let stand until foamy, about 10 minutes. In a saucepan, heat the milk and butter until warm and the butter is melted. Let cool to room temperature. Stir into the yeast mixture. Add the flour, stirring to blend the wet and dry ingredients until a rough dough forms.

Turn out the dough onto a floured work surface and knead until smooth, adding a little more flour if needed, about 6 minutes. Place in a clean bowl; cover with a damp kitchen towel. Let rise in a warm place until doubled in volume, about 45 minutes. Press down and shape into a disc.

On the floured work surface, roll out the dough as thinly as possible, about 1/8 inch (3 mm). If the dough becomes stretchy, let it rest under a damp towel for a few minutes before continuing to roll. Using a round cookie cutter, cut out rounds about 2½ inches (6 cm) in diameter. While cutting, it may be necessary to reroll the dough to keep it as thin as possible. The thinner the biscuit, the finer it will be.

Transfer to prepared pans and prick all over with a fork. (This keeps the biscuits from puffing.) Bake, rotating and switching pans halfway through, until biscuits are light golden, about 20 minutes.

Transfer to a rack to cool. (Make-ahead: Store in airtight containers at cool room temperature for up to 1 week or freeze for up to 1 month.)

Makes about 90 biscuits.

Sally Luns, or Bath Breakfast Cakes: Page 295

Original Recipe

Rub into two pounds of flour half a pound of butter, and mix with it one pint of milk a little warmed, a quarter of a pint of fresh yeast, four well-beaten eggs, and a tea-spoonful of salt; cover it, and let it stand before the fire to rise for three quarter of an hour; make it into thick cakes about the size of the inside of a dinner plate; bake them in a quick oven, then cut them into three, that the middle slice, as also the top and bottom, may be well buttered. Serve them hot.

Modern Version

According to Elizabeth David, in her book English Bread and Yeast Cookery, Sally Lunns (Mrs Dalgairns's recipe title uses the spelling "Luns" and "Lun's") are an English version of French brioche, a soft textured bun made with milk, eggs, and butter. Folk etymology is at work in the name "Sally Lunn." The bun was first called "soleilune" or "solimemne," based on the French "soleil" (sun) and "lune" (moon), words that sounded unfamiliar to English ears. When people encounter an unusual (often foreign) word, the tendency is to change it into something that sounds like the original but is expressed in familiar words. Hence, Sally Lunn. Sound it out – the unfamiliar replaced by the familiar. Likewise, asparagus became known after its arrival in England as sparrow grass. Another example is "girasole," which is Italian for sunflower, and the tubers of this North American sunflower became known as Jerusalem artichokes.

And then there's the story of a real woman, Sally Lunn, who baked these rich breakfast cakes in Bath. The recipe below has been halved.

2 tsp (10 mL) instant dry yeast
1 tsp (5 mL) granulated sugar
¼ cup (60 mL) lukewarm water
3½ cups (875 mL) all-purpose flour, approximate
½ tsp (2 mL) salt
½ cup (125 mL) cold butter, cubed
2 medium eggs, at room temperature
1 cup (250 mL) whole milk, at room temperature

Stir the yeast and sugar into the warm water; let stand until frothy, about 10 minutes. In a large bowl, whisk together the flour and salt. Work in the butter using a pastry blender or fingertips until the mixture is light golden from the butter with an even texture like fresh breadcrumbs. Make a well in the centre.

In a medium bowl, whisk the eggs until foamy; whisk in the yeast mixture and milk. Pour the mixture into the well and, using a wooden spoon, gradually mix together the wet and dry ingredients. The dough will be quite soft and sticky. Cover the bowl and let the dough rise in a warm place until airy and doubled in volume, 45 to 60 minutes. With a floured hand, pat down gently.

Line a baking sheet with parchment paper. On a generously floured work surface and with floured hands, press the dough into a log shape. Divide into 6 equal pieces; shape each into a round, about 1½ inches (4 cm) high. Arrange on the prepared pan about 1 inch (2.5 cm) apart. Cover with a light damp towel and let rise until almost doubled in size, about 30 minutes.

Meanwhile, position an oven rack in the centre of the oven; heat to 350°F (180°C). Bake until golden and hollow sounding when tapped on the bottom, 25 to 30 minutes. Let cool slightly before slicing and serving; note that slicing into 2 layers is fine, rather than 3 layers as instructed in the original recipe. (Make-ahead: Let cool; transfer to a resealable freezer bag and freeze inside a large airtight container for up to 2 weeks.)

Makes 6 buns.

Kitchen Note:

Mrs Dalgairns's marmalade (page 299) is ideal for spreading on buttered Sally Lunns.

PRESERVES – CHAPTER XVI

Another way to make Orange Marmalade: Page 300

Original Recipe

Wash the oranges, and grate off any defective part; to three pounds of fruit allow five of fine loaf sugar; put the oranges into a sauce-pan with plenty of cold water;

cover it closely, and let them boil till a straw or the head of a pin will easily pierce them; take them out, cut them into four, pick out the seeds, and slice them, skin and all, as thin as possible; break the sugar small, and to each pound allow a quarter of a pint of water; stir it till the sugar be dissolved, and when it has boiled a few minutes, take it off the fire; pour in a quarter of a pint of cold water, which will throw up all the refuse; scum it off; put it again on the fire, and if any more scum rises, remove it; add the sliced oranges, and boil for fifteen minutes

Modern Version

It is not surprising that Mrs Dalgairns, a resident of Dundee, Scotland, a city famous for its marmalade, would slip four recipes for marmalade into her cookbook.

3 lb (1.5 kg) Seville oranges, about 10 large, divided
14 cups (3.5 L) granulated sugar, divided

Read "Kitchen Notes" below for preserving tips.

Scrub the oranges in warm sudsy water; drain and rinse well. Trim off the stem end and any blemishes. Place in a large pot (a pasta or stock pot is ideal) and fill with enough cold water to cover the oranges. Cover and bring to a boil; reduce the heat and simmer very gently for 3 hours. The orange skins should be tender enough that they turn to mush when pressed between the thumb and index finger, or "till a straw or the head of a pin will easily pierce them." Reserving the cooking water, scoop the oranges onto a baking sheet and let cool. Meanwhile, place 2 clean plates in the freezer.

Working with half of the oranges at a time, cut them into quarters; pick out and discard the seeds. Slice the oranges – skins, flesh, and tender membranes – crosswise as thinly as possible.

Scrape into a large preserving pot. Stir in 3 cups (750 mL) of the cooking water. Bring to a boil over high heat. Add half of the sugar, stirring constantly, and return to a full rolling boil. Boil, stirring constantly, until set, about 12 minutes.

To test whether the marmalade is set, remove the pot from the heat and one of the cold plates from the freezer. Drop about 1 tsp (5 mL) of the marmalade liquid onto the plate; let the little puddle cool down, about 3 minutes. Run the tip of a spoon through the puddle: if the surface wrinkles, the marmalade is set; if the surface does not wrinkle, return the pot to the heat and continue boiling until set, testing on the second cold plate (return the first plate to the freezer). Repeat as necessary until set.

Pour the marmalade into the jars, leaving a ¼-inch (1 cm) headspace. If any of the marmalade has smeared on the rim of the jars, wipe clean with a moist paper towel. Seal the jars with the lids and bands. Place the jars in the canner; cover and bring to a boil. Boil for 10 minutes. Remove the lid of the canner and turn off the heat to let the boiling water subside; with preserving tongs, lift the jars onto a rack to cool.

Repeat with the remaining oranges, cooking water and sugar.

Wipe and label the jars, checking that they have sealed properly. (If you have new lids and true preserving jars, it is highly unlikely that there will be any lids that have not snapped down to seal). If any jars have not sealed, refrigerate them to enjoy the marmalade within 3 weeks.)

Makes enough for about twelve 1-cup (250 mL) jars.

Kitchen Notes:

Two pots are essential: for boiling the marmalade, use a Maslin pan or other suitable heavy-bottomed preserving pot or Dutch oven, preferably with flared sides; and for processing the marmalade, use a large boiling water canner with a rack to hold the jars.

Before starting to boil the fruit and sugar, wash, rinse, and air-dry the preserving jars. Add water to the boiling water canner until it is two-thirds full; rest the rack on the rim. Place the jars on the rack and lower it into the water, letting the water fill the jars. Place the lid on the canner and set it over low heat to warm the jars. Set 2 plates in the freezer to use when testing the doneness of the marmalade. A few minutes before filling the jars with marmalade, place the new lids in a heat-proof bowl and cover with hot water.

When the marmalade has reached the setting point, remove it from the heat. Use preserving tongs to transfer the jars to a tray. Shake off any water. Fill, seal, and boil the filled jars according to the instructions in the recipe.

VINEGARS – CHAPTER XVII

PICKLES: SUBCHAPTER OF VINEGARS

Mushroom Catsup: Page 324

Original Recipe

Cut off the stalks from the broad flat mushrooms; peel, and break them into small bits; strew salt equally over them, allowing a large table-spoonful to every quart of the pulp. Let them stand twenty-four hours; put all into a sauce-pan, and let it boil gently for three quarters of an hour; strain, and let it stand to settle. The next day pour off the clear part, and to every pint of the liquor add half the quantity of port wine or old strong beer, a few blades of mace, twelve black peppercorns, and the same of allspice, a piece of ginger bruised, and eight cloves. Simmer it for nearly twenty minutes, pour it out, and when cold, bottle it with the spices equally divided.

Modern Version

As a catsup, this is more like Worcestershire sauce than the thick and tangy sweet red ketchup that is the companion of fries, grilled cheese, and more. Like Worcestershire sauce, Mushroom Catsup adds a little oomph, a taste boost, a full-bodied meatiness to a savoury dish. Spices – peppercorns, mace, cloves, allspice, and salt – do their part, but the biggest contribution to flavour enhancement is the main ingredient, mushrooms rich in umami. There are several brands of mushroom catsup for sale in the United Kingdom, and in specialty shops and online in the United States and Canada.

1 lb (500 g) fresh mushrooms such as cremini, rinsed
4 tsp (20 mL) pickling or kosher salt
1/2 cup (125 mL) port wine, approximate
12 black peppercorns
12 whole allspice
8 cloves
2 blades mace
1 piece (1 inch/2.5 cm) fresh ginger, bruised

Chop the mushrooms finely either by hand or in batches in a food processor. Transfer to a bowl and add the salt; cover and let stand for 24 hours.

Scrape the mushroom pulp and liquid into a small saucepan; bring to a very gentle simmer. Simmer, covered, to extract the mushroom flavour, about 45 minutes. Strain into a bowl and let settle for 12 hours. Measure the liquid; it should be about 1 cup (250 mL).

In a small saucepan, combine the mushroom liquid with half its volume of port (about 1/2 cup/125 mL). Add the peppercorns, allspice, cloves, mace, and ginger; bring to a simmer. Cover and simmer very gently for 20 minutes. Pour into a clean jar.

Mushroom Catsup can be stored in the refrigerator for up to 2 weeks. For longer storage, freeze in 1 tbsp (15 mL) portions in ice cube trays; transfer individual frozen cubes to resealable freezer bags and freeze for up to a few months.

Makes about 1 cup (250 mL).

To Pickle Mushrooms: Page 327

Original Recipe

Cut off the stalks, and wash clean, in cold water, some small button mushrooms; rub them with a bit of flannel, then throw them into fresh water, and when perfectly clean, put them into a sauce-pan with fresh cold water, and let them boil eight or ten minutes; strain off the water, lay them into the folds of a cloth. Boil, in a quart of vinegar, a quarter of an ounce of white pepper, the same of allspice, and two or three blades of mace, and a tea-spoonful of salt; put the mushrooms into a jar, and when the vinegar is cold, pour it, with the spices, over them.

Modern Version

Pickled mushrooms make an excellent addition to a contemporary charcuterie board or a piquant garnish for a rich stew such as Beef à la Braise, page 437.

1 lb (500 g) button mushrooms
1 ¼ cups (300 mL) white wine vinegar
½ tsp (2 mL) coarse pickling or kosher salt
½ tsp (2 mL) white peppercorns

½ tsp (2 mL) whole allspice
2 blades mace or ¼ tsp (1 mL) ground mace

Trim the mushroom stems so that they are level with the cap. Rinse the mushrooms well and place in a small saucepan; pour in enough water to cover. Bring to a boil; reduce the heat and simmer until the mushrooms are tender, about 8 minutes. Drain; spread the mushrooms, stem side down, on a clean kitchen towel and let dry for 1 hour.

Meanwhile, bring the vinegar, salt, peppercorns, allspice, and mace to a boil; boil for 1 minute. Let cool. Transfer the mushrooms to a clean 2-cup (500 mL) preserving jar. Pour the seasoned vinegar over top. Seal and refrigerate for at least 1 week before using. (Pickled mushrooms can be stored in the refrigerator for up to 1 month.) Remove from the jar using a clean fork and let drain before using.

Makes 2 cups (500 mL) pickled mushrooms.

To Pickle Beet-Root: Page 327

Original Recipe

Wash it perfectly clean, but do not cut off any of the fibres; put it on in plenty of boiling water with a little salt and boil it for half an hour; if the skin will come off easily, it is done enough. Lay it upon a cloth, and with a coarse one rub off the skin. Cut into slices, put it into a jar, and pour over it vinegar which has become cold, after having been boiled in the proportion of half an ounce of whole black pepper and a race of ginger to a quart. Cover the jar closely when cold.

Modern Version

This pickle is notable because, unlike contemporary pickled beet recipes, it has no sugar – just the strong tastes of pepper, ginger, and vinegar to balance the natural sweetness of beets.

5 large beets, 2 lb (1 kg)
1 tsp (5 mL) pickling or kosher salt
1½ cups (375 mL) white wine vinegar or cider vinegar, approximate

1 slice (¼ inch/5 mm) fresh gingerroot
1 ½ tsp (2 mL) black peppercorns

To clean the beets, brush each lightly in a bowl of cold water; leave the top and narrow root untrimmed. Add beets and salt to a large saucepan of water; cover and bring to a boil over high heat; cook, reducing heat if necessary, until the skins of the beets slip off easily, about 40 minutes. Drain and let cool.

Meanwhile, in a small saucepan, bring the vinegar, ginger, and peppercorns to a boil; boil for 1 minute. Let cool.

Peel and cut the beets into ½-inch (2 cm) thick slices. Fit into two 2-cup (500 mL) jars, halving the slices if necessary to fill the jars comfortably without pressing. Pour enough of the spiced vinegar into the jars to cover the beets, leaving only a ¼-inch (5 mm) headspace. (Add more plain vinegar if necessary to cover.) Refrigerate for at least 1 day before eating or store in the refrigerator for up to 2 weeks.

Makes two 2-cup (500 mL) jars.

WINES – CHAPTER XVIII

Lemon Liqueur, variation of Orange Liqueur: Page 345

Original Recipe

To each orange, one quart of strong spirits, and one pound and a quarter of loaf sugar are allowed; six or eight cloves are to be stuck into each orange, which, with the spirits and sugar, is to be put into a jar. It must be closely covered, and stirred occasionally in the course of two months; it is then to be filtered through blotting paper, and bottled for use.

Lemon Liqueur is made in the same way, substituting lemons for oranges. Instead of mixing the sugar with the other materials in the jar, it may be made into a syrup, and added to the strained or filtered spirits. This, though more troublesome, will be found a better method.

Modern Version

This update offers a less sweet liqueur with a mild lemon flavour.

1 lemon
8 whole cloves
4 cups (1 L) vodka
1 cup (250 mL) granulated sugar
1 cup (250 mL) water

Scrub the lemon well in soapy water; rinse well. Insert the cloves into the peel of the lemon. Place in a clean glass jar; pour in the vodka to cover. Seal and let infuse in a cool dark place, checking from time to time, for 1 month.

In a medium saucepan, bring the sugar and water to a boil; boil for 1 minute. Remove from heat. Stack 2 coffee filters together. Pressing on the lemon to extract the liquid, filter the infused vodka through the doubled filters into a large measuring cup. Discard the lemon. Combine the syrup and infused vodka; pour into clean sterilized jars or bottles and seal. The liqueur can be stored in the refrigerator for up to 1 month.

Makes a generous 4 cup (1 L).

Glossary of Food and Cooking Terms

FOODS

alum – a chemical compound used in pickling as a preservative
angelica – a medicinal herb that can be eaten: leafy parts like celery and stalks are often candied.
barberry – the fruit of an evergreen shrub, used to make jellies
blanquette – refers to the white sauce served with simmered veal breast
burnet – notionally a vegetable resembling a herb such as cilantro (coriander), added to salads
capillaire – a syrup prepared from the maidenhair fern
capsicum – bell pepper
cardoon – a vegetable genetically similar to the artichoke, the stalks and ribs are normally blanched
carmine – food colouring extracted from cochineal (see below)
caveach – a fillet of fish, pickled in vinegar
cedraty – "cedrat" is related to the lemon tree
chine – backbone of animal, cut of meat
chitterlings – see offal
chous – small round cake with sweet filling
cibol – of the onion family, called the Welsh Onion
clary – a medicinal plant grown for its essential oil
cochineal – a pink food colouring, deriving from the cochineal insect
cod sounds – the air bladder of a codfish
collar – to bone, season and roll up
collops – a thin slice of meat
comfits – a confectionary – seed or nut coated in layers of sugar
coratch – a sauce made of catsup, soy, and anchovies

costmary – an aromatic English herb that can be brewed for tea, similar to tansy (see tansy)
crappet – a fish stock based on haddock, onions, and flavourings
crimp – of fish, cut into fillets or slices
croquets – various shapes, such as like a cork
crulla – an Aberdeen crulla is a kind of small Scottish cake or bannock
cuites – an erratum which should read "cullis," the strained juices from cooked meat, or puree of chicken, game, or fish
cullis, or coulis – a meat juice
cutcharee – a kind of sauce served with kebobbed meat
fagadu – an Indian dish, involving lobster or shrimps
flummery – a sweet dish made with milk, beaten eggs, sugar, and flavourings
forcemeat – highly spiced stuffing in general, whether for meats and other foods, and made from lean minced meat, or even fish, as in *The Practice of Cookery*
fore-saye (forsye) – Scottish term for shoulder of beef
fricandeau – a veal fillet, usually sliced from the leg, stewed or fried with a sauce
fricandellans – minced meat rolled up in the form of corks
fricassee – any kind of meat or fish cut up in small pieces for stews
gigot – leg of mutton or lamb
grilse – a young salmon
griskin – the spine, chine, or backbone of pork
hartshorn – shavings of an animal horn
Harvey's Sauce – said to have been first compounded in 1795, and soon called *Lazenbury's Harvey's Sauce*; after 1870 imitations could be sold under "Harvey's Sauce"
hotch-potch – a thin stew, or soup; also a traditional Scottish dish
hyssop – an ancient largely medicinal herb, mentioned in the Old Testament
isinglass – a kind of gelatine made from animal parts, used in sweet and savoury jellies
Jamaica pepper – allspice, grown in Jamaica
knap – Scottish term for parts of the legs of beef
lake – a range of food dyes
laver – a reddish-purple seaweed found off rocky coasts of Britain
ling – a salt cod
maids – or Twaite Shad, a herring-like European coastal and river fish. Because of their bony flesh they were thought to have little economic importance

milts – soft roe of a fish
maigre – applies to dishes made without meat
offal – lights include head, ears, feet, pettitoes, brains, lungs, tongue, sweetbreads, liver, harslet, kidneys, tails, chitterlings, gristles, entrails
olio – a highly spiced stew of various meats and vegetables
pettitoes – pigs' feet
prunella salt – "A substance made by fusing potassium nitrate with sulphur, used in the eighteenth and nineteenth centuries for curing meat" (*Oxford Reference*)
raspings – rough gratings
ratafia – small macaroon biscuits
rennet – enzymes produced in the stomachs of ruminant mammals. Rennet is used in the production of most cheeses.
roux – thickening
salsify – a root vegetable, black on the outside and cream-coloured on the inside
saltpetre – potassium nitrate, a preservative
samphire – a fleshy plant that grows around rocks and sand dunes by sea coasts
scorzonera – a black root vegetable
sea kale – a vegetable with edible shoots, sometimes found near beaches
sippets – small pieces
skirret – long-rooted sweet vegetable
souchy – fish stewed and served in a little water
sowens – an oatmeal porridge
spitchcock (spitcock) – a split eel, prepared for grilling or frying
tansy (Tanacetum vulgare) – an aromatic herb with medicinal properties which tends to run wild
tusk – a North Atlantic cod-like fish

WEIGHTS AND MEASUREMENTS

(Note that weights and measurements were stabilized in Scotland by the Weights and Measurements Act of 1824.)

1 tea-spoonful – 1 teaspoon; 5ml
1 dessert-spoonful – 2 teaspoons; 10ml
1 table-spoonful – 1 tablespoon, or 3 teaspoons; 15ml

1 tea-cupful – 4 fluid ounces; 142ml
1 cup – 8 oz.; 250ml
1 gill – UK: 5 ounces, 142ml; North America: ½ cup or 8 large tablespoons; 118ml
1 pint – In England and Scotland, and PEI at the time, one pint = 20 fluid ounces (568ml). In USA 16 fluid ounces; 500ml
wine glass – ¼ cup; 60ml
1 quart (fluid) – 1.136 litres
1 quart (dry, i.e. flour, sugar, Indian meal) 1 pound, 2oz.; 900ml; 510g
1 pound – 16 oz.; 450g
1 peck – UK 8 quarts / USA 8.81 quarts; 9 litres
butter – 1 cup = ½ pound; 225g
butter the size of a walnut = 1 oz; 30g, or the size of an egg
bread crumbs – 2 ½ cups = 1 pound; 450g
flour – 1 quart = 1 pound; 450g
sugar (white) – 2 cups = 1 pound; 450g
sugar (brown) – 2 2/3 cups = 1 pound; 450g

OVEN TEMPERATURES

	F	C
Very slow oven	225–250	110–130
Cool oven	275–300	140–150
Slow oven	300–325	150–170
Moderate oven	325–350	170–180
Quick oven	375–400	190–204
Brisk oven	400–425	200–220
Hot oven	425–450	220–230

Measurements in The Practice of Cookery *expressed as equal in size to a British coin, or, what it would cost:*

the size of a shilling, the size of a crown-piece; the size of half-a-crown; the size of a crown; pennyworth of cochineal; a penny loaf; two penny loaves; three-penny roll; four pence worth of bones, &c.

KITCHEN UTENSILS AND EQUIPMENT

attelets – ornamental skewers, decorative for the table
dariole moulds – small cylindrical moulds in which food can be steamed, baked, or poached
digester – a cooking pot with a lid, often for soups, equipped with a valve for letting steam out
Dutch oven – a heavy iron pot with three legs, lid, and handle
fagot – a small bundle
firkin – a small cask
girdle – traditional Scottish baking iron, similar to a griddle
gridiron – an iron dish armed with iron bars for broiling
jars, variously named stone jars, stoneware jars, earthenware jars, potting jars, or just small jars
jelly-bag – a bag of made various materials, used for clarifying jellies
mortar – a heavy bowl made of marble, ceramic, or wood, in which food is pounded with a pestle
patty-pan – a pan for making individual puff or short-crust pies
pipkin – a small earthenware pot or pan
salamander – a thick iron plate with a long handle to brown the surface of dishes
stew-pan – thick pan or casserole, usually made of iron, with tight-fitting lid
tammy – a cloth made of woollen material, used as a sieve
thevil – a Scottish term for a stick for stirring butter
wafer-irons – a long-handled pair of iron tongs moulded with a design that is impressed upon the wafer batter in baking

Bibliography

ARCHIVAL SOURCES

All Souls College, Oxford. Codrington Library. "A Guide to manuscripts relating to America in Great Britain and Ireland," by B.R. Crick (1961). Includes correspondence of Margaret Hunter Hall, Captain Basil Hall, and General Martin Hunter, 1829–37.

British Library. 1. Callbeck (Montagu Thomas), correspondence with Sir W. A'Court 1820–21, Add. 41539 ff. 245, 247, 283, 285, 286. C. correspondence as Envoy to Naples and Sicily (41514–41540). 2. Callbeck (Ann), widow of P. Callbeck, Attorney General of Prince Edward Island, letters to the 2nd Earl of Liverpool and other papers 1804, 1817, 38241, vol. 52 (ff. 318) May 1804 to February 1806.

Library and Archives Canada. Neilson Printing firm. MG 24, B1.

Library of Congress. George Washington Papers, Phillip Callbeck and Thomas Wright to George Washington, 7 December 1775, with copy created/published 7 December 1775, MSS 44693, reel 034, series 4, general correspondence, 1697–1799.

National Archives Kew. Will of Phillips Callbeck of Charlottetown Island of Saint John, North America, PROB 11/1202/272, British Library, Archives and Record Office, correspondence and papers, official and private, of the first three Earls of Liverpool, 38190-38489.

National Library of Scotland. Correspondence and papers of the publisher Robert Cadell. MSS.21001–21069. Includes letters to Captain Basil Hall (1824–41), Diaries (1828–31), Misc. accounts (1812–57), accounts (1827–848), notebooks (1826–48), and general correspondence (1802–50).

– Letters of Capt. Basil Hall, 1826–40, MS.3649, fols. 134–1481.

– Xerox copies of letters to Jean, Lady Hunter, from members of the family of Sir James Hall of Dunglass, 1829–41, MS 14196.

– Archive of John Murray, publishers. MS 40504, letters of Basil Hall to John Murray, 1817–39.

National Records of Scotland. Court of Sessions. Sequestrations. Sundry references to Peter Dalgairns, CS230, CS280.

Prince Edward Island Genealogical Society. Cemetery inscriptions.

Public Archives and Record Office of Prince Edward Island (PAPEI). The Island Register; the Macdonald Papers (Z664); St Paul's Anglican Church, Charlottetown, Prince Edward Island; Records of marriages, acc. 3069/1, Supreme Court Fonds, series 5: Case files, Subseries: Case files 1770–1899.

Public Archives of New Brunswick. Martin Hunter Colonial Administrator, RS333, record series A, correspondence.

University of New Brunswick Archives and Special Collections, Winslow Papers, AD 1776–1826. Online at https://www.lib.unb.ca/winslow/about.html. See pages 124–6 re letter from Guy Carleton to Winslow, 21 August 1783, and note re Phillips Callbeck being captured by the Americans.

BOOKS AND ARTICLES

Accum, Frederick. *A Treatise on Adulterations of Food, and Culinary Poisons Exhibiting the Fraudulent Sophistications of Bread, Beer, Wine, Spirituous Liquors, Tea, Coffee, Cream, Confectionery, Vinegar, Mustard, Pepper, Cheese, Olive Oil, Pickles, and Other Articles Employed in Domestic Economy, and Methods of Detecting Them.* London: Longman, 1820. https://publicdomainreview.org/collection/a-treatise-on-adulteration-of-food-and-culinary-poisons-1820.

Asperne, James. *Information to Emigrants: An Account of the Island of Prince Edward with Practical Advice to Those Intending to Emigrate.* London: James Asperne, 1819.

Ayrton, Elisabeth. *The Cookery of England, being a Collection of Recipes for Traditional Dishes of All Kinds from the Fifteenth Century to the Present Day, with Notes on Their Social and Culinary Background.* Harmondsworth, Middlesex: Penguin Books, 1977.

Baird, Elizabeth, and Bridget Wranich. *Setting a Fine Table: Historical Desserts and Drinks from the Officers' Kitchen at Fort York.* Toronto: Whitecap Books, 2013.

Bickel, Walter. *Hering's Dictionary of Classical and Modern Cookery.* Edited, revised, and translated by Walter Bickel. Title of original publication: *Lexikon der Küche* (1907, 1950) by Richard Hering. Giessen: Fachbuchverlag Dr. Pfanneberg and Co., 1958.

Brears, Peter. "Everyday Meals in Regency London." Part 1, "The Household." *Petits Propos Culinaires* 110 (February 2018): 28–49; Part 2, "Changing Circumstances," 111 (June 2018): 22–42; Part 3. "Celebrations," 112 (November 2018): 15–24.

Brillat-Savarin, Jean-Anthelme. *The Physiology of Taste, or Meditations on Transcendental Gastronomy*. Philadelphia: Lindsay and Blakiston, 1854.

Brown, Catherine. *Classic Scots Cookery*. Glasgow: Angels' Share, 2004.

Bumsted, J.M. *Land, Settlement, and Politics on Eighteenth-Century Prince Edward Island*. Montreal and Kingston: McGill-Queen's University Press, 1987.

– "The Origins of the Land Question on Prince Edward Island, 1767–1805." *Acadiensis* 11, 1 (1981): 43–56.

Burnett, David, and Helen Saberi. *The Road to Vindaloo: Curry Cooks and Curry Books*. Totnes, UK: Prospect Books, 2008. Includes Mrs Dalgairns's recipes for Kebbobbed Currie and Cold Fish Currie.

Burnett, Joseph. *About Vanilla*. Boston: The Joseph Burnett Company, 1900.

Callbeck, Lorne C. *The Cradle of Confederation: A Brief History of Prince Edward Island from Its Discovery in 1534 to the Present Time*. Fredericton, NB: Brunswick Press, 1964.

– *My Island, My People*. Charlottetown: The Prince Edward Island Heritage Foundation, 1979.

Cambridge, John. *A Description of Prince Edward Island in the Gulph of Saint Laurence, North America*. 3rd ed. Bristol: Jonathan Baller, 1818.

Campey, Lucille H. *A Very Fine Class of Immigrants: Prince Edward Island's Scottish Pioneers 1770–1850*. Toronto: Dundurn, Natural Heritage Books, 2001.

Chute, Janet E. "Mi'kmaq Fishing in the Maritimes: A Historical Overview." In *Earth, Water, Air and Fire: Studies in Canadian Ethnohistory*, ed. David McNab for Nin.Da.Waab.Jig (Group), 95–113. Waterloo, ON: Wilfrid Laurier University Press, 1998.

Collingham, Lizzie. *Curry: A Tale of Cooks and Conquerors*. New York: Oxford University Press, 2006.

Comfort, Judith. "Some Good! The Maritime Harvest." In *Northern Bounty: A Celebration of Canadian Cuisine*, ed. Jo Marie Powers and Anita Stewart, 195–202. Toronto: Random House, 1995.

Cooke, Nathalie, and Fiona Lucas, eds. *Catharine Parr Traill's "The Female Emigrant's Guide": Cooking with a Canadian Classic*. Montreal and Kingston: McGill-Queen's University Press, 2017.

Cooper-Richet, Diana, and Emily Borgeaud. *Galignani*. English version by Iain Watson. Paris: Galignani, 1999.

Czarra, Fred. *Spices: A Global History*. London: Reaktion Books, 2009. (The Edible Series.)

Dallas, E.S. *Kettner's Book of the Table: A Manual of Cookery, Practical, Theoretical*. London: Centaur Press, 1968 [1877].

David, Elizabeth. *Spices, Salt and Aromatics in the English Kitchen*. Harmondsworth, UK: Penguin Books, 1970.

Davidson, Alan. *The Oxford Companion to Food*. Oxford: Oxford University Press, 1999.

Dickens, Charles. *Life, Letters, and Speeches of Charles Dickens, with Biographical Sketches of the Principal Illustrators of Dickens's Work.* Edited by Edwin Percy Whipple and others. vol. 1. Boston and New York: Houghton Mifflin and Co., 1894.

Dickson-Wright, Clarissa. *A History of English Food.* London: Random House, 2011.

Driver, Elizabeth. *Culinary Landmarks: A Bibliography of Canadian Cookbooks, 1825–1949.* Toronto: University of Toronto Press, 2008.

Drummond, J.C., and Anne Wilbraham. *The Englishman's Food: A History of Five Centuries of English Diet.* Revised by Dorothy Hollingsworth. London: Pimlico, 1991 [1939].

Duncan, Dorothy. *Food, Fellowship and Folklore: Canadians at Table, a Culinary History of Canada.* Toronto: Dundurn Press, 2006.

Dundee in 1793 and 1833: The First and Second Statistical Accounts with an introduction by Annette M. Smith. St Andrews: St Andrews University Library, 1991.

The Dundee Book: An Anthology of Living in the City, edited by Billy Kay. Edinburgh: Mainsteam Publishing, 1990.

Ecott, Tim. *Vanilla: Travels in Search of the Ice Cream Orchid.* New York: Grove Press, 2004.

Eveleigh, David J. *Firegrates and Kitchen Ranges.* Princes Risborough, UK: Shire Publications, 1996. (Shire Album 99.)

Geddes, Olive M. *The Laird's Kitchen: Three Hundred Years of Food in Scotland.* Edinburgh: National Library of Scotland, 1994.

Gotlieb, Sondra. *The Gourmet's Canada.* Toronto: New Press, 1972.

Grant, Elizabeth of Rothiemurchus. *Memoirs of a Highland Lady.* Edinburgh: Canongate Classics, 1988 [1898].

Gray, Hugh. *Letters from Canada Written during a Residence There in the Years 1806, 1807 and 1808.* London: Printed for Longman, Hurst, Rees, and Orme, 1809.

Gringoire, Th. and L. Saulnier. *Le répertoire de la cuisine.* Paris: Flammarion, 1986.

Hall, Basil. *Fragments of Voyages and Travels.* vol. 1. Edinburgh: Robert Cadell, 1831.

– *Fragments of Voyages and Travels.* Second series. 2nd ed. Edinburgh: Robert Cadell, 1832.

– *Travels in North America in the Years 1827 and 1828.* Philadelphia: Carey, Lea and Carey, 1829.

Hartley, Dorothy. *Food in England.* London: Macdonald, 1954.

– *Lost Country Life.* New York: Pantheon Books, 1979.

Hazlitt, W. Carew. *Old Cookery Books and Ancient Cuisine.* London: Elliot Stock, 1902.

Heriot, George. *Travels through the Canadas.* London: Richard Phillips, 1805.

Höfler, Manfred. *Dictionaire de l'art culinaire français: Etymologie et histoire.* Aix-en-Provence: Edisud, 1996.

Holman, H.T. "Phillips Callbeck." In *Dictionary of Canadian Biography,* vol. 4. Toronto: University of Toronto Press, 1979.

Hope, Annette. *A Caledonian Feast.* Edinburgh, London, New York, Melbourne: Canongate, 2002.

Hornby, Jim. *Black Islanders: Prince Edward Island's Historical Black Community.* Charlottetown: Institute of Island Studies, 1991.

Howells, Marion. *Hamlyn's Illustrated Cook's Dictionary.* London, New York, Toronto: Hamlyn, 1969.

Hughes, Kathryn. *The Short Life and Long Times of Mrs. Beeton.* London: Fourth Estate; New York: Knopf, 2006.

Innis, Mary Quayle, ed. *Mrs. Simcoe's Diary.* Toronto: Macmillan of Canada; New York: St Martin's Press, 1965.

Jackson, Gordon, and Kate Kinnear. *The Trade and Shipping of Dundee, 1780–1850.* Dundee: Abertay Historical Society, 1991. (Publication no. 31.)

Jaine, Tom. "Do Cookery Books Tell the Truth?" In *Culinary History*, ed. A. Lynn Martin and Barbara Santich, 87–96. Brompton, South Australia: East Street Publications, 2004.

Johnson, Samuel. *A Journey to the Western Islands of Scotland.* London: W. Strahan and T. Cadell, 1775.

Jones, Orlo, and Doris Haslam, eds. *An Island Refuge: Loyalists and Disbanded Troops on the Island of Saint John.* Charlottetown: Abegeweit Branch of the United Empire Loyalists Association of Canada, 1983.

Kuhnlein, Harriet V., and Nancy J. Turner. *Traditional Plant Foods of Canadian Indigenous Peoples: Nutrition, Botany and Use.* Philadelphia: Gordon and Breach, 1991. (Food and Nutrition in History and Anthropology, vol. 8).

Kurlansky, Mark. *The Big Oyster: History on the Half Shell.* New York: Ballantine Books, 2006.

Lanza, Fabrizia. *Olive: A Global History.* London: Reaktion Books (The Edible Series), 2011.

Larousse Gastronomique: The Encyclopedia of Food, Wine and Cooking. Prosper Montagne with the collaboration of Dr Gottschalk, ed. Nina Froud and Charlotte Turgeon. London: Paul Hamlyn, 1961.

Law's Grocer's Manual: A Practical Guide for Tea and Provision Dealers, Italian Warehousemen, Chandlers, Shipstore Dealers, Bakers, Confectioners, Fruiterers, and General Shopkeepers. Liverpool: J.T. Law, 1896.

Leard, George A. "Rum 'N' Ribbons." *Loyalist Gazette* 21, 1 (1983): 23–4.

Lehmann, Gilly. *The British Housewife: Cookery Books, Cooking and Society in Eighteenth-Century Britain.* Totnes, UK: Prospect Books, 2003

Lochhead, Marion. "The Scot at Table." In *The Scots Household in the Eighteenth Century: A Century of Scottish Domestic and Social Life*, 190–223. Edinburgh: The Moray Press, 1948.

Lupton, L.F.S. "Indians and Islanders: The Micmacs in Colonial Prince Edward Island." *Acadiensis* 6, 1 (1976): 21–42.

Mackenzie, William L. *Sketches of Canada and The United States.* London: Effingham Wilson, 1833.

Mackie, Charles. *Historical Description of the Town of Dundee.* Glasgow: Joseph Swan; London: Smith, Elder and Co., 1836. https://archive.org/details/historicaldescroo mackgoog.

Mancke, Elizabeth. 1995. "At the Counter of the General Store: Women and the Economy in Eighteenth-Century Horton, Nova Scotia." In *Intimate Relations: Family and Community in Planter Nova Scotia, 1759–1800*, ed. Margaret Conrad, 167–81. Fredericton, NB: Acadiensis Press, 1995.

Martin, R. Montgomery. "Prince Edward Island, 1834." In *History of the British Colonies in Five Volumes*, 423–54. Vol. 3: *Possessions in North America.* London: James Cochrane and Co., 1834.

Mason, Laura, and Catherine Brown. *The Taste of Britain.* London: Harper Press, 2006.

Mathew, W.M. *Keiller's of Dundee: The Rise of the Marmalade Dynasty, 1800–1879.* Dundee: Abertay Historical Society, 1998.

McCarthy, James. *That Curious Fellow: Captain Basil Hall, R.N.* Caithness, SCT: Whittles Publishing, 2011.

McNeill, F. Marian. *The Scots Kitchen: Its Traditions and Lore with Old-Time Recipes.* 2nd ed. Glasgow and London: Blackie and Son, 1963 [1929].

McNeill, F. Marian. *The Scots Cellar.* Edinburgh: Richard Paterson, 1956.

Nenadic, Stana. "Middle-Rank Consumers and Domestic Culture in Edinburgh and Glasgow, 1720–1840." *Past and Present* 145 (1994): 122–54.

Morley, Jefferson. *Snow-Storm in August: Washington City, Francis Scott Key, and the Forgotten Race Riot of 1835.* New York: Nan A. Talese/Doubleday, 2012.

Nicol, Walter. *The Scotch Forcing and Kitchen Gardener.* 2nd ed. Edinburgh: Printed for the author, 1798.

Nightingale, Marie. "The Enduring Influence on Today's East Coast Cooking." In *Northern Bounty: A Celebration of Canadian Cuisine.* Ed. Jo Marie Powers and Anita Stewart, 209–16. Toronto: Random House, 1995.

Past and Present of Prince Edward Island, Embracing a Concise Review of Its Early Settlement, Development and Present Conditions, Written by the Most Gifted Authors of the Province. Under the advisory editorship of Hon. D.A. MacKinnon, LLB, KC, and Hon. A.B. Warburton, DCL, KC. Charlottetown: B.F. Bowen [1906?].

Phillips Callbeck. In *Dictionary of Canadian Biography*, vol. 4, 128–9. Toronto: University of Toronto Press, 1979.

Pope-Hennessey, Una. *The Aristocratic Journey: Being the Outspoken Letters of Mrs. Basil Hall, Written during a Fourteen Months Sojourn in America, 1827–1828*. New York: Knickerbocker Press, 1931.

Prince Edward Island. *The Canadian Encyclopedia*, vol. 3, 1474–81 (Edmonton: Hurtig Publishers, 1985).

Raymond, William Odber, and Edward Winslow. *Winslow Papers, AD 1776–1826*. New Brunswick Historical Society. St John: Sun Printine, 1901.

Redmond, Theresa. "'We Cannot Work without Food': Nova Scotia Indian Policy and Mi'kmaq Agriculture, 1783–1867." In *Earth, Water, Air and Fire: Studies in Canadian Ethnohistory*, ed. David McNab, Nin.Da.Waab.Jig (Group), 115–25. Waterloo, ON: Wilfrid Laurier University Press, 1998.

Saberi, Helen, and Alan Davidson. *Trifle*. Totnes, UK: Prospect Books, 2001. (The English Kitchen.)

Sambrook, Pamela A., and Peter Brears. *The Country House Kitchen, 1650–1900*. London: Alan Sutton Publishing in Association with National Trust Enterprises, 1996.

Scottish Economic and Social History Society of Scotland. *Scottish Economic and Social History*. Glasgow: University of Glasgow, Department of Economic History, 1981–. (Online resource.)

Sen, Colleen Taylor. *Curry: A Global History*. London: Reaktion Books, 2009. (The Edible Series.)

Simon, André L. *André L. Simon's Guide to Good Food and Wines: A Concise Encyclopaedia of Gastronomy Complete and Unabridged*. London and Glasgow: Collins, 1960.

Smith, Andrew F., ed. *The Oxford Encyclopedia of Food and Drink in America*. 2 vols. New York: Oxford University Press, 2004.

Smith, Sally. *Cockburnspath: A History of a People and a Place including Cove, Dunglass, Old Cambus, Oldhamstocks, Bilsdean, Tower and Pease*. Cockburnspath: Dunglass Mill Press, 1999.

Speechly, William. *Practical Hints in Domestic Rural Economy, Relating Particularly to the Management of Fruit, Kitchen, Cottage Gardens and Orchards*. London: Longman, Hurst, Rees, Orme, and Brown, 1820.

Stewart, John. *An Account of Prince Edward Island in the Gulph of St. Lawrence, North America*. London: W. Winchester and Son, 1806.

Szezawinski, Adam F., and Nancy J. Turner. *Wild Green Vegetables of Canada*. Ottawa: National Museum of Natural Sciences, 1980. (*Edible Wild Plants of Canada*, no. 4.)

Traill, Catharine Parr. *The Backwoods of Canada: Being Letters from the Wife of an Emigrant Officer, Illustrative of the Domestic Economy of British America*. London: C. Knight, 1836.

Upton, L.F.S. "Indians and Islanders: The Micmacs in Colonial Prince Edward Island." *Acadiensis* 6, 1 (1976), 21–42.

– "Thomas Irwin: Champion of the Micmacs." *The Island* (Fall–Winter 1977): 13–16.

Visser, Margaret. *Much Depends on Dinner: The Extraordinary History and Mythology, Allure, and Obsessions, Perils and Taboos, of an Ordinary Meal*. Toronto: McClelland and Stewart, 1986.

Walsh, Edward. "An Account of Prince Edward's Island, 1803." *Island Magazine*, Spring–Summer, 1984, 9–13.

Watson, Julie V. "Global Marketing of Lobster: A Prince Edward Island Success Story." In *Northern Bounty: A Celebration of Canadian Cuisine*, ed. Jo Marie Powers and Anita Stewart, 203–8. Toronto: Random House, 1995.

Webster, Thomas. *An Encyclopaedia of Domestic Economy*. Books 1–26. London: Longman, Brown, Green and Longmans, 1844. (Facsimile edition, NL: Elibron Classics, 2005.)

Wheaton, Barbara Ketcham. *Savouring the Past: The French Kitchen and Table from 1300 to 1789*. London: Chatto and Windus, The Hogarth Press, 1983.

Whitfield, Harvey Amani. *North to Bondage: Loyalist Slavery in the Maritimes*. Vancouver: UBC Press, 2016.

Whitfield, Harvey Amani, and Barry Cahill. "Slave Life and Slave Law in Colonial Prince Edward Island, 1769–1825." *Acadiensis* 38, 2 (2009): 29–51.

Williamson, Mary F. "The Publication of 'Mrs. Dalgairns' Cookery': A Fortuitous Nineteenth-Century Success Story." *Papers of the Bibliographical Society of Canada* 45, 1 (2007): 43–66.

– "Mrs. Dalgairns' 'The Practice of Cookery' in America." *Food History News* 19, 1 (77, 2008): 1, 5–6.

Willis, H.P., and W. H. Bartlett. *Canadian Scenery Illustrated: From Drawings by W.H. Bartlett, the Literary Department by N.P. Willis, Esq.* Vol. 1. London: George Virtue, 1842.

Wilson, C. Anne. *The Book of Marmalade*. Totnes, UK: Prospect Books, 1999.

– *Eating with the Victorians*. UK: Stroud: Sutton Publishing Ltd., 2004

– "The French Connection." *Petits Propos Culinaires* 2 (August 1979): 10–16, and 4 (February 1980): 8–20.

Wright, Clarissa Dickson. *A History of English Food*. London: Arrow Books, Random House, 2012.

Wright, George. "The Story of an Early Pioneer." In *Who Departed This Life: A History of the Old Protestant Burying Ground, Charlottetown, Prince Edward Island*, 25, 31–6. Charlottetown: Acorn Press, 2005.

EARLY COOKBOOKS

A.B. of Grimsby. *The Frugal Housewife's Manual Containing a Number of Useful Receipts Carefully Selected and Adapted to the Use of Families in General*. Toronto: Guardian Office, 1840.

Acton, Eliza. *Modern Cookery for Private Families*. London: Longman, Brown, Green and Longmans, 1845. (Reprint with Introduction by Elizabeth Ray. Lewes, UK: Southover Press, 1993.)

Bury, Charlotte [Lady]. *The Lady's Own Cookery Book and New Dinner-Table Directory*. 3rd ed. London: Henry Colburn, 1844.

Caird, John. *The Complete Confectioner and Family Cook, Including All the Late Improvements*. Edinburgh: John Anderson, 1809.

Cooke, John Conrade. *Cookery and Confectionary*. London: W. Simpkin and R. Marshall, 1824.

Craig, Elizabeth. *Court Favourites: Recipes from Royal Kitchens*. London: Andre Deutsch, 1853.

Dods, Mistress Margaret of the Cleikum Inn, St Ronan's. *The Cook and Housewife's Manual: A Practical System of Modern Domestic Cookery and Family Management*, 4th ed., revised and enlarged. Edinburgh: Oliver and Boyd, 1829. (Reprint with introduction by Glynn Christian, London: Rosters, 1988.)

Dolby, Richard. *The Cook's Dictionary, and House-Keeper's Directory*. London: Henry Colburn and Richard Bentley, 1830.

Evelyn, John. *Acetaria: A Discourse of Sallets by J.E. S.R.S. Author of the Kalendarium*. London: for Benjamin Tooke, 1699. (Reprint, with an introduction by Tom Jaine, Totnes, UK: Prospect Books, 1996.)

Frazer, Mrs. *The Practice of Cookery, Pastry, Pickling, Preserving, &c*. Edinburgh: Peter Hill; London: T. Cadell, 1791.

Glasse, Hannah. *The Art of Cookery, made Plain and Easy; Which Far Exceeds any Thing of the Kind yet Published*. By a Lady. London: A. Millar, and T. Trye, 1758.

Glasse, Mrs. *The Art of Cookery made Plain and Easy; Excelling any Thing of the Kind ever published*. Alexandria, VA: Cottom and Stewart, 1805. (Reprint, with an introduction by Karen Hess, Bedford, MA: Applewood Books, 1997.)

Kitchiner, William, M.D. *The Cook's Oracle; Containing Receipts for Plain Cookery, on the Most Economical Plan for Private Families*. A new edition. London: Robert Cadell of Edinburgh, 1831.

Ladies' Aid Society, First Methodist Church. *Jubilee Cook Book: Valuable Recipes and Vouched for by the Ladies Whose Names Appear under the Recipes*. Charlottetown, 1897.

Lee, Mrs N.K M. *The Cook's Own Book: Being a Complete Culinary Encyclopedia. By a Boston Housekeeper*. Boston: Munroe and Francis; New York: Charles S. Francis and David Felt; Philadelphia: Carey and Lead, and Grigg and Elliot, 1832. (Reprint, New York: Arno Press, 1972).

MacDonald, Duncan. *The New London Family Cook*. London: James Cundee, 1808.

McClintock, Mrs. *Receipts for Cookery and Pastry-Work*. Glasgow: n.p., 1736. (Reprint of first edition in the Glasgow University Library, with introduction and glossary by Iseabail Macleod, Aberdeen: Aberdeen University Press, 1986.)

Menon. *La cuisinière bourgeoise, suivie de l'office à l'usage de tous ceux qui se mêlent de dépenses de maisons*. Paris: Chez Guillyn, 1746. (Reprint, Luzarches, France: Imprimerie Réunies de Senlis pour Daniel Morcrette, 1977.)

Nightingale, Marie. *Out of Old Nova Scotia Kitchens: A Collection of Traditional Recipes of Nova Scotia and the Story of the People Who Cooked Them*. Halifax: Cystic Fibrosis Society of Nova Scotia, 1970.

Raffald, Elizabeth. *The Experienced English Housekeeper*. Manchester: printed by J. Harrop, for the author, and sold by Messrs. Fletcher and Anderson, in St Paul's Church-Yard, London; and by Eliz. Raffald, Confectioner, near the Exchange, Manchester 1769. (Reprint, with introduction by Roy Shipperbottom. Lewes, UK: Southover Press, 1997.)

Randolph, Mrs Mary. *The Virginia Housewife: or, Methodical Cook*. Baltimore: Plaskitt and Cugle, 1828. (Reprint, Birmingham, AL: Oxmoor House, 1984.)

Rundell, Mrs. *A New System of Domestic Cookery; Formed on Principles of Economy, and Adapted to the Use of Private Families, By a Lady*, London: J. Murray, 1806. (Wellcome Institute, Leeds University Library.)

Simmons, Amelia. *American Cookery or the Art of Dressing Viands, Fish, Poultry and Vegetables, and the best modes of making Pastes, Puffs, Pies, Tarts, Puddings Custards and Preserves*. By Amelia Simmons, an American Orphan. Hartford: Hudson and Goodwin, 1796. (Reprint of first edition, Grand Rapids, MI: William B. Eerdmans Publishing Co. 1965.)

Ude, Louis Eustache. *The French Cook, or, The Art of Cookery Developed in All of Its Various Branches*. London: Printed by J. Ebers, 1815. (Facsimile of the third edition in the Harvard College Library [La Vergne, TN]: Nabu Public Domain Reprints, n.d.)

Index to *The Practice of Cookery* by Mrs Dalgairns

Index to the Introduction and Glossary